Financial Reporting with SAP

 PRESS

SAP PRESS is a joint initiative of SAP and Galileo Press. The know-how offered by SAP specialists combined with the expertise of the publishing house Galileo Press offers the reader expert books in the field. SAP PRESS features first-hand information and expert advice, and provides useful skills for professional decision-making.

SAP PRESS offers a variety of books on technical and business related topics for the SAP user. For further information, please visit our website: *www.sap-press.com*.

Jörg Thomas Dickersbach, Gerhard Keller, Klaus Weihrauch
Production Planning and Control with SAP
2006, approx. 400 pp., ISBN 1-59229-106-6

Martin Murray
SAP MM — Functionality and Technical Configuration
2006, 504 pp., ISBN 1-59229-072-8

Gerd Hartmann, Ulrich Schmidt
Product Lifecycle Management with SAP
2005, 620 pp., ISBN 1-59229-036-1

Michael Hölzer, Michael Schramm
Quality Management with SAP
2005, 538 pp., ISBN 1-59229-051-5

Aylin Korkmaz

Financial Reporting with SAP

Galileo Press

Bonn • Boston

ISBN 978-1-59229-179-3

1st edition 2008

Editor Stephen Solomon
Copy Editor Ruth Saavedra
Cover Design Nadine Kohl
Layout Design Vera Brauner
Production Todd Brown
Typesetting Publishers' Design and Production Services, Inc.
Printed and bound in Canada

Contents at a Glance

Contents

4   Tax Reporting 121

Preface

Dedication

My parents who always told me I could do whatever I set my mind to.

Acknowledgments

This book would not have been possible without the encouragement and support of my dear friends and family who without their efforts and constant support I would not achieve my goal. Thanks are due to all those who supported me.

First and foremost, I'd like to express my most heartfelt thanks to my husband, Bulent, who showed a great deal of understanding and patience for all those hours of our time which I had to invest in the work for this book.

I would also like to thank SAP AG for their commitment, support and contribution to the last chapter. In particular, I would like to express my deepest gratitude to Janet Salmon (Solution Manager, SAP ERP Financials) and Dr. Dirk Braun (Solution Manager, SAP AG) who assisted me with writing the last chapter on the future direction of financial reporting. The content of this chapter would not have been possible on this early date without their contribution and provide me such great support.

I would also like to acknowledge the folks at SAP PRESS for the encouragement, collaboration and support in writing this book.

I wish to extend sincere thank to all my executives and supervisors in Accenture for their leadership and support throughout in my career. I would also like to thank to all my colleagues for their patience and their understanding that while I was writing the book I had less time than usual for them.

Thanks also to Wellesley Information System (WIS) for providing me the various opportunities that they have.

A final thanks to all those not mentioned above who have taken time to share their time and experiences with me.

Foreword

SAP ERP Financials' functionality and related reporting capabilities have significantly evolved in the current versions of the software, enabling organizations to further increase the return on their SAP software investment. Companies that implemented SAP have always significantly focused on the areas of financial reporting and compliance with internal and external regulations and controls. In recent years, however, many organizations have refocused their efforts on driving additional reporting capabilities in order to realize more value from their SAP ERP and SAP NetWeaver BI solutions.

I was delighted when Aylin Korkmaz asked me to contribute to *Financial Reporting with SAP* by writing the Foreword. She is a world-renowned SAP ERP Financials expert, has published numerous articles, and has hands-on SAP implementation experience that is clearly encapsulated in the content you are about to read.

In this book, Aylin provides readers with a single source for exploring and maximizing the reporting capabilities in both SAP ERP Financials and SAP NetWeaver BI. In addition, she covers the latest developments in SAP Reporting & Analytics. A detailed overview of approaches to structuring SAP Financials functionality and related reporting to promote efficient, accurate, and timely execution of financial reporting functions is included within these pages, much of it drawn from direct experience with complex implementations. These functions are capable of providing an organization and all its stakeholders with reliable information and analysis to enhance performance and compliance. They have never been practically detailed and documented in one place before, making their appearance within the pages of this book a novel and unique occurrence in the SAP ERP Financials universe.

Aylin also gives you a fresh look at your existing SAP capabilities by showing you how to discover new areas of improvement and focus on extending financial reporting and compliance with SAP. Even if your organization is not using SAP, you will still find a lot of key concepts covered here that will likely be of interest to you, including governance, risk, & compliance; shortening time to close; improving reporting efficiency; streamlining and simplifying financial processes, and bridging the communication gap between Finance and other areas of the organization. All of these strategies can be used to improve your financial reporting and compliance activities whether you have implemented SAP ERP or not.

The ever-increasing demands from regulatory bodies and internal and external stakeholders are driving organizations to create new capabilities in the area of financial reporting while constantly enhancing the existing ones. We believe that these drivers will continue to have a significant impact in this area, and force finance professionals to think creatively and practically about managing their reporting capabilities. Enterprise Service-Oriented Architecture, or enterprise SOA, will continue to change the way organizations execute financial reporting and improve compliance efficiency. The Securities and Exchange Commission's demands that US public companies speed up their closing processes and shorten the time required to prepare financial statements will continue to force executives to think practically about building best-in-class reporting solutions. International companies subjected to myriad laws requiring them to issue consolidated financial reports compliant with several accounting standards will need to manage their reporting capabilities without incurring redundant costs and processes as they do so. Finally, while collection of and access to detailed information grows almost exponentially every year, many companies continue to struggle to consume and provide information with the depth and breadth necessary to make informed and timely decisions. Getting the right information to employees at the right time and accurately integrating business processes with reporting is of utmost importance in today's fast-changing business environment.

This book contains many excellent examples dealing with many of the real-world SAP ERP and NetWeaver BI challenges. It is a substantial contribution to the success of effective financial reporting and compliance, and I hope that it will extend your knowledge of the practical, and vision for the creative, as you work to build and manage your organization's reporting capabilities.

Chicago, USA, November 2007

Cenk O. Ozdemir, Executive Director, Accenture

1 Introduction

This book is about financial reporting in SAP®. Financial reporting underpins all business transactions. Risks posed by inadequate management of financial information may lead to severe consequences for corporations and their senior executives when completing business transactions, fulfilling organizational objectives or opportunities, or satisfying legislative requirements. These risks include inaccessible and incomplete financial information, inaccuracy of data, and lack of credibility of information.

At the turn of the century, significant and massive business failures—as a result of fraud and a lack of internal control, governance practices, and robust risk prevention—prompted the U.S. Congress to introduce the Sarbanes-Oxley Act (SOX) to help calm financial markets by ensuring that more accountability was in place for senior executives and that accurate information would be provided to investors in the form of financial reports and disclosures. SOX also established requirements for internal control systems related to financial reporting. Section 404 of the act established the requirements for companies to express a view formally on their internal control systems for financial reporting and for external auditors to sign off on these management assessments.

In addition, many international companies are subject to several sets of laws requiring them to issue multiple consolidated financial reports. For example, companies listed in the United States or belonging to a U.S. company must submit their financial statements according to the U.S.'s Generally Accepted Accounting Standards (U.S. GAAP), whereas the European Commission has required that from the end of 2005 all listed European Union companies must report their financial results in accordance with International Financial Reporting Standards (IFRS) to promote internationally comparable financial statements. Transition by the end of 2007 is required for companies that currently apply different internationally recognized standards, such as the U.S. GAAP, for their published financial statements.

Compliance with these regulations forces many companies to publish financial information that is not easily captured and reported with their existing reporting systems. For example, additional information on management reports and interim accounts, measurement of exposure to and the impact of market volatility, new key performance indicators, and additions to annual reporting materials are difficult to capture and report. Cash flow statements also need to be split into operating, investing, and financing activities, with increased levels of precision and control. Forecasting and budgeting processes must generate more consistent results and support scenario analysis. Finally, external reporting with faster timelines and increased data requirements is becoming the standard across industries.

All of these regulations have a significant impact on the construction of financial reports and increase the need for standardized financial processes and reporting. Companies need to streamline their financial reporting processes and automate the many aspects involved in the preparation of their financial reports. Although international accounting standards have done much to promote consistency, the financial reporting process has to be flexible enough to incorporate and adapt to different demands of accounting standards and automate the preparation of the regulatory filing process.

The identification of reporting requirements and the design and implementation of optimal reporting architecture is critical to the effectiveness of financial reporting processes. Most of the effort in designing and implementing an effective reporting architecture is spent in the areas of gathering the reporting requirements and designing the processes in such a way that the data is available for reporting. Streamlined and seamlessly integrated reporting capabilities are critical for companies to meet all these regulations with a minimal amount of work and resource expenditure.

This SAP PRESS Essentials book provides finance and IT teams with best practices for delivering financial reports faster, more accurately, and in compliance with various international accounting standards. Featuring step-by-step coverage of all major SAP ERP Financials reporting functions, including finance subledgers, management accounting, financial supply chain management, governance, risk and compliance, and corporate performance management. This book helps you streamline and simplify financial business processes and automate financial and management reporting in SAP ERP. We also cover financial reporting integration with SAP NetWeaver® Business Intelligence (SAP NetWeaver BI 7.0), SAP xApp™ Analytics, and Duet™, as well as the future direction of SAP financial reporting.

1.1 Who Should Read this Book

This book can be used by a wide audience, including upper management, finance managers, mid-level management, consultants, and business analysts. It will be of most use for those who need to:

▶ Understand the strategies and best practices for delivering financial reports faster, more accurately, and in compliance with regulations

▶ Understand the SAP ERP Financials components, capabilities, and underlying financial processes, with the focus upon key design considerations and work-in best practices

▶ Learn key financial reports in SAP ERP and SAP Netweaver BI

▶ Understand the capabilities and features of SAP ERP's reporting tools, including SAP List Viewer, Report Painter and Report Writer, Drilldown Reporting, and SAP Query

▶ Understand how to use SAP NetWeaver BI Business Explorer (BEx) Suite applications

▶ Understand how to increase the effectiveness of an organization's financial compliance with SAP Governance, Risk, and Compliance (GRC) technology foundation applications

▶ Understand the new SAP Corporate Performance Management (SAP CPM) suite applications and the evolution of SAP Strategic Enterprise Management (SAP SEM®) solutions to SAP CPM solutions

▶ Understand information worker applications such as SAP xApp Analytics™, Duet™, and SAP Interactive Forms software by Adobe

▶ Learn how to improve financial reporting with SAP's innovations

1.2 How to Use this Book

The aim of this book is to demystify effective financial reporting, as well as to guide readers about SAP's financial reporting capabilities. We have written the chapters based on our experience in consulting work and the feedback that we have received from our readers and customers. We have specifically covered the practical issues that managers and business analysts face in today's fast changing and innovative environment. The individual chapters provide the main design considerations and work-in best practices for financial processes and the features and capabilities necessary to generate financial reports in compliance with regulations. Each chapter covers key reports from SAP ERP 6.0 and SAP NetWeaver BI 7.0.

All SAP ERP report examples in our book use sample data from SAP's International Demo and Education System (IDES). IDES represents a model company, which consists of an international group with subsidiaries in a number of countries around the globe. The SAP ERP IDES, regularly updated by SAP AG, can be installed by SAP customers and is typically used for training and demonstration purposes. It contains application data for various integrated business scenarios, and preconfigured business processes designed to reflect realistic business requirements. We use IDES with the objective of providing our readers with universal knowledge without being tied to specific customer or project implementation. By using IDES, you can replicate the reports we illustrate in the chapters. However, keep in mind that reported figures, certain master data, and configurations may be different in your IDES system. For more information about IDES and its current availability, contact your SAP account manager.

With SAP NetWeaver BI 7.0, we concentrate on standard business content, which consists of a collection of preconfigured objects that enable business applications to take advantage of the integration capabilities of SAP NetWeaver and best industry practices and to speed up project implementation. SAP NetWeaver BI business content is continuously being improved and enhanced by both SAP and its partners in close collaboration with SAP customers.

Throughout all the chapters we explain business content objects, data models, data flows, and queries in the financial business content, with the goal of recommending how to utilize standard SAP NetWeaver BI content. Business content, delivered with a wide variety of role-based business packages containing predefined application resources assembled into portal interfaces, as well as predefined reporting and analysis scenarios, is a fundamental building block of each project implementation, especially when it comes to financial reporting. Without doubt, business content enables you to save resources and add significant business value to the implementations. However, note that one-solution-fits-all is not possible due to the multitude of business requirements that companies have to meet. Thus, you may need to model your existing business intelligence scenarios by using business content as a template.

1.3 Structure of the Book

Chapter 2 discusses the best practices and methods for designing financial statements and statutory reports according to international accounting standards and outlines the main integration points of financial data flow across SAP ERP and SAP NetWeaver BI, with the goal of recommending a generic solution that provides leading practices for generating financial statements and statutory reports.

Chapter 3 explains segment reporting compliance, different segment reporting solutions, the design considerations and best practices for simplifying and streamlining segment reporting. The emphasis in this chapter is on recommending the best foundations of segment reporting design.

Chapter 4 describes the tax reporting architecture in SAP ERP and SAP NetWeaver BI. In particular, it focuses on design principles and makes recommendations on how organizations can streamline and automate the tax process and capture the right level of tax data granularity.

An organization might want to increase the efficiency of its accounts payable (AP) and accounts receivable (AR) reporting for a number of reasons. These include a desire to improve the control of AR and AP processes, cost and time efficiencies, and risk management. In Chapter 5 we discuss the design considerations and work-in best practices for AP and AR reporting.

Asset reporting based on standardized processes and transparent data provides timely management information, supports audit processes, and satisfies the high standards of international capital markets. In Chapter 6 we focus on the asset lifecycle process, make recommendations regarding how to streamline and automate the asset lifecycle process, and explain the asset reporting architecture in SAP ERP and SAP NetWeaver BI.

Chapter 7 deals with cash management reporting. One of the biggest challenges in SAP implementation projects is to reflect all cash transactions accurately and on time to produce comprehensive cash management reports that support decisions on funding, investment, and borrowing. This chapter covers SAP's cash management reporting capabilities and explains the design considerations and best practices for cash management reporting.

Chapter 8 covers treasury and risk management reporting. In this chapter we specifically focus on straight-through processing, which can provide the necessary transparency for transaction and position management reporting and market risk management analysis.

Chapter 9 explains the foundations of management accounting reporting. It particularly focuses on overhead cost management reporting architecture and design considerations. Chapter 10 covers product cost controlling and profitability analysis as part of management accounting reporting.

Chapter 11 explains the flexible data modeling of the SAP SEM-BCS solution along with the consolidation design considerations and scenarios. In this chapter we walk through the best practices for harmonizing legal and management consolidation, structuring master data and hierarchies, strengthening the integration of master data across SAP ERP, SAP NetWeaver BI, and SAP SEM-BCS, and automating the consolidating tasks for generating consolidated financial statements accurately and promptly. Note that the future direction of consolidated financial reporting is covered in the CPM section of Chapter 14.

Chapters 12 and 13 provide an overview of the reporting tools in SAP ERP and SAP NetWeaver BI for those who have little or no experience with reporting tools. These chapters include brief descriptions of the report components and formatting options, as well as hints and guidelines for creating customized reports and applications.

We devote Chapter 14 to organizational performance and information worker applications. We first focus on financial compliance, which is heavily centered upon SAP GRC Access Control and SAP GRC Process Control. After that we explain SAP's new CPM strategy and focus on the features and capabilities of new CPM applications and then explain the evolution of SEM solutions to CPM solutions. We also cover SAP xApp Analytics, Duet, and SAP Interactive Forms.

Finally, Chapter 15 deals with SAP's future direction in financial reporting. It first explains SAP Enhancement Package for SAP ERP with a focus upon the new functions and capabilities, and then a focus upon SAP's simplified financial reporting innovation.

What are the major leading practices that will help your organization streamline and improve its financial reporting process? What are the key reporting capabilities to comply with multiple accounting standards? How can you leverage the reporting capabilities of SAP NetWeaver BI to generate financial statements? In this chapter, we address all of these questions and explain how to establish a robust reporting architecture for generating financial statements.

2 Financial Statements and Statutory Reporting

In today's competitive environment, providing financial statements fast and accurately and complying with international accounting standards is not optional, but mandatory. After the *U.S. Security and Exchange Commission (SEC)* demanded shortening the time required to prepare financial statements, submitting financial reports faster became even more important to U.S. public companies and increased the accountability of organizations' executives.

Many international companies are subject to several sets of laws requiring them to issue multiple consolidated financial statements. Companies listed in the United States or belonging to a U.S. company must submit their financial statements according to the United States' Generally Accepted Accounting Standards (U.S. GAAP), whereas the European Commission requires that all listed European Union companies must report their financial results in accordance with International Financial Reporting Standards (IFRS).

In addition to the international accounting regulatory compliances, companies must also comply in accordance with their country's specific requirements and legislation and submit their financial statements to the local government authorities. All of these regulations have a significant impact upon the construction of financial statements and increase the need for standardized financial processes and reporting.

This chapter discusses the key design considerations for designing financial statements and statutory reports and outlines the main integration points of financial data flow across SAP ERP and SAP NetWeaver BI, with the goal of recommending a generic solution that provides leading practices for generating financial statements and statutory reports.

2.1 The Financial Reporting Process

The financial reporting process touches many key financial processes related to different applications in SAP ERP. Streamlining and standardizing the financial reporting process largely depends upon improving and automating these financial processes. Figure 2.1 shows the main processes involved in the financial reporting process.

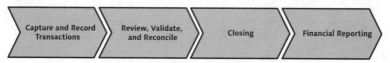

Figure 2.1 Financial Reporting Process

Let's look at each of these processes in detail:

▸ **Capture and Record Transactions**
The financial reporting process is influenced by almost all business processes, and it is imperative to capture and record all transactions resulting in financial values and update the Financial Accounting (FI) component. This is relatively straightforward because the SAP ERP architecture provides a modular but integrated structure. Some components of SAP ERP are directly linked to FI, and financial values are updated in FI simultaneously. For example, all requisition-to-pay (RTP) transactions are recorded in the Materials Management (MM) component, whereas order-to-cash (OTC) transactions are recorded in the Sales and Distribution (SD) component. These components are integrated with Accounts Payable (AP) and Accounts Receivable (AR), which are subcomponents of FI. Both RTP and OTC business processes update FI simultaneously. Some SAP ERP components such as Human Capital Management (HCM) do not but have online integration with FI. Transactions related to salaries and wages, for example, are first calculated and evaluated in HCM and then transferred to FI on a periodic basis.

- **Review, Validate, and Reconcile**

  This process includes the analysis of recorded transactions, the validation of these transactions, and the reconciliation of data. With this process, accounting discrepancies are identified and resolved before closing. It is very important to reconcile financial data, as nonavailability of the right information will cause inaccurate reporting. SAP ERP provides standard reconciliation reports as well as validation and substitution functionalities to define system-built controls to streamline this process.

- **Closing**

  This process covers all closing tasks that should be executed before running financial statements, that is, foreign currency valuation, regrouping of receivables and payables, allocations, and so on. The faster you close the period, the faster you generate and submit financial statements and statutory reports.

- **Financial Reporting**

  This process involves the creation and submission of financial reports to authorities and other regulatory bodies in the required format and timeline. Examples of financial reports include:

  - **Financial statements (balance sheet, income statement, cash flow statement)**

    Financial statements include the balance sheet, income statement, and cash flow statement. The balance sheet shows the financial position of a company at a specific moment in time. The income statement summarizes the results of operations for a specific period of time. Most public companies must also publish a cash flow statement to explain incoming and outgoing cash, together with the income statement and balance sheet. Financial statements, when published, are usually accompanied by accounting policies used for preparation and other explanatory notes.

  - **Statutory reports (country-specific financial statements)**

    Statutory reports are generally referred to as country-specific financial statement reports. Some countries in which the enterprise operates may have specific requirements and legislation related to the financial statements. That is why statutory reports must be prepared in accordance with each country's specific requirements and legislation (for example, 10-K in the United States).

▶ **Tax reports**

Tax reports are classified into two types: indirect tax reports and direct tax reports. The terms *indirect tax* and *direct tax* are related to the way tax authorities collect the tax from the taxpayers. Indirect tax is determined during the RTP and OTC processes, as well as tax related general ledger processes for enterprises such as sales tax and value added tax (VAT). *Direct tax* is the term used for tax that is directly collected by the tax authorities. Direct tax reporting contains direct tax charges and liabilities. Tax reports are prepared in accordance with each country's tax authorities. For example, the Internal Revenue Service (IRS) has established regulations for tax accounting and reporting in the United States. Note that this chapter only focuses on financial statements and statutory reports. We cover tax reporting in Chapter 4.

Now let's take an in-depth look at designing the financial reporting process.

2.2   Designing the Financial Reporting Process

The General Ledger (G/L) is the basis of the SAP financial management environment's ability to provide financial and management information. As illustrated in Figure 2.2, it is the core financial application that supports the company's financial operations and financial reporting. All business transactions resulting in financial value update the G/L, which enables companies to run their financial reports directly from the G/L. Besides, companies can use SAP NetWeaver BI and SAP SEM-BCS to get more flexible and advanced financial reports and consolidated financial statements. The primary customers of financial statements are external parties such as financial market regulators, tax authorities, investors, and auditors.

In this section, we discuss major leading practices and design considerations that will help your enterprise to streamline and improve the financial reporting process. Specifically, we discuss the following:

▶ Master data governance

▶ Harmonizing and unifying the chart of accounts

▶ Standardizing the financial reporting structure

▶ Automating the reconciliation of intercompany transactions

▶ Complying with international accounting standards

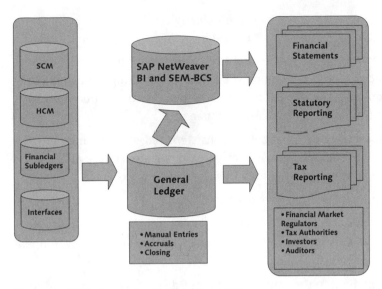

Figure 2.2 G/L as Source for Financial Reporting

2.2.1 Master Data Governance

High-quality data can add significant value to organizations' ability to report financial information accurately and on time. Organizations often have a decentralized master data management strategy, resulting in redundant and inconsistent data, which has a significant impact on financial reporting. To provide accurate and timely financial reporting, it is vital that the underlying finance master data be maintained efficiently. An effective strategy for governing master data for the creation and maintenance of master data prevents unauthorized changes, which could result in fraudulent activity and business risk. Having a controlled master data management approach enables consistent reporting and reduces reconciliation activities. The following list identifies leading practices to govern master data efficiently and effectively:

▶ Data should be owned and maintained by a centralized organization. This organization must be accountable for creating, changing, and archiving data. Without the centralized management of data, each business unit may have a different approach, leading to inconsistent data in the system.

▶ Standardize the master data maintenance process for all master data objects. The master data maintenance process should be driven with the use of a standardized request form, and the process should clearly be defined for validations, acceptance/creation, and rejection/return criteria with a clear responsibility.

▶ Create checklists for master data creation and change requests. Before any master data is created or changed, there must be an understanding of business drivers for the action. Without validation of business need, the number of master data objects can become large and costly to manage.

▶ Identify data gaps and ensure that data is consistent across companies and systems. Inconsistent master data prevents efficient report generation and leads to enormous efforts to find gaps, resulting in significant costs.

▶ Reduce redundant data and improve data quality.

▶ The wrong customization of master data can result in inaccurate reporting results. It can also create complexity when upgrading versions or activating enhancement packages.

▶ Master data maintained in the source system and distributed to target systems (i.e., SAP NetWeaver BI and SAP SEM-BCS) should not be changed in the target systems.

Master data can be maintained in SAP ERP, SAP NetWeaver BI, and SAP SEM-BCS. SAP ERP sends master data into the SAP NetWeaver BI environment. Then, master data is synchronized via standard delivered programs between SAP SEM-BCS and SAP NetWeaver BI. It is imperative to integrate master data across SAP ERP, SAP NetWeaver BI, and SAP SEM-BCS to decrease the effort of reconciliation across these systems and provide financial reports consistently. Although the master data flow from SAP ERP to SAP NetWeaver BI and SAP SEM-BCS seems straightforward, you need to consider many integration points to generate accurate financial statements. In the next two sections we explain the main integration points and design considerations for generating financial statements consistently in SAP ERP and SAP NetWeaver BI.

2.2.2 Harmonizing and Unifying the Chart of Accounts

New regulations and increased pressure on timing to provide financial reports have a large impact upon the design of the *chart of accounts* and posting procedures. A chart of accounts is a logical structure of general ledger accounts used to record, consolidate, and report financial transaction information related to the business. It provides the control framework to capture and record financial transactions. The chart of accounts traditionally served primarily as the means for coding accounting transactions for financial reporting. However, now that enterprise resource planning systems are available and there is better system integration across SAP ERP components such as FI, SCM, and HCM, the chart of accounts has turned into a strategic core performance-reporting data structure.

One of the leading practices for effective financial reporting is to establish a single, global chart of accounts that is used across the enterprise. This promotes standardized financial processes and enables cross-entity reporting. Business analysis will be significantly enhanced through the overall data management discipline that a unified chart of accounts brings culturally to the enterprise. Additionally, you can eliminate duplicate efforts and promote progressive financial practice and compliance. A unified chart of accounts provides the following benefits:

▶ Consistent accounting definitions and account usage across the enterprise

▶ An efficient and consistent data collection mechanism

▶ An efficient data processing flow of information for financial and management reporting

▶ Increased data integrity across different systems

▶ Greater flexibility for financial reporting and analysis

▶ Support for the audit and control of financial transactions

There are three charts of accounts to meet regulatory, group, and local requirements in SAP ERP. The hierarchical structures of G/L accounts for financial statements are defined in financial statement versions per chart of accounts. Refer to Figure 2.3 for a schematic view of the chart of accounts and financial statement versions.

Let's look at each chart of accounts type in more detail:

▶ **Operational Chart of Accounts**
The operational chart of accounts contains the G/L accounts, called *operational accounts*, that are used for recording financial transactions in a company code.

▶ **Group Chart of Accounts**
The group chart of accounts contains the G/L accounts, called *group accounts*, that are used by the entire group for consolidated financial reporting. This allows the enterprise to provide financial reports for the entire group.

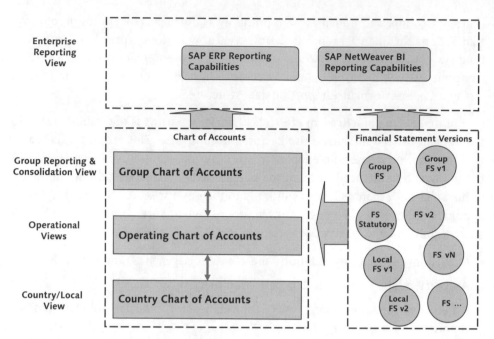

Figure 2.3 Chart of Accounts Definition and Mapping

▸ **Country Chart of Accounts**

SAP allows accounts in the operating chart of accounts to be mapped to country charts in the account master data with G/L accounts, called *alternative accounts*. The country chart of accounts is used for countries that have special country legislation and requirements such as submitting financial statements in a pre-defined format, that is, account number and description. Countries listed below are typical countries that require a country chart of accounts:

▸ Western Europe: Spain, Portugal, France, Belgium, Italy, Norway, Greece, etc.

▸ Eastern Europe: Hungary, Poland, Czech, Slovakia, Greece, some Russian Federation countries, etc.

SAP ERP contains predefined country-specific charts of accounts in the standard business content. These country-specific charts of accounts can be used by companies as a reference to establish their own country-specific charts of accounts.

Leading Design Practices for Standardizing Charts of Accounts

There are a number of leading design practices for standardizing charts of accounts in SAP implementations. The main practices are:

▶ Define group-wide common coding logic.

▶ Implement leading GAAP valuation at operational chart of accounts level across all business entities.

▶ Use natural accounts definitions in the G/L and leverage other coding blocks such as cost centers.

▶ Align the operational chart of accounts with the group chart of accounts.

▶ Do not use hierarchical coding logic (including hard coding) of groupings (i.e., geographical area dependent, country dependent).

▶ Use country-specific charts linked to operational charts when required.

▶ Define consistent accounting adjustment functionality to deliver local GAAPs.

Chart of Accounts Assignment

In the configuration, the group chart of accounts is assigned to the operational chart of accounts. The operational chart of accounts and country chart of accounts are assigned to a company code at the company code definition. Refer to Figure 2.4 for the chart of accounts assignment in SAP ERP. In our example, **group chart of accounts CONS** is assigned to **operational chart of accounts INT**. Both **operational chart of accounts INT** and **country chart of accounts CAES** are assigned to company code **2300** in the global definition of company code.

With this assignment, you can maintain alternative accounts and group accounts in the operational accounts master data so that both alternative accounts and group accounts are updated at the time of posting to operational accounts automatically, resulting in a clear and transparent view for audit. Let's take a closer look at how alternative accounts and group accounts are maintained in the G/L account master data and examine a vendor posting example to see how alternative and group accounts are updated simultaneously.

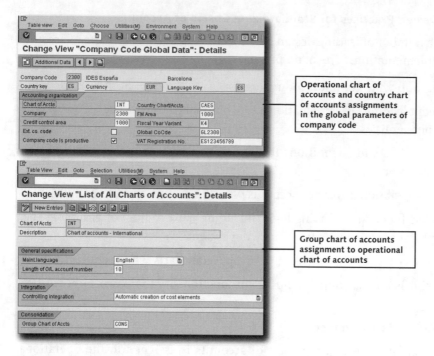

Figure 2.4 Chart of Accounts Assignment in SAP ERP

G/L Account Master Data Definition

As we mentioned above, alternative and group accounts are assigned to operational accounts in the master data. Figure 2.5 illustrates an example G/L account master data in SAP ERP. Alternative account 164000, defined under the country chart of accounts, is assigned to the operational account **160000** at the company code level (left side of the figure). Operational account **160000** is assigned to the **group account 201100** at the chart of accounts level (right side of the figure).

When posting a financial document, all three accounts are updated in the financial document. Figure 2.6 shows an example of a vendor financial posting document. The reconciliation account of vendor 1000 is 160000 in our example. As you can see from the posting, vendor account 1000 is updated with its alternative account (164000) and group account (201100) simultaneously in the invoice. The offsetting entry is posted to the travel expense operational account (474240) that has an alternative account (624000) and group account (312400).

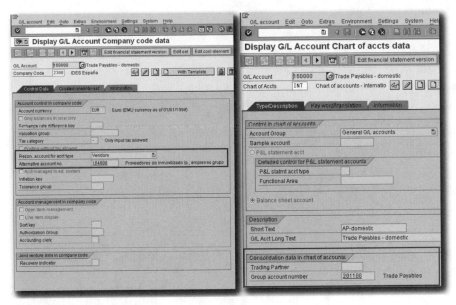

Figure 2.5 G/L Account Master Data Definition

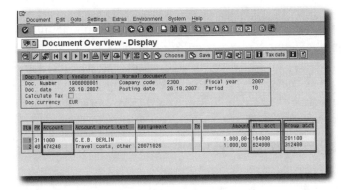

Figure 2.6 Financial Posting Example

Now that we have explained the chart of accounts and the relationship with the chart of accounts, along with how the alternative and group accounts are maintained in the operational account master data, let's examine how to define G/L account master data in SAP NetWeaver BI using the SAP NetWeaver BI business content InfoObject.

G/L Account InfoObject

The business content InfoObject for the G/L account in SAP NetWeaver BI is 0GL_ACCOUNT. Figure 2.7 and Figure 2.8 illustrate the definition of G/L Account InfoObject 0GL_ACCOUNT in SAP NetWeaver BI. You can see how G/L account master data 160000 (how it is defined in SAP ERP was shown in Figure 2.5) is defined in SAP NetWeaver BI with this example. Six tabs are available in the definition of InfoObjects, as follows:

▶ **General**
On the **General** tab, you define basic characteristics of the InfoObject, that is, description, data type (CHAR, NUMC…), length, and so on.

▶ **Business Explorer**
The **Business Explorer** tab is used to specify whether the characteristic appears as a textual description or as a key in SAP NetWeaver BI reports.

▶ **Master Data/Texts**
You identify whether the characteristic has attributes or texts on the **Master Data/Texts** tab. If the characteristic has its own texts, you need to make at least one text selection (short, medium length, long text).

▶ **Hierarchy**
You identify whether the characteristic can have hierarchies and hierarchy settings on the **Hierarchy** tab. Hierarchies are used to depict alternative views of the data in reporting. A hierarchy is like a tree structure that includes nodes and leaves. The nodes represent the sublevels, and leaves are represented by the characteristic values. You can either create hierarchies in SAP NetWeaver BI or extract them from source systems.

You can see the **Master Data/Texts** and **Hierarchy** tabs of InfoObject 0GLAC-COUNT in Figure 2.7.

▶ **Compounding**
A compounding characteristic is needed to define characteristic values uniquely. If there are identical characteristic values describing different objects for the same characteristic in the source system or various source systems, you have to extract the values to SAP NetWeaver BI in such a way that they will be unique. For example, you can create a G/L account in different charts of accounts. To extract the identical G/L accounts created in different charts of accounts, chart of accounts InfoObject (0CHRT_ACCTS) must be defined as a compounding characteristic for InfoObject 0GL_ACCOUNT. In our example, G/L account 160000

is created in CAUS, GKR, and INT charts of accounts. To extract values from account 160000 from different charts of accounts, InfoObject 0CHRT_ACCTS is defined as a compounding characteristic (see highlight 1 and 2 in Figure 2.8).

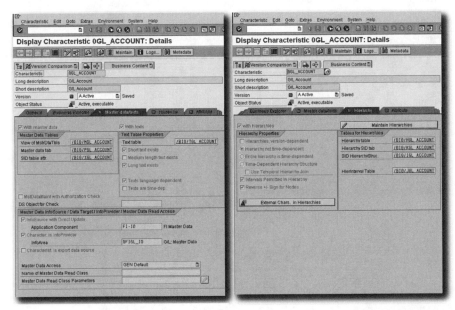

Figure 2.7 Master Data/Text and Hierarchy Tabs of G/L Account InfoObject in SAP NetWeaver BI

▶ **Attributes**

You can assign attributes to the characteristic on the **Attributes** tab. Attributes are used to describe the characteristics in detail. In highlight 3 in Figure 2.8, you see that one of the attributes of the characteristic 0GL_ACCOUNT is financial statement item **InfoObject (0GLACCEXT)**. If you check the **with master data indicator** box in the **Master Data/Texts** tab, you can specify the attributes and details of these attributes together with the characteristic. There are two types of attributes: *display attributes (DIS)* and *navigation attributes (NAV)*.

If you define an attribute as a display attribute, you can only use this attribute as additional information in reporting. In other words, you cannot navigate using this attribute in SAP NetWeaver BI reports. If you define an attribute as a navigation attribute, you can use this attribute to navigate in reporting. In Figure 2.8, the financial statement item (0GLACCEXT) is defined as a display attribute, so it is possible to display financial statement item(s) in SAP NetWeaver BI financial queries that use the 0GL_ACCOUNT InfoObject, but it is not possible to navigate through the financial statement item(s) in these reports. A characteristic that is used as a navigation attribute can also have its own navigation attributes. These are called transitive attributes. You can activate these as well, thus making them available for reporting.

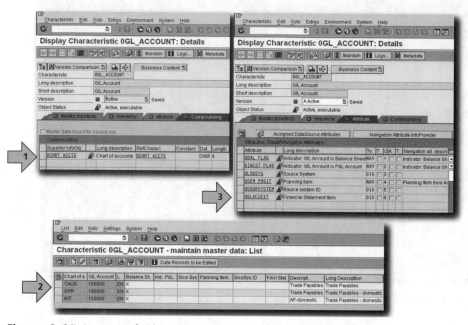

Figure 2.8 G/L Account InfoObject Master Data in SAP NetWeaver BI

Note

If compounding and attribute characteristics are used extensively, the performance of SAP NetWeaver BI queries can be adversely affected.

2.2.3 Standardizing the Financial Reporting Structure

The *financial statement version* determines the format and structure of financial statements in both SAP ERP and SAP NetWeaver BI. Each financial statement version is defined per chart of accounts. You can define the financial statement versions to meet the reporting requirements for your main valuation accounting standards, local financial accounting standards, and group reporting. For example, you can have a local financial statement version using the country chart of accounts and a group financial statement version using the group chart of accounts.

The financial statement version has a hierarchical tree structure. You assign accounts and the range of accounts hierarchically in the structure and determine the totals and subtotals. You can group accounts under headers such as assets, liabilities and equity, and income statement. Under each of these headers, you can create as many descriptors or other nodes as needed for financial reporting and analysis purposes. By default, the nodes are **Assets**, **Liabilities**, **P/L result**, **Net result profit**, **Net result loss**, **Not assigned**, and **Financial statement notes**.

SAP ERP provides predefined financial statement versions with a predefined chart of accounts. You can use SAP-provided financial statement versions or you can create your own financial statement version with reference to predefined ones. Technically, you can create many financial statement versions per chart of accounts in SAP ERP. However, the best practices dictate that you should unify and standardize the financial reporting structure for the main valuation and group accounting requirements. For statutory reporting, you can create country-specific financial statement version(s).

The capabilities of the country-specific versions are as follows:

▶ You can create a financial statement version in a different language, for example, in the language of the country in which the company code is based.

▶ You can change the level of detail of financial statements. A detailed financial statement or grouping might be required for some countries.

Let's take a closer look at how to define financial statement versions.

Financial Statement Version Example

In the financial statement versions, you define which items are to be included in the version and the sequence and hierarchy of these items. G/L accounts not assigned to any nodes are linked automatically to an unassigned node. This is to provide integrity between the chart of accounts and the financial statement version.

Financial statement versions also provide a mechanism to control debit and credit balance display in the financial statements. This is especially important for the balance-dependent position of accounts (also called *contra accounts*). A contra account must be displayed either under assets or liabilities, depending on its balance at the financial statement runtime. For example, the positive balance of a cash account is considered as an asset, whereas the negative balance of a cash account is considered as a liability. By assigning a cash account to a financial statement item on both the assets and liabilities sides of the financial statement version with corresponding debit and credit indicators, you can control the debit and credit balance display in the financial statements. An example of contra account assignment is illustrated in Figure 2.9 and Figure 2.10. In this example, commerzbank accounts are assigned to financial statement item 1044000/24, with a debit indicator on the asset side, whereas they are assigned to financial statement item 2042010/24 on the liabilities side. Thus, the balance of commerzbank accounts will be considered as assets under the node checks, cash on hand, deposit if the accounts have debit balance, whereas the balance of these accounts will be considered as liabilities under due within one year if the accounts have credit balance in the financial statements.

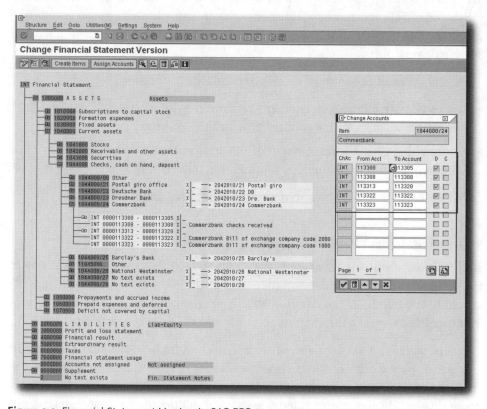

Figure 2.9 Financial Statement Version in SAP ERP

New features of financial statement versions in SAP ERP

As of SAP ERP 5.0, financial statement versions are stored in transparent tables. This new feature of SAP ERP provides the following advantages:

▶ 20 hierarchy levels are available (previously 10).

▶ 1000 subitems are available per item (previously 99).

▶ There are fixed items for financial statement notes.

▶ Financial statement versions can be transported.

The financial statement versions are also used for reporting in SAP NetWeaver BI and SAP SEM-BCS, which promotes consistency for financial statement reports across these systems. The leading practice is to define the financial statement versions in the source SAP ERP system(s) and use them consistently in different system landscapes. Let's examine the financial statement item master data in SAP NetWeaver BI.

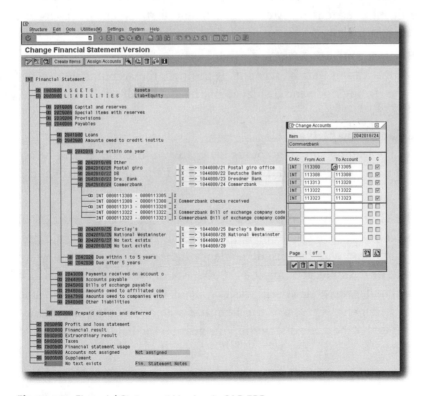

Figure 2.10 Financial Statement Version in SAP ERP

Financial Statement Item InfoObject

The InfoObject for a financial statement item in SAP NetWeaver BI is 0GLACCEXT. The InfoObject 0GLACCEXT is used in SAP NetWeaver BI queries to generate financial statements. We often hear the following questions from SAP customers: Is it possible to use 0GL_ACCOUNT and its hierarchy instead of 0GLACCEXT in SAP NetWeaver BI financial statement reports? Will it show the same values? The answer to these questions is no. Although it is possible to define hierarchical structure for 0GL_ACCOUNT, it is not possible to display contra accounts either under **assets** or **liabilities**, depending on its balance at the financial statement runtime, by using 0GL_ACCOUNT. You can only show the balances in financial statements accurately by using the 0GLACCEXT InfoObject, which contains a special attribute called **balance dependency hierarchy node (0BAL_DEPEND)**. The balance dependency hierarchy node has three values:

▸ **No Balance dependency (" ")**
The financial statement item is always either on the assets side or the liabilities side of the financial statement. Most of the financial statement items are included under this category.

▸ **Suppress Balance if positive ("1")**
If the sum of the leading side of accounts is positive, the accounts will be aggregated to the leading node and displayed on the assets side of financial statements.

▸ **Suppress Balance if negative ("2")**
If the sum of the leading side of accounts is negative, the accounts will be aggregated to the leading node and displayed on the liabilities side of financial statements.

Figure 2.11 shows an example InfoObject 0GLACCEXT hierarchy for financial statement version INT. As you see in the figure, the commerzbank financial statement items are indicated with balance dependency indicator 1 and 2, as they are contra accounts. For example, if account 113000 has a debit balance, its balance will be displayed under the node checks, cash on hand, deposit on the assets side of the financial statement, whereas if the item has a credit balance, its balance will be displayed under the node due within one year on the liabilities side of the financial statement.

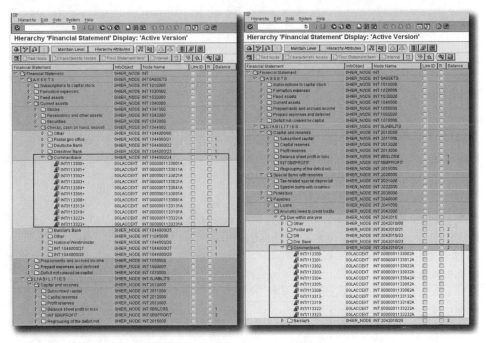

Figure 2.11 Financial Statement Item Hierarchy in SAP NetWeaver BI

Note that 0GLACCEXT is the only InfoObject with a hierarchy that has the hard-coded attribute 0BAL_DEPEND. The financial InfoProviders get data with a special functional module that is hard-coded for InfoObject 0GLACCEXT. Thus, you should not create custom InfoObjects instead of using 0GLACCEXT.

Key Structure for Characteristic 0GLACCEXT

The key field for the characteristic 0GLACCEXT includes several parts. Figure 2.12 illustrates the key structure for the characteristic 0GLACCEXT. As shown in the figure, the first 4 characters correspond to the *chart of accounts*. The next 12 characters represent the *G/L account* or *functional area*. The next character is the *item indicator*. As we explained earlier, the item indicator (balance dependency indicator) shows whether a financial statement item (such as a specific G/L account) is assigned to the assets or liabilities side of the financial statement. The last character corresponds to the *type of financial statement item*. There are two types of financial statement items. A corresponds to accounts, and F corresponds to functional area. The formatting of the technical display in the financial statements is performed using the special conversion exit ACCEX, which is assigned to characteristic 0GLA-CCEXT. For example, the internal key INT 0000001133001A is displayed on the financial statements as financial statement item INT/1130001+.

Name	Chart of Accounts	G/L Account or Functional Area	Item Indicator	Type of Financial Statement Item
Chars	4	12	1	1

Figure 2.12 Key Structure for Characteristic 0GLACCEXT

Transfer Rules for InfoObject 0GLACCEXT

SAP ERP provides a standard DataSource called 0GLACCEXT_T011_HIER for InfoObject 0GLACCEXT. However, the transfer rules for financial statement hierarchies cannot be delivered automatically for technical reasons. You must create the transfer rules manually after you activate the InfoObject 0GLACCEXT. Figure 2.13 illustrates these transfer rules. Note that InfoSource 0GLACCEXT has two segments: hierarchy header and hierarchy node.

Now that we have explained the design considerations and leading practices for the governance of master data, charts of accounts, and financial statement versions, we will look at a case study to illustrate the concepts covered so far in this chapter.

Case Study

Client ABC implemented an SAP system without having an effective governance model or the focus required to deliver the key business processes automatically. As a result, highly distributed ERP enterprise architectures with little to no business integration have been implemented. Each entity had a different local version of chart of accounts according to their local GAAP. The generation of financial statements was taking too much effort and time because of the different level of interpretation of the accounting manual. Significant time was incurred processing low-value invoices. The corporate allocations process was very complex and not transparent. The consolidation and reporting process was manual, which encouraged local control in the closing process. There was no integrated set of data or consistent process flow to support statutory, regulatory, and management reporting. This resulted in client ABC facing major challenges in producing their financial reports.

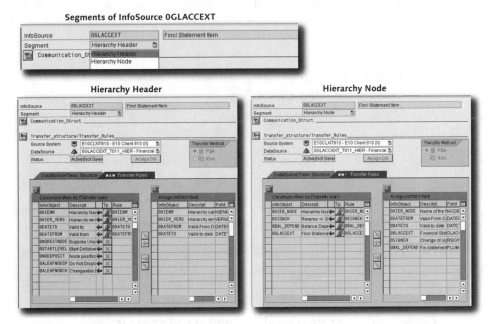

Figure 2.13 Transfer Rules of InfoObject 0GLACCEXT

The organization set a long-term strategy of "harmonize, integrate, expand." They decided to improve usage of SAP standard functionalities and improve the visibility of global accounting (56 legal entities in 12 countries worldwide, 10 business divisions globally, 28,000 G/L account codes, etc.).

The project team first started to harmonize and unify the chart of accounts. The team used the following approach:

▶ Primary GAAP compliance to adopt across entities

▶ Top-down approach from management, legal, and statutory requirements

▶ Bottom-up approach for validation and healthy challenge from country businesses

▶ Congruence analysis overlaying charts of accounts to reduce the number of accounts required

▶ Natural definitions for accounts and a standardized definition and usage of coding blocks

▸ Focus on communication to enable effective change management and obtained ownership from key accounting stakeholders

The result:

▸ Account codes were reduced to 1,500 following a benchmark against the top four competitors in the same industry.

▸ A core set of financial accounting processes was standardized in their SAP ERP system.

▸ Increased control through common coding and reference was achieved.

▸ Faster access to more and transparent financial information was enabled through a common financial language.

▸ Operational efficiency was increased, and more timely and accurate information was provided.

Next, we look at how to comply with international accounting standards.

2.2.4   Comply with International Accounting Standards

Financial reporting design must support financial processes in accordance with different accounting standards as well as for various statutory reporting requirements. Additionally, it is necessary to be able to identify the specific type of adjustments to keep adjustments aligned with the proper category of accounting standards. Parallel financial reporting in the G/L with SAP ERP financials enables you to meet many local and international reporting requirements with two powerful methods:

▸ Account method

▸ Ledger method

Both methods provide capabilities for the reporting of financial statements in accordance with different accounting standards. Note that the account method has been available in previous releases of SAP ERP.

Account Method

The account method enables parallel reporting by using sets of general ledger accounts. There are two main set of accounts: common accounts and GAAP-specific accounts. *Common accounts* are the accounts used for postings that are valid for all accounting regulations. Accounts such as cash, bank, accounts receivables, accounts payables, and material stock are classified using this method as common accounts. *GAAP-specific accounts* are the accounts used only in GAAP-specific postings. GAAP reporting includes these postings in addition to the postings to the common accounts. Accounts such as purchase accounts, statutory depreciation, and GAAP retained earnings are classified as GAAP-specific accounts.

In the account method, common postings are made using the common accounts, and GAAP-specific postings are made using the GAAP-specific accounts. For example, IFRS-specific postings are made to IFRS-specific accounts, whereas all other postings are generated with common accounts. Reporting capability is based on the accounts with this method. When you generate a financial statement for a specific accounting standard, the common accounts and specific accounts for this accounting standard are evaluated. For example, by reporting on common accounts and IFRS-specific accounts, you can generate the financial statement according to IFRS. This means you need to create financial statement versions for each valuation, which includes the common and GAAP-specific accounts such as the IFRS version, U.S. GAAP version and Local GAAP version. The account method requires separate retained earning accounts for each valuation. Profit and loss balances are carried forward through GAAP-specific retained earning accounts. A schematic view of the account method is illustrated in Figure 2.14.

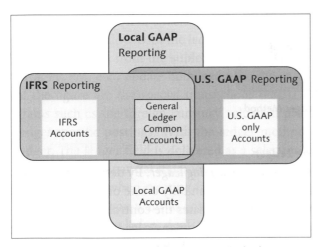

Figure 2.14 Schematic View of the Account Method

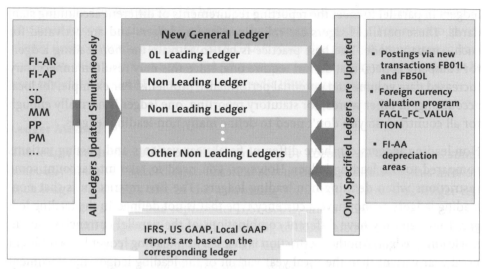

Figure 2.16 Values and Integration Flow with the Ledger Method

---

Special ledger component

Some companies use the special ledger (SL) component to define ledgers for reporting purposes. User-defined ledgers are kept as general ledgers or subsidiary ledgers with various account assignment objects. Account assignment objects can either be SAP dimensions from various applications such as profit center or custom-defined dimensions such as region. The special ledgers enable reporting at various levels using the values from the various components. The functions available in the special ledgers enable you to collect and combine information, create and modify totals, and distribute actual and plan values. The values are transferred to the special ledgers from other SAP applications and external systems.

The ledger method explained in this section is the "ledger method" delivered in the new G/L. You should not confuse this method with the ledger method available in the special ledger component, although the new G/L in SAP ERP uses the special ledger technique to save total values.

If you are already using the special ledger, you can continue to use the ledger method in the special ledger in SAP ERP. However, note that SAP will develop reporting functionalities for the ledger method in the G/L. The new G/L provides one-stop integrated reconciliation of the ledger that combines different ledgers. You can eliminate any need for a separate cost-of-sales ledger, special-purpose ledger, reconciliation ledger, or profit-center ledger.

Example Posting with Ledger Method

Figure 2.17 shows an example of how postings update two ledgers simultaneously. As you can see in the figure, the system updated ledgers in different levels of detail. The posting is updated with the cost center, profit center, and segment details for ledger 0L, whereas none of these dimensions are updated in ledger N1. This control is achieved through a *scenario*, which is a new term introduced to SAP ERP. Scenarios are used to identify the dimensions that should be updated in ledgers. For example, the cost center, profit center, and segment dimensions are updated in ledger 0L, as the relevant scenarios are assigned to this ledger, whereas the document was only updated at the G/L account and company code level in ledger N1, as no scenario is assigned to ledger N1. Six scenarios are delivered in SAP ERP:

- ▶ Segmentation (FIN_SEGM)

- ▶ Cost Center Update (FIN_CCA)

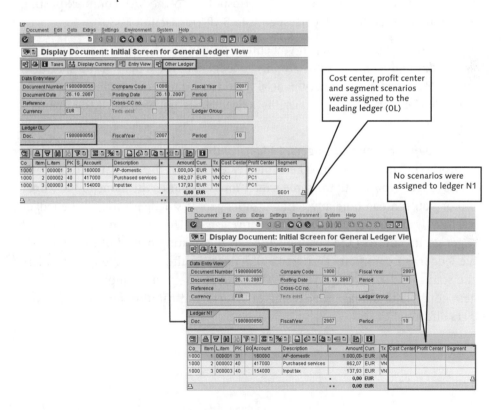

Figure 2.17 Financial Posting Updating All Ledgers

- ▶ Preparation for Consolidation (FIN_CONS)

- ▶ Business Area (FIN_GSBER)

- ▶ Profit Center Update (FIN_PCA)

- ▶ Cost of Sales Accounting (FIN_UK)

A ledger can be assigned to one or more scenarios, or even six at once. There is no rule regarding which scenarios should be assigned to which ledgers. The decision of how many scenarios to assign to the ledger depends on your business requirements and how to set up the ledger method.

Ledger-Specific Postings

As mentioned above, the new G/L provides two new transactions for adjustment and correction postings related to particular accounting principles, FB01L and FB50L, for the ledger solution. FB01L corresponds to the SAP complex posting Transaction FB01, and FB50L corresponds to SAP Transaction FB50.

With these special transactions, if you enter a ledger or ledger group in the ledger group field, the document is posted only to ledgers in the ledger group specified. Figure 2.18 illustrates a special financial posting example in which ledger group N1 only has ledger N1. Thus, only the ledger N1 is updated with the financial posting.

A *ledger group* is a group of ledgers. Ledgers in the ledger group are combined for joint processing in a function. When you create a ledger, the system automatically creates a ledger group with the same name. You can change the name of the ledger group or you can combine any number of ledgers in a ledger group. One ledger in a ledger group has to be the *representative ledger*. The representative ledger of a ledger group controls the posting period. If the posting period of the representative ledger is open, you can post to all ledgers in the ledger group, regardless of the status of their posting period. Thus, we advise you to implement built-in system controls to manage the closing of ledgers and running reports out of the ledgers effectively.

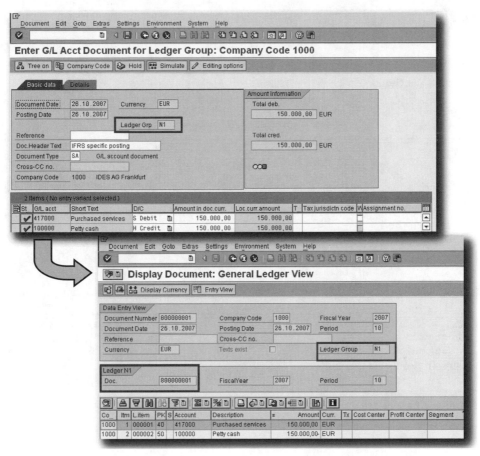

Figure 2.18 Special Transaction Posting

Which Parallel Reporting Method Is Right for Your Organization?

SAP considers both account and ledger methods to be equivalent, and they recommend using the ledger solution method if you have many G/L accounts. You can also use a combination of these two methods. It is not easy to decide which method to use for your enterprise, and a number of factors need to be considered. The decision about the reporting method also depends upon the enterprise culture and existing systems. In Figure 2.19, you can see reporting methods listed with the associated benefits, issues, and risks. This information will help you decide which reporting method best suits your organization.

Options	Benefits	Issues/Risks
Account Method	• Method is well-known by SAP users • All methods of parallel valuation (i.e., value adjustments or results analysis) are supported • Standard reporting is available • Retained earnings account and balance carry forward - a separate retained earnings account for each accounting principle is maintained • Financial statement versions - When you create financial statements, you can select a separate structure for each accounting standards • Complete postings - Perform complete postings in the specific account areas	• It may cause difficulties in controlling the number of G/L accounts in global implementations • It may be difficult to model different fiscal year variants for across various accounting standards • Additional validations are required to ensure that there are no crossover postings between different GAAP accounts
Ledger Method	• Uses fewer G/L accounts and gives better control over the chart of accounts. • The method is transparent and easy to understand. • Different fiscal year variants can be used for parallel ledgers • Different posting control variant can be used for parallel ledgers • Ledgers have complete postings • Currency valuations for different accounting standards will use the same accounts, but post automatically to different ledgers • Adjustment postings for different accounting standards can be posted to the specified ledger • Value adjustments for accounts receivable are also supported by this method • Financial statement version maintenance is easier due to fewer accounts • There is no need to use separate carry forward accounts because each ledger has its own balance	• The data volume could increase dramatically • You need to create a data source to extract data from non-leading ledgers in SAP ERP to SAP NetWeaver BI
Ledger and Account Method Combination	• Using both standard SAP parallel accounting methods together can bring a combined benefit and eradicate the issues/risks related to each method, when used individually. • Starting with the account method and moving to Ledger method is easier than the other way around • Ledger method can be used limited to certain company codes	• Potential risk of overcomplicating the solution methods. • Data extraction to SAP NetWeaver BI has to be adjusted to suit each method

Figure 2.19 Benefits and Issues and Risks of Reporting Methods

2.2.5 Automating the Reconciliation of Intercompany Transactions

The reconciliation of intercompany transactions is a mandatory process, which needs to occur before generating financial statements. The process for the reconciliation of intercompany transactions is often not standard, centralized, or monitored for compliance across the enterprise. This may result in huge imbalances and requires significant time and effort for reconciliation. By introducing automation and centralization, the process becomes more efficient and simpler to use, issues are identified early, and costs are reduced. More importantly, you can generate your financial statements on time.

Program RFICRC20 (Transaction FB2E) was formerly used to check intercompany documents based on business transactions and clear any differences necessary for reconciling the associated companies within the single SAP system. This program is no longer available in SAP ERP. SAP ERP Financials includes a new intercompany reconciliation tool that can load and store documents or totals from both SAP and non-SAP systems in a central database repository.

Cross-System Reconciliation Example

Imagine a company with six systems, in which each system has to reconcile individually with the other systems (left side of Figure 2.20). This type of reconciliation takes enormous time and effort. You can transform this complex reconciliation network into a single centralized reconciliation system (right side of Figure 2.20). The new *cross-system intercompany reconciliation tool* in SAP ERP financials allows documents or totals from SAP and non-SAP systems to be loaded and stored in a central database repository.

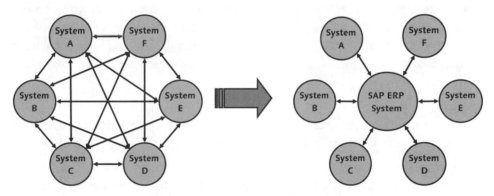

Figure 2.20 Reconciliation of Cross System Intercompany Transactions

With the reconciliation of cross-system intercompany tools, you can match, reconcile, and recall data for reconciliation analysis within SAP ERP and other SAP and non-SAP systems. By doing so, you can achieve streamlined, standardized reconciliation process. These new reconciliation programs provide more functionality and flexibility and let you reconcile data across multiple systems. Figure 2.21 shows an overview of the cross-system intercompany reconciliation process.

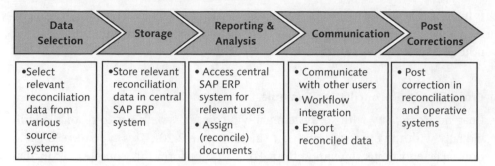

Figure 2.21 Cross-System Intercompany Reconciliation Process

Let's look at each step in more detail, as follows:

▶ **Data Selection**
The first step of the reconciliation of intercompany transactions is to select relevant data from the source systems. With this step, data is selected from both SAP and non-SAP systems for reconciliation. The selected data includes vendor and customer documents for the associated companies, and intercompany G/L account postings.

▶ **Storage**
The system selects the data to be reconciled from the operational systems of the companies and transfers it to the central reconciliation database in SAP ERP.

▶ **Reporting and Analysis**
Once you have transferred the operational data to the reconciliation database, you can automatically reconcile intercompany transactions across all entities and systems.

▶ **Communication**
As a result of the reporting and analysis step, the imbalances are reported to reviewers by means of different communication techniques, such as mail and fax, to operating companies to resolve differences. You can also create notes for any other means of communication and attach any supporting documents centrally in the database. You can update the status as well, that is, in process, on hold, clarification needed, requested correcting posting, and so on (see Figure 2.22).

▶ **Post Corrections**
The last step is the operating company carrying out the required post corrections and adjustments. After the data is corrected in the operating company's system, the data is selected and stored for reconciliation analysis again.

To monitor and reconcile cross-system intercompany transactions effectively, a governance structure should be in place to ensure that the prescribed process and policies are adhered to and that relevant parties are held accountable for any disputes and imbalances. Responsibilities and accountabilities should be clearly defined (i.e., for dispute reconciliation). You can establish a governance structure with a central team, which monitors intercompany transactions and reconciliations. The governance structure should cover all intercompany transactions in order to be effective in reducing the total number of intercompany imbalances and disputes. The authorization concept is another area you need to take into account when designing the cross-system intercompany reconciliation process because the new cross-system intercompany reconciliation tool allows you to drill down the transactions from source system(s).

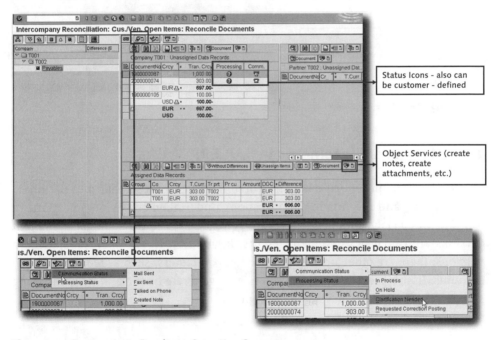

Figure 2.22 Communicate Results to Operating Company

Figure 2.23 shows an example of how to view cross-system postings. Posting document 190000000105 is not reconciled automatically. When you select the document button, you can recall the original document details from the source system. The detail of the original document is illustrated at the bottom of Figure 2.23.

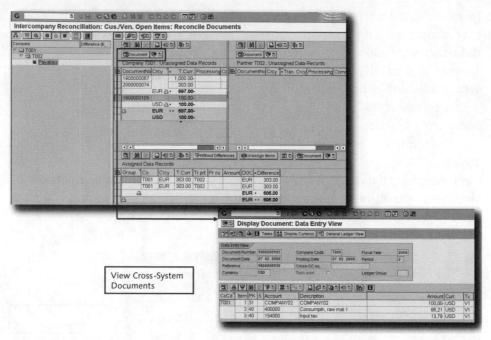

Figure 2.23 View Cross-System Documents

2.3   Financial Statements in SAP ERP

Financial statement reports are a structured financial representation of the financial positions and the financial transactions undertaken by an organization. In SAP ERP, financial statement reports are generated using the financial statement versions with financial statement reports. In addition to the financial statement versions, there are other important selection parameters, such as ledgers and G/L accounts. In this section, we show you how to generate financial statements using standard SAP ERP financial statement reports.

2.3.1   Balance Sheet and Income Statement

The balance sheet presents the financial position of the enterprise. A balance sheet has two main sections: assets and equity and liabilities. Under these sections, additional headings and subtotals are presented, such as current assets, inventories, issued capital, and reserves.

The income statement represents the financial performance of the enterprise. It has components related to the revenues, expenses, and net profit and loss for the period. The expenses are classified according to either their nature or function. The net profit and loss amount for the current period is calculated by the financial statement report and transferred to the balance sheet.

The structure of the balance sheet and income statement and information disclosed vary according to different accounting standards. Figure 2.24 illustrates an example of a balance sheet and income statement with minimum requirements according to IAS 1 presentation of financial statements. On the left side of the figure are the components of the balance sheet and the values represented by X along with comparison values of the previous reporting period. On the right side of the figure is an example of an income statement classified according to the nature of the expenses.

In SAP ERP, the balance sheet and income statements are included within the same financial statement report. In the standard financial statement reports, you do not need to make manual postings to the accumulated profits and losses. The system automatically calculates the profit and loss for the year based on the income statement for the year when you run financial statement reports, carried forward to the retained earnings account(s). Note that retained earnings accounts are defined to capture the balance of profit and loss accounts when the balance sheet accounts are carried forward to the new fiscal year and profit and loss accounts are cleared for the new fiscal year. Note also that all profit and loss accounts should be created for retained earning account of type "X" and hence are carried forward into the retained account automatically.

There are two financial statement reports in SAP ERP. One is the classic financial statement report, and the other is the new financial statement report. The classic financial statement report (program RFBILA00) has been available since SAP R/2 and has been slightly modified with SAP ERP to include a ledger and other dimensions on the selection screen. With the new general ledger (G/L), SAP provided one-stop integrated reconciliation of multiple ledgers. Ledgers such as consolidation staging ledgers, profit center ledgers, and cost of sales ledgers are combined into a one-stop ledger. Thus, the new G/L provides a unified data structure resulting in a single source of truth. The capabilities of the new G/L reporting are based on a unified reporting database. In a single data record, you can include different dimensions, such as profit center, segment, and functional area. As a result of this unified data reporting structure, a new financial statement report has been developed, which is based on the drilldown reporting tool, provides flexible analysis, and easily generates segmented financial statements based on dimensions other than the company code such as segment, profit center, and so on. (Note that we cover segment reporting in Chapter 3.) Let's take a closer look at the capabilities of the New Financial Statement report and Classic Financial Statement report.

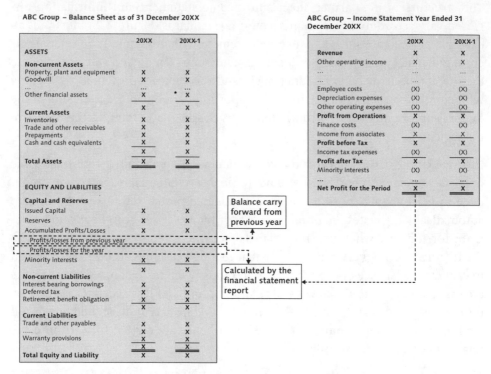

Figure 2.24 Financial Statement Structure and Balance Carry Forward

The New Financial Statement Report

To access the new Financial Statement report, follow the menu path **Accounting • Financial Accounting • General Ledger • Information System • General Ledger Reports (New) • Financial Statement / Cash Flow • General • Actual/ Actual Comparison • Financial Statement Actual / Actual Comparison** (Transaction S_PL0_86000028).

The New Financial Statement report is a *drilldown report*. From the report output screen, you can drill down to the additional dimensions and display balances. Figure 2.25 shows an example of an output of the New Financial Statement report.

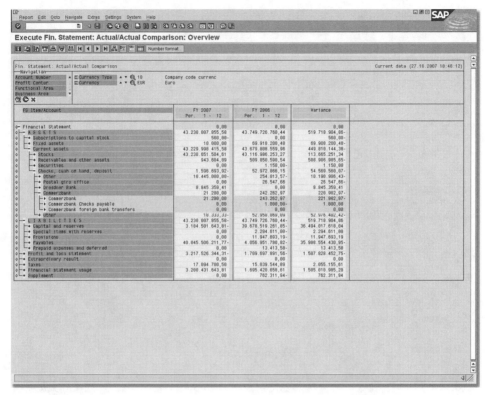

Figure 2.25 New Financial Statement Report with Classic Drilldown Output

The drilldown capabilities allow you to analyze details of account balances with the additional dimensions. In addition, you can call up other reports (i.e., line items) from the line value you are interested in to see the document details. For example, you might want to see the details of commerzbank balance. By clicking on the **commerzbank** line and selecting line items from the **Goto** menu, you can call up the **G/L Account Line Item Display G/L View** report to analyze the details of the account balance, showing the commerzbank balance by account. See Figure 2.26 for an illustration of this detailed line item report.

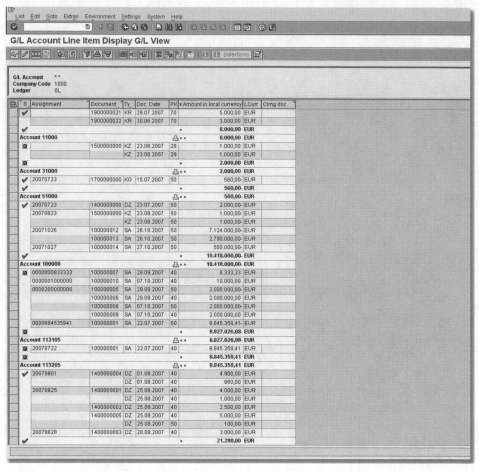

Figure 2.26 Line Items Report Called from New Financial Statement Report

You can also run the New Financial Statement report in graphical report output mode to get a more spreadsheet-like output. This display is based on SAP list viewer (ALV) capability. (Note that we cover the functionalities of ALV in Chapter 12.) Here you can drag and drop objects and easily navigate between the characteristics. You can also call up a Line Items report for the selected line by using **Goto •Line items.** Figure 2.27 illustrates the New Financial Statement report in graphical form and shows the menu path of how to call up the Line Items report.

The Classic Financial Statement Report

When you activate the new G/L, all standard reports in SAP ERP read data from the new G/L tables. Thus, you can also use the Classic Financial Statement report for generating the financial statements. To access the Classic Financial Statement, follow the menu path **Accounting • Financial Accounting • General Ledger • Periodic Processing • Closing • Report • General Ledger Reports (New) • Financial Statements / Cash Flow Reporting • General • Actual / Actual Comparison • Financial Statement Actual / Actual Comparison** (Transaction S_ALR_87012284, standard report RFBILA00).

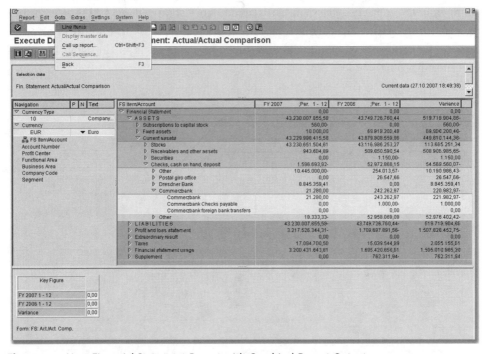

Figure 2.27 New Financial Statement Report with Graphical Report Output

Perhaps the most important difference between the Classic Financial Statement and the New Financial Statement report is that the New Financial Statement report supports segmented financial statements better than the Classic Financial Statement. Although you can specify the segment reporting dimension in the selection screen of both reports (note that the segment reporting dimensions are in the dynamic selection of the Classic Financial Statement report), the Classic Financial Statement report does not show the segment report dimensions in the report output, which may create confusion. Another difference between these two reports is the currency translation. In the Classic Financial Statement report, you can enter the display currency, the key date for translation, and the exchange rate type for translation in the selection screen, and these parameters will be shown in the report output. On the other hand, the currency translation functionality of the New Financial Statement report is based on drilldown reporting functions. You can only translate the amount to another currency in the report output by selecting the exchange rate key and translation key.

Figure 2.28 shows an example of the output of the Classic Financial Statement report with ALV tree control. In addition to ALV tree control, you can generate the Financial Statement in a classical list, grid control list output, and ALV tree control as structured balance list formats. Note that you cannot call up Line Item or other reports from the Classic Financial Statement report, as it is in the New Financial Statement report.

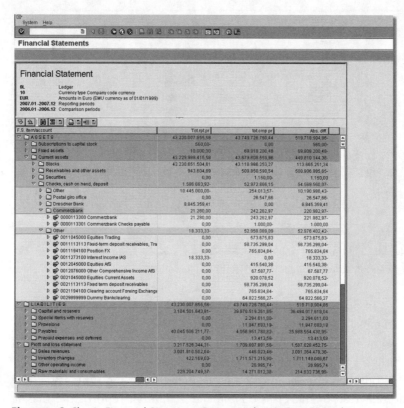

Figure 2.28 Classic Financial Statement Report with ALV Tree Control

2.3.2 Cash Flow Statement

Cash flow statements show the historical changes in cash and cash equivalents, classified for the reporting period as cash flow from operating, investing, and financing activities. Classification by activity provides information for assessing the impact of those activities on the financial position of the company. *IAS 7 Cash Flow Statements* sets the reporting requirements and standards for the cash flow statement representation. Cash flow statement requirements for U.S. GAAP are stated in *FASB Statement No. 95* (SFAS 95: Statement of Financial Accounting Standards No. 95). The amendments of FASB Statement No. 95 are stated in FASB Statement No. 104.

There are three standard cash flow reports in SAP ERP. Note that they have been created as example drilldown reports and only work for company codes using the SAP delivered financial statement version INT. Table 2.1 outlines the standard SAP delivered cash flow reports along with the transaction, report and form names.

Transaction	Report Name	Report	Report Form
S_ALR_87012271	Cash Flow (Direct Method)	0SAPRATIO-04	0SAPRATIO-04
S_ALR_87012272	Cash Flow (Indirect Method) Variant 1	0SAPRATIO-03	0SAPRATIO-03
S_ALR_87012273	Cash Flow (Indirect Method) Variant 1	0SAPRATIO-01	0SAPRATIO-01

Table 2.1 Cash Flow Statement Reports in SAP ERP

As we mentioned above, you will not get any results from these reports unless your company is using the financial statement version INT, as the report definition is hard-coded to the financial statement version INT. However, you can define your own cash flow statement reports by using these predefined cash statement reports as a reference. We will cover how to define your own drilldown report by using an example cash flow statement report in the Drilldown Reporting section of Chapter 12. To access SAP standard delivered cash flow reports follow the menu path **Accounting • Financial Accounting • General Ledger • Periodic Processing • Closing • Report • General Ledger Reports (New) • Financial Statements / Cash Flow Reporting • General • Cash Flow**.

Cash flow statement reports support direct and indirect cash flow methods. With the direct method, major classes of gross cash receipts and gross payments are disclosed. With the indirect method, the cash flow from operating activities is determined by adjusting the net profit or loss.

Figure 2.29 shows an example output of a cash flow statement using the direct method with classic drilldown output. You can see that the cash flow from operations is categorized under sales collection, material disbursement, and personal disbursement.

Note that there are also some country-specific cash flow reports available under the **Financial Statements / Cash Flow Reporting** menu path.

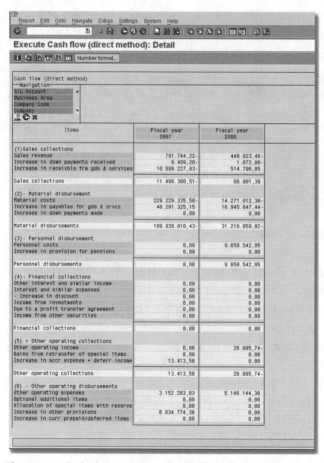

Figure 2.29 Cash Flow Direct Method with Classic Drilldown Output

2.4   Financial Statements in SAP NetWeaver BI

You can use SAP NetWeaver BI for more advanced and flexible reporting. SAP NetWeaver BI business content includes standard InfoProviders and InfoObjects to model financial statement reporting and other G/L reports. Figure 2.30 shows business content InfoProviders for the General Ledger InfoArea in SAP NetWeaver BI.

In addition, SAP delivers new SAP NetWeaver BI content and new reports for general ledger with the enhancement package 3. You can only use this content if you use the enhancement package 3 for SAP ERP 6.0 and have activated the Reporting Financials business function. Note that we explain the SAP enhancement package for SAP ERP, SAP's simplified financial reporting innovation, and show the new reports in Chapter 15.

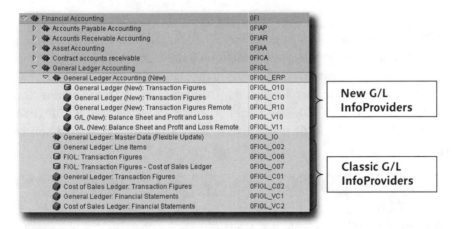

Figure 2.30 G/L Business Content InfoProviders

Let's take a closer look at the InfoProviders delivered for the new G/L:

▶ **General Ledger (New): Transaction Figures DSO**
This DSO (0FIGL_O10) provides delta process for the DataSource General Ledger: Balances, Leading Ledger (0FI_GL_10). It contains all the total records from the leading ledger in the new G/L from the source system(s).

▶ **General Ledger (New): Transaction Figures InfoCube**
This InfoCube (0FIGL_C10) contains all the transaction data from the leading ledger in the new G/L from the source system(s). It is supplied data with Info-

Source 0FI_GL_10, which includes transaction figures from the leading ledger of the new G/L.

▶ **General Ledger (New): Transaction Figures Remote InfoCube**
This InfoCube (0FIGL_R10) contains all the transaction data from the leading ledger in new G/L that was loaded from the source systems. This InfoCube reads data from the source systems in real time. It is not necessary for the data to be replicated in InfoProviders.

Balances from non-leading ledgers

The DataSource 0FI_GL_10 is designed to extract data from the leading ledger. To extract data from the non-leading ledger(s), you need to create a generic DataSource by using Transaction FAGLBW03. You can select the relevant ledger in this transaction to create a ledger-specific DataSource that extracts the total records from a specified ledger in SAP ERP. Note that no content is delivered in SAP NetWeaver BI for the generic DataSource.

Figure 2.31 shows the data flow of the General Ledger (New) Transaction Figures InfoCube and General Ledger (New) Transaction Figures Remote InfoCube. In our example, the data is first extracted to the General Ledger (New) Transaction Figures DSO (0FI_GL_O10) and then loaded to the General Ledger (New) Transaction Figures InfoCube (0FI_GL_C10). The General Ledger (New) Transaction Figures Remote InfoCube (0FI_GL_R10) reads data directly from the connected source systems by means of BAPI.

Line item DataSource

SAP ERP 6.0 does not include the line item data extractor, which is especially required to drill back to line item details for further analysis. The line item data extractor General Ledger Accounting (New): Line Items of the Leading Ledger (0FI_GL_14) is delivered with the enhancement package 3. This DataSource is used to extract line items from the leading ledger in new G/L. To extract line items from other ledgers, you have to create separate DataSources. With the enhancement package 3, you can create a generic DataSource to extract line items from a selected ledger by using Transaction FAGLBW03. You can select the relevant ledger in this transaction to create a ledger-specific DataSource that extracts the line item records from a specified ledger in SAP ERP. Note that no content is delivered in SAP NetWeaver BI for the generic DataSource.

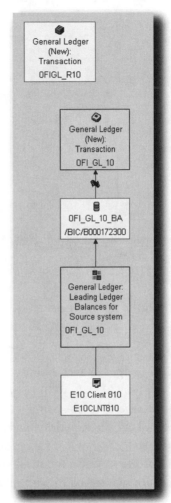

Data Flow of General Ledger (New) Transaction Figures InfoCube

Data Flow of General Ledger (New) Transaction Figures Remote InfoCube

Figure 2.31 Data Flow of General Ledger (New) Transaction Figures and General Ledger (New) Transaction Figures Remote InfoCubes

Figure 2.32 shows the data model of the General Ledger (New) Transaction Figures InfoCube and the General Ledger (New) Transaction Figures Remote InfoCube. As you can see in the figure, the data models of both basic and remote InfoCubes are similar.

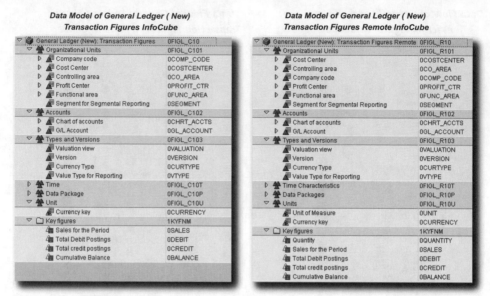

Figure 2.32 Data Model of General Ledger (New) Transaction Figures InfoCube and General Ledger (New) Transaction Figures Remote InfoCube

Let's look at the new G/L virtual InfoProviders, which don't have their own physical data storage in SAP NetWeaver BI. Virtual InfoProviders use a function module instead of DataSource. They are only used for reporting purposes.

▶ **General Ledger (New): Balance Sheet and Profit Loss InfoCube**
This InfoCube (0FIGL_V10) is a virtual InfoCube that is only used for reporting. The InfoCube does not contain any data. Queries based on this InfoCube read data by using the function module, which takes the data from the InfoCube General Ledger (New): Transaction Figures (0FIGL_C10). The function module is used to display the financial statement using a financial statement version and ensure that the contra accounts balances are displayed accurately.

▶ **General Ledger (New): Balance Sheet and Profit Loss Remote InfoCube**
This InfoCube (0FIGL_V11) is similar to the General Ledger (New): Balance Sheet and Profit Loss (0FIGL_V10). It is only used for reporting purposes. The InfoCube does not contain any data. Queries based on this InfoCube read data by using the function module, which takes the data from the InfoCube General Ledger (New): Transaction Figures Remote (0FIGL_R10). The function module is used to display the financial statement using a financial statement version and ensure that the contra accounts balances are displayed accurately.

Figure 2.33 shows the data model of the G/L (New): Balance Sheet and Profit and Loss InfoCube and G/L (New): Balance Sheet and Profit and Loss Remote Info-Cube.

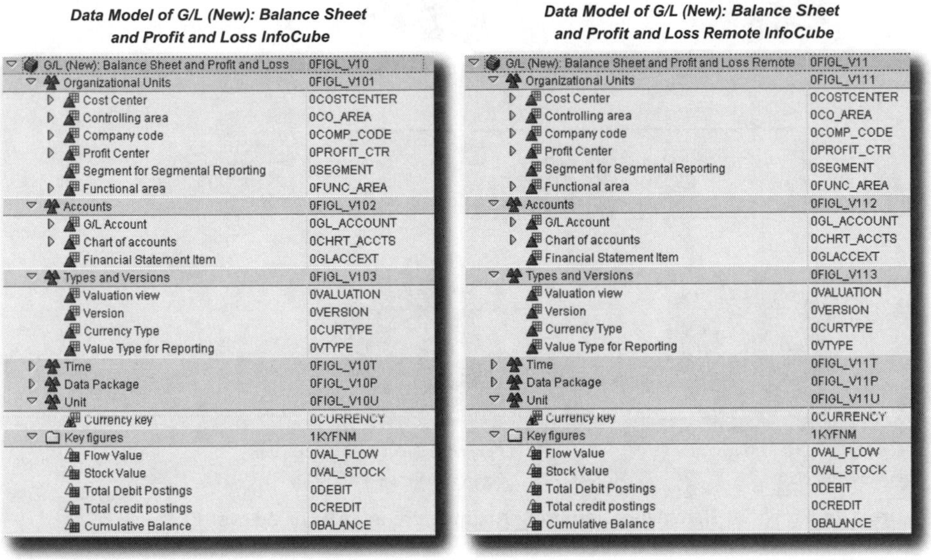

Figure 2.33 Data Model of the G/L (New): Balance Sheet and Profit and Loss InfoCube and the G/L (New): Balance Sheet and Profit and Loss Remote InfoCube

SAP offers a predefined reporting architecture for financial statements by using these virtual InfoProviders. As we explained earlier, the virtual InfoCubes do not contain any data. Queries based on this InfoCube read data by using function modules, which take the data from the InfoCube General Ledger (New): Transaction Figures (0FIGL_C10) and General Ledger (New): Transaction Figures Remote (0FIGL_R10). The function module determines the item indicator in the key for the financial statement items based on the balance in the respective node in the financial statement structure. In addition to displaying the balance of contra accounts accurately, the function module enables the calculation of the net result (retained earnings and losses). The key figure asset value (0VAL_STOCK) corresponds to asset value, and the flow value (0VAL_FLOW) contains the values of the P&L statement. By adding these two key figures, the net result is displayed in the queries based on virtual InfoProviders. Refer to Figure 2.34 for reporting architecture in SAP NetWeaver BI.

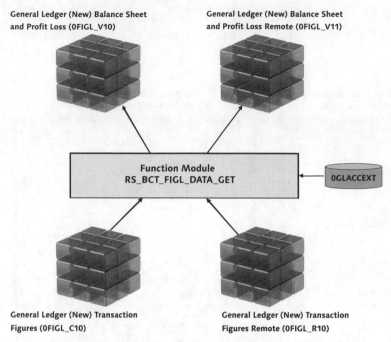

General Ledger (New) Balance Sheet and Profit Loss (0FIGL_V10)

General Ledger (New) Balance Sheet and Profit Loss Remote (0FIGL_V11)

Function Module
RS_BCT_FIGL_DATA_GET

0GLACCEXT

General Ledger (New) Transaction Figures (0FIGL_C10)

General Ledger (New) Transaction Figures Remote (0FIGL_R10)

Figure 2.34 Financial Statements Reporting Architecture in SAP NetWeaver BI

2.4.1 SAP NetWeaver BI Queries for New G/L

SAP NetWeaver BI provides reference queries in the business content for the new G/L based on the InfoProviders explained above. Figure 2.35 shows the available queries in the business content. As shown in the figure, the names of some of the queries are similar. For example, the names of queries based on the General Ledger (New) Transaction Figures and General Ledger (New) Transaction Figures Remote are alike. The difference is that the queries based on the General Ledger (New) Transaction Figures Remote can read the data in real time by means of BAPI.

Let's take a closer look at the Balance Sheet and Profit Loss (New): Actual/Actual Comparison report, which you can use as a reference to create your financial statement reports in SAP NetWeaver BI.

Figure 2.35 Business Content Queries Based on New G/L InfoProviders

Balance Sheet and Profit and Loss (New): Actual/Actual Comparison

In the business content of SAP NetWeaver 7.0 (2004s), you can use the Balance Sheet and Profit and Loss (New) Actual/Actual Comparison (0FIGL_V10_Q0001) query as a reference to create your financial statement reports. This query shows the balance sheet and profit and loss statement for the selected two reporting time frames. It enables you to calculate the net result (retained earnings and losses) as well as assign items in the financial statement version (contra items) on the basis of the balance.

The query reads the data from the InfoCube (G/L): New Balance Sheet and Profit and Loss (0FIGL_V10). There is another query with the same content and structure but based on the remote virtual InfoCube G/L (New) Balance Sheet and Profit and Loss Remote (0FIGL_V11). The name of the query is Balance Sheet and Profit and Loss (New) Actual/Actual Comparison Remote (0FIGL_V11_Q0001). With this query you can create financial statements in real time. It is not necessary for the data to be replicated in InfoProviders. Figure 2.36 shows an example of the output of the 0FIGL_V11_Q0001 query in the Web Analyzer. The query displays the financial statement based on the financial statement version, as illustrated in the SAP ERP financial statement reports (see Figure 2.25, Figure 2.27, and Figure 2.28).

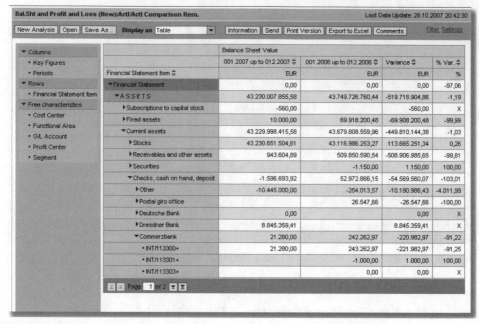

Figure 2.36 Balance Sheet and Profit and Loss (New) Actual/Actual Comparison

You can also use 0FIGL_V10_Q0001 and 0FIGL_V11_Q0001 queries to create segmented financial statements. We cover segmented financial statements in Chapter 3.

2.4.2 Consolidated Financial Statements

In addition to SAP NetWeaver BI, you can use SAP SEM-BCS to generate consolidated financial statements enterprise wide, as well as consolidated statutory reporting. Figure 2.37 shows an overview of the financial reporting process through SAP NetWeaver BI and SAP SEM-BCS.

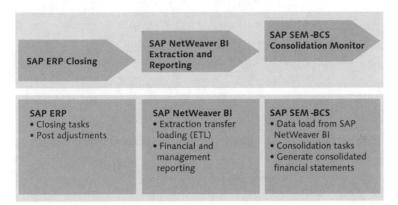

Figure 2.37 Financial Reporting Process through SAP NetWeaver BI and SAP SEM-BCS

Group-consolidated financial reporting requires the consolidation of more than one company code. Financial data from all companies is translated to group currency, intercompany unit eliminations are executed, and financial statements are aggregated. After performing the consolidation tasks, you can use SAP SEM-BCS to generate consolidated financial statements and submit them to stakeholders and regulatory bodies. The convergence of financial data in SAP SEM-BCS enables it to become the single version of truth for an organization's financial reporting. We will cover consolidation reporting with SAP SEM-BCS in Chapter 11 and explain the future direction of consolidated financial reporting in Chapter 14.

2.5 Summary

In today's competitive and regulatory environment, submitting financial statements fast and accurately and complying with international accounting standards is not optional, but mandatory. SAP ERP provides financial statements and statutory reports with the General Ledger Accounting (G/L) component within FI. In this chapter, we first focused on the financial reporting process along with financial reporting architecture in SAP ERP and SAP NetWeaver BI. Then, we discussed the key design considerations and approaches for generating accurate financial statements and statutory reports and outlined the main integration points of financial data flow across SAP ERP and SAP NetWeaver BI. Finally, we explained the SAP ERP financial statement reporting capabilities and the SAP NetWeaver BI business content for the new G/L, along with data flow and modeling examples and the business content queries.

Evaluating the range of options that are available for segment reporting within the SAP ERP system is complex, primarily due to the multitude of possible implementation solutions. Additionally, it is difficult to isolate a decision through the segment reporting approach from overall decisions regarding the integrated reporting strategy and the underlying system architecture. The emphasis in this chapter is on recommending the best foundations of segment reporting design. In addition, we explain the key reports in SAP ERP and SAP NetWeaver BI to comply with segment reporting requirements.

3 Segment Reporting

One of the requirements of *International Financial Reporting Standards (IFRS)* is to provide financial information by line of business and geographical areas to clearly identify the opportunities and risks in these areas, which is known as *segment reporting compliance (IAS 14)*. This compliance applies to companies whose equity and debt securities are publicly traded and to enterprises in the process of issuing securities to the public. In addition, any enterprise voluntarily providing segment information should comply with the requirements of the standard.

A business segment is a distinguishable part of the company that delivers an individual product or service or a group of products or services, which is subject to risks and returns that are different from other business segments. A geographical segment is a distinguishable part of the company that delivers products or services within a particular economic environment that is subject to risks and returns that are different from those of components operating in other economic environments.

Segment reporting requirements for *U. S. Generally Accepted Accounting Principles (U.S. GAAP)* are stated in *FASB Statement No.131 (SFAS 131 — Statement of Financial Accounting Standards No. 131)*. The requirements of SFAS 131 are based on the way the management regards an entity, focusing on information about the components of the business that management uses to make decisions about operating matters. In contrast to U.S. GAAP, IFRS requires the disclosure of the entity's financial statement, divided into segments based on related products and services and on geographical areas.

In spite of convergence initiatives of the accounting standards, accounting regulations using segment reporting still differ. The major differences are in the segment definition, accounting policies, and disclosure of segment information. For example, segment definition is based on risks and return profiles along with internal reporting structure in IFRS, whereas it is based on internally reported operating segments in U.S. GAAP.

Segment reports prepared for the board of directors, CFO, and CEO should normally determine segments for external financial reporting purposes. It is important that you first define the segments according to compliance requirements. You can use the following criteria to define your segments according to IFRS. A segment is a reportable object if a majority of its revenue is earned from sales to external customers and if:

▶ Its revenue from sales to external customers and from transactions with other segments is at least 10% of total sales.

▶ Its profit and loss is at least 10% of the total profit and loss.

▶ Its assets are at least 10% of the total assets of all segments.

In addition, it is important to note that if the total revenue of reportable segments is less than 75% of the total consolidated revenue, additional reportable segments must be added until the threshold is reached.

SAP R/3 provided many different and complex ways of providing segment reporting. With SAP ERP, SAP strengthened reporting capabilities a great deal, especially for segment reporting. By using the new functionalities, organizations no longer have to wait until period end close to build their segment reporting, which is an error-prone and expensive approach. That said, many SAP customers have already implemented their SAP system and want to understand how they can improve their segment reporting in line with the strategic direction of SAP ERP.

In the next section, we look at the design considerations and explain the best practices to simplify and streamline segment reporting. Reviewing the different segment reporting solutions and recommended best practices in this section is crucial to generating segment reporting accurately at your organization.

3.1   Designing Segment Reporting

Evaluating the range of options that are available for segment reporting within the SAP ERP system is complex, primarily due to the multitude of possible implementation solutions. SAP ERP provides a better way of modeling options for segment reporting compliance. The reporting capabilities of SAP ERP are based on the unified data reporting structure. You can capture segment details in each data record. Because segment information is stored at the detailed document level, segment-based financial statements are available within standard reporting in G/L, saving time and minimizing errors. You can review account balances at the segment level and handle periodic activities (e.g., revaluation and balance carry forwards) easily.

You can consider many leading design practices when evaluating segment reporting solutions and approaches. In this section, we discuss these leading design practices and share our experience. We specifically look at:

▶ Determining the right segment reporting solution

▶ Splitting and having balanced books on segment reporting objects

▶ Ensuring that all transactions are updated with segment information

▶ Simplifying allocations

▶ Rationalizing the number of profit centers

▶ Streamlining data flow from SAP ERP to SAP NetWeaver BI

Let's first discuss reporting solutions and approaches so you can determine the best one to meet your segment reporting requirements, which will in turn influence the design of business processes and the modeling of data flow from SAP ERP to SAP NetWeaver BI.

3.1.1   Determining the Right Segment Reporting Solution

SAP ERP offers several reporting solutions to meet segment reporting compliance. The main applications of these solutions are:

▶ Business Area Accounting (FI-BA)

▶ Profit Center Accounting (EC-PCA)

▶ Special Purpose Ledger (FI-SL)

▶ New General Ledger (new G/L)

There are similarities and differences between the core functionalities of each of these solutions, and there are variations in the ways in which these solutions can be implemented in SAP R/3 and SAP ERP. The solutions themselves vary in terms of the level of customization involved, requirements met, and desired capabilities delivered. In addition to these reporting solutions, many reporting objects are available in financial and management accounting. Some of these reporting objects are relevant to only financial accounting, some of them are relevant to only management accounting, and some of them are relevant to both.

Figure 3.1 shows the main reporting objects available in SAP ERP. SAP ERP provides balanced books capability only for dimensions such as the business area, profit center, segment, customer fields, and industry-specific fields such as fund and grant. This means you can generate your segment reporting only for those dimensions. Perhaps the most important question is which reporting solution and dimension is best to use for segment reporting. The answer to this question depends upon the SAP release you are using and your business requirements. In this section, we explain and evaluate each of the segment reporting objects in conjunction with the reporting solution to guide you in determining the right solution for your organization.

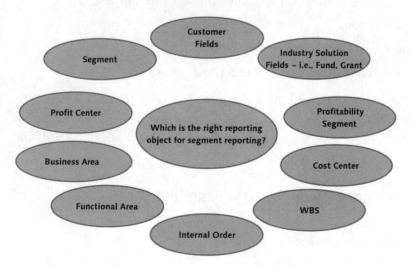

Figure 3.1 Main Reporting Dimensions in SAP ERP

We first look at business area and profit center reporting objects, which were available in the previous releases of SAP ERP. After that we examine the new reporting object segment and other segment reporting dimensions fields such as customer fields and industry-specific fields integrated with New G/L.

Business Area

The business area has been available as a segment reporting object for a long time. Business area accounting operates within the financial component and is integrated with the logistic and management accounting components. You can define business areas according to different segment areas (e.g., product lines, geographical areas, management areas, etc.). The business area definition is not dependent upon any structure or relationship of company codes or controlling areas. They are defined within one client and can be used across all company codes within that client. Business areas are not available in hierarchies and may only be reported in a flat manner within the standard delivered SAP system reports. It is possible to define business area hierarchies using sets with the Report Painter and Report Writer tools of SAP R/3 and SAP ERP. It is also possible to define master data hierarchies for the business area in SAP NetWeaver BI.

In SAP R/3 you can assign balance sheet items such as fixed assets, receivables, payables, and material stock, as well as the majority of profit and loss (P&L) items directly to a specific business area. However, it is only possible to assign cash discounts, equites, and taxes to business areas using indirect methods via periodic adjustment postings in the classic G/L. Also, controlling (CO) postings, which include cross–business area allocations and transactions, are transferred to FI periodically via reconciliation ledger postings. These postings are based on the reconciliation ledger, which is summarized and not easy to reconcile back to individual transactions in CO, resulting in limited visibility within business area reports. For these reasons, it is not easy to create segment reporting at the business area level that would meet international accounting reporting standards in SAP R/3. Although the FI-BA solution is not suitable for producing accurate segment reporting in classic G/L, as required for IFRS and U.S. GAAP, one advantage is that it does provide standard capability for producing financial statements at the business area level, provided that indirect allocations of balance sheet (B/S) items and reconciliation postings are carried out periodically. You can also generate reporting at the business area level in accounts receivable, accounts payable, and asset accounting, for example, to report AP/AR line items by business areas.

Some SAP customers use business areas for their reporting today. If you are an existing customer using business areas for segment reporting in SAP R/3, you can continue to use business areas, as the functionality will be kept in future releases. You can either use your business area solution in SAP ERP as it was implemented in the previous release or integrate the solution with the new G/L. To use your business area solution without any change, a technical upgrade to SAP ERP could be enough. However, to use business areas with the new G/L, the main prerequisite is to activate the *business area update scenario*. In addition, you can eliminate the periodic balance sheet adjustment with the new G/L splitting functionality, which we explain in the next section.

However, our recommendation for SAP customers is to use profit center or segment entities instead of business areas. Originally, FI-BA and EC-PCA were developed as parallel solutions for different purposes. FI-BA was developed for internal and external reporting purposes to produce financial statements, whereas EC-PCA was developed for internal reporting of management performance. Over the years and following releases, SAP continued to work with the EC-PCA to improve its capabilities and encourage the use of EC-PCA as the source behind the internal management reporting, and partially for external reporting. FI-BA was never popular in SAP implementations. With more requests coming from customers and increased regulatory requirements on reporting, SAP decided to make a choice about which approach to develop further. The decision was made to pursue the PCA approach as per SAP Note 321190, which was released in 2002, to do no further development for business areas, and to focus future development on profit centers, although FI-BA would continue to be supported. The rationale behind this suggestion was that EC-PCA had significantly better functionality than FI-BA. For example, EC-PCA has its own allocations, separate ledger, hierarchical reporting, transfer pricing, profit center substitution rules, and integration with planning and SAP Strategic Enterprise Management (SEM). Later on, when SAP ERP introduced the *segment* reporting object, the note was amended to recommend the segment in addition to the profit center in reporting.

Now that we have highlighted some of the important historical developments in the area of business area accounting versus profit center accounting, let's look at the design considerations of using the profit center as a reporting object for segment reporting.

Profit Center

The profit center has also been available as a reporting object for a long time and can be defined in a similar manner to the business areas; that is, it is possible to define and create reporting structures based on product lines, geography, a combination of these, or management areas. Profit centers are created within a controlling area and therefore dependent upon the assignment of company codes to a controlling area. They are then available company-code-wide for the assigned controlling area and can be used by company codes within the controlling area in the postings.

With profit centers, it is possible to create hierarchal structures as groups of profit centers and then to use these hierarchies within reporting. Similar to business areas, profit centers are normally assigned to all CO objects relevant for revenue and expense postings (cost centers, orders, WBS elements, etc.). As a result of these assignments, any postings to the assigned objects are then automatically updated with the corresponding profit center. For example, each cost center has a profit center field on its master record, and as a result, any postings to that cost center also appear in the assigned profit center. Additionally, profit centers are assigned to materials to capture material-related postings, such as change in stock, goods receipts, and good issues.

In the previous releases of SAP ERP, EC-PCA had to be activated to use the profit center as a reporting object. Unlike FI-BA, EC-PCA falls neither within the FI component nor within the CO component but is cross-functional, mirroring the transactions of both. PCA achieves this by lying within the separate enterprise controlling (EC) component, with each EC-PCA posting being a separate and parallel posting to the FI and CO postings.

EC-PCA offers many advanced functionalities needed for segment reporting. For example, it provides substitution tools to create rules for more complex assignments as well as postings via assignments of other objects. In addition, certain allocation techniques are available that allow the creation of EC-PCA–only allocations or postings that do not affect other ledgers. Another feature of EC-PCA that is important for segment reporting is that it recognizes CO transactions. Therefore, reports generated from EC-PCA include all accounts within the chart of accounts and secondary cost elements. EC-PCA also allows the analysis of statistical key figures by profit center. (Statistical key figures are defined to capture measures such as number of employees, square meters, etc. and can be used in allocations and reporting.) Consequently, it is possible to calculate key performance indicators (KPIs) such as return on investment, cash flow, sales per employee, and so on. Because of all these advanced functionalities, EC-PCA is the preferred solution compared to the FI-BA solution. However, if you used EC-PCA for segment reporting, you know that the problems usually arose with balance sheet accounts. Balance sheet accounts are transferred to EC-PCA at the period end. Although you would transfer them as a period end closing task, it was difficult to transfer some balance sheet accounts accurately.

EC-PCA is still available and can be used in SAP ERP. However, with the new G/L, profit center accounting is integrated into the G/L so you no longer need to use the EC-PCA component to report on the profit center; rather, you need to activate the profit center scenario as a main prerequisite. Perhaps it would be much easier to call the new G/L functionality of profit center accounting as FI-PCA. However, the reality is that SAP not only adapted the functionalities of EC-PCA within the G/L, but also provided powerful functionalities for segment reporting.

With the adoption of profit center accounting functionalities, profit center and partner profit center are characteristics in the new G/L tables. Thus, profit center details are updated in the financial transactions simultaneously, which gives the ability to get profit center–based financial statements from the new G/L. The data is not updated in other tables as in the EC-PCA. The new G/L provides the one-stop integrated reconciliation of ledgers. Ledgers such as the profit center ledger, cost of sales ledger, and consolidation staging ledger are combined into the new G/L.

After profit center accounting was drastically improved and integrated into the new G/L, many SAP customers who implemented and used EC-PCA raised questions regarding the future roadmap and strategy for the existing and new implementations. One of the questions we often hear is that they want to know whether they can still use EC-PCA in parallel with the new G/L. The answer is yes, provided that this is an interim solution. We don't recommend keeping EC-PCA in parallel with the new G/L due to increased data volume and the time and effort required for the reconciliation of these two applications.

As we mentioned before, you can also use segment as a reporting object, which is explained below.

Segment

As the name suggests, segment reporting object is introduced for segment reporting compliance. You can use segment as a reporting object by activating the *segment reporting scenario* in the new G/L. Segments are not dependent upon any structure or relationship of company codes or controlling areas. Like business areas, they are defined within one client and can be used across all company codes within that client. Unlike profit centers, it is not possible to create hierarchical structures as groups of segments and then to use these hierarchies in standard reports.

To post, analyze and display segments in the new G/L reports, you need to derive them in the financial transactions. Segments can be derived from profit centers, via a business add-in, or defaulted to a constant value. Figure 3.2 shows a schematic view of segment derivation. Once the new G/L is activated, the segment field appears in the profit center master data automatically so that you can assign segments to relevant profit centers. As a result of these assignments, any postings to the profit centers are then automatically updated in the corresponding segment. Postings without profit centers can be updated by either using business add-in (BAdl) or defaulting to a constant value. In addition, segment information can be manually populated at the time of posting. We recommend that such manual updates be carefully controlled to avoid any mistakes.

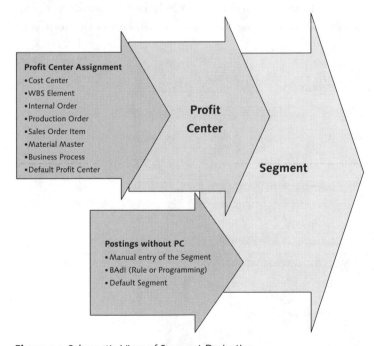

Profit Center Assignment
- Cost Center
- WBS Element
- Internal Order
- Production Order
- Sales Order Item
- Material Master
- Business Process
- Default Profit Center

Profit Center

Segment

Postings without PC
- Manual entry of the Segment
- BAdl (Rule or Programming)
- Default Segment

Figure 3.2 Schematic View of Segment Derivation

Figure 3.3 shows an example of how you can assign segment information in the profit center master data. Once you have assigned the segment to a profit center and saved your changes, the segment field area becomes gray. This means it is no longer possible to change the segment field assignment in the single master data change transaction (Transaction KE52). This ensures consistent balance at the segment level, as any change in segment assignment in the profit center master data can lead to misstatement in segment reporting if postings were already made to the profit center. However, the system does not allow you to make any changes, even if there is no posting to the profit center. In that case, you can implement SAP Note 940721 and change the segment assignment. After you make the changes, we advise implementing SAP Note 1037986 so that it is not possible to change the segment assignment in the profit center. You should not be able to make changes to the assignment of a profit center to a segment, because this may need to be supported with G/L postings and the conversion of open items that have already been posted to the segment or profit center. In contrast to a single master data change, it is possible to change the segment assignment by using the profit center mass maintenance (Transaction KE55). This is a missing functionality in SAP ERP, so our recommendation is to implement SAP Note 940440 to have built-in control functionality so the segment cannot be changed in the profit center master data.

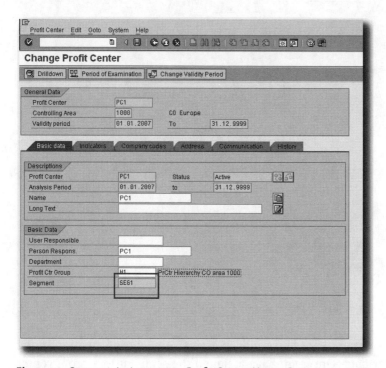

Figure 3.3 Segment Assignment to Profit Center Master Data

A tip on segment reporting scenario

You have a new installation of the SAP ERP system and use the new G/L and CO. If you assign the segment reporting scenario to at least one of your ledger in the new G/L, due to missing functionality, the segment field will not be updated in some CO postings, resulting in miscalculations in overheads or price determination. This would lead to inaccurate product costing and profitability reports. To avoid such a situation, we recommend implementing SAP Note 1024480.

Customer Field

Customer fields can be added to the coding block of the general ledger and used as a reporting object. SAP ERP allows the addition of customer fields to the code block of the general ledger as in the previous releases. Once added, these fields behave like other account assignment fields. In the previous releases, customer fields were used for reporting with the FI-SL. Although the customer field approach can provide segmented financial statements, deriving and populating the customer fields in financial transactions are difficult. In addition, if you choose the customer field reporting solution for reporting, you need to enhance the standard SAP NetWeaver BI extractors for the new G/L. This could complicate the data flow design from SAP ERP to SAP NetWeaver BI. Our recommendation is that the customer field approach is not a practical reporting solution for meeting segment reporting requirements. We recommend not using customer fields before fully exploring the standard reporting objects (segment, profit center, and business area).

Industry Solution Field

SAP ERP introduced industry solutions fields, where you can get full financial statements. For example, you can get financial statements at the grant and fund level in the SAP ERP for Public Sector solution. We recommend using the industry solution fields along with the scenarios and tables to meet your industry-specific requirements.

In addition to the reporting objects we have discussed, some organizations use the company code approach for their segment reporting. We do not recommend using this approach unless it has already been implemented. We explain the company code approach in the note below.

> **Company code approach**
>
> The company code is the smallest organizational unit within SAP for which a complete self-contained set of accounts can be created for the purposes of external reporting. Frequently, the principle is to use one company code per legal entity. To support segment reporting requirements, some implementations have broken this principle and created separate company code for each reporting unit and then consolidated this information for legal entity reporting. Although in this manner a company code approach would provide full financial information by reporting unit, the sharing of facilities between company codes could be difficult. For example, items such as customers, plants, sales organizations, cost centers, and so on are either directly or indirectly assigned to company codes and as a result would necessitate multiple assignments per legal entity for each reporting unit. This would complicate financial transactions and system management where objects are shared across reporting units. This approach would also complicate business processes such as period end closing, where multiple period end closes would be required for each reporting unit. In addition, using the company code approach for purposes different than its original design intention results in little flexibility for future changes and could lead to many unanticipated problems. We do not recommend using this approach unless it has been already implemented.

As discussed earlier, inflexibilities exist for segment reporting in the previous releases of SAP ERP. Each line item in the FI document or PCA document can have only one assignment. In many cases, it is desirable to split transactions between segment reporting objects to update the segments accurately instead of updating them by periodic adjustment postings. To achieve a split using the segment reporting object, separate line items would need to be created in the financial documents. SAP ERP provides this capability with the *splitting functionality* and ensures *balanced book* on segment reporting objects. In the next section, we discuss the splitting functionality, explain how you can have balanced books on splitting characteristics, and give recommendations on splitting design.

3.1.2 Splitting and Having Balanced Books on Segment Reporting Objects

Splitting is a very powerful functionality that was introduced with SAP ERP. It enables line items to be divided for selected dimensions to produce financial statements. As an example of what happens during splitting, consider an invoice from a vendor, which is posted with multiple expense lines to different cost account assignment objects. A comparison of the same documents in split and without split form, along with the segmented balance sheet, is illustrated in Figure 3.4 (for simplicity, not all the details of the postings are illustrated in the figure). On the left side of the figure, a document without splitting is illustrated. The expense lines are posted to relevant profit centers and segments, but the vendor and the tax lines are not posted to the profit center and segment, resulting in unbalanced books for the profit center and segment. On the other hand, vendor and input VAT line items are split based according to the proportion of expense line amounts and posted to the relevant profit centers and segments, resulting in a balanced book entry at the profit center and segment level, as shown on the right side of the figure.

To get segmented financial statements on selected dimension(s), you need to define them as splitting characteristic(s). For example, by defining the profit center and segment as splitting characteristics, a balanced financial statement for these dimensions is generated, as in the example in Figure 3.4.

Splitting characteristics in SAP ERP

You can define business area, profit center, segment, customer fields, and industry-specific fields as splitting characteristics.

Document without splitting

PK Segment	PC	Account	Amount
31		Vendor	1160
40 SEGMENT 1	PC1	Postage Expense	200
40 SEGMENT 2	PC2	Postage Expense	800
40		Input VAT	160

Document with splitting

PK Segment	PC	Account	Amount
31 SEGMENT 1	PC1	Vendor	232
31 SEGMENT 2	PC2	Vendor	928
40 SEGMENT 1	PC1	Postage Expense	200
40 SEGMENT 2	PC2	Postage Expense	800
40 SEGMENT 1	PC1	Input VAT	32
40 SEGMENT 2	PC2	Input VAT	128

Balance Sheet SEGMENT 1

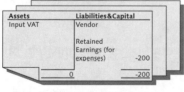

Balance Sheet SEGMENT 1

Balance Sheet SEGMENT 2

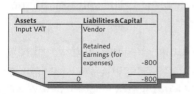

Balance Sheet SEGMENT 2

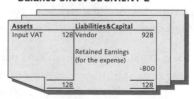

Figure 3.4 Unsplit and Split Comparison

Splitting is facilitated by splitting rules, which are predefined in the standard business content of SAP ERP. Figure 3.5 illustrates a schematic view of the splitting rule definition. To explain splitting rules, we first give detailed definitions of the key terms used.

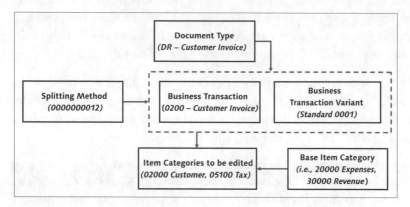

Figure 3.5 Splitting Rule Definition

▶ **Business transaction (BT)**
A business transaction is an event that leads to a value update in financial accounting, for example, customer invoice and vendor invoice. Business transactions are pre-delivered by SAP. You cannot define a new business transaction.

▶ **Item categories**
The item category characterizes the items of an accounting document, for example, customer, vendor, and asset. Like business transactions, you cannot define an item category.

▶ **Business transaction variants (BTV)**
A BTV is a special version of a BT, in which you can further limit the item categories that are specified in the business transactions.

▶ **Splitting method**
The splitting method defines how the split is performed. The splitting method combined with the BT and BTV produce the splitting rules.

Now that we explained the key terms used in splitting, let's look at how splitting rules are defined. Splitting rules determine which item categories will be split, as well as which base can be used for splitting. For example, the customer invoices business transaction (0200) with business transaction variant (0001) will be split along with taxes on sales and purchases items based on item categories 20000 expenses and 30000 revenue, as shown in Figure 3.5.

You can define your own splitting rules. Note, however, that it is recommended that you do not change the standard splitting rules. If you need to change the standard splitting rules, first copy them to your own rules and further modify them according to your business needs.

To understand the splitting mechanism, let's look at a splitting simulation example. Figure 3.6 and Figure 3.7 show how you can simulate the G/L posting to see the splitting rules used in the posting and configuration settings behind. In this example, we allocated cash from profit center PC2, which belongs to segment SEG2, to profit enter PC1, which belongs to segment SEG1. If you navigate to the document menu and select the **Simulate General Ledger** option, the system then shows the details of the G/L view of the document, as shown in Figure 3.6.

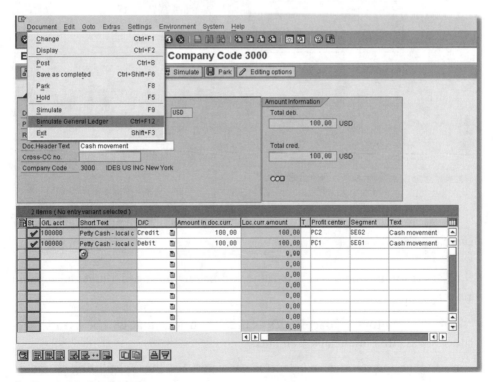

Figure 3.6 G/L Simulation

Figure 3.7 shows the G/L simulation view of the document. Because we activated zero balancing of the segment and profit center dimension, the system generated two additional balancing lines with the clearing account (194500) automatically. This ensures zero balancing of the segment reporting dimension. By pressing the **Expert Mode** button in the application menu bar, you can see the splitting rule details that were used to split the document. For example, the splitting rule consists of splitting method 0000000012, 0000 unspecified posting business transaction, and 0001 BTV, as shown in the **Configuration of Doc. Splitting** box on the left side of the figure.

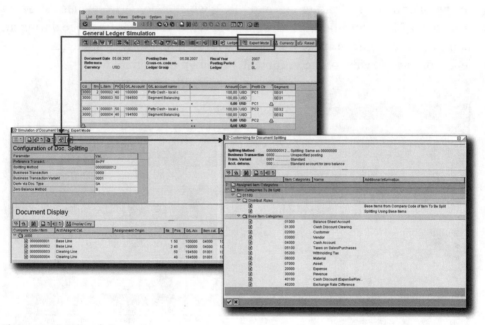

Figure 3.7 G/L Simulation

Below are recommendations on splitting and having balanced books on segment reporting:

▶ Define the splitting characteristics as the dimensions that will be used to produce segmented financial statements.

▶ Ensure that you select zero balancing characteristics for the splitting characteristics. By doing so, balance books are secured for the splitting characteristics.

- ▶ Ensure that you select the mandatory characteristic option for splitting characteristics. By doing so, selected characteristics are populated in each document line.

- ▶ Activate the inheritance option so that if no reporting dimensions are specified, characteristics are populated from the offsetting lines.

- ▶ Ensure that you specify a default assignment for cases where the reporting objects cannot be determined.

- ▶ Ensure that you assign revenue, expense, balance sheet, and bank and cash accounts to the right item categories.

- ▶ Ensure that you assign new document types to BTs and BTVs.

- ▶ Review the splitting rules if you define a customer field as a segment reporting object and splitting characteristic.

By using the splitting functionality and enabling balanced books, you can streamline and simplify your segment reporting. Now let's look at another leading practice for segment reporting, which is to capture and record all transactions with segment information.

3.1.3 Capturing All Transactions with Segment Information

The foundation of supporting segment compliance is the availability of segment relevant data, which is generated as a result of both finance and logistic business processes. Therefore, alignment of those processes and capture of segment information is critical to ensure the generation of accurate reports. In this section we look at the challenges of capturing the derivation of specific items with segment information. As we discussed earlier, the best practice is to use segment or profit center for segment reporting. Let's look at the mechanism of segment derivation and capturing segments in all transactions.

The derivation of segments in transactions is met, broadly, by the following options:

- ▶ **Deriving from profit center**
  You can derive segments from the profit center master data. Profit centers are assigned to cost objects (cost centers, internal orders, WBS elements, etc.), sales orders, and materials. When you post to any of these cost objects, the system automatically updates the profit center and relevant segment simultaneously.

▶ **Using business add-in**

If you are not using profit center master data in your implementation, you can define custom derivation rules with business add-in (BAdI) FAGL_DERIVE_SEGMENT to populate segments automatically. BAdIs do not only include an ABAP routine, but also include rule-based derivation rules similar to finance validation and substitution definitions.

▶ **Using constants for nonassigned processes**

In certain postings, it is not possible to derive or identify the correct account assignments at the time of the posting, as the required information is not available or is too difficult to obtain. Non-assigned processes could cause misstatements in segment reporting. Thus, we recommend using constants, or so-called defaults, for non-assigned postings. In some cases, you need to allocate the non-assigned amounts collected in the constant segment to other segments with allocation cycles. In other cases, it is possible to determine the original correct assignment at a later stage. This may appear a bit confusing at first.

We can explain this mechanism with a cash receipt example, in which a cash receipt from a customer is posted to the company's house bank. When the cash is first received, it is not immediately known which invoices are paid by this cash receipt. Figure 3.8 illustrates the posting journal and FI postings. When you review the postings, you can see how the segment is originated from the customer invoice. In step 1, the customer invoice is captured and recorded in the system with the correct segment. Then a posting from the bank account against the cash receipt is made. As there is no segment information available in the cash receipt, a *default segment* is used. The cash receipt clearing account is debited, and the bank account is credited on a default segment (step 2). Next, the cash receipt account is posted against the customer account during the clearing of the invoice, the correct segment (SEG1) is determined from the cleared invoice, and cash receipt accounts are cleared against each other (step 3). Because both positions are assigned to different segments, corresponding segment balancing lines are generated (step 4). As a result, the receipt clearing account is updated with the correct segment derived from the customer invoice, which was not possible when the cash was first received by the company's house bank.

▶ **Updating segments manually**

Another way of populating segment information is capturing the segment details manually at the time of the financial posting. Note, however, that there is always a risk of populating wrong segment information with this method, resulting in the inaccurate representation of financial information, so we do not recommend updating the segments manually. Nevertheless, if you need to use this method, we recommend increasing the system's built-in controls to reduce the risks associated with a manual update.

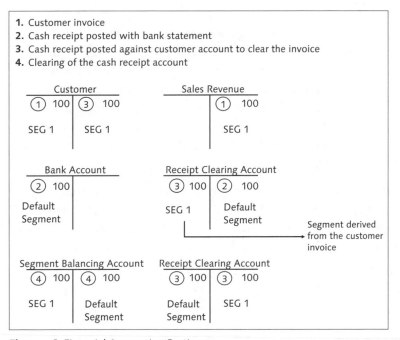

Figure 3.8 Financial Accounting Postings

Profit center assignment to selected balance sheet items

With SAP ERP, profit center assignment functionality is the same as in the previous releases. In addition, SAP ERP allows you to automatically assign a profit center for individual company codes and ranges of accounts. Companies often like to automate the assignment of some balance sheet items to profit centers. This was possible in Transaction 3KEH in SAP R/3. Similar functionality is now available in the new G/L. The new Transaction is FAGL3KEH. In addition to the standard settings, the rule can be extended with the use of BAdIs. The derivation of partner profit centers for consolidation purpose is also supported with the use of BAdIs.

Now that we have explained how to capture all transactions with segment information, we can look at another work-in best practice, which is related to allocation.

3.1.4 Simplifying Allocations

One of the important design considerations for segment reporting is related to allocations. For example, do you need allocations in the new G/L? What happens to CO allocations? With new G/L allocations, will you encounter the same problems as in EC-PCA?

EC-PCA allocations create cross-module reconciliation issues. The new allocation capability introduced within the new G/L in SAP ERP gives the ability to maintain cycles and execute them in the G/L for segment reporting objects. The new allocation cycles create financial postings in the G/L and update the profit center and segment dimensions simultaneously. In other words, there is no longer a reconciliation problem because the transactions are updated in the G/L with all dimensions. The recommended best business practice is to use allocations in the new G/L and define a transparent allocation process.

CO allocations are still in CO and should be performed in CO depending on your cost center accounting architecture. We explain the design considerations for CO allocations with a case study example in Chapter 9. With this example, you can make a decision regarding CO allocations.

The following section introduces another important design decision, which can increase the effectiveness of generating segment reporting.

3.1.5 Rationalizing the Number of Profit Centers

One of the questions we hear frequently from SAP customers is that they want to know how many profit centers they can create without affecting the performance of generating reports.

Regardless of which application you are using (EC-PCA or profit center accounting within the new G/L), you need to consider the right and balanced number of profit centers for your reporting and system performance. The number of profit centers you use depends on your organization structure and the way your business needs to report. Too few profit centers will not give the desired granularity in the reports, and too many could cause confusion and potential misstatements. We cannot determine the balanced amount for your organization but will give you guidance regarding the number of profit centers you can use without creating major system performance problems.

The system performance depends on various factors, such as the system infrastructure and the number of totals records. Among other things, the number of totals records is affected by the number of profit centers. Therefore, the important aspect for performance considerations is always the number of profit centers. If there are too many profit centers, there may be performance problems in the system. SAP has given guidance on the number of profit centers based on existing implementations and performance statistics (the figures are rough estimates):

▶ **Less than 1,000 profit centers**
This is a normal installation where performance problems are not expected.

▶ **1,000 to 5,000 profit centers**
Large global organizations normally have this number of profit centers. Performance problems are not to be expected.

▶ **5,000 to 10,000 profit centers**
This is a lot of profit centers and could cause performance issues. Extensive performance testing should be performed before the production start-up.

▶ **More than 10,000 profit centers**
This is classified as an extremely large number of profit centers. It is recommended to redesign the solution and reduce the number of profit centers.

If the number of profit centers is not carefully controlled, organizations could face the challenge of rationalizing the number of profit centers, so it is vital to design the right and balanced number of profit centers at the beginning.

3.1.6 Streamlining Data Flow from SAP ERP to SAP NetWeaver BI

In previous releases of SAP ERP, finance data was collected via complex data models for segment reporting. The classic G/L does not include all required financial information. For example, it does not have some of the CO transactions (e.g., allocations), which should be included in the segment reporting. Thus, companies get data from different components such as FI-GL, CO, and EC-PCA via complicated update and transfer rules, extensions to the standard data extractor, and so on. The data is then combined and reconciled in SAP NetWeaver BI and SAP SEM.

Organizations using the classic general ledger often use EC-PCA as their main source for segment reporting, with various combinations of other components and data sources. Figure 3.9 illustrates one variation of this case where data flows from EC-PCA to SAP NetWeaver BI and SAP SEM.

EC-PCA is updated with transactions from logistics, classic G/L and controlling. The data from EC-PCA flows to SAP NetWeaver BI with standards extractors. In addition, data from the G/L can further be extracted into SAP NetWeaver BI and combined with EC-PCA using complex data flow with transfer and update rules, depending on functional design. You can then get data to SAP SEM-BCS for consolidation and SAP SEM-BPS for planning. This model requires that EC-PCA is updated with all financial data so that you can use profit center accounting as a single source and the main ledger for segment reporting. If this is not the case, you need to combine the EC-PCA with additional data flow in SAP NetWeaver BI.

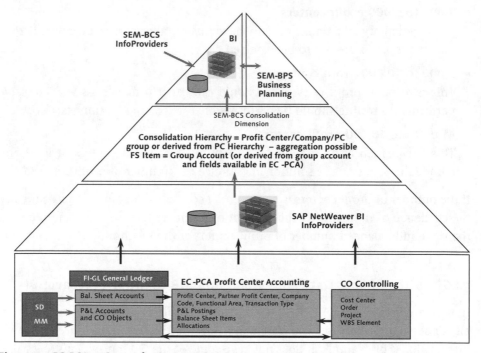

Figure 3.9 EC-PCA as Source for Segment Reporting

Many global organizations use this model, where EC-PCA is the main ledger for segment reporting. They can continue to use the same data model in SAP ERP, provided that this model has already been implemented and they will only technically upgrade to SAP ERP. However, best practices dictate that if the new G/L is used, it is good practice to use the new G/L as the source, simplify the data flow in SAP NetWeaver BI and SAP SEM-BCS, and improve the data model.

Figure 3.10 shows the data flow from the new G/L to SAP NetWeaver BI and SAP SEM-BCS. The new G/L captures all financial transactions with the dimensions required for segment reporting. In addition, the new G/L DataSources include the transaction data at the segment reporting objects level, so there is no longer any need for complicated update and transfer rules in data flow. This model makes the architecture more transparent, and because all financial transactions are captured and recorded in one source, reconciliation activities are reduced and data flow is simplified. In addition, a single version of the data source can be provided with this model, which is a very important aspect according to the Sarbanes-Oxley Act (SOX).

Next, we look at a case study to illustrate the concepts covered in this section.

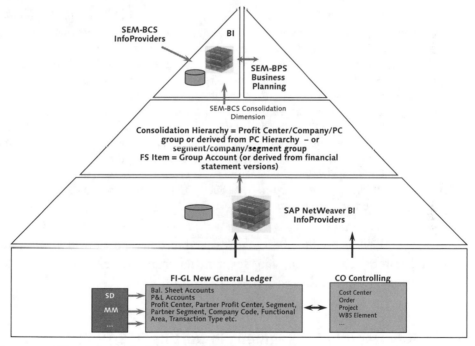

Figure 3.10 G/L as a Source for Segment Reporting

Case study

Here is a real-world example. The global organization ABC, which operates across numerous geographical regions, lacked an integrated view of its segmented financial information. Significant challenges were encountered during data capturing, which resulted in deriving many crucial data items from other applications and spreadsheets, rather than generating reports directly from a single source. In addition, different SAP ERP systems were implemented by various business units, all with different data standards and reporting objects. These and other issues resulted in extensive manual effort to provide management with reliable data, frustration with the lack of the timeliness of reliable information, and general concern about the quality of the financial information.

To overcome the problems in segment reporting, as well as to improve the overall reporting architecture, ABC set out a strategy of "having one source of truth." To achieve this goal, they decided to implement SAP ERP for their core business, SAP SEM-BCS for consolidation, and SAP NetWeaver BI for their reporting, and to standardize their reporting solution enterprise wide (45 legal entities in 14 countries worldwide, 9 business divisions globally, etc.).

The project team first carried out a detailed analysis to collect the business requirements, including legal and country business requirements. Then they evaluated the available reporting solutions and decided to use profit center accounting in the new G/L. Profit center and segment reporting objects are used as reporting dimensions for segment reporting. They mapped their legacy-reporting objects into profit centers and segments. Some legacy systems were using the EC-PCA module, and this added more complexity to the project implementation due to the new logic of the G/L and paradigm of the existing profit center accounting solution. A total of 12 segments along with approximately 150 profit centers were created. All financial transactions are captured in the new G/L, which is then linked to SAP NetWeaver BI for reporting. After the implementation, a benefit realization study related to reporting KPI showed that organization ABC reduced reporting costs by up to 30% due to the high-quality data at source and the ability to report accurately and on time.

Now that you have learned the best practices and recommendations that will serve as a solid foundation for improving segment reporting, we can look at the key reports available in SAP ERP and SAP NetWeaver BI.

3.2 Key Reports for Segment Reporting in SAP ERP

IAS 14 and FASB 131 have detailed guidance on which items of revenue and expense are included in segment reporting so that all companies will report a standardized measure of segment results. Disclosures relating to segmental reporting include the following:

- Revenue from sales to external customers and to other segments
- The amount of depreciation and amortization for the period and other noncash expenses
- Share of the profit or loss of equity accounted entities and their relevant investment balances
- Segment result between continuing and discontinued operations
- Goodwill, total assets, and total liabilities
- Capital expenditure
- The nature and amount of any material items of segment revenue and expense that is relevant to explain the performance of a segment

Reports vary depending on the approach that we discussed in the previous section. As mentioned earlier in the chapter, splitting and balanced books capability combined with the right reporting solution and object allows you to get segmented financial statements from the new G/L.

3.2.1 New Financial Statement Report

The main report that you can use for the segmented financial statement is the New Financial Statement report. To access this report, follow the menu path **Accounting • Financial Accounting • General Ledger • Information System • General Ledger Reports (New) • Financial Statement/Cash Flow • General • Actual/ Actual Comparison • Financial Statement Actual/Actual Comparison** (Transaction S_PL0_86000028).

As shown in Figure 3.11, direct selection by standard characteristics is possible in the entry screen of the New Financial Statement report. You can choose the segment reporting dimension in the selection parameters, that is, segment, profit center, business area, and so on. You can also select your reporting financial statement version along with the comparison time frame. Three output types can be selected. We have selected the graphical report output option for this drilldown report to provide greater flexibility and a better visual effect. With that option, several views of the report are shown on the screen (i.e., the drilldown list and detail list). You can run the report using various combinations of selection criteria and drill down to the desired detail level. For example, you can run the report for several company codes and drill down to the segment reporting dimension.

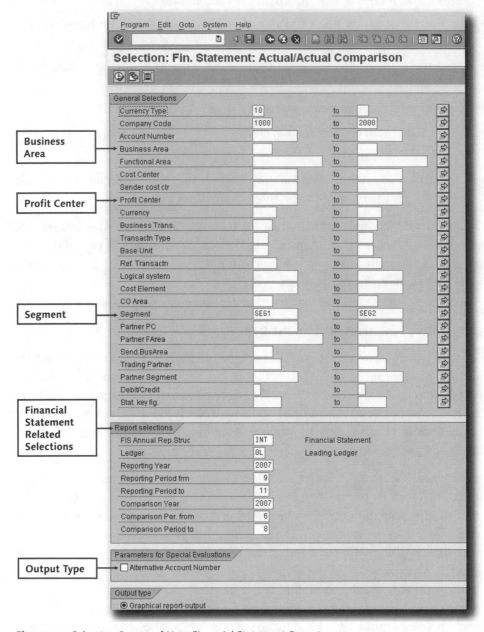

Figure 3.11 Selection Screen of New Financial Statement Report

The flexibility comes from the ability to navigate through all characteristics. From the report output, you can easily investigate additional data on any suspect balance by drilling down into the balance in question. This allows you to determine the accounts affected and the reasons for the transaction in question.

An example of the Balance Sheet report with a graphical output is illustrated in Figure 3.12 and Figure 3.13. Figure 3.12 is a segmented financial statement report without drilldown, showing values for all selection parameters. The graphical report output has a navigation toolbar containing buttons such as report parameters and download report. Below the toolbar is an information area, where you can show your company logo and other information using HTML templates. In the navigation area you can navigate to other dimensions by double-clicking on the desired dimension. The drilldown of that dimension is then displayed in the drilldown area. At the bottom of the report, you can see the key figure details.

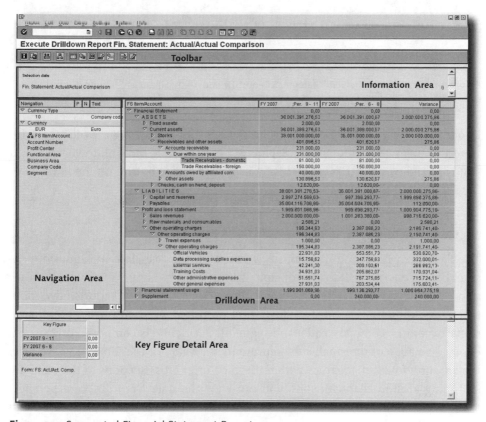

Figure 3.12 Segmented Financial Statement Report

By dragging and dropping a *trade receivables-domestic* item from the drilldown area to the segment characteristic in the navigation area, you can see the details of trade receivables-domestic per segment, as shown in Figure 3.13.

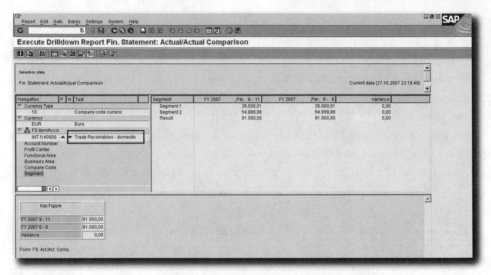

Figure 3.13 Segmented Financial Statement Report Drilldown by Financial Statement Item/Account

In addition, you can drill down to the segment level, as shown in Figure 3.14. Here the financial statement for Segment 1 is shown in the drilldown area, and you can navigate to other segments by using the arrow button on the left side of the segment in the navigation area.

Drilldown Reporting Mechanism

The drilldown reporting mechanism is based on the principle of a multidimensional data set. The drilldown principle is illustrated in Figure 3.15, which shows a three-dimensional data set represented by a cube. Normally, reports have more than three dimensions, but for illustration purposes we used only three dimensions: accounts, company code, and segment. Each cube is composed of 27 small cubes. The edge of the small cube represents the value of the dimension. You can look at individual small cubes within the cube or at cross-sections of the cube. By swapping around characteristics, you can view the data from different perspectives. We explain how you can create drilldown reporting and further drilldown functionalities in Chapter 12.

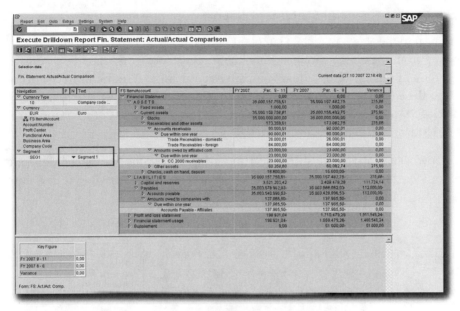

Figure 3.14 Segmented Financial Statement Report Drilldown by Segment

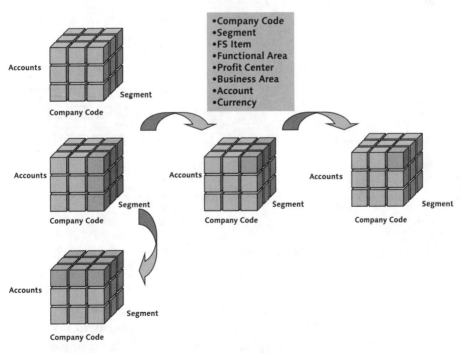

Figure 3.15 Drilldown Mechanism for Segment Reporting

3.2.2 Classic Financial Statement Report

In addition to the New Financial Statement report, you can generate your segment reporting from the Classic Financial Statement report. To access the Classic Financial Statement report, follow the menu path **Accounting • Financial Accounting • General Ledger • Information System • General Ledger Reports (New) • Financial Statement/Cash Flow • General • Actual/Actual Comparison • Financial Statements** (Transaction S_ALR_87012284).

Note, however, that you need to select reporting dimensions from the dynamic selections button in the Classic Financial Statement report, as shown in Figure 3.16.

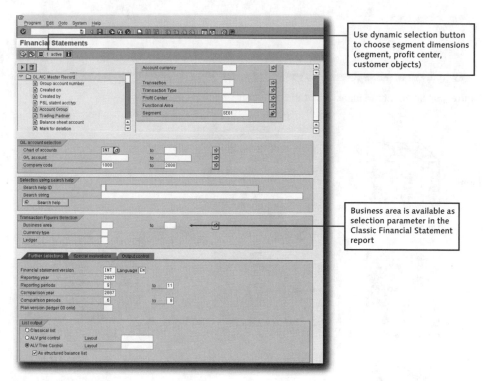

Figure 3.16 Selection Screen of Classic Financial Statement Report

The Classic Financial Statement report is not a drilldown report, so it is less flexible than the New Financial Statement report. The ALV tree control format output of the Classic Financial Statement report is shown in Figure 3.17. Although the segment is selected in the selection parameters, it is not possible to see segment information in the output.

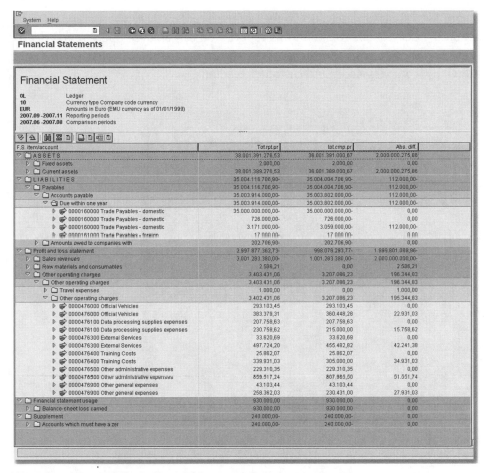

Figure 3.17 Output of Classic Financial Statement Report

3.2.3 Other Reports for Segment Reporting

The new G/L provides four new drilldown reports in the information system: Profit Center Receivables, Profit Center Payables, Receivables Segment, and Payables Segment. With these reports, you can analyze the line items of accounts receivables and accounts payables per segment and profit center. To access these new drilldown line item reports, follow the menu path **Accounting • Financial Accounting • General Ledger • Information System • General Ledger Reports (New) • Line Items • Open Items**.

Figure 3.18 shows the selection screen of the Segment Receivables report (Transaction S_PCO_36000218). With this report, you can analyze open items, cleared items, or all items of accounts receivable postings for the selected profit center hierarchy, company code, and customer accounts.

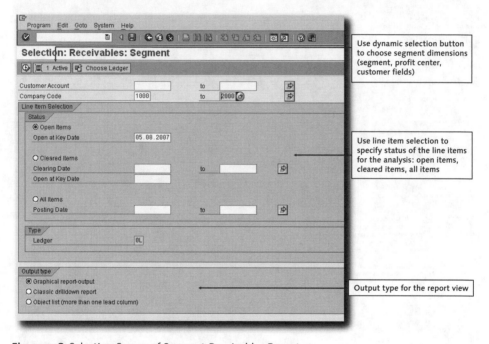

Figure 3.18 Selection Screen of Segment Receivables Report

The output can be graphical, drilldown, or object list form. A graphical report output type is selected in the example shown in Figure 3.19. You can navigate through profit centers and drill down to line items.

New Account Balances and Transaction Figures Reports

SAP ERP also introduces the new G/L Account Balances report and Transaction Figures Account Balance report for the new dimensions. To access these new reports, follow the menu path **Accounting • Financial Accounting • General Ledger • Information System • General Ledger Reports (New) • Account Balances • General • G/L Account Balances • G/L Account Balances (New) and Transaction Figures** (Transaction S_PL0_86000030 for G/L Account Balances report and Transaction S_PL0_86000031 for Transaction Figures Account Balance report).

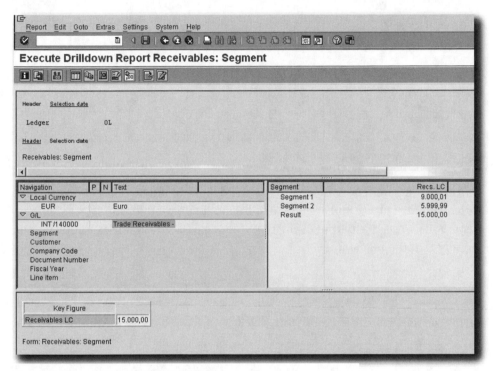

Figure 3.19 Output of Segment Receivables

Both of these reports are drilldown reports and support multiple views of segment information. Figure 3.20 illustrates an example of G/L Account Balances report.

In our example, we showed account balances per segment and currency type. You can further drill down to the profit center level. In addition, you can call up other reports by selecting a particular cell, navigating to the **GoTo** menu, and selecting line items or calling up the report option. The system calls up other reports and displays values of the selections.

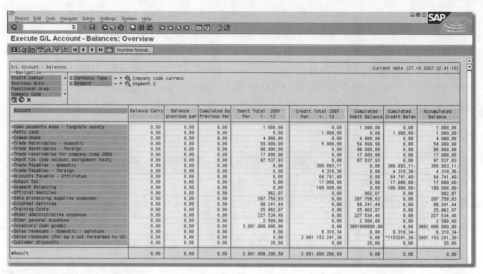

Figure 3.20 G/L Account Balances Report

Transaction Figure report is used to see the debit and credit transactions and the corresponding balance and accumulated balance per period for the selected dimensions. You can see the output of the report in Figure 3.21. In our example, we run the report at the segment level.

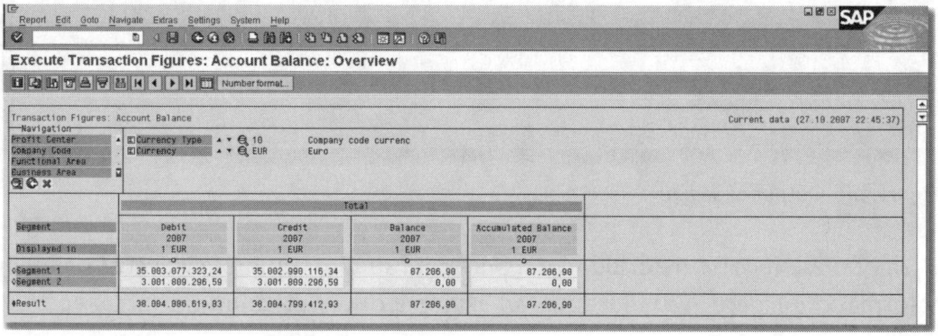

Figure 3.21 Transaction Figures Account Balance Report by Segment

Segmented Line Item and Balance Display Reports

In addition to the reports that we explained, the new display line item report (Transaction FAGLL03) is introduced and available in the menu of G/L accounting. With this report, you can analyze the line items per segment and other G/L reporting objects of one or more G/L accounts per ledger. In the selection screen of the report, you can switch between entry view and G/L view. You enter the company code and the account status of the line items in the selection screen. You can further restrict the selection parameters, such as the segment or profit center, in the dynamic selection. This report replaces the old line item report in the classic G/L, which only shows the entry view of the G/L line items (Transaction FBL3N).

Figure 3.22 shows the output of the report in ALV format. Segment and profit centers of the general ledger line items are displayed along with the other line item information. Double-clicking on the line items does not take you to the document level. To analyze the document of the line item, click on the line, navigate to the environment, and select the document option.

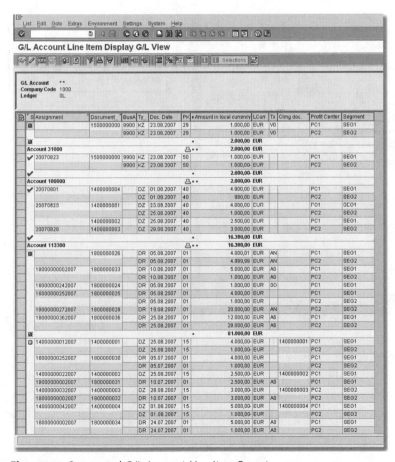

Figure 3.22 Segmented G/L Account Line Item Report

You can also display individual or a range of G/L account balances at the segment or for other reporting dimensions. To do so, use the Display Balances (New) report (Transaction FAGLB03). This report replaces the old Account Balances report (Transaction FS10N) in SAP ERP. You can see an example output of the Account Balances report for Segment 1 in Figure 3.23.

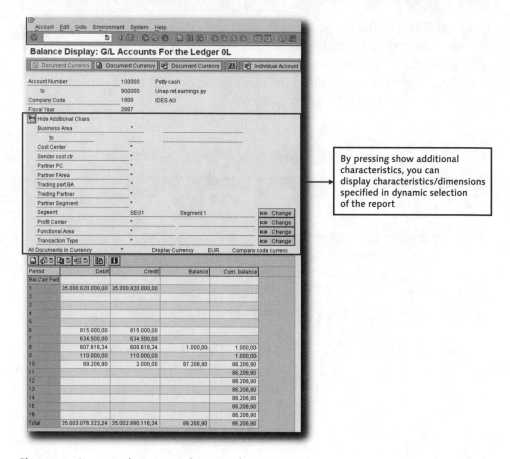

Figure 3.23 Segmented Account Balance Display

The characteristics available as additional characteristics when displaying balances are set in the configuration. You can specify up to five characteristics per ledger. To identify characteristics as selection parameters, follow the configuration menu path **Financial Accounting (New) • General Ledger Accounting (New) • Information System • Define Balance Display**.

Figure 3.24 shows the configuration menu path and an example of balance display settings. In our example, we defined segment (**SEGMENT**) and profit center (**PRCTR**) as additional characteristics for balance display.

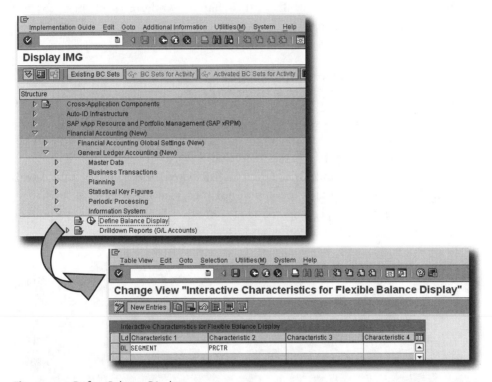

Figure 3.24 Define Balance Display

Now that we have explained the key reports for segment reporting in SAP ERP, we can look at the SAP NetWeaver BI queries.

3.3 Key Reports for Segment Reporting in SAP NetWeaver BI

You can use SAP NetWeaver BI for more advanced and flexible reporting. SAP NetWeaver BI business content includes standard InfoProviders and InfoObjects to model segment reporting. Note that we covered the business content for the new G/L InfoArea in SAP NetWeaver BI. In this chapter, we look at business content queries for segment reporting.

3.3.1 G/L (New) Balance Display Report

As the name suggests, the G/L (New) Balance Display (0FIGL_C10_Q0001) query provides an overview of G/L account balances. With this query, you can drill down and set filters by using the characteristics Segment, Profit Center, Value Type, Functional Area, Cost Center, G/L Account, and Fiscal Year/Period. Figure 3.25 shows an example of the output of G/L (New) Balance Display query in the web analyzer. The query displays the total debit postings, total credit postings, balance, and accumulated balance per selected characteristics. We filtered the output for characteristics segment, G/L account, and fiscal year/period.

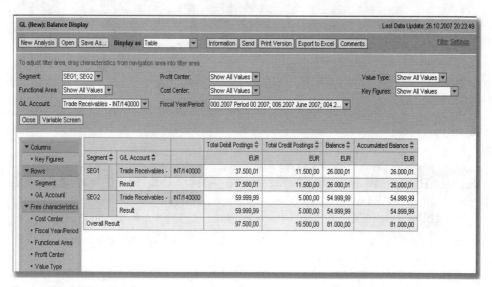

Figure 3.25 G/L (New) Balance Display Report Output

Figure 3.26 shows another output of this query. In this example, the segment characteristic is a free characteristic and filtered to SEG1 value.

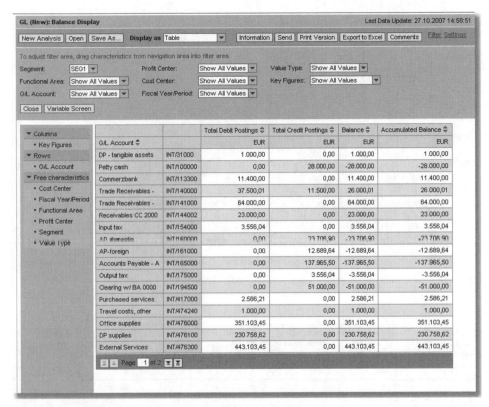

Figure 3.26 G/L (New) Balance Display Report Output

3.3.2 Balance Sheet and Profit and Loss (New): Actual/Actual Comparison

As we mentioned in Chapter 2, the Balance Sheet and Profit and Loss (New) Actual/Actual Comparison (0FIGL_V10_Q0001) query can be used as a reference to create your own financial statement reports. This query shows the balance sheet and profit and loss statement for the two selected reporting time frames. The query allows you to drill down and set filters by using the characteristics Segment, Profit Center, Value Type, Functional Area, Cost Center, G/L Account, and Fiscal Year/ Period. By selecting your segment reporting dimension (segment, profit center), you can generate a segmented financial statement report. Figure 3.27 and Figure 3.28 show examples of segmented financial statements.

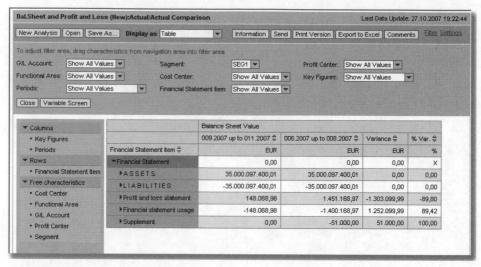

Figure 3.27 Balance Sheet and Profit and Loss (New) Actual/Actual Comparison by Segment

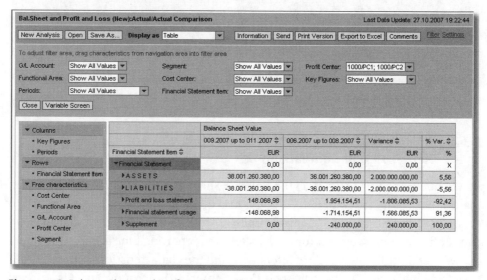

Figure 3.28 Balance Sheet and Profit and Loss (New) Actual/Actual Comparison by Profit Center

3.4   New Segment Reports Available with the Enhancement Package 3

The enhancement package 3 for SAP ERP 6.0 provides the following new standard reports for segment reporting:

- PC Group Plan-Actual Difference
- PC Group Plan/Plan/Actual
- Profit Center Group: Key Figures
- Profit Center Comparison Return on Investment
- Segment Plan-Actual Difference
- Segment Plan/Plan/Actual
- Segment: Key Figures
- Segment Comparison Return on Investment

These reports can be used for performing analysis either for an individual profit center, for a range of profit centers, for a profit center group, or for an individual segment or range of segments. You can drill down by profit center, partner profit center, segment, and partner segment. With Enhancement Package 3, SAP also delivers a migration tool so that you can automatically migrate existing Report Painter and Report Writer reports built on the EC-PCA ledger (ledger 8A) to the new G/L.

In addition, SAP delivers new SAP NetWeaver BI content and POWER lists for segment reporting with the enhancement package 3. You can only use this content if you use the enhancement package 3 for SAP ERP 6.0 and have activated the Reporting Financials business function. Figure 3.29 shows the new reports with the descriptions. Note that we explain enhancement package for SAP ERP as well as SAP's simplified financial reporting innovation in Chapter 15.

best practices, and approaches for tax reporting process design, along with the tax reporting capabilities of SAP ERP and SAP NetWeaver BI.

4.1 Designing the Tax Reporting Process

Tax processes have multiple touch points with all business transactions, even if transactions have no immediate tax impact. Because of this, you need to design your tax reporting process as an integral part of the entire implementation. By doing so, you can manage the tax framework to minimize the business's tax exposure and prevent wrong tax determination and calculation to avoid fines or penalties. It is important to involve the tax department in the project implementation from the early stages to capture all tax requirements. Tax reporting can be classified into two main categories:

▶ Indirect tax reporting
▶ Direct tax reporting

The terms *indirect tax* and *direct tax* are related to the way tax authorities collect the tax from the taxpayers.

4.1.1 Indirect Tax Reporting

Indirect tax is determined during the requisition-to-pay and order-to-cash processes, as well as tax-related G/L processes for enterprises. Sales and use tax, value added tax (VAT), and goods and services tax (GST) are different types of indirect taxes. Figure 4.1 illustrates the indirect tax reporting process.

The indirect tax reporting process facilitates two main outcomes: the tax return and tax payment to tax authorities. When a customer invoice is produced, output tax is calculated on revenue and collected with the customer payment. It is likely that when the vendor's invoice is received, input tax is recorded and later paid to the vendor. The indirect tax process for a given reporting period starts with tax collection from the customers and tax payment to the vendors and ends when the tax liabilities to the tax authorities are settled. The tax liabilities are posted to the corresponding tax accounts and reported to the tax authorities through a tax return. The output tax amount is typically greater than the input tax amount for companies, which means companies need to pay the difference between the output and input tax amount to the tax authority. In contrast, when the input tax amount is greater than the output tax amount, the difference is refunded by the tax authority.

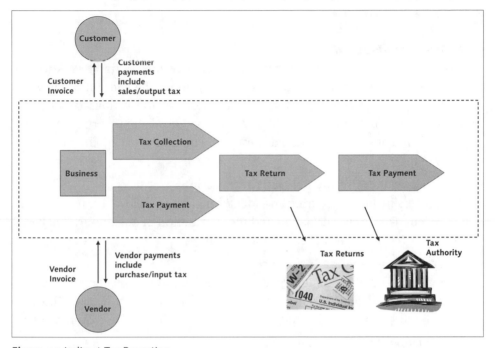

Figure 4.1 Indirect Tax Reporting

4.1.2 Direct Tax Reporting

Direct tax is the other tax category and is tax that is directly collected by the tax authorities. It covers the process of capturing and reporting the information necessary to calculate direct tax charges and liabilities and their presentation in consolidated financial statements. For example, corporate tax, tax on assets, payroll taxes, and withholding tax are classified as direct tax for companies.

As illustrated in Figure 4.2, the direct tax reporting process has four main steps: maintain tax framework, capture and identify tax-relevant transactions, report and analyze tax information, and post tax entries. Now we look at each of these steps.

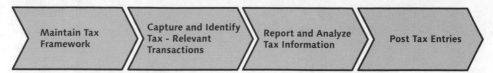

Figure 4.2 Direct Tax Reporting

▶ **Maintain Tax Framework**
This process is intended to determine and maintain the tax framework for the organization. The objective of this step is to establish the connection between the tax reporting system and the tax framework of the various countries in which the organization operates. With this step, you ensure that rules and compliances are constantly monitored, captured, and addressed by the tax reporting system.

▶ **Capture and Identify Tax-Relevant Transactions**
This process includes capturing and identifying the tax-relevant transactions in the system. Direct tax calculation and the preparation of a tax return are based on the tax-relevant transactions in the system.

▶ **Report and Analyze Tax Information**
The report and analyze tax information process retrieves direct tax information from the G/L and subledgers and presents it in the necessary format. This process provides information to fulfill the following tax reporting requirements:

  ▶ Calculating the tax for tax return

  ▶ Calculating tax provisions reported in the financial statements and other regulatory reports

  ▶ Supporting other tax processes such as the estimation of tax payments

  ▶ Supporting tax audit activities

▶ **Post Tax Entries**
This process involves journal bookings of the tax entries and the payment of tax to the tax authorities.

Now that we have explained the indirect and direct tax processes, we can move to the design considerations of tax reporting.

4.2 Tax Reporting Design Considerations

Tax processes, particularly those that are direct tax related, traditionally have been manual in nature, with limited automation and controls. Tax controls often rely on the skills and experience of the individuals performing the process, so problems often arise due to the limited process transparency and the lack of effective process monitoring. Skilled individuals, often with support from tax consultants, tend to compensate for poor tax processes and systems, resulting in organizations being dependent on the quality of the human factors involved. In this section, we discuss best practices and approaches to help your enterprise streamline and automate the tax reporting process to generate accurate tax reporting. Specifically, we look at:

▶ Developing a common approach for tax calculation and tax determination

▶ Integrating all tax requirements into the design

▶ Tax data granularity

▶ Automating tax determination and calculation

▶ Capturing tax-exempt transactions

▶ Meeting data retention and archiving requirements for tax reporting

4.2.1 Developing a Common Approach for Tax Calculation and Tax Determination

The tax reporting process has to achieve two main objectives: compliance with group tax reporting and reporting for local tax jurisdictions. In many countries there is a requirement to generate and submit periodic tax estimates and payments (United States: monthly, United Kingdom: quarterly, etc). One way to increase efficiency in tax reporting is to integrate local and group tax reporting so that they complement each other, enabling an improved audit trial of tax reporting to the local authorities and reconciled local and group tax figures. This can be achieved by developing a common design approach for tax determination and tax calculation processes that is robust and flexible enough to support the country-specific requirements.

Multiple factors influence tax calculations and tax determination. In SAP ERP, tax determination and tax calculation for indirect tax are controlled across multiple components, as illustrated in Figure 4.3. The Financial Accounting (FI) component holds the configuration settings, including country tax procedures, condition types, and tax codes. The other settings necessary to determine tax on sales and purchase transactions are set up in Material Management (MM) and Sales and Distribution (SD) components, for example, creation of tax-specific procedures and entry information in the customer and vendor master data. You can enhance the standard functionality, that is, when external tax calculations are used, by activating and developing various tax enhancements.

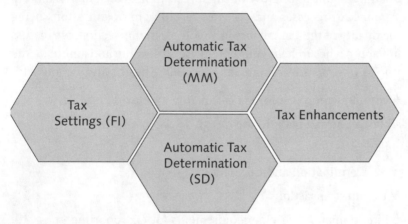

Figure 4.3 Indirect Tax Calculation Settings

The most important setting for tax determination and calculation in FI is the *tax calculation procedure*. Tax calculation procedures are typically defined for each country and then assigned to the country master data. Each calculation procedure consists of the specifications required to calculate and post tax on sales and purchases. In addition, each calculation procedure contains several *tax types*, which are called condition types (such as input or output tax). The *condition type* specifies the base amount on which the tax is calculated and the account key that is used to determine the tax-related G/L accounts in financial transactions. The specifications necessary for calculating and posting tax are defined by the condition types and account keys. SAP ERP provides preconfigured tax calculation procedures for many countries. Figure 4.4 shows the configuration settings of the tax calculation procedure TAXD (Sales Tax–Germany). The procedure includes a list of all common tax types with rules for tax calculation. You can use the preconfigured tax calculation procedures and change existing settings if necessary. Generally, it is not necessary to change the preconfigured procedures, as they have been tested and implemented by numerous customers.

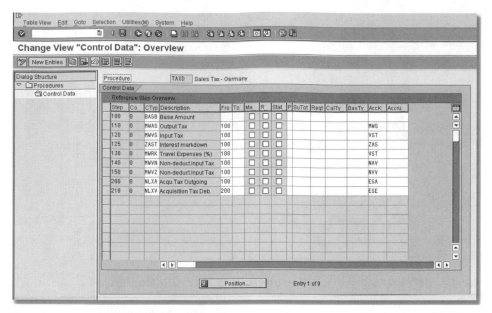

Figure 4.4 Tax Calculation Procedure

Another important setting is to define *tax codes*. You need to define tax on sales and purchases codes for each country. Each code includes one or more tax rates for the different tax types. SAP ERP provides preconfigured tax codes for many countries. Figure 4.5 shows an example of tax code settings in SAP ERP. Each tax code has tax percentage rate and a G/L account for automatic tax posting. In our example, tax code A1 has an output tax percentage rate of 15% and is assigned to G/L account 175000.

We advise checking the delivered tax codes for the countries and changing them if necessary. Best practices dictate that tax codes and the corresponding G/L accounts be used consistently across the organization; even different tax procedures are used. For example, if tax code A1 is used as the output tax in one country, if used in other countries' tax procedures, it is a good practice to define A1 as the output tax. This makes automatic account determination easier and prevents inconsistent situations in reporting.

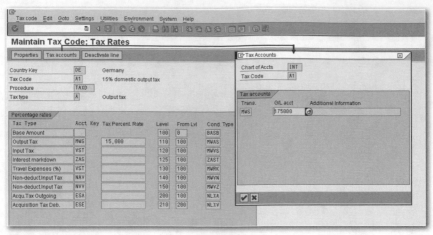

Figure 4.5 Tax Code Settings

4.2.2 Integrating All Tax Requirements into the Design

Additional work-in best practice is to integrate SAP certified third-party tax solutions into the design rather than building the tax jurisdiction rules in the SAP ERP system. This is particularly a good practice for countries such as the United States that have a large number of sales and use tax jurisdictions (taxation authority) in which different tax requirements and rules apply.

SAP ERP provides two methods for calculating sales and use tax for countries with many jurisdictions: jurisdiction method and jurisdiction method with third-party solution. With the jurisdiction method, the configuration of tax determination and calculation for each jurisdiction requires significant configuration and ongoing maintenance. In addition, manual data entry efforts can be time consuming and error prone. To simplify this, many global U.S. companies use third-party tax package solutions with a combination of SAP ERP standard functionality to support countries and requirements that are not included in the scope of the selected third-party tax package solutions.

Tax procedures for jurisdiction codes are predelivered in the system. For example, SAP ERP provides the tax procedure TAXUSJ for the jurisdiction method and TAXUSX for the jurisdiction method with external tax calculation. Each method has the same final goal of applying appropriate tax percentages to line items in SD, MM, and FI. The jurisdiction method with third-party solution establishes tax rates separately in these areas using tax codes, whereas jurisdiction method uses jurisdiction codes in addition to tax codes to determine the tax rates.

The tax procedure is assigned to a country, as shown in Figure 4.6. Once the accounting system is set as productive, it is difficult to switch between the methods; therefore, deciding which method to use is critical in the early stages of implementation.

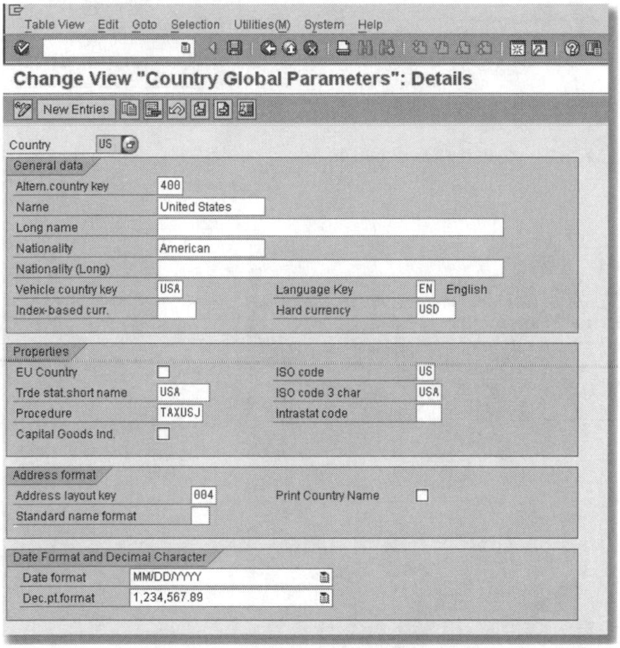

Figure 4.6 Assign Tax Procedure to Country Global Parameters

Figure 4.7 shows the SAP system integration with third-party tax package tool. As it is illustrated in the figure, third-party tax package tools can provide the tax repository, jurisdiction tax database, compliance requirements, and tax calculation engine.

Communication with the external tax calculation system is enabled via the SALESTAX interface in SAP ERP. The interface determines the tax jurisdictions based on the master data elements of customers, vendors, cost centers, and plants. To activate the external tax calculation, follow the configuration menu path **Financial Accounting (New)** • **Financial Accounting Global Settings (New)** • **Tax on Sales/Purchases** • **Basic Settings** • **External Tax Calculation** • **Activate External Tax Calculation**. The activation of the interface screen is illustrated in Figure 4.8.

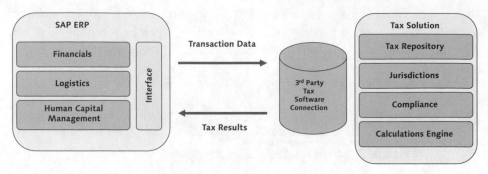

Figure 4.7 SAP System Integration with Third-Party Tax Package Tool

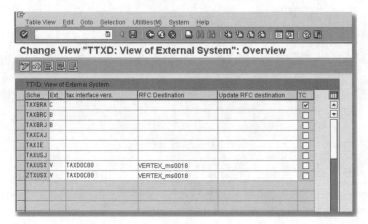

Figure 4.8 Activate External Tax Calculation

Here you specify the connection of the tax schema to the tax interface and the server of the external tax system (remote function call [RFC] destination and update RFC destination).

4.2.3 Automating Tax Determination and Calculation

Another best practice is to automate the tax determination and seamlessly integrate it into the SAP system based on parameters such as customer, vendor, material, and country of destination to reduce the manual interventions. By automating tax determination and calculation, you can avoid fines and penalties that result from incorrect tax-related transactions. SAP provides a mechanism to automate the tax determination of calculations.

The Sales and Distribution (SD) component can automatically calculate sales taxes by taking into account several factors. First, the system determines whether the transaction is domestic or foreign from the customer's ship-to party country and the legal entity generating the sale. In addition, the customer's and material's tax classifications per country are evaluated. For example, a customer can be liable for tax, but the material can be tax-exempt or have a reduced tax rate, or both customer and material can be tax liable. Figure 4.9 shows customer and material master data tax-related segments. Customer **300627** is liable for tax and material **P-100** subject to full tax. Taking into account these criteria, the tax rate per item is automatically determined in the sales order. The tax-related condition types are defined per tax rate in SD condition type records. Figure 4.10 shows condition records for VAT tax. The highlighted line displays the tax classification for customers and materials and the corresponding condition record MWST value of 16% along with the country DE.

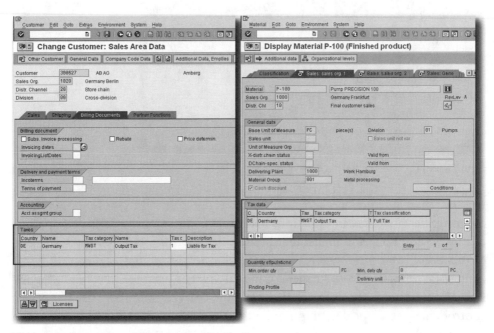

Figure 4.9 Customer and Material Tax Classification

In purchasing, the tax code can be automatically determined during the price-determination process based on various factors such as material group and type of consumption. This is determined in the item conditions within the purchase order, quotation, or an outline agreement and is updated in the tax key fields of the items. When the vendor's invoice is received, the tax code from the purchase order is copied to the invoice and can be used to verify calculation of the tax base amount.

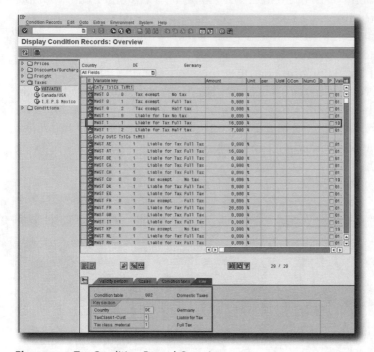

Figure 4.10 Tax Condition Record Overview

In addition to automation, there are built-in system controls to prevent users from entering inaccurate tax information. Because a comprehensive, detailed analysis of how to automate and implement built-in system controls is beyond the scope of this book, we concentrate here on several examples of master data settings to control tax information in financial transactions. For example, the **tax category** field and **posting without tax indicator** in the G/L account master are important control parameters for determining the right tax data at the time of posting (see Figure 4.11).

Input and output tax accounts use the tax categories *input tax account* represented by "<" and *output tax account* represented by ">" in the G/L account master data. By specifying the relevant tax categories in the G/L account master record, you can avoid inaccurate tax postings to these accounts. For example, you should set indicator "-" for accounts only relevant to input tax so that only input tax codes are allowed for these accounts in financial postings. You can further restrict the use of tax codes by specifying a particular tax code in the tax category field of the master data of the G/L account. In doing so, users can only input the tax code specified in the G/L account master data when posting to this account.

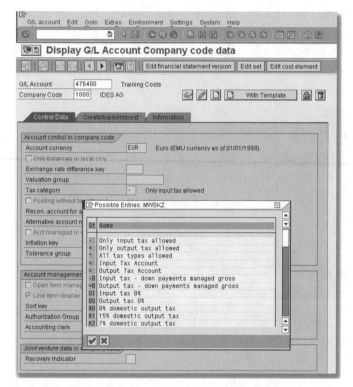

Figure 4.11 G/L Account Master Data Tax-Relevant Information

4.2.4 Capturing Tax-Exempt Transactions

One of the most important design considerations for tax reporting is to make sure that all tax transactions are captured regardless of whether the transaction is tax exempt. For example, in the European single market, there is no individual tax frontier between European Union (EU) countries. Delivery of goods and goods movements are tax exempt, with tax levied in the destination country. However, each organization has to report deliveries to their tax authorities in the form of the European Community (EC) sales list quarterly and annually. The EC sales list should include information on tax-exempt deliveries within the EU and goods movements to registered organizations made in the reporting period. This means that even the transaction has no taxable results; it should be captured in the system as a tax-exempt transaction. This requires using tax-exempt codes for those transactions. Because those transactions are tax-exempt, there is the likelihood that companies fail to record them in their system. You should ensure that tax-exempt codes are configured, properly identified, and recorded. Figure 4.12 shows an example of EU tax-exempt code settings. As shown in the figure, ensure that the relevant **EU code** is selected.

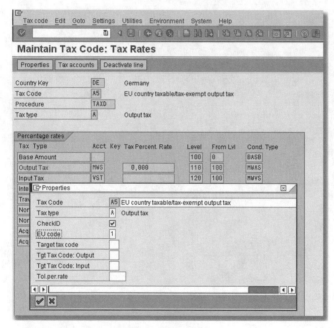

Figure 4.12 Tax-Exempt Tax Code Definition

4.2.5 Tax Data Granularity

Tax-relevant data in the transactions are the foundation of tax reporting and compliance. You must get all the tax-related information from the posted documents and complete the prerequisites for tax returns. Best practices dictate that you should allow correct and accurate tax treatment of underlying transactions by determining the right level of tax data granularity. Populating the financial transactions with the right level of information allows the appropriate treatment to be applied for tax compliance. Without the necessary tax granularity, this information would be obtained through manual analysis of transactions and supporting documents, which could be an arduous and error-prone task.

For global system implementations, it is important to determine the level of tax data granularity, due to the numerous tax frameworks and requirements involved. For direct tax reporting data granularity, the key is to determine both the nature and the purpose of transactions. For example, you should determine whether service fees were incurred for acquisition or disposal or for revenue purposes. Having identified the need to capture the necessary tax information on the transactions, the question is then how to proceed. The answer to this question largely depends on using the right objects with the right level of detail. Let's look at the major design solutions to capture the right level of granularity for direct tax reporting in SAP ERP:

▶ **Chart of accounts**

You can capture additional tax-relevant information about the transaction by using additional G/L accounts in the chart of accounts. The G/L accounts are typically used to capture the nature rather than the purpose of the transaction. Thus, expanding the chart of accounts serves to capture the additional tax information to a certain extent. However, this may be feasible only for a few tax frameworks involved, because this solution may significantly increase the number of G/L accounts for large implementations, resulting in an increased burden on the chart of accounts and risk of inaccuracies.

▶ **Existing field**

You can capture additional tax information by utilizing an existing field that is not used for any other purpose. In other words, you can use an existing element of coding block in SAP ERP to capture the transaction detail required for direct tax reporting. Note that this field should only be used for the purposes of tax data capturing and recording.

▶ **Customer field**

Another way of achieving data granularity is to create a customer field in the new G/L to capture additional tax information (see Figure 4.13). The customer field dedicated entirely to tax information capturing and recording provides the necessary details for direct tax reporting.

Note, however, that you should set up derivation rules to automate updating the customer field or existing field in the financial transactions. Users can enter the relevant tax information when posting the financial documents as well. In that case, you should ensure that users get the required tax information from the invoice details or assistance from the tax department. We advise you to have built-in system controls to ensure that tax information is updated accurately and consistently in financial transactions.

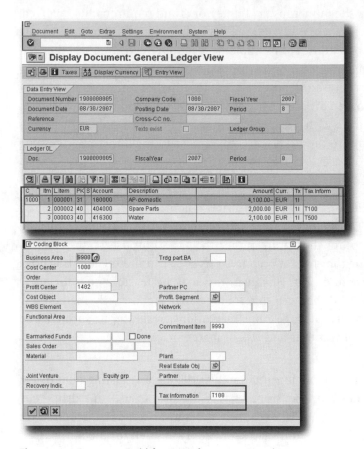

Figure 4.13 Customer Field for Tax Information Details

Note that the customer or existing field can also be populated with the additional tax information for direct tax reporting by using the roll-up ledger at the period end. The roll-up ledger functionality of the new G/L provides great flexibility to derive necessary tax information for existing or customer fields.

4.2.6 Meeting Data Retention and Archiving Requirements for Tax Reporting

Data retention and archiving is crucial to tax reporting. Companies have different policies on record retention and archiving of financial data. Section 802 of the Sarbanes-Oxley Act requires the archiving and retention of data records relevant for audit and review purposes. The Act requires records to be retained for seven years after audit is completed. The historical tax data must be readily accessible for auditors when required.

Each country has its own rules and regulations on record archiving and retrieving. For example, IRS Revenue Procedure 98-25 sets the guidance regarding data retention and archiving compliance in the United States. Some of the IRS Revenue Procedure 98-25 retention requirements are:

▶ Retain "machine-sensible" records that may be or may become material to Internal Revenue Law.

▶ Establish the audit trail, authenticity, and integrity of retained records relative to source document.

▶ Retain at a minimum until expiration of period of limitations.

Having different rules and regulations can be challenging for international businesses. Thus, compliance with all the rules must be carefully considered, and a well-defined archiving approach that covers all geographical areas should be pursued. Data archiving and retention requirements are often not considered during the SAP ERP design stage, resulting in tax record archiving and retention being overlooked. This could create the risk of not complying with rules and having a huge database of records with potential performance issues.

Today data archiving and retention compliance is a growing concern for companies. Many companies that implemented SAP ERP systems in the late 1990s are now facing system performance issues as a result of increased data in the system. IT departments can address this issue by increasing storage space, purchasing faster processors and servers, and so on. In most scenarios, however, the rate of data growth could outpace the system's ability to handle it. Eventually, system performance problems are likely to be encountered. The leading practice is to integrate the archiving, retention, and reporting requirements within the SAP ERP solution and design a comprehensive global tax record retention solution to increase internal controls and streamline tax audit and compliance processes. Failing to implement the right archiving and retention approach puts companies at risk of noncompliance with data archiving and retention requirements, resulting in additional cost and penalties. For example, lack of documentary support may result in deductions not being allowed, and this could lead to increasing the company's tax burden retroactively and subjecting it to interest and penalties. The tax authority may take the position that there was an incomplete filing. In that case, the tax authority could assess income tax on the gross income of the company, without allowing any deductions.

SAP developed the *DART (Data and Retention Tool)* for data retention. With DART, you can periodically extract and retain tax-relevant transaction data from finance and logistic applications. DART was originally developed to meet legal data retention requirements for tax audit purposes, especially to comply with U.S. tax laws (Rev. Proc. 98-25). The extract is in the form of sequential file and can be viewed in various ways. During the past few years, DART has been continuously enhanced to meet new international legal requirements. In addition to DART, several SAP partner products are available for data retention.

Figure 4.14 shows the data extract setup of the DART tool. To go to the extract setup, follow the menu path to access DART tool SAP ERP: **Tools • Administration • Administration • Data Retention Tool • Configuration • Data Extracts** (Transaction FTWP).

Here you determine data extract sources and file storage folders and archive link connections.

Before extracting data for retention, you first need to archive the data. SAP Archiving is the activity of removing data from the SAP database for the purpose of deletion or storage for later retrieval. SAP ERP provides the *Archive Development Kit (ADK)* for data archiving. With ADK programs, you can remove transactional and master data from the system. In addition to data archiving, you can image the documents. Document imaging is the ability to store an SAP document image prior to removal of the data for that document from system. ADK retrieval programs and third-party document imaging tools provide the means to display archived data necessary to fulfill legal and business retention requirements.

You need to take into account many considerations for the archiving and retention of data for tax purposes. Once SAP ERP data is archived, the data is stored in a format optimized for storing the data. Thus, while some of the required tax data can be saved in flat file format, the tax function may no longer be able to drill down to the detail level to answer specific questions posed by the IRS or other auditors. Such risks are significant and constitute one of the primary efforts to substantiate and document tax controls in relation to the Sarbanes-Oxley Act. The reporting views, which you create with the query tool, may not be sufficient to satisfy all tax reporting requirements. Standard delivered views may not be adequate to join the data across application areas or provide a full view of the transaction (in other words, linking purchase order to invoice and payment information). In Figure 4.15 you can see the selection screen of a standard delivered Sales and Use Tax query (query technical name is 0SAP_SUTAX). With the involvement of company tax specialists, you need to create your custom views to support the tax reporting requirements. You can find details regarding how to create SAP ERP queries in Chapter 12.

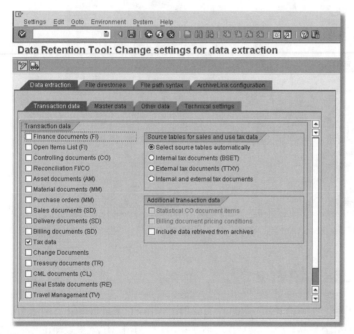

Figure 4.14 DART Data Extraction Settings

Many organizations rely on the IT function and finance to generate and store historical information. However, technical problems with the archiving system or any changes to technology or storage protocols could result in separation between tax and the historical information required to substantiate audits and close off returns. In addition, there could be issues with the system providing too much tax data during the tax audit. If you don't want the tax auditor to have a field day conducting a "fishing expedition" within your tax database, you need to design a comprehensive global tax record archiving and retention solution.

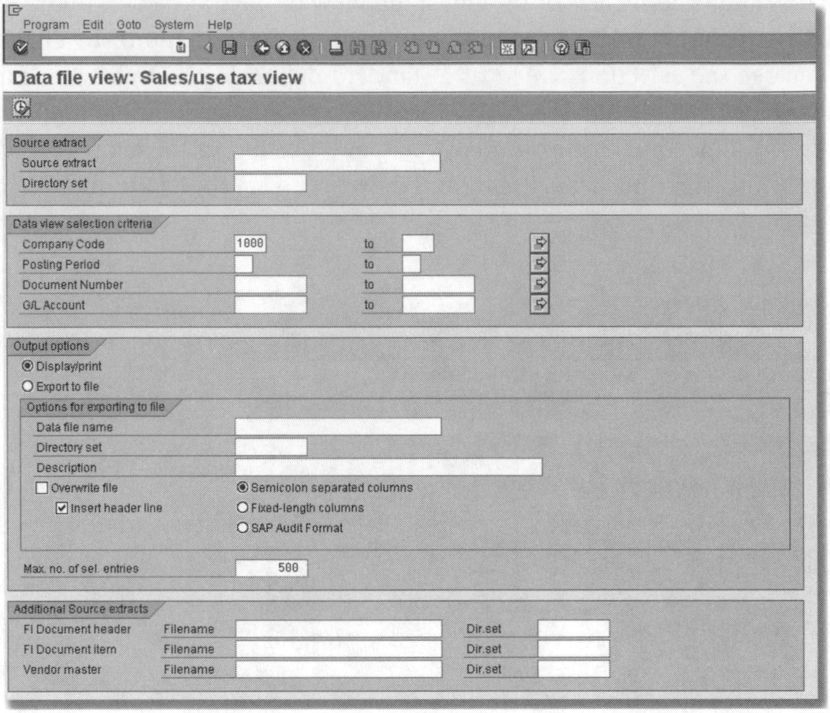

Figure 4.15 Dart Query for Sales and Use Tax

4.3 Tax Reports in SAP ERP

In SAP ERP, although there are many country-specific reports for country-specific requirements and legislation, we can classify tax reporting into five sections:

▸ General sales and purchase tax reporting

▸ Deferred tax reporting

▸ EC sales tax list

▸ Withholding tax reporting

▸ Sales and use tax reporting

Tax reports are listed under the reporting section of financial accounting, except for withholding and property tax reports. You can access tax reports by following the menu path **Financial Accounting • General Ledger • Reporting**. Figure 4.16 shows tax reports available under this menu path. In this section, we examine tax reports that we classified into five sections. Note that property tax reports are examined in Chapter 6.

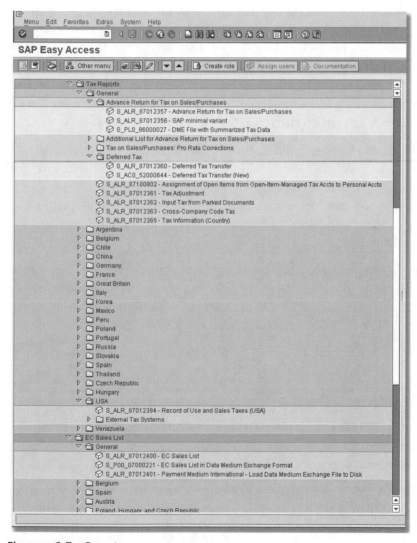

Figure 4.16 Tax Reports

4.3.1 General Sales and Purchase Tax Reporting

Companies registered for sales and purchase tax are liable to provide tax return on sales and purchases sourced from financial transactions. As discussed earlier, SAP ERP provides standard functionality to record sales and purchase tax on procurement and sales transactions as well as on transactions recorded directly in financial accounting.

Sales and purchase tax reporting is generally based on country-specific requirements. The countries in which there is no deferred tax or jurisdiction tax requirements can create a tax return by using the Advance Return for Tax on Sales Purchases report (Transaction S_ALR_87012357). To access the Advance Return for Tax on Sales Purchase report, follow the menu path **Financial Accounting • General Ledger • Reporting • Tax Reports • General • Advance Return for Tax on Sales/Purchases • Advance Return for Tax on Sales/Purchases.**

The report reads data from each line item and provides information on sales and purchase tax for tax analysis. After evaluating the output data of the report, you can automatically generate the tax closing postings and generate the payable to the tax authority, and then you can submit the return to the tax authorities. Figure 4.17 shows the selection screen of the Advance Return for Tax on Sales and Purchases report.

You can specify a range for the company code, document number, fiscal year, posting date, and document reference in the selection parameters. In addition, you can use more selection parameters in the **Further selections** section to restrict reported data. These selection parameters are explained in Table 4.1.

With this report, you can create the tax payable transfer postings via batch input. If you choose the field batch input session required in the tax payable posting parameters as shown in Figure 4.18, the system creates a financial posting with a credit entry to the purchase tax account, debit entry to the sales tax account, and balancing entry to the tax authority payable account. This posting is created with the document type and the posting date and posting period specified in the tax payable posting parameters.

Sales tax (output tax) is generally greater than the purchase tax (input tax) for companies. In that case, the tax authority payable account is credited. With the automatic payment run, payment is made to the tax authority vendor account. The due date for the tax payable account is also specified in the tax payable posting parameters. In our example, a tax posting is created automatically with document type SA and posting date 15.08.2007 via a batch input session called RFUMSV00. We specified the due date of the tax payable account as 15.09.2007.

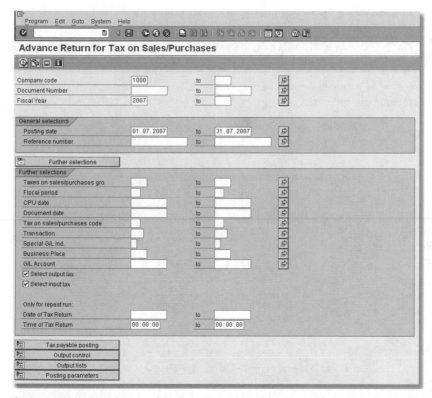

Figure 4.17 Selection Screen of the Advance Return for Tax on Sales and Purchases Report

> **Note**
>
> The account determination of the tax authority payable account can be specified in table T030 with transaction key UMS.

Another important parameter of this report is to update the document field in the posting parameter section as shown in Figure 4.18. If you select this parameter, the date and time of the execution will be updated in the tax line items when you execute the report. In doing so, you can identify tax line items with the tax report execution time and date. This gives you the capability to exclude the previous period run input data in the subsequent run. Note that this is an optional step. You can still create your postings without updating the date stamp. In that case, you need to make sure the selection does not overlap with the previous return, so it is advisable to update documents with report execution time. Note, however, that the run time of the report increases if you stamp tax postings with date and time fields.

Further Selection Parameter	Description
Taxes on sales/ purchases grouping	This parameter is used in some countries such as Belgium, Germany, and Russia when generating the tax return.
Fiscal period	You can restrict your report to a specific fiscal period from the fiscal year variant.
CPU date	CPU date represents the entry date of the document. In some countries, the entry date of the document is required when submitting a tax return.
Document date	As the name suggests, document date represents the data for which the financial document is created. In some countries, the document date is required when submitting a tax return.
Tax on sales/ purchases code	Tax on sales/purchases code field is used to restrict the reported data to specific tax codes such as A1, A2, A3, etc.
Transaction	The transaction key is used to determine the accounts or posting keys of the line items.
Special G/L ind.	Special G/L indicator is used to select special G/L transactions.
Business place	Business place represents an organizational unit below the company code level used for tax reporting purposes in some countries such as Thailand.
G/L account	In the report, you can specify the sales and purchases tax accounts.
Select output tax	By selecting this option, you can generate a Tax on Sales/Purchases report for only output tax.
Select input tax	By selecting this option, you can generate a Tax on Sales/Purchases report for input tax only.
Date of tax return	Date of tax return indicates the last date the tax return was made. This parameter is used to prevent double reporting.
Time of tax return	Time of tax return represents the time at which the tax return was made. This parameter is used to prevent double reporting.

Table 4.1 Further Selection Parameters

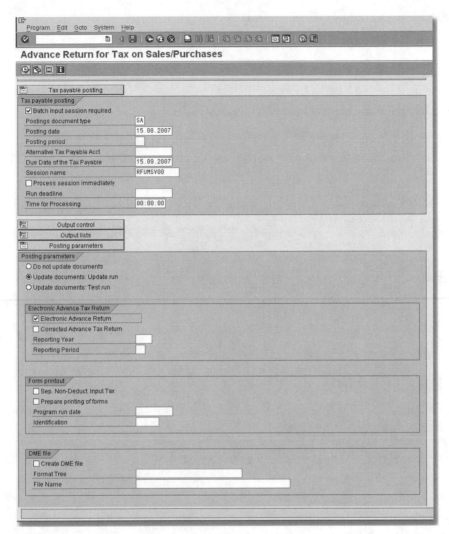

Figure 4.18 Tax Payable Postings and Posting Parameters in the Selection Screen of the Advance Return for Tax on Sales and Purchases Report

The output of the report shows each tax type at the line item level. You can suppress the line item details on the output selection of the report. Note, however, that the system continues to read data from each financial line item. The output of the reported data can be presented in lists with different summarization levels:

▸ Line item list with output tax per company code

▸ Summary list of output tax per company code

- ▶ Line item list with input tax per company code

- ▶ Summary list of input tax per company code

- ▶ Line item list of documents with tax differences per company code

- ▶ Summary list of tax balances per company code

- ▶ Summary list of tax balances for all company codes

Figure 4.19 shows an example of the Advanced Tax on Sales/Purchases report output by line item list with input and output tax per company code.

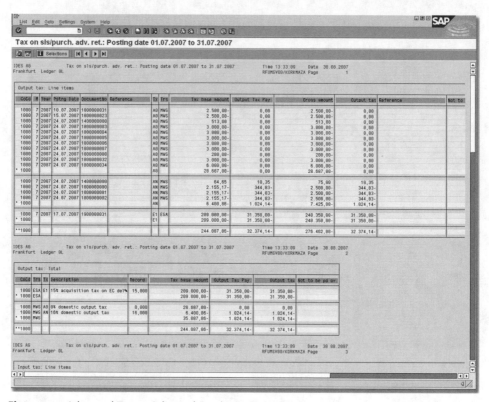

Figure 4.19 Advanced Tax on Sales and Purchases Report Output

Another important parameter for Advanced Tax on Sales/Purchases report is to select the output type and format required by tax authorities. There are four options for providing a tax return to the tax authorities:

▶ **Send a print format**

You can update tax balances per company code, debit and credit indicator, transaction key, tax on sales and purchases, date, and time in the corresponding tables. After that, you can use the print report for printing the tax return from these tables.

▶ **Send XML format**

You can provide the tax on sales and purchases report in XML format. XML is usually the preferred solution for data transfer, as it is very flexible compared to other formats.

▶ **Send as DME**

You can save the tax output as data medium exchange (DME) and send it to tax authorities.

▶ **Send electronically**

With this option, the tax return is sent to tax authorities electronically.

We now explore how you can submit your tax return electronically. The first prerequisite is to select the **Electronic Advance Return** box in the selection screen as shown in Figure 4.18. To use this functionality, ensure that the reporting period corresponds with the declaration period of the tax return. In addition, you need to define the tax transfer procedure and forms required by the tax authority. Once you have done all required settings, the report will create an electronic advance return for tax on sales and purchases. You can then send this electronic form of report output directly to the tax authorities. To access the Administration Data Transmission report, follow the menu path **Financial Accounting • General Ledger • Reporting • Electronic Communication with Authorities • Administration Report Data Transmission** (Transaction FOTV).

Figure 4.20 shows the selection screen of the Electronic Data Transmission report. You first need to select the output data created with the report Advance Return for Tax on Sales and Purchases. After doing this, you can send the data to the tax authorities electronically by using SAP Exchange Infrastructure (XI) technology.

In addition to the Advance Return for Tax on Sales and Purchases report, SAP ERP provides the Additional List for Advance Return for Tax on Sales and Purchases (Transaction S_ALR_87012359) report. This report uses G/L account balances as a tax base, whereas the Advance Return for Tax on Sales and Purchases report reads each financial line item.

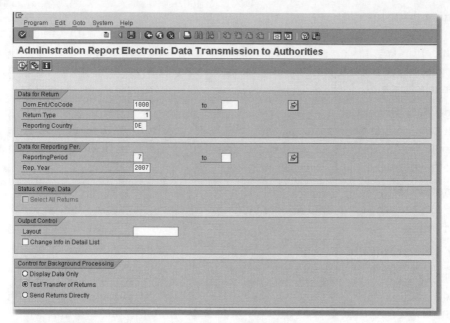

Figure 4.20 Electronic Data Transmission to Authorities Administration

Country-specific tax on sales and purchases reports

The reporting section of the general ledger menu has additional tax reports for some countries. These have been developed to comply with country-specific requirements and legislation.

4.3.2 Deferred Tax Reporting

Tax on sales and purchases is typically reported when an invoice is issued. The tax payable amount is calculated as the balance of the input and output tax and cleared by the payment program as described in the Advance Return for Tax on Sales and Purchases report. However, sometimes the tax is calculated and posted but not accepted for deduction from the tax authorities until a specific event occurs. In such cases the sales and purchases tax is called *deferred tax*. For example, purchase tax cannot be claimed until the vendor has been paid, or the sales tax is not paid until the customer pays the invoice or the goods are shipped. Deferred tax is common in France, Italy, and some east European countries. Deferred tax shows variations from country to country. For example, France has deferred tax for both sales and purchases, whereas Italy has deferred tax only for purchases.

SAP has developed several general deferred tax reports and deferred report variations for country-specific requirements. The most common report used for deferred tax is the Deferred Tax Transfer report (program RFUMSV25). This report is used to evaluate customer and vendor invoices posted with deferred tax codes and generates tax postings with the target tax codes to which deferred tax codes are linked. For example, the deferred tax code W3 for France is assigned to tax code V3, as illustrated in Figure 4.21. This means Deferred Tax Transfer report evaluates the financial postings posted with W3 and generates postings with the target tax code V3. After deferred tax codes are transferred to the target tax codes, the Advance Return for Tax on Sales and Purchases report is used for the tax return. Note that SAP ERP provides country-specific deferred tax reports.

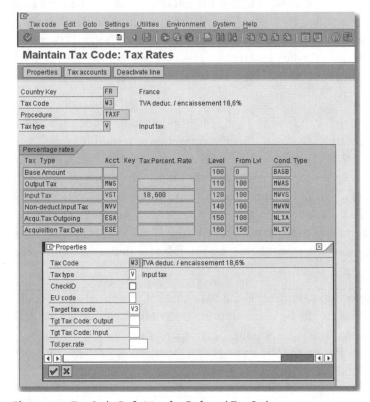

Figure 4.21 Tax Code Definition for Deferred Tax Code

4.3.3 EC Sales Tax List

The EC Sales Tax List provides a list of all tax-exempt deliveries of goods within the EU and goods movements to EU-registered companies in the reporting period. Companies registered within the EU with these kinds of transactions must submit an EC sales tax list to the tax authorities. The report is generally required quarterly or yearly.

In SAP ERP, you can generate the EC Sales Tax List using the EC Sales List report (program RFASLM00). Alternatively, you can use the EC sales list in the data medium exchange format report (program RFASLD20) to provide the report output in DME format (Transaction S_P00_07000221). The EC Sales List is structured in SAPscript form. Country-specific SAP delivered forms are available in SAP ERP. For example, the default form for the German EC sales list is F_ASL_DE (see Figure 4.22). In addition, SAP ERP provides the F_ASL_DE_LISTE form to issue the address of the customer. Note, however, that the parameter import address data should be selected to include the address details in the output. Other country-specific formats are also available, such as Denmark, Finland, Ireland, Portugal, and Austria. To access the EC Sales List report, follow the menu path **Financial Accounting • Reporting • EC Sales List • General • EC Sales List** (Transaction S_ALR_87012400).

In the selection screen, you can specify a range for the company code, document number, fiscal year, posting date, and document reference. In addition, you can specify additional restrictions on the data such as reporting quarter, reporting period, reporting country, output tax code, and tax on sales or purchase group. If you select the line item display, the report shows the information at the document level as shown in Figure 4.23. You can get totals per VAT registration number of the customer or per company code in the report output. You can also list the triangular deals in the EC Sales List report if you set the relevant indicator in financial postings.

Another important selection parameter is the base amount. If you select this indicator in the selection screen, the base amounts are determined from the tax items rather than the line items. This is important for companies that post a net tax base amount, as the Advance Return for Tax on Sales and Purchases report and EC Sales List report show the same base amount.

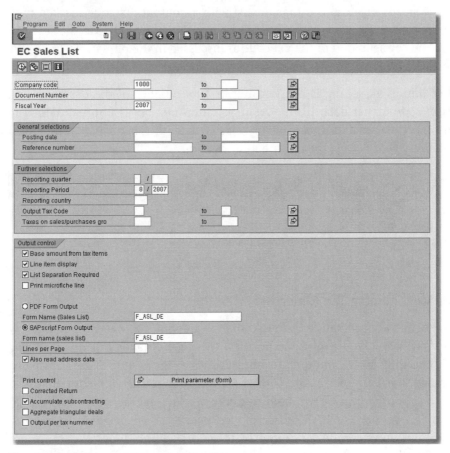

Figure 4.22 EC Sales List Report Selection Screen

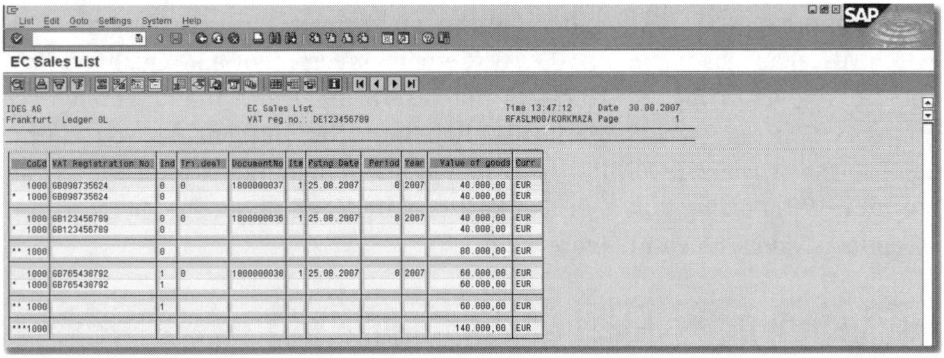

Figure 4.23 EC Sales List Report Output

The report reads financial postings posted with an output tax code marked with an EU code with a value of 1 or 3. Thus, it is important to choose the relevant value in the configuration of the tax code as discussed in the previous section (see Figure 4.12).

Another important setting is the VAT registration number of the customer and company code master data. If the VAT registration number is not maintained in the customer master data and company master data, the report will generate an error message and not list the required information.

Plants abroad functionality

Plants abroad functionality is taken into account when generating the EC Sales List report. The number of tax reports including the Advance Return for Tax on Sales and Purchases report and the Deferred Tax Transfer report support the plants abroad functionality.

4.3.4 Withholding Tax Reporting

In some countries, companies withhold the tax amount that needs to be paid by another payee and report to tax authorities. This type of tax is called *withholding tax*. Withholding tax is common in countries such as the United States, Germany, and France. For example, in the United States, legal entities are sometimes required to submit returns of withholding tax to the Internal Revenue Service (IRS) on behalf of vendors such as self-employed people or nonresident foreigners. Legal entities are typically only required to report withholding tax and are not obliged to collect or pay it. The vendor is liable for paying the withholding tax amount to the IRS. Legal entities must submit a withholding tax return to the IRS and withholding tax liable vendors by using preprinted forms such as the 1099 Misc (Miscellaneous Income), 1099-G (Certain Government and Qualified State Tuition Program Payments), 1099-INT (Interest Income), and 1042S (Foreign Person's U.S. Source Income Subject to Withholding). SAP ERP enables you to print these forms or generate DME files to submit a withholding tax return to tax authorities. Withholding tax reports in SAP ERP are listed under the menu path of accounts payable shown in Figure 4.24.

Note

Legal entities pay withholding tax to tax authorities in some countries such as the United Kingdom.

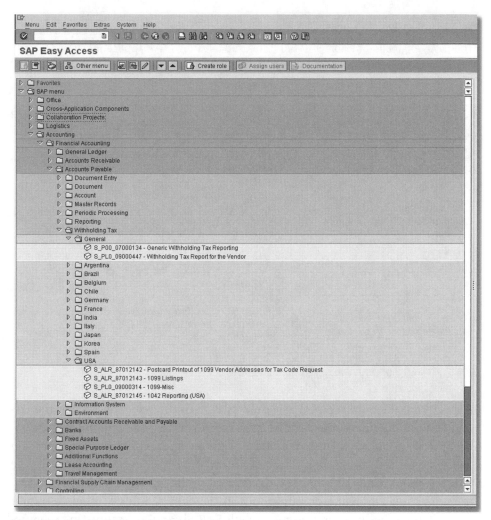

Figure 4.24 Withholding Tax Reports

You can create DME files and print 1099 and 1042S forms using the generic withholding tax report (Transaction S_P00_07000134). The report generates return forms using SAP smart forms and creates files using the data medium format from the DME engine. You can specify where to save the files on your file system in the selection parameters of the report. The forms and DME tree for files used for IRS returns are specified in Table 2.

> **Note**
>
> The DME engine is a flexible SAP ERP tool used in various SAP applications to generate DME files in any format without a need for programming.

IRS Return	Transaction/Form	DME Tree for Files
1099-MISC (Miscellaneous Income)	S_P00_07000134 (Program RFI-DYYWT) with form IDWTCERT_US_1099MISC	IDWTFILE_US_1099
1099-G (Certain Government and Qualified State Tuition Program Payments)	S_P00_07000134 (Program RFI-DYYWT) with form IDWTCERT_US_1099G	IDWTFILE_US_1099G
1099-INT (Interest Income)	S_P00_07000134 (Program RFI-DYYWT) with form IDWTCERT_US_1099INT	IDWTFILE_US_1099INT
1042S (Foreign Person's U.S. Source Income Subject to Withholding)	S_P00_07000134 (Program RFI-DYYWT) with form IDWTCERT_US_1042S	IDWTFILE_US_1042

Table 4.2 Forms and DME Trees Used for IRS Returns

By specifying the output group and process type in the selection screen, the Generic Withholding Tax report can be used for generating the withholding tax returns listed in table 2. In the definition of output group and process type, you specify the form that is used in the printout and the DME format tree used for the DME file, along with the other settings related to the tax items to be selected by the report. You can define output groups in the configuration. To define output groups, follow the configuration menu path **SAP Financial Accounting (New) • Financial Accounting Global Settings (New) • Withholding Tax • Extended Withholding Tax • Generic Withholding Tax Reporting • Define Output Groups** (See Figure 4.25).

Another important setting for generating withholding tax returns is withholding tax codes. Withholding tax codes are used to identify the tax rates, the tax base, and any exemptions in the withholding tax reports. SAP ERP provides predefined withholding tax codes. If you create a company code using the U.S. company code template, some of the withholding tax codes are created automatically. Note, however, that you must create others manually. Figure 4.26 illustrates the settings of withholding tax code **07**. As shown in the figure, the withholding tax rate, currency, minimum amount, percentage subject to tax, and so on are set up in the withholding tax code configuration.

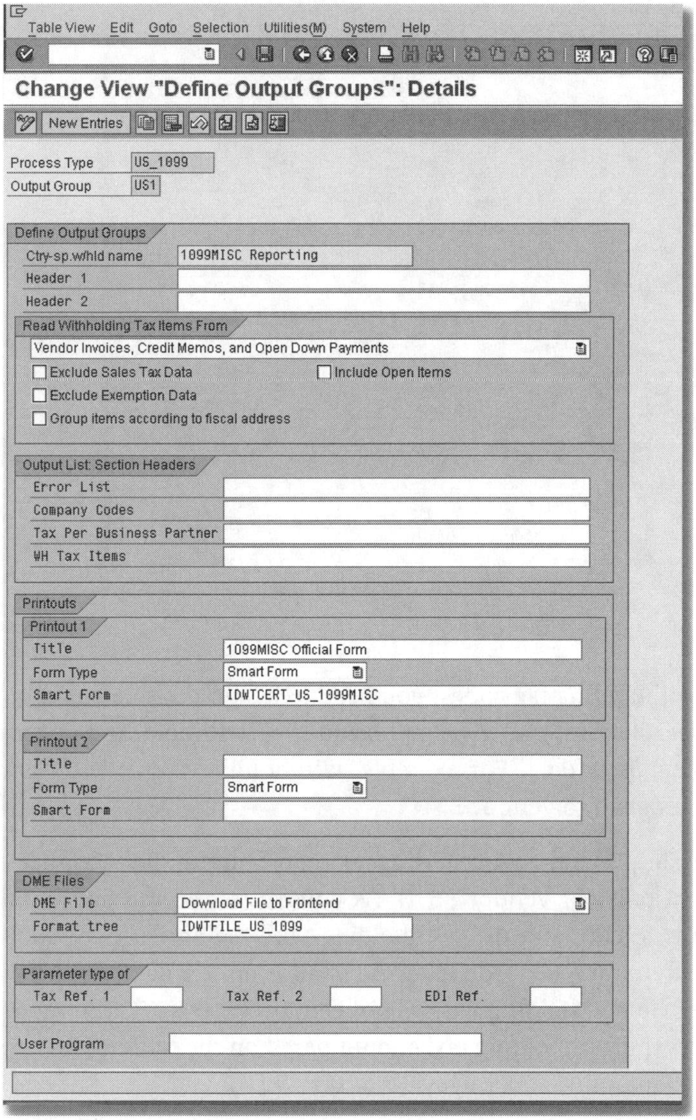

Figure 4.25 Define Output Groups

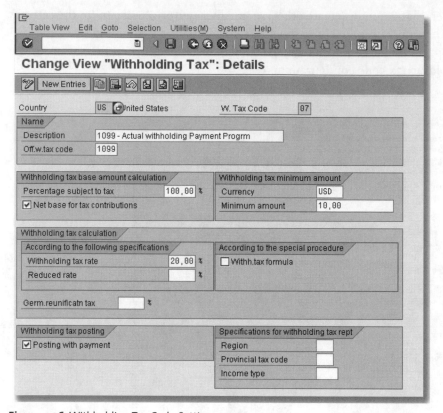

Figure 4.26 Withholding Tax Code Setting

Once you set up the withholding tax codes, you need to assign them in customer and vendor master data. Figure 4.27 gives an example of withholding tax code settings in the vendor master data. For example, withholding tax code **07** and recipient type **01** are assigned to vendor **3510**.

Figure 4.28 gives an example of the withholding tax report output. For simplicity, we executed the report only for vendor 3510. As you can see in the figure, the total invoice amount is **$9000**, and the withholding tax base amount is **$1000**. The report gets the withholding tax code from the vendor master data. As shown in the previous figure, the withholding tax code of vendor 3510 is 07. The report automatically calculates the withholding tax amount based on the withholding tax rate of 20% of the base amount $1000, which is $200.

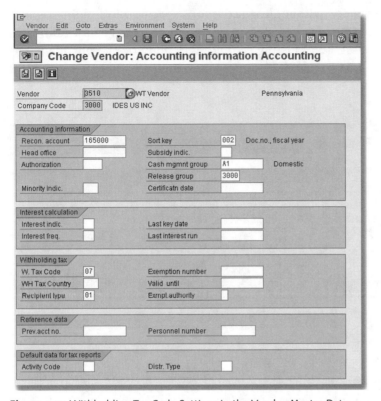

Figure 4.27 Withholding Tax Code Settings in the Vendor Master Data

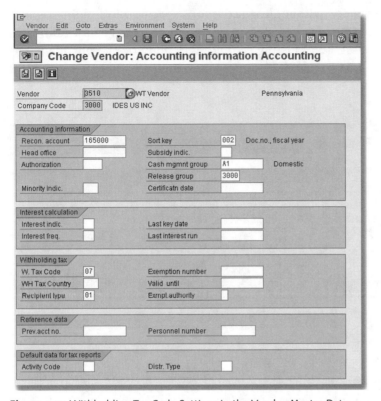

Figure 4.28 Generic Withholding Tax Reporting Output

In addition to the generic withholding tax report, specific withholding reports are delivered for the United States: Postcard Printout of 1099 Vendor Addresses for a Tax Code Request, 1099 Listings, 1099 Misc, and 1042 Reporting (USA) as shown in Figure 4.24. Figure 4.29 shows an example of 1099 Listings report output.

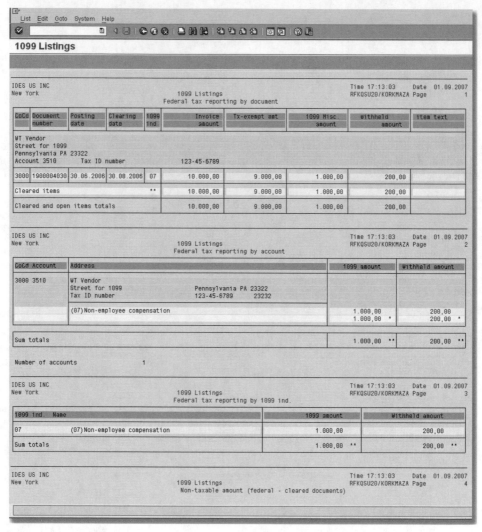

Figure 4.29 1099 Listings Report Output

Note that you have to use the *extended withholding tax functionality* to prepare the 1099-G and 1099-INT reports from SAP ERP, whereas the 1099-MISC report can be prepared by using classic or extended withholding tax functionality. Thus, we recommend using extended withholding tax functionality for modeling withholding tax reporting.

> **Extended withholding functionality**
>
> Extended withholding functionality enables you to carry out withholding tax from both the vendor and the customer. In accounts payable, the vendor is subject to tax, and the company code is obligated to deduct withholding tax. In accounts receivable, the company code is subject to tax, and a customer doing business with this company is obligated to deduct withholding tax. For new implementations, we recommend using the extended withholding tax functionality. For existing implementations, the withholding tax changeover tool available in SAP ERP can be used to convert classic withholding tax to the extended withholding tax functionality. Note that we showed the classic withholding tax functionality in our examples. Also note that classic and extended withholding tax functionality cannot be used at the same time.

4.3.5 Sales and Use Tax Reporting

Tax on sales and purchases is known as sales and use tax in the United States. If you purchase a taxable good within the state, *sales tax* is imposed on the sale. The vendor collects and remits tax to the jurisdiction. If you purchase a taxable good from another state, the vendor does not charge sales tax. In that case, you are obliged to remit *use tax* to the tax authority where the goods are consumed. Transactions are exposed to sales or use tax but not both.

As discussed in the previous section, SAP ERP provides two methods for countries that have many jurisdictions with different tax requirements: the jurisdiction method and the jurisdiction method with external third party. In this section, we look at the Record of Use and Sales Taxes (USA) report designed for the jurisdiction method. Figure 4.30 shows the selection screen of the Record of Use and Sales Taxes report. As shown in the figure, you can specify the company code, fiscal year, posting date, jurisdiction code, and so forth.

With the Record of Use and Sales Tax report, you can display the documents per customer and vendor in the output of the report (program RFUTAX00). In addition, you can take a total by tax code and jurisdiction with reference to the tax base and amount. An example of the report output is given in Figure 4.31.

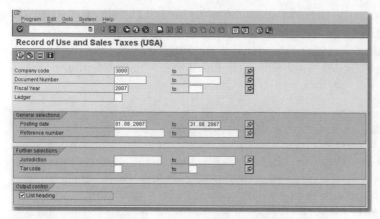

Figure 4.30 Record of Use and Sales Taxes Selection Screen

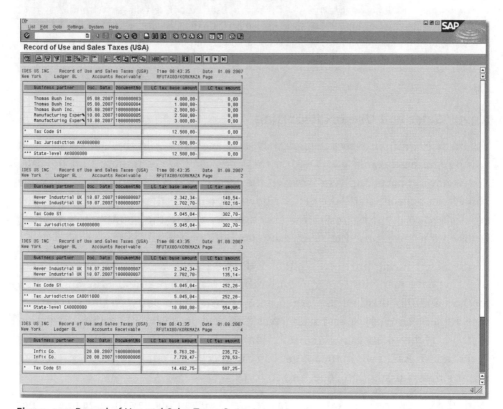

Figure 4.31 Record of Use and Sales Taxes Output

Corporate Tax Reporting

SAP ERP does not provide corporate tax reporting that you can provide directly to tax authorities. You can model corporate tax reporting with the reporting tools described in Chapter 12.

Data Flow of Taxes on Sales/Purchases DSO   *Overview of Taxes on Sales/Purchases DSO*

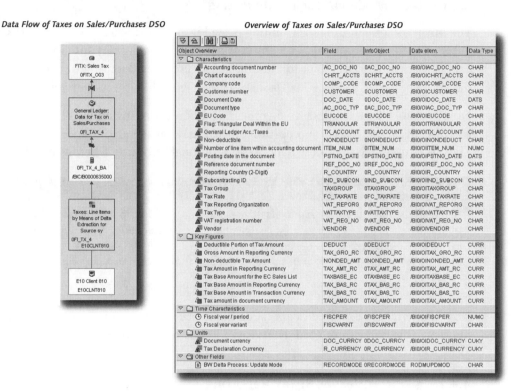

Figure 4.32 Data Flow of Sales Tax Data DSO along with the Object Overview

4.4   Tax Reports in SAP NetWeaver BI

SAP NetWeaver BI reporting primarily supports tax reporting for management information purposes. In the business content, a standard data storage object (DSO) and InfoObjects are delivered for tax reporting. You can model your tax reporting architecture in SAP NetWeaver BI by using these standard objects. However, it is important to note that you should carefully check whether the preconfigured solution fulfills all of your tax reporting requirements. Also note that you should reconcile and verify tax postings with SAP ERP before generating tax reports to ensure accuracy and completeness. In this section, we focus exclusively on business content for tax accounting. Let's first look at the data modeling scenario using the business content objects.

4.4.1 Data Modeling for Tax Reporting

The business content in tax accounting provides the FITX: Sales Tax Data (0FITX_003) DSO for tax reporting. The object is supplied with data by InfoSource 0FI_TAX_4 General Ledger: Data for Tax on Sales/Purchases. Figure 4.32 shows the data flow of the FITX: Sales Tax Data DSO along with the object overview.

Note that this modeling example is for illustration purposes only. When carried out directly in the DSO, the reporting process may cause performance problems. Thus, it is advisable to update data in the additional InfoCube when using DSO.

> **Tax type InfoObject (0VATTAXTYPE)**
>
> The Tax Type InfoObject is used to classify tax as input and output. In the business content, the field tax type is delivered unassigned in the data modeling. We strongly recommend checking whether the tax type is filled when extracting data into SAP NetWeaver BI if you require this field in your tax reporting and use the business content as a reference template.

Now that we have explained data modeling for tax reporting, let's continue with queries delivered with the SAP NetWeaver BI business content.

4.4.2 SAP NetWeaver BI Tax Reporting

SAP NetWeaver BI provides three queries based on the DSO FITX: Sales Tax Data:

- Advance Sales Tax Return–General
- EC Sales List–General
- Advance Return for Tax on Sales and Purchases in Italy & Spain

In this section, we only look at the Advance Sales Tax Return—General and the EC Sales List–General (see Figure 4.33).

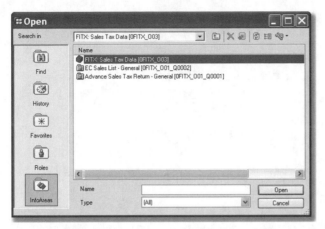

Figure 4.33 Tax Queries in SAP NetWeaver BI

Advance Sales Tax Return–General

In the business content, you can activate the Advance Sales Tax Return—General (0FITX_O01_Q0001) query for tax on sales and purchases reporting. The query reads data from the DSO FITX: Sales Tax Data (0FITX_O03). The report is similar to the SAP ERP Advance Return for Tax on Sales and Purchases report described in the previous section. Note, however, that you cannot generate tax postings to the tax authority with this query or any other query you designed for reporting tax in SAP NetWeaver BI. However, SAP NetWeaver BI offers greater flexibility for analyzing tax figures. Figure 4.34 shows an example of the Advance Sales Tax Return–General report output in Web Analyzer. In the report output, you can swap tax type with company code, document number, fiscal year variant, fiscal year period, item, posting date, reference, tax group, and tax rate.

EC Sales List–General

In the business content, you can activate the EC Sales List–General (0FITX_O01_Q0002) query for EC sales list reporting. The query reads data from the DSO FITX: Sales Tax Data (0FITX_O03). The report shows many similarities to the SAP ERP EC Sales List report described in the previous section. Figure 4.35 shows the output of the EC Sales List- General query in Web Analyzer. You can swap the company code with the document number, EU code, fiscal year variant, fiscal year/period, indicator: triangular deal, item, posting date, sales tax ID, subcontracting ID, and tax declaration currency.

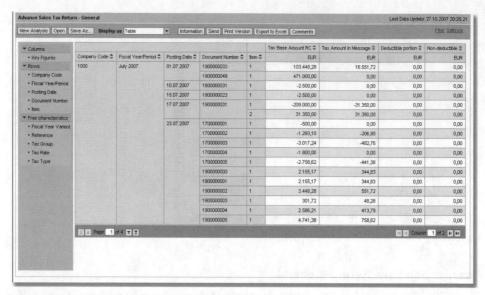

Figure 4.34 Advance Sales Tax Return–General Output

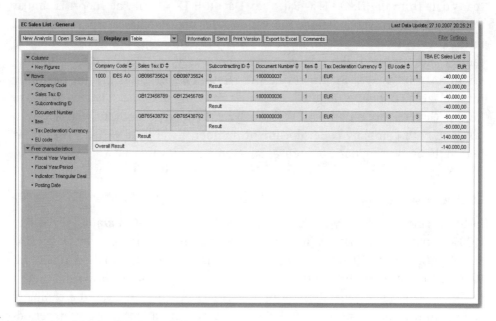

Figure 4.35 EC Sales List–General Output

4.5 Summary

SAP ERP enables automatic calculation and tax postings. When posting a document, the system automatically determines the tax amounts and assigns the amounts to the corresponding accounts and retains the information for reporting. Enterprises might consider improving the tax reporting design process for many reasons. These include a desire to improve risk management, cost and time efficiencies, or the need to comply with new or changing regulatory requirements. If the right approach and design considerations are taken into account, benefits can be realized in all these areas. In this chapter, we discussed the most important design considerations and approaches for the tax reporting process. In addition, we examined the SAP ERP tax reporting capabilities and discussed SAP NetWeaver BI business content for tax reporting.

Corporate fraud and new regulatory requirements have increased the importance of all subprocesses within requisition to pay and order to cash, especially in the area of revenue and expense recognition. In this chapter, we address process design considerations and best practices to improve accounts payable and accounts receivable reporting. We also explain the key SAP ERP reports along with the SAP NetWeaver BI business content for accounts payable and accounts receivable.

5   Accounts Payable and Accounts Receivable Reporting

Accounts payable is part of the *requisition to pay (RTP)* process, and accounts receivable is part of the *order to cash (OTC)* process. Leading organizations review, reassess, and streamline their processes across all aspects of the business, including accounts payable and accounts receivable. Corporate fraud and new regulatory requirements have increased the importance of all subprocesses within RTP and OTC. The bankruptcy of Enron and other large corporation failures have highlighted the importance of *accounts payable (AP)* and *accounts receivable (AR)* processes, especially in the area of revenue and expense recognition. It is not possible to isolate AP and AR processes and make improvements in these areas without addressing overall end-to-end RTP and OTC processes. For example, the purchasing process has a direct impact upon the efficiency of the AP process. By the same token, the billing process has a direct impact upon AR process. However, AP and AR can be streamlined and standardized. Improvements in AP and AR can be used as a series of improvement steps toward overall RTP and OTC end-to-end process improvement.

An organization might want to increase the efficiency of AP and AR reporting for multiple reasons. These include a desire to improve the control of AP and AR processes, cost and time efficiencies, and risk management. Benefits can be realized in all of these areas if the right considerations and approaches are taken into account in the design and improvement of AP and AR reporting processes. In this chapter, we discuss the design considerations and work-in best practices for AP and AR reporting. In addition, we examine the key reports in SAP ERP and the SAP NetWeaver BI business content of AP and AR.

5.1   Accounts Payable Reporting

AP transaction processing and AP reporting process are closely interrelated. To give you a better understanding of AP reporting, we first present an overview of AP transaction processing. Vendor business transactions are captured and recorded in the Accounts Payable (AP) component, which is a subledger of the G/L. When you post business transactions to AP, the system updates the G/L simultaneously. This means you can get financial statements at any time without having to transfer balances and reconcile from AP to the G/L. As part of the RTP process, AP is also integrated with the purchasing application of the Materials Management (MM) component. Accounts payable information captured in MM flows immediately into the AP subledger. The SAP ERP system offers a number of analytical reports for AP transaction processing, such as vendor open items, due date analysis, vendor master data control reports, and vendor evaluations. In addition, you can use SAP NetWeaver BI for more comprehensive analysis of AP processes. Figure 5.1 illustrates the AP reporting process in relation to AP transaction processing. AP processes are transactional processes, so the associated reports are designed to report information mainly on transactional operations.

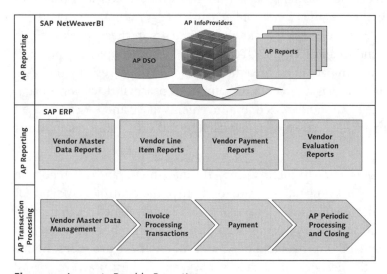

Figure 5.1 Accounts Payable Reporting

AP transaction processing can be classified in four subprocesses:

▶ **Vendor master data management**
This process includes the activities of managing vendor master data, that is, creating, changing, and deleting the vendor master data. Each vendor has a unique identification code in SAP ERP, which is called vendor account. This code is required for all AP transaction processing. For example, you need to enter the vendor code when posting vendor business transactions in both AP and MM components.

▶ **Invoice processing transactions**
This process involves capturing and recording invoices and credit memos in the system. In SAP ERP, you can process the invoices and credit memos either in AP or MM components. If it is not possible or practical to use a purchase order (for product transactions) or a request for services (for non-product transactions), you can generate the invoice in the AP component. Companies allow invoice transactions without a purchase order or request for services in limited cases such as utility bills. In that case, you have to establish a tight control procedure to get the invoices approved before processing the invoice and payment so that you can prevent fraud. If the transaction requires a purchase order or request for services, you need to process the invoices and credit memos with MM invoice verification after generating the purchase order or request for service. The use of purchase orders and requests for services and the integrated approval process provide a documented understanding of the terms and prices of an agreement and the account assignment objects, thereby making postings into AP and the G/L more accurate.

▶ **Payment**
In this process, all outstanding due payables are settled after being reviewed and approved. In SAP ERP all standard payment methods are supported in both printed (such as checks and transfers) and electronic (data medium exchange on disk and electronic data interchange) media.

▶ **AP periodic processing and closing**
AP periodic processing and closing are composed of many subprocesses such as balance confirmation, foreign currency valuation, and balance carry forward. These subprocesses are required to close the AP subledger and generate financial statements from the G/L.

As mentioned earlier, the AP reporting process runs in parallel with transaction processing. Vendor master data reports are executed to control and monitor vendor master data. Vendor line item reports are used to analyze AP transactions such as invoices and credit memos. After the payments are generated you can use payment reports and line item reports to monitor payments. In addition to line item and payment reports, vendor evaluations can be used to further analyze vendors, especially as part of your period end closing process. Thus, AP reporting is a crucial step for each AP subprocess. Now that we have explained the key components of AP transaction processing and AP reporting, we will explain the design considerations and approaches of each of these processes to generate accurate and consistent AP reports.

5.1.1 Vendor Master Data Management

Multiple records often exist for the same vendor in the system during system upgrade or conversion activities. This situation typically arises due to a lack of control procedures that prevent multiple vendor master data creation, which can lead to deficiencies in the ability to track and manage vendor business transactions. A vendor used by more than one organization unit within the enterprise should have only one master record; no duplicates should be allowed. However, implementing effective controls is not an easy task because vendor master data management can be spread across multiple departments and responsibilities within the organization. Master data in SAP ERP is stored on three different levels: client level, company code level, and purchasing organization level (see Figure 5.2).

- ▶ **General data (client level)**
  The actual identity of a vendor (vendor number, name, address, communication language, phone, fax number, etc.) is stored on the highest level, the client-dependent level. This information is maintained only once and is available for all company codes and purchasing organizations. The client is the highest organizational unit within SAP systems and represents the owner of the system. Any changes to data on this level affects all companies using the specific vendor.

- ▶ **Company code data (company code level)**
  The second level of data is company code dependent. The data stored on this level can differ from one company code to another for the same vendor. For example, the G/L reconciliation account, payment methods, payment terms, and vendor correspondence details are kept in the company code data. This information is valid only for the company code it is maintained for and can differ

based on different company codes. Changes of data on this level only affect the company for which the change is carried out.

▶ **Purchasing data (purchasing organization level)**
Master data used for purchasing (MM-PUR) are stored on the third level. A company code assigned to several organizational objects in purchasing can thereby contain different data for a vendor, depending on the purchasing organization. Purchasing details such as ordering currency, contact person, partner roles, and payment methods are kept in the purchasing data.

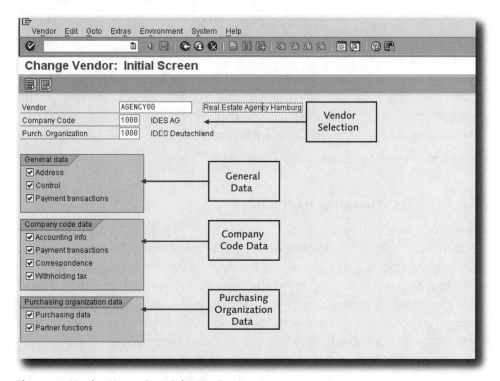

Figure 5.2 Vendor Master Data Selection Screen

Vendor master records are used in many departments and business units across the enterprise. The best practices dictate that vendor accounts should have the same identification number for all company codes. This can be achieved by managing vendor master data centrally. By doing so, you can manage vendor master data consistently throughout your organization and avoid risks of inconsistencies. With well-defined master data management procedures, you can increase data integrity and improve supplier analysis for better procurement opportunities, as well as prevent fraud. The key design considerations for vendor master data management process are:

- ▶ Use consistent identification coding.

- ▶ Implement rigid checks for duplicate vendors.

- ▶ Use business partner functionality to support the procurement process. Partner functionality is based on various roles of the business partner. For example, the purchase order is placed when the vendor takes the ordering address role. Then, when goods are received, the vendor takes the supplier of goods role. After the invoice is received, the vendor takes the invoicing party role, followed by the payee role during the payment. This is achieved by assigning corresponding partner roles in the vendor master record.

- ▶ Use the segregation of duties principle when creating and changing the vendor master records. SAP ERP supports confirmation scenarios when vendor creation or change transactions must be confirmed by another authorized user before being released for AP transaction processing.

- ▶ Block, delete, and archive obsolete vendors.

5.1.2 Invoice Processing Transactions

For invoice processing transactions, automation is the key. Automation in AP transaction processing undoubtedly brings numerous benefits to organizations. The methods of storing and channeling information gathered during the RTP process are critical to minimizing the manual interventions and automating the tasks of invoice processing, payment, and reconciliation. Scanning incoming invoices, routing the digital images, and generating paperless communication is one method of automation. It is a good practice to use digital communication whenever possible instead of printing vendor communications and placing them in an envelope because these steps require significant and unnecessary manual interventions. Digital communication can significantly increase communication speed and impact positively upon the organization's ability to optimize working capital. Thus, printing hard copy and then mailing it in an envelope or faxing it should be replaced with automated emailing or faxing of the digital image of the document straight from the system.

Another way of increasing automation is to use *electronic data interchange (EDI)* for AP transactional processing. SAP ERP offers powerful capability and functionality to support and use EDI technology. By linking your suppliers with EDI, you can receive and book invoices electronically. This practice gives you the ability to reduce and eliminate paper flows and associated issues, as well as to increase transactional efficiency and accuracy. Note that *optical character recognition (OCR)* can be integrated with EDI technology to process digitally scanned documents. This can significantly automate incoming invoice processing because information from the paper invoice will be converted into posted invoices.

Our experience has shown that incoming invoice processing can be centralized, in which case, vendors send invoices and credit memos to a central location, where incoming documents are scanned and parked for approval. With workflow technology, the approver of the invoice receives a digital image of the invoice. Once the invoice is approved, it is posted, and subsequent process steps are triggered. OCR technology can be deployed in the central location, and digitally scanned invoices can be converted into parked documents waiting for approval. You can use an OCR application to read invoices and pull the required information from the purchase order number to the material code. SAP ERP has a standard open interface to upload the OCR invoice data into the AP component.

By increasing the use of electronic communication, you can eliminate most of the manual effort and reduce the overall workforce. Your organization will ultimately join the emerging trend toward more standard electronic invoice delivery and processing.

5.1.3 Payment Processing

SAP ERP provides many advanced functionalities in the area of vendor payment process. Two important functionalities can be used to improve the payment process. The first functionality is related to the payment processing, the second one is related to the payment medium.

▸ Automate the payment program.

▸ Use the Data Medium Exchange (DME) engine to generate payment mediums.

The *automatic payment program* (Transaction F110) in SAP ERP enables you to automatically select the open invoices to be paid (or incoming payments to be collected), generate payment documents, and create payment mediums. What is not automatic in the payment program is the execution of the program itself. To reduce the potential errors, you can take a further step and automate the payment program execution as well. To do so, you need to use the SAP ERP delivered report for the automatic scheduling of the *payment program* (program RFF110S/ Transaction F110S) within the automatic scheduler such as the schedule manager, closing cockpit, or background job scheduler. If you want to automate the execution of the payment program, you should define two variants: one for running the proposal run and the debit balance check and one for executing payment run. In other words, the program needs to be scheduled first for executing the proposal run excluding vendors with debit balances, and then for executing the payment run.

SAP ERP delivers many standard payment medium programs starting with the letters RFFO. These programs support standard international formats as well as country-specific payment mediums and payment methods. Generating payment mediums with these programs, especially when frequent changes to the payment format have to be applied, is not an easy task. You need to utilize user exists or copy and modify existing programs. A better and more flexible way of generating various payment medium files is by using the *DME engine*, which offers a number of benefits:

▶ It is flexible in adjusting to different payment formats.

▶ It does not necessarily require programming skills.

▶ It offers better performance in mass payments.

▶ It provides clear understanding of output medium structure.

▶ It offers flexibility when generating payment advice.

▶ A single program can be used for all the different payment mediums generated with the DME engine. The program name is *SAPFPAYM*.

So far, we have covered key design considerations and best practices for AP processes to generate accurate reporting. In the next section we explain the AR reporting process in conjunction with AR processes and discuss how to improve the efficiency of the AR reporting process.

5.2 Accounts Receivable Reporting

AR transaction processing and AR reporting process are closely interrelated. To give you a better understanding of AR reporting, we first give you an overview of AR processes. Customer business transactions are captured and recorded in the

Account Receivable (AR) component, which is a subledger of the G/L. When you post business transactions to the AR subledger, the system updates the G/L simultaneously. This means you can get financial statements at any time without having to transfer balances and reconcile from the AR subledger to the G/L. As part of the OTC process, AR is also integrated with the Sales and Distribution (SD) component. AR information captured in SD flows simultaneously into the AR subledger. AR component is not only used for AR transaction processing, but also provides the data required for effective credit management, as well as information for the optimization of liquidity planning.

The SAP ERP system offers many AR analytical reports for monitoring AR transaction processing, such as customer open items, due date analysis, customer master data control reports, and customer evaluations. In addition, SAP NetWeaver BI offers comprehensive reporting capabilities for AR reporting.

Figure 5.3 shows the AR reporting process in connection to AR transaction processing. AR processes are mostly transactional processes, so the associated reports are designed to mainly report information on transactional operations.

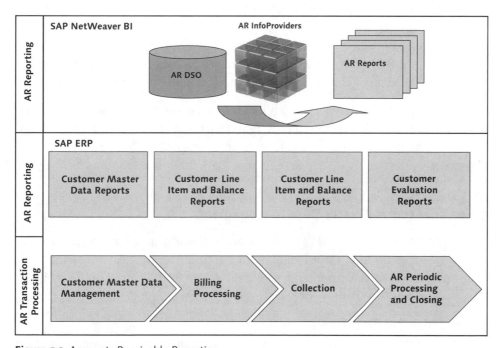

Figure 5.3 Accounts Receivable Reporting

AR transaction processing can be classified in four subprocesses:

▶ **Customer master data management**
This process includes the activities of managing customer master data that is, creating, changing and deleting customer master data. Each customer has a unique identification code in SAP ERP, which is called customer account. This code is required for all AR transaction processes. For example, you need to enter the customer code when posting customer business transactions in both AR and SD components.

▶ **Billing processing**
This process involves capturing and recording billing invoices and debit memos in the system. In SAP ERP, you can process billing invoices and debit memos in either the AR or SD components. If it is not possible or practical to use the SD component for billing, you can run the billing process in AR component.

▶ **Collection**
In this process, all outstanding receivables are collected. This is achieved with customer payments or direct debit collection methods.

▶ **AR periodic processing and closing**
AR periodic processing and closing is composed of many subprocesses, including balance confirmation, foreign currency valuation, value adjustment, transferring payables, and balance carry forward. These subprocesses are required to close the AR subledger and generate financial statements from the G/L.

AR reporting is a crucial part of each of these subprocesses. In the next section, we explain the key design considerations and best practices that organizations can adopt to deliver overall improvement in the efficiency and effectiveness of the AR processes.

5.2.1 Customer Master Data Management

Effective customer master data management enables organizations to achieve strategic advantage through improvements in customer service, cash management, and reduction in costs. Customer master data in SAP ERP is stored on three different levels: client level, company code level, and sales area level.

▶ **General data (client level)**
The identity of a customer (customer number, name, address, communication language, phone, fax number, etc.) is stored on the highest level, the client-

dependent level. This information is maintained only once and is available for all company codes and sales organizations. This means the data is shared and is not dependent upon any organizational objects such as company code, controlling area, and sales organization. Any changes to data on this level affect all companies using the specific customer.

▶ **Company code data (company code level)**
The second level of data is company code dependent. The data stored on this level can differ from one company code to another for the same customer. For example, G/L reconciliation account, payment methods, payment terms, dunning information, and customer correspondence details are kept in the company code data. This information is valid only for the company code it is maintained for and can differ in different company codes. Changes of data on this level only affect the company for which the change is carried out.

▶ **Sales area data (sales area level)**
Master data used for SD is stored on the third level. A company code assigned to several organizational objects in SD can contain different data for a customer depending on the sales organization. Sales details such as ordering currency, contact person, partner roles, and payment methods are kept in the sales data.

The general data of the customer master data is displayed in Figure 5.4 along with the button to access the company code and sales area level.

To achieve high data quality and efficient credit management, a single customer should only be created once in the system on the client level. The basic concept is to have one customer represented by one and only one customer number. To achieve the objective of having single entries for customers on the client level, one must thoroughly analyze current data before a new record is created. It is therefore essential that creation of master data on the client level is coordinated and managed as a centralized function. Since changes to data on the client level affect all units using that record, it is also crucial that changes are coordinated and centralized. The company data and sales area data only affect the local organizational objects for which the data has been created. The data might differ from different business establishments and contain information such as payment terms, partner functions, and contact persons. Although the procedures and policies are client specific, there are several key design considerations that you can use for effective customer master data management:

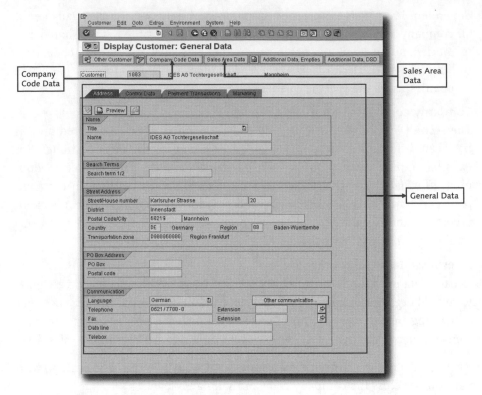

Figure 5.4 Customer Master Data

- ▶ Use consistent identification coding.

- ▶ Implement rigid checks for duplicate customers.

- ▶ Use business partner functions to support sales processes. This is achieved by assigning corresponding partner roles in the customer master record. To send invoices, shipment, and so on to different addresses, partner functions in SD component should be used.

- ▶ Follow the segregation of duties when creating and changing the customer master records. SAP ERP supports confirmation scenarios when customer creation or change transactions must be confirmed by another authorized user before being released for use.

- ▶ Block, delete, and archive obsolete customers.

- ▶ To prevent fraud, the critical identity information must be validated via letter or fax or other official documents from the customer. Examples of critical fields include, but are not restricted to, names/addresses, bank sort codes and account numbers, tax details, and direct debit mandate.

5.2.2 Automate Collection Management

The key process in AR is to collect debt after customers have been billed for goods or services. Companies face the risk of not collecting customer payments on time. The reasons for this include missing invoices or sales orders with inaccurate details, inconsistency in the customer's purchasing system related to the payment terms, or simply missing communication details. If these issues are not addressed properly, your enterprise could lose cash flow, mistakenly overpay sales commissions, and incur high costs for order processing and reworking and fixing billing errors. Customer dissatisfaction may lead to unnecessary concessions and suboptimal decision-making. All these consequences could adversely affect the enterprise's ability to compete in the market.

The collection management process can be enhanced by the utilization of electronic commerce, in particular, EDI, electronic mail, electronic funds transfer (EFT), and electronic catalog systems, to allow buyers and suppliers to transact business by exchanging information between their systems. EDI links with customers ensure that customer orders are taken quickly and accurately. SAP ERP can store documents electronically and allow enquiries to drill down to the source document and clear up points as necessary (i.e., re-invoice). In addition, electronic invoicing can speed up transaction time and reduce the incidence of errors that delay payment. By using electronic workflow functionality, you can pull up a required invoice on demand and eliminate paper flows and associated issues. Electronic functionality greatly speeds up query resolution.

Another way to enhance the collection management process is by utilizing *automatic dunning functionality*. The automatic dunning functionality enables you to check overdue receivables and then issue a payment reminder or dunning notice to remind these business partners of their outstanding debts. The automatic generation of dunning notices increases the available collector time. The dunning program selects the overdue open items, determines the dunning level in accordance with the number of days in arrears, and generates a dunning notice. The dunning data is then saved in the corresponding customer accounts. Dunning data parameters are updated in the company code of the customer master record, as dunning is not a practice in some countries. Thus, this functionality can be used for selected countries. For example, customers are typically not dunned in the United States.

5.2.3 Improve Dispute Management

Improving the dispute management process is an effective approach to improving debt collection. Technology has to be used together with a well-defined dispute management process to improve customer dispute management, reduce the total number of imbalances and disputes, and drive standardization.

SAP ERP provides *Dispute Management application* under Financial Supply Chain Management (FSCM) that enables the enterprise to establish a successful dispute management process. By using this application you can control and streamline the dispute management process. The Dispute Management application enables you to identify, monitor, and report AR disputes.

For effective dispute management, reports showing individual transactions that are out of balance and the reason for the imbalance should be regularly produced to understand the root causes of problems and allow those accountable to proactively follow up to achieve resolution.

5.2.4 Credit Management

Credit management enables you to recognize credit risks early so you can control your receivables. Credit problems usually appear in financial statements when the lost receivables affect the operating profits. Thus, increasing sales does not help companies increase profit if there is no effective credit control management. With the *SAP Credit Management* application under FSCM, you can store both internal and external credit information within the customer master data. You can automate the credit storage of customers or calculate credit limits for customers via credit rules in SAP ERP. In addition, you can set rules to increase the credit controls. SAP Credit Management application supports credit decision support for customers.

5.3 Intragroup Accounts Payables and Accounts Receivables

Intercompany transactions are managed in AP and AR subledgers. The company organization unit is used to represent affiliated companies within a corporate group. Trading partner is used to identify the business partner at the group level. Each affiliated company assumes the role of trading partner when assigned to the AP or AR accounts. Therefore, when creating customer and vendor accounts for affiliated companies, the trading partner has to be specified to identify the affiliated company account. In posting transactions, the trading partner field identifies if a posting is an intercompany transaction.

The most common challenges in intragroup and capital management process occur from a lack of common corporate direction and approach and standardized processes and systems. Intercompany transactions must be readily identifiable in the accounting systems and balanced across all ERP systems for effective interunit elimination during consolidation. For effective and efficient control, the recording, settlement, and balancing of all intercompany transactions should be automated. This can be achieved by automating intercompany transactions via a hub and controlling all intercompany transactions with a central group with overall responsibility for the intragroup process and accountability for imbalances.

To support the hub concept, SAP has developed the *intercompany processing hub* application, which supports the electronic processing of intercompany invoices and intercompany payments across multiple systems via a common platform. The solution architecture is illustrated in Figure 5.5. The concept is to automate intercompany transactions via a central hub. A purchase order created in the purchasing company for the intercompany vendor is transferred to the selling company, where the sales order is created automatically (step 1). The AP posting in the purchasing company is generated and automated through AR posting in the selling company (step 2). With the payment run, open AP items are cleared and payment advice is generated and transferred to selling company (step 3). All these intercompany transactions are routed through the intercompany processing hub.

Although this solution has yet to be implemented, leading organizations use the hub concept to streamline their intercompany process and eliminate imbalances between group companies, improve the integrity of financial statements, and reduce reconciliation work. The key design considerations that you need to take into account to increase the effectiveness of the process are:

▶ A reduction in the number of group reporting entities and the complexity of the legal entity structure so that the number and complexity of intercompany transactions are minimized.

▶ Upfront agreement on charges and terms to allow purchasers to agree on details before placing an order for goods or services, leaving fewer disputes from the misunderstanding of terms and hence reducing the number of disputes.

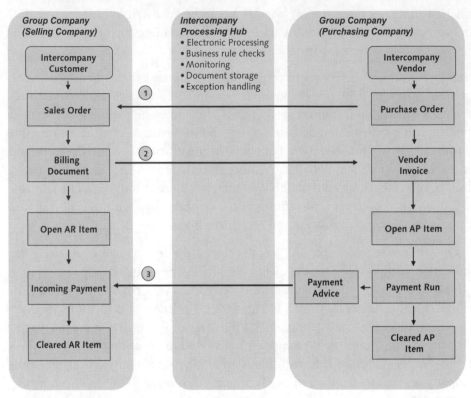

Figure 5.5 Intercompany Process Solution Architecture

▶ After the upfront agreement of terms, all bookings resulting from the intercompany transactions should be automated.

▶ A standard process for transaction postings, issue resolution, and settlements should be implemented to ensure consistency across the group and ensure that all users understand the process. This should be clearly documented and supported by effective training coupled with enforcement by the governance team. Adherence to a standard process drives data quality through a better understanding of the process to be used.

Note

Note that we discuss leading practices for the intragroup settlement process in Chapter 7 and the intragroup reconciliation process in Chapter 2.

5.4   AP and AR Reports in SAP ERP

The AP and AR information systems provide an extensive combination of variables and the classification of reports for AP and AR reporting. As a comprehensive analysis of all these reports exceeds the scope of this book, we examine the key selected AP and AR reports in this section.

5.4.1   Accounts Payable Reports

AP reports enable the detailed monitoring of the AP transaction process. By using these reports, you can also generate key performance indicators (KPIs) in relation to vendor open items and payment transactions.

Figure 5.6 shows AP reports available in SAP ERP. The standard AP reports are listed under the AP information system folder. To access the AP information system folder, follow the menu path **Accounting • Accounts Payable • Information System • Reports for Accounts Payable Accounting.** In addition to the AP information system, there are useful transactions to analyze AP transactions such as Display Vendor Balances (Transaction FK10N) and Display/Change Line Items (Transaction FBL1N). There are also evaluation reports and queries for further analysis and reporting.

In this section we cover key AP reports from each of the areas highlighted in Figure 5.6. Let's start with AP master data reports.

Vendor Master Data Reports

As discussed earlier, vendor master data management plays a crucial role in AP reporting. Any unauthorized creation or change in the vendor master data can lead to fraud or misstatement. SAP ERP provides three important control reports that can be used for vendor master data management. You can use the **Vendor List** report to identify new vendors created in the system, the **Display Changes to Vendors report** to identify all updates to the vendor master data, and the **Display/Confirm Critical Vendor Changes** report to see confirmation information on sensitive fields of vendor master data.

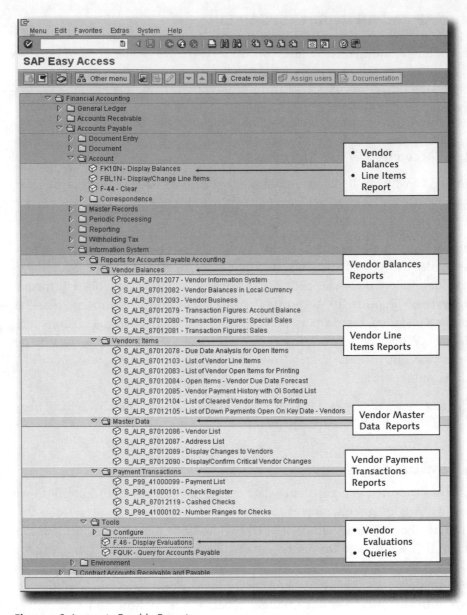

Figure 5.6 Accounts Payable Reports

Vendor List Report

The Vendor List report (Transaction S_ALR_87012086) is used primarily for information and documentation purposes. It shows all vendors with the search term, account group, created by, and created date information. You can use different selection parameters to restrict the number of vendors to be reported in the output. For example, you can specify the vendor account number, company code, search term, or intervals of these parameters. In the further selection criteria, you can choose additional fields to be shown in the report output, for example, tax info and references, additional VAT reg. numbers, payment data, and bank data. Output control parameters are used to determine the volume of information. With the parameter additional heading, a page header for the report could be issued. The selection screen of this report is shown in Figure 5.7. As illustrated in the figure, vendor accounts range from 1000 to 2000 for company code 1000, and tax info and references are selected in the selection screen of the report. We also specified an additional heading for the output of the report called Vendor List for Company Code 1000 in the selection screen.

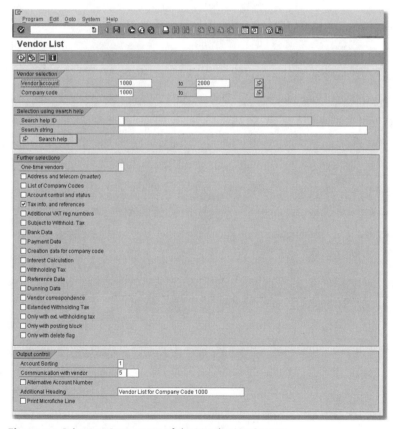

Figure 5.7 Selection Parameters of the Vendor List Report

Figure 5.8 shows the output of the Vendor List report. Vendors in the range of 1000 to 2000 for the company code 1000 with the tax information and general data such as search criteria, account group, created by, and created on are listed in the report output.

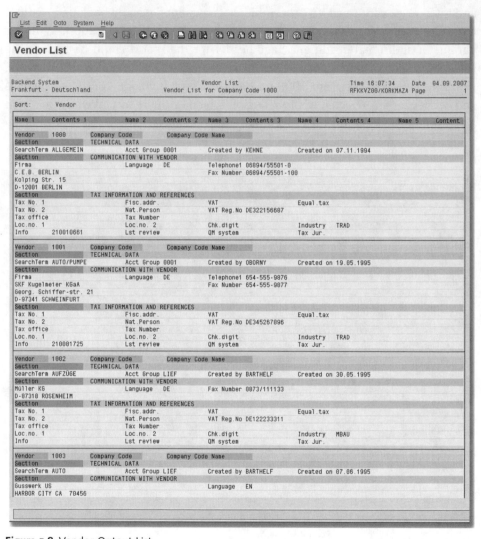

Figure 5.8 Vendor Output List

Display Changes to Vendors Report

The Display Changes to Vendors (Transaction S_ALR_87012089) report shows changes in the vendor master data. In the selection parameter, you specify whether you want to see the changes to the general data, the company code data, or the purchasing data. Figure 5.9 shows the selection screen and the output of this report.

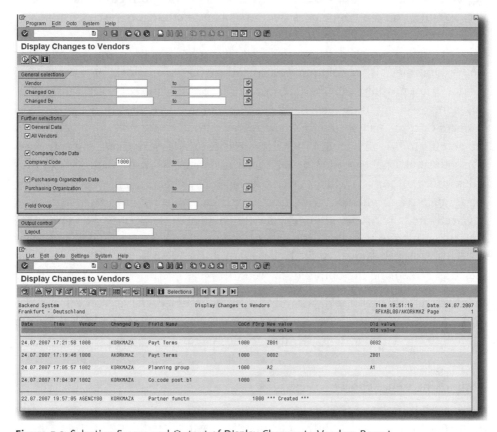

Figure 5.9 Selection Screen and Output of Display Changes to Vendors Report

Display Confirm Critical Changes Report

SAP ERP provides Display Confirm Critical Changes (Transaction S_ALR_87012090) report to analyze the information regarding the confirmation of critical changes to vendor master data. You can use *confirm changes functionality* to increase the control of vendor master data maintenance to avoid the risk of fraud and misstatements. With this functionality, once a creation or change is carried out by a user, another authorized user should confirm the changes to sensitive fields. Sensitive fields are defined in the configuration. To define sensitive fields, follow the configuration menu path **Financial Accounting (New) • Accounts Receivable and Accounts Payable • Vendor Accounts • Master Data • Preparations for Creating Vendor Master Data • Define Sensitive Fields for Dual Controls Vendors**. For example, you can define bank fields, payment method, interest indicator, and cash management fields as sensitive fields. When a change is made to a sensitive field, a payment run block is activated for that vendor, and the confirmation status "to be confirmed" is set. With this status and payment run block, payment to this vendor is not possible until the authorized user confirms the change. Confirmation can be made either individually or by calling up the list generated by the Display/ Confirm Critical Changes report. In the report output, you need to double click on the vendor to be confirmed. When the confirmation is carried out, the confirmation status field in the vendor master data is updated. The confirmation status provides information as to whether sensitive fields have been changed in the vendor master record and whether the changes have been confirmed or rejected. After you have activated the confirmation functionality for a dual check, the system provides a message that the change must be confirmed for each sensitive field change. Figure 5.10 shows the sensitive fields definition in the configuration along with the selection screen and the output of the report.

In addition to the master data control reports discussed above, you can use the Address List Report to see whether there are any vendors created with the same address to check duplicate master data in the system.

Vendor Line Item Reports

Invoices and credit memos that are not processed in a timely manner can cause late payments, unrecorded liabilities and potential negative credit ratings. Therefore, it is important to constantly analyze invoice and payment information and control the invoice to payment process. SAP ERP provides many reports for AP invoice processing analysis. A list of these reports is illustrated in Table 5.1.

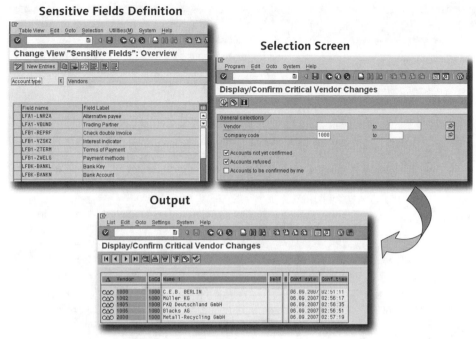

Figure 5.10 The Sensitive Fields Definition along with Selection Screen and Output of Display/Confirm Critical Vendor Changes Report

Report Name and Transaction	Report Description
Display/Change Line Items (FBL1N)	This report provides line items of a selected vendor or range of vendor accounts. You can display open, cleared, or all line items for a selected date. In the report output, you can change individual items or carry out a mass change.
Due Date Analysis for Open Items (S_ALR_87012078)	This report enables you to analyze unpaid invoices split between due and not due items divided into 30-day periods. The report can be executed for a vendor or range of vendors at any specific date.
List of Vendor Line Items (S_ALR_87012103)	This report provides details of all standard line items for a specific vendor or range of vendors to the selected period. It is not possible to drill down in the report output, but you can export the report output to Excel. The program name is RFKEPL00.

Table 5.1 Vendor Line Item Reports

Report Name and Transaction	Report Description
List of Vendor Open Items for Printing (S_ALR_87012083)	This report provides an open items list for a specific vendor or group of vendors at a specified date. It is not possible to drill down in the report output, but you can export the report output to Excel. The program name is RFKEPL00.
Open Items Vendor Due Date Forecast (S_ALR_87012084)	This report sorts vendor open items by the due date for net payment per company code and business area. A totals sheet (created individually upon request) displays the sorted list totals cumulatively for all selected vendors. Because this report presents a forecast, it does not include overdue items.
Vendor Payment History with OI Sorted List (S_ALR_87012085)	This report provides the payment history of a selected vendor or range of vendors with a sorted list of open items. With this report, you can analyze whether vendors pay on time or are in arrears. You can specify up to five different due date intervals in the selection screen of the report.
List of Cleared Vendor Items for Printing (S_ALR_87012104)	This report provides a cleared items list for a specific vendor or range of vendors at a given time interval. It is not possible to drill down in the report output, but you can export the report output to Excel.
List of Down Payments Open on Key Date Vendors (S_ALR_87012105)	This report shows the list of down payment documents with the net amount and tax amount details. In the selection screen, you can specify special G/L accounts and tax on sales and purchase codes to restrict the output to certain down payment types and tax-relevant information.

Table 5.1 Vendor Line Item Reports (cont.)

Display/Change Line Item Report

The Display/Change Line Item (Transaction FBL1N) report generates lists of vendor transactions in classic list or ALV format. You can display the items for a specific vendor or group of vendor accounts, regardless of whether the vendors belong to the same company code or not. You can configure the information displayed in the report output with layouts. The report is used not only for displaying the vendor line items, but also to change individual documents or carry out mass changes to selected items in the report output.

Figure 5.11 shows the selection screen of the Vendor Line Item Display report. As shown in the selection screen, you need to specify the vendor accounts and company codes and select the line items you want to report, such as open items, cleared items, or all items. In addition, you need to specify the type of the line items. In the selection screen, you can also specify a layout for the report output.

If the report is run without a display layout, either standard SAP variants or a default variant is selected. It is possible to select a new layout or update the selected layout after running the report. In the SAP standard layout, the items are sorted and summarized according to the vendor account and company code. Open, cleared, and parked items are grouped by colored status icons.

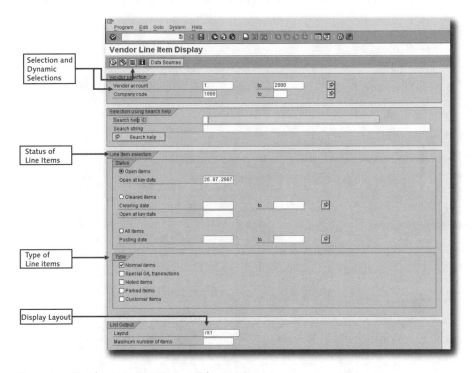

Figure 5.11 Vendor Line Item Report Selection Screen

Line item type

Line item types are used to restrict the output of the report with respect to the relationship between the subledger and the G/L. Normal items are vendor items that update the G/L with the vendor reconciliation account. Vendor items with the special G/L transactions item type are postings that update the G/L with a reconciliation account tied to a special G/L indicator. Noted items are statistical postings that do not update the G/L until processed with subledger transactions such as payment run. Parked items are vendor items that do not update the G/L because they are parked in the G/L. Customer items are used to display all the payable items of a customer that are also defined as vendor. The item type is often not selected correctly, causing misstatements in the report output.

The fields that can be used in the report output are from the table structure RF-POSXEXT. From the field list on the menu bar, you can add new fields for further analysis such as indicating the due date for net payment and the cash discount deadline for open items. In addition to these fields, you can define additional fields called special fields for the report output. You can access the special fields from the menu **Settings • Special Fields** in the report output, as shown in Figure 5.12.

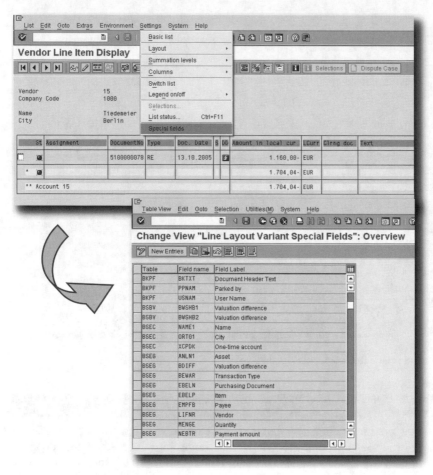

Figure 5.12 Line Layout Variant Special Fields

You can configure the display of the header rows in the layout of the report. To do so, use the menu path **Settings • Current Layout • Current Header Rows**, as illustrated in the classic view of the report output in Figure 5.13. By double-clicking on the line items, you can call up the details of the line item and display the underlying document. When you are displaying the details of the items, you can jump to the next and previous items by clicking on the arrow buttons on the menu bar. In addition, you can jump to the vendor master data and call up the Account Balances report from the report output. To do so follow the menu path **Environment • Display Balances • Account Master Record.**

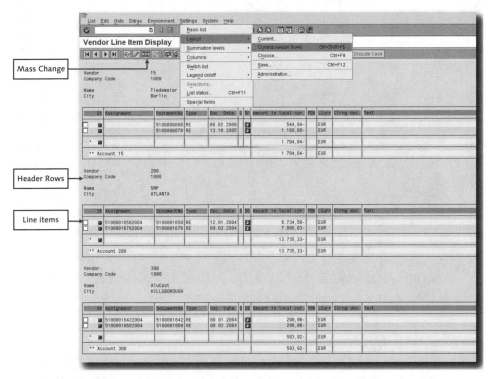

Figure 5.13 Vendor Line Item Display Classic Layout

From the settings menu you can switch the list to view the report in ALV format, as illustrated in Figure 5.14.

If you have the necessary authorization you can change a single line item or carry out a mass change in the line report output. To do so, select the item(s) to be changed and press the button for mass change indicated in Figure 5.13.

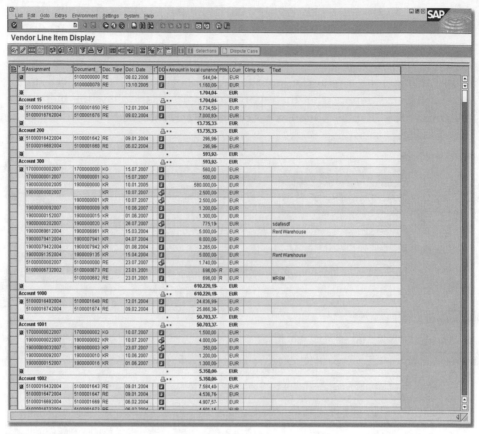

Figure 5.14 Vendor Line Item Display in ALV Format

Due Date Analysis for Open Items

This report shows the total of due items, the total of not due items, and the total open items for selected vendor(s) divided into 30-day periods. The report can be executed for a vendor or group of vendors at any specific date. As shown in Figure 5.15, you can specify the vendor account(s) and company code(s) that you want to analyze on the selection screen. The due date is used to identify the date from which open items will be selected. You can use the **Dynamic Selection** button for further restriction of the report output.

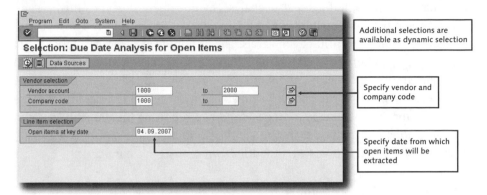

Figure 5.15 Selection Screen of the Vendor Due Date Analysis for the Open Items Report

The report output provides the information of unpaid invoices split between due and not due, divided into 30-day periods. Figure 5.16 shows the report output.

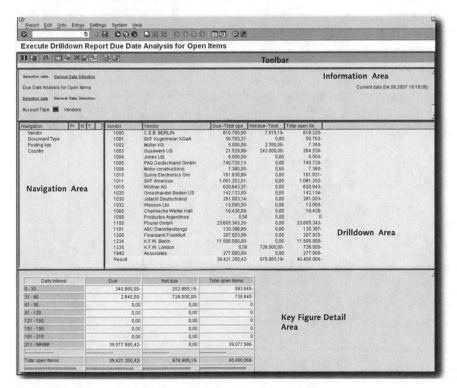

Figure 5.16 Output of Due Date Analysis for Open Items Report

You can navigate through the due date analysis by document type, posting key, and country in the report output. In the key figure area, you can see due, not due, and total open items divided into 30-day intervals. The drilldown area shows total due, not due, and total open item per vendor. In addition, you can call up other reports such as line item, transaction figures, and master data reports. To call up another report, use the **Goto** menu and select the report that you want to call up. Because the due date analysis for the open item report has drilldown reporting functionality, you can create exceptions and conditions that add to the flexibility of the report. (We explain how you can create your own SAP ERP drilldown reports in Chapter 12.)

Vendor Account Balances Reports

The vendor account balances reports are listed in Table 5.2.

Report Name and Transaction	Report Description
Vendor Balance Display (FK10N)	This report provides the debits, credits, balance, cumulative balance and sales/purchases of a single or a range of vendors per period. From the report output, you can call up the line item report.
Vendor Balances in Local Currency (S_ALR_87012082)	With this report, you can analyze the vendor balances in the currency of the company code, with various options for output and sort sequence. The report shows the balance carry forward, credit, debit, and accumulated balance for the selected period. The end of the report displays totals per company code and final total across all company codes for each local currency. The report can also display special G/L transactions such as down payment. You can use different sorting methods and summarization and display the output in ALV format.
Vendor Business (S_ALR_87012093)	This report displays vendor purchases in a list in company code currency. There is an option to convert to another currency with fixed date conversion in the selection parameter.
Transaction Figures: Account Balance (S_ALR_87012079)	This report shows debit totals, credit totals, balances, and cumulative balances for the selected vendors and company codes.
Transaction Figures: Special Sales (S_ALR_87012080)	This report provides the special G/L transactions for the selected vendors and company codes.
Transaction Figures: Sales (S_ALR_87012081)	This report provides the purchase amounts or turnovers for the selected vendors and company codes.

Table 5.2 Vendor Account Balances Reports

In the next section, we examine the Transaction Figures: Account Balance report.

Transaction Figures: Account Balance Report

The Transaction Figures: Account Balance report (Transaction ALR_87012079) provides information on vendor accounts debit totals, credit totals, balances, and cumulative balances, with period, fiscal year, and company code breakdown. You can navigate through the vendor account, fiscal year, and company code. You can also call up other reports such as Transaction Figures Sales, Transaction Figures Special Sales, and Line Item reports. The report can be run in classic drilldown, graphical output, or object list format. You can create exceptions and conditions that add to the flexibility of the report. With SAP drilldown reporting functionality, you can copy the report and the underlying form and create your own reports. The selection screen and output of the Transaction Figure Account Balance report in classic drilldown is shown in Figure 5.17.

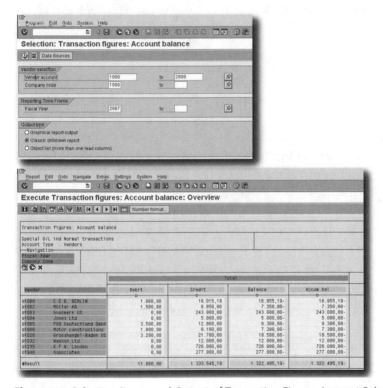

Figure 5.17 Selection Screen and Output of Transaction Figures Account Balance Report

Vendor Payment Transaction Reports

The vendor payment transaction reports are listed in Table 5.3.

Report Name and Transaction	Report Description
Payment List (S_P99_41000099)	This report provides details of payment proposal and payment run.
Check Register (S_P99_41000101)	This report provides the list of all check registers that belong to one paying company code. You can sort the report output by payment method and check number with manually voided checks at the start and manually issued checks at the end.
Cashed Checks (S_ALR_87012119)	This report provides the list of checks that were cashed by vendors. The report reads data for the cashed checks delivered by a bank payment file.
Number Ranges for Checks (S_P99_41000102)	This report provides check lots with the corresponding check number ranges and the current check number.

Table 5.3 Vendor Payment Transaction Reports

In this section, we examine the Payment List report.

Payment List Report

The Payment List report (Transaction S_P99_41000099) is used to analyze the payment proposal and payment run of the payment run program. The report displays information about the invoices that are due for payment and any exception items. You can run this report after a proposal run and use it as a basis for processing proposals or after an update run to use it for reconciliation with the payment results. You can create your own layouts and use them when running the report. This can be done before or after running the report. Figure 5.18 shows an example of Payment List report output. Reasons for exceptions are displayed as error codes and explained at the end of the report output.

Vendor Evaluations

Vendor Evaluations provide comprehensive analyses of vendor transactions. They provide more advanced reporting functionalities compared to the other transaction reports. You can analyze company code, business area, country, planning group with the vendor accounts, and drill down from the totals level to the individual documents level.

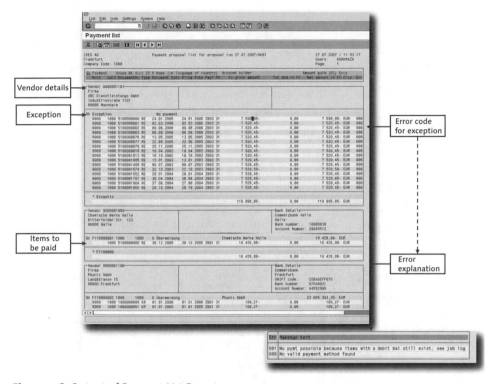

Figure 5.18 Output of Payment List Report

Evaluations are delivered within SAP ERP. Note, however, that you need to activate and fill them with data before using them. Unlike the other transactional reports, evaluation reports have their own database tables that have to be populated on a regular basis. Typically the update has to be scheduled daily or several times per day during the period end closing. Companies often do not use evaluation reports because either the configuration is not done or the daily update job is not scheduled.

The report RFKRRSEL is used to create the vendor information system and retrieve data. The data volume to be retrieved is determined for every evaluation view via a selection variant. The report RFKRRGEN, started in batch, calls up the data. The selected data records are transferred to the reports to create different evaluations. Just like any other SAP standard report, you can define the data that you want returned from the table by limiting parameters such as company code, vendor account, document type, and posting key. You can set up a different selection variant for each view of the data. SAP ERP provides the following evaluations:

► Due Date Analysis (RFKRRE01)

► Currency Analysis (RFKRRE03)

► Overdue Items (RFKRRE04)

These programs update RFRR for display at a later stage. The data records required for this are transferred by the data retrieval (RFKRRSEL) report. Variants are predefined for each of these programs. The variant determines the data grouping, sort order, and what to create the evaluations for. Vendor evaluations are displayed in a tree-like structure from which you can access each evaluation. Figure 5.19 shows the overdue items evaluation by company code and drilldown to overdue item level. You can drill down to the detailed level by double-clicking until you reach the lowest level of detail, which is usually the underlying financial accounting document.

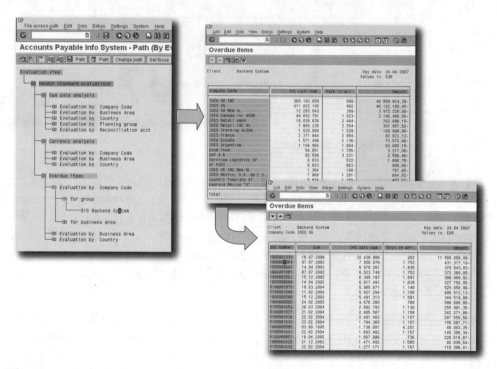

Figure 5.19 Vendor Evaluations and Drilldown to Detailed Level

SAP ERP also provides country-specific AP reports. You can access these reports by following the menu path **Accounting • Financial Accounting • Accounts Payable • Reporting.**

Note

AP withholding tax reports are explained in Chapter 4.

5.4.2 Accounts Receivable Reports

AR reports enable detailed monitoring of AR transaction reporting, such as overdue items, customer cash discount analyses, and customer payment history. These reports also allow the generation and analysis of key performance indicators (KPIs) in relation to customer open items and payment transactions.

Figure 5.20 shows AR reports available in SAP ERP. The standard AR reports are listed under the AR information system folder. To access the AR information system folder, follow the menu path **Accounting • Accounts Receivable • Information System • Reports for Accounts Receivable Accounting**. In addition to reports under the AR information system, there are useful transactions for analyzing AR transactions such as Display Customer Balances (FD10N) and Display/Change Line Items (FBL5N). There are also customer evaluations and queries for further analysis and reporting.

As a comprehensive analysis of all these reports exceeds the scope of this book, we examine the key selected reports from each section highlighted in Figure 5.20.

Customer Master Data Reports

Customer master data management plays an important role in accurate AR reporting. Any unauthorized creation or change in the customer master data can lead to fraud or misstatement. SAP ERP provides four important control reports that you can to use to control customer master data records. You can use the **Customer List** report to identify new customers created in the system, the **Display Changes to Customers** report to identify changes in customer master data, the **Display/ Confirm Critical Customer Changes** report to see confirmation information on sensitive fields of customer master data, and the **Customer Master Data Comparison** report enables analysis of which accounts have been maintained in the AR and SD component.

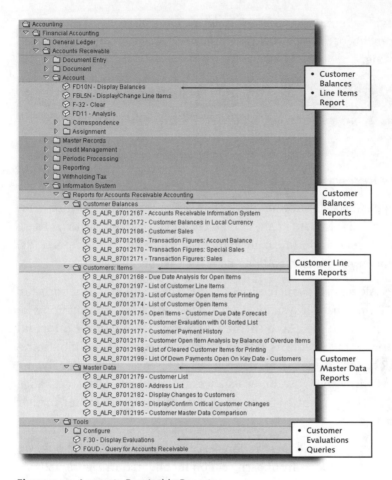

Figure 5.20 Accounts Receivable Reports

Customer List Report

The Customer List report (Transaction S_ALR_87012179) is used for displaying and printing customer master data. The list can be used for information and documentation. You can narrow down the number of customers to be printed using selection criteria. This includes, for example, the account number of the customer, the company code, a search term, or an interval for the selection criteria. However, only customers for whom company code–dependent master data exist are displayed. Output control parameters are used to determine the volume of information. With the parameter additional heading, a page header for the report could be issued. The selection screen of this report is shown in Figure 5.21. As indicated in the figure, customer accounts range from 1000 to 1500 for company code 1000, specified with further selections account control and status, bank data, payment data, and dunning data.

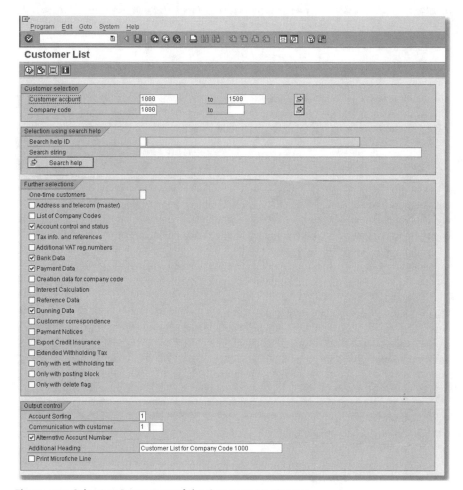

Figure 5.21 Selection Parameters of the Customer List Report

The report output is illustrated in Figure 5.22. As shown, you can see the customer list with the details specified in the further selection screen.

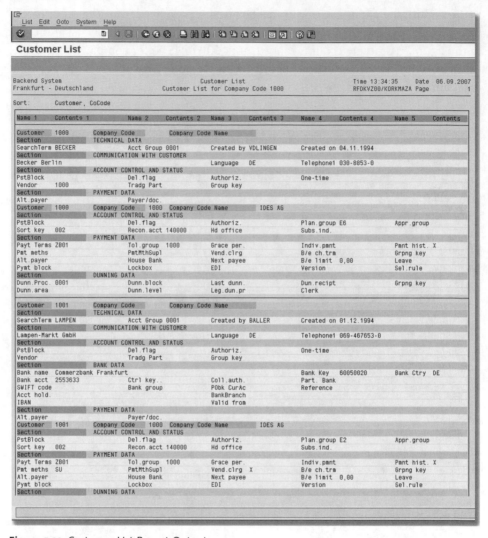

Figure 5.22 Customer List Report Output

Display Changes to Customers

The Display Changes to Customers (Transaction S_ALR_87012182) report shows changes to the customer master record data across accounts. Select options exist concerning the customer, the change date, the name of the person changing, and the field group. Additionally, you can choose whether you want to see the changes for the general data, the company code data, or the sales area data. Within each data range, you can set limits according to the organizational form. Figure 5.23 shows the selection screen and the output of display changes to Customer Report.

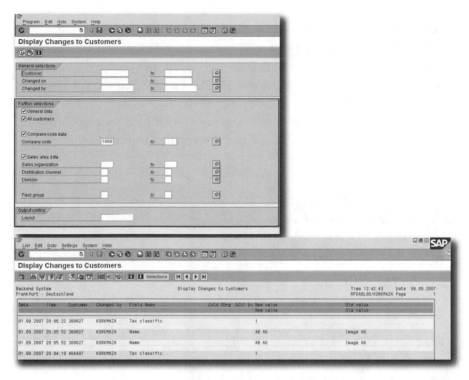

Figure 5.23 Selection Screen and the Output of Display Changes to Customer Report

Display Confirm Critical Changes Report

Another important report to control customer master data changes is the Display Confirm Critical Changes (Transaction S_ALR_87012183) report to see information regarding the confirmation of critical changes of customer master data. You can use *confirm changes functionality* to increase the control of customer master data maintenance to avoid the risk of fraud and misstatements. Once a creation or change is carried out by a user, another authorized user should confirm the changes to sensitive fields. Sensitive fields are defined in the configuration. To define a sensitive field for customer master data, follow the configuration menu path **Financial Accounting (New) • Accounts Receivable and Accounts Payable • Customer Accounts • Master Data • Preparations for Creating Customer Master Data**

• **Define Sensitive Fields for Dual Controls Customers**. For example, you can define bank fields, dunning level, interest indicator, and cash management fields as sensitive fields. When a change is made to a sensitive field, the confirmation status "to be confirmed" is set.

Display Customer Master Data Comparison Report

The Customer Master Data Comparison (Transaction S_ALR_87012195) report is used for reconciling customer master data. With this report, you can display which accounts have been maintained in AR and SD. As discussed in the AR reporting process section, one of the reasons for wrong master data maintenance is the involvement of different users from finance and sales and distribution departments. Figure 5.24 shows the selection screen and the report output of the Customer Master Data Comparison report.

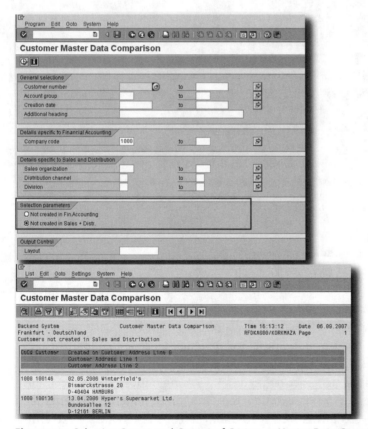

Figure 5.24 Selection Screen and Output of Customer Master Data Comparison Report

In addition to these control reports, you can use the Address List report to see whether any customers have been created with the same address to check for duplicate master data in the system.

Customer Line Item Reports

Invoices and debit memos that are not processed in a timely manner can cause late collections. SAP ERP provides many AR reports for the analysis of the invoice to collection process. A list of these reports is illustrated in Table 5.4.

Report Name and Transaction	Report Description
Display/Change Line Items (FBL5N)	This report lists the open items and cleared items for a selected customer or customer group. You can drill down into the FI and SD documents in the report output.
Due Date Analysis for Open Items (S_ALR_87012168)	This report shows the total of due items, the total of not due items, and the total of open items per customer document type and sorts them into 30-day due date intervals.
List of Customer Line Items (S_ALR_87012103)	This report provides details of all standard line items for a specific customer or a range of customers for the selected period. It is not possible to drill down into the report output, but you can export the report output to Excel. The program name is SAPLKKBL.
List of Customer Open Items for Printing (S_ALR_87012173)	This report is another sort of the program SAPLKKBL. You can list open customer receivables sorted by key date. The user can display only balances by suppressing line items and can analyze customer receivables based on a variety of parameters. The report offers sorting options ranging from the A/R reconciliation account to the industry group of the customer to the accounting clerk who entered the item. It is not possible to drill down in the report output, but you can export the report output to Excel.
List of Customer Open Items (S_ALR_87012174)	This report is another sort of the program SAPLKKBL. The same functionalities of the list of customer open items for printing apply to this report.
Open Items Customer Due Date Forecast (S_ALR_87012175)	This report sorts customer open items by the due date for net payment per company code and business area. A totals sheet (created individually upon request) displays the sorted list totals cumulatively for all selected customers. Since this report presents a forecast, it does not include overdue items.

Table 5.4 Customer Line Item Reports

Report Name and Transaction	Report Description
Customer Payment History with OI Sorted List (S_ALR_87012176)	This report provides information on the payment history of a selected customer or range of customers with a sorted list of open items. With this report, you can analyze whether customer payments are on time or in arrears. The report can help identify which customers require special credit monitoring.
Customer Payment History (S_ALR_87012177)	This report provides detailed analysis of the customer payment history details of the selected customer or range of customers. It also contains a forecast of payment volumes and payment arrears, based on existing payment history.
Customer Open Item Analysis by Balance of Overdue Items (S_ALR_87012178)	This report enables you to select and analyze the customer open items for all customers whose overdue items exceed a predefined amount. If there is no need to report on the balance of the overdue items, you can use the vendor payment history with OI sorted list report. It provides overdue analysis and executes faster than this report.
List of Customer Cleared Items for Printing (S_ALR_87012198)	This report shows the cleared items for a customer or range of customers for a specified period. You cannot drill down to the individual items, but you can download the report output into Excel.
List of Down Payments Open on Key Date (S_ALR_87012199)	This report lists down payment documents with the net amount and tax amount details. In the selection screen, you can specify the special G/L account and tax on sales and purchase code to restrict the output.

Table 5.4 Customer Line Item Reports (cont.)

In this section we examine the Customer Payment History report.

Customer Payment History

The Customer Payment History (Transaction S_ALR_87012177) report provides detailed analysis of the customer payment history details of the selected customer or range of customers. It also contains a forecast of payment volumes and payment arrears, based on existing payment history. Note that the information on the payment history of a customer is only stored if you select the reconciliation payment history field in the customer master data. Figure 5.25 shows the selection screen and the payment history and forecast details based on payment history.

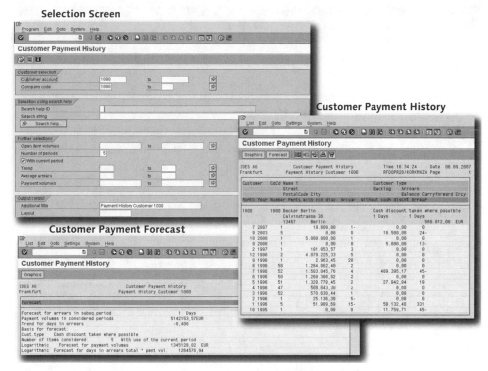

Figure 5.25 The Selection Screen and the Output of the Customer Payment History Report

Customer Account Balances Reports

The customer account balances reports are listed in Table 5.5. In this section we examine the Customer Balances in Local Currency report.

Customer Balances in Local Currency Report

The Customer Balances in Local Currency (S_ALR_87012172) report displays balances by customer account number and reconciliation account in company code currency. The report provides carry forward balances and current debit and credit balances for each customer in the period selected. This report offers a variety of selection options, as illustrated in Figure 5.26. In our example, we selected customer account 1000 and company code 1000 in fiscal year 2007. We further restricted the output for period 08 and selected only normal and special G/L balances.

Report Name and Transaction	Report Description
Customer Balance Display (FD10N)	This report provides the debits, credits, and balances in local currency of a single or a range of customers per period. The report also provides carry forward balances from the previous year and balances of special G/L transactions (e.g., down payments). From the report output, you can call up the line Item Report.
Customer Balances in Local Currency (S_ALR_87012172)	This report lists balances by customer account number and reconciliation account. The report provides carry forward balances and current debit and credit balances for each customer in the period selected. The end of the report displays totals per company code and final total across all company codes for each local currency. You can use different sorting methods and summarization and display the output in ALV format.
Customer Sales (S_ALR_87012186)	This report displays customer sales in a list in company code currency. There is an option to convert to another currency with fixed date conversion in the selection parameter.
Transaction Figures: Account Balance (S_ALR_87012169)	The report provides information on accounts debit totals, credit totals, balances, and cumulative balances for the selected customers and company codes.
Transaction Figures: Special Sales (S_ALR_87012170)	This report provides the special sales volumes for the selected customers and company codes.
Transaction Figures: Sales (S_ALR_87012171)	This report provides the sales volumes for the selected customers and company codes.

Table 5.5 Customer Account Balances Reports

As shown in Figure 5.27, the report output shows the balance carry forward, total debits, total credits, and accumulated balances by customer and reconciliation accounts. The end of the report displays totals per company code and a final total across all company codes for each local currency. You can use a different sorting method and summarization and display the output in ALV format.

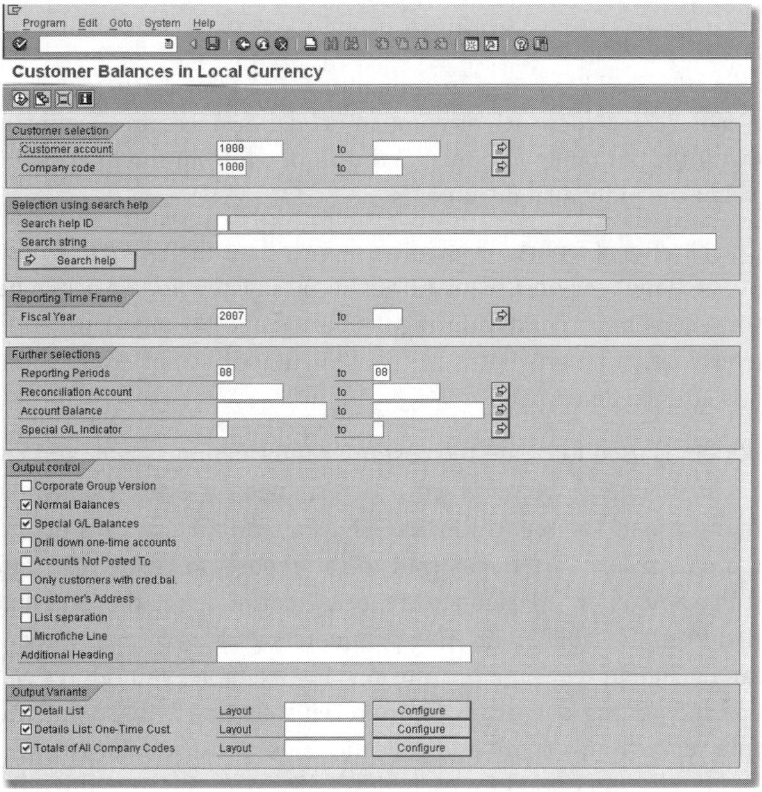

Figure 5.26 Selection Screen of Customer Balances in Local Currency

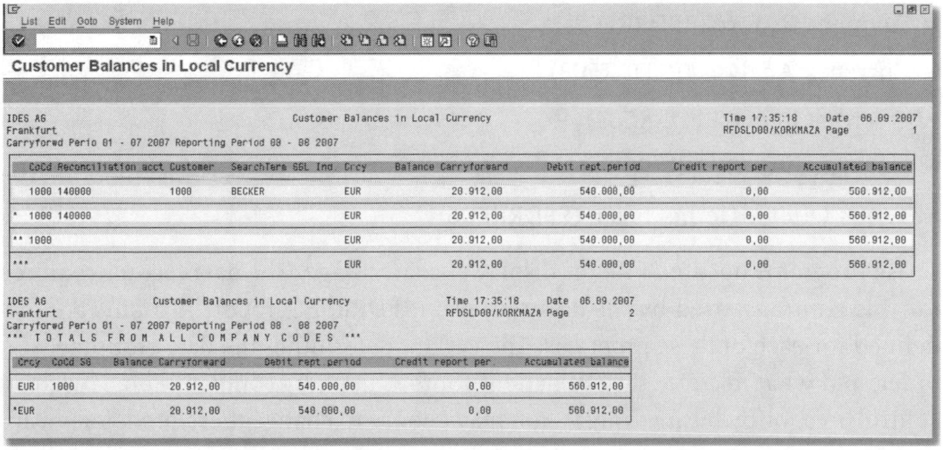

Figure 5.27 Output of the Customer Balances in Local Currency Report

Customer Evaluations

Customer evaluations provide comprehensive analyses of customer transactions. They provide more advanced reporting functionalities than the other transaction reports. You can analyze analytics such as company code, business area, country, planning group with the customer accounts, and drill down from the totals level to the details level of the individual documents.

Unlike the other transactional reports, evaluation reports have their own database tables that have to be populated on a regular basis. Typically, the update has to be scheduled daily or several times per day during the period end closing. Companies often do not use evaluation reports because the configuration is not done or the daily update job is not scheduled.

The report RFDRRSEL is used to create the customer information system and retrieve data. The data volume to be retrieved is determined for every evaluation view via a selection variant. The report RFDRRGEN, started in batch, calls up the data. The selected data records are transferred to the reports to create different evaluations. Just like any other SAP standard report, you can define the data that you want returned from the table by limiting parameters such as company code, customer account, document type, and posting key. For example, you can restrict the document type and posting key to only return receivables line items so that the reports make more sense from a credit and collections point of view for AR. You can set up a different selection variant for each view of the data. SAP ERP provides the following evaluations:

- ▶ Due Date Analysis (RFDRRE01)
- ▶ Payment History (RFDRRE02)
- ▶ Currency Analysis (RFDRRE03)
- ▶ Overdue Items (RFDRRE04)
- ▶ DSO Analysis (RFDRRE05)
- ▶ Terms Offered/Terms Taken (RFDRRE06)

These programs update RFRR for display at a later stage. The data records required for this are transferred by the data retrieval (RFDRRSEL) report. Variants are predefined for each of these programs. The variant determines the data grouping, sort order, and what to create the evaluations for (by client, by company code, by credit control area, or by business area). You may choose to change these predefined variants or create new ones.

SAP ERP also provides country-specific AR reports. You can access these reports by following the menu path **Accounting • Financial Accounting • Accounts Receivable • Reporting.**

5.5   AR and AP Reporting in SAP NetWeaver BI

SAP NetWeaver BI reporting provides comprehensive AP and AR reports. In the business content, standard InfoProviders and InfoObjects are delivered for both AP and AR reporting. In this section, we focus exclusively on the business content for AP and AR accounting. It should be noted that the data modeling examples in this section are for illustration purposes only. You can model your AP and AR reporting architecture by reference to predelivered business content objects. Note, however, that you should check whether the preconfigured solution fulfills all of your business requirements.

In addition, SAP delivers new SAP NetWeaver BI content and new AP and AR reports with the enhancement package 3. You can only use this content if you use the enhancement package 3 for SAP ERP 6.0 and have activated the Reporting Financials business function. Note that we explain SAP enhancement package for SAP ERP, SAP's simplified financial reporting innovation and show the new reports in Chapter 15.

5.5.1   Accounts Payable Data Modeling

The business content in AP provides two InfoCubes and three data storage objects (DSOs) for AP reporting. Figure 5.28 shows data flow examples with the predelivered business content objects. In our data modeling examples, data to InfoCubes is supplied with DSOs. Note, however, that you can get data to InfoCubes directly from InfoSources without connecting DSOs. Let's examine these InfoCubes and DSOs.

▶ **FIAP Line Item InfoCube (0FIAP_C03)**
This InfoCube contains AP line items that are extracted from the connected source systems. In our example, it is supplied with data by FIAP Line Item DSO (0FIAP_O03), and the DSO gets data using the Accounts Payable Line Item Info-Source (0FI_AP_4). You can also use the Accounts Payable Line Item InfoSource (0FI_AP_3). Note that you can get data to this InfoCube directly from the line item InfoSource without connecting the line item DSO.

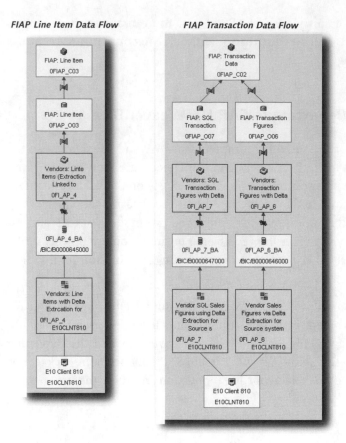

Figure 5.28 AP Data Flow Examples

▶ **FIAP Transaction Data InfoCube (0FIAP_C02)**

This InfoCube contains AP total transaction figures that are extracted from the connected source systems. In our example, it is supplied with data by FIAP Transaction Figures DSO (0FIAP_O06) and FIAP SGL Transaction DSO (0FIAP_O07). FIAP SGL Transaction Figures DSO (0FIAP_O07) contains AP special G/L transactions that are extracted from the connected source systems. The data is supplied with data by the InfoSource Accounts Payable Special General Ledger Transaction Figures using Delta Procedure (0FI_AP_7). FIAP Transaction Figures DSO (0FIAP_O06) contains transaction figures extracted from the connected source systems using the InfoSource called Accounts Payable Transaction Figures using Delta Procedure (0FI_AP_6). Alternatively, you can extract data directly by InfoSource Accounts Payable Transaction Figures (0FI_AP_1).

Note

You can use either OFI_AP_3 or OFI_AP_4 as an AP line item data extractor. The Info-Source OFI_AP_4 enables a more advanced extraction mechanism than OFI_AP_3. It accesses tables directly instead of accessing the AP records during the data extraction. The communication structure of the old line item InfoSource OFI_AP _3 and the new one OFI_AP_4 is the same. This means the update rules for data targets can be kept. The migration from InfoSource OFI_AP_3 to InfoSource OFI_AP_4 is described in SAP Note 410797.

5.5.2 Accounts Payable Reports

In the business content, SAP NetWeaver BI provides only one query for vendor transaction analysis, as illustrated in Figure 5.29. You can create your own queries based on the InfoProviders explained above.

Figure 5.29 AP Queries

Vendors Overview

The Vendors Overview (0FIAP_C02_Q0001) query is used for the analysis of AP transactions. The query reads data from the FIAP Transaction Data (0FIAP_C02)

InfoCube. You can analyze the total debit postings, total credit postings, balance (debit-credit), cumulative balance (balance+cumulative balance of the previous period), and sales volume by vendor for the selected company codes and periods. Figure 5.30 shows an example of the output of this query.

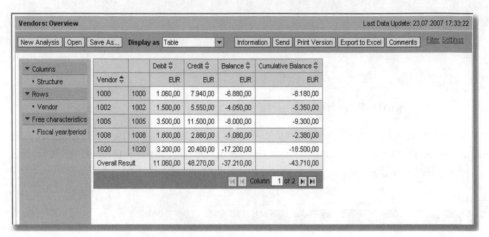

Figure 5.30 Output of Vendor Overview Report

5.5.3 Accounts Receivable Data Modeling

The business content in AR provides three InfoCubes and six DSOs for AR reporting. Figure 5.31 shows data foow examples with the pre-delivered business content objects.

▸ **FIAR Line Item InfoCube (0FIAR_C03)**
   This InfoCube contains AR line items that are extracted from the connected source systems. In our data modeling example, data is supplied by FIAR Line Item DSO (0FIAR_O03), and the DSO gets data with the InfoSource Accounts Receivable Line Items InfoSource (0FI_AR_4). You can also use the Accounts Receivable Line Item InfoSource (0FI_AR_3). Note that you can get data to this InfoCube directly from the line item InfoSource without connecting the Line Item DSO.

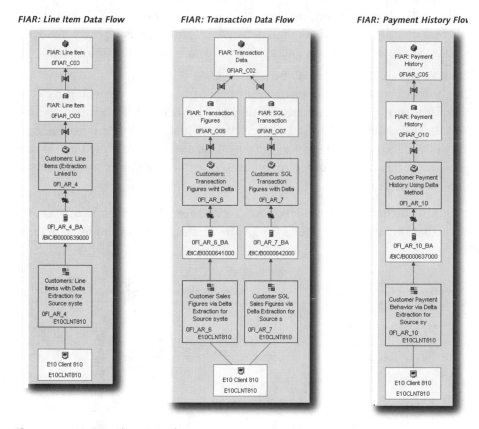

Figure 5.31 AR Data Flow Examples

▶ **FIAR Transaction Data InfoCube (0FIAR_C02)**

This InfoCube contains AR total transaction figures that are extracted from the connected source systems. The key figures of the InfoCube are total debit postings, total credit postings, cumulative balance, and sales for the period. The data is supplied by FIAR Transaction Figures (0FIAR_O06) and FIAR SGL Transaction (0FIAR_O07). FIAR SGL Transaction DSO (0FIAR_O07) contains AR special G/L transaction figures that are extracted from the connected source systems by using the InfoSource called Accounts Receivable Special General Ledger Transaction Figures using Delta Procedure (0FI_AR_7). FIAR Transaction Figures DSO (0FIAR_O06) contains transaction figures extracted from the connected source systems using the InfoSource called Accounts Receivable Transaction Figures using Delta Procedure (0FI_AR_6). Alternatively, you can extract data to the InfoCube directly with InfoSource Accounts Receivable Transaction Figures

(0FI_AR_1). Note, however, that 0FI_AR_6 provides a delta upload mechanism, whereas 0FI_AR_1 uploads the full data. We recommend using this InfoSource to extract transaction figures and upload the data to InfoCube 0FIAR_C02.

▶ **FIAR Payment History InfoCube (0FIAR_C05)**
This InfoCube contains the payment history of customers per company code and fiscal year period. The data is supplied by DSO FIAR Payment History (0FIAR_O05). This DSO contains the payment history (payment volume and days in arrears) of customers per company code and fiscal year period. It is supplied with data by InfoSource Accounts Receivable Payment via Delta Extraction (0FI_AR_10).

In addition to these InfoProviders, SAP NetWeaver BI provides two DSOs for credit management reporting. Figure 5.32 provides data flow examples with these DSOs.

Figure 5.32 Credit Management DSOs

5.5.4 Accounts Receivable Reports

In the business content, SAP Netweaver BI provides AR queries based on these InfoProviders explained above. Figure 5.33 shows the SAP NetWeaver BI queries delivered within the business content. Let's first look at key DSO queries based on FIAR Transaction Data InfoCube (0FIAR_C05).

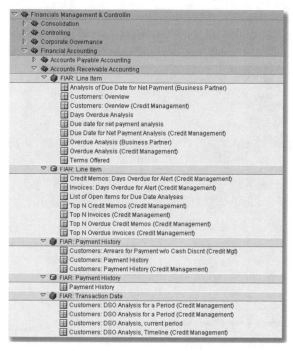

Figure 5.33 AR Queries

DSO Analysis Queries

The day sales outstanding (DSO) analysis provides a comprehensive measure of an organization's efficiency in collecting its outstanding receivables. DSO analysis provides the average time organizations take to turn their outstanding AR debts into cash. The DSO analysis is always carried out within a specific period and is always measured in days. In SAP NetWeaver BI, DSO is calculated as total outstanding receivables (open customer items) for the current period analyzed divided by average sales for the previous period, times the number of days in the period analyzed (30 days). We can represent the calculation of DSO with the following formula:

Outstanding receivables / average sales for the previous period × 30

In the business content, you can activate the DSO Analysis for a Period (0FIAR_C02_Q0001) query for detailed DSO analysis. This query reads data from the InfoCube FIAR Transaction Data (0FIAR_C02). It shows the balance of the current period and sales in the previous period and automatically calculates DSO by each customer for the current period. The report output is illustrated in Figure 5.34.

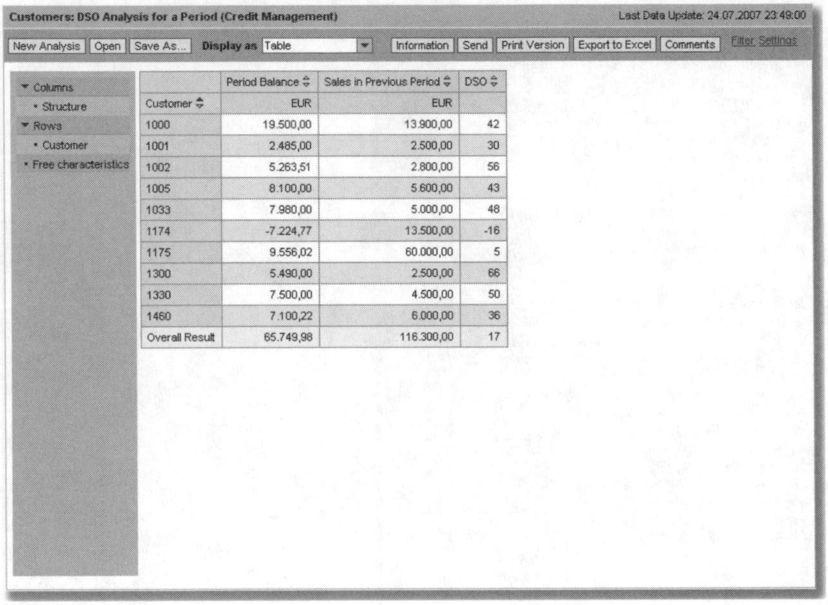

Customers: DSO Analysis for a Period (Credit Management)			Last Data Update: 24.07.2007 23:49:00
	Period Balance ⇕	Sales in Previous Period ⇕	DSO ⇕
Customer ⇕	EUR	EUR	
1000	19.500,00	13.900,00	42
1001	2.485,00	2.500,00	30
1002	5.263,51	2.800,00	56
1005	8.100,00	5.600,00	43
1033	7.980,00	5.000,00	48
1174	-7.224,77	13.500,00	-16
1175	9.556,02	60.000,00	5
1300	5.490,00	2.500,00	66
1330	7.500,00	4.500,00	50
1460	7.100,22	6.000,00	36
Overall Result	65.749,98	116.300,00	17

Figure 5.34 Output of Day sales outstanding Analysis for a Period (Credit Management) Report

In the report output, you can filter and drill down the DSO analysis to company code. You can swap the customer characteristic with structure. By carrying out further analysis with the reporting functionalities, you can identify the root cause for high DSO figures. With a clear audit trail, you can reduce payment delays and bad debts to reduce DSO. Let's assume a company with approximate monthly revenue of $500 million. If 30% of their customers fail to pay their bills on time, the company has an additional credit of $150 million monthly. Reducing DSO by two days saves the company approximately $33 million. The $33 million represents additional free capital, which can be invested in the business. This increases the capital turnover rate, which presents a high value for companies. For example, by investing this money back into the business, the company can slash their interest rate on debt by 5%, accumulating an additional savings of $20 million yearly.

The Customers DSO Analysis for a Period Credit Management (0FIAR_C02_Q1002) query provides DSO analysis for the last 12 periods. You can swap the customer with structure and time series. The report output shows the last 12 period DSO figures by customer or company code. The report output is illustrated in Figure 5.35.

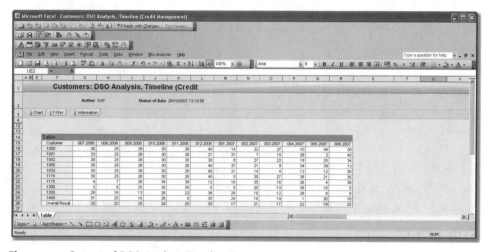

Figure 5.35 Output of DSO Analysis Timeline Report

We will now look at the queries based on FIAR Payment History InfoCube (0FIAR_C05). As the name suggests, this InfoProvider provides reports for AR payment history.

Payment History

The Payment History (0FIAR_C05_Q1001) query provides payment and arrears volumes per fiscal year period for a chosen customer. You can see payments with cash discount, payments without cash discount, arrears with cash discount, and arrears without cash discount per fiscal year. The number of payments is also shown in this report. You can use this report for payment history KPIs. For instance, you can use the ratio of cash discount payments to payment without cash discount for your analysis to develop the payment history of a customer. In the report output, you can swap the customer characteristic with fiscal year/period and structure. Figure 5.36 shows an output example of the report.

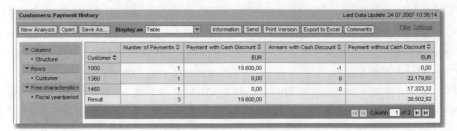

Figure 5.36 Output of Payment History (Credit Management) Report

In the next section, we will look at the queries based on FIAR Line Item InfoCube (0FIAR_C03).

Due Date for Net Payment Analysis

The Due Date for Net Payment Analysis (0FIAR_C03_Q0002) query shows open items by due date for selected company codes. You can display cumulative totals for all selected customers, as shown in Figure 5.37. The due date for net payment is calculated as the due date for net payment minus the key date. You can swap the customer characteristic with credit control area, document type, dunning area, dunning block, dunning key, dunning level, key figures, or posting key. In addition, you can drill down to the credit control area, document type, dunning area, dunning block, dunning key, dunning level, or posting key.

Customer ⇕	Balance ⇕ EUR	0 Days, Posting Date <= Key Date, Open items ⇕ EUR	0 Days ⇕ EUR	1 - 15 days ⇕
1000	21.612,04		21.612,00	21.612,00
1001	3.267,38		3.267,40	3.267,40
1002	5.117,55		5.117,55	5.117,55
1005	8.100,00		8.100,00	8.100,00
1012	0,00			
1032	457.694,31		457.694,30	457.694,30
1033	281.106,10		281.106,14	281.106,14
1034	0,00			
1050	3.696.022,20		3.696.022,16	3.696.022,16
1100	0,01			
1111	0,00			
1170	0,01			
1171	1.113,70		1.171,48	1.171,48
1172	36.435,18		36.435,19	36.435,19
1173	0,01			
1174	1.618.533,67		1.618.533,67	1.618.533,67
1175	251.550,01		251.550,00	251.550,00

Figure 5.37 Output of Due Date for Net Payment Analysis Report

Overdue Analysis

The Overdue Analysis (0FIAR_C03_Q0005) query is used to identify customers whose credit limits need to be monitored intensively as a result of considerable arrears. The overdue amounts of each customer are sorted by the number of days overdue. Figure 5.38 shows an example of an Overdue Analysis report.

Days Overdue Analysis			Balance		0 Days	
▼ Columns		Credit Control Area	1000	Overall Result ⇕	1000	Overall Result ⇕
• Key Figures			1000		1000	
• Credit Control Area	Customer ⇕		EUR	EUR		
▼ Rows						
• Customer	1000	1000	21.612,00	21.612,00		
▼ Free characteristics	1001	1001	3.267,40	3.267,40		
• Account Type	1002	1002	5.117,55	5.117,55		
• Document Type	1005	1005	8.100,00	8.100,00		
• Posting Key	1032	1032	457.694,30	457.694,30		
• Special G/L Indicator	1033	1033	281.106,14	281.106,14		
	1050	1050	3.696.022,16	3.696.022,16		
	1171	1171	1.171,48	1.171,48		
	1172	1172	36.435,19	36.435,19		
	1174	1174	1.618.533,67	1.618.533,67		
	1175	1175	251.550,00	251.550,00		
	1300	1300	6.141,74	6.141,74		
	1330	1330	7.500,00	7.500,00		
	1360	1360	86.721,86	86.721,86		
	1390	1390	40.600,00	40.600,00		
	1460	1460	215.876,36	215.876,36		
	Overall Result		6.737.449,85	6.737.449,85		

Figure 5.38 Output of Overdue Analysis Report

Terms Offered

The Terms Offered (0FIAR_C03_Q0001) query is used for the analysis of the cash discount history (days agreed/days taken) of the chosen customers. It shows how the customer has used the payment conditions you offered him. Starting from a starting date, a period in the past is analyzed, normally 30 days. All invoices that are posted in this period are included in the evaluation. It does not matter whether they have been cleared or not. The invoices are sorted according to the payment conditions offered into net, discount 1, and discount 2.

Depending on the payment conditions offered, customers can fall into one, two, or all of these categories. The evaluation of payments made by the customer in the period analyzed depends on the number of days that the customer took to pay and the payment method. The total number of days is calculated from the monthly amounts and the total interest divided by 100. The interest (amount × days / 100) is a value that contains pieces of information, the length of time and the amounts.

5.6 Summary

An organization might want to increase the efficiency of AP and AR reporting for multiple reasons. These include a desire to improve the control of AR and AP processes, cost and time efficiencies, and risk management and prevent fraud. SAP ERP provides AP and AR reports with the AP and AR subcomponents within FI. In this chapter, we first focused on the design considerations and work-in best practices for AP and AR reporting. Then we explained the key SAP ERP AP and AR reports. Finally, we explained the SAP NetWeaver BI business content for AP and AR along with data flow and modeling examples and the business content queries.

How can organizations improve their asset lifecycle process? What are the key touch points of the asset lifecycle process with other financial processes? How can you ensure that all assets available for depreciation are accurately reported in your tax reporting system? This chapter focuses on the best practices to standardize and streamline the asset lifecycle process to enhance the accuracy of asset reporting. We also explain the key asset reports in SAP ERP along with the SAP NetWeaver BI business content for asset accounting.

6 Asset Lifecycle Reporting

One of the fundamental requirements of achieving accurate financial reporting is to have a robust asset lifecycle process that complies with tax and regulatory requirements. For companies operating in capital-intensive industries, the fixed asset items of the balance sheet are often the largest portion of the assets in their financial statements. The income and cash flow statements are also influenced by fixed asset depreciation and revaluation. Our experiences show that organizations often do not consider improving the asset lifecycle and reporting process to be a priority. Often fixed asset register and depreciation postings are not complete and accurate, which leads to the misstatement of cost and depreciation in financial statements, without the awareness of the CEO or CFO.

One of the reasons for this kind of situation is that these organizations do not apply standardized processes and procedures to the asset lifecycle process. This lack of standardization results in significant discrepancies across the physical inventory, the fixed asset register, and the accounting system, as well as the limited ability of asset reporting and analysis.

Reporting requirements related to fixed assets for International Financial Reporting Standards are stated in IAS 16 (Property, Plan, and Equipment), IAS 36 (Impairment of Assets), and IAS 38 (Intangible Assets). The objective of IAS 16 is to advise on the accounting treatment for property, plant and equipment. In summary, the principal gives guidance on asset recognition, carrying amounts, and depreciation charges. IAS 36 states the principles related to an asset's recoverable amounts. The accounting treatment for intangible assets is prescribed in IAS 38. The standard specifies the criteria to be met for recognizing an intangible asset, as well as the carrying amount and other disclosures related to intangible assets. With the convergence initiatives of the accounting standards, FASB Statement No. 153 (SFAS No. 153 – Exchanges of Non-monetary Assets—an amendment of APB Opinion No. 29) was issued by FASB. With this statement, the main asset reporting differences between U.S. GAAP and IFRS were largely eliminated to improve cross-border financial reporting.

> **Asset accounting and SOX**
>
> Asset capitalization misstatement was one of the fraudulent accounting techniques that caused business failures such as Enron. As a result, the U.S. Congress passed the Sarbanes-Oxley Act (SOX) to ensure more accountability for senior executives at companies for the information provided to investors, by establishing requirements for internal control systems related to financial reporting.

By standardizing, simplifying, and automating the asset lifecycle process, organizations can have a consistent and accurate asset register and record keeping and effectively comply with the reporting requirements of accounting standards and regulatory organizations' rules. In this chapter, we focus on the key design considerations of the asset lifecycle and reporting process. In addition, we examine the asset reporting architecture along with the key SAP ERP and SAP NetWeaver BI reports.

6.1   The Asset Lifecycle and Reporting Process

The traditional asset lifecycle process starts with asset acquisition and ends with asset retirement when the asset is sold or scrapped. Leading organizations have extended the boundaries of the traditional asset lifecycle process by integrating the capital and investment management process into the asset lifecycle process. By doing so, organizations monitor capital investment during the asset lifecycle and analyze return on investment. In this section, we explain the asset lifecycle process and its integration with the capital and investment management process.

Figure 6.1 illustrates the main steps of the asset lifecycle process. The asset lifecycle starts with the capital and investment management process. Organizations first perform capital planning and budgeting. Once the capital budgeting is approved and capital is allocated, capital investment projects are created. Costs are first captured and recorded in the capital investment projects. They are then settled to assets and assets under constructions (AUCs). With the settlement, fixed assets are capitalized and asset transactions such as transfer and retirement can be performed. On a periodic basis, assets are depreciated, balance sheets are revaluated, and investment grants are recorded. Asset reporting is a fundamental part of each step in the end-to-end asset lifecycle process.

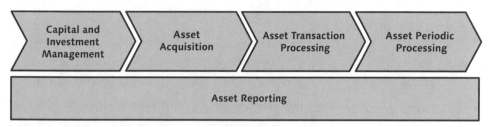

Figure 6.1 The Asset Lifecycle and Reporting Process

Let's look at each of these steps in detail:

- **Capital and investment management**
  The first step of the capital and investment management process is capital planning and budgeting. Capital planning and budgeting is prepared before procuring assets or undertaking capital projects. Planning is an important part of the capital and investment management process and is usually performed in several iterations, typically with the wider involvement of regions and locations of the organization. Budget approval and capital allocation follow this step to make sure that expenditures are properly authorized. The capital and investment management process can be monitored by using the Investment Management (IM) component in SAP ERP. With the IM information system, you can analyze your investment plans, budgets, and capital allocated to projects.

- **Asset acquisition**
  Once the budget is released and capital is allocated, the asset acquisition process starts. With the use of investment measures such as capital project or order, the expenditure incurred to acquire assets is first accumulated in the projects or orders. During this stage asset master data can be created and connected to the capital projects and orders. Depending on the nature of the asset, you can either create a fixed asset or an AUC in the Asset Accounting (AA) component, which is a subcomponent of FI in SAP ERP. Note that it is also possible to auto-

matically create an AUC from a project in AA. The accumulated expenditures in the projects or orders are settled to assets when the assets are placed in service or actively utilized, in other words, when the assets are capitalized.

▶ **Asset transaction processing**
Once the asset acquisition is completed and the asset is capitalized, asset transaction processing can begin. Asset transaction processing includes daily asset transactions, for example, asset transfers, asset retirements, post capitalization, and asset master data maintenance.

▶ **Asset periodic processing**
This process covers all asset periodic postings that should be executed before running financial statements, for example, depreciation calculation and posting, conducting physical asset inventory, and revaluation for the balance sheet.

Asset reporting is a fundamental part of the asset lifecycle process. It involves monitoring and analyzing all processes within the entire capital base. Best practices dictate that asset lifecycle reporting should cover the total cost of ownership, the value realized from investments, and the analysis of capital investments across multiple reporting entities. This can be achieved by establishing robust asset reporting architecture that provides information transparency for the end-to-end asset lifecycle process.

6.2 The Asset Reporting Architecture

Asset Accounting (AA) component is the basis of the SAP financial management environment's ability to track the asset register and asset-related information. All asset business transactions are captured in AA, which provides the ability to generate asset reports directly from the AA component, for example, asset transaction report, depreciation report, period values, asset history sheet, and asset inventory list. As we explained in the previous section, leading organizations exceed the boundaries of the traditional asset lifecycle process by integrating the capital and investment management process with the asset lifecycle process. The IM component provides numerous reports for analyzing the investment measures across the entire asset lifecycle. In addition to AA and IM, organizations can use SAP NetWeaver BI to create more flexible and advanced asset accounting reports. The asset reporting architecture is illustrated in Figure 6.2. In this figure, you can see how multiple components are integrated within SAP ERP.

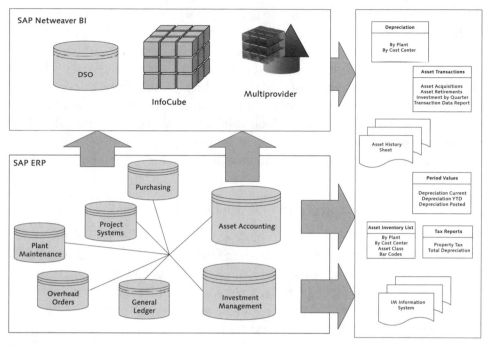

Figure 6.2 Asset Reporting Architecture

The AA component is very well integrated with the IM, Project Systems (PS), and Overhead Cost Controlling—Overhead Orders (CO-OM-OPA) components. The IM component enables capital and investment management processing, including planning, budgeting, capital allocation, and approval for capital investments. The expenditures incurred to acquire assets are recorded in either the G/L or the purchasing component. This information is available immediately in the IM component with the investment measures. The investment measure is not a separate object type in SAP ERP, so there is no separate investment measure master data. Instead, investment measures are represented by either work breakdown structure (WBS) elements managed in PS or investment orders managed in CO-OM-OPA, which are linked to assets and AUCs. In other words, investment measures are special internal orders or projects with properties integrating AA and IM. Such connection provides a mechanism that captures expenditure in investment measures, available in PS or CO-OM-OPA. With the settlement process, the investment measure costs are transferred from WBS elements or investment orders to AUCs. When an investment is completed, settlement is again performed, but this time from an AUC to a fixed asset. Settlement also supports direct capitalization, which allows costs to be settled directly to fixed assets.

Integration is of utmost importance to the asset lifecycle process. Reporting should be built on a well-integrated asset lifecycle process to enable that information to be seamlessly available for the reporting process at the desired level of detail. Now that we have explained the foundation of the reporting architecture, let's look at the best practices and approaches that would help organizations streamline and standardize the asset lifecycle process to enhance asset reporting accuracy. In the rest of this section, we specifically look at how to incorporate the capital and investment management process into the asset lifecycle process and design considerations of asset master data management and asset transfer process.

6.2.1 Integrating Capital and Investment Management

Developing a common solution to capture capital and investment information at the source and enable source applications to integrate with the asset lifecycle process has many benefits, including improving assurance and providing transparency of information to support audit and compliance. SAP ERP provides a modular but integrated structure to support the end-to-end asset lifecycle process. The integration points of the asset lifecycle process are best articulated in Figure 6.3.

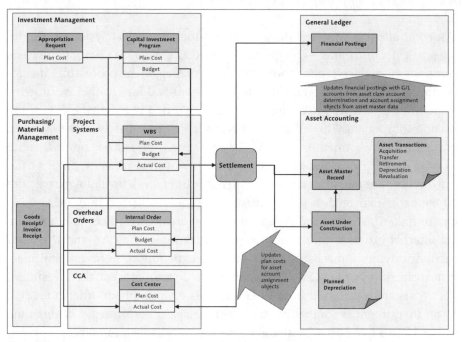

Figure 6.3 Integration Points of the Asset Lifecycle

The *capital investment program* provides a complete overview of the investments in the enterprise. It has a hierarchical structure where *investment measures* are assigned to the hierarchy nodes. You can make planning on the investment program nodes bottom-up and budgeting on them top-down. The plan values from investment measures or *appropriation requests* can be rolled up to the investment program. The appropriation requests are investment requests that can be planned and later, if appropriate, converted into investment measures. Once planning is complete and budgets are updated in the investment program nodes, you can distribute budgets from investment program nodes to the assigned investment measures.

Actual costs on investment measures originate from AP invoices, G/L postings, goods movements and purchases in MM, and certain transactions such as internal activity allocation and settlement in management accounting (CO).

With settlement, investment measures are credited and the costs are transferred to *fixed assets* or AUCs for capitalization. Settlement information is immediately available in G/L, AA, and CO components. Operating costs that are not capitalized are settled to cost centers, which could update the G/L depending on your real-time integration settings. Note that we cover real-time integration from CO to FI in Chapter 9.

Once the assets are capitalized, asset transactions such as transfers, retirements, depreciation, and revaluation are carried out in AA, simultaneously updating the G/L.

With the integrated asset accounting and cost planning, you can transfer planned depreciation and interest from assets to cost centers, investment measures, and capital investment programs. This is so that the planning information is fed back to IM and CO to complete the planning cycle with more accurate asset forecast information. The best practices dictate that you should incorporate your investment management process into your asset lifecycle process so that you can monitor capital and investment through the end-to-end asset lifecycle process.

The asset master data design plays a crucial role in establishing integration of the end-to-end asset lifecycle process. In the following section, we examine design considerations of asset master data for reporting.

6.2.2 Design Considerations for Asset Master Data Management

Consistent and transparent asset master data is not only required for the integrated solution architecture but also ensure accurate reporting. The asset master data should be well defined in such a way that the asset transactions can be automated and asset information streamlined through the end-to-end asset lifecycle process. In SAP ERP, asset master data records offer a lot of flexibility and options, with the capability to capture a lot of asset-related information. We recognized in our experience that often little attention is paid to which fields are used and the purpose of using those fields in the asset master record. Figure 6.4 illustrates the key fields in the asset master record.

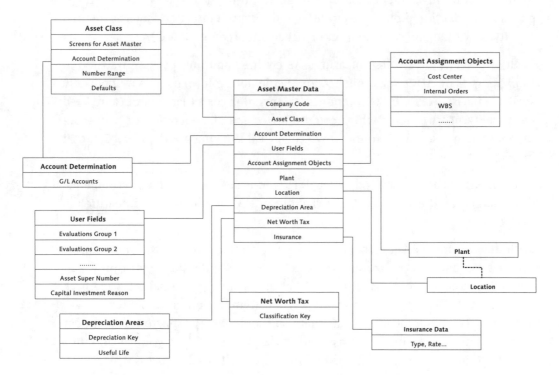

Figure 6.4 Key Asset Master Data Fields

▶ **Asset class**

The first key data field of the asset master data is the asset class. Asset class defines the classification of assets and holds the asset's G/L account determination, screen layout, and default depreciation terms and determines the asset numbering. Asset classes are structured to classify assets and their depreciation treatments for accounting and tax purposes. Account determination specifies the G/L accounts used in the asset transaction processing. When creating assets, you first specify the company code and the asset class.

▶ **Account assignment objects**

The account assignment objects specify the business ownership of the assets and control depreciation and balance sheet postings. The account assignment objects typically used are cost centers, internal orders, and WBS elements. With the account assignment objects, assets are integrated with other SAP ERP components.

▶ **Plant and location**

Plant and location are used to identify the physical whereabouts of assets. They facilitate the confirmation and validation of the existence of assets. The assignment of plant and location enables asset tracking. Additional fields can also be populated to further identify the asset whereabouts, for example, cost center and room. Physical asset inventory is normally conducted at the plant and location level. You need to ensure that all of the assets to be counted are listed in the inventory list report. To do so, you need to activate the checkbox for the inventory list in the master record of assets. The assignment of plant and location is important to track the location of assets. Furthermore, plant and location are linked to tax jurisdictions. You should consider tax reporting requirements when designing the location list to be used in the asset master records. Specifically, the tax jurisdiction code of the location has to be aligned with the tax location to enable accurate tax reporting, as the information directly feeds tax fillings. With validation and substitution rules for asset master data creation or change, you can create built-in system controls to increase the accuracy of the asset transaction processing.

▶ **User fields**

You can use SAP delivered user fields, that is, evaluation groups, asset super number, reason for capital investment, and so on, for the logical grouping of assets for reporting purposes and classifications. These user fields are delivered by SAP ERP, and you can define the field value content and change, if required, such as the field description and evaluation groups. For example, you can change the name of Evaluation Group 1 to Asset Type and Evaluation Group 2 to Asset Subclass. By doing so, you can track the asset type and asset class by using evaluation groups.

Asset reporting requirements vary from country to country, dependent upon local statutory and operational requirements. User fields can be used for meeting these diverse asset reporting requirements. However, it is important to define and use them consistently enterprise-wide so that they are not misused.

▶ **Depreciation areas**

A chart of depreciation comprises depreciation areas, which represent different asset books for statutory, tax, and business requirements. The decision on the number of depreciation areas to be used is important for statutory, tax, and business requirements. SAP ERP delivers a number of predefined charts of depreciation that you can use as a reference in your implementation. For consistent reporting there are two important design considerations in the definition of the depreciation area. The first design consideration is that you need to define depreciation areas across the charts of depreciation consistently. For example, if one depreciation area is used for special tax depreciation in one chart of depreciation, that depreciation area should be used for the same purpose in other charts of depreciation. This is especially important in cross-entity asset reporting. The next aspect of the depreciation area is populating the correct depreciation area information in the asset master data. For example, information such as the depreciation key and the useful life are critical for asset depreciation. The depreciation key is the main control parameter used for calculating depreciation amounts along with the useful life of the asset. You can default these fields from the asset class to automate their update in the asset master and avoid user entry-related errors. Furthermore, you can use built-in system controls to ensure accuracy and consistency in the depreciation area fields of the asset master data.

▶ **Net worth tax**

Property tax reporting requirements are very important, but often little attention is paid to capturing the required fields in the asset master data, resulting in tax reporting challenges. You can capture property law requirements in the asset master data and classify assets according to net worth tax criteria in SAP ERP, rather than relying on offline records. As discussed in Chapter 4, one of the leading practices for successful tax reporting is to involve the tax department in tax-related design decisions. In that respect, you need to have strong representation from the tax department to ensure that all tax-relevant data is correctly updated in the asset master records.

▶ **Insurance data**

Insurance data is another set of fields that provides useful management information. You can capture the asset insurance details such as insurance type, insurance company, and agreement number in the asset master record.

We advise you to have a single global set of asset master data screen layout rules to standardize the asset master data management and minimize the full lifecycle cost of maintenance. Our experience has shown us that one of the leading practices of master data management is to define the critical fields for your business, legal, and statutory requirements as mandatory fields and have built-in system controls such as validations and substitutions.

Incomplete asset report

You can still make some fields mandatory after you have implemented asset accounting and actively started to use it. SAP ERP provides the Incomplete Asset Detail List report (Transaction AUVA) that you can use to determine the assets that are not incomplete with respect to the mandatory fields. You can update missing mandatory fields directly from this report.

Now that we have examined the asset master data, we can move on the design aspects of reporting asset transaction processing. Our experience shows that most of the reporting problems arise from inaccurate asset transfers. In the next section, we look at design considerations for the asset transfer process.

6.2.3 Asset Transfer Process

Asset transfers can be classified into two main categories:

▶ **Intercompany asset transfer**
Intercompany asset transfer is used to transfer assets from one company code to another. It is important to assign the right asset transaction types to ensure that these postings are eliminated in the consolidation process and reported accurately in consolidated financial statements.

▶ **Intracompany asset transfer**
Intracompany asset transfer is used to transfer assets within the company code. There are two cases for intracompany asset transfers. The first one is moving

the asset location without changing the account assignment object. You can make this transfer by changing the location field directly in the asset master record. The second case is when the asset is moved to a location with different account assignment objects such as cost centers. It is important to make such transfers by using the asset transfer transaction, not by changing the account assignment field in the asset master record. Doing so enables the balances to be updated with the correct segment information and enables accurate segment reporting, which is discussed in Chapter 3.

You can post both transfer types either manually or automatically. By automating transfers, you can reduce the steps involved in the process and the number of manual interventions. Automation is especially important in some dynamic industries such as the chemical industry, where having the ability to mass asset transfer due to business mergers and demergers is important.

Asset transfer methods

In SAP ERP, many methods are delivered. For example, you can use either the net value or the gross value transfer method. With the gross value method, the receiver asset is capitalized with the total reserve and the accumulated depreciation from the sender asset. In contrast, with the net book value method, only the net book value is transferred. Depending on your business needs, you can also define your own transfer method. Profit and losses resulting from intercompany asset transfers must be eliminated in consolidation to reflect a true picture of the accurate consolidation of financial information.

Now that we have explained the design considerations and best practices to establish a robust reporting architecture, we can examine the standard asset lifecycle reports. We first look at the standard SAP ERP reports.

6.3   Asset Reporting in SAP ERP

The asset information system includes a number of asset reports for management information requirements as well as tax reporting requirements. Asset accounting reports allow the analysis of asset transactions such as transfer, depreciation, and retirement and enable detailed monitoring of both fixed assets and AUCs. These reports focus primarily on financial impacts on asset transactions such as acquisition, depreciation, and retirement. You can use the asset management reports to control the asset lifecycle process, fill out tax reports, and support management business decisions and audits. These reports can also be used to generate key performance indicators (KPIs) in relation to asset management. The perspective gained from these analyses should be incorporated into the capital management process for further investment planning and decision-making. In this section, we explain the key reports from IM and AA information systems.

6.3.1   Investment Management Information System

To perform comprehensive analysis of capital investment, the IM information system provides many analytical reports to monitor capital investments. This section only focuses on two key reports available under the IM information system. The standard investment management reports are available under the IM information system folder in SAP ERP. To reach the IM system information folder, follow the menu path **Investment Management • Programs • Information System • Investment Management Reports • Fixed Assets**.

List of Origins of Asset Charges Report

The List of Origins of Asset Charges report (Transaction S_ALR_87012930) provides information about asset acquisitions. It displays the sources of asset acquisitions that you need during the asset lifecycle. With this report, you can analyze capitalized assets by source transactions and trace them to the original documents. This report also displays the settlement of actual costs from investment measures, AP invoices directly posted to assets, goods receipt of assets, and asset transfers. For example, in Figure 6.5, the origin of asset 2303 is vendor invoice 1900000021. From the output of this report, it is possible to call up the Asset Explorer, which we explain later in this section.

The report displays a question mark if it is not possible to obtain clear proof of origin regarding the source of acquisition. For example, an acquisition that was posted first to a clearing account appears as a question mark in the output of the report. In that case, you need to carry out further analysis by navigating to the original documents. Note that you do not need to use the full IM functionalities to execute this report, although it is under the IM information system.

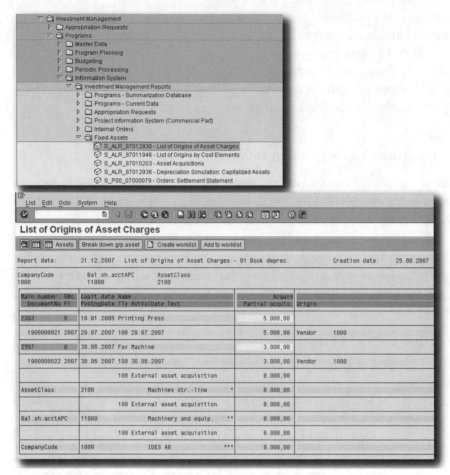

Figure 6.5 Selection Screen and Output of List of Origins of Asset Charges Report

Total/Annual Budget in Measures Report

The Total/Annual Budget in Measures report (Transaction S_ALR_87012820) displays overall and yearly budget figures in investment measures assigned to program nodes. The investment program is displayed in a hierarchical structure, with investment measures assigned to the program nodes. With the report-to-report interface, you can jump up to another report called Project: Budget/Actual/ Commitments/Remaining Plan/Allotted to view the project details. Figure 6.6 illustrates the output of this report in ALV format.

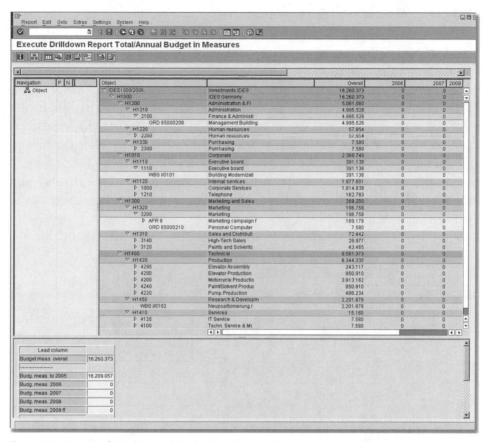

Figure 6.6 Output of Total/Annual Budget in Measures Report

6.3.2 Asset Accounting Information System

The standard asset accounting reports are available under the AA information system folder in SAP ERP. To reach the AA information system folder, follow the menu path **Accounting • Asset Accounting • Information System • Reports for Asset Accounting**.

In this section, we look at the key asset accounting control and tax reports.

Changes to Asset Master Records Report

Incorrect or incomplete changes to asset master data lead to poor-quality asset master record and potential errors in transaction processing and reporting. You can use built-in system controls such as validation rules to control the consistency of asset master record changes. In addition, you can monitor the changes using the Asset Master Data report (Transaction S_ALR_87012037). The changes are displayed in sequential order, as shown in Figure 6.7. You can restrict the selection of the report by asset, date of change, user name of the person who made the change, and the name of the changed field as it is in the selection screen of the report. It is also possible to show the newly created assets, provided that the **Display new assets also?** checkbox is selected in the selection parameters. The report can be displayed in ALV format.

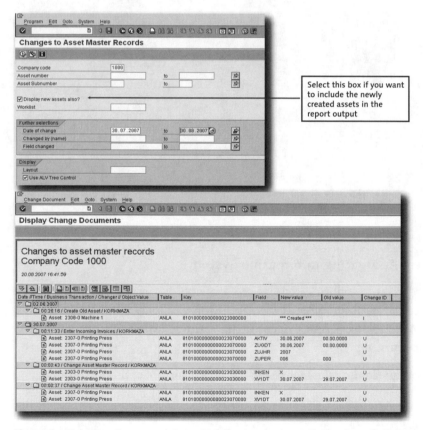

Figure 6.7 Selection Screen and Output of Changes to Asset Master Records Report

Inventory Management Reports

The inventory management reports are used when conducting a physical asset inventory. SAP ERP provides the inventory list reports by cost center, location, plant, or asset class. The inventory list reports are based on the SAP ERP query reporting tool. Thus, they can be easily copied and modified according to your business needs. These reports can be displayed in ALV format and downloaded to different file formats. The menu path, selection screen and the output of the Inventory List by Cost Center report in ALV format is illustrated in Figure 6.8.

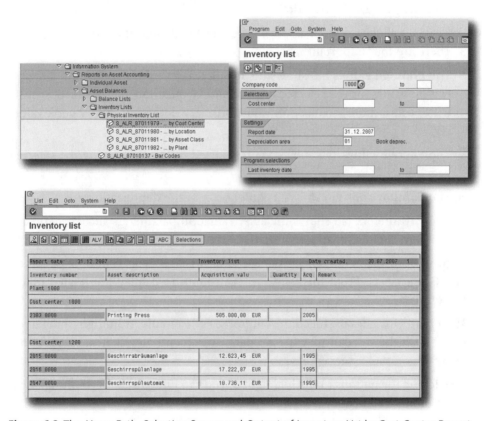

Figure 6.8 The Menu Path, Selection Screen and Output of Inventory List by Cost Center Report

Note

The SAP ERP query reporting tool is explained in Chapter 12.

Asset Explorer Report

The Asset Explorer report (Transaction AW01N) shows all the values of an individual asset master record. Figure 6.9 illustrates an example of asset explorer output. Five important sections are highlighted in the report output:

▶ Highlight 1 is the selection parameters area, where you specify asset, asset subnumber, and company code. You can switch to another asset without exiting the transaction by specifying the parameters of the other asset.

▶ Highlight 2 shows the available depreciation areas. The report displays the values for the selected depreciation area.

▶ You can see all the values of assets for the selected depreciation area in highlight 3. There are four important tabs:

  ▶ The **Planned values** tab shows the detailed asset values and planned depreciation values for the selected asset record: acquisition and production costs (APC) transactions, acquisition value, ordinary depreciation, net book value, etc.

  ▶ The **Posted values** tab shows figures posted to the G/L during the selected year.

  ▶ The **Comparisons** tab shows a comparison of the depreciation areas.

  ▶ The **Parameters** tab shows the asset valuation parameters such as depreciation key, useful life, and depreciation start date.

▶ Highlight 4 displays the objects related to the asset, such as vendor, cost center, and G/L account. From this view, you can jump to display the related object master data.

▶ Highlight 5 includes useful control buttons. For example, from right to left, you can refresh the view, display master data, switch currency, activate simulation, and call up other asset reports.

▶ By clicking the buttons in the highlight 6, you can jump to the accounting document or all documents.

The Asset Explorer uses ALV grid control for the output format. You can also activate Excel in place functionality for the ALV grid control to view the values in Excel.

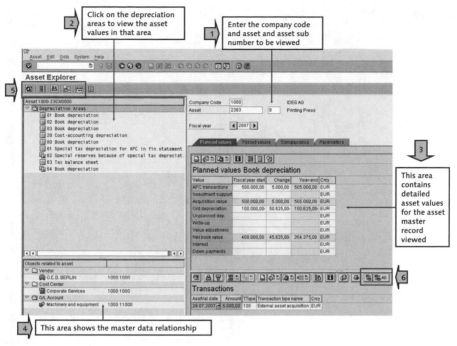

Figure 6.9 Asset Explorer Report

Asset History Sheet Report

The Asset History Sheet (Transaction S_ALR_87011990) is perhaps the most comprehensive report showing the complete picture of assets transactions and balances within a specified period of time. The Asset History Sheet is a legally required report in many countries and is used for financial statement reconciliations. It provides information on all asset transactions in a single report. The report shows beginning balances, ending balances, and asset transactions such as acquisitions, depreciation, transfers, and retirements. Figure 6.10 shows the menu path and selection screen of the Asset History Sheet report.

Let's examine the important selection parameters to get a meaningful output of Asset History Sheet report.

▶ **History sheet version**

The history sheet version is perhaps the most important parameter of this report. It is selected in the selection parameters of the report and structures the form and content of the report.

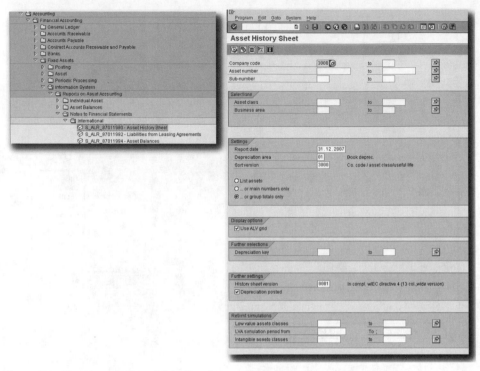

Figure 6.10 The Menu Path and Selection Screen of the Asset History Sheet Report

▶ **Sort version**

The sort version determines the fields to be displayed with the sort levels and the summation levels of the report output. It plays an important role in the overall output of the report. The sort version can be used in many asset reports. SAP delivers many predefined sort versions that can be used as references. You can also define your own sort versions. It is important to give a name starting with an allowed customer character such as Z or Y to ensure that your sort versions are not overwritten by the SAP standard delivery during a release change.

▶ **Report date**

It is important to set the date to end of period date for any period of the current year that you are interested in. When you run the report for the past closed years and future years, always use the last day of the year.

▶ **Depreciation posted**

This checkbox controls the display of posted and planned depreciation. Select the **Depreciation posted** checkbox to display posted depreciation; otherwise the report will show planned depreciation. You need to be aware of this setting because the net book value displayed in the report of the asset is calculated based on this parameter.

The Asset History Sheet report can be run by any sort version and show totals on group levels. A list without individual asset information can be easily generated if you select the **... or group totals only** option in the selection screen. If you select the **List assets** option, you can display the Asset History Sheet by assets.

Now that we have explained the key parameters of the Asset History Sheet report, let's dive in to the configuration of the history sheet version and sort version parameters. The settings of these two parameters are very important to generate a meaningful report output.

History Sheet Version

The history sheet version is the foundation of the line and column structure of the Asset History Sheet report. SAP ERP delivers predefined history sheet versions according to international accounting standard requirements, as well as country-specific requirements. For example, asset history sheet in compliance with EC directives, depreciation by depreciation type, acquisition values, transferred values, special reserves, and so on are predelivered history sheet versions within SAP ERP. You can use these versions or design your own versions according to your business needs. One of the important design considerations is that the new history sheet version key should begin with a custom letter such as Z or Y to ensure that it is not overwritten by the SAP standard delivery during a release change. To define the history sheet version, follow the configuration menu path **Financial Accounting (new)** • **Asset Accounting** • **Information System** • **Asset History Sheet** • **Define History Sheet Version**.

Figure 6.11 shows the asset history version **0001**, **In compl. w/EC directive 4 (13 col.,wide version)**, which is delivered by SAP ERP. By double-clicking on the **Acquisition** cell highlighted with the step 1 arrow, you can see the details of the cell **Acquisition** (column 10, line 2), where you select the transactions that are shown in the report for asset acquisitions (step 2 arrow). Indicator X means the transaction is included in the history sheet version.

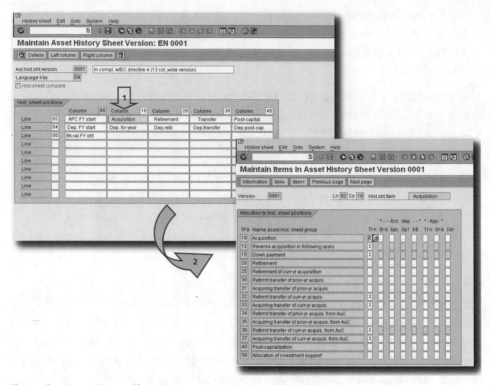

Figure 6.11 Asset History Sheet Version

> ### Incomplete history sheet version
>
> When you create your own history sheet and save it, the system checks whether the definition of the history sheet version is complete. The history sheet version is complete when all value categories (asset balances, value adjustments, depreciation, etc.) are assigned to a cell in the history sheet version. If the history sheet version you are using is not complete, it means some value categories are missing from the definition. Note that it is important to assign all value categories so that the Asset History report displays the correct values. If the Asset History sheet version is not complete, it is indicated in the header of the report output.

Figure 6.12 illustrates the ALV output format of the Asset History Sheet report. By double-clicking on the lines you can call up the Asset Explorer to see the details of the asset. In addition, from the menu bar by using **Goto • Reports menu**, you can call up other asset reports including asset balances, asset acquisitions, intracompany asset transfers, asset retirement, depreciation, posted depreciation, and so on.

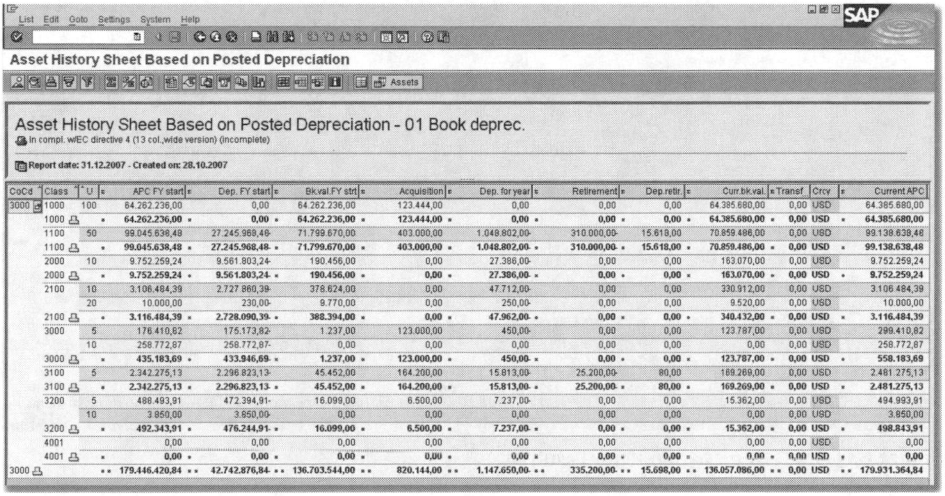

CoCd	Class	U	APC FY start	Dep. FY start	Bk.val.FY strt	Acquisition	Dep. for year	Retirement	Dep.retir.	Curr.bk.val.	Transf	Crcy	Current APC
3000	1000	100	64.262.236,00	0,00	64.262.236,00	123.444,00	0,00	0,00	0,00	64.385.680,00	0,00	USD	64.385.680,00
	1000		64.262.236,00	0,00	64.262.236,00	123.444,00	0,00	0,00	0,00	64.385.680,00	0,00	USD	64.385.680,00
	1100	50	99.045.638,48	27.245.968,48-	71.799.670,00	403.000,00	1.048.802,00-	310.000,00-	15.618,00	70.859.486,00	0,00	USD	99.138.638,48
	1100		99.045.638,48	27.245.968,48-	71.799.670,00	403.000,00	1.048.802,00-	310.000,00-	15.618,00	70.859.486,00	0,00	USD	99.138.638,48
	2000	10	9.752.259,24	9.561.803,24-	190.456,00	0,00	27.386,00-	0,00	0,00	163.070,00	0,00	USD	9.752.259,24
	2000		9.752.259,24	9.561.803,24-	190.456,00	0,00	27.386,00-	0,00	0,00	163.070,00	0,00	USD	9.752.259,24
	2100	10	3.106.484,39	2.727.860,39-	378.624,00	0,00	47.712,00-	0,00	0,00	330.912,00	0,00	USD	3.106.484,39
		20	10.000,00	230,00-	9.770,00	0,00	250,00-	0,00	0,00	9.520,00	0,00	USD	10.000,00
	2100		3.116.484,39	2.728.090,39-	388.394,00	0,00	47.962,00-	0,00	0,00	340.432,00	0,00	USD	3.116.484,39
	3000	5	176.410,82	175.173,82-	1.237,00	123.000,00	450,00-	0,00	0,00	123.787,00	0,00	USD	299.410,82
		10	258.772,87	258.772,87-	0,00	0,00	0,00	0,00	0,00	0,00	0,00	USD	258.772,87
	3000		435.183,69	433.946,69-	1.237,00	123.000,00	450,00-	0,00	0,00	123.787,00	0,00	USD	558.183,69
	3100	5	2.342.275,13	2.296.823,13-	45.452,00	164.200,00	15.813,00-	25.200,00-	80,00	169.269,00	0,00	USD	2.481.275,13
	3100		2.342.275,13	2.296.823,13-	45.452,00	164.200,00	15.813,00-	25.200,00-	80,00	169.269,00	0,00	USD	2.481.275,13
	3200	5	488.493,91	472.394,91-	16.099,00	6.500,00	7.237,00-	0,00	0,00	15.362,00	0,00	USD	494.993,91
		10	3.850,00	3.850,00-	0,00	0,00	0,00	0,00	0,00	0,00	0,00	USD	3.850,00
	3200		492.343,91	476.244,91-	16.099,00	6.500,00	7.237,00-	0,00	0,00	15.362,00	0,00	USD	498.843,91
	4001		0,00	0,00	0,00	0,00	0,00	0,00	0,00	0,00	0,00	USD	0,00
	4001		0,00	0,00	0,00	0,00	0,00	0,00	0,00	0,00	0,00	USD	0,00
3000			179.446.420,84	42.742.876,84-	136.703.544,00	820.144,00	1.147.650,00-	335.200,00-	15.698,00	136.057.086,00	0,00	USD	179.931.364,84

Figure 6.12 Asset History Sheet Report Output

Total Depreciation Report

The Total Depreciation report (Transaction S_ALR_87012004) shows the planned and posted depreciation values. The report shows individual asset or grouping asset values based on the sorting variant selected in the selection screen. As shown in Figure 6.13, the report output displays beginning and ending balances, current year depreciation separately from prior accumulated depreciation, ordinary, unplanned, and special depreciation, useful life of the assets, acquisition value, and so on. The Total Depreciation report is used in many countries for asset tax reporting. For example, you can use this report as a basis for IRS tax form 4562 (Depreciation and Amortization) in the United States.

Analysis of Retirement Revenue Report

The Analysis of Retirement Revenue report (Transaction S_ALR_87012066) is used for tax reporting in the United States. To access the report, follow the menu path **SAP Menu • Accounting • Financial Accounting • Fixed Asset • Information System • Reports on Asset Accounting • Taxes • Country Specific • USA.**

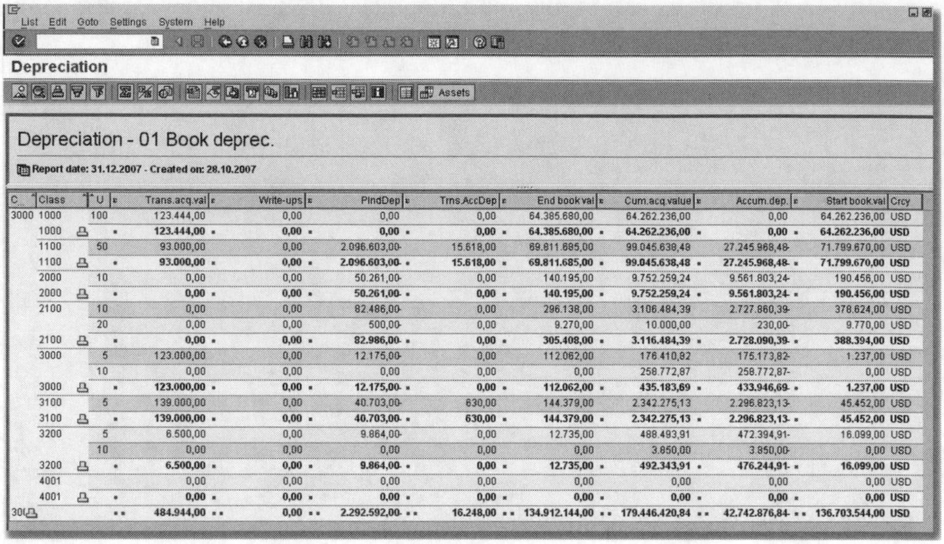

C	Class	U	Trans.acq.val	Write-ups	PlndDep	Trns.AccDep	End book val	Cum.acq.value	Accum.dep.	Start book val	Crcy
3000	1000	100	123.444,00	0,00	0,00	0,00	64.385.680,00	64.262.236,00	0,00	64.262.236,00	USD
	1000		**123.444,00**	**0,00**	**0,00**	**0,00**	**64.385.680,00**	**64.262.236,00**	**0,00**	**64.262.236,00**	**USD**
	1100	50	93.000,00	0,00	2.096.603,00-	15.618,00	69.811.685,00	99.045.638,48	27.245.968,48-	71.799.670,00	USD
	1100		**93.000,00**	**0,00**	**2.096.603,00-**	**15.618,00**	**69.811.685,00**	**99.045.638,48**	**27.245.968,48-**	**71.799.670,00**	**USD**
	2000	10	0,00	0,00	50.261,00-	0,00	140.195,00	9.752.259,24	9.561.803,24-	190.456,00	USD
	2000		**0,00**	**0,00**	**50.261,00-**	**0,00**	**140.195,00**	**9.752.259,24**	**9.561.803,24-**	**190.456,00**	**USD**
	2100	10	0,00	0,00	82.486,00-	0,00	296.138,00	3.106.484,39	2.727.860,39-	378.624,00	USD
		20	0,00	0,00	500,00-	0,00	9.270,00	10.000,00	230,00-	9.770,00	USD
	2100		**0,00**	**0,00**	**82.986,00-**	**0,00**	**305.408,00**	**3.116.484,39**	**2.728.090,39-**	**388.394,00**	**USD**
	3000	5	123.000,00	0,00	12.175,00-	0,00	112.062,00	176.410,82	175.173,82-	1.237,00	USD
		10	0,00	0,00	0,00	0,00	0,00	258.772,87	258.772,87-	0,00	USD
	3000		**123.000,00**	**0,00**	**12.175,00-**	**0,00**	**112.062,00**	**435.183,69**	**433.946,69-**	**1.237,00**	**USD**
	3100	5	139.000,00	0,00	40.703,00-	630,00	144.379,00	2.342.275,13	2.296.823,13-	45.452,00	USD
	3100		**139.000,00**	**0,00**	**40.703,00-**	**630,00**	**144.379,00**	**2.342.275,13**	**2.296.823,13-**	**45.452,00**	**USD**
	3200	5	6.500,00	0,00	9.864,00-	0,00	12.735,00	488.493,91	472.394,91-	16.099,00	USD
		10	0,00	0,00	0,00	0,00	0,00	3.850,00	3.850,00-	0,00	USD
	3200		**6.500,00**	**0,00**	**9.864,00-**	**0,00**	**12.735,00**	**492.343,91**	**476.244,91-**	**16.099,00**	**USD**
	4001		0,00	0,00	0,00	0,00	0,00	0,00	0,00	0,00	USD
	4001		**0,00**	**0,00**	**0,00**	**0,00**	**0,00**	**0,00**	**0,00**	**0,00**	**USD**
30(			**484.944,00**	**0,00**	**2.292.592,00-**	**16.248,00**	**134.912.144,00**	**179.446.420,84**	**42.742.876,84-**	**136.703.544,00**	**USD**

Figure 6.13 Total Depreciation Report Output

This report is used for filling IRS tax form 4797 (Sales of Business Property). As shown in the report output in Figure 6.14, capital gains are displayed in the **Capital gain** column. Capital gains are calculated by subtracting the APC value of the asset from the sales revenue. Gains that are less than the APC value of the asset are shown in the column labeled **Ordinary gain**. Capital losses occur when the sales revenue is less than the net book value of the assets.

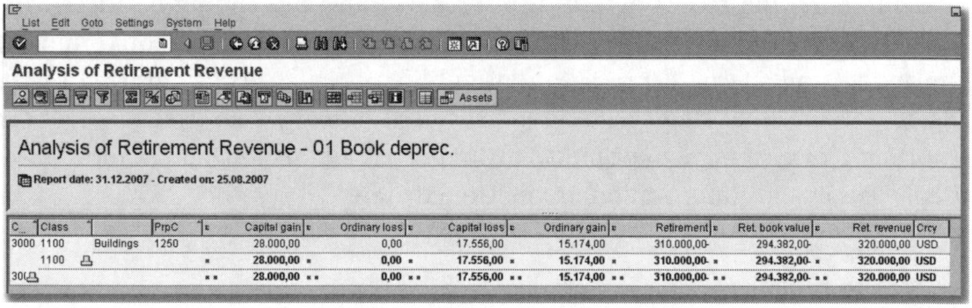

C	Class		PrpC	Capital gain	Ordinary loss	Capital loss	Ordinary gain	Retirement	Ret. book value	Ret. revenue	Crcy
3000	1100	Buildings	1250	28.000,00	0,00	17.556,00	15.174,00	310.000,00-	294.382,00-	320.000,00	USD
	1100			**28.000,00**	**0,00**	**17.556,00**	**15.174,00**	**310.000,00-**	**294.382,00-**	**320.000,00**	**USD**
30(				**28.000,00**	**0,00**	**17.556,00**	**15.174,00**	**310.000,00-**	**294.382,00-**	**320.000,00**	**USD**

Figure 6.14 Analysis of Retirement Revenue Report Output

Net Worth Valuation Report

The Net Worth Valuation report (Transaction S_ALR_87012028) displays asset values for determining net worth tax so that you can determine property tax values.

To access the report, follow the menu path **SAP Menu • Accounting • Financial Accounting • Fixed Asset • Information System • Reports on Asset Accounting • Specific Valuations • International.** In the report output, all values for the reporting year are always displayed. The work-in best practices to use this report in the most efficient manner are the followings:

▶ **Depreciation area**

Determine the depreciation area for net worth valuation for each company code.

▶ **Property classification key**

You need to create values for the property classification key for property types, for example, 1250 buildings. In addition, you should include the property classification key in the definition of the sort indicator to structure the columns of the report. Figure 6.15 shows the output of the report along with definition of the sort key with the fields company code, asset class, and property classification key.

▶ **Reason for manual valuation**

This key is used when the asset value is replaced with the net worth updated in the asset master data. For example, in the report output for asset 1146, the acquisition value is US $20,000, manually valuated at US $25,000. The reason for manual valuation specified is 003—Assessed value.

In the columns there are important fields such as depreciation key, asset capitalization date, acquisition value at the beginning of the current fiscal year, cut off value, planned net worth value, and planned net book value. For assets with the net worth value set manually, the cutoff percentage and cutoff value cannot be determined by the report, and this is shown as nil in the report output.

Asset Transactions Report

The Asset Transaction (Transaction S_ALR_87012048) report lists all asset transactions in the reporting year by asset or higher level per depreciation area. To access this report, follow the menu path **SAP Menu • Accounting • Financial Accounting • Fixed Asset • Information System • Reports on Asset Accounting • Day-to-Day Activities • International.** The report shows the change in APC, value adjustment, and asset transactions used. In addition, you can display settlements from investment measures if you specify in the selection screen. The output of the report is shown in Figure 6.16.

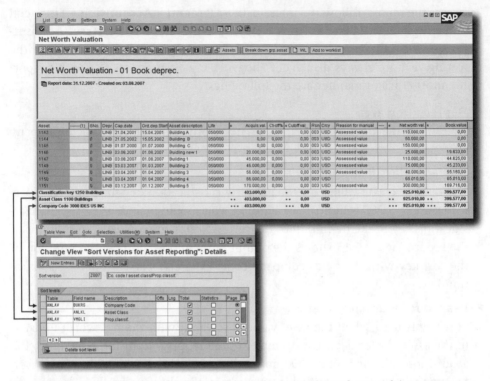

Figure 6.15 Output of Net Worth Valuation Report along with the Definition of the Sort Version Used in the Report

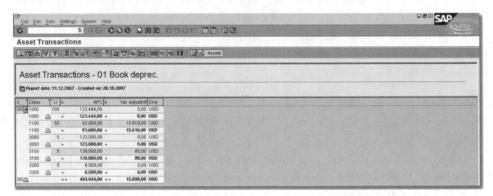

Figure 6.16 Asset Transactions Report Output

Asset Acquisitions (Mid-Quarter-Convention) Report

The Asset Acquisition (Mid-Quarter-Convention) report (Transaction S_ALR_87012047) lists asset acquisitions according to U.S. tax mid-quarter convention per quarter. To access the report follow the menu path **SAP Menu • Accounting • Financial Accounting • Fixed Asset • Information System • Reports on Asset Accounting • Preparation for Closing • Country Specific • USA.**

With this report, you can compare actual acquisitions against planned capital investments. This is specified in the selection screen of the report where sort version, company code, report date, and other selection parameters are entered. In the columns of the report the values of asset acquisitions for each quarter are shown as in Figure 6.17. In addition, the maximum amount for asset acquisitions according to the mid-quarter convention is displayed in the column **Max. amt. acc. to MQC** (maximum amount according to Mid-Quarter-Convention). The maximum amount is calculated as 40% of total acquisitions in the reporting year. If total acquisitions exceed 40% limit in the last quarter, the report displays a warning in the message column: "MQC total is already exceeded."

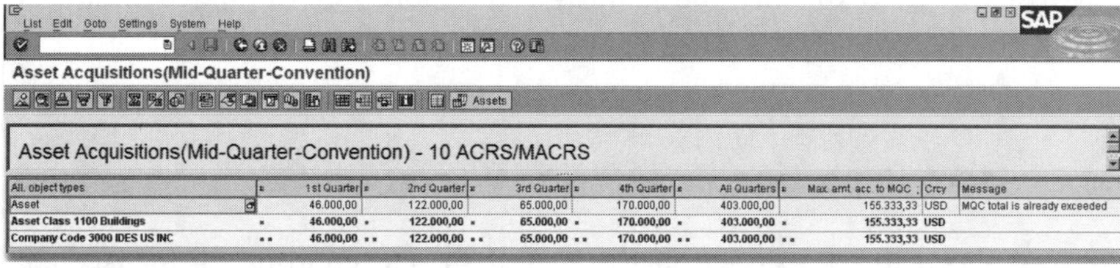

Figure 6.17 Asset Acquisitions (Mid-Quarter-Convention) Report Output

SAP Queries for Asset Accounting

SAP delivers a number of standard queries for asset accounting that can be used for reporting in addition to standard asset reports. Some of these queries, for example the inventory lists, are already added to the asset information system. You can see the list of SAP delivered queries assigned to user group asset manager (AM) in Figure 6.18. SAP queries can be used as a generic data source for SAP NetWeaver BI.

> **Note**
>
> The SAP ERP query reporting tool is explained in Chapter 12.

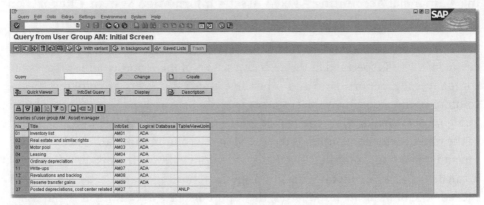

Figure 6.18 SAP Delivered Asset Queries for User Group AM

Now that we have explained the standard SAP reports, we can move on to asset reporting in SAP NetWeaver BI.

6.4 Asset Reporting in SAP NetWeaver BI

SAP NetWeaver BI reporting primarily supports asset reporting for management information purposes. In the business content, standard InfoProviders and Info-Objects are delivered for asset accounting. You can model your asset reporting architecture in SAP NetWeaver BI by using these standard objects. However, it is important to note that you should carefully check whether the preconfigured solution fulfils all of your business requirements.

In this section, we focus exclusively on the business content for asset accounting. Let's first look at the data modeling scenarios that use the business content objects.

6.4.1 Data Flow and Modeling for Asset Accounting

The business content in asset accounting provides four InfoCubes, three data storage objects (DSOs), and three MultiProviders. Figure 6.19, Figure 6.20 and Figure

6.21 show data flow examples with the predelivered business content objects. It should be noted that the data flow examples in these figures are for illustration purposes only. Figure 6.19 illustrates data flow examples with asset accounting InfoCubes. Now, let's examine each of these InfoCubes:

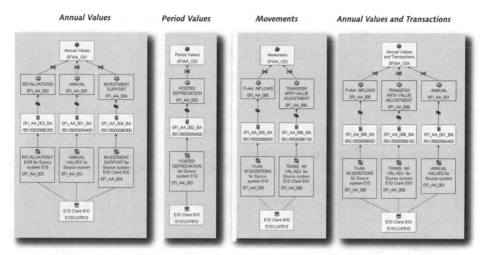

Figure 6.19 Data Flow of Asset Accounting InfoCubes

▶ **Annual Values (0FIAA_C01)**
This InfoCube contains all of the annual asset values that are extracted from the connected source system(s) based on planned depreciation. It is supplied with data by InfoSources Annual Values (0FI_AA_001), Revaluation/Year (0FI_AA_003), and Investment Support (0FI_AA_004).

▶ **Period Values (0FIAA_C02)**
This InfoCube contains periodic asset values that are extracted from the connected source system(s) based on posted depreciation. It is supplied with data by InfoSource posted depreciation (0FI_AA_002).

▶ **Movements (0FIAA_C03)**
This InfoCube contains all asset accounting line items that are extracted from the connected source system(s). It is supplied with data by InfoSources Acquisitions (0FI_AA_005) and Transactions w/ Value Adjustments (0FI_AA_006).

▶ **Annual Values and Transactions (0FIAA_C04)**
This InfoCube contains all annual values that are extracted from the connected source system(s) based on planned depreciation and line items. This InfoCube

primarily serves for the generation of the Asset History Sheet report. It includes the planned depreciation values from InfoCube 0FIAA_C01 and the line items from InfoCube 0FIAA_C03. It is supplied with data by InfoSources Annual Values (0FI_AA_001), Acquisitions (0FI_AA_005), and Transactions w/ Value Adjustments (0FI_AA_006).

In the business content, the field 0ASSET_AFAB is delivered unassigned in the data modeling. We strongly recommend that you check whether the depreciation area InfoObject 0ASSET_AFAB is filled from the InfoObject 0DEPRAREA in the update rules. The asset queries in the business content based on these InfoCubes use 0ASSET_AFAB. If you require this field in your reports and use the business content as a reference template, ensure that the depreciation area field is correctly populated in SAP NetWeaver BI.

> **Data extraction into InfoCubes**
>
> To upload data into the Asset InfoCubes described above, you first need to delete the existing data, as the system adds it to the existing values each time. Note that the delta InfoCubes are delivered for the annual values, period values, and asset movements: Annual Value Delta (0FIAA_C12), Cumulated Movements Delta (0FIAA_C11), and Period Value Delta (0FIAA_C13).

Now that we have explained data modeling with InfoCubes, let's continue with data modeling based on DSOs. Figure 6.20 illustrates data modeling examples with business content DSOs.

▶ **Transactions Delta (0FIA_DS11)**
This DSO contains all asset transactions and annual values. The InfoSource of this DSO is FI:AA Movements (0FI_AA_11).

▶ **Annual Value Delta (0FIA_DS12)**
This DSO contains the annual values for assets. The annual values are calculated from the annual value information posted in DSO Transactions Delta.

▶ **Period Value Delta (0FIA_DS13)**
This DSO contains the period values for assets. It has the same structure as the Annual Values Delta DSO. Note, however, that the values are kept periodically. The object is supplied with data from both DSO object 0FIA_DS11 and InfoSource 0FI_AA_12. In other words, period values are calculated by using the annual values and transactions in the Transactions DSO, and the depreciation values are extracted directly from the source systems.

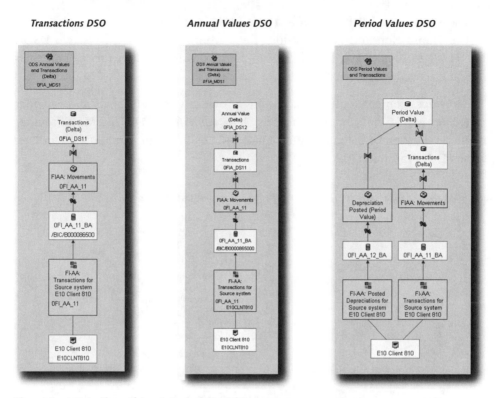

Figure 6.20 Data Flow of Asset Accounting DSOs

> **Note**
>
> For DSOs, you should always remember that the reporting process carried out directly in the DSO may cause performance problems. It is advisable to update data in the additional InfoCube when using DSO. For example, you can supply data from Transactions DSO to Transactions InfoCube.

The business content in asset accounting provides three MultiProviders to optimize the data flow. Figure 6.21 illustrates data flow examples with the business content MultiProviders.

- ▶ **Transaction and Annual Values Delta (0FIA_MDS1)**

    The Transaction and Annual Values Delta MultiProvider connects 0FIA_DS11 and 0FIA_DS12 DSOs. You can use this MultiProvider for annual values and transactions reporting.

▶ **Transaction and Period Values Delta (0FIA_MDS2)**
The Transaction and Period Values Delta MultiProvider connects two DSOs, OFIA_DS11 and OFIA_DS13. You can use this MultiProvider for period values and transactions reporting.

The business content for asset accounting provides one additional MultiProvider called Annual Values and Transactions Delta (0FIAA_MC1). This MultiProvider connects the Annual Value Delta InfoCube (0FIAA_C12) and the Cumulated Movements Delta InfoCube (0FIAA_C11).

Annual Values and Transactions   *Period Values and Transactions*

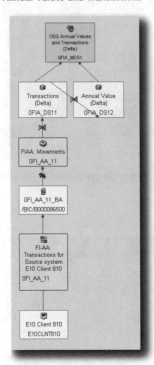
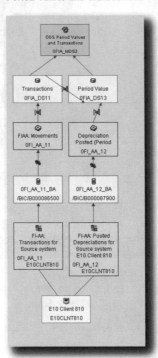

Figure 6.21 Data Flow of Asset Accounting MultiProviders

> **Note**
>
> Before you can use the delta extraction, you have to activate the FIAA_BW_DELTA_UP-DATE BAdI. This BAdI ensures that the change tables BWFIAA_AEDAT_TR, BWFIAA_AEDAT_AB, and BWFIAA_AEDAT_AS are updated when you update transactions or create and change master data and annual values for assets.

Now that we have explained the data flow and modeling of asset accounting in SAP NetWeaver BI, let's look at the asset queries delivered within the business content.

6.4.2 SAP NetWeaver BI Asset Reports

The preceding section covered data flow and modeling with the business content objects for asset accounting. In this section, we look at the business content queries for asset accounting. To examine the asset queries more easily, we have categorized them into four areas, as shown in Figure 6.22: Asset History Sheet, Asset Transactions, Asset Annual Values, and Depreciation.

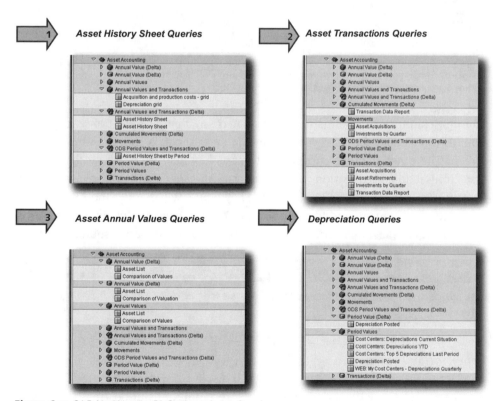

Figure 6.22 SAP NetWeaver BI Content Asset Queries

Because a comprehensive, detailed analysis of each asset query exceeds the scope of this book, we concentrate here on selected queries from each of these categories. Let's start with asset history sheet queries (see highlight 1 in Figure 6.22).

Asset History Sheet Queries

Acquisition and Production Cost Report

The Acquisition and Production Cost - Grid (0FIAA_C04_Q001) query displays the fiscal year start acquisition and production costs, acquisition, retirement, transfer postings, and current year acquisition and production costs. Figure 6.23 shows an example output of the Acquisition and Production Cost query.

		Acquisition and production costs FY start ⇕	Acquisition ⇕	Retirement ⇕	Current acquisition and production costs ⇕
Asset class ⇕		$	$	$	$
Overall Result		179.476.420,84	820.144,00	-335.200,00	179.961.364,84
4001	AuC for Measures	0,00			0,00
3200	Personal computers	492.343,91	6.500,00		498.843,91
3100	Vehicles	2.342.275,13	164.200,00	-25.200,00	2.481.275,13
3000	Fixture and fitting	435.183,69	123.000,00		558.183,69
2100	Machines str -line	3.116.484,39			3.116.484,39
2000	Machines decl. depr.	9.752.259,24			9.752.259,24
1100	Buildings	99.075.638,48	403.000,00	-310.000,00	99.168.638,48
1000	Real estate	64.262.236,00	123.444,00		64.385.680,00

Figure 6.23 Acquisition and Production Cost Report Output

The first column corresponds to the calculated key figure acquisition and production (APC) value for the fiscal year and the depreciation area chosen in the selection screen. The other columns correspond to basic key figures and show the relevant asset transactions: acquisition, retirement, and transfer posting. The last column, current APC, corresponds to the calculated key figure, which totals the APC FY start, acquisition, retirement, and transfer posting. You can execute this report for the selected asset class and then drill down to company, asset, and asset subnumbers.

> **Note**
>
> Be aware that "asset characteristic" is called "attachment" in some SAP NetWeaver BI queries.

Depreciation Report

The Depreciation query (0FIAA_C04_Q002) displays the depreciation FY start, inflow depreciation, outflow depreciation, depreciation transfer posting, and closing balance depreciation. Figure 6.24 shows an example output of the Depreciation report.

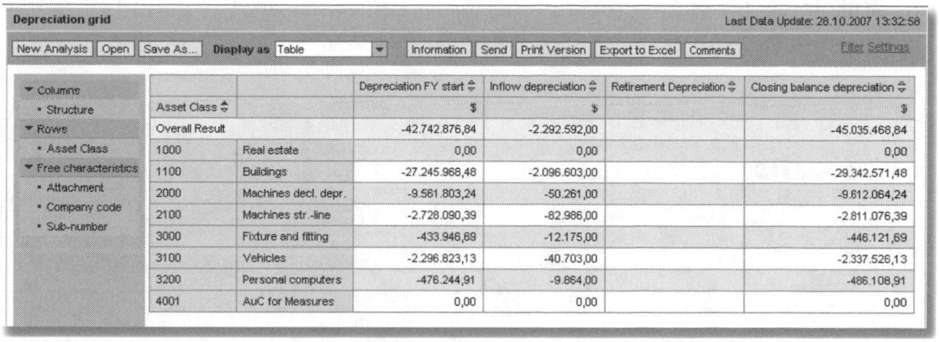

		Depreciation FY start	Inflow depreciation	Retirement Depreciation	Closing balance depreciation
Asset Class		$	$		$
Overall Result		-42.742.876,84	-2.292.592,00		-45.035.468,84
1000	Real estate	0,00	0,00		0,00
1100	Buildings	-27.245.968,48	-2.096.603,00		-29.342.571,48
2000	Machines decl. depr.	-9.561.803,24	-50.261,00		-9.612.064,24
2100	Machines str.-line	-2.728.090,39	-82.986,00		-2.811.076,39
3000	Fixture and fitting	-433.946,69	-12.175,00		-446.121,69
3100	Vehicles	-2.296.823,13	-40.703,00		-2.337.526,13
3200	Personal computers	-476.244,91	-9.864,00		-486.108,91
4001	AuC for Measures	0,00	0,00		0,00

Figure 6.24 Depreciation Report Output

The first column corresponds to the calculated key figure depreciation FY start value for the fiscal year and depreciation area chosen in the selection screen. The inflow depreciation is the total of the value adjustments on acquisitions and planned annual depreciation. The outflow depreciation and depreciation transfer posting show the value adjustments on transactions limited to transactions in the retirement history sheet groups. The last column, closing balance depreciation, shows the total amount of depreciation FY start, inflow depreciation, outflow depreciation and transfer depreciation.

Note that the Acquisition and Production Cost report and Depreciation report together form the Asset History Sheet. They provide the details of all asset values and transactions. If you model asset accounting by using MultiProviders, you can generate Asset History Sheets by using the queries based on these MultiProviders.

Now that we have explained the asset history sheet queries, let's move on to asset transactions queries (see highlight 2 in Figure 6.22).

Asset Transactions Queries

Asset Acquisitions Report

The Asset Acquisitions query displays the asset acquisitions. As shown in the report output in Figure 6.25, you can list asset acquisitions by asset class for the fiscal year and depreciation area chosen in the selection screen. You can swap asset class with characteristics such as asset, company code, cost center, fiscal year/period, key figures, line item, subnumber, and transaction type in the report output. You can drill down to asset, company code, cost center, fiscal year/period, line item and subnumber.

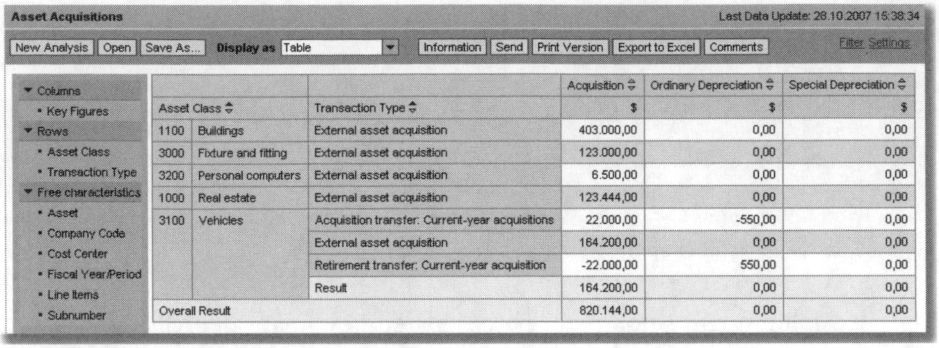

Asset Acquisitions			Last Data Update: 28.10.2007 15:38:34		
			Acquisition $\Diamond$	Ordinary Depreciation $\Diamond$	Special Depreciation $\Diamond$
Asset Class $\Diamond$		Transaction Type $\Diamond$	$	$	$
1100	Buildings	External asset acquisition	403.000,00	0,00	0,00
3000	Fixture and fitting	External asset acquisition	123.000,00	0,00	0,00
3200	Personal computers	External asset acquisition	6.500,00	0,00	0,00
1000	Real estate	External asset acquisition	123.444,00	0,00	0,00
3100	Vehicles	Acquisition transfer: Current-year acquisitions	22.000,00	-550,00	0,00
		External asset acquisition	164.200,00	0,00	0,00
		Retirement transfer: Current-year acquisition	-22.000,00	550,00	0,00
		Result	164.200,00	0,00	0,00
Overall Result			820.144,00	0,00	0,00

Figure 6.25 Asset Acquisitions Report Output

Investment by Quarter Report

The Investment by Quarter query displays all asset acquisitions in a given fiscal year and provides quarterly summaries of the values. You can swap asset class with characteristics such as asset, company code, key figures and subnumber. You can drill down to asset, company code, and subnumber. Figure 6.26 shows an example of the report output.

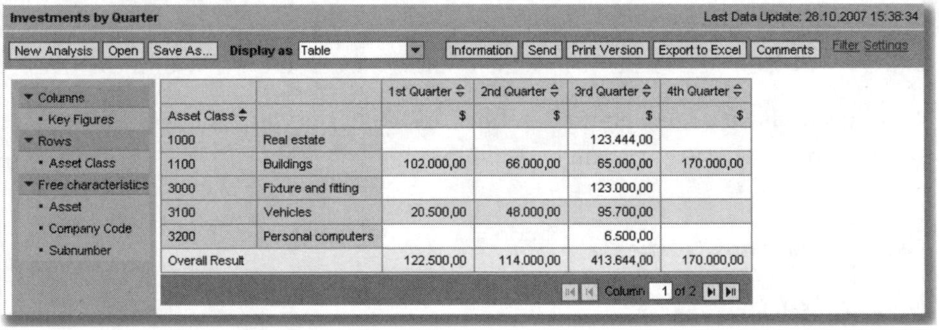

Investments by Quarter			Last Data Update: 28.10.2007 15:38:34			
		1st Quarter $\Diamond$	2nd Quarter $\Diamond$	3rd Quarter $\Diamond$	4th Quarter $\Diamond$
Asset Class $\Diamond$		$	$	$	$
1000	Real estate			123.444,00	
1100	Buildings	102.000,00	66.000,00	65.000,00	170.000,00
3000	Fixture and fitting			123.000,00	
3100	Vehicles	20.500,00	48.000,00	95.700,00	
3200	Personal computers			6.500,00	
Overall Result		122.500,00	114.000,00	413.644,00	170.000,00

Figure 6.26 Investments by Quarter Report Output

Asset Retirements Report

The Asset Retirements query displays all asset retirements in a given fiscal year. As shown in the report output in Figure 6.27, you can display the asset retirement values by asset class. You can swap asset class with characteristics such as asset, company code, cost center, fiscal year/period, key figures, line item, transaction type and subnumber. In addition, you can drill down to asset, company code, cost center, fiscal year/period, and subnumber. This report provides details of asset retirements for both management information and to support audit processes, particularly during asset inventory count.

Let's continue with selected asset annual values queries highlighted in section 3 in Figure 6.22.

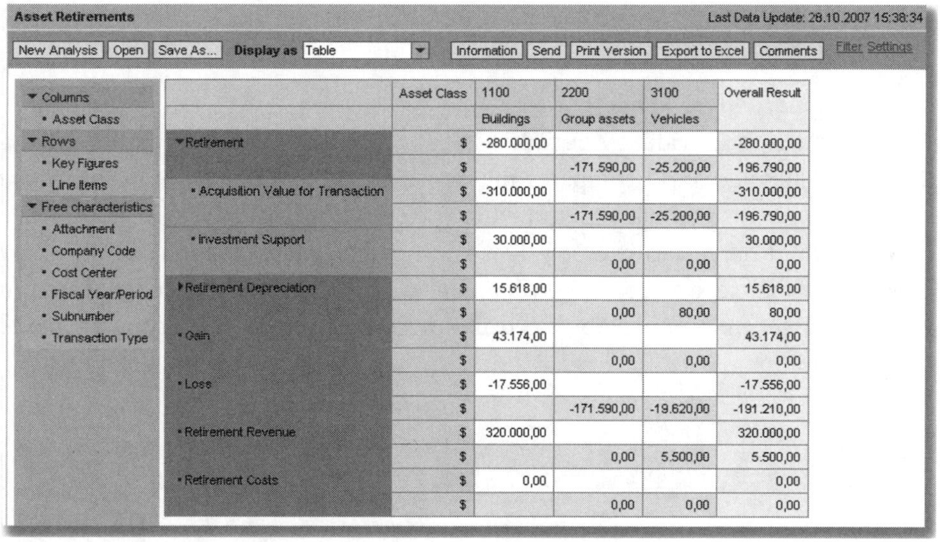

		Asset Class 1100	2200	3100	Overall Result
		Buildings	Group assets	Vehicles	
Retirement	$	-280.000,00			-280.000,00
	$		-171.590,00	-25.200,00	-196.790,00
Acquisition Value for Transaction	$	-310.000,00			-310.000,00
	$		-171.590,00	-25.200,00	-196.790,00
Investment Support	$	30.000,00			30.000,00
	$		0,00	0,00	0,00
Retirement Depreciation	$	15.618,00			15.618,00
	$		0,00	80,00	80,00
Gain	$	43.174,00			43.174,00
	$		0,00	0,00	0,00
Loss	$	-17.556,00			-17.556,00
	$		-171.590,00	-19.620,00	-191.210,00
Retirement Revenue	$	320.000,00			320.000,00
	$		0,00	5.500,00	5.500,00
Retirement Costs	$	0,00			0,00
	$		0,00	0,00	0,00

Figure 6.27 Asset Retirements Report Output

Asset Annual Values Queries

Asset List Report

The Asset List query displays the current asset values, including acquisition value, value adjustment, net book value, and depreciation value in percentage by asset class for the selected depreciation area and fiscal year. You can swap asset class with characteristics asset, company code, cost center, structure, and subnumber. You can drill down to asset, company code, cost center and subnumber in the report output. An example of the report output is illustrated in Figure 6.28.

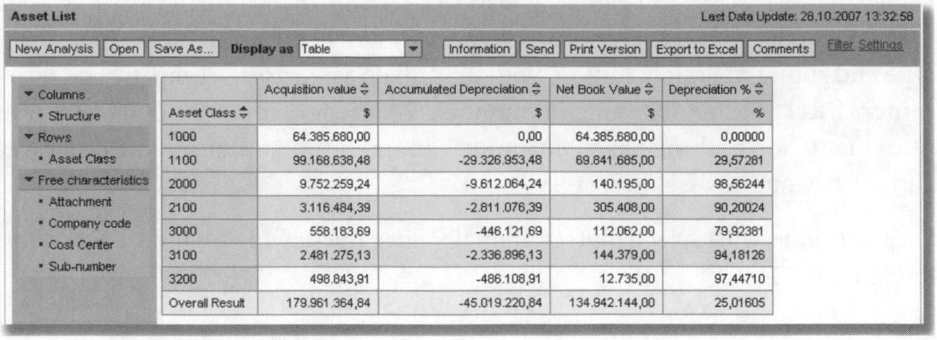

	Acquisition value	Accumulated Depreciation	Net Book Value	Depreciation %
Asset Class	$	$	$	%
1000	64.385.680,00	0,00	64.385.680,00	0,00000
1100	99.168.638,48	-29.326.953,48	69.841.685,00	29,57281
2000	9.752.259,24	-9.612.064,24	140.195,00	98,56244
2100	3.116.484,39	-2.811.076,39	305.408,00	90,20024
3000	558.183,69	-446.121,69	112.062,00	79,92381
3100	2.481.275,13	-2.336.896,13	144.379,00	94,18126
3200	498.843,91	-486.108,91	12.735,00	97,44710
Overall Result	179.961.364,84	-45.019.220,84	134.942.144,00	25,01605

Figure 6.28 Asset List Report Output

Comparison of Values Report

The Comparison of Values query is used for the comparison of two depreciation areas. It selects and compares the depreciation and net book values of the depreciation areas you have identified in the selection parameters. It allows easy comparison of depreciation area values and related details. Figure 6.29 shows an example of this report. You can swap asset class with company code, structure, asset, and asset subnumber. You can drill down according to asset, company code, and subnumber.

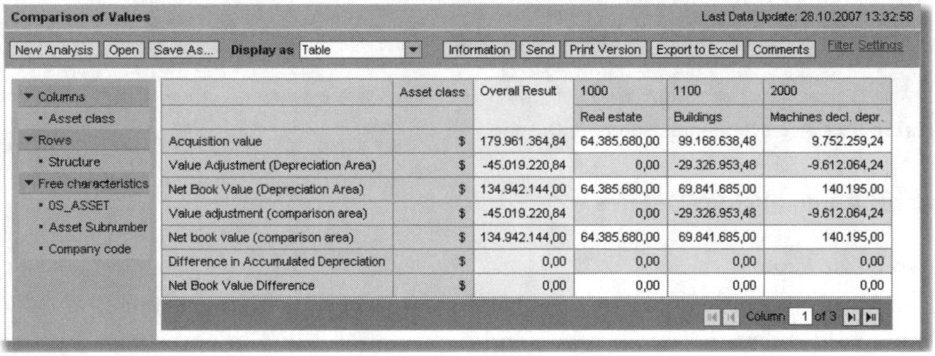

	Asset class	Overall Result	1000	1100	2000
			Real estate	Buildings	Machines decl. depr.
Acquisition value	$	179.961.364,84	64.385.680,00	99.168.638,48	9.752.259,24
Value Adjustment (Depreciation Area)	$	-45.019.220,84	0,00	-29.326.953,48	-9.612.064,24
Net Book Value (Depreciation Area)	$	134.942.144,00	64.385.680,00	69.841.685,00	140.195,00
Value adjustment (comparison area)	$	-45.019.220,84	0,00	-29.326.953,48	-9.612.064,24
Net book value (comparison area)	$	134.942.144,00	64.385.680,00	69.841.685,00	140.195,00
Difference in Accumulated Depreciation	$	0,00	0,00	0,00	0,00
Net Book Value Difference	$	0,00	0,00	0,00	0,00

Figure 6.29 Comparison of Values Report Output

Let's move on to depreciation queries (see highlight 4 in Figure 6.22).

Depreciation Queries

Depreciation Posted Report

The Depreciation Posted query shows posted depreciation broken down by cost center for the selected fiscal year and depreciation area chosen in the selection screen. You can swap cost center with characteristics such as asset, asset class, company code, key figures, and subnumber in the report output. You can drill down to asset class, asset, and company code and subnumber. A drilldown report output example is shown in Figure 6.30.

Now that we have examined our selected asset queries in SAP NetWeaver BI content, we will look at one example query for the capital and investment management process. As we have pointed out throughout the chapter, it is important to incorporate the capital and investment management process into the asset lifecycle process. SAP NetWeaver BI provides flexible and advanced reporting capabilities for investment and capital management.

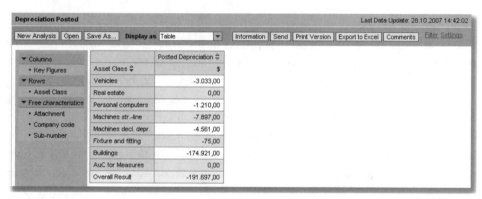

Figure 6.30 Depreciation Posted Report Output

Budget for Program and Measures

The Budget for Program and Measures query shows the budget per program position and the corresponding investment measure for the fiscal year chosen in the selection screen. You can swap program position with appropriation request, order, WBS element, budget, fiscal year, and detail for value type. You can drill down to appropriation request, detail for value type, fiscal year, order, and WBS element. The report shows the budget and budget measures by program positions, as shown in Figure 6.31.

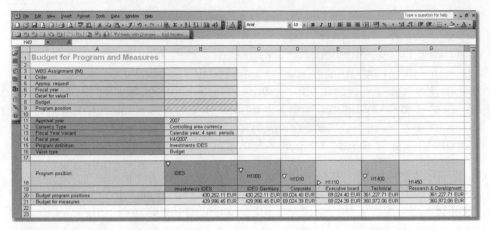

Figure 6.31 Budget for Program and Measures Report Output

6.5 Summary

Asset reporting based on standardized processes and transparent data provides timely management information, supports audit process, and satisfies the high standards of international capital markets. Enhancing the accuracy of asset reporting can only be achieved by a robust reporting architecture. In this chapter, we focused on the asset lifecycle process along with the asset reporting architecture in SAP ERP and SAP NetWeaver BI. We first explained the most crucial points of generating accurate asset reporting and made recommendations regarding how to streamline and automate the asset lifecycle process along with the key asset reports in SAP ERP. Then we explained the business content for asset accounting and showed modeling examples for asset reporting architecture in SAP NetWeaver BI. Finally, we examined the business content query examples.

One of the biggest challenges in SAP ERP implementation projects is to reflect all cash transactions accurately and on time to produce comprehensive cash management reports to support decisions on funding, investment, and borrowing. Managing cash flow with the right balance of functionality, flexibility, security, and efficiency is the ultimate goal of companies in today's competitive economy. In this chapter, we explain the design considerations and best practices for cash management reporting. In addition, we examine the key cash management reports in SAP ERP and SAP NetWeaver BI business content for Cash and Liquidity Management (CLM).

7 Cash Management Reporting

The growing capital market has put enormous pressure on treasurers to generate comprehensive cash position and liquidity forecast reports on time to make the right investment decisions. With the *Sarbanes-Oxley Act (SOX) section 404*, corporate treasurers are faced with new responsibilities and therefore need consistent solutions for cash management reporting. The SOX requires the implementation of sound internal controls and the disclosure of all material deficiencies in controls to the auditor, as well as certification that the financial reports reflect no misleading statements.

In the past, analyzing and forecasting cash flow involved collecting information from various sources into spreadsheets. Although spreadsheets are easy to use and provide flexible ad hoc reporting, it is not easy to implement controls and ensure the integrity of the financial reporting. One of the problems with using spreadsheets is establishing an effective audit trial, because the updating and accessing of the spreadsheets by employees cannot be easily controlled and in some cases is impossible. Outdated information is another problem related to the use of spreadsheets. Thus, treasurers increasingly need tools that provide real-time (or close to real-time) information. Today, companies that have historically relied upon spreadsheets to manage their treasury operations are looking into implementing technology that incorporates the necessary controls and functionalities.

An infrastructure that enables real-time integration can provide the transparency for SOX compliance and other regulatory demands to control cash positions and operational risks. SAP ERP provides that infrastructure with the *Cash and Liquidity Management (CLM)* application of *SAP Financial Supply Chain Management (SAP FSCM)*. The CLM application enables timely, accurate, and reliable cash forecasts to help treasurers better manage debt and investment portfolios and reduce operational risks.

In this chapter we discuss how to integrate cash and cash-relevant data for cash management reporting and outline the key integration points of financial transaction data flow across other SAP ERP components to the CLM application and from the CLM application to SAP NetWeaver BI. In addition, we examine the key cash management reports in SAP ERP as well as the CLM business content queries delivered within SAP NetWeaver BI.

7.1 Designing the Cash Management Reporting Process

For effective cash management reporting, you need access to all cash-relevant transactions and the ability to structure and present this information. By improving and automating the cash management reporting process, treasurers gain better insight into the cash flow. Figure 7.1 shows three key steps involved in the cash management reporting process. Let's have a look at each of these steps in detail:

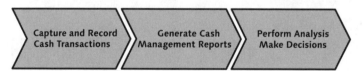

Figure 7.1 Cash Management Reporting Process

▶ **Capture and Record Cash Transactions**
The recording of cash inflow and outflow transactions facilitates analysis of the cash and funding requirements of the business. This step includes capturing and recording all cash-relevant transactions in the system.

▶ **Generate Cash Management Reports**
This step comprises the generation of cash management reports. The information for cash management reports is taken from daily business activities, such as procurement of materials and sales of products, which are recorded as in-

voices and billing documents. In addition, incoming and outgoing payments affect the cash balances. Examples of cash management reports include:

▶ **Cash Position**
The Cash Position report shows the short-term trends in the bank and cash accounts. In the report, you can analyze all cash movements within a short time frame, usually one or two days.

▶ **Liquidity Forecast**
The Liquidity Forecast report shows medium-term trends in the subledger accounts. The time frame of the report varies typically from 3 to 21 days.

▶ **Cash planning and budgeting reports**
Cash planning and budgeting reports shows the medium- and long-term trends of cash flow.

▶ **Perform Analysis and Make Decisions**
In this step, you analyze the cash management reports for investment decisions and ensure that the funding and liquidity requirements are met. The financial instrument transactions resulting from investment decisions can be captured and recorded in SAP ERP and will be available for the cash management reports. Note that processing of financial instrument transactions and treasury and risk management reporting are explained in Chapter 8.

The cash management reporting process touches many key financial processes related to different components of SAP ERP. Improving the cash management reporting process largely depends upon integrating these financial processes with the CLM application in SAP ERP. Now let's take an in-depth look at the cash management reporting architecture.

7.2 Cash Management Reporting Architecture

The CLM application is the basis of the SAP financial management environment's ability to provide the cash and liquidity position of the enterprise in SAP ERP. All business transactions resulting in cash value update the CLM application, which enables companies to run their cash management reports for individual business entities, as well as consolidated cash reports at the group level. CLM functions are linked to SAP NetWeaver BI to generate more flexible and advanced cash management reports. The cash management reporting architecture is illustrated in Figure 7.2.

The Liquidity Forecast report receives information from the sales and distribution, accounts receivable, purchasing, accounts payable and SAP FSCM applications. The information from these sources is converted into a liquidity forecast at each step based on the transaction information and the corresponding configuration settings. Let's look at how the transactions are updated in the CLM reports with the requisition to pay process. Once a *purchase requisition* is created, the amount of the transaction and the delivery date are used to forecast the payment amount and the payment date, and this information is displayed in the Liquidity Forecast report. After the purchase requisition is followed by a *purchase order*, the forecast is updated based on the vendor's payment terms and the amount of the purchase order. The Liquidity Forecast report receives more accurate information as the business process moves into financial accounting. When the vendor invoice is received, the forecast is updated based on payment terms and the amount of the *invoice*. Finally, when the vendor invoice is settled with the *outgoing payment*, the cash transaction information is passed to the Cash Position report. In other words, with the payment transaction, the forecast information becomes available for the Cash Position report based on the value date of the financial transaction.

For the order to cash process, *sales quotation* or *sales order* transaction details such as the delivery date, sold to party payment terms, and amount are first used in the liquidity forecast. When the goods or services are delivered, the liquidity forecast is updated with more accurate information, and once the *billing* document is generated, the amount and the payment terms of the billing document are used in the Liquidity Forecast report. When the customer payment is updated with the incoming *bank statement*, the cash transaction information is passed to the Cash Position report.

Memo records, which are created in the CLM application, are used as planning items to reflect expected cash inflows and outflows that are known but are not reflected in transactions. They are used in both Liquidity Forecast and Cash Position reports. The memo records are either archived or replaced with the corresponding actual transactions later on.

The Cash Position report has three main sources of information:

▶ Cash and cash-relevant transactions in the G/L and postings from the G/L interfaces.

▶ Memo records updated in the CLM application itself.

► Financial transactions from other SAP FSCM applications (e.g., deposits, foreign exchange transactions).

The cash and liquidity transactions from SAP ERP and other systems can be extracted to SAP NetWeaver BI at regular intervals or in real-time to generate more flexible and advanced cash management reports.

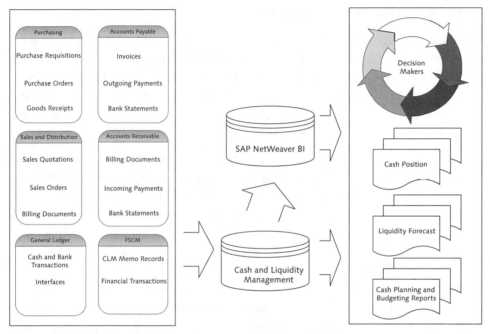

Figure 7.2 Cash and Liquidity Management as a Source for Cash Management Reporting

Identification of cash data requirements and establishment of an efficient and consistent cash data flow mechanism to the CLM application is critical to the effectiveness of generating cash management reports in SAP ERP. Most of the effort in designing and implementing effective cash management reporting is spent in the areas of cash data requirement identification and building a robust reporting architecture. Failures in these critical areas could cause material misstatements in the cash management reports. In this section, we discuss the key design considerations and best practices and approaches for building a robust cash management reporting architecture. We specifically discuss the following:

- Centralizing cash management
- Standardizing the structure of bank G/L accounts
- Automating the reconciliation of bank statements
- Integrating cash data with the CLM application

7.2.1 Centralizing Cash Management

Organizations often have decentralized cash management with significant local autonomy, where treasurers have a lack of visibility of a significant portion of cash balances across the enterprise due to information gaps relating to the local operations. That kind of situation can lead to difficulties in presenting cash flow reports accurately and on time and result in a limited ability to consolidate multiple cash positions effectively.

A cash management model with a centralized control, standard procedures, and limited local autonomy is a path that leading organizations choose in today's global economy. Improved visibility of cash flow across enterprises, better cash concentration and investing of cash, rationalizing bank accounts and bank partners, and netting are strong driving forces toward centralized cash management. Improved visibility gives better control over the cash position of the enterprise and enables organizations to produce timely and more accurate cash management reports. Establishing a cash management relationship with a small number of banks and bank partners simplifies *cash concentration* and enables an optimized cash position. *Netting*, or the so-called *internal payment clearing* process for intercompany receivables and payables, can further optimize the cash position and result in significant cost savings. Other benefits of centralized cash management are:

- Improved control by ensuring a consistent cash management approach with standardized procedures enterprise-wide
- Reduced time and effort spent on collecting and preparing cash information
- Improved working capital management by enabling increased visibility and access to cash, which can be used to reduce borrowing or increase investment returns
- Netting of currency exposures that could have been hedged if not combined
- Potential for developing stronger relationships with a core banking partner, which could lead to a number of benefits including decreasing interest cost and increasing interest income

▶ Improved overall negotiation capabilities due to economies of scale and central expertise

> **Note**
>
> Creating a cash management model with centralized controls should be strongly supported with a well-defined and established relationship between corporate treasury and local entities, resulting in constant cooperation and interaction, so that cash management reports reliability is constantly improved.

Centralized Cash Management with SAP ERP

The CLM application provides the required platform to realize the benefits of centralized cash management practice. Even though a single ERP system makes centralizing cash management easier, to have centralized cash management does not necessarily mean having a single ERP system. Distributed system scenarios are supported in the CLM application, which means you can have a number of SAP and non-SAP ERP systems interconnected in one SAP ERP system to centralize cash management. This is facilitated with the functionality of the CLM application called *Treasury Workstation*. The Treasury Workstation can be used in various application link enabling (ALE) scenarios. A treasury workstation connects the local treasury systems to one central system or creates links between operative components such as purchasing, AP, AR, and SD to the central cash management system. In both scenarios, the transactions and reports are based on ALE technology. Flows that are relevant for financial accounting are also transferred from the Treasury Workstation back into the operative system using ALE technology.

The configuration steps for distributed cash management are shown in Figure 7.3.

To access the CLM distributed application, follow the menu path **Accounting** • **Financial Supply Chain Management** • **Cash and Liquidity Management** • **Cash Management** • **Tools** • **Distribution**.

> **Note**
>
> SAP Note 823358 contains technical information on distributed cash management.

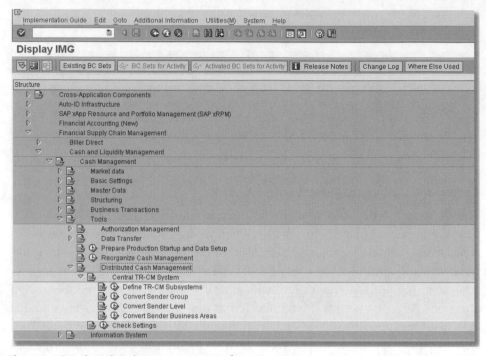

Figure 7.3 Distributed Cash Management Configuration Steps

As discussed earlier, cash concentration and netting are important driving forces for centralized cash management. Let's now look at how SAP ERP supports cash concentration and netting.

Cash Concentration

Cash concentration is used to leverage funds, increase return on investment, and improve working capital. This can be combined with rationalizing the bank's relationships by pruning relationships with smaller local banks and building strong relationships with core banks.

In SAP ERP, cash concentration can be automated. The balances from various bank accounts are moved to one target account, keeping a specified minimum balance at the source accounts. Cash concentration is performed in several key steps:

► Create cash concentration proposal.

► Generate payment advice.

► Generate payment requests from payment advice.

► Execute payment request payment program.

To access CLM cash concentration transactions, follow the menu path **Accounting • Financial Supply Chain Management • Cash and Liquidity Management • Cash Management • Planning • Cash Concentration** (Transaction FF73).

All bank accounts that you cash pool are linked together in a grouping structure that is defined in the configuration of cash concentration. The cash concentration proposal is generated based on this grouping structure. The proposal contains the day-end balances and the cash planning results, which are the expected account balances for transfer. You can adjust the proposal at any stage of the cash concentration. See Figure 7.4 for an example of a cash concentration proposal.

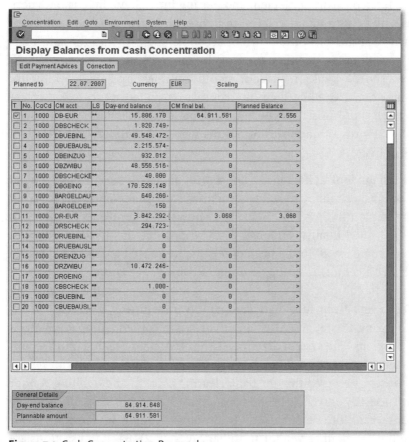

Figure 7.4 Cash Concentration Proposal

Cash concentration makes account transfers by using payment advice notes. The payment advice notes correct the cash balances based on the value date and can subsequently be converted to payment requests that are processed with the payment request payment program (Transaction F111). The payment request program generates the financial postings of the cash concentration and generates the payment orders for the banks.

Netting

Companies with many overseas subsidiaries and significant intragroup transactions use various netting solutions. Netting solutions have been used to reduce foreign exchange risks and to formalize intercompany settlements. SAP has recently developed a solution to replace intercompany settlement netting solutions by moving the intercompany settlement and netting into a new dimension where the in-house bank plays a vital role. The in-house bank manages the settlement of intercompany transactions of the current accounts and provides the subsidiaries with bank statements as confirmation of the movements on those accounts, in the same way that a bank or financial institution does. By using an in-house bank, companies can streamline their intercompany payment process and create cost savings for the enterprise by reducing banking fees and the number of bank accounts. SAP ERP provides a means to do this with the *In-House Cash (IHC)* application in SAP FSCM.

Let's take an in-depth look at how the in-house bank manages the current accounts of its customers, makes money transfers, generates bank statements, receive bank statements, and so on in SAP ERP. Figure 7.5 shows an example to give you an overview of IHC functionality. Suppose your head office has two subsidiaries, company A and company B. In the head office, the in-house bank (also called the in-house cash [IHC] center) is set up, and the FI component is used. Company A renders services to company B, and company B makes a payment to company A. The invoice is sent from subsidiary company A to company B. The invoice is received at company B (step 1). After the invoice is recorded, company B starts the payment program. The system determines the open items, taking into account the payment terms and the specified bank details, and the payment run generates financial postings by crediting the bank clearing account and debiting vendor subsidiary A. The IHC center has been identified as the vendor bank of company A and the house bank of company code B. Company code B instructs its house bank to make the payment to vendor subsidiary A (step 2). Bank transactions are executed within the IHC center, where funds are moved from the current account of subsidiary B into the current account of subsidiary A. In other words, the current account of subsidiary B is debited $100 and the current account of subsidiary A is credited $100 (step 3). After that, the IHC center sends bank statements to both subsidiary A and subsidiary B and clears out the open items (step 4). With the daily closing of the IHC center, IHC payables and IHC receivables are updated in the FI component of the headquarters accounting system (step 5).

> **Note**
>
> The in-house bank can be used for third-party payments as well.

Centralizing cash management is similar to any other investment decision and should be treated as such. Thus, we strongly advise you to carry out a cost–benefit analysis for having centralized cash management. Once the benefits are quantified for your organization, you have stronger arguments and motivation for change. However, keep in mind that qualitative factors such as improved process controls and better reporting can be equally important consideration factors.

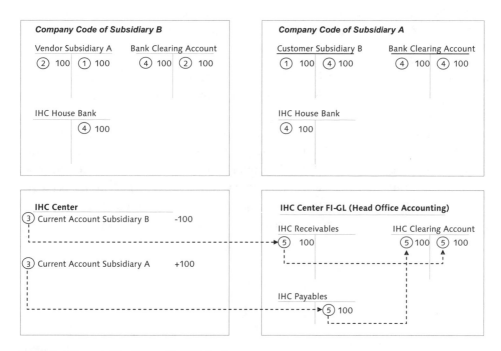

Figure 7.5 Financial Postings with IHC Center

7.2.2 Standardization of the Structure of Bank G/L Accounts

The bank G/L account structure determines how bank accounting postings are displayed in the Cash Position report. The bank account structure is the foundation of the ability to generate transparent cash management reports. Organizations often have unstructured bank accounts, which leads to a limited ability to generate a clear view of the cash position. This could lead to difficulties in setting up the cash position and interpreting the results of the cash management reports. Standardization of the bank account structure increases the visibility of the cash flows by each business entity, makes it easier to analyze the Cash Position report, and reduces the effort of setting up the reports in the system. Furthermore, when the organization expands into new regions, there is significant cost savings in rolling new company codes for the consolidated view of the cash position enterprise-wide.

Bank G/L accounts are created for each active bank account of the enterprise. For each bank G/L account, it is a good practice to have a set of clearing accounts. The selection of the best coding for the bank G/L account structure involves defining the key cash flow data views required while taking full advantage of the features available in the SAP ERP system. Although there is no standard rule for structuring the bank G/L accounts, we recommend that the bank G/L account structure be consistently created for each active bank account and currency. An example bank G/L account structure can be found in Table 7.1.

In the first column of the table, the last three digits of the G/L accounts are shown. The second column describes the bank G/L accounts. In our example, the last digit of the account is used to classify the G/L account according to the purpose of the account, such as current account, check clearing account, and so on. The currency dimension is represented by the last two digits of the accounts. Finally, the last three digits identify the bank dimension of the bank G/L account. With this bank account structure, accounts ending with 0 are current accounts, accounts ending with 00 are local currency current accounts, and accounts ending with 200 are bank B local currency current accounts, where local currency is the currency of the company code.

Last Three Digits of the Bank G/L Account	Purpose of the G/L account
100	Bank A (current account—domestic—currency local)
101	Bank A (outgoing checks)
102	Bank A (outgoing bank transfers, domestic)
103	Bank A (outgoing bank transfers, foreign)
104	Bank A (automatic deposit)
105	Bank A (miscellaneous interim postings)
108	Bank A (incoming checks)
109	Bank A (customer cash receipts)
1..	Bank A (other provisional postings)
1..	Bank A (account bill of exchange)
130	Bank A (current account—domestic—currency EUR)
131	Bank A (outgoing checks EUR)
....	
200	Bank B (current account—domestic—currency local)
201	Bank B (outgoing checks)
202	Bank B (outgoing bank transfers, domestic)
203	Bank B (outgoing bank transfers, foreign)
204	Bank B (automatic deposit)
205	Bank B (miscellaneous interim postings)
208	Bank B (incoming checks)
209	Bank B (customer cash receipts)
2..	Bank B (other provisional postings)
2..	Bank B (account bill of exchange)
300	Bank C (current account—domestic—currency local)
....	

Table 7.1 Bank Accounts Structure

The standardized bank G/L account structure not only improves the cash transparency of the cash management reports but also provides the following key benefits:

▸ Provides a standardized G/L account structure across the organization

▸ Simplifies the configuration of the bank statement and makes processing bank statements easy and error free

▸ Makes it easy to identify bank source transactions

7.2.3 Automating the Reconciliation of Bank Statements

The bank reconciliation process is performed to match the bank transactions and the transactions recorded in your books. Let's look at the details of the process.

After the bank institutions receive transaction orders from their customers, they execute the transactions and update their system. After that they provide bank statements for reconciliation and filing purposes. There is usually a time lag between these two steps: getting the order and executing the order. The order execution is reflected in the bank statements. Thus, you have to make sure that all bank transactions in your books are reconciled with the cash movements in your bank accounts after you receive the bank statements.

Bank accounting transactions update the bank, bank clearing, and subledger accounts. For example, when funds are transferred to your bank accounts, you need to debit the bank G/L accounts and credit bank clearing accounts. When your customers make fund transfers to your bank accounts to clear out their bills, you should debit bank clearing accounts and credit customer accounts with clearing. All these bookings can be automated with the processing of bank statements in SAP ERP. Bank statements can be processed either manually or automatically.

Manual Bank Statement

The manual bank statement is a fast entry tool that can be utilized to update the bank transactions in the system. By using a manual bank statement, you only need to enter the bank statement items and not the entire posting records. The system then automatically makes the postings with a batch input session to the bank account, bank clearing account, and subledger accounts. The manual bank statement can be effectively used for a relatively small number of bank transactions.

If many bank transactions need to be updated, we advise you to use an electronic bank statement, as processing manual bank statements requires significant time and effort.

Electronic Bank Statement

SAP ERP supports automatic processing of *electronic bank statements (EBS)* in various banking formats. With EBS, a daily electronic file that includes detailed activity, along with the ending balance transmitted from the bank, is uploaded automatically into the SAP system. Automatic clearing of the bank clearing accounts and the subledger accounts can also be processed at this stage. It is also possible to post-process the bank statements if any error occurs or the clearing cannot be performed. EBS introduce automation and reduce the errors associated with manual bank statements. With bank statement automation, the reconciliation process becomes more efficient, and processing costs are significantly reduced. More importantly, you can generate your cash management reports in real-time (or almost real-time) and accurately reflect the cash position.

The electronic bank statements are imported with the *Bank Communication Software (BCS)*. A number of banking file formats are supported by SAP ERP. You need to get the file from BCS and import it into your SAP ERP system tables. This can be done by using the bank statement various formats transaction (Transaction FF_5). When you execute this transaction, the system automatically creates postings in the G/L and subledgers. These postings depend on the transaction codes given by banks and reflected in the bank statements. Typically, payment postings update bank G/L accounts, bank G/L clearing accounts, customer accounts, and vendor accounts, where appropriate (see Figure 7.6).

If immediate postings are not performed (for example, when clearing is not possible or when the bank transaction code is not assigned to a posting rule in SAP ERP), the file is further processed through the post-processing transaction FEBA_BANK_STATEMENT.

The electronic bank statement functionality, when properly utilized, results in more efficient and timely processing for bank reconciliation. The error rate for the account reconciliation process is significantly reduced, and processing time is shortened.

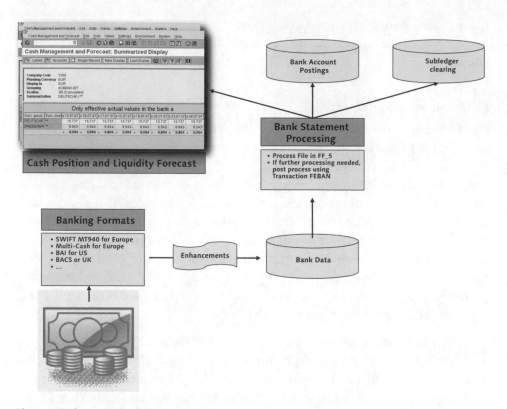

Figure 7.6 Electronic Bank Statement Process

> **Note**
>
> Once the bank statements are loaded in the system, you can print them out at any time (Transaction FF_6).

7.2.4 Integrating Cash Data with the CLM application

The key to generating accurate and transparent cash management reports is integrating the cash data with the CLM application. This can be achieved by linking the underlying cash data and automating the flow of cash transactions to the CLM application. In this section we explain the integration points for generating accurate cash position and liquidity forecast reports.

Planning Levels

The planning level indicates the type of transaction. The granularity and visibility of the cash management reports are based on the planning levels. SAP ERP provides the following predefined levels:

▶ Level F0 for bank accounts

▶ Level F1 for purchasing and sales (vendors and customer)

▶ Level FF for down payment requests

▶ Level FW for bills of exchange

▶ Levels B1 to BN for bank clearing accounts

▶ Level CP for confirmed payment advice notes

▶ Level UP for unconfirmed payment advice notes

▶ Level NI for noted items

Levels starting with F or B are used for bank accounting postings. F levels are used for bank accounts, customers, and vendors, and B levels are used for bank clearing accounts. CP, UP, and N1 are reserved for manually created payment advice notes or planned items. For example, you can analyze the actual bank account postings with level F0 and plan postings with other levels in the Cash Position report if you use the predefined planning levels.

You can either use these predefined levels or you can create your own levels according to business needs. To define the planning level, follow the configuration menu path **Financial Supply Chain Management • Cash and Liquidity Management • Cash Management • Master Data • G/L Accounts • Define Planning Levels.**

After you define the planning levels, you need to assign them to cash-relevant G/L accounts so that cash transactions stream into the CLM application. Planning levels are updated in the **Create/bank/interest** tab of the G/L account master data. Figure 7.7 and Figure 7.8 show examples of different planning level assignments in the master data of the G/L accounts. Bank account 113100 is assigned to planning level F0 (posting to bank accounts), whereas bank clearing account 113101 is assigned to planning level B1 (outgoing checks). It is important to set up a planning level as a required entry for cash and bank G/L accounts. In addition to the planning level, you also need to cross-check the **Cash management relevant** button in the G/L account master data to make sure that cash transactions stream into the CLM application.

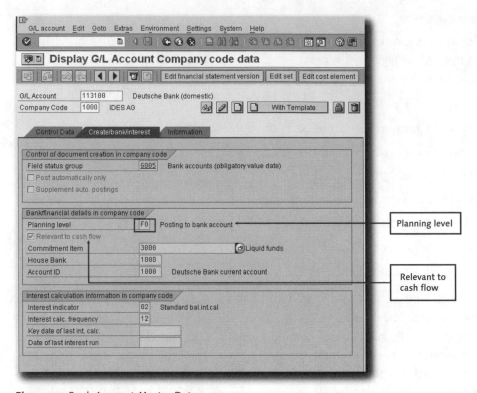

Figure 7.7 Bank Account Master Data

Additional cash management settings in the G/L account

There are two additional important settings for accurate cash flow. These settings are defined in the **Control Data** tab of the G/L account master data. The first setting is to determine whether the cash account is *open item management* or not. Bank clearing accounts must always be open item managed, as there is an offsetting entry to be made against when you post to the bank clearing account. On the other hand, bank accounts should not be set up as open item managed.

The second important setting is to define the sort key of the bank and cash-relevant accounts. We recommend defining the value date (027) as the sorting key in the bank accounts. The sorting key of the cash clearing accounts should be set as a local value (005). Defining the sort key in that way is not a mandatory task, but it will provide valuable information in the assignment field of the corresponding general ledger line item. This information can be used during clearing open items and reporting.

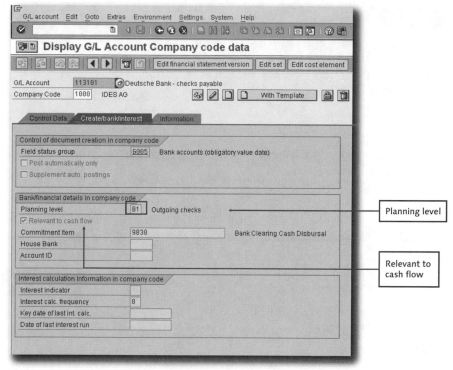

Figure 7.8 Bank Clearing Account Master Data

Planning Groups

Planning groups indicate specific characteristics or risks of the customers and vendors. For example, customer and vendor groups can be defined based on cash flow expectations and risks or type of business relationship. SAP provides predefined planning groups, for example, domestic customers, foreign customers, and high-risk customers. Figure 7.9 shows an example of planning group assignment in the customer master data.

You can either use these predefined cash management groups or create your own groups according to your business needs. To define planning groups, follow the configuration menu path **Financial Supply Chain Management • Cash and Liquidity Management • Cash Management • Master Data • Subledger Accounts • Define Planning Groups**.

> **Note**
>
> You need to activate **historic payment record** in the customer master data for better liquidity forecast reports. This indicator is used to record the payment history of the customers. If you activate this indicator, you can carry out evaluation of the payment history of customers.

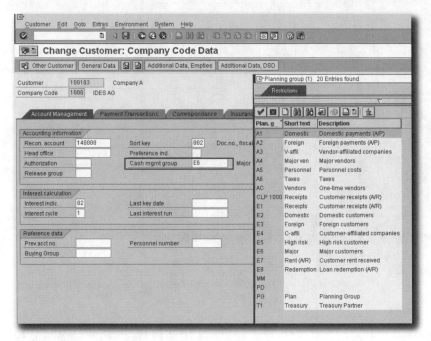

Figure 7.9 Customer Master Data

Value Date

Value date indicates the average number of days it takes a payment or deposit recorded in the bank. Cash positions are always managed by value date. Thus, the value date must be recorded in all postings to the bank accounts. This can be achieved by defining the value date field as a required entry in the field status group. The value date is the date that drives the display of the balances in the cash management reports.

SAP ERP provides reports to compare the accuracy of the value date for the cash position. You can compare the value dates with actual dates for bank postings with the Compare Value Date with Bank Posting (Transaction FF/2) report. The value dates with actual clearing dates can be compared with the report Cashed Checks per Bank Account (Transaction FF.3).

> **Note**
>
> You can find recommendations on settings regarding value dates in SAP Note 24883.

7.3 Cash Management Reports in SAP ERP

Cash management reports are structured financial representations of the cash and liquidity position of organizations. The structure of the cash management reports is defined in the configuration. Grouping and summarization levels are the basis of how cash management reports are displayed. Figure 7.10 shows a schematic view of the cash management report structure.

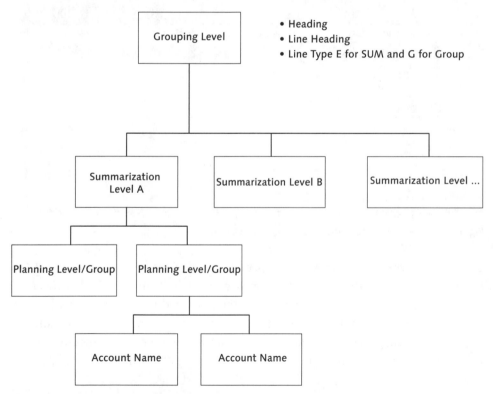

Figure 7.10 Schematic View of Cash Management Report Structure

It is a good practice to standardize the structure of the cash reports across the enterprise. *Groupings* are used to determine which levels and accounts should be displayed in the cash management reports. *Headings* are defined with the groupings. They are used to identify the cash positions and for the description of the cash reports. To define groupings with the headings, follow the configuration menu path **Financial Supply Chain Management • Cash and Liquidity Management • Cash Management • Structuring • Groupings • Define Groupings and Maintain Headers**.

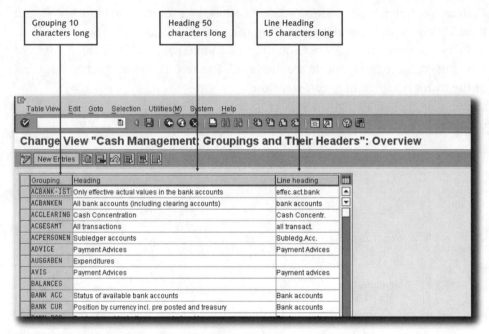

Figure 7.11 Define Heading and Line Headings with Groupings

You can see where groupings and respective headers are defined in Figure 7.11. For example, the *ACBANK-IST* grouping is defined with the heading *"only effective actual values in the bank accounts"* and the line heading *"effect act. bank."* This means that when you select the grouping ACBANK-IST in the selection parameter of the cash management reports, the report header will be "only effective actual values in the bank accounts" and the line heading will be "effect act. bank."

The second important key for the structure of cash management reports is to maintain grouping structures. Grouping structures determine which accounts are included and which ones are excluded in the cash management reports. If you want the report output to be as detailed as possible, SAP recommends selecting all levels for each grouping. This can be achieved by masking the entry with ++. Note that you should enter account numbers with leading zeros as shown in Figure 7.12.

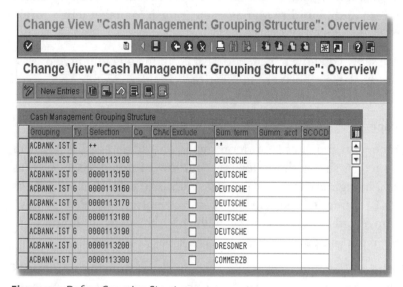

Figure 7.12 Define Grouping Structures

By using the *summarization* term, you can combine the level lines and the group lines of one grouping for the display of cash position and liquidity forecast. If no summarization term is specified, the system creates a line for each account, *planning level*, or *planning group*. The line type E stands for level and G for the account or planning group.

Another term used in cash management reports is the *cash management account name*. Cash management account names are defined at the company code level. The account name is used with the cash management reports instead of the account number. If required, you can report the cash position with the account number details as well.

Now that we have explained the structure of the cash management reports, we can look at cash management reports in depth.

7.3.1 Cash Management Reports

Cash management reports are available under the CLM information system. To access the CLM information system, follow the menu path **Financial Supply Chain Management • Cash and Liquidity Management • Cash Management • Information System** (see Figure 7.13).

In this section, we show you how to generate Cash Position and Liquidity Forecast reports. The other available reports are summarized in Table 7.2.

Cash Position Report

The Cash Position report provides short-term trends of cash and cash equivalent movements. The report shows the inflow and outflow of liquid assets such as bank, cash, check, foreign exchange deals, and so on. The data for the report is taken from the G/L postings on the respective cash accounts. Nonintegrated postings such as memo records, which are made only within the CLM application, are also shown in the report output.

To access the Cash Position report, follow the menu path **Accounting • Financial Supply Chain Management • Cash and Liquidity Management • Cash Management • Information System • Reports for Cash Management • Liquidity Analyses • Cash Position** (Transaction FF7A).

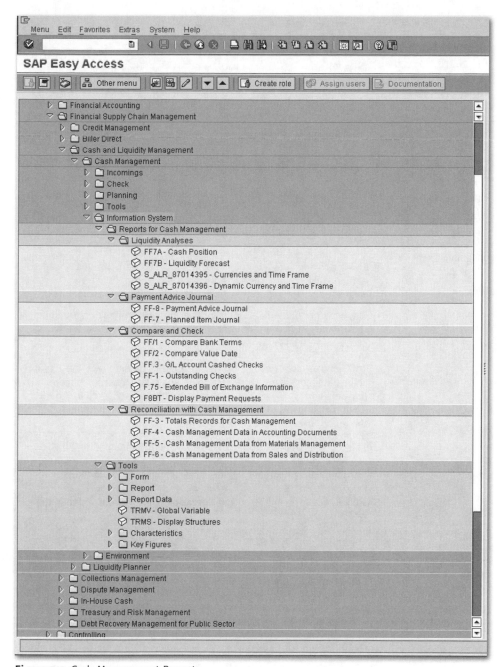

Figure 7.13 Cash Management Reports

Report Name and Transaction	Report Description
Currencies and Time Frame (S_ALR_87014395)	This report provides the analysis of foreign currency amounts in selected currencies for the three weeks following the last working day. You can display the amounts at company code, planning group, planning level, planned currency, planning date, business area, and G/L account level.
Dynamic Currency and Time Frame (S_ALR_87014396)	This report provides planned amount per planned currencies for three weeks following the last working day.
Payment Advice Journal (FF-8)	This report provides a list of all payment advice that was recorded, changed, deleted, or reactivated for a specified date. It is useful for analyzing cash position.
Planned Item Journal (FF-7)	This report provides a list of all planned payment advice for a specified date. It is useful for analyzing liquidity forecasts.
Compare Bank Terms (FF/1)	This report provides a list of interest terms, cash management account status, and G/L account monthly debits and credits for selected bank accounts on the key date specified.
Compare Value Date (FF/2)	This report is used to compare the planned value date with the actual value date. For each item cleared in a bank clearing account, the report finds the corresponding balance sheet account posting and lists both items if their dates differ. If several clearing items exist for one item, the report always considers the first item found.
G/L Account Cashed Checks (FF.3)	This report is used to display the average period outstanding for checks already cashed and not yet cashed. In addition, it displays the outstanding number and amount of checks. You can also use this report to compare value dates with actual clearing dates for checks. To do so, you must specify the option **Deviation from planning date** in the selection screen.
Extended Bill of Exchange Information (F.75)	This report shows all open bill of exchange information with the dates. If you specify the **cleared bills of exchange** option in the selection screen, you can also display the cleared bills. The report output shows bills of exchange receivable and bills of exchange payable with the important bill of exchange data.
Display Payment Requests (F8BT)	This report shows the open payment requests for the selected company codes. If you select the **cleared** option in the selection screen, you can also display the cleared payment requests.

Report Name and Transaction	Report Description
Totals Records for Cash Management (FF-3)	This report (program RFFDIS40) shows the summary records in cash management. The report output is used to compare and reconcile the cash management figures with the actual FI postings. You can compare summary records with the output of the report Cash Management Data in Accounting Documents (program RFFDEP00). Note, however, that you cannot compare the bank amounts with the figures supplied with RFFDEP00 because the bank account amounts may not include cash management information details.
Cash Management Data in Accounting Documents (FF-4)	This report shows the summary records for accounting documents in cash management. The summary record is made up of open items from customer and vendor accounts as well as the open items from G/L accounts. The Totals Records for Cash Management and Cash Management in Accounting Documents reports have the same sorting criteria, which makes comparison of these two reports easier.
Cash Management Data from Materials Management (FF-5)	This report (program RFFDMM00) shows the materials management line items updated in cash management. The report output can be compared with the summary records produced by the Totals Records for Cash Management report.
Cash Management Data from Sales and Distribution (FF-6)	This report (program RFFDSD00) shows the sales and distribution line items updated in cash management. The report output can be compared with the summary records produced by the Totals Records for Cash Management report.

Table 7.2 Cash Management Reports (cont.)

Figure 7.14 shows the selection screen of the Cash Position report. The cash position indicator is a default parameter in the selection screen. Note that the Liquidity Forecast indicator must not be selected for the Cash Position report. As shown in the selection screen, you need to specify company codes, groupings, and the starting date of the account forecast (**Display as of**) that you want to report.

Let's look at other key selection parameters. There are two important currency parameters in the selection screen: planned currency and display in currency. The *Planned Currency* is the currency of the transaction, which is the document currency of the underlying accounting document. However, when posting to G/L cash accounts that are not open item managed and have currency different than the company code currency, the planned currency is updated by the G/L account currency. To get your cash report split by planned currency, leave that field blank in the selection parameters. The **Display in** field is used to indicate the currency of the report output.

Note, however, that to generate report output in the display currency specified in the selection screen is not enough. You also need to click on the **Display in currency** button in the output of the report to see the values in the selected currency. In addition to report currency, you can also specify the *exchange rate* for the translation from the planned currency to the display currency in the selection parameters. If exchange rate type and conversion ratios (e.g., **FC/LC Exchange Rate**) are not specified, the average rate is used for currency translation.

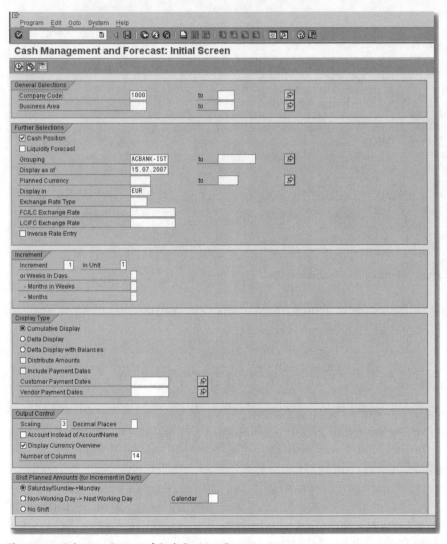

Figure 7.14 Selection Screen of Cash Position Report

There are additional selection parameters in the increments part of the selection screen. For example, you can specify the required time increment of the report. Optional displays include cash position on a daily, weekly, and monthly basis as well as cumulative, delta or delta with balance views. Option T (daily) is selected for daily increment in our example. With this option, the report displays daily transactions.

In the display part, you can choose whether you want to have cumulative, delta display, or delta display with amounts in the report output. Delta display helps you to analyze intraday cash movements, whereas the cumulative display shows the total balance.

In the output control parameters, if you select the indicator **Account Instead of Account Name**, the Cash Position report shows the accounts instead of the cash management account names. You can control the total number of displayed columns by using the **Number of Columns** parameter. In addition, in the output control parameters, you can specify the scaling and decimal places of figures in the output of the report.

The report shows cash and cash-equivalent transaction details with the value date. You can also see manual memo records and the anticipated cash flow of short-term financial instrument transactions in the report output. The first several days from current date include the most important cash position information that you can use in short-term funding and investment decisions. Figure 7.15 shows an example of the output of the Cash Position report with daily increments. By clicking on the **New Display** button, you can change the *time scaling* of the report without reexecuting. It is also possible to have a combination of time increments in the report. To do this, leave the increment and unit blank in the new display and enter days, weeks, or months.

You can analyze the information in the Cash Position report along with multiple dimensions, such as currency, grouping, account, account name, value date, and company code. The output of the report is structured with groupings. The groupings determine which accounts are shown in the report. Drilldown capability is available from the report through to individual transactions, providing a complete audit trail of all cash and cash-related transactions. For example, you can drill down to underlying transactions, and find reasons for any discrepancy. You can also drill down through the cash position to the underlying document by double-clicking on the respective cell. There are several drilldown levels before reaching the source transactions. You can first drill down to the summarization group from the cash position by currency (see Figure 7.16).

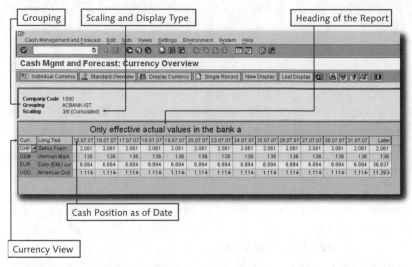

Figure 7.15 Output of Cash Position by Currency

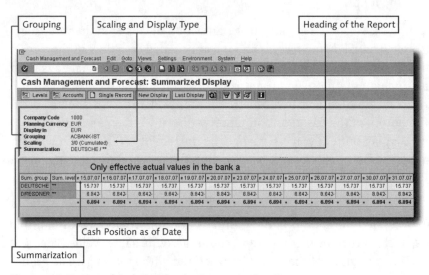

Figure 7.16 Output of Cash Position by Summarization Group

You can then drill down to planning-level details from the summarization group and display the cash position for each planning level (see Figure 7.17). From the planning level view you can further drill down to see source transactions, for example, international transfers transactions, check transactions, deposits/loans (see Figure 7.18). The lowest level of the drilldown either displays a particular financial accounting document or the transaction data for a specific financial instrument transaction.

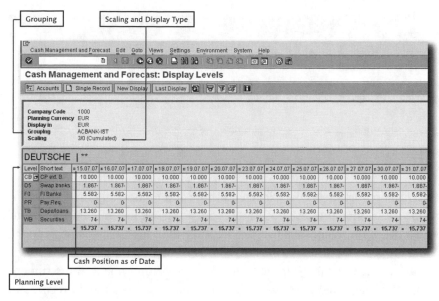

Figure 7.17 Output of Cash Position by Planning Level

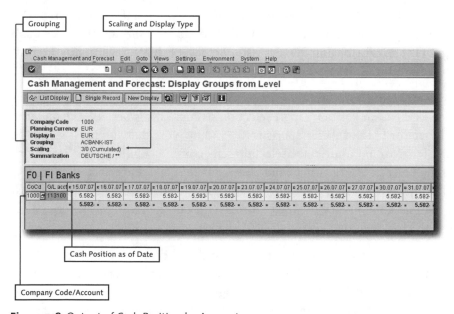

Figure 7.18 Output of Cash Position by Account

Alternative views of the reports

As an alternative to the SAP list viewer view is to switch to the Excel, Lotus Notes, or Crystal Reports views or display the graphic of the report. This is done by using the views menu in the menu bar. Alternatively, the report can be exported to a local folder in various formats such as spreadsheet, Word, XML, and so on.

Liquidity Forecast

The Liquidity Forecast report shows mid-term trends of cash and cash-equivalent movements. The report shows the expected inflow and outflow of liquid assets for a longer time frame than the Cash Position report. Typically the time frame is up to 24 weeks, so the liquidity forecast has less accuracy than the Cash Position report. The data for the report is taken from transactions in materials management, sales and distribution, accounts payable, accounts receivable, and financial instrument transactions. Nonintegrated postings such as manually entered memo records in the CLM application are also shown in the report.

To access the Liquidity Forecast report, follow the menu path **Accounting • Financial Supply Chain Management • Cash and Liquidity Management • Cash Management • Information System • Report for Cash Management • Liquidity Analyses • Liquidity Forecast** (Transaction FF7B).

As shown in Figure 7.19, the selection screen of the Liquidity Forecast report is the same as the Cash Position report selection screen. This is because the underlying program for both of these reports is RFTS7000. Note that you must select the Liquidity Forecast indicator in the selection screen of the Liquidity Forecast report. In the selection screen, you can include the payment dates and select for customer and vendor payment dates. You can use these dates to change the liquidity forecast display so that amounts are no longer displayed as of the relevant planning date, but as of the payment date.

The Liquidity Forecast report also supports powerful drilldown functionality, allowing you to move from the currency display view to drill down to the planning group (see Figure 7.20). From the planning group you can drill down further and see source transactions, for example, customer and vendor open items, material management, and sales and distribution transactions.

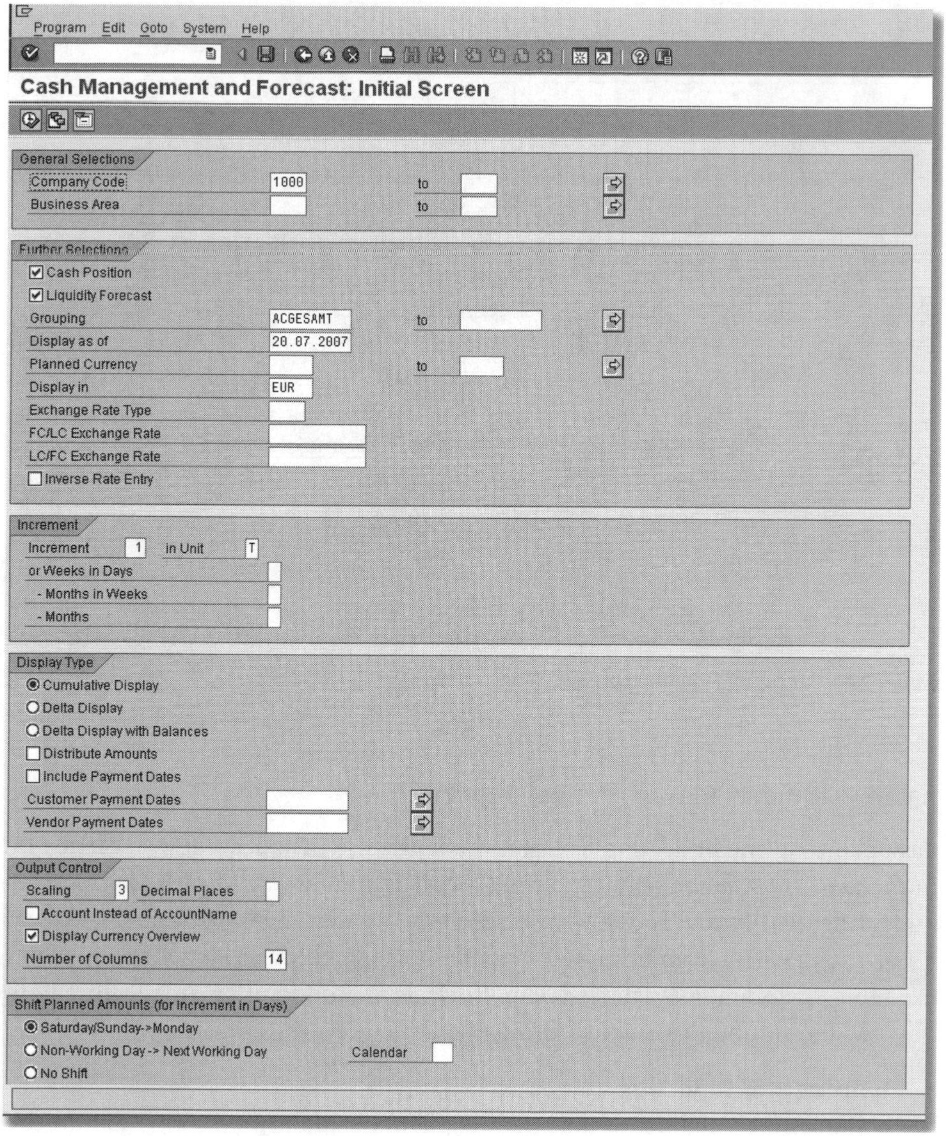

Figure 7.19 Selection Screen of Liquidity Forecast Report

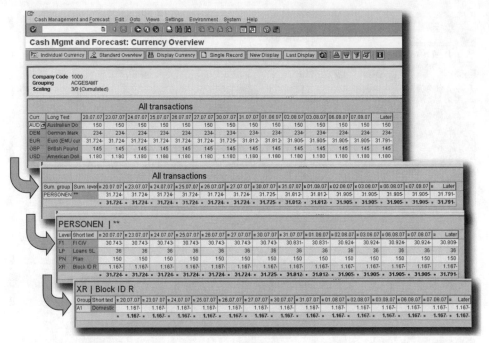

Figure 7.20 Output of Liquidity Forecast Report Drilldown

7.3.2 Liquidity Planner Actual Reports

Cash planning and budgeting, which is the long-term cash flow view, is carried out in the *Liquidity Planner* application of CLM. The time frame of cash planning and budgeting usually covers one year. However, note that the time period for liquidity planning varies from business to business. The Liquidity Planner application is used to plan and monitor the payment flows. From the solution architecture point of view, the solution consists of two parts:

▸ **Planning and reporting**
Planning functionalities of the liquidity planning application are within the SAP Strategic Enterprise Management Business Planning Simulation (SAP SEM-BPS) product. In other words, liquidity planning is carried out in SAP SEM-BPS. SAP SEM-BPS is based on SAP Business Warehouse. Liquidity planning business content was first delivered with SEM 3.0, BW 2.1C. As of BW release 3.5, liquidity planning is integrated with core BW. Note that we cover the evolution of SEM solutions to CPM solutions in Chapter 14.

► **Actual data and liquidity calculation**
Liquidity calculation for actual data is carried out in the CLM Liquidity Planner application of SAP ERP.

You can find information about the functions of the liquidity calculation and how to set up the Liquidity Planner in SAP Note 412605. In this section, we focus on the reports provided by the information system of the Liquidity Planner. To access the liquidity planner information system, follow the menu path **Accounting • Financial Supply Chain Management • Cash and Liquidity Management • Liquidity Planner • Information System**.

The CLM liquidity planner reports shown in Figure 7.21 are based on actual data. Let's examine the Payment report, from which you can drill down to the Totals List, Line Items, and Line Item History reports.

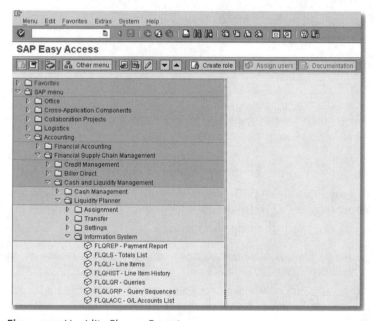

Figure 7.21 Liquidity Planner Reports

Payment Report

Liquidity calculation provides a classification of payments in accordance with their use and origin. This classification is carried out by programs that assign payments to liquidity items. The *liquidity item* is a new term introduced with the CLM Liquidity Planner application. They are used to indicate the origin and use of payments and are similar to cost elements in CO or commitment items in Cash Budget Management component.

The Payment report (Transaction FLQREP) shows the payments recorded for the liquidity calculation. In the selection screen, you need to specify the payment date intervals. You can restrict the output of the report by specifying the paying company codes and the liquidity items. The report output is illustrated in Figure 7.22. In our example we classified payments according to two liquidity items: INIT_IN for incoming payments and INIT_OUT for outgoing payments.

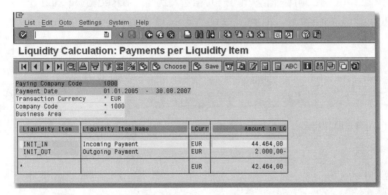

Figure 7.22 Output of Payments per Liquidity Item Report

By double-clicking on a row, you can go to the Totals List report. From there you can drill down to the Line Item List report, and you can further drill down to the Line Item History report (Figure 7.23). By double-clicking on the row on the Line Item History report, you can reach the original posting.

Cash Budget Management or Liquidity Planner
SAP first introduced the Cash Budget Management component for mid- to long-term cash planning and budgeting. However, the performance of the component did not meet the expectations of SAP customers. In 2001, SAP introduced the Liquidity Planner application for cash planning and budgeting. Cash Budget Management component is supported until R/3 Release 4.7 inclusive. SAP ERP only includes the Liquidity Planner application for cash planning and budgeting. The Cash Budget Management component is no longer available in SAP ERP. You can find a detailed comparison of Cash Budget Management and the Liquidity Planner in SAP Note 412606.

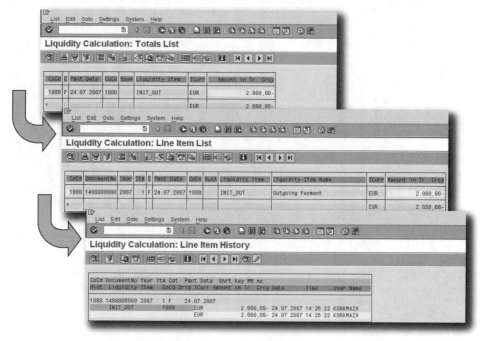

Figure 7.23 Totals List, Line Item List, and Line Item History List

7.4 Cash and Liquidity Management Reporting in SAP NetWeaver BI

SAP NetWeaver BI allows flexible and advanced reporting capabilities for cash management. In this section, we focus exclusively on the business content of CLM and provide data flow examples and queries based on standard InfoProviders. Note that the data flow examples are for illustration purposes only.

7.4.1 Cash and Liquidity Management Data Flow

The business content in CLM provides three InfoProviders for cash and liquidity management reporting: the Planned Amounts InfoCube (0TRCM_C01), the Current Planned Amounts InfoCube (0TRCM_R01), and the Planned Amounts Comparison (0TRCM_MC1). Figure 7.24 shows the data flow of the InfoCube Planned Amounts (0TRCM_C01) along with the data model.

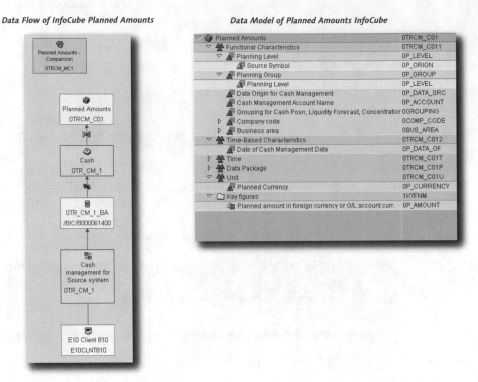

Data Flow of InfoCube Planned Amounts

Data Model of Planned Amounts InfoCube

Figure 7.24 Data Flow of the Planned Amounts InfoCube along with the Data Model

The Planned Amounts InfoCube (0TRCM_C01) contains the cash- and liquidity-relevant transactions that are extracted from the connected source systems. It is supplied with data by InfoSource 0TR_CM_1, which includes the key figure planned amount in the planned currency.

In addition to the Planned Amounts InfoCube, SAP NetWeaver BI provides the Current Planned Amounts InfoCube (0TRCM_R01) and the Planned Amounts Comparison (0TRCM_MC1) MultiProvider. Figure 7.25 shows the data flow of the Current Planned Amounts InfoCube and Planned Amounts Comparison MultiProvider. Note that the Current Planned Amounts InfoCube is a VirtualProvider, which means it can read data in real time from SAP ERP.

Data Flow of Current Planned Amounts InfoCube   *Data Flow of Planned AmountsComparison MultiProvider*

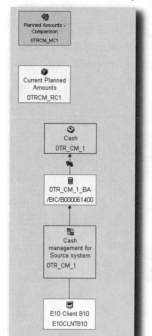 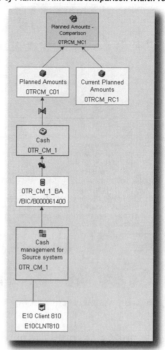

Figure 7.25 Data Flow of Current Planned Amount InfoCube and Planned Amount Comparison MultiProvider

Now that we have explained the InfoProviders for cash and liquidity management, let's examine the queries delivered in the business content based on these InfoProviders.

7.4.2 Cash and Liquidity Management Reports in SAP NetWeaver BI

SAP NetWeaver BI provides queries within the business content of CLM based on the InfoProviders explained above. Figure 7.26 shows the available queries for CLM in the business content. As shown in the figure, the name of the queries based on the Planned Amount InfoCube and Current Planned Amount InfoCube are similar. The difference is that the queries based on the Current Planned Amounts InfoCube can read the data in real time, as the Current Planned Amounts InfoCube is a VirtualProvider.

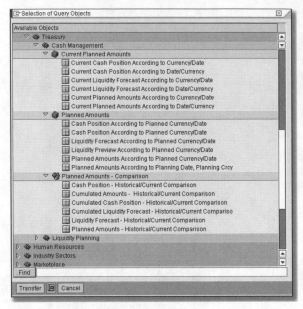

Figure 7.26 Cash Management Queries

Let's look closely at some of these queries.

Cash Position According to Planned Currency/Date Report

The Cash Position According to Planned Currency/Date (OTR-CM-TFS-2) report shows the planned amount and calendar day by planned currency for the chosen grouping and cash management date. You can swap currency characteristic with business area, cash management account name, calendar day, company code, planning level, and structure. You can drill down to business area, CM account name, company code and planning level. The query is based on InfoCube 0TRCM_C01.

The Cash Position According to Planned Currency/Date (OTR-CM-TFS-1) query (Figure 7.27) shows the same data in a different output format. It displays the planned currency and planned amount by calendar day.

Liquidity Forecast According to Planned Currency/Date Report

The Liquidity Forecast According to Planned Currency/Date (OTR-CM-LIQ-1) report shows planned currency and amount by calendar day. You can swap calendar day with business area, CM account name, calendar day, company code, planning level, or structure and drill down to business area, CM account, company code, or planning level. Figure 7.28 shows the output of the Liquidity Forecast According to Planned Currency/Date.

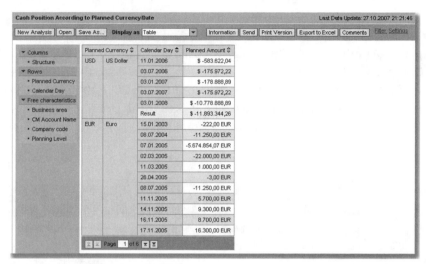

Figure 7.27 Output of Cash Position According to Planned Currency/Date Report

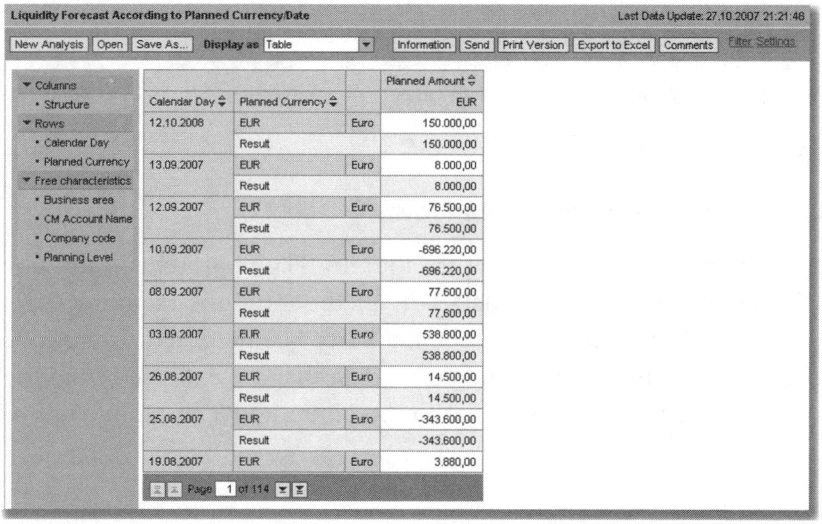

Figure 7.28 Output of Liquidity Forecast According to Planned Currency/Date Report

Cumulated Cash Position Historical Comparison Report

The Cumulated Cash Position Historical Comparison report shows the cumulated historical amount, cumulated current amount, and the difference between the current and historical values as an amount and percentage by planned currency. You can swap planned currency with business area, company code, key figure, planned group, and planning level. You can drill down to planning group and planning level. This query is based on MultiProvider Planned Amounts Comparison (0TRCM_MC1). As shown in Figure 7.25, the MultiProvider is supplied with data by the Planned Amounts InfoCube (0TRCM_C01) and Current Planned Amounts InfoCube (0TRCM_R01). The cumulated current amount is read in real time from the source system. Figure 7.29 shows an output of this report.

Cumulated Cash Position - Historical/Current Comparison   Last Data Update: 27.10.2007 21:21:46

	Planned Currency	Company Code			Cumulated Amount - Historical	Cumulated Current Amount	Absolute Variance	Percentage Variance
								%
	CHF	Swiss Franc	1000	IDES AG	2.060.833,33 CHF	2.060.833,33 CHF	0,00 CHF	0,00000 %
			Result		2.060.833,33 CHF	2.060.833,33 CHF	0,00 CHF	0,00000 %
	EUR	Euro	1000	IDES AG	44.517.636,33 EUR	44.517.636,33 EUR	0,00 EUR	0,00000 %
			Result		44.517.636,33 EUR	44.517.636,33 EUR	0,00 EUR	0,00000 %
	USD	US Dollar	1000	IDES AG	$ -34.357.425,21	$ -34.357.425,21	$ 0,00	0,00000 %
			Result		$ -34.357.425,21	$ -34.357.425,21	$ 0,00	0,00000 %
	Overall Result				*	*	*	0,00000 %

Figure 7.29 Output of Cumulated Cash Position Historical Comparison Report

7.4.3 Liquidity Planner Actual Data Flow

The business content in CLM provides the Liquidity Planning Actual InfoCube (0TRLP_C01). Figure 7.30 shows the data flow of the InfoCube Liquidity Planning Actual along with the data model. The Liquidity Planning Actual InfoCube contains the liquidity item planning and actual data that are extracted from the connected source systems. It is supplied with the Liquidity Planning InfoSource 0TR_LP_1.

*Data Flow of Liquidity Planning
Actual InfoCube*

*Data Model of Liquidity Planning
Actual InfoCube*

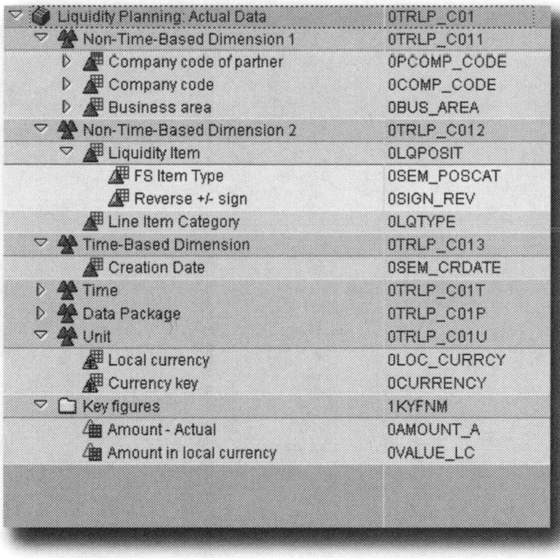

Figure 7.30 Data Flow of InfoCube Liquidity Planning Actual along with the Data Model

7.4.4 Liquidity Planner Reports in SAP NetWeaver BI

The planning application of the Liquidity Planner is part of SAP SEM-BPS. The planning application consists of the standard SAP SEM-BPS planning functionalities and an InfoCube (0SEM_C12) dedicated to a specific planning scenario. InfoCube 0TRLP_C01 saves the actual data, which extracts actual data from the Liquidity Planner application of the CLM. The business content in SAP NetWeaver BI provides a MultiProvider (0SEM_MC1) that combines both actual and plan data. Queries for plan/actual comparisons are executed in this MultiProvider, which contains both aforementioned InfoCubes. Figure 7.31 shows the data flow of the MultiProvider Liquidity Planning Plan/Actual along with the data model.

Data Flow of Liquidity Planning Plan/Actual MultiProvider

Data Model of Liquidity Planning Plan/Actual MultiProvider

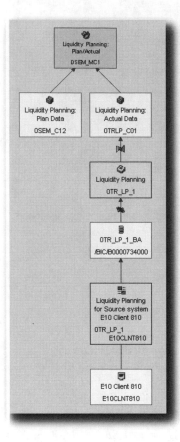

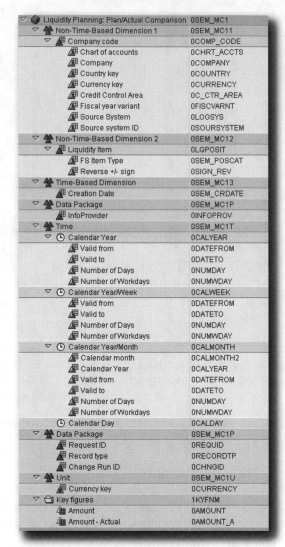

Figure 7.31 Data Flow of MultiProvider Liquidity Planning Plan/Actual along with the Data Model

In this section, we focus on queries based on the Liquidity Planner Actual Info-Cube (see Figure 7.32).

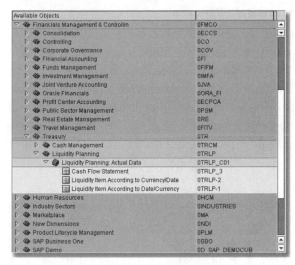

Figure 7.32 Liquidity Planning Queries

Cash Flow Statement Report

The Cash Flow Statement (OTRLP_3) report shows the amounts per liquidity item. In the selection screen, you specify the creation date and periods to be analyzed. You can swap the liquidity item characteristic with calendar year/month, calendar year/week, key figures, or partner company code. You can drill down to calendar year/month, calendar year/week, and partner company code. Figure 7.33 illustrates an example of a cash flow statement. As described earlier, we used two liquidity items, INIT_IN and INIT_OUT, for the classification of payments.

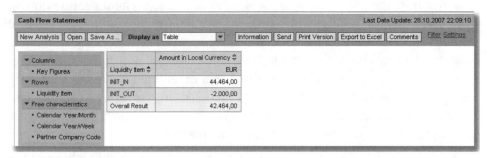

Figure 7.33 Output of Cash Flow Statement Report

Liquidity Item According to Currency/Date Report

The Liquidity Item According to Currency/Date (0TRLP-2) report shows the liquidity amounts per currency. In the selection screen, you need to specify the creation date. You can swap the currency characteristic with calendar day, company code, key figures, line item category, liquidity item, or partner company code. In addition, you can drill down to company code, line item category, liquidity item, and partner company code. The report output is illustrated in Figure 7.34. This query shows similarities to the payment report in the Liquidity Planner application of SAP ERP discussed earlier.

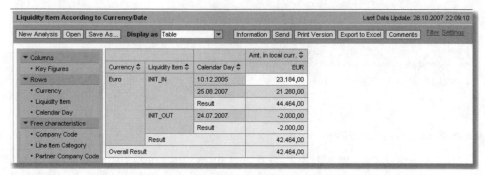

Figure 7.34 Figure 7.34 Output of Liquidity Item According to Currency/Date Report

7.5 Summary

Improving cash management reporting is an important part of corporate governance legislation compliance. Accurate and timely cash information creates a competitive advantage and is crucial to investment decisions on funding, investment, and borrowing. SAP ERP provides cash management reports with the Cash and Liquidity Management (CLM) application within SAP FSCM. Multiple company codes can be consolidated into a single view for cash position and liquidity forecast reports in the CLM application. Drilldown capability is available from cash management reports through to individual transactions, providing a complete audit trail of all financial transactions. In this chapter we explained the design considerations for cash management reporting architecture in SAP ERP and gave recommendations on how to structure and analyze the cash information. In addition, we explained the SAP NetWeaver BI business content of CLM along with data flow and modeling examples and gave example queries from the business content.

Managing financial instrument transactions with the right balance of functionality, flexibility, security, and efficiency is the ultimate goal of today's competitive economy. An infrastructure that facilitates straight-through processing (STP) can best support these goals and provide the transparency on reports that international accounting standards and compliances demand. SAP provides that infrastructure with Treasury and Risk Management (TRM), an application of SAP FSCM. This chapter covers transaction and position management reporting and market risk management analysis.

8 Treasury and Risk Management Reporting

In today's global economy, increasing numbers of companies are making financial investments and hedging their positions. With new accounting regulations, the shifting economic environment, and market globalization, organizations must find ways of managing risk effectively and ensure that their treasury and risk management reporting complies with the Sarbanes-Oxley Act (SOX), other regulations, and accounting standards and rules.

Traditionally, in many organizations the treasury department has acted as an isolated unit, often with inadequate board and senior management oversight, excessive risk-taking, and poor internal controls. However, this changed after SOX. With SOX, there is more emphasis upon risk management and the disclosure of risk management capabilities and approaches. In addition, financial analysts who evaluate the performance of organizations are increasingly focusing upon risk management as part of their analysis. Effective treasury and risk management has become a fundamental and core process that plays a vital role in the success of organizations.

In SAP ERP, the TRM application is designed to manage the treasury and risk management processes of organizations. The TRM application enables organizations to automate treasury functions, continuously monitor treasury processes, and manage risks effectively. The TRM application consists of four subapplications:

- Transaction Manager (TRM-TM)
- Market Analyzer (TRM-MR)
- Credit Risk Analyzer (TRM-CR)
- Portfolio Analyzer (TRM-PA)

The TRM-TM application enables an organization to manage financial investments and treasury operations. With TRM-TM, companies do not have to use spreadsheet or nonintegrated treasury software to record the investments, and they do not have to resort to manual processes or interfaces to post to FI. The financial transactions can be monitored and evaluated by using the analyzer applications of TRM.

Perhaps the most critical factor of treasury functions is market risks evaluation and management. Both investment decisions and treasury operations are affected by market risks, which eventually have an inextricable effect upon the timing of payment flows and the cash amounts of the enterprise. To manage financial transactions and other treasury activities effectively, it is important to have well-established risk management processes and capabilities to monitor risks. This can be achieved by using the TRM-MR application.

In this chapter, we first explain the reporting architecture of TRM. Then we focus upon the financial investment process—the so-called transaction and position management process in SAP ERP—and market risk analysis. We then examine the key reports for monitoring financial transactions and evaluating market risks. The last section of the chapter deals with the business content for TRM in SAP NetWeaver BI.

8.1   Treasury and Risk Management Reporting Architecture

Through implementing integrated treasury and risk management reporting architecture, you can add significant value to your organization. You can have better and more reliable forecasting, which eventually results in better yields on investments. The SAP TRM application enables integrated planning, transaction processing, and risk management, which is the foundation of integrated reporting architecture. The treasury and risk management reporting architecture in SAP ERP is illustrated in Figure 8.1.

TRM applications are integrated with the Cash and Liquidity Management (CLM) and In-House Cash (IHC) applications of FSCM. All financial transactions captured in the TRM application are automatically reflected in Cash Position and Liquidity Forecast reports. IHC center acts as an in-house bank, and transactions posted in IHC center are updated in both TRM and CLM applications. (We cover cash and liquidity management reporting in Chapter 7.) The TRM subapplications are also integrated with each other. This integration provides the ability to analyze and evaluate financial transactions captured in the TRM-TM application by using the TRM analyzer applications. (Note that TRM is also an application of SAP FSCM.) When it comes to SAP NetWeaver BI, business content InfoProviders for the transaction manager and analyzer are delivered within the Corporate Finance Management (CFM) InfoArea. You can load financial transactions data to these InfoProviders from different source systems for enterprise-wide position analysis and reporting.

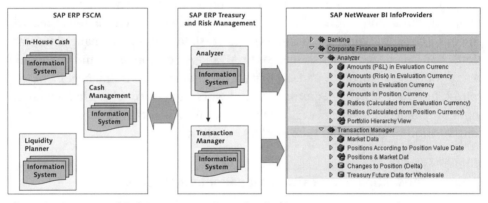

Figure 8.1 Treasury and Risk Management Reporting Architecture

Now that we have provided an overview of the treasury and risk management reporting architecture, we can take a closer look at the TRM-TM application.

8.2   Transaction Manager

The TRM-TM application enables companies to update the treasury financial transactions directly to FI without the need to keep additional accounting entries in the treasury workstation. It provides better operational and process controls, as well as increased automation and workflow so that companies have a much greater ability to assess what is going on in their business. In addition to process controls and automation, TRM-TM supports SOX and other compliances such as International

Financial Reporting Standards (IFRS) and U.S. Generally Accepted Accounting Principles for the United States (U.S. GAAP).

One of the questions we often hear from SAP customers is that they want to know why they can't just use the Accounts Receivable (AR) and Accounts Payable (AP) components for managing their financial transactions and risks. Unlike TRM-TR, the AR and AP components are not flexible enough to facilitate treasury functions or provide flexible reporting capabilities. For example, you cannot calculate the interest on fixed-term deposits or automatically update cash management for the future return of the investment. Measuring financial risk involves integrating your operational cash flows, financial transactions, and market data for comprehensive analyses. It is difficult to carry out this analysis by only using AR and AP. Thus, you may lose transparency and efficiency if you follow your financial transactions in AR and AP, as you would need to rely on work-around solutions as a basis of your financial transaction reports. In addition, you would need to create memo records in your CLM application to post the expected cash flow from the financial transactions. You cannot perform risk analysis in AP and AR components, and you would need to pull your financial transactions data to an external risk management system. Using so many adapted programs and workarounds could cause integration and compliance problems. Let's have a look at how you can manage transaction and position management in the TRM-TM application.

8.2.1 Transaction and Position Management Process

When it comes to transaction and position management process, STP is the key. STP integrates all aspects of financial transactions and makes the processing of transactions more efficient because data progresses automatically from one step to another without being manually reentered at each step. SAP TRM-TM facilitates STP by eliminating parallel structures to create transparency and streamline the financial process. Below are the key master data definitions to understand the transaction and position management process.

Product Categories and Product Types

TRM-TM supports a range of financial products, including money market, foreign exchange (FX), securities, derivatives, and debt management. The product category is a system-level classification of the financial products in TRM-TM. By using money market and FX product categories, you can manage liquidity and risks in the short term. Money market product categories are used for liquidity deficits and surpluses. FX product categories are used to hedge foreign exchange exposures. In the medium to long term, securities and loan product categories are used. In addition to these product types, the TRM-TM application also supports derivative product categories for managing interest rate and currency risks. Product categories are predefined in the system and cannot be modified. Each product category is further classified into product types in SAP ERP according to the organization's needs. Table 8.1 lists the main financial instruments and product categories in SAP ERP TRM-TM.

Financial Instrument	Product Categories
Money market	Fixed-term deposits Deposits at notice Commercial papers Repurchase agreements (Repos) Floating rate
Foreign exchange (FX)	FX spot transactions Forward FX transactions FX swaps FX options FX futures
Securities	Bonds Dual currency bonds Index-linked bonds Drawable bonds Warrant bonds Stocks Shareholdings Subscriptions rights Investment certificates Repurchase agreements (Repos) Reverse repurchase agreements Security lending
Derivatives	Caps/Floors Forward rate agreements (FRAs) Swaps Derivatives

Table 8.1 Financial Instrument and Product Categories in SAP ERP TRM-TM

Transaction Category and Transaction Type

The financial transaction category determines which transaction categories can be executed within a certain product category. The basic transaction categories are delivered within SAP ERP and should not be changed.

A financial transaction type determines the type of transaction executed with a specific product type. It controls the transaction and position management process. For example, the fixed-term deposits product type has two transaction types: investment and borrowing. You can refine the transaction types according to business requirements on the basis of transaction categories.

Business Partner

The business partner is an organization or person executing financial transactions on behalf of the company. Business partners should be created, released, and authorized before processing financial transactions. If your business partner is the house bank of your organization, there is no need for active payment. The house bank makes the corresponding posting to the company's bank account via a bank statement. If the business partner is not the company's house bank, the FI program should make the active payment. In this case, you should create the business partner either as a customer in AR or vendor in AP and link it to the business partner. You can make the link between the business partner and customer or vendor via Transactions FLBPD2 or FLBPC2.

Now that we have explained the key master data used in the TRM application, let's examine the transaction and position management process (see Figure 8.2).

In SAP ERP, financial transactions for each product type progress through different stages called *activities*. Activities depend upon the nature of the product, compliances, and the company's procedures. The sequence of activities is called the *transaction and position management process*, which is divided into three areas:

- *Trading area*, which includes functions for maintaining financial transactions
- *Back office area*, where transactions are settled
- *Accounting area*, where the G/L and subledgers are updated

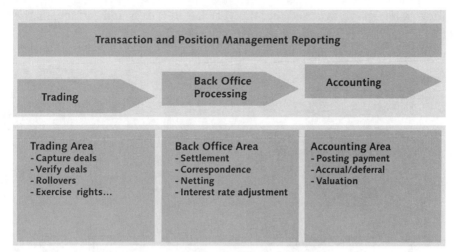

Figure 8.2 Transaction and Position Management Process

The functionalities of TRM-TR support the trading activities involved in preparing and entering transactions in addition to the back office and accounting activities, such as settlement, accounting, payment control, and transaction analysis.

Many steps in the transaction and position management processes are automated, and the status of a financial transaction can be evaluated and monitored at any time. Let's examine the process more closely and see how transactions are processed in the end-to-end process. In our example, company code 1000 has a liquidity surplus and invests this surplus amount with business partner 1000 in a fixed-term deposit. Business partner 1000 is the house bank of the company code.

Trading

The first step of the transaction and position management process is trading. The treasury responsible for working in the trading area, called the trader, maintains direct contact with the business partners, negotiates and executes transactions or orders, exercises options and other rights, and enters transactions and positions.

Figure 8.3 shows an example of the structure of fixed-term deposit transaction. EUR 2,000,000.00 has been invested in a 30-day fixed-term deposit with a 6% interest rate and Act/360 interest calculation methods. Interest is paid on maturity of the 30-day term. The interest rate calculation methods are predefined in SAP

ERP. In our example, we assumed that the year has 360 days and Act means the number of actual days between the start date and the finish date.

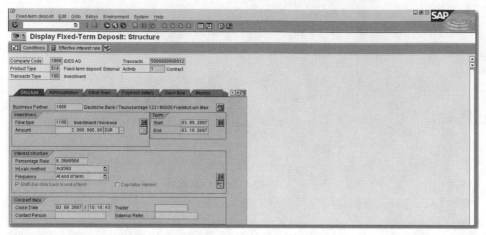

Figure 8.3 Structure of Fixed-Term Deposit

SAP ERP determines the cash flow in chronological order via the flow types. The expected cash flow of the fixed term deposit is shown in Figure 8.4. Payment flows for the cash flow and postings are indicated by (+) and (–) indicators in the D (direction) column. The flow types are defined in the configuration and assigned to the product and transaction types. In our example, EUR 2,000,000.00 was invested in a 30-day fixed-term deposit on September 3. Full repayment upon maturity and nominal interest will create a cash inflow on October 3. The positive flow of the nominal interest is shown on a separate line. Nominal interest and repayment will be posted to different accounts based on the flow types. Flow types allow you to clearly identify the cash flows. You can also define additional flow types for bank charges or commissions. These flow types are then recorded with each transaction. This way, you can increase the transparency of the cash flow in your reports.

Back Office

The back office activities are split into two parts. The first one is related to the immediate processing of deals entered in the trading area. The back office processor's role is to confirm and check transaction activities carried out by the trader in the trading area. This role also includes managing business partners and master agreements as well as entering and transferring payment flows. The back office area includes correspondence functions, such as the function for automatically generating confirmations. Correspondence output data is generated via print, fax, email, and IDocs.

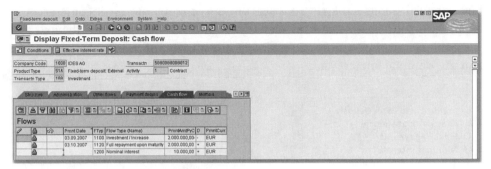

Figure 8.4 Cash Flow of Fixed-Term Deposit

The second part of back office tasks is related to periodic activities such as interest rate adjustments and FX fixing. A financial transaction goes through various activities during its processing. For example, when the contract is first created in the trading area, the activity status is set to contract. Settling alters the status of the activity from contract to contract settlement.

Accounting

The staff accountant role takes on the transactions that have been processed by the back office staff and carries out the postings, accruals, deferrals, and valuations. The accounting area includes posting activities that do not result directly from trading and back office processes. Examples of these are incoming payment postings (such as interest earned or dividends) or depreciation postings that result from a position valuation.

The accounting area features automatic posting functions for transferring data to FI and can update the G/L on a real-time basis. It also contains flexible functions for processing payment transactions and facilities for valuation and accrual and deferral. Reporting functions, such as the posting journal and the posting overview, support these features. Figure 8.5 shows the posting journal and FI postings related to our example. Note that because we have used the company's house bank, there is no active payment transaction. When the fixed-term deposit is settled to accounting, the fixed-term deposit account is debited and the bank clearing account is credited (step 1). When the first bank statement is received, the bank clearing account is debited and the bank main account is credited (step 2). After the 30-day term ends and the fixed-term deposit is transferred to the current bank account, the bank clearing account is debited and the fixed-term deposit account is credited (step 3). Without taking the tax into account, the nominal interest on the fixed-term deposit debits bank clearing account and credits interest income account (step 4). Finally, the second bank statement current bank account is debited and the bank clearing account is credited with the amount of the fixed-term deposit and the nominal interest rate.

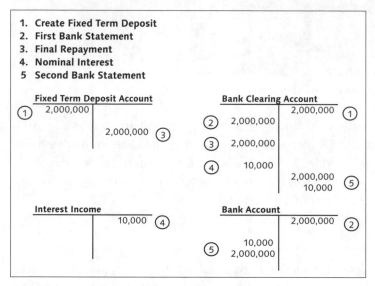

Figure 8.5 Financial Accounting Postings

Reporting and analysis is a fundamental process in the end-to-end transaction and position management process. With this process you can monitor the cash and profit and loss position across the enterprise, track payment schedules, evaluate financial transactions, and manage risks. Let's now look at two important aspects of transaction and position management reporting:

▸ Parallel Position Management

▸ Hedge Management

8.2.2 Parallel Position Management

A position is the smallest unit that you can analyze in the balance sheet accounts within the TRM application. Valuations are carried out, and derived flows are generated based on positions. The TRM-TM application allows for managing parallel positions to comply with the reporting requirements of different accounting regulations. It is possible to define parallel *valuation areas* and set various *position management procedures* according to different accounting standards to cover the reporting requirements of local accounting, IFRS, and U.S. GAAP.

The valuation results are posted to each valuation area in accordance with the reporting requirements. Parallel accounting with the valuation areas can be set up using two methods: the account method and the parallel ledger method. (Note that we cover these two methods in Chapter 2 for parallel accounting with the new G/L.) In this section we specifically look at how position management is achieved with the use of valuation areas within the TRM application.

Valuation areas provide different classifications to meet accounting regulations. For example, you can define *general valuation classes (GVCs)* and *special valuation classes* for each valuation area and assign these classes to each other. GVCs are used by traders to group financial investments. For example, you can classify your investments as short term, medium term, and long term by using GVCs. Doing so will give a high-level grouping of financial position. Valuation areas are used to determine the structure of financial statements. Let's assume you must prepare financial statements according to IFRS (valuation area 001) and local GAAP (valuation area 002). We defined GVCs as short term, medium term, and long term. For simplicity, we assume that IFRS has three valuation classes: trading, held to maturity, and available for sales. Local GAAP has two valuation classes: fixed assets and current assets. In the configuration, GVCs are assigned to valuation area and valuation classes. Table 8.2 illustrates an example of such assignments.

GVC	Valuation Area	Valuation Class
Short term	001	Trading
Short term	002	Current asset
Medium term	001	Held to maturity
Medium term	002	Fixed asset
Long term	001	Available for sales
Long term	002	Fixed asset

Table 8.2 GVC, Valuation Area, and Valuation Class Assignment

The assignment of GVC, valuation area, and valuation class plays a very important role in parallel position management. For example, if a trader assigns a position to the GVC short term, then the position is classified as trading in valuation area 001 IFRS, whereas it is recognized as current assets according to valuation area 002 local GAAP.

Another important concept for position management is *differentiation criteria*, which determines how positions are shown in the reports. The financial transactions, loans, listed options, and futures have fixed differentiation terms. For example, valuation area, valuation class, accounting code and transaction number are differentiation terms for financial transactions. Note that the accounting code represents the company code in position management. There is a one-to-one relationship between accounting code and company code.

You can define additional differentiation terms for security positions such as portfolio and lot. A *portfolio* is an organizational element that is used to group transactions for reporting. *Lot* refers to the consumption unit used in lot accounting (single position management). You can activate single positions for securities and listed derivatives and manage them either as LIFO (last in first out) or FIFO (first in first out). For example, if you choose the FIFO method, the first position bought is sold first.

As we mentioned earlier, you can define various position management procedures to comply with different accounting regulations. With the *position management procedures*, you can define how positions are valued and reported. Once you define the position management procedures, you should assign them to relevant characteristics such as accounting code, valuation areas, and valuation class.

The position management settings are defined in the configuration. The system has default settings that can be used as a reference. To go to position management settings follow the configuration menu path **Financial Supply Chain Management • Treasury and Risk Management • Transaction Manager • Accounting • Settings for Position Management**.

8.2.3 Hedge Management

A hedge is an investment to lower or neutralize the risk in another investment. One of the biggest challenges for treasurers is not having real-time performance measurement and risk management across the enterprise, which results in high operational costs and ineffective hedging.

To manage interest rate and currency risks, derivative financial instruments are used as hedging transactions. Traditionally, derivatives have not been fairly recognized on financial statements. The main reason for this is that when the derivative financial instrument was recorded in the accounting system, there was either no initial net investment or little investment relative to the total amount of the contract. However, the derivative has a positive (asset) or negative (liability) value as time passes and the value of risks changes. For example, interest rate or currency rate changes result in positive or negative values for derivatives.

Both IFRS and U.S. GAAP require all derivatives to be recognized in financial statements at fair value, although they have special accounting rules for managing derivatives and hedging. The main disclosures related to financial instruments for IFRS are stated in IAS 39 Financial Instruments: Recognition and Measurement. The accounting and reporting standards of derivatives and hedging activities for U.S. GAAP are established by FASB Statement No. 133 (SFAS 133 — Accounting for Derivative Instruments and Hedging Activities). The SAP TR-TRM application supports managing derivative financial instruments and hedging relationships according to both IFRS and U.S. GAAP.

Let's take a closer look at the hedging requirements of U.S. GAAP. According to SFAS 133, a company can postpone the earnings impact of changes in the fair value of the derivative, provided that the derivative is designated to hedge in order to minimize the exposure of a certain specified risk, which is known as *qualifying for hedge accounting*. However, note that you have to meet certain criteria for all hedges to qualify for hedge accounting. One of the main criteria is to link the hedged item (underlying exposure) and the hedging instrument (derivative). This can be achieved by creating a *hedging relationship* in the TRM application. A hedging relationship also forms a *hedge strategy*, which is used to assess and measure the effectiveness of the hedging relationship. A hedge strategy consists of a series of rules that determines how effectiveness is tested. For example, how to calculate the changes in the fair value of a hedged item and hedging instrument and the allowed range of the effectiveness ratio are defined in the hedge strategy. After the hedging relationship has been defined, you can use the *effectiveness test* to determine whether the derivative effectively hedges the value changes of the underlying exposure.

Hedging is based on the principle that cash market prices and futures market prices tend to move up and down together. This is used to lessen the risk of a loss in the cash market by taking an opposite position in the futures market. Taking opposite positions allows losses in one market to be offset by gains in the other.

Let's have a look at the key reports used for hedge management. For simplicity, we examine the reports with one derivative transaction used as a hedging transaction. In our example, company 1000 intends to invest US $300,000, which is planned for January 2008. Without the protection of hedging, if the dollar strengthens, the company would need a greater amount of euros to pay for the investment in U.S. dollars. In contrast, if the dollar value weakens, the company would pay less in euros for the investment in U.S. dollars. Because there is uncertainty in the exchange rate volatility, the company would like to minimize its currency exposure with the use of hedging. Without hedging, the appreciation of the U.S. dollar against the euro at the time of the investment settlement would lead to currency loss due to exposure.

To hedge the exchange risk, the company decides to buy a forward contract on U.S. dollars/euros in the derivatives market. By hedging when the dollar appreciates, the company realizes its gains in forward transactions, which will offset any loss in the spot transaction at the time of the investment settlement. When the dollar weakens against the euro, the loss in the forward transaction will be offset by the gain in the spot market transaction. By doing so, risk will be hedged.

In our example, a derivative transaction is recorded as a hedge transaction, with US $300,000.00 exposure on the contract date October 10, 2007, which is the date when the contract is conducted. The total value of exposure is designated as the hedge volume. In our example, the 90-day euro/U.S. dollar future contract rate is 1.4174, the spot rate is 1.4134, and the swap is 0.0040 (see Figure 8.6). The exchange rate is 1.4100 when the future is concluded.

The hedge management relationship is entered on the hedge tab of the derivative transaction. Figure 8.7 shows the hedging relationship of derivative transaction 4000000005903.

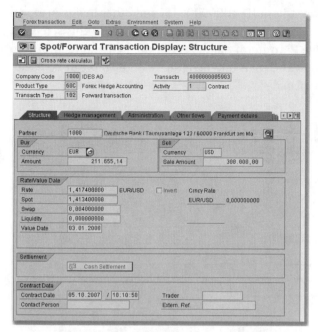

Figure 8.6 Structure of the Derivative

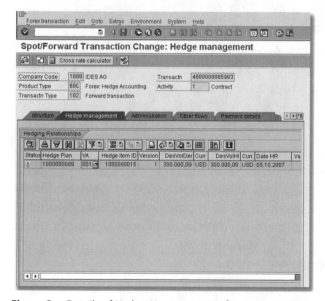

Figure 8.7 Details of Hedge Management Information

Hedge plan 1000000009, hedged item ID 1000000015, and other hedge management information are displayed in the **Hedge management** tab. In this screen, if you double-click on the **Hedge Plan** item, the details of the hedging relationship are displayed (see Figure 8.8). More than one hedging relationship can be established within the same hedge plan.

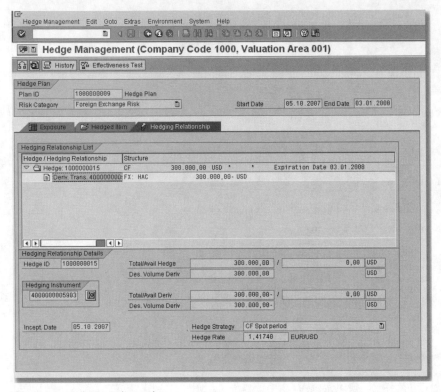

Figure 8.8 Hedging Relationship

The effectiveness test and other hedge accounting reports are listed under the hedge management information system. To access the hedge management information system, follow the menu path **Accounting • Financial Supply Chain Management • Treasury and Risk Management • Transaction Manager • Hedge Management • Information System**.

Effectiveness Test Report

The Effectiveness Test (Transaction THM80) report is used to determine whether hedging instruments effectively hedge value changes of the underlying exposure for the selected company codes. The report can carry out retrospective and prospective effectiveness testing. The check is carried out by determining the net present value changes of the underlying and hedge transaction between two points in time and putting them in relation to each other. In our example, we made a prospective effectiveness test with scenario SC_RDB, in which the exchange rate from euros to U.S. dollars was 1.35100, and the bid rate and ask rates were 1.35300.

The report calculates the effectiveness by dividing the price (or cash flow) change for the hedging instrument by the price (or cash flow) change of the hedged item. The report displays the delta amounts and totals for the derivative and the hedged item, along with the effectiveness ratio and an indicator showing whether the hedging relationship is effective or not. Figure 8.9 shows the effectiveness test of derivative 4000000005903.

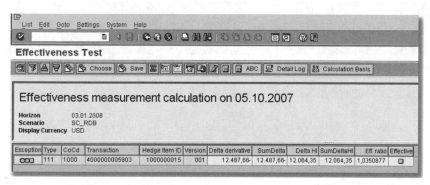

Figure 8.9 Effectiveness Test Report Output

The price change for the hedging instrument is calculated as US $12,487.66, the price change of the hedge item is calculated as US $12,064.35, and the effectiveness ratio is calculated as 1.0350877 (12,487.66/12,064.35). The effectiveness test uses the market risk analyzer price calculators. The details of effectiveness ratio calculation can be analyzed in the detailed log. You can see the detailed log by either double-clicking on the line item or selecting the detailed log box in the application tool bar.

Refer to Table 8.3 and Table 8.4 for the calculation of delta and the total value of derivative and hedge items. Note that the difference between the value of designated derivatives with the current accounting rate (exchange rate type M) and scenario rate is set as the delta value of the designated derivative. Thus, the value of the designated derivate is calculated as US $-12,487.66 (-14,053.91 - [-1,566.25]). The same calculation applies to the calculation of the value of the designated hedge item.

Date	Value	Rate	Value in displayed currency	Value of entire derivative	Value of designated derivative
05/10/07	211,655.14	1.4100	298,433.75	-1,566.25	-1,566.25
03/01/08	211,655.14	1.3510	285,946.09	-14,053.91	-14,053.91

Table 8.3 Calculation of the Entire Value and Designated Value of the Derivative

Date	Value	Rate	Value in displayed currency	Value of entire hedge item	Value of designated hedge item
05/10/07	-211,655.14	1.4100	-298,433.75	1,566.25	1,566.25
03/01/08	-211,655.14	1.3530	-286,369.40	13,630.60	13,630.60

Table 8.4 Calculation of the Entire Value and Designated Value of the Hedge Item

Hedge Plan Overview Report

The Hedge Plan Overview (Transaction THM82) report provides an overview of hedge plans for selected company codes. In the selection parameter, you should specify whether you want to display the FX plan or interest exchange plan. The individual plans are shown in a hierarchical view where all hedge management objects are listed: hedged items, exposures, transactions, and the assigned derivative contracts. You can also analyze the details of each object in the report output (see Figure 8.10).

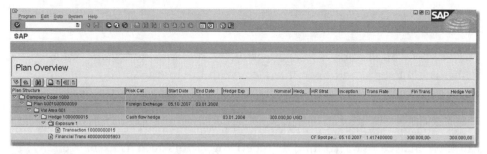

Figure 8.10 Hedge Plan Overview

Hedging Relationships per Derivative Report

The Hedging Relationships per Derivative (Transaction THM83) report is used to analyze the hedging relationships per derivative for selected company codes. In other words, you can display the relationship of derivatives. Figure 8.11 shows an example of this report output executed with the hierarchical list option.

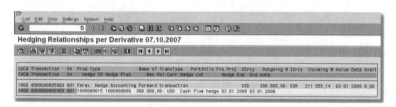

Figure 8.11 Hedging Relationships per Derivative as Hierarchical List

8.3 Market Risk Analyzer

Market risk is the risk that the fair value or cash flows of an investment will change due to changes in market prices, making organizations vulnerable to financial loss. Changes in FX rates, interest rates, and stock and commodity prices have a profound effect upon future earnings, cash flows, and the fair market values of assets and liabilities.

To control and manage risks, it is necessary to capture and record all risk-related transactions. The TRM-MR application provides the foundations to measure and evaluate the risks of financial transactions. With TRM-MR, you can keep all risk-related data and carry out methodological risk analysis and evaluation of financial transactions.

The TRM-MR application is fully integrated with the real-time *data feed interface*, which is a universal and open interface. With the interface, you can transfer or import exchange rates, swap rates, security price information (stocks and bonds), reference interest rates, and volatilities (for exchange rates, interest rates, security prices, and indexes) data into TRM-MR from various market data providers. You can then analyze risk according to underlying factors such as exchange rates, interest rates, prices, and volatilities. In addition, you can carry out risk analysis for interest and currency exposure and value-at-risk analysis, which are classic risk control methods. The application also supports various risk calculation methods.

Risk hierarchies, *portfolio hierarchies*, and *maturity bands* determine how the evaluations of risks take place (see Figure 8.12). Let's take a closer look at these terms.

▶ **Risk Hierarchy**
Market risk is divided into five categories for more comprehensive risk management and control: interest rate risk, currency risk, index risk, volatility risk, and price risk. Each risk category can then be further split into subrisks. For example, interest area can be split into swaps, bonds, money market transaction risk, and so on. The risk hierarchy defines how the market risk is split into its categories. Risk hierarchies provide detailed information of different risk factors in the evaluations. In the evaluations, the individual risks that form the risk hierarchy can be analyzed.

▶ **Portfolio Hierarchy**
Risk analysis can be carried out on an aggregated level. Portfolio hierarchy is used to define aggregation methodology. It is a grouping of financial characteristics (e.g., company code, currency, contract, etc.) on which risk analysis can be based.

▶ **Maturity Band**
Maturity bands determine the sequence of time periods and are used in evaluation reports to identify in which time periods the analysis is carried out.

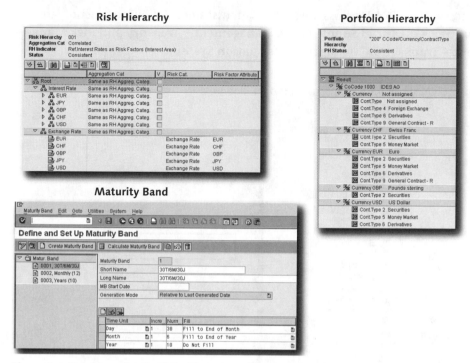

Figure 8.12 Risk Hierarchy, Portfolio Hierarchy, and Maturity Band

8.4 Treasury and Risk Management Reporting in SAP ERP

You can view your company's financial transactions, positions, and portfolios with predefined and flexible reports available in the information system of TRM. The link to the SAP drilldown reporting tools allows you to define your own reports in addition to those provided by the TRM application.

8.4.1 Transaction Manager Reporting in SAP ERP

The TRM-TR application provides information for each transaction type category as well as a cross-area information system. In other words, each financial instrument has its own information system in addition to a cross-area information system where you can monitor and analyze all types of financial investments. Figure 8.13 shows the money market information system and cross-area information system.

To access the TRM-TR cross-area information system, follow the menu path **Accounting • Financial Supply Chain Management • Treasury and Risk Management • Transaction Manager • Information System**.

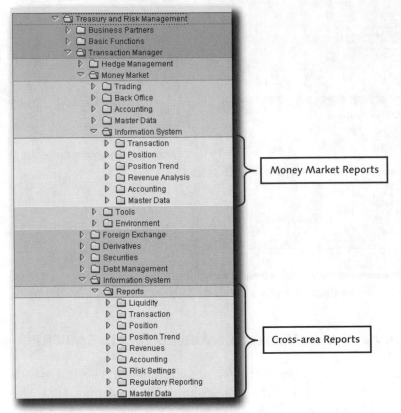

Figure 8.13 TRM-TR Information System Structure

The TRM-TM cross-area information system includes liquidity analysis reports from the Cash and Liquidity Management application, cross-TM reports for analyzing positions and revenues, reports for risk analysis from the market risk analyzer, and regulatory reports. In this section, we examine the key cross-area TM reports. In the next section, we look at risk analysis reports available in the information system of TRM-MR. (Note that we covered cash and liquidity management reporting in Chapter 7.)

Journal of Financial Transactions Report

The Journal of Financial Transactions (Transaction TJ01) report is used to analyze transactions recorded in the system using various selection parameters. For example, you can specify product group, transaction type, business partner, trader, and so on, in the selection screen of the report. Figure 8.14 shows an example of report output. The report output shows only the key data related to financial transactions. By double-clicking a line or selecting the magnifying glass on the application tool bar, you can see the details of the transaction in question.

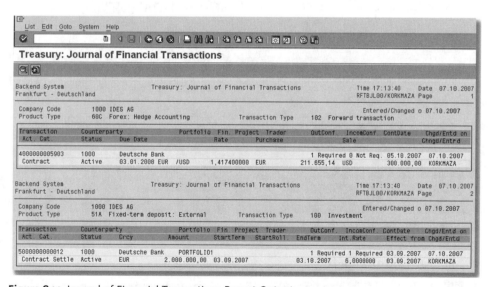

Figure 8.14 Journal of Financial Transactions Report Output

The Short Journal (Transaction TJ10) report is also used to analyze financial transactions according to specified selection parameters. Note that the Short Journal report is displayed in ALV format and has the standard ALV controls as well as the application-specific controls (see Figure 8.15).

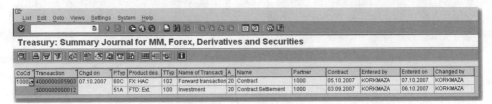

Figure 8.15 Short Journal of Financial Transactions Output

Transactions with Cash Flows Report

The Transactions with Cash Flows (Transaction TJ12) report provides cash flow information as well as the status of selected financial transactions. This report is typically used to evaluate which flows become due in the future. Figure 8.16 shows an example the Transactions with Cash Flows report output.

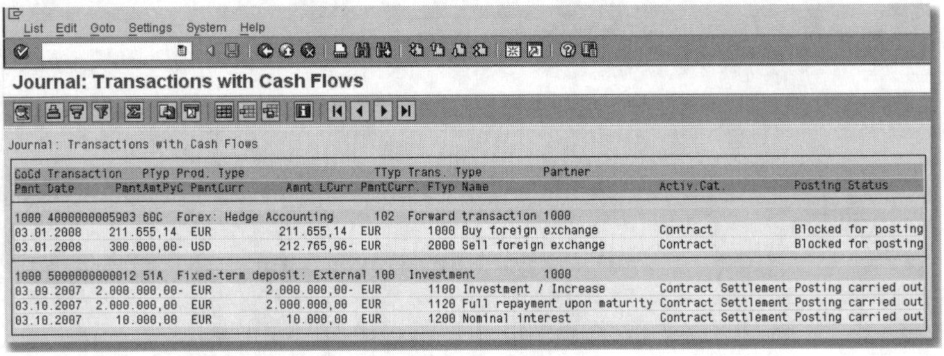

Figure 8.16 Transactions with Cash Flow Report Output

Payment Schedule Report

The Payment Schedule (program RFTBFL02) report is executed at regular intervals to prevent late payments. With this report, you can analyze which payments have been made and which are still due. The report also contains information on the corresponding business partners and bank details. The payment schedule report is included under each financial instrument's information system. In the selection screen, you need to specify the open item buttons to report all unpaid transactions. If you choose the paid items, the report will also show the paid items. Figure 8.17 shows an example output of this report.

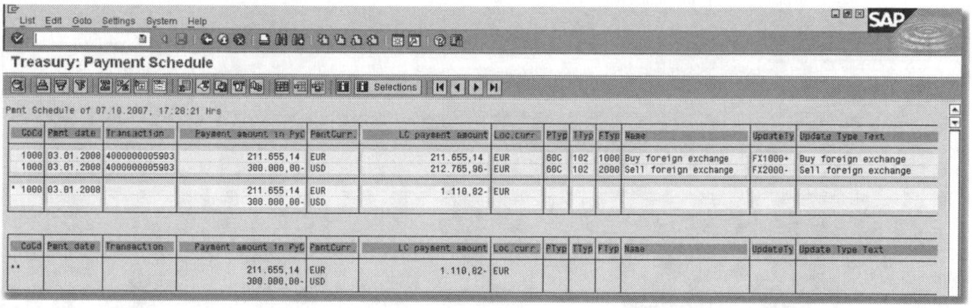

Figure 8.17 Payment Schedule Report Output

To use payment reporting, you first need to assign the payment-relevance indicator to the relevant update types. Update types that are flagged as payment-relevant are selected by the logical database fti_tr_cash_flows. After you flag the relevant update types for payment, you should generate the proposal for payment for these update types. Doing so will take out the operative valuation area and other position-management-relevant parameters from the fti_tr_cash_flows logical database. Thus, payments can be made independent of valuation areas. These two steps are carried out in configuration. To define the settings for payment reporting, follow the menu path **Financial Supply Chain Management • Treasury and Risk Management • Transaction Manager • General Settings • Information System • Payment Reporting**.

Overview Positions Report

The Overview Positions (Transaction TPM12) report provides a list of positions from securities, loans, listed derivatives, and over-the-counter (OTC) transactions (MM, foreign exchange, OTC derivatives), with the values of the position on a key date specified in the selection screen. Figure 8.18 shows an example of the report output.

The report output is displayed in ALV format and has the standard ALV controls as well as the application-specific controls. There are many control buttons on the application toolbar menu. For example, you can display securities account groups, position indicator, position management procedure, security detail view, and so on. By selecting the **Security: Detail View** button, the system will display the differences in the position and valuation currencies, including the price/rate in the position currency and exchange rate for the selected securities position with the differentiation characteristic details, as shown in Figure 8.19.

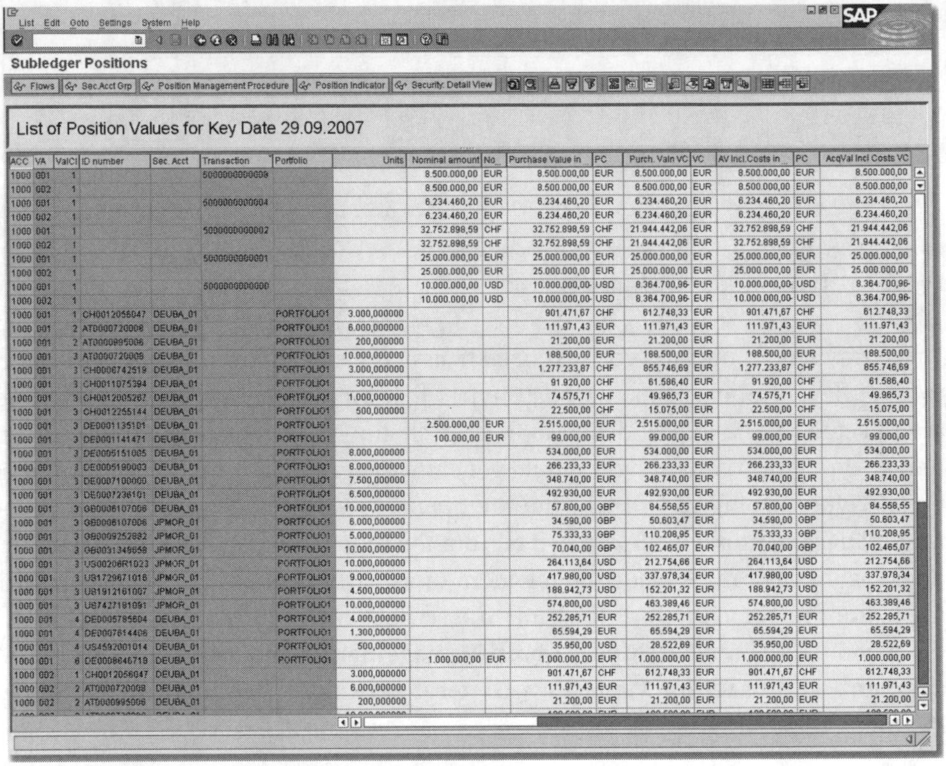

ACC	VA	ValCl	ID number	Sec. Acct	Transaction	Portfolio	Units	Nominal amount	No_	Purchase Value in	PC	Purch. Valn VC	VC	AV Incl.Costs in	PC	AcqVal Incl Costs VC
1000	001	1			5000000000003			8.500.000,00	EUR	8.500.000,00	EUR	8.500.000,00	EUR	8.500.000,00	EUR	8.500.000,00
1000	002	1						8.500.000,00	EUR	8.500.000,00	EUR	8.500.000,00	EUR	8.500.000,00	EUR	8.500.000,00
1000	001	1			5000000000004			6.234.460,20	EUR	6.234.460,20	EUR	6.234.460,20	EUR	6.234.460,20	EUR	6.234.460,20
1000	002	1						6.234.460,20	EUR	6.234.460,20	EUR	6.234.460,20	EUR	6.234.460,20	EUR	6.234.460,20
1000	001	1			5000000000002			32.752.898,59	CHF	32.752.898,59	CHF	21.944.442,06	EUR	32.752.898,59	CHF	21.944.442,06
1000	002	1						32.752.898,59	CHF	32.752.898,59	CHF	21.944.442,06	EUR	32.752.898,59	CHF	21.944.442,06
1000	001	1			5000000000001			25.000.000,00	EUR	25.000.000,00	EUR	25.000.000,00	EUR	25.000.000,00	EUR	25.000.000,00
1000	002	1						25.000.000,00	EUR	25.000.000,00	EUR	25.000.000,00	EUR	25.000.000,00	EUR	25.000.000,00
1000	001	1			5000000000000			10.000.000,00	USD	10.000.000,00-	USD	8.364.700,96-	EUR	10.000.000,00-	USD	8.364.700,96-
1000	002	1						10.000.000,00	USD	10.000.000,00-	USD	8.364.700,96-	EUR	10.000.000,00-	USD	8.364.700,96-
1000	001	1	CH0012056047	DEUBA_01		PORTFOLIO1	3.000,000000			901.471,67	CHF	612.748,33	EUR	901.471,67	CHF	612.748,33
1000	001	2	AT0000720008	DEUBA_01		PORTFOLIO1	6.000,000000			111.971,43	EUR	111.971,43	EUR	111.971,43	EUR	111.971,43
1000	001	2	AT0000995006	DEUBA_01		PORTFOLIO1	200,000000			21.200,00	EUR	21.200,00	EUR	21.200,00	EUR	21.200,00
1000	001	3	AT0000720008	DEUBA_01		PORTFOLIO1	10.000,000000			188.500,00	EUR	188.500,00	EUR	188.500,00	EUR	188.500,00
1000	001	3	CH0006742519	DEUBA_01		PORTFOLIO1	3.000,000000			1.277.233,87	CHF	855.746,69	EUR	1.277.233,87	CHF	855.746,69
1000	001	3	CH0011075394	DEUBA_01		PORTFOLIO1	300,000000			91.920,00	CHF	61.586,40	EUR	91.920,00	CHF	61.586,40
1000	001	3	CH0012005267	DEUBA_01		PORTFOLIO1	1.000,000000			74.575,71	CHF	49.965,73	EUR	74.575,71	CHF	49.965,73
1000	001	3	CH0012255144	DEUBA_01		PORTFOLIO1	500,000000			22.500,00	CHF	15.075,00	EUR	22.500,00	CHF	15.075,00
1000	001	3	DE0001135101	DEUBA_01		PORTFOLIO1		2.500.000,00	EUR	2.515.000,00	EUR	2.515.000,00	EUR	2.515.000,00	EUR	2.515.000,00
1000	001	3	DE0001141471	DEUBA_01		PORTFOLIO1		100.000,00	EUR	99.000,00	EUR	99.000,00	EUR	99.000,00	EUR	99.000,00
1000	001	3	DE0005151005	DEUBA_01		PORTFOLIO1	8.000,000000			534.000,00	EUR	534.000,00	EUR	534.000,00	EUR	534.000,00
1000	001	3	DE0005190003	DEUBA_01		PORTFOLIO1	8.000,000000			266.233,33	EUR	266.233,33	EUR	266.233,33	EUR	266.233,33
1000	001	3	DE0007100000	DEUBA_01		PORTFOLIO1	7.500,000000			348.740,00	EUR	348.740,00	EUR	348.740,00	EUR	348.740,00
1000	001	3	DE0007236101	DEUBA_01		PORTFOLIO1	6.500,000000			492.930,00	EUR	492.930,00	EUR	492.930,00	EUR	492.930,00
1000	001	3	GB0006107006	DEUBA_01		PORTFOLIO1	10.000,000000			57.800,00	GBP	84.558,55	EUR	57.800,00	GBP	84.558,55
1000	001	3	GB0006107006	JPMOR_01		PORTFOLIO1	6.000,000000			34.590,00	GBP	50.603,47	EUR	34.590,00	GBP	50.603,47
1000	001	3	GB0009252882	JPMOR_01		PORTFOLIO1	5.000,000000			75.333,33	GBP	110.208,95	EUR	75.333,33	GBP	110.208,95
1000	001	3	GB0031348658	JPMOR_01		PORTFOLIO1	10.000,000000			70.040,00	GBP	102.465,07	EUR	70.040,00	GBP	102.465,07
1000	001	3	US00206R1023	JPMOR_01		PORTFOLIO1	10.000,000000			264.113,64	USD	212.754,66	EUR	264.113,64	USD	212.754,66
1000	001	3	US1729671016	JPMOR_01		PORTFOLIO1	9.000,000000			417.980,00	USD	337.978,34	EUR	417.980,00	USD	337.978,34
1000	001	3	US1912161007	JPMOR_01		PORTFOLIO1	4.500,000000			188.942,73	USD	152.201,32	EUR	188.942,73	USD	152.201,32
1000	001	3	US7427181091	JPMOR_01		PORTFOLIO1	10.000,000000			574.800,00	USD	463.389,46	EUR	574.800,00	USD	463.389,46
1000	001	4	DE0005785604	DEUBA_01		PORTFOLIO1	4.000,000000			252.285,71	EUR	252.285,71	EUR	252.285,71	EUR	252.285,71
1000	001	4	DE0007614406	DEUBA_01		PORTFOLIO1	1.300,000000			65.594,29	EUR	65.594,29	EUR	65.594,29	EUR	65.594,29
1000	001	4	US4592001014	DEUBA_01		PORTFOLIO1	500,000000			35.950,00	USD	28.522,69	EUR	35.950,00	USD	28.522,69
1000	001	6	DE0008646719	DEUBA_01		PORTFOLIO1		1.000.000,00	EUR	1.000.000,00	EUR	1.000.000,00	EUR	1.000.000,00	EUR	1.000.000,00
1000	002	1	CH0012056047	DEUBA_01			3.000,000000			901.471,67	CHF	612.748,33	EUR	901.471,67	CHF	612.748,33
1000	002	2	AT0000720008	DEUBA_01			6.000,000000			111.971,43	EUR	111.971,43	EUR	111.971,43	EUR	111.971,43
1000	002	2	AT0000995006	DEUBA_01			200,000000			21.200,00	EUR	21.200,00	EUR	21.200,00	EUR	21.200,00

Figure 8.18 Overview Positions Report Output

Posting Journal Report

The Posting Journal (Transaction TPM20) report provides details on the posted flows of selected transaction(s). The report output has two sections: transaction data information and posting data information. In the transaction data information, you can see transaction details such as transaction number, account assignment reference, and update type. The posting information section contains information on the related flows, such as financial posting document number, and G/L accounts. Figure 8.20 shows the report output for our example Transaction

5000000000012 in ALV format. You can select different characteristics from the field selection button from the application tool bar for further details. In addition to posted flows, you can analyze the flows that have been flagged for reversal or reversed flows.

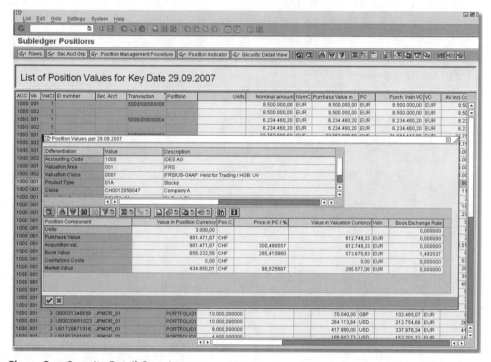

Figure 8.19 Security Detail Overview

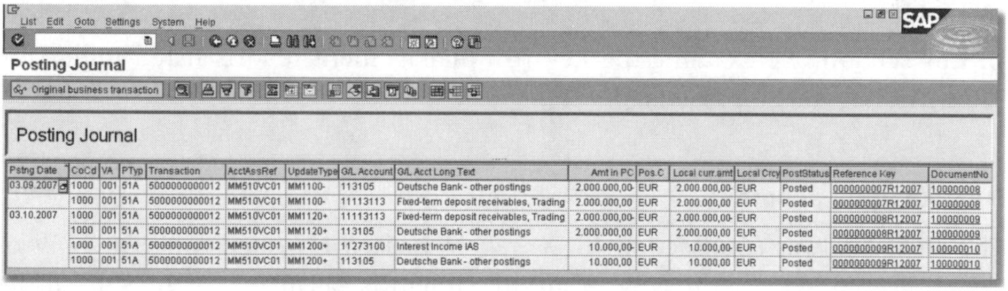

Figure 8.20 Posting Journal Report Output

8.4.2 Market Risk Analysis in SAP ERP

The main objective of market risk analysis is to evaluate financial transactions in accordance with current market data and risks and to identify potential losses. The TRM-MR information system has market risk analysis reports, which include risk analysis functions such as net present value (NPV) analysis, and value at risk analysis. Figure 8.21 shows risk management information system reports. To access the TRM-MR information system, follow the menu path **Financial Supply Chain Management • Treasury and Risk Management • Market Risk Analyzer • Information System**.

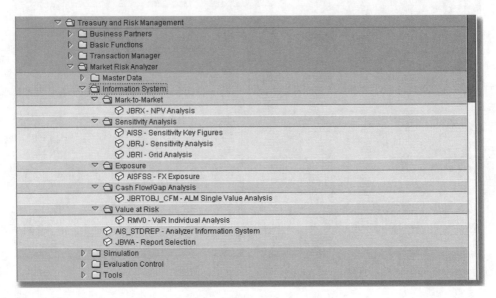

Figure 8.21 Information System of Market Risk Analysis

In this section, we examine the key risk management reports listed under the TRM-MR information system.

NPV Analysis Report

The NPV Analysis (Transaction JBRX) report is used for calculating the NPV of financial transactions. The NPV of an investment is calculated as the sum of the present value of the annual cash flows minus the initial investment. To have an accurate financial and risk situation, it is important to analyze the financial investments according to their current market value. NPV analysis is one of the most robust financial risk management analysis methods used to manage the risks of investments. It is possible to store the calculated NPVs to meet with the requirements of international accounting standards such as FASB Statement No. 133 and IAS 39. Figure 8.22 shows an example output of an NPV Analysis report where you can see the NPV values of transactions and the selection parameters. Let's first look at the important selection parameters that affect NPV analysis:

- **Evaluation type**
  The evaluation type determines the market and valuation parameters of risk management evaluation reports.

- **Evaluation date**
  Market risk analysis reports select the transaction data and market data according to the evaluation date.

- **Horizon of evaluation**
  In SAP ERP, you can calculate NPVs at the current date or a future date. The horizon of evaluation identifies the date on which the NPVs are calculated. You can either select the horizon date as the evaluation date or after the evaluation date.

- **Scenario**
  The scenario determines the market data (e.g., exchange rates, exchange rate volatilities, security prices, etc.) that are used in the report. You can either maintain the scenario with the current market data or probable market situation data.

- **Market data shift rule**
  The market data shift rule determines the shifts in risk management, related to one or more risk factors that determine market prices.

As illustrated in the report output, we executed the report output for portfolio hierarchy 200 on the same evaluation and horizon of evaluation date (01/10/2007), with the current market data scenario without any market data shifts. This means that all future cash flows are calculated based on 01/10/2007 using the current market data. By navigating the characteristics of the portfolio hierarchy on the result area, you can display the NPV values per company, currency, contract type, and transaction. In our example, we navigated to **Cont.type 2** in **Currency EUR**. From the report output, you can reach the market data by selecting calculation bases, as shown in Figure 8.23.

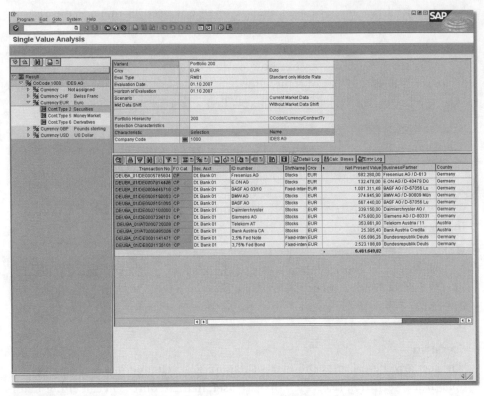

Figure 8.22 NPV Analysis Report Output

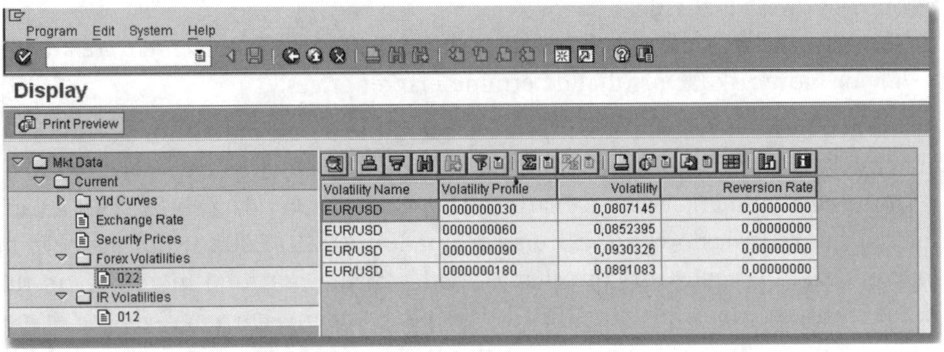

Figure 8.23 Market Data

Sensitivity Key Figures Report

The Sensitivity Key Figures (Transaction AISS) report calculates different key figures based on NPVs to measure the sensitivity of selected portfolio hierarchies or portfolios. With this report, you can analyze the sensitivity key figures macaulay duration, fisher-weil duration, convexity, and basis point sensitivity. These key figures are referred to as interest rate risk figures and are typically used in the sensitivity analysis of securities. Figure 8.24 illustrates an example of the Sensitivity Key Figures report output.

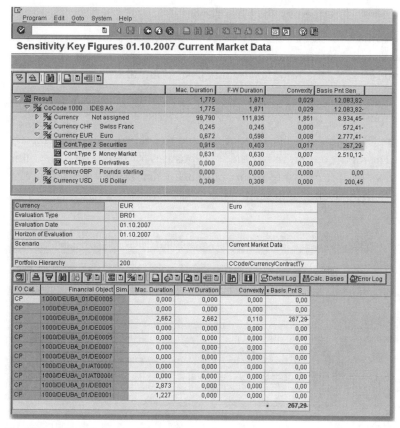

Figure 8.24 Sensitivity Key Figures Report Output

The sensitivity key figures are calculated based on NPVs:

▶ **Macaulay duration**

Macaulay duration is a sensitivity key figure calculated as a weighting based on the present value of each cash flow of the investment divided by the price. Macaulay duration can be interpreted as the average commitment period in years of the invested capital.

▶ **Fisher-Weil duration**

Fisher-Weil duration describes the elasticity of the NPV to interest rate changes.

▶ **Convexity**

The convexity is the key figure that describes the sensitivity of NPV to the changes in the interest rate described by the price curve.

▶ **Basis point value**

The basis point value corresponds to the change in market value for an increase in market interest rates for all terms, by one basis point (0.01%).

FX Exposure Report

The FX Exposure (Transaction AISFSS) report is used to analyze and hedge foreign currency risks. The report output shows the FX exposures for selected transactions. Figure 8.25 shows the FX exposure report output for derivative transaction that we used in the hedging example in section 8.2.3.

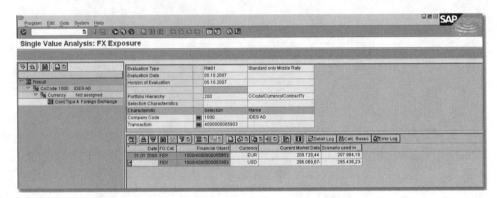

Figure 8.25 FX Exposure Report Output

ALM Single Value Analysis Report

The ALM Single Value Analysis (Transaction JBRTOBJ_CFM) report is used to analyze position and maturity volumes, cash flows, and liquidities for selected key dates or periods. With this report, you can analyze gap positions, interest rate risk, currency risk, and liquidity risk. Figure 8.26 shows an example of the currency liquidity analysis of this report, where you can have a clear overview of currency liquidity. The currency liquidity is listed separately for each currency along in-payments, disbursement, liquidity gap, and accumulated liquidity gap on maturity band dates.

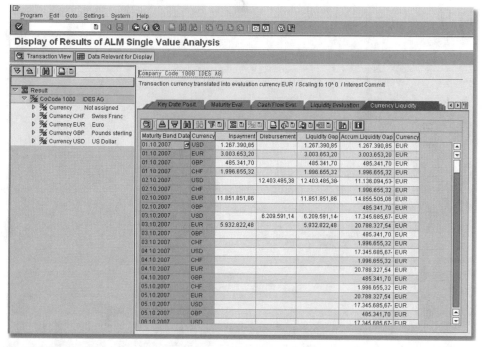

Figure 8.26 ALM Single Value Analysis Report Output

Value-at-Risk Analysis

The Value-at-Risk Analysis (Transaction RMV0) report shows the probable losses, which are reflected as the net value in the report output before the position is hedged or liquidated. The report is based on the value-at-risk figures. Figure 8.27 shows an example of the Value-at-Risk Analysis report output.

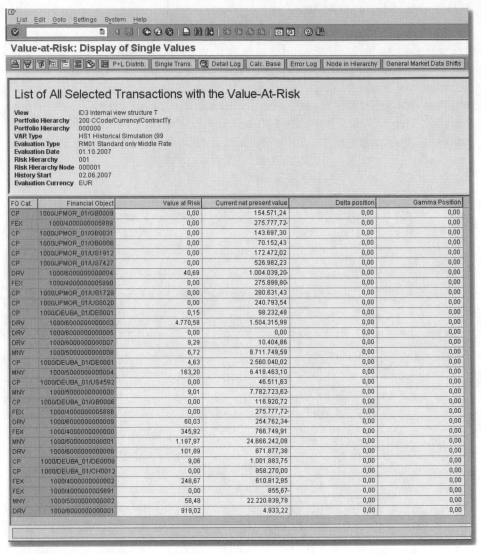

Figure 8.27 Value-at-Risk Analysis Report Output

8.5 Treasury and Risk Management Reporting in SAP NetWeaver BI

As mentioned earlier, TRM is an application of the FSCM application in SAP ERP. In SAP NetWeaver BI content, FSCM objects are grouped under Corporate Finance

Management (CFM). CFM's name comes from the history of the TRM application. The CFM application was first introduced as an add-on for SAP R/3. The main objective of CFM was to manage financial resources and analyze and optimize financial business processes. Applications such as Transaction Manager and Cash Management were originally part of the SAP CFM application. As of SAP ERP 2004, CFM is no longer used as a name for SAP ERP's treasury functions. TRM and other applications of the SAP CFM are now applications of FSCM. However, SAP NetWeaver BI content objects for TRM still keep the CFM name and are located under financial services in SAP NetWeaver BI. The business content InfoProviders for TRM are categorized into two areas: Transaction Manager and Analyzer. In the following pages, we examine the business content and reporting aspects of each area.

8.5.1 Transaction Manager Reporting in SAP NetWeaver BI

Transaction and position management flow and data model in SAP Netweaver BI are illustrated in Figure 8.28. Note that not all of the key figures are shown in the data model due to the large number. Let's have a closer look at the data flow of the Positions & Market MultiProvider (0CFM_MC2).

The data is supplied from two InfoCubes: Positions According to Position Value Date (0CFM_C10) and Market Data (0CFM_C11).

- **Positions According to Position Value Date**
  This InfoCube contains the key figures of positions. The key figures are updated with the local currency, position currency, and valuation currency. The InfoCube is supplied with data from the Changes to Position Delta DSO (0CFM_O01) and the CFM Positions Initialization Only InfoSource (0CFM_POSITIONS). The DSO is used to manage the large amount of data extracted from source systems. It has its own initialization DataSource.

- **Market Data**
  This InfoCube contains the key figures for NPVs, market values, effective interest rates, nominal values of swap, and FX transactions that are extracted from the connected source systems. The key figures are updated with local currency, position currency, and valuation currency. In addition, nominal currency is updated for swap transactions.

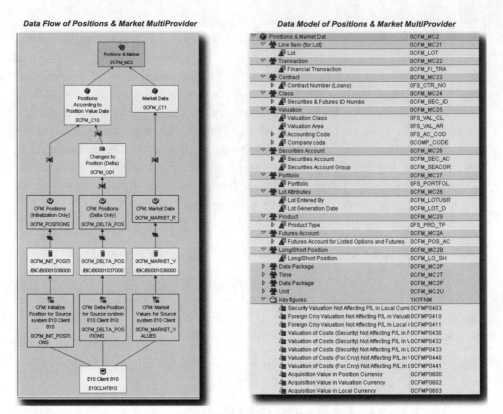

Figure 8.28 Data Flow and Data Model of Positions & Market MultiProvider

No business content queries are delivered for TRM-TM in SAP NetWeaver BI, as such, that you can use as a reference. You can build your queries based on the Positions According to Position Value Date InfoCube, the Market Data InfoCube, or the Positions & Market MultiProvider.

These InfoProviders can be used to analyze and run evaluations for differentiation characteristics, as well as characteristics such as class, product type, update type, business transaction category, securities and future transactions ID number, lot, and their attributes. Refer to Figure 8.29 for the characteristics that are delivered in the data model of the Positions According to Position Value Date InfoCube and the Market Data InfoCube. Note that not all of the key figures are shown in the data model of these InfoCubes due to the large number.

Figure 8.29 Data Models of Positions According to Value Date and Market Data InfoCubes

8.5.2 Market Risk Analysis in SAP NetWeaver BI

SAP NetWeaver business content provides six InfoCubes and one MultiProvider for the analyzer area (see Figure 8.1). Let's have a closer look at the Portfolio Hierarchy View MultiProvider (0CFM_MC1), which consists of three InfoCubes: Ratios Calculated from Evaluation (0CFM_C01), Amounts in Evaluation Currency (0CFM_C03), and Risks in Evaluation Currency (0CFM_C05). These InfoCubes contain data for risk management analysis. You can carry out evaluations based on the portfolio hierarchy and risk hierarchy with the queries based on these Info-Providers. Refer to Figure 8.30 for the data flow and data model of the Portfolio Hierarchy View MultiProvider.

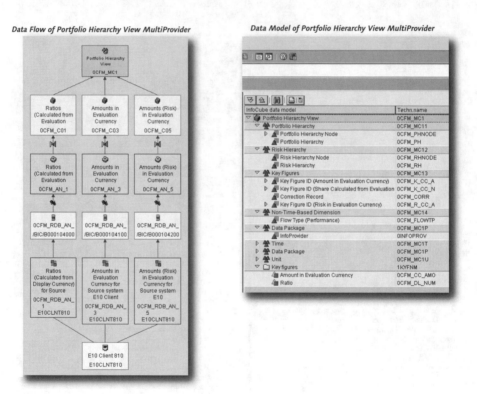

Figure 8.30 Data Flow and Data Model of the Portfolio Hierarchy MultiProvider

SAP NetWeaver BI Queries for Market Risk Analyzer

In the business content, reference queries based on the market risk analyzer InfoProviders are delivered (see Figure 8.31). With these queries, you can evaluate financial positions for selected portfolio hierarchies and risk hierarchies.

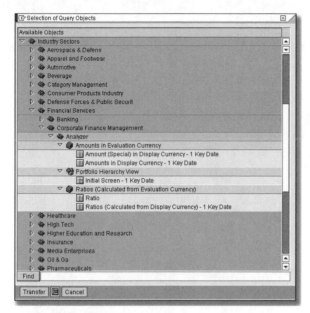

Figure 8.31 SAP NetWeaver BI Queries

8.6 Summary

With new accounting regulations, the shifting economic environment, and market globalization, organizations must find ways of managing risk effectively and ensure that their treasury and risk management reporting complies with SOX, other regulations, and accounting standards and rules. SAP ERP provides TRM application within SAP FSCM to manage treasury and risk management and reporting process. In this chapter, we first focused on the design considerations and work-in best practices for treasury and risk management and reporting process. Then we explained the key SAP ERP reports. Finally, we explained the SAP NetWeaver BI business content for treasury and risk management reporting along with data flow and modeling examples.

Consistent management accounting reporting enables organizations to more effectively plan, analyze, and manage their business and make informed decisions. In this chapter, we explain the foundations of management accounting, focusing particularly on overhead cost management reporting architecture and design considerations. In addition, we examine the key overhead cost management reports in SAP ERP and SAP NetWeaver BI. The subsequent chapter covers the product cost controlling and profitability analysis part of management accounting reporting.

9 Management Accounting Reporting

Management accounting reporting is the process of monitoring, controlling, and analyzing costs through operational and financial information. Management accounting reports are compiled for internal stakeholders and hold a wide variety of performance and profitability information. This information is collected and presented to help and support business decision-making. Management accounting reporting helps answer questions such as "How is the business performing compared to planned targets?" "How are the organization's strategies met?" "What else can be done to achieve operational and strategic targets?"

Management accounting reporting takes a different approach to viewing the financial reporting information compared to financial reporting. Management accounting reports, which are analyzed by internal stakeholders, are comprehensive information views of the enterprise's situation, typically representing different time slices, for example, weekly, monthly, month-to-date, and year-to-date. Financial reports are compiled for external stakeholders and must comply in accordance with statutory and accounting standards regulations. Note that we covered financial statements and statutory reporting in Chapter 2.

The management accounting reporting is performed in the *Controlling (CO)* component of SAP ERP. The CO component provides an organization with the information required for controlling, monitoring, and analyzing costs and value flows within the organization and consists of three subcomponents:

- ▸ Overhead Cost Controlling (CO-OM)

- ▸ Product Cost Controlling (CO-PC)

- ▸ Profitability Analysis (CO-PA)

The CO-OM component enables an organization to plan, allocate, monitor, and control overhead costs. The information provided by CO-OM forms a building block for calculating the cost of products in CO-PC and carrying out profitability analysis in CO-PA. This chapter focuses exclusively on management reporting foundations and overhead cost controlling reporting with CO-OM. Chapter 10 covers management reporting with CO-PC and CO-PA.

9.1 Overhead Cost Controlling Reporting Architecture

There are two types of costs: direct costs and indirect costs. Direct costs are the costs that can be directly traced and allocated to projects, products, or services. Indirect costs, also referred to as *overhead costs*, are the costs that are incurred to support and administer an enterprise's activities. The *CO-OM component* provides the foundation to control, monitor, and analyze overhead costs, such as expenses that are not directly associated to a particular part of the work or product.

The CO-OM component is further classified into four subcomponents. Let's have a closer look at each of them.

- ▸ **Cost Element Accounting (CO-OM-CEL)**
  Cost element accounting enables you to control costs and revenues that are incurred within the organization. This component is the interface between financial accounting (FI) and management accounting (CO), and ensures that FI and CO are reconciled.

- ▸ **Cost Center Accounting (CO-OM-CCA)**
  Cost center accounting enables the controlling and monitoring of costs in cost centers. A cost center represents the source assignment of the costs. In other words, it represents where the costs were incurred. Cost centers are used to collect costs to facilitate planning, reporting, and decision-making.

- ▸ **Internal Orders (CO-OM-OPA)**
  Internal orders are used to plan, collect, and settle the costs of internal jobs requests, tasks, and assignments.

▶ **Activity-Based Costing (CO-OM-ABC)**

Activity-based costing enables the analysis and control of the cost of cross-departmental business processes. Activity-based costing has complementary functions enhancing traditional cost center accounting. Compared to CO-OM-CCA, activity-based costing provides a cross-functional view of the overheads, whereas cost center accounting provides a cost view of the locations and departments.

Now that we have explained the subcomponents of CO-OM, let's look at how they are integrated with other SAP ERP components and SAP NetWeaver BI. Figure 9.1 illustrates the schematic view of CO-OM data flow and reporting architecture. Overhead costs can be captured and recorded in source components such as MM, SD, HR, and FI, as well as via interfaces. All the postings are first updated in FI, and then via CO-OM-CEL, flowing simultaneously to other subcomponents of CO-OM. The main purpose of CO-OM-CEL is to record and classify the data that forms the basis for cost accounting. In addition to the flow of costs from source components and external interfaces, there is also cost value flow between subcomponents of CO-OM, such as the settlement of costs from internal orders to cost centers. As illustrated in the SAP ERP Overhead Cost Controlling box in Figure 9.1, the Project System (PS) component can also be used for overhead cost management. With the PS component, you can plan, control, and analyze overhead costs.

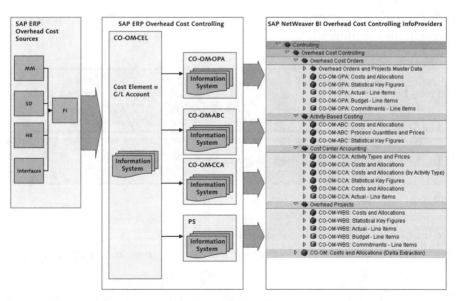

Figure 9.1 CO-OM Data Flow and Reporting Architecture

Each CO-OM subcomponent and PS has its own information system that includes analytical reports. With the business content, SAP NetWeaver BI provides Info-Providers for overhead cost orders, activity-based costing, cost center accounting, and overhead projects. The business content includes many queries based on these InfoProviders.

Now that we have explained CO-OM data flow and reporting architecture, let's look at the overhead cost management process.

9.2 Overhead Cost Management Process

Overhead cost management starts with the *master data maintenance* process. Master data maintenance includes tasks for creating, changing, deleting, and monitoring the changes to overhead cost management master data. *Planning* is the process of planning and forecasting for future business operations. It provides a baseline measurement against actual results. Planning is managed with versions that can be used for different planning scenarios. *Actual posting* is the process of capturing and recording actual costs and revenue. Transactions such as the allocation and settlement of costs are carried out for the further classification of data in overhead cost controlling during the *period end closing* process. Reporting and analysis is a fundamental process in the end-to-end overhead cost management process (see Figure 9.2). With this process you report, monitor, and analyze overhead cost management information.

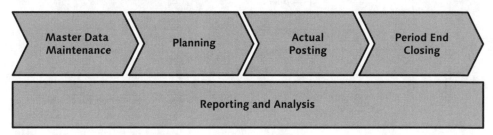

Figure 9.2 Overhead Cost Management Process

To have an effective overhead cost management process, it is important to standardize associated processes and establish robust reporting architecture. In this section, we discuss design considerations and best practices that help organizations achieve these goals. We specifically cover the following areas:

▶ Management accounting organizational structure

▶ Master data management for overhead cost controlling

▶ Real-time integration from CO to FI

▶ Integrated planning

9.2.1 Management Accounting Organizational Structure

Management accounting in SAP ERP is founded on an organizational unit called *controlling area*. Company code organization objects of FI have to be assigned to controlling areas to establish connection between FI and CO organizational structures. All account assignment objects that are accounted for in management accounting are assigned to controlling areas. Perhaps the most important design consideration is whether to establish management reporting with one controlling area or multiple controlling areas. The decision about controlling area design depends largely on the organization's management structure and management reporting requirements.

In a single controlling area model, all company codes are assigned to one controlling area, which allows the use of cross-company code overhead cost accounting, enterprise-wide. In other words, you can carry out planning, allocations, and reporting across the organization. The prerequisites for a single controlling area are as follows:

▶ Single operational chart of accounts used in all company codes

▶ Same fiscal year variant in all company codes

Multiple controlling areas are required if the management accounting approach and procedures are highly diverse and independent within the enterprise. If you model your management accounting with multiple controlling areas, you cannot carry out cross-controlling area cost allocations, planning, and reporting.

You can model management accounting reporting architecture on either a single controlling area or multiple controlling areas. Both approaches should be evaluated based on your organization's management structure and management accounting reporting requirements. Our experience shows that leading organizations implemented a single controlling area to harmonize and standardize management reporting enterprise-wide.

> **Operating concern**
>
> An operating concern is another management accounting organizational unit, which is set up above controlling areas and defined in CO-PA. We explain the operating concern structure in Chapter 10.

9.2.2 Master Data Management for Overhead Cost Controlling

Master data elements and structures determine how data is presented in the output of management reports. Accurate and effective management accounting reporting cannot be realized and sustained without reliable master data elements and structures. To improve information consistency and reliability, you must standardize the master data elements and structures and ensure that master data records are correctly recorded in SAP ERP and SAP NetWeaver BI. Key benefits of standardizing are:

- More efficient data capture and information flow
- Common structures across the organization
- Easier cost analysis enterprise-wide
- Process improvements to reduce transaction processing costs
- Improve staff productivity—focus effort on business decision support and analysis

Overhead Cost Management Master Data in SAP ERP

The overhead cost management master data elements and their structures in SAP ERP are illustrated in Figure 9.3. Each master data used for overhead cost management has its individual coding structure, groups, and hierarchies. It is important to have a well-defined master data management process and to standardize the master data coding structure, groupings, and hierarchies for accurate and effective reporting.

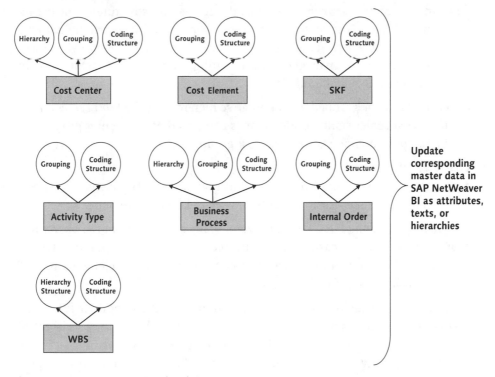

Figure 9.3 Master Data in Overhead Cost Management

Each master data has a description, unique identifier or coding structure that represents the master data record in SAP ERP. Overhead cost management master data elements, except WBS elements, have master data groups, which are used in cost processing transactions, planning, customizing, and reporting. Cost centers and business processes have special groups called hierarchies. WBS elements are created with hierarchical structures. Let's examine each master data element in detail:

▶ **Cost center**
A cost center is an object used to collect costs in order to facilitate cost planning, reporting, and decision-making. A cost center represents the source assignment of the cost. In other words, it represents the location where the cost was incurred.

Standard cost center hierarchy represents the cost center structure of the organization in SAP ERP. Cost centers have to be assigned to the hierarchy nodes of the standard cost center hierarchy. A harmonized standard hierarchy enables a common platform for management accounting reporting and facilitates comparison across individual units.

Cost centers can be grouped into alternative hierarchies called *cost center groups*. In fact, a cost center standard hierarchy is composed of cost center groups, and the hierarchy's top node is a special cost group itself.

▶ **Cost element**
A cost element corresponds to the classification of costs. There are two types of cost elements: primary cost elements and secondary cost elements.

A primary cost element is a cost- or revenue-relevant account in the operational chart of accounts. For each primary cost element, one corresponding G/L account exists in the operational chart of accounts. Primary cost elements and G/L accounts have the same coding structure.

Secondary cost elements are used only within the CO component for certain cost controlling transactions such as internal activity allocation, overhead calculation, and internal settlement. Secondary cost elements have unique coding structures that have to be different from any G/L account code in the operational chart of accounts.

Cost elements can be grouped into *cost element groups*.

▶ **Activity type**
Activity types are used to represent activities produced and consumed within the business. With the activity allocation functionality costs can be allocated to receivers based on activity quantity consumptions. Activity types can be grouped into *activity type groups*.

▶ **Statistical key figure**
Statistical key figures (SKFs) are figures that provide measurement or statistics related to the cost objects (e.g., cost center, internal order, business process, etc.) to which they belong. SKFs can be grouped into *statistical key figure groups*.

▶ **Business process**
A business process is a cross-functional object that consumes resources from multiple cost objects within the organization. Business processes operate across

cost center boundaries. In other words, multiple cost centers can execute the same business process.

Business processes have to be assigned to a *standard hierarchy* that represents a business process structure of the organization. In addition to the standard hierarchy, business processes can be grouped into *business process groups*.

► **Internal order**
Internal orders are flexible cost objects that are used to record costs and revenues. They are classified by order type and can be used for different purposes. Overhead orders, investment orders, and revenue orders are examples of order types. Overhead cost orders are used for monitoring and recording of overhead costs. Investment orders are used for monitoring and recording investment costs that are capitalized and settled to fixed assets. Revenue orders are used to record revenue and costs for specific tasks or customer orders. Internal orders can be grouped into *internal order groups*.

► **Overhead WBS element**
A work breakdown structure (WBS) is a model of the work to be performed in a project organized in a hierarchical structure within the PS component. The individual elements within the WBS represent activities, called WBS elements. From a management accounting perspective, the WBS element is a cost object that is used for monitoring and recording costs and revenues. WBS elements and *WBS hierarchy structures* are created within the same transaction.

Each WBS element has a unique identifier or coding structure that offers great flexibility when naming the WBS elements.

Compared to internal orders, WBS elements offer much greater functionality and flexibility for designing, modeling and reporting enterprise processes. Thus, we recommend that you use WBS elements instead of internal orders.

Overhead Cost Management Master Data in SAP NetWeaver BI

Now that we have explained the overhead cost management master data in SAP ERP, let's look at how they are defined in SAP NetWeaver BI. There are three types of master data for an InfoObject in SAP NetWeaver BI: attributes, master data text, and hierarchy. Attributes are characteristics of an InfoObject and are classified into two groups: display attributes (DIS) and navigation attributes (NAV). If you define an attribute as a display attribute, you can only use this attribute as additional information in SAP NetWeaver BI reporting. If you define an attribute as a navigation attribute, you can use this attribute to navigate in reporting. Figure 9.4 shows the master data of cost center CC2 in SAP ERP and SAP NetWeaver BI, along with the attribute master data type of the cost center InfoObject (0COSTCENTER). For example, the profit center is a navigation attribute and the business area is a display attribute.

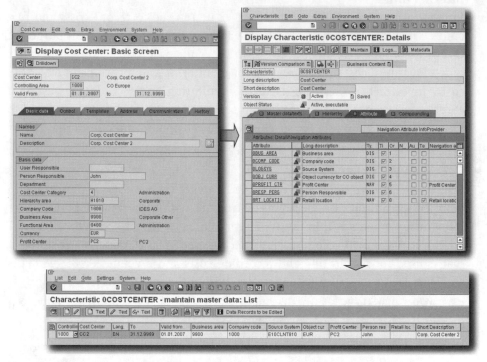

Figure 9.4 Cost Center Master Data in SAP ERP and SAP NetWeaver BI along with Attribute Master Data Type of Cost Center InfoObject

When master data is loaded from SAP ERP or other source systems to SAP NetWeaver BI, the data is passed via the *transformation* process. With the transformation process you can consolidate, cleanse, and integrate data. Figure 9.5 shows the transformation for the cost center InfoObject (0COSTCENTER). Refer to the figure for the assignment of DataSource 0COSTCENTER_ATTR to the target InfoObject 0COSTCENTER. DataSource fields are assigned to the target InfoObjects via rules. For example, the source field for the CO Area (KOKRS) is assigned to the Controlling area (0CO_AREA) InfoObject in SAP NetWeaver BI by a rule-type direct assignment. If the source fields are not assigned to the target InfoObjects, they are not updated, and no transformation takes place.

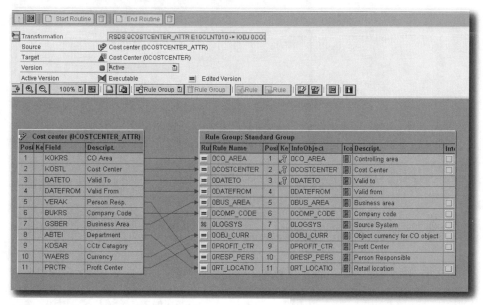

Figure 9.5 Transformation for the Cost Center InfoObject

Master data groups and hierarchies in SAP ERP are loaded as *hierarchies* to SAP NetWeaver BI. In other words, master data groups are also called hierarchies in SAP NetWeaver BI. In both SAP ERP and SAP NetWeaver BI, you can navigate within the master groups and hierarchies in reports that are designed to use groups and hierarchies. In addition, you can create subtotals and grand totals at the group or hierarchy level. It is important to ensure that master data groups and hierarchies are consistent across source SAP ERP systems and SAP NetWeaver BI for accurate and consistent reporting. Figure 9.6 illustrates an example of a cost center hierarchy in SAP ERP and SAP NetWeaver BI.

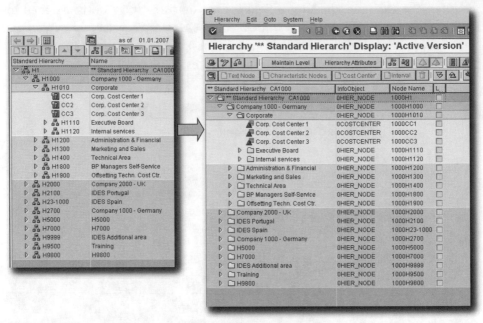

Figure 9.6 Cost Center Hierarchy in SAP ERP and SAP NetWeaver BI

9.2.3 Real-time Integration from CO to FI

Real-time integration from FI to CO has been available since SAP R/2. However, real-time integration from CO to FI is available only in SAP ERP. In the previous releases, when a posting involved cross-company codes or business areas, this information was stored initially in CO and transferred to FI at the period end by reconciliation ledger postings. By enabling real-time integration from CO to FI in the new G/L, you can eliminate the reconciliation ledger postings. By doing so, postings from CO are automatically posted in the G/L at the appropriate level. Real-time CO to FI integration process flow is shown in Figure 9.7.

On the left side of the figure is the CO component where there are various CO cost objects such as cost centers, internal orders, WBS elements, and profitability segments (note that we cover profitability segments in Chapter 10). These cost objects are assigned to other objects such as profit center, company code, business area, and functional area. CO transactions are recorded with primary or secondary cost elements using CO cost objects, for example, periodic CO allocations such as assessment, distribution, and transfer posting. In the previous releases of SAP ERP, if these postings involved cross objects such as cross-company code or cross-business area, they were first updated in CO and transferred back to FI with the reconciliation ledger postings at the period end. With the real-time integration functionality, it is possible to reflect specified CO postings in FI to keep CO and FI reconciled and synchronized.

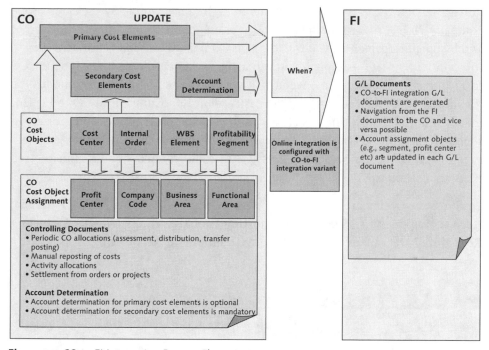

Figure 9.7 CO to FI Integration Process Flow

The accounts used to update the G/L as a result of CO postings are specified in the account determinations, which are classified into primary and secondary. Account determination for primary cost elements is optional, because if it is not set up, the documents in the G/L are updated with the primary cost elements. Account determination for secondary cost elements is mandatory because secondary cost elements do not have corresponding G/L accounts in the operational chart of accounts.

In FI, financial postings are generated simultaneously as a result of CO transactions. You can navigate from FI documents to the CO documents and vice versa. In the financial postings, account assignment objects (e.g., segment, profit center, etc.) are updated.

The real-time integration is controlled with the CO to FI integration variant. An example of the configuration settings of a CO to FI integration variant is illustrated in Figure 9.8. In the variant, you select document lines for real-time integration. This can be done by using checkboxes, defining BAdIs, or rules. By selecting **Update All CO LIs FI**, you can update all CO line items in FI, but this may create an undesirably large number of documents in FI. In our example, we selected cross-company code, cross-profit center, and cross-segment in the integration variant and assigned document type CO. Note that CO document type is not delivered in the standard system. Although you can assign a standard document type for CO to FI integration documents, we advise you to create a specific document type for these transactions so that you can easily identify postings from CO to FI. This means that if a CO posting is a cross-company code, cross-profit center, or cross-segment, then the posting will be simultaneously updated in FI with the document type CO. The integration variant is assigned to the company codes after the settings are completed.

To access the CO integration variant, follow the configuration menu path **Financial Accounting (New) • Financial Accounting Global Settings (New) • Ledgers • Real-time Integration of Controlling with Financial Accounting**.

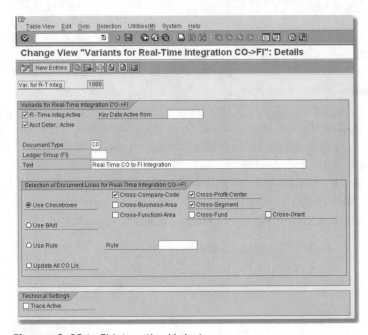

Figure 9.8 CO to FI Integration Variant

CO to FI reconciliation ledger postings
After activating the new G/L, if you try to execute the CO to FI reconciliation posting transaction (Transaction KALC), an error message will appear ("new general ledger is active. See long text"), and you have to exit the transaction. The reason for this error message is that you need to consider using the real-time CO to FI integration functionality of the new G/L. You can still perform reconciliation ledger postings with Transaction KALC by deactivating this error message. However, reconciliation ledger postings do not update the profit center and segment details in FI, so the profit center and segment dimension cannot be reconciled if KALC is used. In addition, misstatement occurs if segmented financial statements are generated from the G/L. Thus, we recommend activating real-time integration instead of reconciliation ledger postings.

9.2.4 Integrated Planning

The SAP ERP integrated planning and forecasting process is an end-to-end cycle involving multiple components and requires cross-functional involvement of an organization's units. At each stage of the planning process, plan data can be adjusted after receiving input from the previous stage. Each SAP ERP planning component has a number of functionalities that automate the planning process, such as copying plan values, revaluing plan values, and top-down distribution. The integrated planning process cycle is illustrated in Figure 9.9.

The integrated planning and forecasting process starts with *sales planning*. Sales planning is the planning step in which sales volumes are planned. Sales planning can be performed both in the Sales Information System (SIS) and CO-PA. SIS and CO-PA are integrated, and plan volume data can be transferred between these two components. Sales volumes are valuated with future sales prices, and planned revenue is generated.

After sales volumes are planned, plan volumes are transferred to *production planning*. In the production planning sales and operation planning component (PP-SOP), detailed production resource planning is performed, and scheduled activity information is transferred to CO-OM-CCA and CO-OM-ABC.

In these two components, plan activity quantities are created according to the scheduled activity information received from production planning. Production *cost planning* is performed on cost centers and business processes. Additional plan overhead costs can be transferred from Asset Accounting (AA) and Human Capital Management (HCM) components. Manual planning functions can be performed at this stage. Then plan activity prices are calculated and transferred to product cost planning. Plan costs that are not related to products can be transferred to CO-PA for profitability planning via plan assessment process.

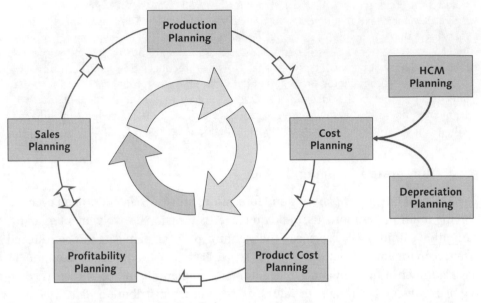

Figure 9.9 Integrated Planning Process Cycle

Plan activity prices are used in *product cost planning* for the product cost estimate with the use of bills of material and routings (quantity structures) and to generate product cost plans and estimates. Finally, product cost estimates are transferred to profitability planning to be valuated with sales volumes and to generate the planned cost of goods sold to complete the *profitability planning*. This completes the integrated planning process cycle, which can be executed as many times as needed until the planning process generates the desired results.

Planning is always carried out within a plan version. Once the plan results are approved, the corresponding version should be blocked for changes. In the planning process, you can use different versions with different planned values. Versions have certain settings that are relevant for each controlling area and fiscal year. Figure 9.10 shows an example of the settings of the version for each fiscal year. In the fiscal year definition, planning-specific parameters are set, such as whether copying the version is allowed, if planned data for the version is locked (cannot be changed), or whether the version is available for integrated planning. Further planning parameters are also specified in the version settings. For example, you can determine the receiver version for sales planning data or specify the exchange rate type.

Version 0 is created automatically when a controlling area is created. All actual values are updated in version 0. Thus, version 0 is used for plan and actual value comparisons.

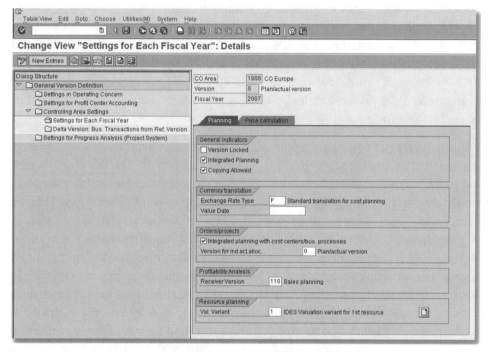

Figure 9.10 Version Settings in Configuration

9.3 Overhead Cost Management with the New G/L

As we explained in Chapter 3, *scenario* is a new term introduced with SAP ERP's new G/L. It identifies the fields updated in the G/L during financial postings. For example, if you want to update the cost center in the G/L, you should assign the cost center update scenario (FIN_CCA) to ledgers. SAP ERP provides six scenarios:

▶ Segmentation (FIN_SEGM)

▶ Cost Center Update (FIN_CCA)

▶ Preparation for Consolidation (FIN_CONS)

▶ Business Area (FIN_GSBER)

▶ Profit Center Update (FIN_PCA)

▶ Cost of Sales Accounting (FIN_UK)

There is no universal rule for scenario assignments to the new G/L. You can assign more than one scenario (even all six standard scenarios) to the ledgers. In addition to scenarios, customer fields can be assigned to ledgers. We advise that you only activate the scenarios needed so that you can avoid unnecessary data volume and poor performance. Customer fields added to the G/L can also increase the data volume and cause poor performance. Other complexities exist with the use of customer fields. For example, business content data sources for extracting data from SAP ERP to SAP NetWeaver BI should be appended.

From an overhead cost management reporting perspective, the decision to assign the cost center update scenario plays an important role in data flow and modeling in SAP NetWeaver BI. Let's take a closer look at the design considerations for cost center scenario assignment to ledgers in the new G/L. With the new G/L you can produce cost center reports in FI. This design decision should be carefully validated, and you need to ensure that all business requirements are met. Refer to Figure 9.11 for a comprehensive visual look at design solutions for cost center accounting reporting design options: cost center reporting in the new G/L (design A) and cost center reporting in CO (design B). The two solutions vary in the level of customization involved, the requirements met, and the preferred capabilities delivered. If you are planning to use cost center accounting for only simple cost center transaction processing, where you define your cost center structure (perhaps running basic cost allocations) and do not require advance cost transaction processes such as product costing, activity cost allocation, and so on, design A would serve cost center reporting where you assign the cost center update scenario to the new G/L, carry out cost center allocations, and generate your cost center accounting reports from the new G/L. In this model, you use the new G/L as a source for cost center reporting in SAP NetWeaver BI. This approach has potential benefits for companies with simple cost center accounting requirements. However, you need to take the following considerations into account:

▶ Potential reconciliation problems between CO and FI if the system generates reconciliation objects in financial postings, as reconciliation objects are not updated in the new G/L. Reconciliation objects are objects that receive postings automatically from the system to keep FI and CO reconciled, for example, when posting revenue without specifying revenue-bearing objects including WBS elements, internal orders, and profitability segments.

▶ CO-OM-CCA information system reports are not delivered within the new G/L. Instead, SAP ERP has delivered a library called the new G/L (0F), from which you can create cost center reports in Report Painter or Report Writer.

▶ If you only activate the Cost Center Update (FIN_CCA) scenario in the new G/L, cost objects such as internal orders, WBS elements, activity types, and business processes will not be updated in the new G/L.

If you have more advanced management reporting requirements, we advise you to carry out cost allocations and other controlling activities as well as generating reports in CO-OM, as diagrammatically illustrated with design B in Figure 9.11. Design B does not require the cost center update scenario to be updated in the new G/L. The advantage of applying design B is that you can use full CO capabilities in CO-OM, as well as the CO-OM-CCA information system, which provides many analytical reports for cost accounting. SAP NetWeaver BI also provides many analytical reports for cost accounting based on CO-OM-CCA InfoProviders, which can be used as a reference when modeling your cost center reporting in SAP NetWeaver BI. In both designs, cost center master data management is carried out in CO.

In addition to these designs, you can have a design where both G/L and cost center accounting tables are updated with cost center information. With this design, there will be data redundancy because cost accounting data will reside in both the G/L and cost center accounting tables. In this case, to avoid any reconciliation difference, integration variants should be set in such a way that the CCA and G/L are reconciled on the document level. Configuring the integration variant for this purpose creates additional data redundancy, so we advise you to carefully check the design options.

What about the other overhead cost management objects, including internal orders, WBS elements, and business processes? There is no standard scenario that can be used to update them in the new G/L. If there is a requirement to update them in the new G/L, you should create them as customer objects in the coding block and assign them to ledgers directly. Note, however, that standard data sources for extracting data from SAP ERP to SAP NetWeaver BI do not contain customer objects, so you need to enhance them to get data to SAP NetWeaver BI from source systems. In addition, reports under the information system of CO-

OM-OPA, PS and CO-OM-ABC are not delivered in the new G/L. You need to create them by using the Report Painter or Report Writer tools. As mentioned earlier, additional fields increase data volume and can lead to poor performance. Thus, we recommend that you use design B so that you can leverage all the functionalities delivered in SAP ERP and SAP NetWeaver BI.

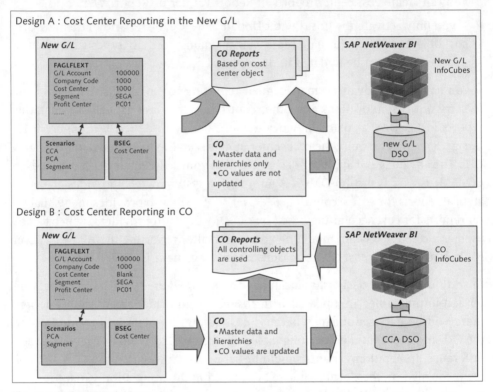

Figure 9.11 Cost Center Reporting

Segmentation and cost of sales accounting scenarios

If you activate the cost of sales accounting or assign the segmentation scenario to ledgers in the new G/L, the functional area and segment field will not be updated in some CO postings, resulting in miscalculations in overhead cost calculation or price determination. This would lead to inaccurate product costing and profitability reports. To avoid such a situation, you need to apply SAP Note 1024480.

9.4 Overhead Cost Controlling Reporting in SAP ERP

The CO-OM information system includes many analytical reports for overhead cost controlling. These reports can also help generate key performance indicators (KPIs) in relation to overhead cost management. In this section, we explain the key reports from each subcomponent of CO-OM.

9.4.1 Cost Element Accounting Reports

The cost element accounting reports are available under the CO-OM-CEL information system folder in SAP ERP. The CO-OM-CEL information system provides analysis for all other CO-OM subcomponents, as it acts as an interface between FI and CO. To reach the CO-OM-CEL information system folder, follow the menu path **Accounting • Controlling • Cost Element Accounting • Information System**.

As shown in Figure 9.12, cost and revenue element accounting reports are listed in two nodes: cost and revenue reports for the classic general ledger, and cost and revenue reports for the new general ledger. Some reports are listed for both, such as the master data indices reports, CO documents actual cost reports, etc. Reports based on the reconciliation ledger are only relevant to the classic general ledger. The cost and revenue reports for the classic general ledger enable you to display the values of the accounts in the general ledger and the values of cost elements. Thus, you can compare the figures for FI and CO, analyze the costs by object type, and control the costs flows within the organization. If you use the new G/L, the reports that select data from the reconciliation ledger do not display any data. The design considerations for enabling reconciliation from CO to FI have been discussed in the previous section.

In the following pages we examine the Cost Elements Breakdown by Company Code report, which is delivered with the new G/L.

Cost Elements Breakdown by Company Code Report

The Cost Elements Breakdown by Company Code (Transaction S_SL0_21000007) report displays the costs incurred for selected company codes and periods. In the selection screen, you can specify the cost elements on which you want to report. The report output shows the values for the selected period and the total values up to the selected period and takes the subtotals by all cost objects posted. This report can be used to compare FI and CO by company codes, cost objects, and cost elements.

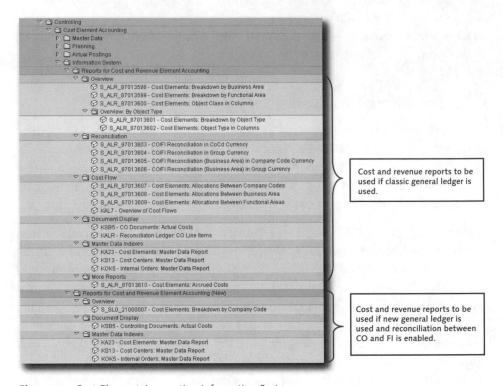

Figure 9.12 Cost Element Accounting Information System

You can navigate through company codes and cost elements in the variation area by selecting a corresponding characteristic value. You can use the **Office Integration** option in the **Application** toolbar to integrate the report output with Excel. An example of the report output in Excel is illustrated in Figure 9.13. In our example, the report output shows subtotals for cost centers, orders, and WBS elements for period 8. This means that all postings from FI during period 8 are only made to these cost objects. Note that postings to reconciliation objects can only be analyzed with this report.

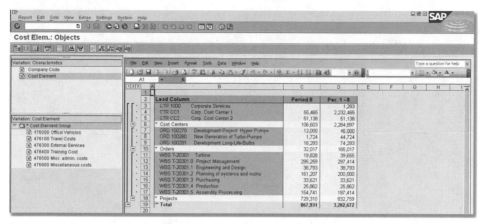

Figure 9.13 Cost Element Breakdown by Company Code Report Output

9.4.2 Cost Center Accounting Reports

The CO-OM-CCA information system provides comprehensive analysis capabilities for controlling the cost flow within the organization. With the reports provided within the CO-OM-CCA information system, you can analyze all costs online and drill down to the line items and original documents.

The cost center accounting reports are available under the CO-OM-CCA information system folder in SAP ERP. To reach the CO-OM-CCA information system folder, follow the menu path **Accounting • Controlling • Cost Center Accounting • Information System** (see Figure 9.14).

Selection parameters allow the filtering of output based on certain conditions in cost center reports. They vary from report to report. The main selection parameters are cost center, cost center group, cost element, cost element group, fiscal year, period from, period to, and version. If you run the report for cost center groups, you can navigate within a group in the report output. All the cost center accounting reports can be executed in the background, which is particularly helpful for a large volume of data.

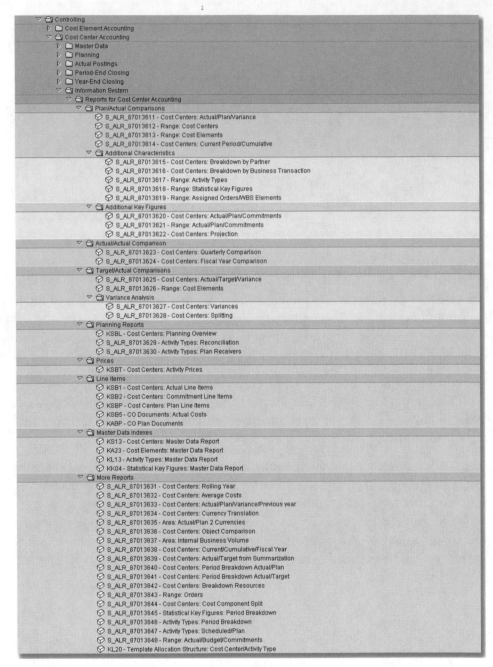

Figure 9.14 Cost Center Accounting Information System

Most CO-OM-CCA reports are designed with the Report Painter and Report Writer tools. You can use these tools to create your own reports or enhance the existing ones. We cover Report Painter and Report Writer tools in Chapter 12.

Some of the key CO-OM-CCA reports are explained below.

Cost Centers: Actual/Plan/Variance Report

The Cost Centers: Actual/Plan/Variance (Transaction S_ALR_87013625) report is used to compare actual and plan costs for selected cost center groups or individual cost centers. The report output shows actual costs, plan costs, absolute variance and percentage of variance per cost element. This report also shows the actual and plan comparison for statistical key figures. An example of report output is illustrated in Figure 9.15. You can navigate within the cost center group by selecting an individual cost center in the variation area. From the report output, you can call up other reports for further analysis. To do so, follow the menu path **Edit • Call Up Report** in the menu bar, as shown in the figure.

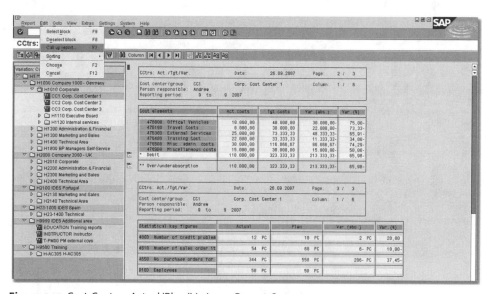

Figure 9.15 Cost Centers Actual/Plan/Variance Report Output

Cost Centers: Actual Line Items Report

The Cost Center Actual Line Items (Transaction KSB1) report is used to analyze the actual line items posted. In the report selection you can select cost centers or cost center groups, cost elements or cost elements groups, and posting date or posting date interval and specify the report output layout. You have more selection criteria if you want to further restrict output per document, organization units, values, quantities, and technical fields. The report is displayed in ALV format and has the standard ALV controls as well as the application-specific controls and standard header. With the control buttons in the application toolbar, you can access master records and underlying documents for any line item. You can call up the master record of the cost element or vendor. By selecting the **Master Record** button and specifying the cost element or vendor in the line items, you can go to the cost element or vendor master record. The report shows details of selected actual line items, for example, posting date, cost element, document type, value in reporting currency, offsetting account type, and offsetting account. Figure 9.16 shows an example of the report output.

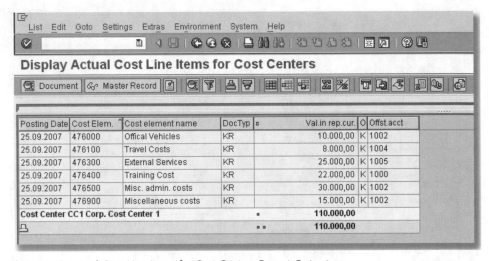

Figure 9.16 Actual Cost Line Items for Cost Centers Report Output

There are other standard ALV functionalities in the application toolbar. You can change the layout or add new fields to the report layout, for example, document number and reference document type. In addition, you can select the line and click on the **Document button** in the application toolbar to go to the original document. The original document of the first line item of the report is shown in Figure 9.17. As you can see in the figure, a vendor (1002) invoice was posted to expense account 476000 Official Vehicles with document type KR on 25/09/2007 in FI and was simultaneously updated in CO.

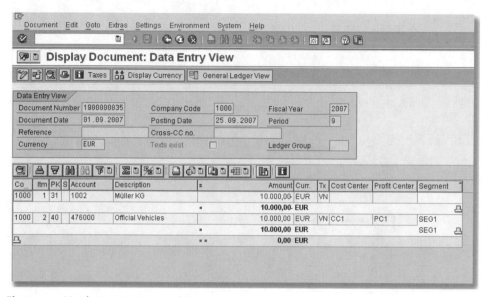

Figure 9.17 Vendor Invoice Financial Posting

If you have the necessary authorization, you can make repostings for the selected line items in the report output. To make a reposting, follow the menu path **Extras • Enter Reposting** in the menu bar.

9.4.3 Internal Order Reports

The internal order accounting reports are available under the CO-OM-OPA information system folder in SAP ERP. To reach the CO-OM-OPA information system folder, follow the menu path **Accounting • Controlling • Internal Orders • Information System** (see Figure 9.18).

The internal order information system enables you to control and analyze internal orders. In the following pages we explain the Orders: Actual/Plan/Commitments report.

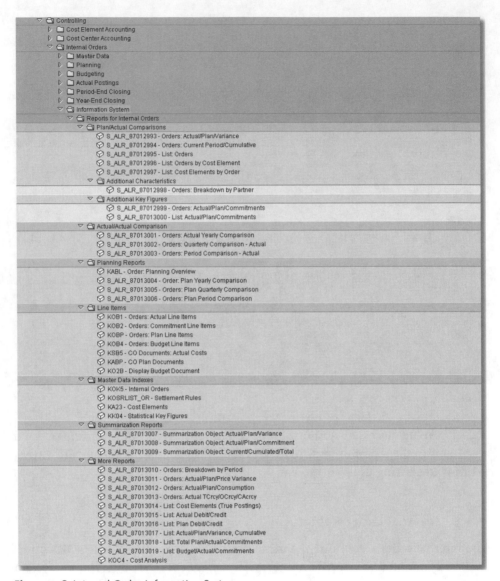

Figure 9.18 Internal Order Information System

Orders: Actual/Plan/Commitments Report

The Orders: Actual/Plan/Commitments (Transaction S_ALR_87012999) report is used to analyze actual costs, plan costs, and commitments for order groups or individual orders in specified period(s), fiscal year and version. An example of report output is illustrated in Figure 9.19. The report output has three sections displayed on pages 2, 3, and 4. Section 1 shows postings of actual costs, plan costs and commitments, and calculation of the available cost. Section 2 shows commitment categories, for example, commitments created by purchase requisition, purchase order, and reserved funds. Section 3 (page 4) shows down payments on the internal orders. It compares the total of actual values and down payments against the plan and calculates absolute variance.

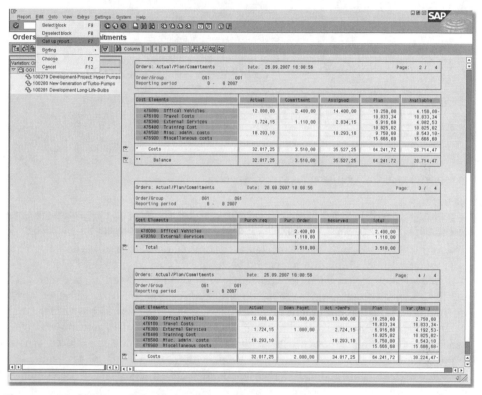

Figure 9.19 Orders: Actual/Plan/Commitments Report Output

From the report output, you can call up other reports for further analysis. To do so, follow the menu path **Edit • Call up report** in the menu bar, as shown in the figure. Figure 9.20 shows the Actual Cost Line Items for Orders (Transaction KOB1) report that we called up from the report output. The Actual Cost Line Item report shows the line items that are created when posting actual costs to internal orders. The Line Item report output shows the document number, cost element, actual cost, offsetting type, offsetting account, and the text from financial postings. The report functionalities are similar to Actual Cost Line Items for Cost Center reports.

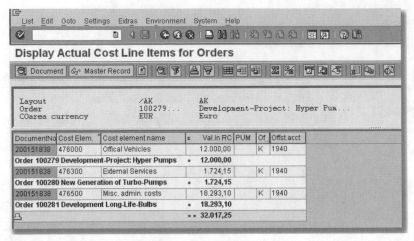

Figure 9.20 Actual Cost Line Items for Orders Report Output

Commitment Management

Commitments are items that are expected to become actual costs and are not reflected in FI when created. Commitments provide valuable information for the expected actual values. They are summed up with actual values and compared against plan values in CO reports. Commitment items are updated for objects such as cost centers, internal orders, and WBS elements. Business transactions such as purchase orders and purchase requests create commitments in CO if commitment management is active. When actual postings are recorded, commitments are reduced. For example, when goods receipts based on purchase orders are generated, the commitments generated by purchase orders are reduced. When goods receipts are completed, the commitments value becomes 0.

Commitment management is activated in the configuration settings of the controlling area. Afterward, they are activated for individual objects. For example, if you want to use commitment management for cost centers and orders, it has to be activated for order types and cost center categories. Commitment management is automatically activated for WBS elements once it is activated in the controlling area. Commitments are reported from the information system of CO-OM-CCA, CO-OM-OPA, and PS components.

9.4.4   Activity-Based Costing Reports

The CO-OM-ABC reports are available under the CO-OM-ABC information system folder in SAP ERP. To reach the CO-OM-ABC information system folder, follow the menu path **Accounting • Controlling • Activity-Based Costing • Information System** (see Figure 9.21).

The CO-OM-ABC reports provide detailed information on costs of business processes. By using these reports, you can carry out a detailed analysis of the usage of business processes, the costs of business processes, and so on.

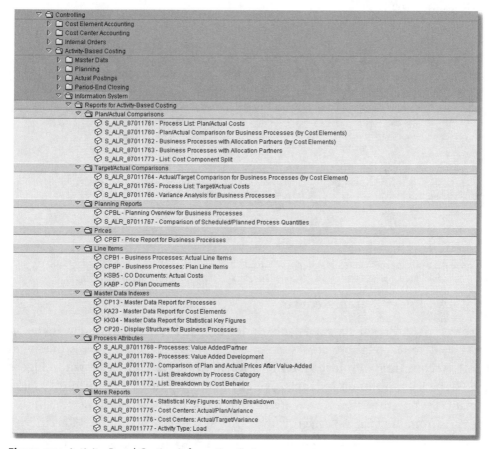

Figure 9.21 Activity-Based Costing Information System

Let's have a look at the Business Process Price List report available in the CO-OM-ABC information system.

Business Process Price Report

The Business Process Price (Transaction CPBT) report shows the unit prices of business processes. With this report, you can analyze the price details of business processes in the controlling area currency. Standard ALV functionalities can be accessed via the application toolbar. You can change the layout or add new fields to the report layout, for example, value type. An example of report output is illustrated in Figure 9.22.

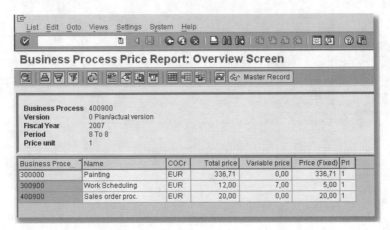

Figure 9.22 Business Process Price Report Output

9.4.5 Project System Reports

Project system reports are available under the PS information system folder in SAP ERP. To reach the project system information system folder, follow the menu path **Accounting • Project System • Information System**. As shown in Figure 9.23, the PS information system is divided into seven categories: structures, claim, financials, progress, resources, material, and tools. In this section, we explain two reports from the financial category: the Costs/Revenues/Expenditures/Receipts report and the Budget/Actual/Variance report.

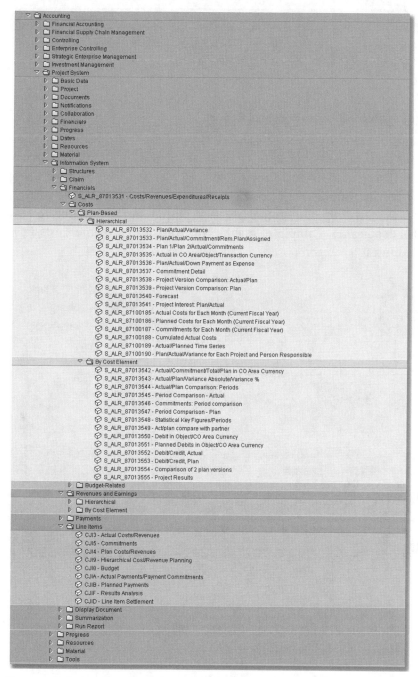

Figure 9.23 Project System Information System

> **Note**
>
> *Hierarchical* reports in the PS information system are drilldown reports and cost element reports are either Report Painter or Report Writer reports (see Figure 9.23).

Costs/Revenues/Expenditures/Receipts Report

Detailed analysis of individual projects and WBS elements is carried out by using the Costs/Revenues/Expenditures/Receipts (Transaction S_ALR_87013531) report. In the selection screen, individual projects or WBS elements are specified using selection profiles and variants. You also need to specify the report output format, either classic drilldown report or graphical report output, in the selection screen. Figure 9.24 illustrates an example of graphical report output of the Costs/Revenues/Expenditures/Receipts report.

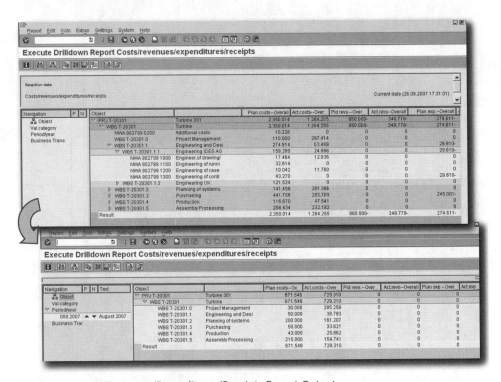

Figure 9.24 Costs/Revenues/Expenditures/Receipts Report Output

With this report, you can compare plan and actual values at projects, WBS elements, and network levels. In the report output, you can navigate to WBS elements/projects, value category, period/year, and business transaction. The values of the selected characteristics are displayed in the drilldown list on the right side of the figure. Object drag-and-drop functions are supported when moving characteristics from the navigation area into the drilldown list area. In our example, we drilled down to **Period/year** and selected the values for WBS element T-20301 for period 8/2007. From the report output, you can call up the line items report by following menu **Goto • Line Items**.

You can define exceptions to sort through large volumes of data to identify exceptions and trends. To define an exception, you should first select a column or a cell in the drilldown list area and then follow the menu **Extras • Exceptions**.

Networks

Networks are typically used for planning, analyzing, controlling, and monitoring costs and dates during the lifecycle of a project. Networks represent the flow of a project or of a task within a project and are the lowest-level functionality within the PS component. All costs posted to networks are automatically rolled into the assigned WBS element for settlement. Networks consist of activities. The network assignment to WBS elements can be defined at the header, ensuring all network activities post to the same WBS element, or the activities are individually assigned to a WBS element.

Budget/Actual/Variance Report

The Budget/Actual/Variance (Transaction S_ALR_87013557) report is used to compare budget and actual values. With this report, you can compare the actual and budget value on a regular basis so that budgets can be managed efficiently and any projected over- or under-spending can be easily monitored and investigated. This report can be used for passive availability control. The format of the report output is specified in the selection screen, either as classic drilldown or graphical report output. Figure 9.25 shows an example report output in the classic drilldown format.

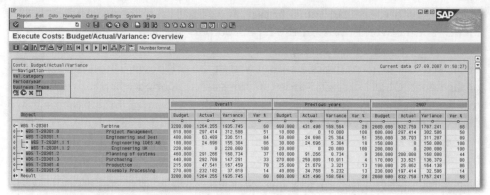

Figure 9.25 Budget/Actual/Variance Report Output

Budget and availability control

A budget is a device used by management to approve and control the plan costs over a given timeframe. The budget in SAP ERP is a value category that is binding. It provides the "ceiling" for expenditure and can be used to set expenditure limits and controls that cannot be changed without approval from a higher authority within the organization. Budgets are created at any level within the WBS structure and for internal orders. Cost centers do not have budgets in SAP ERP.

Both CO-OM-OPA and PS provide availability control functionality. There are two types of availability controls: active and passive. With the use of active availability control, expenditures can be actively compared with budget values and various messages is-sued when budgets are exceeded. In addition, budget increase request actions can be triggered, and the budget manager can be informed via email. With passive availability control, actual values are compared against budget values with reports only. The active availability control is a very effective way of controlling and preventing over-commit-ments against approved budgets and to automatically notify budget holders when com-mitments reach predetermined levels.

9.5 Overhead Cost Controlling Reporting in SAP Netweaver BI

SAP NetWeaver BI provides 21 InfoProviders for overhead cost management and hundreds of queries based on these InfoProviders. Refer to Figure 9.1 for SAP NetWeaver BI content InfoProviders. These InfoProviders and queries can be used as a reference when building overhead cost management reporting architecture in SAP NetWeaver BI. To explain all SAP NetWeaver BI InfoProviders and queries delivered for overhead cost management far exceeds the scope of this book. Thus, we only explain the data modeling and flow of the CO-OM Costs and Allocations InfoCube, which is a general InfoCube that can be used for modeling all reports for overhead cost management depending on your reporting requirements. In the queries section, we first explain queries delivered based on this InfoProvider and then look at other key business content queries based on InfoProviders that are component specific, such as overhead cost orders and overhead cost projects.

In addition, SAP delivers new SAP NetWeaver BI content and new cost center and internal order reports with the enhancement package 3. You can only use this content if you use the enhancement package 3 for SAP ERP 6.0 and have activated the Reporting Financials business function. Note that we explain SAP enhancement package for SAP ERP, SAP's simplified financial reporting innovation and show the new reports in Chapter 15.

9.5.1 Overhead Cost Controlling Data Modeling and Flow

The CO-OM Costs and Allocations InfoCube (0COOM_C02) contains all the costs and quantities on cost centers, internal orders, WBS elements, networks, network activities, and network activity elements that are extracted from the source systems using the delta extraction method. Figure 9.26 shows the data flow of the CO-OM Costs and Allocations (Delta Extraction) InfoCube.

The CO-OM Costs and Allocations InfoCube can be supplied data from 11 Info-Sources, as shown in Figure 9.26. There is a special data extraction for this Info-Cube. Let's have a look at the data extraction for cost center reporting. Cost center values are supplied data from the Cost Centers Costs (0CO_OM_CCA_1) and Cost Centers: Actual Costs through Delta Extraction (0CO_OM_CCA_9) InfoSources. To avoid double figures on reports, SAP recommends the following procedure:

▶ Load actual data with InfoSource 0CO_OM_CCA_9. This can be done with or without the delta process. If you load data with the delta process, you can load actual data at any time. If you load data without the delta process, you need to specify the period and load data after processing the period end closing process.

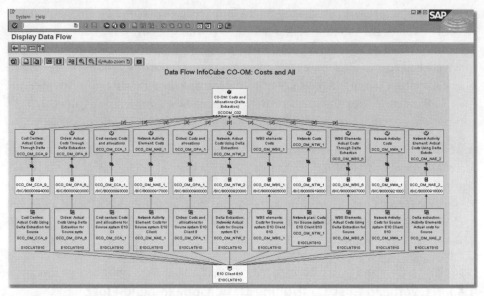

Figure 9.26 Data Flow of CO-OM Costs and Allocations (Delta Extraction) InfoCube

- If you use delta extraction, you can extract the plan, target, and period end closing data with the InfoSource 0CO_OM_CCA_1. Note that 0CO_OM_CCA_1 also includes actual data, so you should restrict the data selection during extraction so that actual values are not doubled. This can be done by restricting the value type, which identifies the type of data. Refer to Figure 9.27 for value types that are used to identify data during extraction.

Value type	Lang.	Descript.	Medium Description
10	EN	Actual	Actual
20	EN	Plan	Plan
30	EN	Target	Target
40	EN	Commitments	Commitments
50	EN	Budget	Budget
60	EN	Forecasting	Forecasting
70	EN	Variance	Variance
80	EN	Selection	Selection
85	EN	Accrual Plan	Accrual Plan
90	EN	Control Costs	Control Costs/Quantities

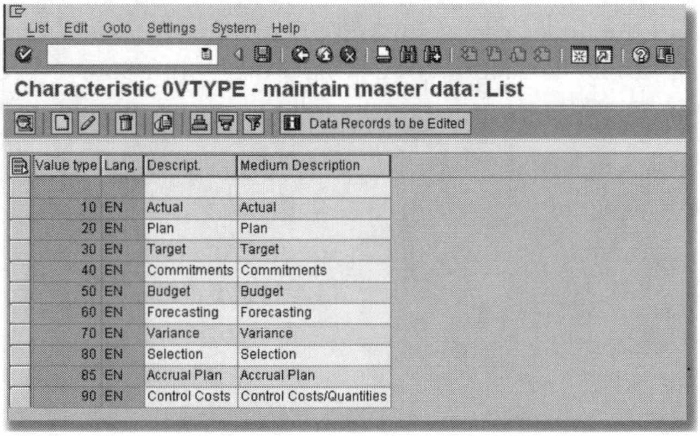

Figure 9.27 Value Types

Now that we have explained the special data extraction procedure for the CO-OM Costs and Allocations InfoCube, let's have a look at its data model. As shown in Figure 9.28, the data model of the CO-OM Costs and Allocations InfoCube includes the cost center, WBS element, order number, project definition, network, activity element, activity type, and network activity account assignment objects, as well as grant, fund, and functional area objects. Thus, you can use this InfoCube for modeling the overall overhead cost management of your enterprise if you do not use activity-based costing.

9.5.2 Overhead Cost Controlling Queries

The queries in SAP NetWeaver BI content differ in terms of content and purpose. Some of them are designed for quick analysis to identify values beyond a certain threshold value or criteria, whereas others provide more detailed and flexible analysis.

In general, the name of the query specifies the details and the purpose of the query. Queries that include *range* in their name provide information on multiple objects, whereas queries that include *detail* in their name provide more specific information. *WEB* queries are designed for the purpose of reporting in web cockpits of the enterprise's portal. However, they can be accessed from the BEx reporting tools. The *PSM* queries are used for management reporting on funds and grants, which are typically used in the public sector. The other queries, for example, *list* queries, are designed to carry out detailed analysis for specific objects such as cost centers and WBS elements.

Numerous queries are delivered in the business content for overhead cost management reporting. You can use these queries as a reference to model your reports in SAP NetWeaver BI. However, note that they are provided only as a reference. You should check the definition of queries and change the definition if required according to your business needs when you copy them. For example, some of these queries have predefined exception conditions. If the values are unusual in reports, they are highlighted in different colors. Exceptions are useful to sort through large volumes of data to identify values that are beyond a certain threshold value or criteria. If you copy business content queries, you can modify or delete the predefined exception conditions according to your business needs.

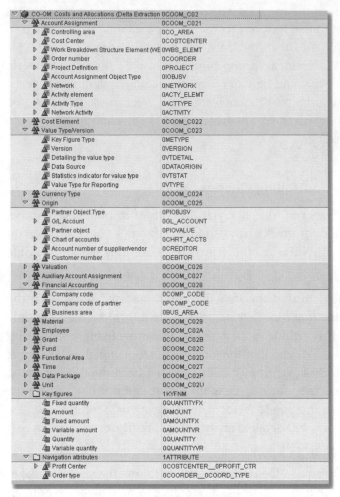

▽ 🌐 CO-OM: Costs and Allocations (Delta Extraction 0COOM_C02	
▽ 🔺 Account Assignment	0COOM_C021
▷ 🔳 Controlling area	0CO_AREA
▷ 🔳 Cost Center	0COSTCENTER
▷ 🔳 Work Breakdown Structure Element (WE	0WBS_ELEMT
▷ 🔳 Order number	0COORDER
▷ 🔳 Project Definition	0PROJECT
🔳 Account Assignment Object Type	0IOBJSV
▷ 🔳 Network	0NETWORK
▷ 🔳 Activity element	0ACTY_ELEMT
▷ 🔳 Activity Type	0ACTTYPE
▷ 🔳 Network Activity	0ACTIVITY
▷ 🔺 Cost Element	0COOM_C022
▽ 🔺 Value Type/Version	0COOM_C023
🔳 Key Figure Type	0METYPE
🔳 Version	0VERSION
🔳 Detailing the value type	0VTDETAIL
🔳 Data Source	0DATAORIGIN
🔳 Statistics indicator for value type	0VTSTAT
🔳 Value Type for Reporting	0VTYPE
▷ 🔺 Currency Type	0COOM_C024
▽ 🔺 Origin	0COOM_C025
🔳 Partner Object Type	0PIOBJSV
▷ 🔳 G/L Account	0GL_ACCOUNT
🔳 Partner object	0PIOVALUE
▷ 🔳 Chart of accounts	0CHRT_ACCTS
▷ 🔳 Account number of supplier/vendor	0CREDITOR
▷ 🔳 Customer number	0DEBITOR
▷ 🔺 Valuation	0COOM_C026
▷ 🔺 Auxiliary Account Assignment	0COOM_C027
▽ 🔺 Financial Accounting	0COOM_C028
▷ 🔳 Company code	0COMP_CODE
▷ 🔳 Company code of partner	0PCOMP_CODE
▷ 🔳 Business area	0BUS_AREA
▷ 🔺 Material	0COOM_C029
▷ 🔺 Employee	0COOM_C02A
▷ 🔺 Grant	0COOM_C02B
▷ 🔺 Fund	0COOM_C02C
▷ 🔺 Functional Area	0COOM_C02D
▷ 🔺 Time	0COOM_C02T
▷ 🔺 Data Package	0COOM_C02P
▷ 🔺 Unit	0COOM_C02U
▽ 🗋 Key figures	1KYFNM
📊 Fixed quantity	0QUANTITYFX
📊 Amount	0AMOUNT
📊 Fixed amount	0AMOUNTFX
📊 Variable amount	0AMOUNTVR
📊 Quantity	0QUANTITY
📊 Variable quantity	0QUANTITYVR
▽ 🗋 Navigation attributes	1ATTRIBUTE
▷ 🔳 Profit Center	0COSTCENTER__0PROFIT_CTR
🔳 Order type	0COORDER__0COORD_TYPE

Figure 9.28 Data Model of CO-OM Costs and Allocations (Delta Extraction) InfoCube

The business content queries for overhead cost management may also include redundant selection parameters such as controlling area. Because controlling area is a customer-specific field and it is possible to model overhead cost management reporting with multiple controlling areas, controlling area is a selection parameter in business content overhead cost management queries. If you model your overhead cost management with a single controlling area, you can default the controlling area when you copy the business content queries.

In this section we first look at queries based on the CO-OM Costs and Allocations InfoCube (see Figure 9.29). Then we will give example queries based on InfoProviders that are specifically designed for overhead cost orders, overhead project orders, and business processes analysis.

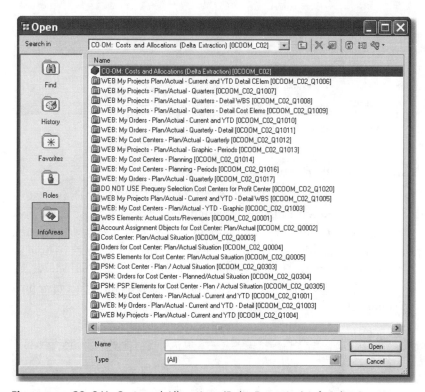

Figure 9.29 CO-OM: Costs and Allocations (Delta Extraction) InfoCube Queries

Cost Center: Plan/Actual—Situation Report

The Cost Center Plan/Actual—Situation (0COOM_C02_Q0003) query displays actual and plan costs of the current period along with the variance (%) for selected cost centers and controlling areas. The percentage variance between actual and plan cost is calculated as (actual – plan)/plan. The report output also shows the cumulative actual and plan values up to the current period and the percentage variance of these values. Figure 9.30 shows an example of the report output.

Cost Element		Actual Costs 009.2007	Planned Costs 009.2007	Variance 009.2007	Actual Costs 2007 YTD	Plan Costs 2007 YTD	Variance 2007 YTD
476000	Official Vehicles	10,000.00 EUR	40,000.00 EUR	- 75.00000 %	323,586.21 EUR	360,000.00 EUR	- 10.11494 %
476100	Travel Costs	8,000.00 EUR	30,000.00 EUR	- 73.33333 %	223,000.00 EUR	250,000.00 EUR	- 10.80000 %
476300	External Services	25,000.00 EUR	73,333.33 EUR	- 65.90909 %	425,862.07 EUR	660,000.00 EUR	- 35.47544 %
476400	Training Cost	22,000.00 EUR	33,333.33 EUR	- 33.99999 %	327,000.00 EUR	340,000.00 EUR	- 3.82353 %
476500	Misc. admin. costs	30,000.00 EUR	116,666.67 EUR	- 74.28572 %	800,086.21 EUR	950,000.00 EUR	- 15.78040 %
476900	Miscellaneous costs	15,000.00 EUR	30,000.00 EUR	- 50.00000 %	242,931.00 EUR	250,000.00 EUR	- 2.82760 %
Overall Result		110,000.00 EUR	323,333.33 EUR	- 65.97938 %	2,342,465.49 EUR	2,810,000.00 EUR	- 16.63824 %

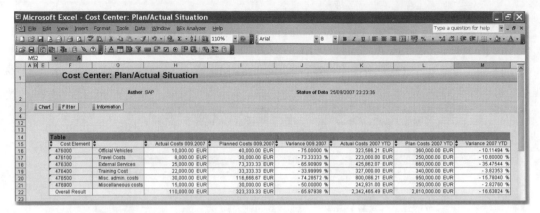

Figure 9.30 Cost Center: Plan/Actual Situation Report Output

WEB: My Cost Centers—Plan/Actual—Quarterly Report

The WEB My Centers—Plan/Actual—Quarterly (0COOM_C02_Q1017) query displays the actual values, planned values, and variance quarterly for a selected cost element hierarchy and controlling area. In the report output, you can exchange the cost element characteristics with cost center, costs, and quarters. It is possible to drill down to cost centers. Figure 9.31 shows an example of a report output where we drilled down to the cost center level. For simplicity, we filtered the report output to cost center CC1.

		007.2007 - 009.2007			004.2007 - 006.2007			001.2007 - 003.2007			010.2006 - 012.2006		
		Actual	Plan	Variances	Actual	Plan	Variances	Actual	Plan	Variances	Actual	Plan	Variances
Cost Center	Cost Element	EUR	EUR	%	EUR	EUR	%	EUR	EUR	%	EUR	EUR	%
Corp. Cost Center 1	Overhead Costs	712,465.49	970,000.00	-27	810,000.00	920,000.00	-12	820,000.00	920,000.00	-11	903,000.00	920,000.00	-2
	Official Vehicles	123,586.21	120,000.00	3	100,000.00	120,000.00	-17	100,000.00	120,000.00	-17	130,000.00	120,000.00	[illegible]
	Travel Costs	78,000.00	90,000.00	-13	70,000.00	80,000.00	-13	75,000.00	80,000.00	-6	70,000.00	80,000.00	-13
	External Services	45,862.07	220,000.00	-79	200,000.00	220,000.00	-9	180,000.00	220,000.00	-18	210,000.00	220,000.00	-5
	Training Cost	72,000.00	100,000.00	-28	130,000.00	120,000.00	8	125,000.00	120,000.00	4	118,000.00	120,000.00	-2
	Misc. admin. costs	280,086.21	350,000.00	-20	250,000.00	300,000.00	-17	270,000.00	300,000.00	-10	250,000.00	300,000.00	-17
	Miscellaneous costs	112,931.00	90,000.00	25	60,000.00	80,000.00	-25	70,000.00	80,000.00	-13	125,000.00	80,000.00	56
Overall Result		712,465.49	970,000.00	-27	810,000.00	920,000.00	-12	820,000.00	920,000.00	-11	903,000.00	920,000.00	-2

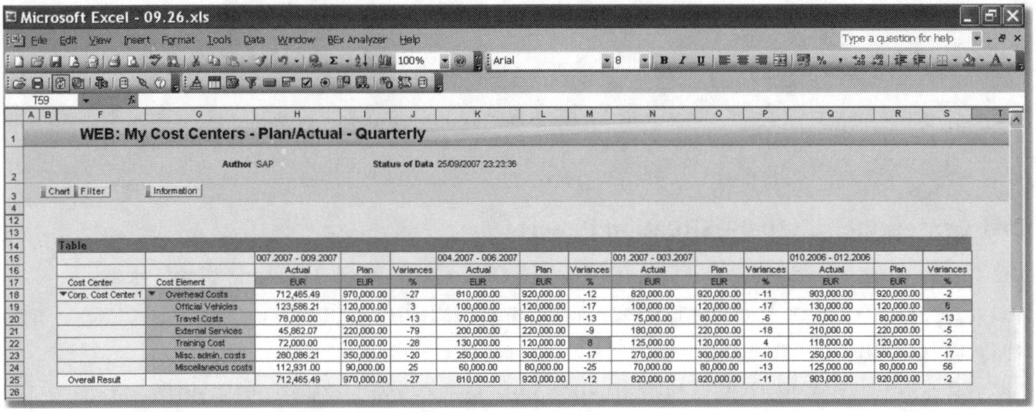

Figure 9.31 WEB: My Cost Centers—Plan/Actual—Quarterly Report Output

Internal Orders (Group): Plan/Actual Formatted Report

The Internal Orders (Group): Plan/Actual Formatted (0OPA_C11_Q0002_CR) query shows the plan values, actual values, and variance (%) for the selected period or fiscal year, order hierarchy, and controlling area. The report output also shows the values of individual internal orders. The query has a drilldown characteristic called request. You can select attributes of this characteristic as additional information in the report output. Responsible cost center, order type, and BW status are default selections in the query definition. In our example we selected profit center and order type as additional attributes (see Figure 9.32).

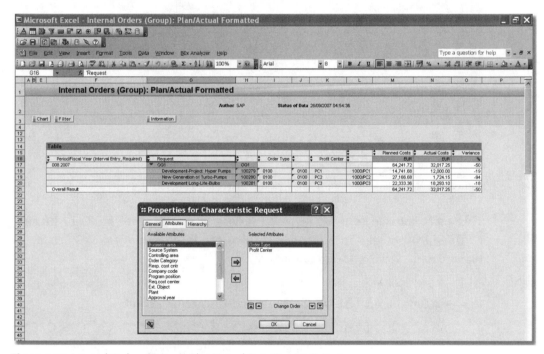

Figure 9.32 Internal Orders (Group): Plan/Actual Data Report Output

This query is based on the CO-OM-OPA: Costs and Allocations InfoCube (0OPA_C11), which provides information of all costs and quantities of internal orders that are extracted from source systems.

WBS Elements (List): Overall Planning/Actual/Commitment Report

The WBS Elements (List): Overall Planning/Actual/Commitment (0WBS_C11_Q0003) query shows the overall planning, actual values and commitments, and allotted and available budget for the current year and throughout the reporting time frame for selected WBS elements. Allotted value is calculated as the total of commitments and actual costs. An example report output is illustrated in Figure 9.33.

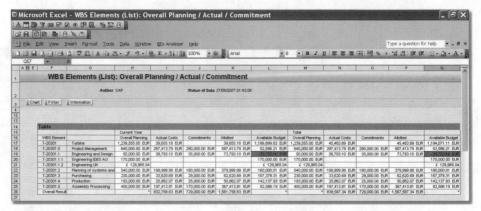

Figure 9.33 WBS Elements (List): Overall Planning/Actual/Commitment Report Output

This query is based on the CO-OM-WBS: Costs and Allocations InfoCube (0WBS_C11), which provides information on all costs and quantities for WBS elements that are extracted from source systems.

Process (Detail): Analysis—Process Costs Plan/Actual Report

The Process (Detail): Analysis—Process Costs Plan/Actual (0ABC_C06_Q0017) query shows the planned costs, actual costs, and variance (%) for selected business processes for a specified time period. Figure 9.34 illustrates an example of the report output.

This query is based on the CO-OM-ABC: Costs and Allocations InfoCube (0ABC_C06), which provides information on all costs and quantities for business processes that are extracted from the source systems. The InfoCube also provides a complete set of information on variances as well as information on allocations. Business process allocations are similar to cost center allocations. Costs or quantities are allocated from sender business processes to receiver business processes.

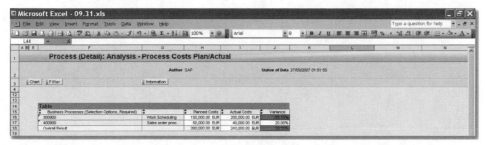

Figure 9.34 Process (Detail): Analysis—Process Costs Plan/Actual Report Output

9.6 Summary

Management reporting is needed to make better-informed business decisions. Management reporting requirements vary from organization to organization. Some examples of management reports are overhead cost management, customer, organizational, profitability and performance, exception, product, and market reports. Standardized performance analysis and reporting improve information consistency and reliability and enable better decision-making. In this chapter we covered the overhead costs management reporting architecture and discussed the design considerations. We also explained the key overhead cost management reports both within SAP ERP and SAP NetWeaver BI. In the next chapter, we focus on product costing and profitability analysis reporting.

This chapter deals with product cost controlling reporting and profitability analysis. It first describes the product cost reporting envisioned by a case study to illustrate how data flows in the end-to-end product costing (CO-PC) process. An introduction to profitability analysis (CO-PA) reporting architecture and how CO-PA is integrated with other SAP components follows. We then explain the key reports delivered with a predefined operating concern in SAP ERP. The last section of the chapter covers the SAP NetWeaver BI business content of CO-PC and CO-PA for reporting.

10   Product Cost Reporting and Profitability Analysis

Product costing and profitability analysis processes cover the most critical activities of management accounting. *Product Cost Controlling (CO-PC)* is the component of SAP ERP in which you calculate, plan, and cost the materials and control the costs in the end-to-end production process. *Profitability Analysis (CO-PA)*, as it is called in SAP ERP, is a tool for making decisions regarding how much of a discount to offer, which product, location, customer, or trade to invest, and so on. Product costing in SAP ERP is based on the *standard costing* cost calculation method. Thus, variances typically occur during the period. At the end of the period, the standard costs are compared with the actual costs to calculate the variances, which are then transferred to CO-PA for analysis. Furthermore, it is possible to calculate the actual price of materials and update in CO-PA for more accurate analysis.

The most frequent request we get from SAP customers is that they want to understand how to analyze reports in the end-to-end product costing process and transfer product costing results to CO-PA. Thus, we explain product costing reporting by envisioning a case study and explain the common errors of product cost calculation. With the case study example, analysis of product costing reports that you may be struggling with should become clearer. After that, we focus on CO-PA reporting architecture and explain how CO-PA is integrated with the CO-PC and other SAP ERP components. In addition, we explain the design considerations of CO-PA and key reports delivered with the predefined operating concern Quickstart

(S_GO). The last section of the chapter deals with the business content of CO-PC and CO-PA.

10.1 Product Costing Process and Reporting

The costs of products are calculated and controlled during the lifecycle of a product through the product costing process. Figure 10.1 illustrates the processes of product costing and reporting.

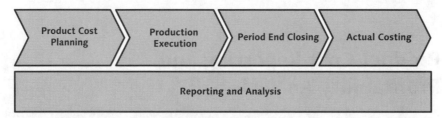

Figure 10.1 Product Costing and Reporting Process

The product costing starts with the product cost planning process. The cost of each product is calculated during the cost planning process. In SAP ERP, product costing is based on the standard cost estimate calculation method. Product costing is carried out and product prices are valuated with a standard price in the Product Cost Planning (CO-PC-PCP) component. Once the prices of the products are set, the production execution process starts. During production execution, the material and other production-related costs are collected in cost objects (e.g., product cost collectors, manufacturing orders, etc.). The actual costs that are not captured during the production execution process are allocated to cost objects during the period end closing. Production execution and period end closing processes are carried out in the *Cost Object Controlling (CO-PC-OBJ)* component of SAP ERP. Afterward, actual material prices are calculated, and stock values are updated with actual values. This can be achieved by using the *Actual Costing/Material Ledger (CO-PC-ACT)* component.

Reporting and analysis is a fundamental part of each process in end-to-end product costing. Reports are executed at each stage of the processes to control, monitor, and analyze costs. Let's take a closer look at each process and examine the key SAP ERP reports in the end-to-end product costing process.

10.1.1 Product Cost Planning

Product cost planning enables you to plan and calculate the cost of a product for the entire product lifecycle. At the start of the product's lifecycle, you can carry out an initial cost estimate for a new product for which there is no master data in SAP ERP via the method called *reference and simulation costing*. The costing is made by creating a *base planning object* as a reference to the new product. The cost of the new product is planned and calculated by using base planning objects.

When the material is created in SAP ERP, you can use the Material Cost Estimate without Quantity Structure method to calculate the cost of the product. The Material Cost Estimate without Quantity Structure enables you to calculate the costs and set the prices for materials without having complete logistic master data. In other words, material costs are calculated without using the bills of materials (BOM) and routings.

When the complete master data is available in the system, you can calculate costs by using the Material Cost Estimate with Quantity Structure method, which calculates the product cost based on BOM and routings. Figure 10.2 illustrates an example of a Material Cost Estimate with Quantity Structure (Transaction CK13N). In this section, we look at how the product costing reports are updated in the end-to-end product costing process by using product P-104.

During the material cost estimate calculation, you can generate different cost component views such as cost of goods manufactured and cost of goods sold. Cost of goods manufactured represents the manufacturing cost of a product. In this example the cost of goods sold is calculated by adding administrative overheads and sales overheads to the cost of goods manufactured. As in Figure 10.2, the cost of goods manufactured for P-104 is calculated as EUR 4,770.97, and the cost of goods sold is calculated as EUR 5,641.89 for costing lot size 10.

The cost estimate of goods manufactured typically consists of three main parts: material costs, production costs, and production overhead costs.

▸ **Material costs**
Material costs are calculated based on planned quantities and prices of raw materials, purchased parts, and semi-finished products required during production. The required materials and their quantities are defined in the BOM of the product for which cost is calculated. During this, materials are valuated based on their price in the material master data. If no price is available for materials,

the price can be determined from the *purchasing info records*. For example, if you require a subcontracting material, you can valuate the subcontracting material based on the purchasing info record.

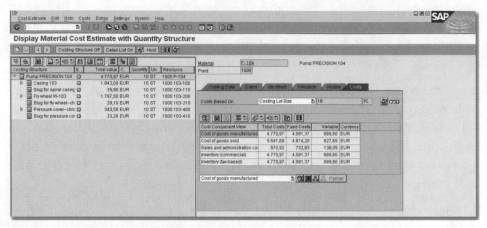

Figure 10.2 Material Cost Estimate with Quantity Structure

▶ **Production costs**

Production costs are calculated based on planned usage of production resources (e.g., labor and machinery) and the prices of these resources. The resources are often represented by *activity types* in SAP ERP. The unit prices of activity types are planned for the required production *cost centers* in cost center planning. Production cost centers are assigned to *work centers*, which is the physical location, such as production machine or line, where the production step is executed. The time planned for resources in the production step is set in a *routing or a master recipe*. Thus, production costs are calculated based on resource (activity type) usage defined in a routing or a master recipe and the unit activity prices planned in production cost centers.

▶ **Overhead costs**

The production costs that are not directly related to a specific product are called overhead costs. These costs are allocated to products using various costing methods. For example, you can allocate overhead costs to products by using *costing sheets*. To do so, you need to specify the material and production cost G/L accounts as the *calculation base* in the costing sheet. In addition, you need to determine whether the overhead is allocated on a percentage basis or on a quantity basis and set the respective settings such as planned overhead rate and the cost objects to be credited at the actual posting.

Now that we have explained the main parts of the cost of goods manufacturing, let's look at how cost estimates can be analyzed. The costing results can be displayed by itemization or cost components views:

▶ **Cost components view**

This view enables you to display the material cost estimate broken down into cost components such as raw material costs, production labor costs, and production set up costs. With the cost component view of the cost estimate, you can analyze the costing results in two levels: lower and upper. The cost of the lower level is composed of raw materials and purchased materials costs, whereas the upper level is composed of activity and overhead costs. The cost estimate is broken down to cost components with the *cost component structure*, where you assign cost elements to cost components and identify how the costs are displayed (fixed, variable, full) for each cost component in the reports.

▶ **Itemization view**

The itemization view is used to show detailed information on the resources of the product cost estimate. Note that you need to select the itemization indicator when saving the cost estimate if you want to display the itemization view of the product costing result.

To call up the cost component view or itemization view from the Material Cost Estimate with Quantity Structure (Transaction CK13N), go to the application toolbar **Costs** menu and select the **Display Cost Components** or **Itemization** option. Figure 10.3 shows the itemization and cost component views of the cost of goods manufactured for product P-104.

The itemization and cost component views can also be accessed from the CO-PC-PCP information system. To access the product cost planning information system, follow the menu path **Accounting • Controlling • Product Cost Controlling • Product Cost Planning • Information System** (see Figure 10.4).

The product cost planning information system provides many analytical reports for product cost planning, including material cost estimates (with and without quantity structure) and base planning objects.

Itemization View

Itemization for material P-104 in plant 1000

ItmNo	I	Resource	Cost Eleme	=	Total Value	=	Fixed Value	Curn	Quantity	Un
1	E	4230 1310 1422	625000		4,63		4,63	EUR	0,667	15M
2	E	4230 1310 1420	620000		44,38		37,46	EUR	1,667	H
3	E	4230 1310 1421	619000		9,86		8,63	EUR	0,333	H
4	M	1000 103-100	890000		1.943,00		1.557,00	EUR	10	PC
5	M	1000 103-110	400000		35,80		0,00	EUR	10	PC
6	M	1000 103-200	890000		1.797,50		1.743,80	EUR	10	PC
7	M	1000 103-210	400000		28,10		0,00	EUR	10	PC
8	M	1000 103-400	890000		343,50		269,70	EUR	10	PC
9	M	1000 103-410	400000		33,20		0,00	EUR	10	PC
10	E	4230 1320 1422	625000		4,63		4,63	EUR	0,667	15M
11	E	4230 1320 1420	620000		22,18		18,72	EUR	0,833	H
12	E	4230 1320 1421	619000		49,38		43,19	EUR	1,667	H
13	E	4230 1906 1422	625000		6,93		6,93	EUR	0,250	H
14	E	4230 1906 1420	620000		98,74		74,89	EUR	3,333	H
15	E	4230 1906 1421	619000		24,67		21,58	EUR	0,833	H
16	E	4220 1904 1422	625000		16,79		16,79	EUR	0,050	H
17	E	4220 1904 1420	620000		113,86		104,25	EUR	1,667	H
18	E	4220 1904 1421	619000		44,24		40,49	EUR	0,833	H
19	E	4230 1905 1422	625000		4,63		4,63	EUR	0,667	15M
20	E	4230 1905 1420	620000		44,38		37,4			
21	E	4230 1905 1421	619000		88,86		77,7			
22	X	000000300900	629000		12,00		5,0			
23	X	000000400900	629000		0,00		0,0			
24	G	4130 655100	655100		9,71		4,8			
25	G	4130 655300	655300		0,00		0,0			
26	G	4130 655400	655400		0,00		0,0			
				*	4.770,97	*	4.081,3			

Cost Component View

Cost Components for Material P-104 Plant 1000

C.	Name of Cost Comp.	=	Overall	=	Fixed	=	Variable	Crcy
10	Raw Materials		464,20				464,20	EUR
20	Purchased Parts							EUR
25	Freight Costs							EUR
30	Production Labor		1.038,41		916,72		121,69	EUR
40	Production Setup		2.329,21		2.329,21			EUR
50	Production Machine		917,44		825,58		91,86	EUR
60	Production Burn-In							EUR
70	External Processing							EUR
75	Work Scheduling							EUR
80	Material Overhead		9,71		4,86		4,85	EUR
90	Equipment Internal							EUR
95	Equipment External							EUR
120	Other Costs							EUR
200	Process "Production"		12,00		5,00		7,00	EUR
210	Process "Procurement"							EUR
		*	4.770,97	*	4.081,37	*	689,60	EUR

Figure 10.3 Itemization and Cost Component Views of Cost Estimate

The information system is categorized into five sections: **Summarized Analysis**, **Object List**, **Detailed Reports**, **Object Comparisons**, and **More Reports**. Let's look at each category.

▶ **Summarized Analysis**

When calculating a cost estimate for many products, product cost planning is typically managed by a *costing run*. The reports listed under **Summarized Analysis** provide an overview of costing run results. With the Results of the Costing Run report, you can analyze the results of costing runs. The Price vs Cost Estimate report enables you to compare the prices of materials with the calculated cost estimates. If you need to compare costing runs, you can use the Variances Between Costing Runs report.

▶ **Object List**

The reports listed under **Object List** are used to check the existing cost estimates for materials and base planning objects in the system. For example, the Analyze/Compare Cost Estimate report displays all the cost estimates for a chosen product. In the report output, you can call up a detailed display for cost estimates, such as the itemization view and the cost component view.

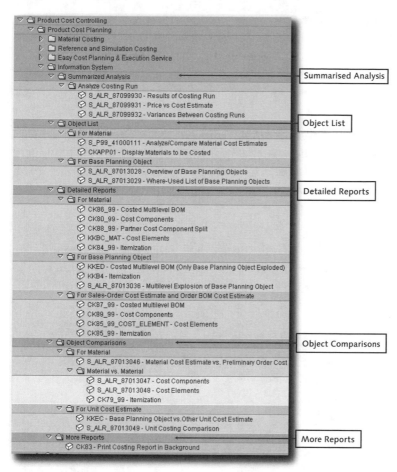

Figure 10.4 Product Cost Planning Information System

▶ **Detailed Reports**

As the name suggests, **Detailed Reports** show the details of existing cost estimates of materials, base planning objects, and sales orders. The itemization, cost components, cost elements, and costed multilevel BOM reports are included in the detailed report category. For example, you can analyze the details of resources that make up the cost estimate by using the Analyze Itemization (Transaction CK84_99) report. Figure 10.5 illustrates an example output of the Itemization report. As shown in the figure, depending on the item category detail, you can analyze costing items that include the item category, resource, total value, currency, quantity, unit of measure, cost element, cost center, plant, work center, activity type, material, and business process. You can add new fields for further analysis, such as BOM item and purchasing info record from the field list in the menu bar. This report shows the cost estimate results for the base quantity specified in the selection screen. In our example we specified the base quantity as 1 in the selection screen.

- **Object Comparisons**
  The reports listed under **Object Comparisons** are used to compare one material cost estimate with another material cost estimate or with the preliminary cost estimate of a product cost collector such as an order. The same comparison can be carried out for base planning objects with the object comparison reports for unit cost estimates.

- **More Reports**
  The only report in this category is the Print Costing Report in Background. The report is used to print costing results. This report is particularly helpful if the result is a long list. It is possible to print costing results in the background.

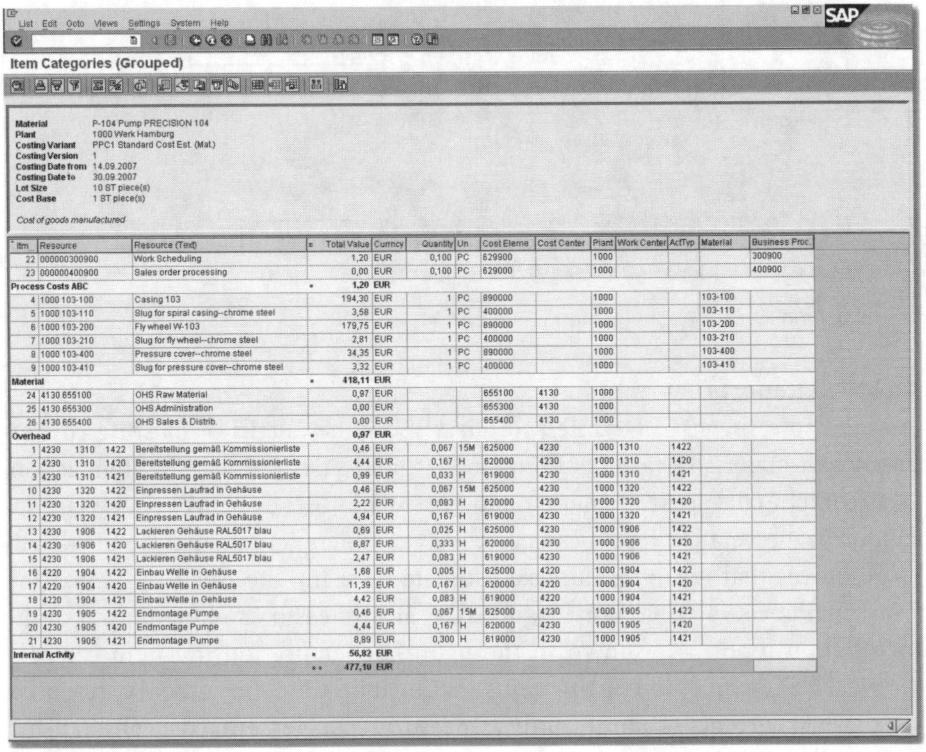

Itm	Resource	Resource (Text)	Σ	Total Value	Currncy	Quantity	Un	Cost Eleme	Cost Center	Plant	Work Center	ActTyp	Material	Business Proc.
22	000000300900	Work Scheduling		1,20	EUR	0,100	PC	629900		1000				300900
23	000000400900	Sales order processing		0,00	EUR	0,100	PC	629000		1000				400900
Process Costs ABC			*	**1,20**	**EUR**									
4	1000 103-100	Casing 103		194,30	EUR	1	PC	890000		1000			103-100	
5	1000 103-110	Slug for spiral casing--chrome steel		3,58	EUR	1	PC	400000		1000			103-110	
6	1000 103-200	Fly wheel W-103		179,75	EUR	1	PC	890000		1000			103-200	
7	1000 103-210	Slug for fly wheel--chrome steel		2,81	EUR	1	PC	400000		1000			103-210	
8	1000 103-400	Pressure cover--chrome steel		34,35	EUR	1	PC	890000		1000			103-400	
9	1000 103-410	Slug for pressure cover--chrome steel		3,32	EUR	1	PC	400000		1000			103-410	
Material			*	**418,11**	**EUR**									
24	4130 655100	OHS Raw Material		0,97	EUR			655100	4130	1000				
25	4130 655300	OHS Administration		0,00	EUR			655300	4130	1000				
26	4130 655400	OHS Sales & Distrib.		0,00	EUR			655400	4130	1000				
Overhead			*	**0,97**	**EUR**									
1	4230 1310 1422	Bereitstellung gemäß Kommissionierliste		0,46	EUR	0,067	15M	625000	4230	1000	1310	1422		
2	4230 1310 1420	Bereitstellung gemäß Kommissionierliste		4,44	EUR	0,167	H	620000	4230	1000	1310	1420		
3	4230 1310 1421	Bereitstellung gemäß Kommissionierliste		0,99	EUR	0,033	H	619000	4230	1000	1310	1421		
10	4230 1320 1422	Einpressen Laufrad in Gehäuse		0,46	EUR	0,067	15M	625000	4230	1000	1320	1422		
11	4230 1320 1420	Einpressen Laufrad in Gehäuse		2,22	EUR	0,083	H	620000	4230	1000	1320	1420		
12	4230 1320 1421	Einpressen Laufrad in Gehäuse		4,94	EUR	0,167	H	619000	4230	1000	1320	1421		
13	4230 1906 1422	Lackieren Gehäuse RAL5017 blau		0,69	EUR	0,025	H	625000	4230	1000	1906	1422		
14	4230 1906 1420	Lackieren Gehäuse RAL5017 blau		8,87	EUR	0,333	H	620000	4230	1000	1906	1420		
15	4230 1906 1421	Lackieren Gehäuse RAL5017 blau		2,47	EUR	0,083	H	619000	4230	1000	1906	1421		
16	4220 1904 1422	Einbau Welle in Gehäuse		1,68	EUR	0,005	H	625000	4220	1000	1904	1422		
17	4220 1904 1420	Einbau Welle in Gehäuse		11,39	EUR	0,167	H	620000	4220	1000	1904	1420		
18	4220 1904 1421	Einbau Welle in Gehäuse		4,42	EUR	0,083	H	619000	4220	1000	1904	1421		
19	4230 1905 1422	Endmontage Pumpe		0,46	EUR	0,067	15M	625000	4230	1000	1905	1422		
20	4230 1905 1420	Endmontage Pumpe		4,44	EUR	0,167	H	620000	4230	1000	1905	1420		
21	4230 1905 1421	Endmontage Pumpe		8,89	EUR	0,300	H	619000	4230	1000	1905	1421		
Internal Activity			*	**56,82**	**EUR**									
			**	**477,10**	**EUR**									

Figure 10.5 Item Categories (Grouped) Report Output

As we mentioned, the product cost planning process is typically managed with costing run (Transaction CK40N) for a large volume of materials. The costing run has six main steps, as illustrated in Figure 10.6.

In the *selection* step, materials to be included in the costing run are selected. The quantity structures of the materials are determined with the *structure explosion* step. Next, *costing* is carried out to calculate the cost estimate. Master data settings and the integration of master data play a very important role in the product cost planning process. Missing or incorrect master data leads to costing errors and warnings in the costing run. Common errors for costing are summarized below:

▶ Missing price for a raw material (material master/info record)

▶ Missing *No Costing* indicator in the costing view of raw materials

▶ Missing *With Qty Structure* and *Material Origin* indicators in the costing view of semi-finished and finished products

▶ Missing price for subcontracting materials (info record)

▶ Incomplete or missing BOM

▶ Incorrect routing or BOM in the costing view of semi-finished and finished products

▶ Incomplete or missing routing or master recipe

▶ Incorrect or missing activity type in a routing or work center

▶ Missing planned activity price in a cost center

▶ Incorrect cost center assignment in a work center

Once you have corrected the errors of the costing run, you should *analyze* the costing results by comparing the calculated price with the current valuation price of the material. This analysis can be carried out directly in the costing run or by using the Analyze/Compare Material Cost Estimates report that is listed under the summarized list category in the information system. Figure 10.7 illustrates an example of costing results analysis. In this analysis, you need to check and analyze the value and percentage differences between the current and calculated price of the materials. In particular, you should analyze *anticipated revaluation*, which will be reflected in stock values once the cost estimate is updated in the material master data. The anticipated revaluation is calculated as (cost estimate value per price unit × total stock quantity) — value of entire valuated inventory. In our example, the cost estimate per unit of P-104 is EUR 477.10 in plant 1000 (see Figure 10.5).

Note that when the product cost planning is carried out, calculation rounding occurs in the cost estimate results. The anticipated revaluation is EUR 876.48, which is calculated as (477.10 × 166)—4,718.20.

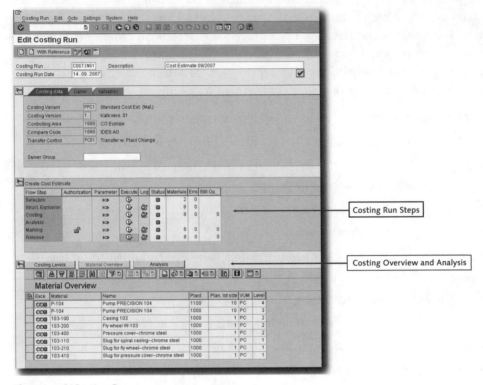

Figure 10.6 Costing Run

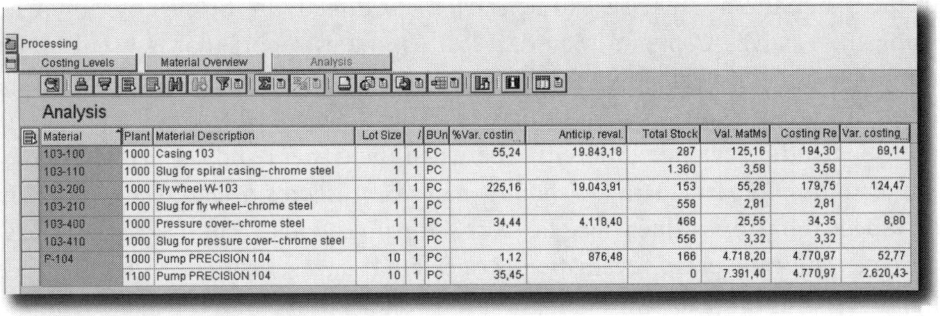

Figure 10.7 Analysis of Costing Run

Costing analysis enables you to find out which cost estimate results greatly differ from the current material price. For example, product P-104 in plant 1100 has a EUR 2,620.43 (35.45%) variance between its current value and planned cost estimate. The reason for the variance is that we reduced the activity unit price used in the routing of this product in plant 1100. It is important to analyze and understand the reasons for the variances. As long as there is a valid business explanation of variances, there is no issue, but sometimes the variances are caused by incorrect master data or inconsistent values that you need to correct before the stock values are valuated, as inaccurate stock values lead to misstatements in tax reports and financial statements. Below is a summary of possible causes of such variance:

▶ Incorrect price in raw material master data or purchasing info records

▶ Incorrect unit conversion in the material master data

▶ Incorrect costing lot size in the material master data

▶ Incorrect base quantity in the BOM or routing

▶ Incorrect activity price

▶ Incorrect overhead rate

▶ Incorrect formula or method in the template

The next step of the costing run is *marking* the cost estimates. With this step, the future planned price in the material master data is updated with the cost estimate. The last step of costing is to *release* the cost estimate. When you release the cost estimate, the current price field in the master data is updated with the planned price. As a result of the release, the stock values in *financial statements* are updated. The release is carried out in the period corresponding to the valid from-date of the cost estimate and can be executed only once.

10.1.2 Production Execution

In the production execution process, the costs incurred from production are assigned to cost objects (e.g., production orders, process orders). As mentioned earlier, the production execution process is carried out in the CO-PC-OBJ component in SAP ERP. The CO-PC-OBJ component supports cost controlling for all types of production. Production types are generally classified into two main categories:

▶ **Make-to-stock production**
In make-to-stock production, costs are managed by orders (e.g., production orders, process orders) by production cost collectors. If costs are managed by

production cost collectors, costs are collected periodically. Production cost collectors can be created for materials or a combination of materials and production versions.

▶ **Sales-order-related production**
In sales-order-related production, materials are produced with reference to sales documents items such as items in sales orders. Both the costs and revenues are collected in the sales documents item.

In this chapter, we focus on the make-to-stock production process and explain how production order costs are controlled. The production order execution process starts with the creation of orders. The costs can be planned for orders when they are created. Alternatively, you can manually initiate preliminary costing. *Preliminary costing* is based on planned cost estimate and planned quantity.

After the order is released, the actual material and other direct production costs are collected on orders through confirmation steps, which are typically executed simultaneously. The costs of orders can be analyzed using the Target/Actual Comparison (Transaction KKBC_ORD) report. Figure 10.8 illustrates an example of the report output. In our example, we created the production order 60003314 to produce 100 units of product P-104. In the rest of the section, we use this report to show how costs are updated during production execution.

Target costs are based on planned cost estimate and actual quantity. *Actual costs* are costs posted during production execution. The costs are collected with confirmation steps: *material consumption*, *activity allocation*, and *goods receipt*. These steps can be executed independently. Note, however, that you can execute activity allocations, goods issues and goods receipts together with Transaction CO15. Let's examine each step in detail and look at how actual costs are accumulated on orders.

▶ **Material consumption**
In this step, confirmation is carried out on how many materials have been consumed in production. Once the confirmation is saved, materials are issued from a warehouse to production. Each material issued for production is valuated with the current price of the material being used, generates automatic financial accounting posting to orders, and updates actual material cost on orders (see highlight number 1 in Figure 10.8).

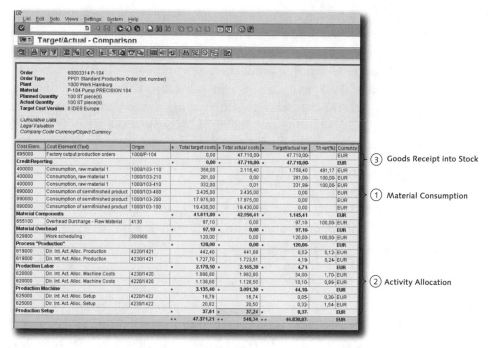

Figure 10.8 Target/Actual Comparison after Confirmation and Goods Receipt into Stock

▶ **Activity allocation**

In this step, the quantity of activities (such as labor, machine, and set-up hours) required for production is confirmed. This creates activity allocation from the production cost centers to orders based on the planned activity unit price (see highlight number 2 in Figure 10.8). In our example, the confirmed actual quantity is equal to the planned quantity, which is specified in material recipe and routing. Note, however, that there are some rounding differences on actual activity allocation values because production lot size is different from costing lot size.

▶ **Goods receipt**

In this step, the quantity of products (yield) that have been produced is confirmed. This creates a goods receipt from production to warehouse. The goods receipt is valuated at the standard price and updated as a credit on a production order. For example, a goods receipt of 100 units of P-104 credited the production order EUR 47,710.00 (see highlight number 3 in Figure 10.8).

10.1.3 Period End Closing

The remaining costs of the production orders, such as overheads, are calculated during the period end closing process. In other words, actual costs that are not captured directly on orders during production execution are allocated to orders. Next, work-in-process (WIP) and variances are calculated and settled to financial accounting and CO-PA. These processes are part of the period end closing process and carried out in the CO-PC-OBJ component. Let's look at the steps to allocate the remaining costs to orders.

▶ **Overhead calculation**
Production overheads are typically allocated by using costing sheets. With costing sheets, production overheads are calculated based on material and production actual costs collected on orders during production execution. Overhead calculation generates overhead allocation from cost centers to production orders (see highlight number 4 in Figure 10.9).

▶ **Template allocation**
Template allocation is used for more accurate overhead allocation to orders. With template allocation, business process cost objects are used to collect and allocate overheads. Overheads are assigned to the business processes according to the resources used and allocated to orders during the period end closing. Template allocation is a sophisticated overhead cost allocation method based on resource usage and cost drivers. Orders are valuated with the business process quantities and prices with the template allocation (see highlight number 5 in Figure 10.9).

▶ **Revaluation at actual prices**
Revaluation at actual prices is carried out to update the activity allocation values with the actual activity prices calculated and set in production cost centers. For simplicity, we used the planning price as an actual price in our example. Thus, no revaluation is posted to order 60003314.

Now that all the remaining costs are allocated to orders, we can calculate the WIP or variance.

▶ **WIP calculation**
In this step, the value of incomplete orders is calculated. The difference between the target and actual costs of orders that are not complete at period end is called *WIP* or *reserves*. If the actual cost of the order is greater than the credit from the goods receipt amount, the balance on the order is called WIP. If the

actual credit from the goods receipt amount is greater than the actual cost, the balance is called reserves for unrealized cost. You can post WIP to financial accounting during settlement.

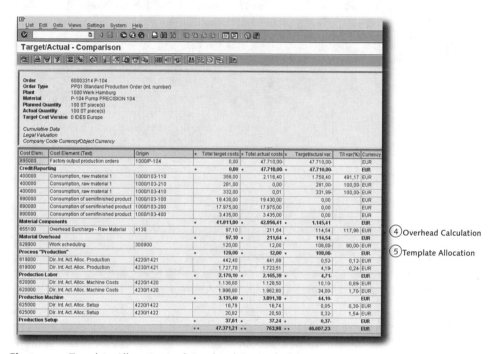

Figure 10.9 Template Allocation and Overhead Cost Calculation

► **Variance calculation**

The difference between the target and actual cost of the completed orders is production *variance*. You can calculate the variance based on variance categories for further analysis. For example, you can categorize variances as input price variance, input quantity variance, scrap variance, resource usage variance, and so on. When the variance calculation is carried out, the target cost of the product is updated in reports (see highlight 6 in Figure 10.10). Variances are posted to financial accounting during settlement. You can also transfer the *total variance* or *individual variance categories* to CO-PA for further analysis and reporting of the contribution margin. We explain how variances are updated in CO-PA in the next section.

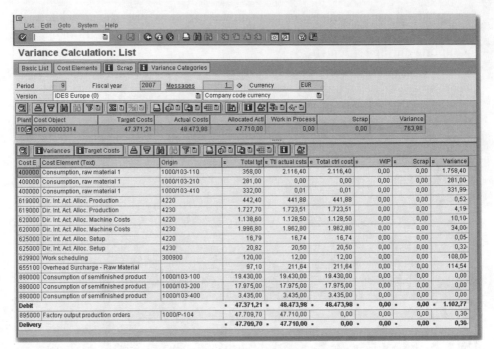

Figure 10.10 Target/Actual Comparison after Variance Calculation

► **Settlement**

As explained above, the difference between the debit and credit of orders is transferred to financial accounting in the settlement process. In doing so, the balance of the order becomes zero (see highlight 7 in Figure 10.11). In our example, the total variance of EUR 763.98 is settled to financial accounting by crediting the production order with the G/L account 895000 (factory output production orders) and debiting the price difference account.

The CO-PC-OBJ component provides many control reports to analyze the costs allocated to cost objects during production execution and period end closing. Our experience shows that the difficulties in cost object controlling often arise due to a lack of understanding of how production and period end closing steps update the costs on cost objects. Thus, we have focused particularly on one report and explained how product cost planning is used during production and illustrated the allocation of costs on orders.

The CO-PC-OBJ information system provides control reports according to the type of production, such as product cost by period reports and product cost by orders. To access the information system of product cost by order, follow the menu path **Accounting • Controlling • Product Cost Controlling • Cost Object Controlling • Product Cost by Order • Information System**.

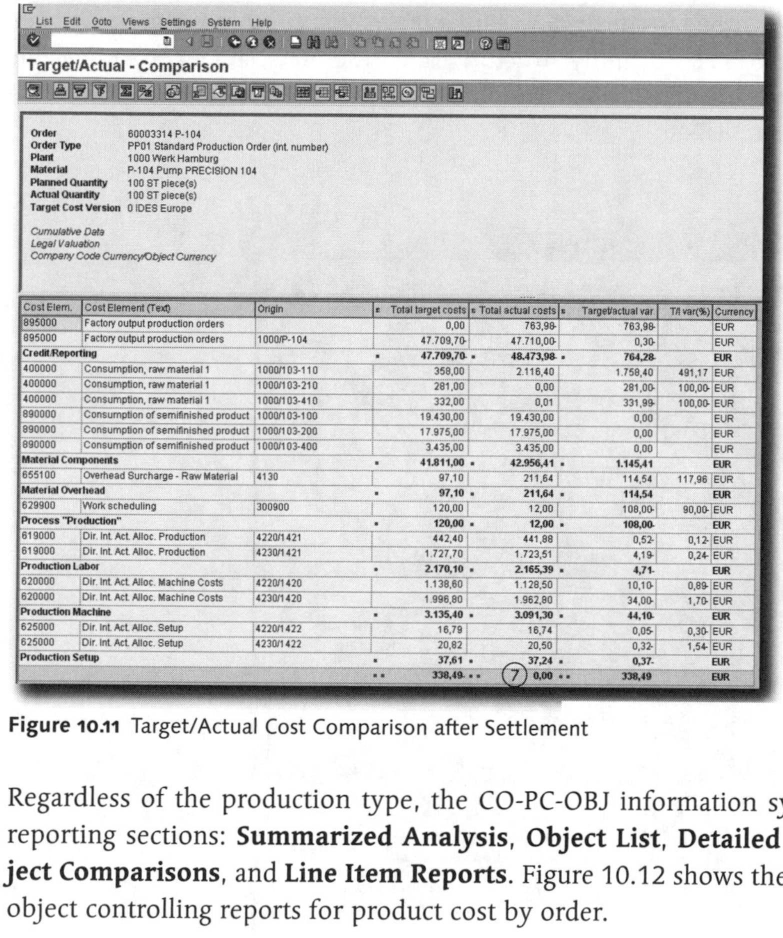

Cost Elem.	Cost Element (Text)	Origin	Total target costs	Total actual costs	Target/actual var	T/I var(%)	Currency
895000	Factory output production orders		0,00	763,98-	763,98-		EUR
895000	Factory output production orders	1000/P-104	47.709,70-	47.710,00-	0,30-		EUR
Credit/Reporting			**47.709,70-** •	**48.473,98-** •	**764,28-**		**EUR**
400000	Consumption, raw material 1	1000/103-110	358,00	2.116,40	1.758,40	491,17	EUR
400000	Consumption, raw material 1	1000/103-210	281,00	0,00	281,00-	100,00-	EUR
400000	Consumption, raw material 1	1000/103-410	332,00	0,01	331,99-	100,00-	EUR
890000	Consumption of semifinished product	1000/103-100	19.430,00	19.430,00	0,00		EUR
890000	Consumption of semifinished product	1000/103-200	17.975,00	17.975,00	0,00		EUR
890000	Consumption of semifinished product	1000/103-400	3.435,00	3.435,00	0,00		EUR
Material Components			**41.811,00** •	**42.956,41** •	**1.145,41**		**EUR**
655100	Overhead Surcharge - Raw Material	4130	97,10	211,64	114,54	117,96	EUR
Material Overhead			**97,10** •	**211,64** •	**114,54**		**EUR**
629900	Work scheduling	300900	120,00	12,00	108,00-	90,00-	EUR
Process "Production"			**120,00** •	**12,00** •	**108,00-**		**EUR**
619000	Dir. Int. Act. Alloc. Production	4220/1421	442,40	441,88	0,52-	0,12-	EUR
619000	Dir. Int. Act. Alloc. Production	4230/1421	1.727,70	1.723,51	4,19-	0,24-	EUR
Production Labor			**2.170,10** •	**2.165,39** •	**4,71-**		**EUR**
620000	Dir. Int. Act. Alloc. Machine Costs	4220/1420	1.138,60	1.128,50	10,10-	0,89-	EUR
620000	Dir. Int. Act. Alloc. Machine Costs	4230/1420	1.996,80	1.962,80	34,00-	1,70-	EUR
Production Machine			**3.135,40** •	**3.091,30** •	**44,10-**		**EUR**
625000	Dir. Int. Act. Alloc. Setup	4220/1422	16,79	16,74	0,05-	0,30-	EUR
625000	Dir. Int. Act. Alloc. Setup	4230/1422	20,82	20,50	0,32-	1,54-	EUR
Production Setup			**37,61** •	**37,24** •	**0,37-**		**EUR**
			338,49- ••	**0,00** ••	**338,49**		**EUR**

Figure 10.11 Target/Actual Cost Comparison after Settlement

Regardless of the production type, the CO-PC-OBJ information system has five reporting sections: **Summarized Analysis**, **Object List**, **Detailed Reports**, **Object Comparisons**, and **Line Item Reports**. Figure 10.12 shows the available cost object controlling reports for product cost by order.

10.1.4 Actual Costing

Once all period end closing tasks are completed for cost objects in CO-PC-OBJ, you can calculate the actual price of materials by using the material ledger in the CO-PC-ACT component. The calculation is carried out in two steps:

► **Single-level price determination**
Single-level price determination is used to calculate the actual cost of raw materials, purchased parts, and trading goods based on the transaction and good movements data.

► **Multi-level price determination**
Multi-level price determination is used to calculate the actual cost for semi-finished and finished products. SAP ERP enables you to store the goods movements on a particular quantity structure called the material ledger so that the actual costs of semi-finished and finished products can be calculated and stock values can be updated.

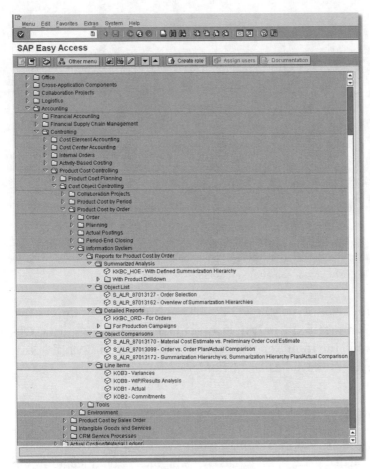

Figure 10.12 Cost Object Controlling Information System

Actual costs can be monitored and analyzed with the Material Price Analysis report. Figure 10.13 illustrates an example of the report output. In the report, you can see the value and quantity information for the categories **Beginning Inventory**, **Receipts**, **Cumulative Inventory**, **Consumption**, and **Ending Inventory** for the chosen period. The value information is composed of the preliminary valuation, the price difference, and the exchange rate difference. The actual prices are calculated based on these figures.

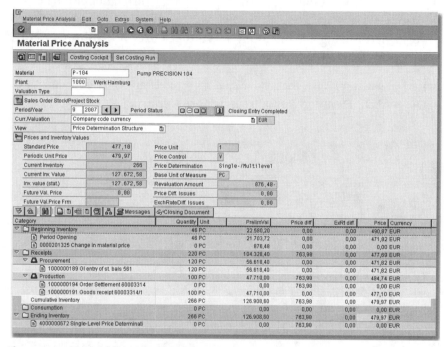

Figure 10.13 Material Price Analysis Report Output

Let's examine the report in detail. We first calculated the cost estimate of product P-104 as EUR 477.10. Stocks were revaluated at EUR 876.48 when we released the cost estimate. Next, we created a production order to produce 100 units of P-104. During the production variances EUR 763.98 occurred, which we settled to financial accounting and CO-PA. The material ledger stored all these movements in the end-to-end product costing process and calculated the actual price as EUR 479.97. In other words, variances are allocated to stocks. The actual price is called the *periodic unit price* in the material ledger and calculated as (price difference / total stock) + standard price. When you carry out closing postings, two accounting documents are created. The price difference account is credited, and the stock value is debited for the current period. The opposite posting is created for the next period. These postings can be displayed by clicking on the **Closing Document** button in the report output. You can update the periodic unit price in the material master data as the current price, which is used as the valuation price until the new periodic unit price is calculated. The material ledger also updates the actual cost of cost components if this feature is activated in configuration.

Material price analysis and other actual costing reports are listed under the CO-PC-ACT information system. To access the actual costing information system, follow the menu path **Accounting • Controlling • Product Cost Controlling • Actual Costing/Material Ledger • Information System**.

As illustrated in Figure 10.14, the actual costing reports are classified into three sections: **Object List**, **Detailed Reports**, and **More Reports**.

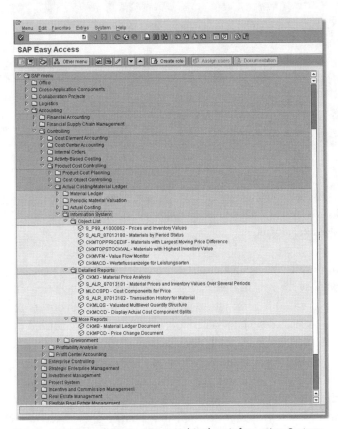

Figure 10.14 Actual Costing/Material Ledger Information System

> **Stock valuation with parallel currency**
>
> The stock values are always valuated in the local currency (company code currency). The material ledger can be used to valuate the stock in two parallel currencies in addition to the local currency. This functionality can be particularly useful for global companies that want to valuate their inventory in group currency with historical exchange rates. Activating parallel currencies in the material ledger increases reporting efficiency and avoids building custom reporting solutions. Valuating stock values with historical exchange rates helps companies comply with foreign currency exchange requirements for financial reporting stated in FASB Statement No. 52 for U.S. GAAP and IAS 21 for IFRS.

10.2 Profitability Analysis and Reporting

Perhaps the most important process in management accounting is the profitability and sales analysis process, which provides critical information about current and future profitability performance to sales, marketing, planning and management functions of the enterprise to support decision-making. Profitability and sales analysis is carried out in the CO-PA component of SAP ERP. CO-PA provides a sophisticated mechanism for the evaluation and analysis of an enterprise's marketing segment's profitability. Figure 10.15 illustrates the key steps of CO-PA reporting and analysis.

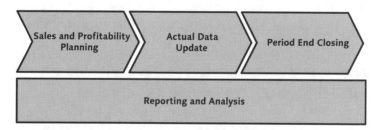

Figure 10.15 Profitability and Sales Analysis Process

▶ **Sales and profitability planning**
The planning process enables the sales and profitability planning information of marketing segments to be updated or generated automatically. With the integrated planning capabilities, plan data is transferred to CO-PA from other SAP ERP components, or vice versa. In addition, plan data can be retracted from SAP NetWeaver BI Integrated Planning to CO-PA.

▶ **Actual data update**
This is the process of collecting and updating actual values and quantities in CO-PA during the accounting period. The profitability-related transactions are

collected from other components such as SD, FI, and MM. These transactions are updated in CO-PA as profitability documents. You can also transfer profitability-related transactions from external interfaces. Actual data is transferred to CO-PA simultaneously and periodically.

▶ **Period end closing**
Period end closing in CO-PA starts with the periodic update of actual data from other modules to CO-PA. The periodic update of actual data is performed with cost settlements and allocations from other CO components. Production variances are settled from production orders, and revenues or costs collected on internal orders or projects are also settled as part of the period end closing. In addition, costs can be allocated to CO-PA segments via assessment, direct and indirect activity allocation, or template allocation methods.

After actual costs are updated in CO-PA, correction postings such as the manual entry of line items or the reposting of line items are performed. Finally, special CO-PA functions such as realignment, periodic valuation with costing or conditions, and top-down distribution are performed.

Reporting and analysis is the process of analyzing the multidimensional profitability data set. It is the process of executing the reports and evaluating and analyzing the contribution margins of marketing segments to support management decision-making. As part of this process, data monitoring and reconciliation reports are executed. The reporting and analysis process is executed through the whole profitability cycle.

Now that we have explained the CO-PA profitability and sales analysis process, our next topic is profitability analysis reporting architecture.

10.2.1 Profitability Analysis Reporting Architecture

Operating concern is the organization structure in CO-PA where the profitability model is created and maintained. The dimensions (*characteristics*) and the values that you want to evaluate are defined in the operating concern. Figure 10.16 illustrates a schematic view of the reporting architecture and the value flow of CO-PA.

The characteristics can be related to customers, products, organization structures, and markets that need to be analyzed with respect to enterprise sales, profits, or contribution margins. In the definition of the operating concern, there are three types of characteristics: fixed characteristics, technical fields, and customer-defined characteristics. *Fixed characteristics* are automatically generated in each operating concern (e.g., product, company code, customer, etc.). In addition to fixed characteristics, you can create your own characteristics called *customer-defined characteristics* (e.g., material group, customer group, etc.). *Technical fields* (e.g., document number, debit/credit indicator, etc.) are automatically created when you generate an operating concern. The combination of characteristics forms a multidimensional profitability segment, for which you can analyze profitability by comparing its costs and revenues.

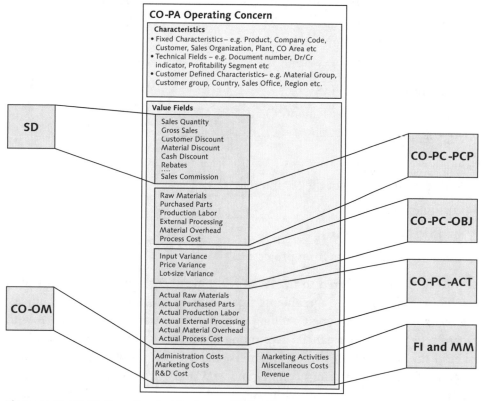

Figure 10.16 CO-PA Reporting Architecture and Value Flow

There are two types of profitability analysis: *costing-based* and *account-based*. In costing-based CO-PA, costs and revenues are grouped according to customer-defined *value fields*, whereas in account-based CO-PA, results are analyzed using *G/L accounts*. You can activate both costing- and account-based CO-PA at the same time. However, note that account-based CO-PA has potential performance issues for large data values because it uses the same line item and total tables as CO-OM and does not offer the flexibility of value fields. Thus, many SAP customers only use costing-based CO-PA. Detailed comparison between these two methods can be found in SAP Note 69384.

As illustrated in Figure 10.16, CO-PA is updated with data from other SAP ERP components. Understanding and correctly setting up the value flow from source components to CO-PA is vital for generating accurate, complete, and high-quality reporting results. Data records, when transferred or entered directly in CO-PA, have special identifiers specifying the data source of the CO-PA records. This special identifier is called *record type*. System-delivered record types are listed in alphabetical order as follows:

▸ Incoming sales orders (A)

▸ Direct postings from FI (B)

▸ Orders and projects settlement (C)

▸ Cost center costs (D)

▸ Single transfer costing (E)

▸ Billing documents from the SD interface (F)

▸ Customer agreements (G)

▸ Statistical key figures (H)

▸ Transfer of sales orders from projects (I)

Sales orders are transferred to CO-PA in real time and generate documents with record type A. Customer agreements from SD are transferred to CO-PA, updating records with record type G. Billing documents are transferred to CO-PA with record type F after the financial accounting document is generated. You can also transfer the costs from cost centers, orders, and projects, as well as the costs and revenues from direct postings from FI and MM. Costs from cost centers are allocated to profitability segments with assessment cycles and updated in CO-PA with record type D. Orders and projects are settled to profitability segments, updating CO-PA with record type C. Direct postings to profitability segments create line items with record type B.

An interface program is available to transfer external data to CO-PA. You can also manually create postings in CO-PA. You need to create your own record types when generating manual postings in CO-PA or receiving data from interfaces. The naming convention for customer-defined record types has to be X, Y, Z or numbers from 0 through 9.

Perhaps the most important information for accurate profitability and sales analysis is the most recent material price and sales-related information such as customer discounts. This information is automatically updated in incoming sales orders and billing documents via *valuation* functionality. Sales information such as discount and rebate is updated from condition types from SD. The cost of sales is determined from the product cost estimate when a sales transaction is posted to CO-PA. You can have a value field for each cost component of the cost estimate in CO-PA for a more detailed breakdown of the cost of sales information in profitability analysis, which is typically required in the manufacturing industry.

As discussed in the previous section, production variances are transferred to CO-PA by settlement at the period end for a correct representation of profitability analysis. You can either settle the production variances as a total, or you can settle the variance categories. If you use material ledger for actual costing, the cost of sales is updated with the actual costs for the actual representation of costs. In that case, valuation is executed at the period end for posted line items to adjust valuation or add the actual cost of goods manufactured. Figure 10.17 shows how actual costing is updated in CO-PA. As you remember, the unit price of product P-104 is calculated as EUR 479.97. When we first create a sales order with 10 PC, the standard cost estimate cost components are updated in CO-PA. After valuation, the cost of sales is updated with the unit price calculated in CO-PC-ACT. By using the material ledger to calculate the actual costs of cost components, you can update the actual costs of cost components in CO-PA such as production labor and material overhead.

The most common problem of value flow in costing-based CO-PA is the discrepancy between costs of goods manufactured recorded in FI and CO-PA. In costing-based CO-PA, the cost of sales is valuated and recorded when the billing document is generated in SD. When a goods issue is carried out in SD, this generates a financial posting for the cost of sales and only updates FI. If the goods issue and billing take place in different periods, there can be a discrepancy between the cost of sales recorded in FI and CO-PA. This causes reconciliation and reporting problems. Best practices dictate that this kind of discrepancy should be prevented. There are a number of ways to avoid such reconciliation differences and ensure that the cost of sales is the same in both FI and CO-PA. We recommend that you implement the built-in system controls so that the goods issue accounting document and billing accounting document are always posted within the same accounting period by using the same cost estimate or material price.

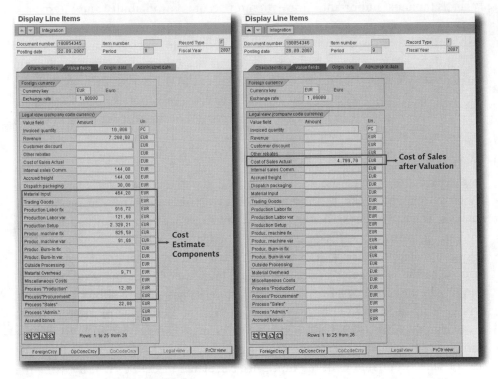

Figure 10.17 Actual Costing in CO-PA

Now that we have explained the reporting architecture and value flow of CO-PA, we will explain key work-in best practices for CO-PA reporting:

▶ Designing correct CO-PA building blocks

▶ Integrating CO-PA and SAP NetWeaver BI for enterprise profitability reporting

▶ Speeding up CO-PA implementation with SAP ERP templates

Designing Correct CO-PA Building Blocks

The fundamental design consideration in CO-PA starts with questions related to sales and profitability reporting requirements. What are the profitability dimensions? What are the profitability elements for each dimension? Once these questions are answered and addressed, it is vital to decide on correct building blocks to meet business requirements. You need to decide whether a dimension is a characteristic or value field. In many cases it is obvious from the dimension itself. Our experience indicates that in some implementations there are problems in this area. Consider the situation when there is a need to analyze net sales by geographical area. In this case, a separate net sales value field for each geographical area (e.g., net sales Europe, net sales Asia, etc.) should not be created. Only one net sales value field with a country-characteristic hierarchy is enough to report net sales by geographical area. Thus, we advise that you do not create value fields for dimensions that can be described by characteristics or characteristic hierarchies.

> **Technical limits of the CO-PA data structure**
>
> In one operating concern it is possible to have a maximum of 50 characteristics and 120 value fields. In addition to 50 characteristics, there are 19 fixed characteristics. As of the basis 6.20 support package 25, you can have up to 200 value fields. Refer to SAP Notes 758420 and 1029391 for more details.

Integrating CO-PA and SAP NetWeaver BI for Enterprise Profitability Reporting

Best practices dictate that profitability analysis is effectively analyzed by using both SAP ERP CO-PA and SAP NetWeaver BI capabilities. Both solutions are compatible and should be used together to achieve complete profitability reporting. SAP ERP CO-PA forms the foundation of profitability information with an established business model for contribution margins reporting of the market segments. SAP NetWeaver BI provides a sophisticated reporting solution for profitability analysis enterprise-wide. With SAP NetWeaver BI, multiple SAP R/3, SAP ERP, and non-SAP systems can be consolidated, providing an enterprise-wide view of profitability information. Figure 10.18 illustrates the schematic view of consolidated profitability reporting architecture. Consolidated profitability can also be achieved when profitability methods in the sources systems show variations in generating a profitability view. With data retraction, you create a connection between data generated in SAP NetWeaver BI and the data stored in sources systems. You can use data retraction functions to retract both plan and actual data from SAP NetWeaver BI to SAP ERP.

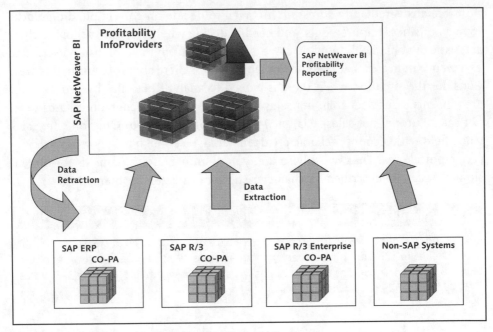

Figure 10.18 Consolidated Profitability Reporting Architecture

Speeding Up CO-PA Implementation with SAP ERP Templates

SAP delivers four predefined operating concern templates. By using these templates as a reference you can speed up your CO-PA implementation and achieve the preferred profitability model faster. It is a good practice to use these templates during the design phase to increase the understanding of CO-PA reporting and analysis capabilities so that you can accommodate business requirements in the design of the profitability model. The following operating concerns are delivered as templates:

- ▶ Template for Route Profitability (S_AL)
- ▶ Quickstart Template (S_GO)
- ▶ Consumer Goods Industry Template (S_CP)
- ▶ Model Bank (E_B1)

To use predefined operating concern templates, follow the menu path **Controlling • Profitability Analysis • Structures • Define Operating Concern • Sam-**

ple Operating Concerns • **Use SAP Operating Concern Template** (Transaction KETE).

After executing Transaction KETE, you need to select the operating concern that you want to use as a reference. For example, we selected the operating concern Quickstart Template (S_GO). Figure 10.19 shows all preconfigured customizing steps for the selected operating concern. In addition, you can prepare application examples by generating example data. The transaction also provides information about each step, which you can access by clicking on the **Information** button. Once you review and test the predefined operating concern template, you can copy the definition and configuration settings to your operating concern for baseline configuration. To do so, select the step **Copy operating concern template** that is shown at the bottom of Figure 10.19. Alternatively, you can use Transaction KECP to copy and customize the operating concern. SAP-delivered operating concerns should not be used in productive environments because SAP can change the customizing settings and data structures with new releases.

In the next section, we look at the example reports provided in the predelivered operating concern Quickstart (S_GO).

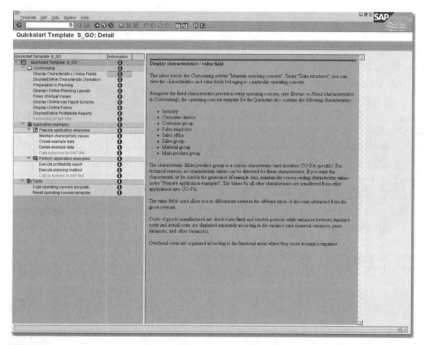

Figure 10.19 Manage Operating Concern Templates

10.2.2 Profitability Analysis Reports in SAP ERP

The data structure of CO-PA depends upon the operating concern, which is specific for each customer implementation. Thus, only a few standard reports are available for profitability analysis. In this section, we explain four standard delivered reports that can be used for all operating concerns and two examples of drilldown reports delivered for operating concern S_GO.

Line Items Reports

There are two line items reports in CO-PA: the Actual Line Items (Transaction KE24) report and the Plan Line Items (Transaction KE25) report. These reports are ALV reports. To access the line items reports follow the menu path **SAP Menu • Accounting • Controlling • Profitability Analysis • Information System • Display Line Item List • Actual or Plan**.

Figure 10.20 shows the selection screen of the Actual Line Items report. The Actual Line Items report has to be executed with special care, because the large data set of line items can cause performance issues and long run times for both foreground and background execution. Thus, we recommend that you restrict the data in the selection screen as much as possible. In our example, we restricted the report output by specifying the record type C, the product P-104, and period 09.2007. Another good practice is to use layouts to control the column structure of the report output. This is particularly useful when executing the report in the background. By selecting the **Read as posted** option in the mode of access, actual line items are read without taking *realignments* into account.

Realignment in CO-PA

Realignment is a function of CO-PA that allows retrospective changes to the assignment of characteristic values. It is used to activate master data changes for all existing data. For example, when a customer moves to a new sales district, the realignment function allows existing postings to be reported in the new district, even though they were posted when the customer belonged to the previous sales district. After executing realignment, only the line items report has the option to read data as it was posted. All other CO-PA reports read the data with realignments.

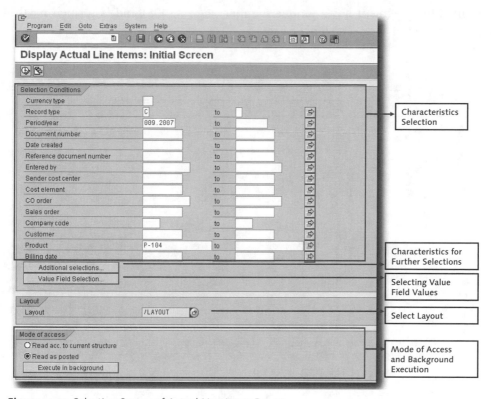

Figure 10.20 Selection Screen of Actual Line Items Report

Figure 10.21 illustrates an example of output the Actual Line Items report. The report is displayed in ALV format and has the standard ALV controls as well as the application-specific controls. The selection parameters of the report are displayed at the header level. With the control buttons in the application toolbar, you can access master data, the profitability segment, and underlying documents for line items. By selecting the line and the corresponding button, you can view the master data of characteristics such as customer and material and jump into other documents or view the profitability segment.

The profitability segment of the first line is shown in Figure 10.21. Note that production variances (e.g., input variances, lot size variance, price variance, quantity variance, etc.) for order 60003314 are transferred to CO-PA in our example. The profitability segment has a unique number (e.g., 73008) and is formed by the combination of the characteristic values.

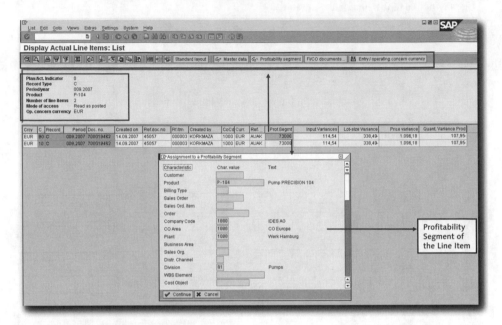

Figure 10.21 Output of Actual Line Items Report

Reconciliation Control Reports

Two reports are delivered to help reconcile figures of CO-PA with other SAP ERP components. The first one is used to reconcile figures among SD, FI, and CO-PA components, and the second one is used to reconcile WBS element and sales order settlements to CO-PA. To access these reports follow the SAP menu path **Accounting • Controlling • Profitability Analysis • Tools • Analyze Value Flows • Check Value Flow in Billing Document Transfer** (Transaction KEAT) **and Check Value Flow from Order/Project Settlement** (Transaction KEAW).

Figure 10.22 illustrates the output of the report Check Value Flow in Billing Document Transfer. You can use this report to compare the actual data in CO-PA to the corresponding postings made in FI and the value flow from SD. The report runs in two formats: ALV grid display and ALV list. The report output shown in Figure 10.22 is in ALV grid display format. The report can only be executed for one company code and one currency type. Thus, you need to execute the report separately for each company code and currency type.

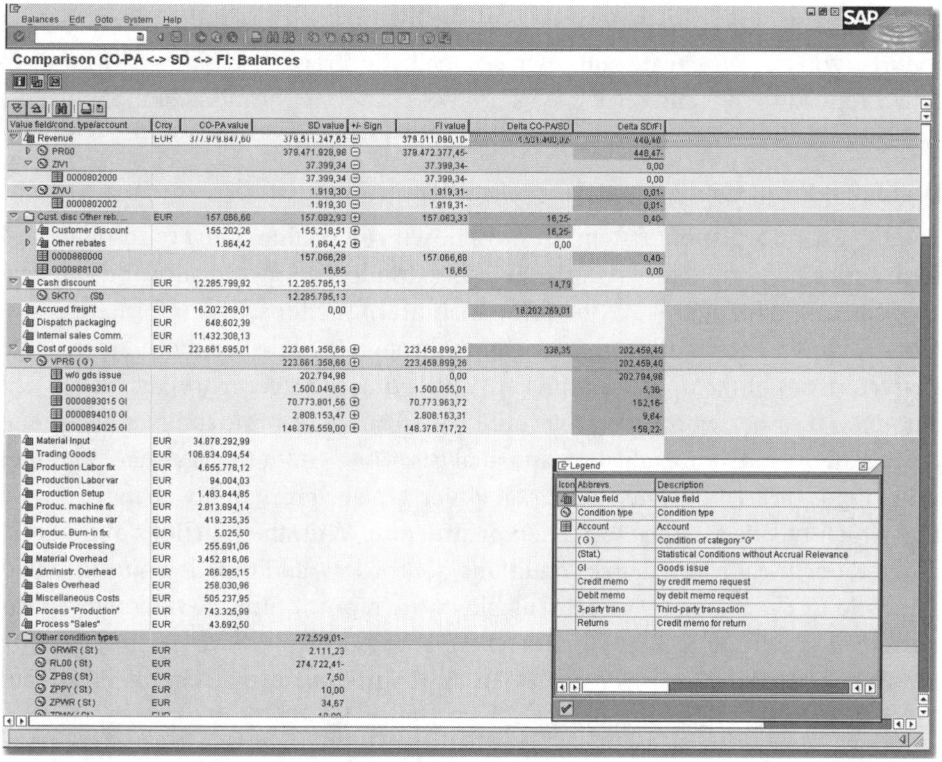

Figure 10.22 Comparison of CO-PA, SD, and FI Balances Report Output

Values in billing documents are assigned to condition types in SD, accounts in FI, and value fields in CO-PA. The first column of the report shows the CO-PA value field along with the corresponding SD condition types and G/L accounts. The legend of the report is shown at the bottom right of the figure with the icons denoting each object. The subsequent columns show currency, CO-PA value, SD value, +/- sign, and FI value. If the value in the **+/- Sign** column is minus, it denotes that there is a difference that exceeds the tolerance limits set in the selection screen. In contrast, a positive sign in the **+/- Sign** column shows that there is no difference or that the difference is less than the tolerance limits specified in the selection screen. After these columns, two delta columns show differences between the values in

CO-PA and SD (**Delta CO-PA/SD**), and between SD and FI (**Delta SD/FI**). By clicking on the difference value, you can display the list of billing documents making up that difference with the delta values.

You cannot change or configure these reports. If you need additional reconciliation reports, you have to create your own reconciliation reports with the CO-PA drilldown reporting tool and reconcile values with other application components.

Drilldown Profitability Reports

The CO-PA information system uses drilldown report functionality to build customer-specific profitability reports. By using drilldown functionality you can analyze existing data online and perform analytical functions. The information system drilldown reports allow for navigation through the selected multidimensional characteristics of the operating concern, displaying selected figures and calculated amounts. In other words, you select the data from your profitability data set and display the results for evaluation and analysis. The system displays data in either value fields or accounts, depending on which type of profitability analysis is used and which type is assigned to the report structure. With the functions of the drilldown reporting you can define conditions, sort orders, and drill down to any characteristic or characteristic value available in the report output. Drilldown reports are executed within SAP ERP or via a web-enabled graphical user interface with SAPGUI for HTML. With web-enabled GUI, reports can also be executed via your Internet browser. This function is available as of release SAP R/3 4.6c.

If you create your operating concern without copying from the delivered templates, no drilldown reports will be available for your operating concern. Creating drilldown reports does not require technical programming skills and is a relatively straightforward task. We cover drilldown reporting fundamentals in Chapter 12. In this section, we examine drilldown reports delivered with the operating concern Quickstart. To access these reports use the menu path **Accounting • Controlling • Profitability Analysis • Information System • Execute Report** (Transaction KE30).

Analysis of Operating Profit Report
The Analysis of Operating Profit report is used to compare the actual and plan data for the selected time interval on the selection screen of the report. With this

report, you can compare the values for the selected periods of the previous and the current year for the entire contribution margin. Figure 10.23 shows the output of the report in graphical report output format.

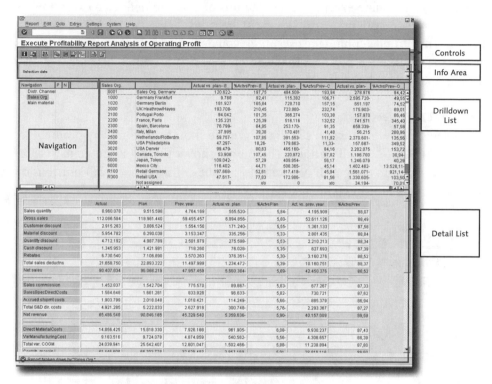

Figure 10.23 Analysis of Operating Profit Report Output

The user interface of CO-PA drilldown reports is user-friendly. Like the other CO-PA drilldown reports, the Analysis of Operating Profit report has a section for various controls to view the report parameters, export the report output to local files, perform currency translation, and so on. Below the controls area is an info area where report information such as name and execution data is displayed. In this area you can load HTML files with which, for example, you can add your company logo. In the navigation area you can navigate between the characteristics and restrict the characteristic values. For example, you can navigate (drilldown) to characteristics such as distribution channel, sales organization, and main material group. Drag-and-drop functions are supported when moving characteristics from the navigation area into the drilldown list area. The details list is always updated for the characteristic values selected in the navigation area.

The report shows the entire contribution margin scheme in the detail list section. It is possible to define exceptions for columns or cells. To define an exception select a column or a cell in the drilldown list area and then go to the menu **Extras • Exceptions**. When defining the exception, you need to define the value thresholds and then assign different colors to the exception. The drilldown list and the detail list are updated with the settings of **Exceptions**.

Analysis CM II Report

The Analysis CM II report is used to analyze the short-term company profitability without CO-OM-CCA allocations. The report shows the plan and actual values up to contribution margin II. An example output of the Analysis of Contribution Margin II report is shown in Figure 10.24.

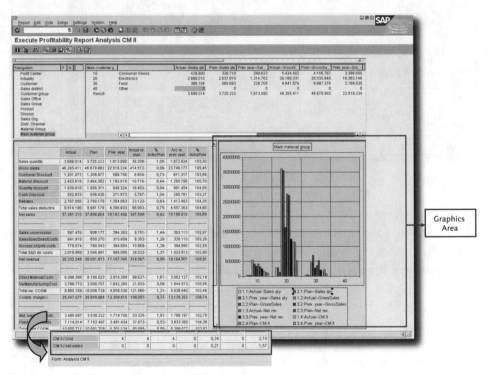

Figure 10.24 Profitability Analysis CM II Report Output

Two calculated key figures related to sales in the report output are displayed at the bottom of the detail list: **CM II/Unit** and **CM II/net sales**. In the report output you can drill down to characteristics such as profit center, industry, customer, sales district, customer group, sales office, sales group, product, division, sales organization, distribution channel, material group, and main material group.

The output control is used to control the components displayed in the output of drilldown reports. For example, the Analysis of CM II report output is shown with graphics, whereas the Analysis of Operating Profit report output is displayed without graphics. This is because the option containing the graphics is selected for the Analysis of CM II report. Figure 10.25 shows the output type settings for the Analysis of CM II report (Transaction KE32).

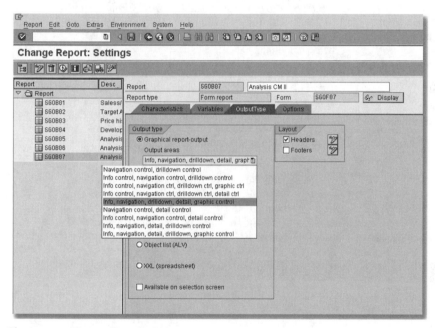

Figure 10.25 Output Type Settings

Five more drilldown reports are available with the operating concern Quickstart (S_GO), listed in Table 10.1.

Report Name and Transaction	Report Description
Sales/Sales Revenues/ Discount (SGOB01)	This report allows you to analyze the short-term sales and volume figures of plan and actual values. For example, you can run an analysis at the customer or product level and compare various discounts with sales revenue. The period and plan actual indicator is specified in the selection screen.
Target Achievement (SGOB02)	This report is used to compare plan and actual sales revenue and volumes, as well as to show the extent to which the planned targets have been attained. You can drill down to characteristics such as customer group, sales group, sales organization, distribution channel, material group, industry, and profit center in the report output.
Price History (SGOB03)	This report shows the gross and net price history for a given fiscal year. The price history is available for both plan and actual data. You can drill down to characteristics such as material and material group.
Development of Customer Sales (SGOB04)	This report is used to analyze customer sales figures for a period of 12 months. The development of the sales can be viewed as a graphic in the report output. When you drill down to characteristics such as customer group, period, sales district, and customer, the output in the graphic area changes accordingly.
Analysis of Incoming Orders (SGOB06)	This report is used to compare the incoming sales orders in the selected period interval with the same interval of the previous year. It displays the contribution margin scheme up to contribution margin II. The report can be used as an indication of the future sales and anticipated sales based on actual sales orders. You can drill down to characteristics such as industry, customer, customer group, division, sales organization, distribution channel, material group, and main material group in the report output.

Table 10.1 Drilldown Reports Delivered with the Operating Concern Quickstart

10.3 Product Costing and Profitability Analysis in SAP NetWeaver BI

SAP NetWeaver BI provides flexible and advanced reporting capabilities for product costing and profitability analysis. In this section, we focus exclusively on the business content for CO-PC and CO-PA and provide data flow and modeling examples for product costing and profitability analysis. In addition, we examine the key product costing and profitability analysis queries based on business content InfoProviders. Note that the data flow and modeling examples are for illustration purposes only.

10.3.1 Data Modeling and Reporting of Product Cost Planning

The business content in product costing provides two InfoProviders for product cost planning reporting: the All Cost Estimates InfoCube (0COPC_C08) and the Released Cost Estimates InfoCube (0COPC_C09). Figure 10.26 shows the data flow of these InfoCubes along with the data model of the All Cost Estimates InfoCube (0COPC_C08).

> **Note**
>
> SAP delivers new SAP NetWeaver BI content and new product costing reports with the enhancement package 3. You can only use this content if you use the enhancement package 3 for SAP ERP 6.0 and have activated the Reporting Financials business function. Note that we explain SAP enhancement package for SAP ERP, SAP's simplified financial reporting innovation and outline the new reports in Chapter 15.

The All Cost Estimates InfoCube (0COPC_C08) contains the values of the cost components split for all existing material cost estimates that are extracted from the connected source systems. It is supplied with data from the All Cost Estimates InfoSource (0CO_PC_PCP_01).

The Released Cost Estimates InfoCube (0COPC_C09) contains the values of the cost components split for released cost estimates that are extracted from the connected source systems. It is supplied with data from the Released Cost Estimates InfoSource (0CO_PC_PCP_02).

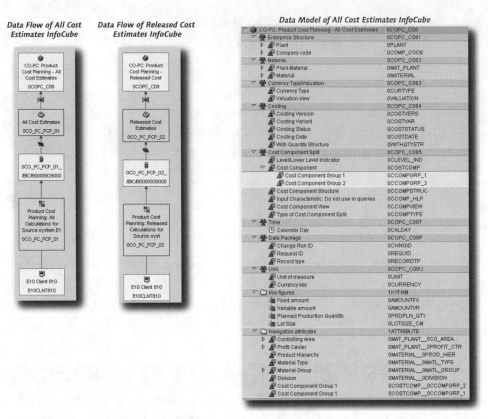

Figure 10.26 Data Flow of the All Cost Estimates and Release Cost Estimates InfoCube along with the Data Model of the All Cost Estimates InfoCube

Below is a summary of the recommendations for InfoObjects specific to these InfoProviders:

▶ The Plant Material (0MAT_PLANT) InfoObject is contained in the data models of both InfoProviders. You can use the attributes of 0MAT_PLANT in queries such as purchasing group.

▶ Both the Costing Date (0COSTDATE) and Calendar Day (0CALDAY) InfoObjects are updated with the costing date. If you need to display the costing date in queries, you should use the Costing Date (0COSTDATE) InfoObject.

▶ Key Figure Lot Size (0LOTSIZE_CM) and Planned Production Quantity (0PRD-PLN_QTY) are included in all cost components in the cost estimate data records. When summing the cost components these key figures are also summed, which creates an inconsistent lot size and a planned production quantity in the queries. This inconsistency can be avoided by exception aggregation. The Input Characteristics (0CCOMP_HLP) InfoObject is a technical InfoObject that connects the Cost Component Structure, Cost Component, and Level/Lower Indicator InfoObjects for exception aggregation. However, note that this InfoObject should not be used in queries.

Figure 10.27 shows the queries delivered based on the All Cost Estimates and Released Cost Estimates InfoProviders.

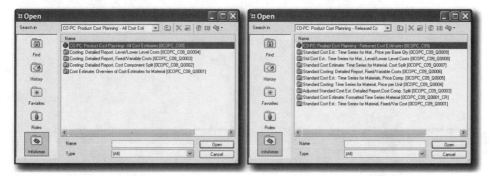

Figure 10.27 Queries Based on All Cost Estimates and Release Cost Estimates InfoCubes

You can analyze and control material cost estimates with these queries. If you want to analyze the cost estimate that updates the material price, we advise you to use the queries based on the Released Cost Estimates InfoCube (0COPC_C09). Let's examine some of these queries based on the Released Cost Estimates InfoCube.

Standard Costing: Detailed Report, Fixed/Variable Costs Report

This query shows the fixed and variable costs as well as the total released costs for a chosen material in a plant for selected periods. You can analyze the cost component split by drilling down to cost components or cost component group 1. The report output along with the drilldown to cost component split is illustrated in Figure 10.28.

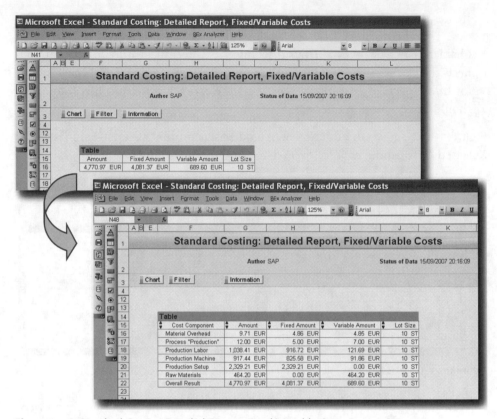

Figure 10.28 Standard Costing Detailed Report, Fixed/Variable Costs Report Output

Standard Cost Estimate: Time Series for Material, Price per Base Quantity Report

This query shows the released cost estimates for base quantity specified in the selection screen. You can analyze the cost component split by drilling down to cost components or cost component group 1, as shown in Figure 10.29.

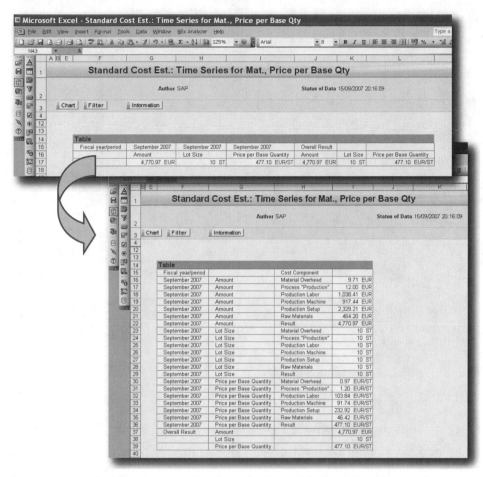

Figure 10.29 Standard Cost Estimate: Time Series for Material, Price per Base Quantity Report Output

Standard Cost Estimate: Time Series for Material, Level/Lower Level Costs Report

This query shows the released costs estimate in two parts: lower level and level. The level indicates whether the costs are incurred in the lower level or deeper manufacturing levels. You can analyze the cost component split at the lower level and level by drilling down to cost components or cost component group 1, as shown in Figure 10.30.

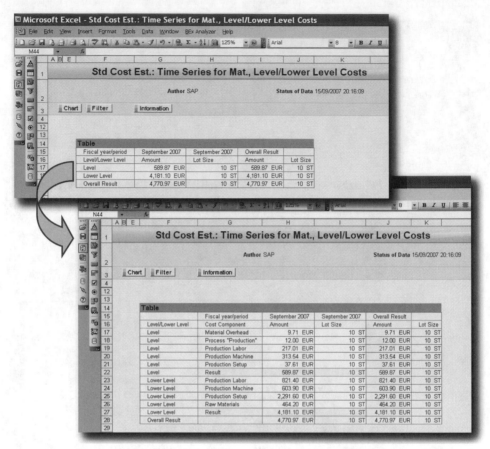

Figure 10.30 Standard Cost Estimate: Time Series for Material, Level/Lower Level Costs Report Output

10.3.2 Data Modeling and Reporting of Cost Object Controlling

The business content in product costing provides the InfoProvider CO-PC Cost Object Controlling (0PC_C01). This InfoCube contains the transaction data for orders that are extracted from the connected source systems. It is supplied data with the InfoSources Cost Object Controlling Plan/Actual Data (0CO_PC_01) and Cost Object Controlling Period End Closing (0CO_PC_02). Figure 10.26 shows the data flow of the CO-PC Cost Object Controlling InfoCube along with the data model.

Data Flow of CO-PC Cost Object Controlling InfoCube   *Data Model of CO-PC Cost Object Controlling InfoCube*

Figure 10.31 Data Flow of Cost Object Controlling InfoCube along with the Data Model

With the queries delivered based on this InfoProvider, you can analyze costs during the production execution and period end closing processes such as plan costs, target costs, actual costs, WIP, and variances. Figure 10.32 shows the business content queries delivered based on the CO-PC Cost Object Controlling InfoCube.

Production: Detailed Order Target/ Actual Report

The Production Detailed Order Actual query shows a detailed target and actual comparison at the material level. The report displays target costs, actual costs, scrap variances, total input variances, total output variances, total variances, and the percentage of total variances against target costs per cost element. Total input variance includes input price variance, input quantity variance, resource usage variance, and remaining input variance. Total output variance includes output price variance, mixed price variance, lot size variance, and remaining variance.

Figure 10.33 illustrates an example of the Production Detail Order Target/Actual report.

Figure 10.32 Cost Object Controlling Queries

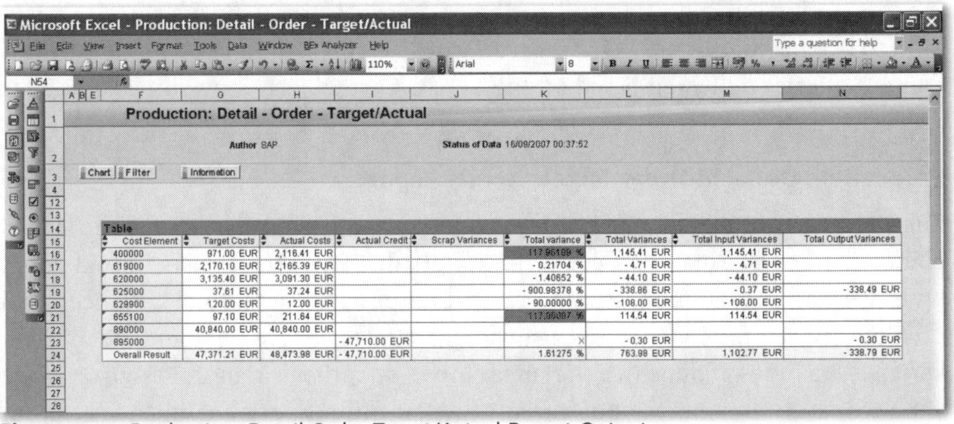

Figure 10.33 Production: Detail Order Target/Actual Report Output

10.3.3 Data Modeling and Reporting of Actual Costing

The business content provides two InfoProviders for actual costing: the Actual Costing/Material Ledger-Costs InfoCube (0COPC_C02) and the Actual Costing/Material Ledger-Cost Component Split InfoCube (0COPC_C07). Figure 10.34 shows the data flow of the Actual Costing/Material Ledger InfoCubes along with the data model example of the Actual Costing/Material Ledger-Costs InfoCube.

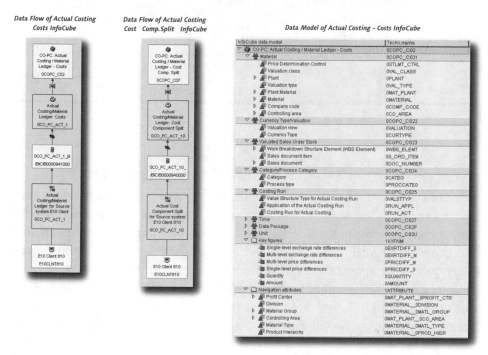

Figure 10.34 Data Flow of Actual Costing InfoCubes along with the Data Model of the Actual Costing/Material Ledger Costs InfoCube

The Actual Costing Costs InfoCube (0COPC_C02) contains the transaction data of the material ledger, which includes the value and quantity information for each material. It is supplied with data from the InfoSource Actual Costing/Material Ledger-Costs (0CO_PC_ACT_1).

The Actual Costing Cost Component Split InfoCube (0COPC_C07) contains the split transaction data of the material ledger, which includes the value and quantity information for each material. It is supplied with data from the InfoSource Actual Costing/Material Ledger-Costs Component Split (0CO_PC_ACT_10).

Figure 10.35 shows the queries delivered based on these InfoProviders. In the following pages we explain two of them.

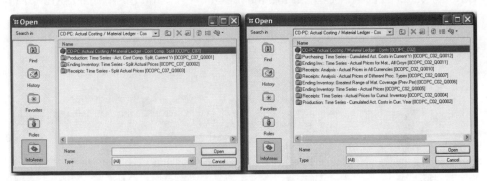

Figure 10.35 Actual Costing/Material Ledger Queries

Receipts: Analysis—Actual Prices of Different Process Types Report

As explained earlier, the material ledger keeps the value and quantity information for the categories beginning inventory, receipts, cumulative inventory, consumption, and ending inventory. The receipts and consumption are further classified into process categories. The Receipt Analysis Actual Prices of Different Process Types query displays detailed information of receipts categories by process type. For example, we first put 120 units of P-104 into stock with the previous period unit price EUR 471.82, which is categorized under process type B+. The goods receipt during the production execution is categorized under process type BF (see Figure 10.36).

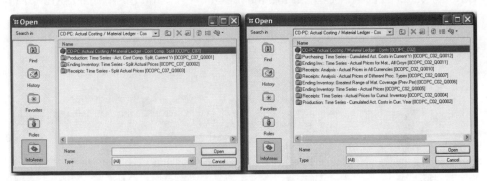

Figure 10.36 Receipts: Analysis—Actual Prices of Different Process Types Report Output

Ending Inventory: Time Series—Actual Prices Report

This query shows the period unit price calculated during actual costing for the chosen materials. Figure 10.37 shows an example of the report output. You can use this report to analyze the period unit prices of materials for the selected period and plant.

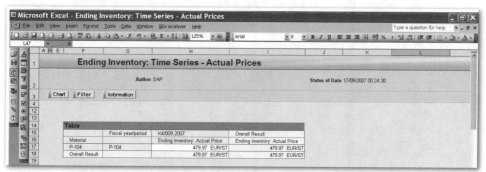

Figure 10.37 Ending Inventory: Time Series—Actual Prices Report Output

10.3.4 Data Modeling and Reporting of Profitability Analysis

The business content of CO-PA is different from the business content of other components because data structures for CO-PA in SAP ERP are customer specific and generated according to business needs. In SAP ERP there is no business content delivered DataSource for your operating concern, as the structures and tables are generated when the operating concern is defined. Thus, you need to create your own DataSource to extract data from source systems to SAP NetWeaver BI.

The business content of CO-PA provides six InfoProviders for profitability analysis and reporting: the Published Key Figures InfoCube (0COPA_C01), CRM Marketing Figures InfoCube (0COPA_C02), Quickstart S_GO InfoCube (0COPA_C03), Consumer Good Industry S_CP InfoCube (0COPA_C04), Route Profitability S_AL InfoCube (0COPA_C05), and MultiProvider CRM Marketing (0COPAMP01). Figure 10.38 shows the data flow of the InfoCube Quickstart S_GO (OCOPA_C03) along with its data model.

The data is updated from the CO-PA Quickstart S_GO InfoSource (0CO_PA_03). In our data flow example, for simplicity, we have not used a DSO. You can implement a scenario where DSO is updated from the InfoSource and InfoCube is updated from DSO.

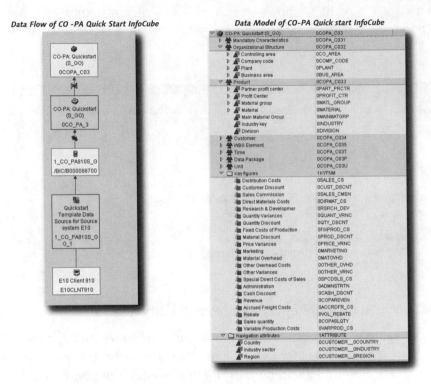

Figure 10.38 Data Flow of the CO-PA Quickstart InfoCube along with Data Model

Create CO-PA DataSource in the SAP ERP system

As we mentioned above, the tables and structures of the operating concern are generated when the operating concern is defined in customizing. Thus, there is no standard data source to extract data from source system(s) to SAP NetWeaver BI. You have to create your own custom DataSource that matches the data structure of your operating concern. Once you create the DataSource, you should replicate it in SAP NetWeaver BI to use it for transferring data from SAP ERP to SAP NetWeaver BI. To create a CO-PA DataSource, follow the configuration menu path in SAP ERP: **Integration with Other mySAP.com Components • Data Transfer to the SAP Business Information Warehouse • Settings for Application-Specific Data-Sources (PI) • Profitability Analysis • Create Transaction Data DataSource** (Transaction KEBO).

Figure 10.39 shows DataSource 1_CO_PA810S_GO_1, which we created to extract data from operating concern Quickstart (S_GO). Characteristics, value fields, and fields from key figure schemes are included in the DataSource.

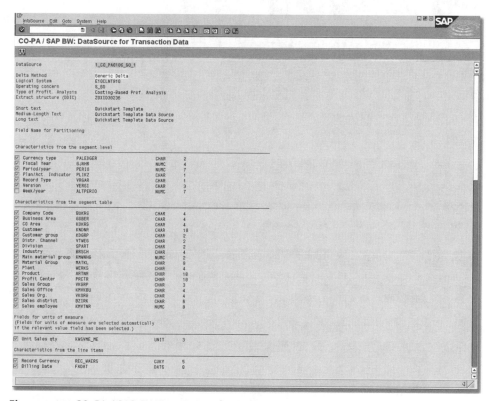

Figure 10.39 CO-PA / SAP BW DataSource for Transaction Data

Profitability Reporting in SAP NetWeaver BI

In this section, we focus on key business content queries based on the InfoProvider Quickstart S_GO (0COPA_C03), which is shown in Figure 10.40.

Product Profitability Report

The Product Profitability (0COPA_C03_Q0011) query provides profitability on products, customers, and other marketing dimensions (e.g., distribution channel). As illustrated in Figure 10.41, you can see net sales, net revenue, contribution margin 1, contribution margin 2, and contribution margin 3 in the report output. You can swap the product characteristic with customer, fiscal year variant, material group, fiscal year/period, distribution channel, and key figures. You can drill down to customer, fiscal year variant, material group, fiscal year/period and distribution channel.

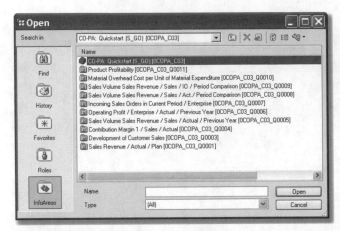

Figure 10.40 CO-PA Quickstart S_GO Queries

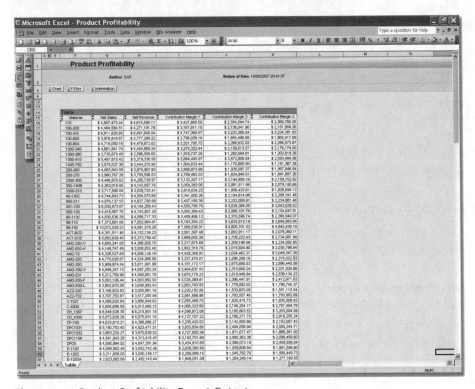

Figure 10.41 Product Profitability Report Output

Contribution Margin 1 / Sales / Actual Report

The Contribution Margin 1 / Sales / Actual (0COPA_C03_Q0004) query provides an actual and plan comparison for profitability analysis down to contribution margin 1. You can see net sales, discounts, material related costs, and contribution margin 1 (see Figure 10.42). In the report output, you can drill down or filter to customer, sales employee, sales group, sales office, and sales organization. You can swap axes to have the key figures in the columns and plan/actual comparison structure in the rows of the report.

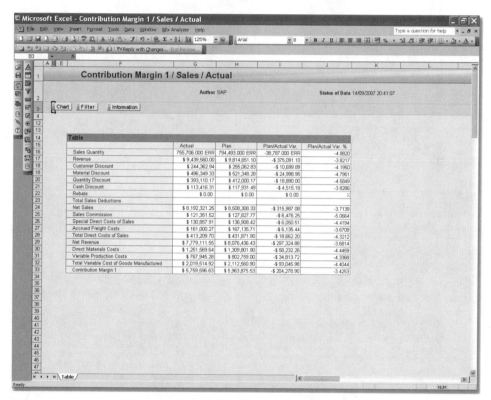

Figure 10.42 Contribution Margin 1 / Sales / Actual Report Output

10.4 Summary

SAP ERP provides CO-PC and CO-PA components for product costing and profitability analysis. The most frequent question we hear from SAP customers is that they want to understand how to analyze reports in the end-to-end product costing process and transfer product costing results to CO-PA. In this chapter, we first explained the product costing reporting by envisioning a case study and discussed the common errors of product cost calculation and showed you how to analyze CO-PC reports. Then we focused on how to transfer product costing results to CO-PA, the reporting architecture of CO-PA as well as the design considerations and work-in best practices for profitability analysis. Finally, we explained the SAP NetWeaver BI business content for product costing and profitability analysis along with data flow and modeling examples and the business content queries.

What are the key design considerations for the consolidation process to ensure that it supports legal and management reporting requirements? What are the key touch points of consolidation processes with other financial processes? How can you leverage the reporting capabilities of SAP NetWeaver BI to generate consolidation financial statements? We address all of these questions in this chapter by explaining our selected leading practices and giving real-world examples. This chapter also discusses how to streamline and simplify the consolidation process and establish a robust consolidation reporting architecture strategy along with the explanation of key financial statement reports.

11 Consolidated Financial Statements

Consolidated financial statements comprise consolidation of the accounts enterprise-wide. The objective of consolidated financial statements is to provide comparable, reliable, and transparent information to regulatory bodies for analyzing the corporate group as if it were a single economic entity. In today's regulatory environment, providing consolidated financial statements fast and accurately and complying with international accounting standards is not optional, but mandatory.

The financial consolidation reporting process starts with data collection. Once the financial data is collected, it is validated and summarized for each reporting entity. Consolidated financial statements at the corporate group level are prepared by combining the financial statements of each reporting entity within the group on a line by line basis. This is accomplished by adding together items such as assets, liabilities, equity, income, and expenses. The consolidation process also involves many subprocesses such as elimination of interunit balances and elimination of interunit profit balances.

The main disclosures related to consolidated financial statements are stated in IAS 27—Consolidated Financial Statements and Accounting for Investments in Subsidiaries, IAS 28—Accounting for Investment in Associates and IFRS 3—Business Combinations. The IFRS/IAS consolidation financial reporting requirements included in these sections have been subject to significant changes.

The requirements of consolidated financial statements for U.S. GAAP are stated in FASB Statement No. 94 (SFAS 94 — Consolidation of all majority-owned subsidiaries) and FASB Statement No. 141 (SFAS 141 — Business Combinations). In spite of convergence initiatives for the accounting standards, accounting regulations for consolidated financial statements still differ. The major differences are the basis of the consolidation policy, the presentation of minority interest, and accounting investment. For example, investment in subsidiaries could be accounted for using the equity method according to the U.S. GAAP, whereas it is carried at cost or accounted for as available assets according to IFRS. The equity method was prohibited in IFRS with the revision of IAS 27 in December 2003.

It is absolutely critical that consolidated financial statements are produced on time and accurately, as well as in accordance with international accounting standards. Many consolidation systems offer the ability to consolidate financial data and enable the generation of consolidated financial statements. However, not all of them are integrated very well with SAP ERP, nor do they provide advanced functionalities to comply with regulations, resulting in incorrect and incomplete financial results. By using SAP ERP, organizations can generate consolidated financial statements accurately and in a consistent, timely, and efficient manner.

Throughout this chapter we examine the design considerations for establishing consolidation reporting architecture, best practices and approaches to standardize and streamline the consolidation reporting process, and real world solutions and issues. Let's start by taking a quick look at the history of SAP's consolidated financial reporting evolution and point out SAP's long-term strategy on consolidation product.

11.1 Evolution of SAP Consolidated Financial Reporting

As the different business requirements are hammered out, SAP has aggressively released new versions of SAP consolidation components and introduced new consolidation products over the years and releases. This has given SAP customers various options of which product to invest in for the long haul. So, which ones will fall by the wayside and which ones should organizations really care about in the future? Figure 11.1 illustrates the evolution of SAP consolidated financial reporting.

In the early releases, SAP offered a tool called Legal Consolidation (FI-LC), which was released in 1993. FI-LC was the first one designed to allow consolidation of the financial data and the generation of consolidated financial reports. This consolidation tool was based on a special ledger. FI-LC was supported until the release SAP R/3 4.6C, and only existing FI-LC implementations were maintained up until SAP R/3 4.6C. In other words, FI-LC was no longer supported for new implementations with SAP R/3 4.6C.

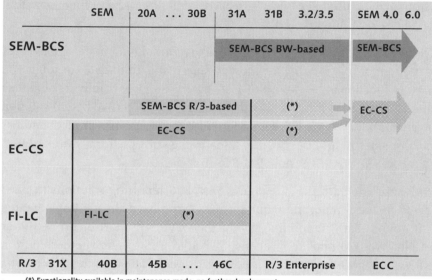

(*) Functionality available in maintenance mode, no further development

Figure 11.1 Evolution of SAP Consolidated Financial Reporting

In 1997, a more advanced product, Enterprise Controlling Consolidation (EC-CS), was introduced. The product roadmap that SAP published at that time identified EC-CS as the consolidation solution to be implemented and enhanced. Thus, many SAP customers implemented the EC-CS or migrated from FI-LC to EC-CS. EC-CS has been the consolidation solution on the market since then.

After EC-CS was introduced, SAP started to develop the Strategic Enterprise Management Business Consolidation SEM-BCS (R/3-based), which was an intermediate version of consolidation within SEM based on EC-CS. As to the consolidation functionalities, EC-CS and SEM-BCS (R/3-based) were identical. SEM-BCS (R/3-based) offered additional data exchange possibilities with Business Information Warehouse (BW). Thus, the consolidation logic of SEM-BCS (R/3-based) resided within

SAP R/3. For reporting purposes, SEM-BCS (R/3-based) was connected to BW. Consequently, the reporting was based, among others, on BW's Business Explorer (BEx) Suite reporting tools, which provided advanced reporting functionalities. In SAP ERP, SEM-BCS (R/3-based) and EC-CS were merged and now run under the common name EC-CS. Since this merge, all of the functionalities developed in SEM-BCS (R/3-based) were featured in EC-CS in SAP ERP, such as read data from BW InfoProviders and real-time reporting of EC-CS data via VirtualProviders. The consolidation solution SEM-BCS (R/3-based) is therefore no longer available in SAP ERP. Customers who used SEM-BCS (R/3-based) will not lose any functionality if they upgrade to SEM-BCS in SAP ERP.

SEM-BCS (BW-based) is the most current consolidation solution in the evolution of consolidation reporting, offering the most advanced and up-to-date consolidation and reporting functionalities. SEM-BCS (BW-based) provides a fully flexible data model and is completely integrated with BW. The SEM-BCS (BW-based) solution is now available with release 6.0 within SAP ERP as an analytics product and has been available since June 2006. Because it shares the same platform with SAP ERP, it is now called SAP SEM-BCS, not SEM-BCS (BW-based).

Today, SAP supports both EC-CS and SAP SEM-BCS reporting solutions to meet consolidated financial reporting requirements. If you have already implemented EC-CS and found that it is limiting you in the way you report or process your financial data, we recommend evaluating SAP SEM-BCS to see whether you can remove these restrictions. If you are a new customer and want to implement a consolidation tool, it is important to keep in mind that SAP's strategic direction is toward SAP SEM-BCS. To support this strategy, SAP enhanced the migration tools so that customers using EC-CS can easily migrate to SAP SEM-BCS. In addition, SAP SEM-BCS is one of the analytics extending the ERP scope to provide strategic insight for better decision-making. It provides more advanced functionalities and flexibility in consolidation reporting architecture. For example, while EC-CS is limited with respect to enhancing the data model with customer-specific attributes, SAP SEM-BCS overcomes these boundaries.

Figure 11.2 provides a summary of the comparison between SAP SEM-BCS and EC-CS with respect to important aspects of the consolidation process.

In our experience, we have seen that some SAP customers who implemented the early releases of SEM-BCS struggled with many missing functionalities and inconsistencies. However, the product has been drastically improved over the years and releases. SAP has strengthened consolidation reporting capabilities to increase process efficiency and data transparency.

At the time we were writing this book SAP AG acquired OutlookSoft Corporation and renamed the OutlookSoft software as SAP Business Planning and Consolidation (SAP BPC). The main reason for this acquisition was to deliver a more flexible solution than SAP SEM-BCS to carry out corporate consolidation activities. The SAP BPC is an application of Corporate Performance Management (CPM).

The area of the comparison	SAP SEM-BCS	SAP EC-CS
Data Model	Flexible	Fixed table set
Segment Reporting	Based on matrix organization	Based on consolidation unit
Versions	Arbitrary number of version characteristics	Only one version characteristic
Subassignments	Arbitrary number of subassignments	Only up to 5 subassignments possible
Automated Consolidation Functions	Role concept for defining semantics for key figures and characteristics	Functions implemented on predefined database
Periods	No restrictions	Up to 16 periods
Group Currency	Characteristic in the data basis	Property of the ledger
Master Data Integration	Integrated with SAP NetWeaver BI	Master data has to be extracted from source system
Transaction Data Integration	Transaction data in one place – SAP NetWeaver BI	Transaction data stored in source system and extracted to SAP NetWeaver BI

Figure 11.2 Comparison of SAP SEM-BCS and EC-CS

The emphasis in this chapter is on recommending the best foundations of consolidation reporting design in SAP SEM-BCS. Generating the consolidated financial statements on time and accurately depends on establishing robust data modeling and consolidation reporting architecture and streamlining the consolidation reporting process. In the next section we explain the design considerations of how best to structure data modeling in SAP SEM-BCS. This includes optimum data model set-up best practices, consolidation implementation scenarios, and key integration points across SAP ERP, SAP NetWeaver BI, and SAP SEM-BCS. Chapter 14 covers how SAP SEM-BCS and SAP BPC applications will be merged into one robust consolidation reporting solution. Note that SAP will protect the investment made by its customers choosing either solution so that you don't need to reinvest in the product.

11.2 Consolidation Data Modeling

In SAP SEM-BCS, consolidation functionalities are based on the data model, where required characteristics (e.g., company, profit center, transaction type, etc.) and key figures (e.g., transaction currency amount, local currency amount, group amount, quantity, etc.) along with their roles in the consolidation are identified.

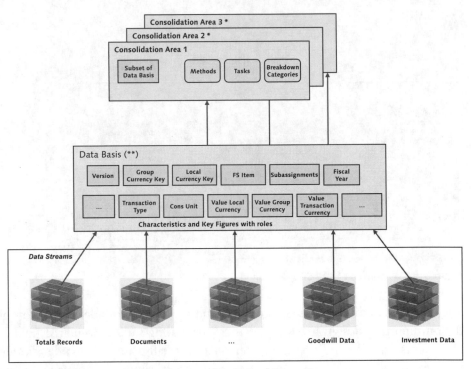

(*) Additional consolidation areas are optional, depending on consolidation implementation scenario

(**) Multiple data basis can be used depending on consolidation implementation scenario

Figure 11.3 Consolidation Data Model

As shown in Figure 11.3, the data model consists of data basis, data streams, and consolidation area:

► **Data Basis**

The data basis is the foundation of the data model. It includes data streams, characteristics, and key figures for the totals records and the associated roles of each characteristic and key figure. Consolidation functions are not designed for any specific fixed model but are based on the *roles* assigned to characteristics and key figures. In other words, the roles define the semantics of characteristics and key figures that provide the basis for consolidation. When defining the data basis, you assign specific roles to characteristics and key figures. The role assignment is very important, as the consolidation functions use the roles for processing. For example, the interunit elimination task is processed with the role of the consolidation unit. If you assign a company to the consolidation unit role, the interunit elimination task is processed with the company characteristic. Figure 11.4 illustrates the role assignment in the data basis. In our example, we allocated the consolidation unit role to company and profit center. This means interunit eliminations are carried out either on the company or profit center dimension or both. This is further controlled in the definition of the consolidation area.

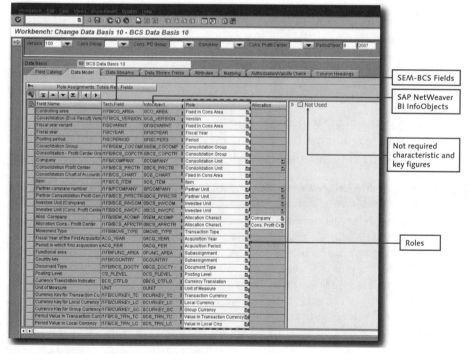

Figure 11.4 Role Assignment in the Data Basis

Roles significantly enhance integration with SAP ERP and SAP NetWeaver BI and the flexibility of the consolidation system. In the following pages, we describe the main roles in the consolidation process.

The **Version** role enables parallel consolidation with various value categories. You can assign more than one characteristic to the version role, for example, valuation view and accounting principles.

The **Consolidation unit** role represents the smallest element of the corporate group structure that can be used as the basis for performing consolidation. In our example, we allocated the consolidation unit role to the company and consolidation profit center characteristics.

The **Consolidation group** role represents the grouping of consolidation units and consolidation groups for the purposes of consolidation and reporting. Multiple consolidation groups can be arranged in a hierarchy.

The **Partner unit** role represents a unit that has a business relationship with a specific consolidation unit. In our example, we allocated the partner unit role to the partner company and the partner consolidation profit center characteristics.

The **Subassignment** role can be used to further differentiate or break down the values of the characteristic. The subassignment can be optional or required depending on the analytical needs. Examples of subassignments are movement types, trading consolidation units, transaction currency, unit of measure quantity, and so on.

The **Item**, or **Financial Statement (FS) item**, role forms the basis for data entry, posting, and reporting of financial data. Financial statement items are the equivalent of G/L accounts in the financial accounting.

Minimum roles to be assigned to the data basis

The following roles must be assigned to at least one characteristic or key figure in the data model: version, group currency, consolidation unit, consolidation group, partner unit, item, document type, posting level, fiscal year and period, and value in group currency. You may require other characteristics and key figures depending on the consolidation functions used. For example, when performing currency translation from local currency or transaction currency to the group currency, you require the local and the transaction currency values to use them in translation. Thus, you need to assign **value in local currency** role and **value in transaction currency role** to relevant characteristics.

▶ **Data Streams**

Data streams identify the storage location for consolidation data. You can use multiple data streams, for example, totals records, documents, goodwill data, and investment data, depending on your business needs. The respective Info-Providers for data streams are defined in SAP NetWeaver BI. The data streams are connected to these InfoProviders in SAP NetWeaver BI where data is written and read from. You can define the InfoProviders in SAP NetWeaver BI and then assign them to data streams. Alternatively, you can get the system to generate the respective InfoProviders automatically, except for the data target InfoProvider for the totals records data stream. To automatically generate a data target in SAP NetWeaver BI, you should select generated indicator of the respective data stream and click on the **Generate** button, as in Figure 11.5. In our example, we generated the virtual InfoProvider ZBCS_DV11 for the documents data stream. If you do not specify the name of the InfoProvider when generating an InfoProvider, the system will propose a name automatically. Note, however, that you should be careful with naming conventions in order not to overwrite an existing object.

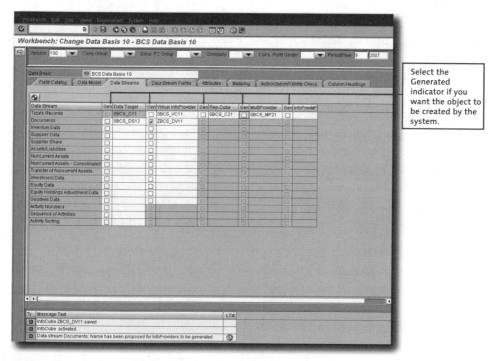

Figure 11.5 Data Streams Definition

When it comes to the data target of the totals records data stream, which is the heart of the consolidation process, the system uses the settings on the **Field Catalog** tab. That is why the data target for the totals records field is gray in the data stream configuration. In our example, InfoProvider 0BCS_C11 is the data target of the totals records. We specified the relevant settings in the **Field Catalog** tab as in Figure 11.6.

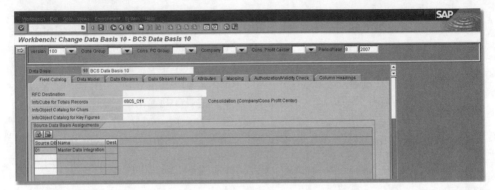

Figure 11.6 Field Catalog

SAP NetWeaver BI provides standard InfoProviders delivered within the business content for business consolidation in SAP SEM-BCS. The standard delivered business content InfoProviders are a great jump-start for building the data model. To create the totals records InfoCube in SAP SEM-BCS, you can activate standard delivered InfoCubes such as 0BCS_C10 and 0BCS_C11. The selection of the characteristics and key figures that are used for the consolidation in the data model is limited to those characteristics that are available in these InfoProviders. Additional characteristics cannot be used in the definition of the data model. Table 11.1 outlines the business content InfoProviders for totals records and documents data streams. Note that SAP ERP provides business content InfoProviders for other data streams such as inventory data, investment data, and goodwill data.

You can modify the standard InfoProviders by adding or deleting the InfoObjects according to your business needs. Note, however, that modifying the totals records InfoProvider should be done very carefully to avoid any inconsistency in the data basis. We strongly recommend checking SAP Note 753688 if you want to use standard business content InfoProviders in the data basis.

InfoProvider	Description
Consolidation Company/Profit Center) (0BCS_C10)	This InfoCube contains total items that are extracted from the connected source system. Virtual InfoCube 0BCS_VC10—Consolidation (Company/Profit Center) is used for reporting.
Consolidation (Company/ Consolidation Profit Center) (0BCS_C11)	This InfoCube contains total items that are extracted from the connected source system. Virtual InfoCube 0BCS_VC11—Consolidation (Company/Consolidation Profit Center) is used for reporting. The difference between 0BCS_C10 and 0BCS_C11 is that the profit center hierarchy and the company hierarchy are dependent on version and time period characteristics in InfoCube 0BCS_C10.
Documents Consolidation (0BCS_DS12)	This DSO contains all transaction data that is generated as a result of consolidation postings. The virtual InfoProvider for documents consolidation is the virtual InfoCube 0BCS_VC12.

Table 11.1 Content InfoProviders

SAP customers often want to know which data streams should be defined in addition to the data target of totals records during consolidation. The answer to this question depends on your business requirements and consolidation reporting architecture. For example, you need to define data targets of data streams for investee equity data, investment data, equity holdings adjustments, goodwill data, activity numbers, and sequence of activities to carry out the consolidation of investment functionality. When it comes to virtual InfoCube, reporting InfoCube, and MultiProvider, the performance plays an important role in the decision, which we explain in detail in the consolidation reporting architecture section.

▶ **Consolidation Area**

A consolidation area is a subset of characteristics and key figures available in the data basis. You can define more than one consolidation area within a data basis. Figure 11.7 illustrates an example of consolidation area settings. In the consolidation area, you can define the permanent parameters, fixed parameters, and characteristics that are displayed in the header of all consolidation screens.

Figure 11.7 Consolidation Area

Permanent parameters are mandatory parameters that affect subsequent activities in the consolidation process. One of the permanent parameters is the consolidation area itself. Version and time characteristics are predefined permanent parameters. In addition to version and time characteristics, you can set some other status-relevant characteristics as permanent parameters by selecting the **Permanent Parameter** box. For each permanent parameter, you can define whether it is displayed in the header of all consolidation screens by selecting the **Display Parameter Page Header** box. In our example, we defined **Consolidation Unit**, **Consolidation Group**, and **Group Currency** as permanent parameters, in addition to version and time characteristics. If you define a single value for the permanent characteristic, it cannot be modified. For example, we defined USD value for the group currency permanent parameter. This means it is not possible to modify the group currency during the consolidation process. Another setting related to characteristics is fixed characteristics. Default values such as **Consolidation Chart of Accounts**, **Controlling Area**, and **Fiscal Year Variant** can be predetermined and fixed by selecting the **Fixed Characteristic** box. In our example, we fixed **Controlling Area** to 1000, **Fiscal Year** to K4, **Consolidation Chart of Accounts** to 01, and **Currency Key for Group Currency** to USD.

Now that we have explained the three important parts of the data model, we can discuss the design considerations to optimize the data model. There are two important design aspects for optimizing the data model.

The first aspect is related to the definition and content of the data streams. We recommend that you first check the business content delivered consolidation Info-Providers. You need to ask analysis questions to find out which characteristics and key figures are relevant to your business and financial reporting requirements. In some cases, information details on characteristics can be viewed without adding the characteristic to the consolidation InfoCube. This can be done by using the *query call up* functionality of SAP NetWeaver BI reporting. For example, you need to check whether you really require reporting cost center details, or could it be that the call up from the company to cost center is enough in SAP NetWeaver BI reporting.

The other important aspect is to determine how to design the legal and management consolidation reporting. Financial data collection reconciliation from different dimensions is an important part of the consolidation process. Consolidation on various levels and dimensions might be required to meet the legal and business requirements. This includes dimensions such as legal entities, geographical areas, product lines, and management areas. In the rest of this chapter, we refer to consolidation of legal entities as legal consolidation and consolidation of geographical areas, lines of products, management areas, and so on as management consolidation. In SAP SEM-BCS, three implementation scenarios are possible for legal and management consolidation. In Table 11.2 we list the consolidation implementation scenarios along with the required set up options in the area of data basis, consolidation area, and consolidation unit:

▶ **Legal and management consolidation in sequence**
In this scenario, legal consolidation and management consolidation are run in sequence. To do so, you need to define two consolidation areas in one data basis: the legal consolidation area and the management consolidation area. The consolidation unit role is assigned to the company characteristic in the legal consolidation area, whereas profit center or another management reporting

characteristic, for example, segment, is assigned to the consolidation unit role in the management consolidation area.

▶ **Legal and management consolidation in parallel**

In this scenario, legal and management consolidation are run in parallel. This can be achieved by defining a separate data basis, and consequently a separate consolidation area, for legal and management consolidation reporting. In the legal consolidation area, the consolidation unit role is allocated to the company characteristic, whereas profit center or another management reporting characteristic, for example, segment, is assigned to the consolidation unit role in the management consolidation area.

▶ **Simultaneous legal and management consolidation**

In this scenario, you run legal and management consolidation simultaneously in one consolidation area. You can achieve integrated legal and management consolidation reporting by allocating the consolidation unit role to company and management reporting characteristics in the same consolidation area.

Implementation Scenario	Data Basis	Consolidation Area	Consolidation Unit
Legal and management consolidation in sequence	Single data basis	Two separate consolidation areas	Two consolidation units: ▶ Company characteristic for legal consolidation ▶ Profit center or another management reporting characteristic for management consolidation
Legal and management consolidation in parallel	Two data bases	Two separate consolidation areas	One consolidation unit per consolidation area: ▶ Company characteristic for legal consolidation ▶ Profit center or another management reporting characteristic for management consolidation
Simultaneous management and legal consolidation	Single data basis	Single consolidation area	Matrix organization consolidation unit. Consolidation unit role is allocated to both company and profit center characteristics (or another management reporting characteristic) in a single consolidation area.

Table 11.2 Legal and Management Consolidation Implementation Scenarios

Both the first and second implementation scenarios can result in data redundancy in SAP NetWeaver BI and SAP SEM-BCS. In addition, these two scenarios require reconciliation between legal and management consolidation results, which can lead to extended time to period end close. Our experience shows that the last scenario is the optimum design solution for designing the data basis and consolidation area. In the next section, we further explore the topic, explain the importance of integrating legal and management consolidation reporting, and discuss the best practices for integrating legal and management consolidation.

11.3 Integrating Legal and Management Consolidation

Traditionally, most companies have two separate processes for consolidation: the legal consolidation reporting process and the management consolidation reporting process. The legal consolidation reporting process provides financial statements according to legal and statutory requirements, whereas the management consolidation reporting process generates consolidated financial statements based on management reporting areas (e.g., profit center, segment). This dual consolidation reporting approach could lead to inconsistent legal and management information, resulting in a lot of time and effort in reconciliation. In today's regulatory environment, it is important to produce both the legal and management consolidation reporting in a consistent, timely, and efficient manner. Companies can make significant cost savings by integrating legal and management consolidation reporting processes.

As mentioned above, SAP SEM-BCS provides the capability to integrate legal and management consolidation via a single data basis and a single consolidation area. The flexible data model allows capturing multiple views of financial information and provides a *single version of truth* for both legal and management data information.

> **Single version of truth**
>
> The Sarbanes-Oxley Act (SOX), among other requirements, mandates publicly traded companies to accelerate the Securities and Exchange Commission (SEC) filings and executive management to certify the accuracy of these results. Without an integrated approach for managing legal and management consolidation reporting, organizations may have to spend a significant amount of time and effort to reconcile financial information reported to the SEC and financial information reported to management. By harmonizing the legal and management consolidation reporting in a common consolidation area, organizations have one data basis that provides a single version of truth for both legal and management reporting. This approach can drastically decrease the closing of the reporting cycle and increase compliance with SOX.

With the introduction of *matrix organization* functionality, SAP SEM-BCS increases the capabilities to support integration of legal and management consolidation. The matrix organization is articulated in Figure 11.8.

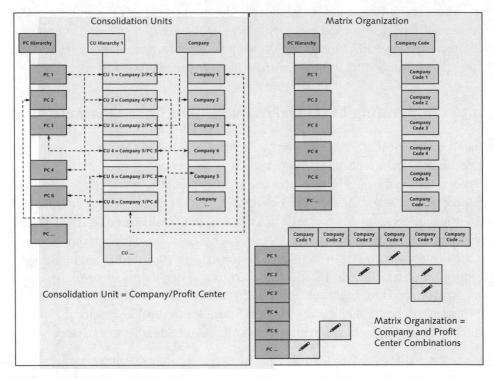

Figure 11.8 Matrix Organization Structure

As mentioned earlier, a consolidation unit is an organization unit where a balanced trial balance is populated for group consolidation. In EC-CS and the earlier version of SAP SEM-BCS, arbitrary numbers of hierarchies are defined for the combination of consolidation units, as shown on the left side of the figure. This model is highly complex and requires great effort in maintaining the consolidation unit groups and hierarchy structures.

With matrix organizations, you can define two consolidation units. For example, one consolidation unit could be the company for legal consolidation, and the other could be the profit center for management consolidation. The concept of matrix organizations is often not very well understood and creates lots of design discussions in the blueprint phase of the project. We advise SAP customers to evaluate whether they truly require one consolidation unit or two. The key question that needs to be answered and agreed upon is whether interunit transactions should be eliminated at the management reporting dimension or be the expected financial consequences of specific actions for management reporting. If the former is the case, matrix organization will serve you well, but if the latter is believed to be disclosed in the consolidated management reports, it is adequate for organizations to define one consolidation unit (e.g., legal entity) and build the consolidated management reports from legal consolidation details by defining management reporting dimension as a sub-assignment. In other words, you need to consider options of aggregation before defining the matrix organization. For example, reporting for profit center groups can be achieved through aggregation when interunit elimination is not required. You should never forget that more characteristics involved in the data model generally means more records to process, which could lead to potential performance issues.

If a matrix approach is used, each characteristic has its own hierarchies. In our example, company characteristic has company hierarchy, whereas profit center has its own hierarchy. Once you have created the hierarchies, you need to define which profit center belongs to which company in the configuration by following the menu path **SEM-BCS: Master Data • Consolidation Units • Combinations of Consolidation Units** (see Figure 11.9).

Matrix organization can serve very well to meet both legal and management consolidation reporting requirements, provided that partner fields are captured and recorded in the source system. However, it is often the case that the partner field for the management reporting dimension is not captured and recorded in the source system. Note that it is not possible to carry out the interunit eliminations without having partner fields populated in the financial data. In that case, it does not make sense to have matrix organization.

Partner derivation for the management reporting dimension is set up via BAdI in SAP ERP. We recognize that it is a big challenge to convince the core ERP team that such a setting is truly required. The core ERP team is typically not positioned to push the use of a partner field and ask the consolidation team to populate the partner field during the data takeover into the SAP SEM-BCS. However, it is not preferred that the data be modified in the consolidation system. Usually, it takes the integration architect or project manager to solve the issue. If you don't want to find out too late that you cannot eliminate interunit eliminations because of the settings in ERP, it is critical to capture and record the partner field for the required transactions in the source systems.

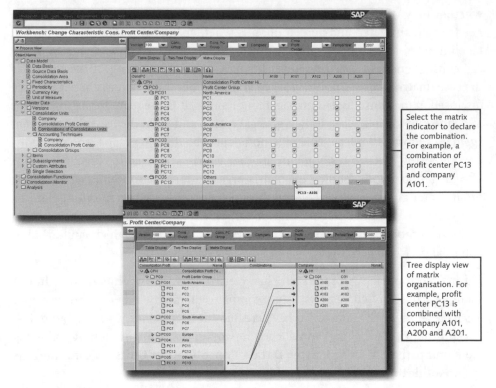

Figure 11.9 Combinations of Consolidation Units

Partner profit center and segment derivation

To define partner segment derivation, follow the configuration menu path **Financial Accounting (New) • Consolidation Preparation (New) Profit Center: Preparations for Consolidation • Derive Partner Profit Center**. If you use segment as consolidated management reporting dimension, you can define segment derivation by following the configuration menu path: **Financial Accounting (New) • Financial Accounting Global Settings (New) • Tools • Customer Enhancements • Business Add-ins (BAdIs) • Segment Derivation**.

According to IAS 14 and FASB 131, the total segment revenues, segment profit or loss, and other amounts disclosed for segments must be stated in consolidated financial statements. You can use either profit center or segment as the reporting dimension for consolidated financial statements. For details regarding which reporting object should be used in segment reporting, see "Determining the Right Segment Reporting Solution" in Chapter 3. In our example above, we used profit center as the management reporting dimension in the matrix organization.

Another design consideration for matrix organization is the required dimensions that you need to consolidate upon. The greater the consolidation unit number, the greater the time required to load data and process consolidation tasks. It is generally advisable to have fewer than 10,000 consolidation units for performance reasons. Let's take a real-world example. Global organization ABC has 800 legal entities, 12 segments, 1,500 profit centers, and 180 profit center groups. In Table 11.2, you can see the impact of using profit center, profit center group, or segment as a consolidation unit in the matrix organization.

Matrix Organization Scenario	Maximum Number of Consolidation Units	Impact
Use company and profit center	1,200,000 (800 × 1,500)	Heavy performance issues Difficulties in master data management Extended time to close
Use company and profit center groups	144,000 (800 × 180)	Performance issues Difficulties in master data management Extended time to close
Use company and segment	9,600 (800 × 12)	Harmonized legal and management reporting Reduced time to close

Table 11.3 Matrix Organization Scenarios

Now that we have explained the design considerations of data modeling for consolidation, we can move to the consolidation process and explain the work-in best practices and the approaches to standardize and streamline the consolidation reporting process.

11.4   The Consolidation Reporting Process

Regardless of the SAP consolidation product that is used, the consolidation reporting process has four main steps: maintain master data, collect financial data, consolidate, and report and analyze. Figure 11.10 shows the main steps of the consolidation reporting process.

Figure 11.10 Consolidation Process Overview

We will now look at each of these steps based on the SAP SEM-BCS product:

▶ **Master data maintenance**
The first step is to prepare and maintain master data and hierarchies to model your corporate structure in the consolidation system. Even though master data remains stable over time and certain master data tasks can be automated, it is important to establish rigorous control and status management of master data. You need to check the master data such as financial statement items, consolidation units, consolidation groups, and transaction types if they are required to be maintained in SAP SEM-BCS before collecting the financial data into SAP SEM-BCS.

▶ **Collect financial data**
In this step, financial data from each reporting entity is taken to SAP SEM-BCS. We can further categorize this step into three:

  ▶ **Data collection**
  There are various data collection methods. You can automatically collect data from SAP NetWeaver BI InfoProviders or other connected SAP systems with loading data from data streams. In addition, you can use manual data entry with data entry layouts, or data can be uploaded from flat files with the flexible upload data collection method. Alternatively, you can post manual entries, for example, to standardize the reported data to meet the accounting and valuation requirements. Other data collection methods such as manual copying and deletion can also be used for data collection.

  ▶ **Validation**
  The validation process provides the ability to avoid inconsistent data throughout the consolidation process. In addition to data collection, you can implement validation rules for consolidation tasks such as the elimination of interunit transactions and additional financial data for investment and equity. One of the common examples of validation used in data collection is to check whether the total value of assets is equal to the total value of liabilities in balance sheets.

▶ **Currency translation**

The currency translation step is processed when the currency of the submitted financial data differs from the group currency. With this step, financial data reported by each reporting entity is translated into the group currency. During this step, rounding differences are also cleared.

▶ **Consolidate**

Depending on your business needs and reporting requirements, different steps are involved in the consolidation of financial data. We will only describe the main steps.

▶ **Interunit elimination**

Interunit elimination is used to eliminate interunit transactions within the selected corporate group based on values and quantities. When viewing the corporate group as a single entity, the group cannot have, for example, receivables and payables from and to itself. It is very important that the interunit transactions are reconciled for any discrepancies before executing this step. We describe the best work-in practices of how to automate and streamline the reconciliation process of group payables and receivables in Chapter 2.

▶ **Consolidation of investments**

This step is required to eliminate the group internal equity holdings (ownership) of the reporting entities. With this process, you eliminate the investments of the higher-level units with their proportionate shares in the stockholders' equity of the reporting unit that belongs to the same consolidation group. During the process, values such as associate profit and loss, minority interest, any goodwill in first acquisition or additions of share ownership, and goodwill amortization are calculated.

▶ **Reclassification**

You can use reclassification to automatically repost or adjust reported financial data and financial postings occurring during consolidation. For example, the consolidated financial statements of a corporate group often need to disclose the retained earnings of the parent unit within the enterprise. With this process, you can reclassify the retained earnings of reporting units as appropriations.

▶ **Allocation**

In this step, you assess or distribute values from sender items to receiver items, for example, to allocate standardized data. Allocations are performed using the distribution or assessment method. When performing allocations, the balance of the sender item is decreased, whereas the balance of the receiver item is increased.

▶ **Report and analyze**
Once you consolidate the financial data, you can create, analyze, and submit the financial statements to stakeholders, authorities, and other regulatory bodies.

Every applicable function is stored as a task in SAP SEM-BCS. The tasks are grouped into a consolidation task hierarchy. In the hierarchy, task dependencies can be specified so that subsequent tasks cannot start if previous ones have not yet been completed. Once you complete the consolidation hierarchy, you can use the consolidation monitor to execute and control all tasks, starting with the initial data take over from the individual consolidation units, over to the availability of standardized financial statement data that has been validated, translated and adjusted to meet the group's consolidation reporting requirements. The consolidation monitor provides sophisticated control over the entire consolidation process across enterprise-wide. Figure 11.11 illustrates the consolidation monitor.

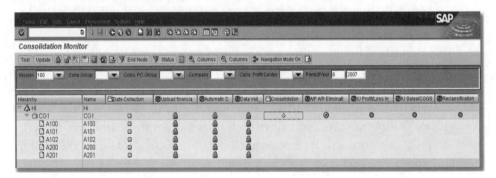

Figure 11.11 Consolidation Monitor

There are several leading design practices for streamlining and simplifying the consolidation reporting process. In the following sections, we discuss these leading design practices. We specifically look at:

▶ Automating the consolidation tasks

▶ Integrating master data

▶ Determining the right structure for consolidation master data

Let's start with the automation of consolidation tasks. Consolidated financial statements must reconcile with SAP ERP systems and be fully auditable, so it is imperative that consolidation tasks are automated.

11.4.1 Automating the Consolidation Tasks

Our experience shows that leading organizations automate the consolidation tasks wherever possible and reduce risks by minimizing the manual interfaces and interventions. With the latest release of SAP SEM-BCS, SAP increased the capabilities of automating the consolidation tasks. In this section, we concentrate on the enhanced functionalities to increase the automation of the consolidation process:

▶ Flexible upload

▶ Interunit profit elimination

▶ Consolidation of investments

Section 302 of the SOX

Risks posed by inadequate management of the consolidation of financial data can lead to severe consequences for corporations and their senior executives in fulfilling organizational objectives, opportunities, or legislative requirements. These risks include inaccessibility of records, inaccuracy of data, lack of credibility of information, and incomplete records and information. Section 302 of the SOX established the requirement for companies to automate postings wherever possible to reduce risk of these errors.

▶ **Flexible upload**

As mentioned earlier, data can be collected by flexible upload or data load from SAP NetWeaver BI InfoProviders. It is possible to upload reported financial data and consolidation master data with the flexible upload method. With SAP SEM-BCS 6.0, flexible upload capabilities have been extended to include additional financial data and documents: investment, equity, equity holding adjustments, goodwill, inventory data, and supplier data. In addition, you can use the program RFBILA00 (Classic Financial Statement report) to download transaction financial data to a file. Then you can use flexible upload in the SAP SEM-BCS system to upload the file as reported financial data.

▶ **Interunit profit elimination**

IFRS 3 Business Combinations requires bringing separate entities together or businesses into one reporting entity. Profits and losses resulting from interunit transactions must be eliminated. With SAP SEM-BCS 6.0, you do not have to post manual elimination documents; instead you can automatically eliminate profit from the interunit transactions. Two new consolidation tasks are available in SAP SEM-BCS:

  ▶ Elimination of interunit profit and loss in transferred assets

  ▶ Elimination of interunit profit and loss in transferred inventory

▶ **Consolidation of investments**

Further efficiencies can be realized by automating the consolidation of investment function, which is a manual effort in many organizations today. SAP SEM-BCS provides automated accounting for investments. For example, you can eliminate investments against equity at acquisition, accounting for minority interests, and equity pickup in which consolidated entities are accounted for under the equity method. As stated earlier, the IFRS consolidation financial reporting requirements included in these sections have been subject to significant changes in recent years due to convergence initiatives of the accounting standards. The functionalities of SAP SEM-BCS are enhanced with the latest release to support the recent changes in IFRS.

By automating the consolidation tasks, you can standardize and streamline the consolidation reporting process in a consistent and efficient manner and provide consolidated financial statements promptly and accurately. In addition to the automation of consolidation tasks, master data integration plays an important role in standardizing and streamlining the consolidation reporting process. In the next section, we discuss the functionalities available in SAP SEM-BCS 6.0 to increase the consolidation master data integration across SAP ERP, SAP NetWeaver BI, and SAP SEM-BCS.

11.4.2   Integrating Consolidation Master Data

Consolidation master data inconsistency across systems prevents efficient consolidated financial report generation and leads to off-line ad hoc analysis efforts. These ad hoc efforts may seem inconsequential, but they can become very costly, as they can cause misstatements in the consolidated financial statements. Regarding master data best practices, consistency and standardization are the keys. Consistent and standard master data eliminate a lot of future headaches.

Master data problems usually arise with the distributed master data approach. Based on application and design requirements, consolidation master data can be maintained in SAP NetWeaver BI, SAP SEM-BCS, or both. Three options are available to prepare master data in SAP SEM-BCS with the distributed master data approach in the early releases:

▶ **Maintain the master data in SAP NetWeaver BI**
All of the consolidation master data and hierarchies for consolidation are maintained in SAP NetWeaver BI and then synchronized to SAP SEM-BCS. With this method, you must manually synchronize the master data; otherwise, characteristic values of InfoObjects and their hierarchies may differ in SAP SEM-BCS, resulting in inconsistency.

▶ **Maintain the master data directly in SAP SEM-BCS**
All of the master data and hierarchies for consolidation are maintained centrally in SAP SEM-BCS. With this method, master data and hierarchies are automatically updated for the corresponding characteristics in SAP NetWeaver BI.

▶ **Maintain the master data partly in SAP SEM-BCS and partly in SAP NetWeaver BI**
It is possible to maintain some of the characteristics in SAP SEM-BCS and populate some of them from SAP NetWeaver BI. Because part of the consolidation master data is maintained in SAP NetWeaver BI, this method requires manual synchronization of master data between SAP NetWeaver BI and SAP SEM-BCS systems.

Regardless of the methods, SAP customers have challenges to build master data integration in SAP SEM-BCS. Although SAP provides predelivered programs to synchronize data between SAP SEM-BCS to SAP NetWeaver BI or vice versa, it is not easy to manage these programs. We advise well-established control on authorizations to execute the synchronization programs, as incorrect usage can cause greater damage than advantage. You can find details regarding how to execute the synchronization programs in SAP Notes 689229 and 578348.

SAP recommends using SAP SEM-BCS as the lead system to maintain consolidation master data; otherwise, manual processing (synchronization) is required to ensure that SAP SEM-BCS tables and SAP NetWeaver BI tables are aligned. The difficulty associated with this method is that you need to create the master data and hierarchies manually or prepare master data flat files to maintain the master data using the flexible file upload function. Both of these options require enormous time and effort.

SAP developed the integration of master data very well in SAP SEM-BCS 6.0. With this release, SAP provided two powerful methods to increase master data integration across SAP ERP, SAP NetWeaver BI, and SAP SEM-BCS. Figure 11.12 illustrates these two methods.

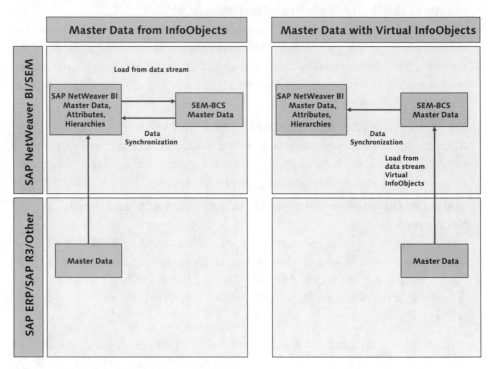

Figure 11.12 Integrated Master Data

- **Master data from InfoObjects**

    The first method is to load master data from SAP NetWeaver BI InfoObjects. SAP SEM-BCS 6.0 provides the ability to read master data from an SAP NetWeaver BI InfoObject. In other words, master data of an SAP NetWeaver BI InfoObject is first replicated in SAP NetWeaver BI from any SAP NetWeaver BI DataSource and then transferred to SAP SEM-BCS. Figure 11.13 shows an example of data load from data stream. In this example, the method DS01 is defined to load consolidation profit center master data via SAP NetWeaver BI InfoObject 0BCS_PRCTR.

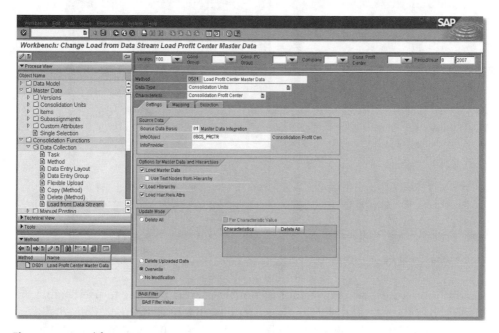

Figure 11.13 Load from Data Stream

The new load function provides the following subfunctions: source selection condition, target selection condition, mapping of sources to target, and BAdI for custom logic.

▶ **Master data with virtual InfoObjects**
The second method is to load master data with virtual SAP NetWeaver BI InfoObjects. SAP SEM-BCS 6.0 provides the ability to read master data of a virtual SAP NetWeaver BI InfoObject from the original location in SAP ERP. With this method, when master data is transferred to SAP SEM-BCS, it is directly extracted from the SAP NetWeaver BI DataSource and simultaneously loaded into SAP SEM-BCS. This method enables integrated master data between SAP ERP and SAP SEM-BCS 6.0 (see Figure 11.14).

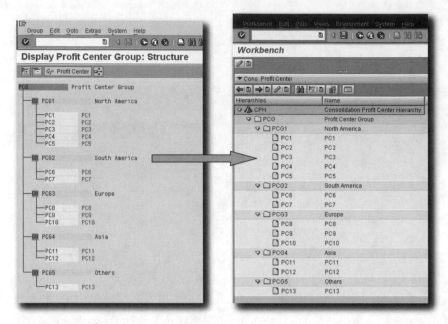

Figure 11.14 Profit Center Hierarchy

In addition to these two powerful functionalities, it is possible to use flexible upload to load the SAP SEM-BCS master data files that have been downloaded from FI-GL and EC-PCA, despite their format in SAP SEM-BCS 6.0. You can also use mapping functions or BAdI as well.

11.4.3 Determining the Right Structure for Consolidation Master Data

Determining the right structure for the consolidation master data plays a very important role in the consolidation reporting process. It is imperative to carry out detailed analysis on the hierarchy structure of consolidation master data such as items, consolidation groups, and consolidation unit hierarchies. In this section, we explain the design considerations of consolidation items, which are also known as financial statement items.

Consolidation items are used to post and analyze amounts and quantity in SAP SEM-BCS. They are the equivalent of G/L accounts in financial accounting. A consolidation item not only allows postings of accounting-related amounts or quantities to the balance sheet and income statement, but also allows statistical amounts and key figures and ratios to be posted. Thus, each consolidation item should be classified under one of the following item types:

▶ Balance sheet

▶ Income statement

▶ Statistical: balance

▶ Statistical: flow

An example of a consolidation item is illustrated in Figure 11.15.

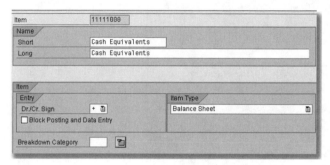

Figure 11.15 Consolidation Item Master Data

The consolidation items are created in the consolidation chart of accounts, which is structured in accordance with the legal and management reporting requirements. In the consolidation chart of accounts, the consolidation items are grouped together in logical groupings and hierarchies. These hierarchies are created based on the reporting needs, such as the various sections and classifications within the balance sheet or income statement.

An example of a consolidation item hierarchy is illustrated in Figure 11.16.

The structure of the consolidation items, item groups, and hierarchies should be robust enough to facilitate the following consolidation steps:

▶ Various reporting formats (IFRS, U.S. GAAP) and currencies

▶ Currency translation

▶ Interunit eliminations

▶ Consolidation of investments

▶ Reclassification

- ▸ Aggregate reporting
- ▸ Audit trail from consolidation items to operational chart of accounts

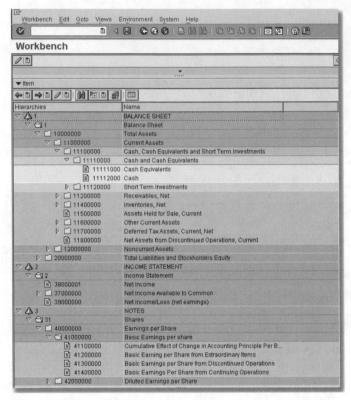

Figure 11.16 Consolidation Item Hierarchy

Now that we have explained the design considerations and the best practices for the consolidation reporting process, we can move to the consolidation reporting architecture.

11.5 Consolidation Reporting Architecture

SAP SEM-BCS is structured to provide a consolidated view of group financial data and to allow for the creation of consolidated financial statements at the group and company level, as well as to present reports for other organization units (segment and profit center) for management. In this section, we explain the SAP SEM-BCS reporting architecture and the fundamentals of SAP SEM-BCS reporting. Reporting data is immediately available when data is loaded or processed in SAP SEM-BCS. From the consolidation statements, you can drill back or jump to the underlying consolidation postings or original source system documents. In other words, SAP SEM-BCS provides an audit trail, which is required by the SOX.

The reporting architecture of SAP SEM-BCS is illustrated in Figure 11.17.

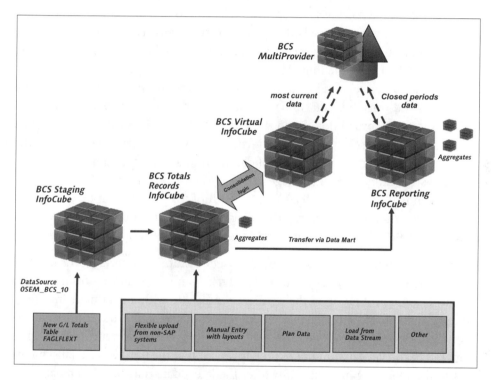

Figure 11.17 Consolidation Reporting Architecture

In this illustration, financial transaction data flows to the SAP SEM-BCS staging InfoCube via standard DataSource 0BCS_SEM_10, which has been especially designed to get totals records from the new G/L. The data is then transferred from an SAP SEM-BCS staging InfoCube to an SAP SEM-BCS totals records InfoCube. In addition to transactional data coming from the SAP SEM-BCS staging InfoCube, data from non-SAP sources and other SAP NetWeaver BI components and data streams flow into the SAP SEM-BCS totals records InfoCube, which is connected to both the SAP SEM-BCS virtual InfoCube and the SAP SEM-BCS reporting InfoCube.

> **Note**
>
> The latest information about integrating the new G/L and SAP SEM-BCS can be found in SAP Notes 852971 and 935370.

The virtual SAP SEM-BCS InfoCube is one of the main components of reporting consolidated data. It has the same data model as the transactional InfoCube, but it does not store any data. It reads the data from the totals records InfoCube when the consolidation reports are executed and applies consolidation logic to take into account consolidation functions. This mechanism provides the capability of generating consolidated reports in real-time, based on the most current consolidation master data and consolidation configuration settings. The data flows from the SAP SEM-BCS totals records InfoCube to the virtual SAP SEM-BCS InfoCube in such a way that the system selects the original data records with regard to characteristics such as the consolidation entity, consolidation unit, and partner unit in full detail and the system cannot take advantage of one of the most important functionalities of BI, which is the use of aggregates. As a result of this, the system may have low performance when generating reports. Nevertheless, it is important to note that the SAP SEM-BCS virtual InfoCube provides real-time consolidation reporting.

The reporting InfoCube is a basic InfoCube used to store the totals records in a format suitable for reporting. The consolidated data can be transferred from the SAP SEM-BCS staging InfoCube to the reporting InfoCube with a data mart interface. The data mart interface prepares the data for reporting. You can optimize the reporting InfoCube by aggregation functionality so that it has shorter response times compared to the virtual InfoCube. Note, however, that the most recent data change flows to the reporting InfoCube only after the latest data transfer. This means you can generate near real-time reporting depending on the data update frequency from the totals record InfoCube to the reporting InfoCube. Perhaps the most important question to ask is "Why do we need to maintain an additional InfoCube for reporting if the virtual InfoCube provides real-time reporting?" The answer to this question is that you can drastically reduce the response time of a report generated by using a reporting InfoCube instead of using the SAP SEM-BCS virtual InfoCube. This is especially important for organizations with high data volume.

Now that we have clarified the use of the totals records InfoCube and reporting InfoCube, let's looks at the MultiProvider role in the consolidation reporting architecture. For performance-optimized real-time reporting, SAP recommends using the virtual InfoCube and the reporting InfoCube in a MultiProvider. The approach of using a MultiProvider is to store data as much as possible in the reporting InfoCube, to make it available as quickly as possible, and to only read the most current changes from the virtual InfoProvider, so that you can generate real-time reporting.

Now that we have explained the reporting architecture of SAP SEM-BCS, we can move on the consolidation reporting capabilities of SAP SEM-BCS.

11.5.1 Consolidation Reporting and Analysis

SAP SEM-BCS works seamlessly with the reporting functions of SAP NetWeaver BI and offers comprehensive reporting and analysis of consolidated financial statements. After you have run all of the consolidation tasks successfully, you can generate analytical reports and financial statements utilizing the full reporting capabilities of SAP NetWeaver BI. We examine the SAP SEM-BCS reports in three categories: business reports, technical reports, and financial statements.

Business Reports

Standard business content contains several consolidation queries. Once you activate business content queries, you can explore them with the SAP Business Explorer (BEx) reporting tools. By using business content queries as a reference, you can create your business reports based on the SAP SEM-BCS virtual InfoCube or SAP SEM-BCS MultiProvider. Custom reports and analysis can be created with SAP BEx Query Designer, BEx Analyzer, BEx Web Application Designer, and BEx Report Designer tools. The BEx suite reporting tools has comprehensive functions for online analytical processing (OLAP) reporting in Microsoft Excel or web-based environments. Figure 11.18 and Figure 11.19 provide the list of business content queries based on the virtual InfoCube 0BCS_VC11 and the MultiProvider 0BCS_MP21 in SAP SEM-BCS 6.0 /SAP NetWeaver BI 7.0. You can use these queries as an example for creating your reports.

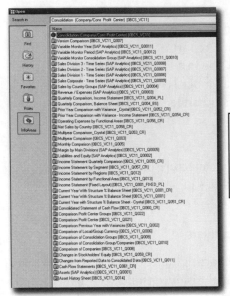

These queries are based on virtual InfoProvider 0BCS_VC11 and delivered as business contents for analytical reports in SAP SEM-BCS 6.0/BI 7.0

Figure 11.18 Analytical Reports Based on the Virtual InfoCube oBCS_VC11

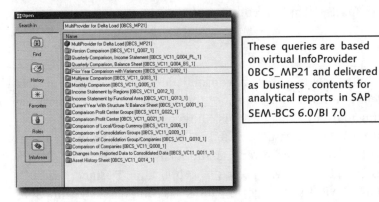

These queries are based on virtual InfoProvider 0BCS_MP21 and delivered as business contents for analytical reports in SAP SEM-BCS 6.0/BI 7.0

Figure 11.19 Analytical Reports Based on the MultiProvider oBCS_MP21

You can use the predelivered queries to model your own reports according to business needs. Figure 11.20 shows an illustration of a consolidated balance sheet report. The query shows the consolidated quarterly balances for the consolidation group CG1 for the fiscal year 2007.

	A	B	C	D	E	F	G	H
9								
10	Controlling area	1000						
11	Cons Chart of Accts	10						
12	Item	Balance Sheet						
13	Version	100						
14	Posting period	#.12						
15	Fiscal Year Variant	K4/2007						
16	Cons Group	CG1						
17								
18	Item		Quarter1	Quarter2	Quarter3	Quarter4	Yearly Balance	
19	▽ 1	Balance Sheet	$0.00	$0.00	$0.00	$0.00	$0.00	
20	▽ 10000000	Total Assets	$ 904,726,000.00	$ 298,897,915.82	-$ 13,380,794.81	-$ 237,835,165.71	$ 952,407,955.30	
21	▽ 11000000	Current Assets	$ 339,241,000.00	$ 302,001,020.60	-$ 13,380,794.81	-$ 135,000.00	$ 627,726,225.79	
22	▷ 11100000	Cash and Short Term	$ 132,650,000.00	$ 109,396,048.36			$ 242,046,048.36	
23	▷ 11200000	Receivables, Net	$ 185,091,000.00	$ 105,460,397.81	-$ 13,230,794.81		$ 277,320,603.00	
24	▷ 11400000	Inventories, Net	$ 16,500,000.00	$ 3,173,722.31	-$ 150,000.00	-$ 135,000.00	$ 19,388,722.31	
25	▷ 11700000	Def.TaxAss.,Curr.	$ 5,000,000.00	$ 1,821,522.34			$ 6,821,522.34	
26	▽ 12000000	Noncurr. Assets	$ 565,485,000.00	$ 205,649,252.23		-$ 237,700,165.71	$ 533,434,086.52	
27	▷ 12100000	Prop.,Plant,Equip.	$ 292,905,000.00	$ 124,699,199.94		-$ 393.33	$ 417,603,806.61	
28	▷ 12300000	Investments	$ 270,000,000.00	$ 117,901,838.05		-$ 270,000,000.00	$ 117,901,838.05	
29	▷ 12400000	Intangible Assets	$ 2,580,000.00	$ 408,884.12		$ 32,300,227.62	$ 35,289,111.74	
30	▽ 20000000	Total Liab./Equity	-$ 904,726,000.00	-$ 364,606,488.42	$ 13,380,794.81	$ 237,835,165.71	-$ 1,018,116,527.90	
31	▽ 21000000	Liabilities	-$ 348,486,000.00	-$ 28,535,058.30	$ 13,244,504.82		-$ 363,776,553.48	
32	▷ 21100000	Curr. Liabilities	-$ 188,955,000.00	-$ 86,735,666.58	$ 13,244,504.82		-$ 262,446,161.76	
33	▷ 21200000	Noncurr. Liabilities	-$ 159,531,000.00	-$ 149,243,318.29			-$ 308,774,318.29	
34	▽ 24000000	Minority Interest				-$ 61,040,227.62	-$ 61,040,227.62	
35	▷ 24100000	Min.-Equity				-$ 61,040,227.62	-$ 61,040,227.62	
36	▽ 25000000	Shareholder's Equity	-$ 556,240,000.00	-$ 370,820,031.03	$ 136,289.99	$ 298,875,393.33	-$ 628,048,347.71	
37	▷ 25100000	Treasury Stock	-$ 10,000,000.00	-$ 6,349,090.19		$ 10,000,000.00	-$ 6,349,090.19	
38	25200000	Preferred Stock	-$ 76,000,000.00	-$ 36,969,588.51		$ 76,000,000.00	-$ 36,969,588.51	
39	25300000	Common Stock	-$ 80,000,000.00	-$ 76,595,834.15		$ 80,000,000.00	-$ 76,595,834.15	
40	25400000	Share Subscriptions	-$ 150,000,000.00	-$ 300,746.60			-$ 150,300,746.60	
41	25500000	Add. Paid In Capital	-$ 118,000,000.00	-$ 87,632,971.47			-$ 205,632,971.47	
42	▷ 25700000	Retained Earnings	-$ 122,240,000.00	-$ 61,621,008.05	$ 150,000.00	$ 132,875,393.33	-$ 50,835,614.72	
43	▷ 25800000	Acc.Oth.Compr.Inc.,N		$ 0.00	-$ 13,710.01		-$ 13,710.01	
44								
45								

Figure 11.20 Consolidated Balance Sheet Query Example

By using the *report-report interface*, you can drill through in the query from group values to reported operational data using posting levels or drill down to another query or jump further to source component SAP ERP on the individual documents. This strong integration across SAP ERP, SAP NetWeaver BI, and SAP SEM-BCS provides the ability to show an audit trail. This capability is very important in consideration of the SOX. We explain how to use the report-report interface in Chapter 13.

Technical Reports

SAP SEM-BCS also provides technical reports and lists either with a database list in the analysis section of the consolidated workbench or with SAP NetWeaver BI queries that are based on standard InfoCubes for consolidation. Figure 11.21 shows the available technical reports in the consolidation workbench along with an example of the Totals Records report output.

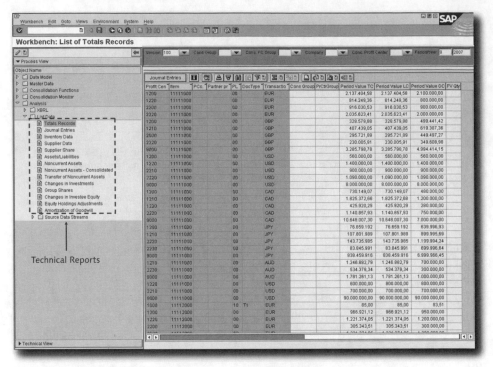

Figure 11.21 Available Technical Reports along with the Totals Records Report Output

---

Database list of source data streams

SAP ERP 6.0 provides the details of the data streams contained in the data basis along with the data fields broken down into data streams.

Financial Statements

SAP SEM-BCS enables you to create and publish individual statements and consolidated statements in *eXtensible Business Reporting Language* (*XBRL*) format. XBRL is a standard language for the creation, publication, analysis, and comparison of information about business enterprises, with a special focus on financial statements. It is supported by the XBRL non-profit organization, which is a consortium of many companies and agencies worldwide working together to build the XBRL language and promote and support its adoption. Since 1998 the organization has produced a variety of specifications and taxonomies to support standard XML-based language for digitizing business reports in accordance with the rules of accounting standards and reporting (check their website: *www.xbrl.org/*).

With the use of XML-based data tags, XBRL is becoming a common standard to describe financial statements and electronic language for financial information, reporting, and analysis.

SAP AG is a member of the XBRL organization, and with SAP SEM you can load XBRL taxonomy and map elements in the taxonomy to the financial statement items, converting the consolidation data into publishable XBRL instance documents. Figure 11.22 shows an XBRL set-up in the consolidation workbench. On the left side of the figure, under the assignment box, you can see the name of the taxonomy. On the right side of the figure, mapping of the taxonomy elements to financial statement items is displayed. You can easily perform the mapping with the use of drag-and-drop functionality. With the use of XBRL it is easy to publish the reports on the website or send them directly to financial analysts, investors, and regulatory authorities.

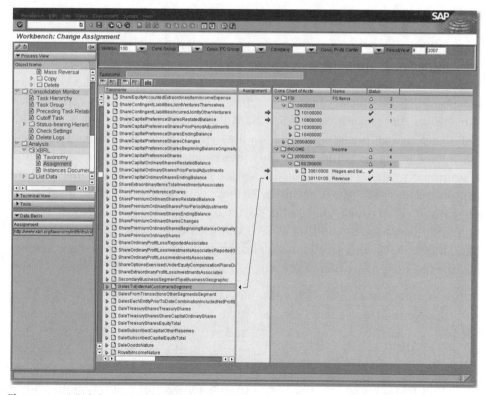

Figure 11.22 XBLR Set-up in SAP SEM-BCS

Taxonomies can be downloaded from the Internet and imported into SAP SEM-BCS. You can download IFRS financial reporting taxonomy from *www.xbrl.org/taxonomy/int/fr/ifrs/ci/2003-07-15/*.

Once you download the taxonomy and upload it to SAP SEM-BCS, you can assign items from any consolidation chart of accounts to the elements of taxonomy. Once you complete the mappings, you can create financial statements as documents in XBRL format based on the SAP SEM-BCS totals records InfoCube. Finally, you can publish instance documents over the Internet, portal, PDF, and so on. Because the logical structure of the data always remains the same, mapping has to be prepared only once, enabling your organization to publish and communicate consolidated financial reports more efficiently, or exchange them reliably with business partners or regulatory bodies.

11.6 Summary

As the business environment becomes increasingly global, the need for providing consolidated financial statements on time and accurately intensifies. SAP has strengthened consolidation reporting capabilities to clearly provide capability, increased process efficiency, and data transparency over the years and releases. Especially with the latest release, SAP SEM-BCS 6.0 delivered as part of SAP ERP, SAP developed enhanced consolidation functionalities to support both legal and management consolidation reporting requirements. You can increase the automation and process efficiency of the consolidation process and model a robust consolidation reporting architecture with these enhanced capabilities. In addition, organizations can reduce total cost of ownership (TCO) due to platform consolidation and integration capabilities of SAP SEM-BCS 6.0. More than anything else, TCO determines which solution provides faster (ROI) and significant cost savings for organizations at the end of the day.

In this chapter, we explained the flexible data modeling of SAP SEM-BCS along with the consolidation design considerations and scenarios. We walked through the best practices for harmonizing legal and management consolidation, structuring the master data and hierarchies, strengthening the integration of master data across SAP ERP, SAP NetWeaver BI, and SAP SEM-BCS, and automating the consolidating tasks. We cover how SAP SEM-BCS and SAP BPC applications will be merged into one robust consolidation reporting solution in Chapter 14.

The purpose of this chapter is to provide an overview of SAP ERP reporting tools for those who have little or no experience with reporting tools. This chapter offers brief descriptions of the report components and formatting options, as well as hints and guidelines for creating reports. All SAP ERP reporting tools covered in this chapter are used in various report developments, and each of them has its own features and capabilities.

12   SAP Reporting Tools

SAP ERP provides various reporting capabilities, available through standard reports or reporting tools. It offers a full suite of predefined reports within each of its components. These standard reports consist of a predefined row and column format yet allow the user the flexibility to report on different data elements or hierarchies within that component.

In previous chapters we have covered the main design considerations for financial processes to generate financial reports accurately and on time. In addition, we have explained the standard SAP ERP reports and business content queries delivered within SAP NetWeaver BI, as well as data flow and data modeling. In this chapter we take you through the reporting tools available in SAP ERP to guide you through reporting tools functions and capabilities for financial reports. With the basic but solid knowledge that you gain in this chapter, you will be able to take your skills further and master the area you are most interested in. The examples we provide are not customer specific, and you can easily replicate them in your own system to build your own reporting solutions, or simply use them as a learning example. We cover the reporting tools for SAP NetWeaver BI in the next chapter.

12.1   SAP ERP Reporting Tools

SAP ERP provides various tools for building reports, including SAP List Viewer (ALV), Report Painter and Report Writer, ABAP, SAP Query, and Drilldown Reporting, as illustrated in Figure 12.1. Each reporting tool has its own special features and capacities. These reporting tools are also used in SAP ERP to create standard delivered reports. For example, many standard financial reports can be executed in ALV format. Except for ABAP, these reporting tools do not necessarily require technical programming skills to build and use the reports. In this section we explain the features and capabilities of each reporting tool and provide useful examples.

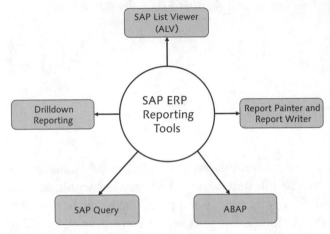

Figure 12.1 Overview of SAP Reporting Tools

Let's first have a look at which reporting tools are typically used in each financial component. Table 12.1 provides an overview of SAP ERP reporting tools and their most common application areas.

SAP ERP Reporting Tools	Application Areas
SAP List Viewer	Used in most financial reports
Drilldown Reporting	Financial Accounting (Classic and New G/L)
	Accounts Payable
	Accounts Receivable
	Profitability Analysis
	Profit Center Accounting
	Special Purpose Ledger
	Executive Information System
	Project Systems
	Consolidation
	Treasury
	Investment Management

Table 12.1 Summary of Reporting Tools by Financial Component

SAP ERP Reporting Tools	Application Areas
Report Painter and Report Writer	Financial Accounting (Classic and New G/L)
	Cost Center Accounting
	Internal Orders
	Profit Center Accounting
	Special Purpose Ledger
	Project Systems
	Product Costing
	Industry Solutions (SAP for Oil & Gas, SAP for Public Sector, etc.)
	Custom tables and views
SAP Queries	Financial Accounting (Classic and New G/L)
	Accounts Payable
	Accounts Receivable
	Asset Accounting
	Treasury

Table 12.1 Summary of Reporting Tools by Financial Component (cont.)

It is important to understand reporting tool functionalities and capabilities in order to use them effectively or create customized reports. In the rest of this section we examine the functionalities of each reporting tool.

12.1.1 SAP List Viewer

SAP List Viewer (ALV) is a list display tool that is used in many standard SAP financial reports. It is a reporting tool in the sense that you can create a customized list based on an existing list structure. Our experience has shown that this powerful functionality is often overlooked and not effectively used when running financial reports due to lack of knowledge and training. We have often recognized that either custom reports were built rather than formatting the reports in ALV display, or users were instructed to download the report output into Excel for formatting such as sorting or generating totals and subtotals. We will now show you the basic functions of ALV so that you can effectively use it when analyzing SAP financial reports.

ALV is used to generate the financial report outputs in simple and flexible format. Reports using ALV are not static outputs, because ALV enables the use of interactive functions such as sorting, filtering, summation, and moving or hiding columns. The columns displayed in the list form the layout of the report.

There are two types of ALV: ALV classic list and ALV grid control. As the name implies, ALV classic list is the older version of the list viewer. It simplifies and unifies the use of lists. Figure 12.2 shows an example of the G/L Account Line Item Display G/L View report (Transaction FAGLL03) in the ALV classic list.

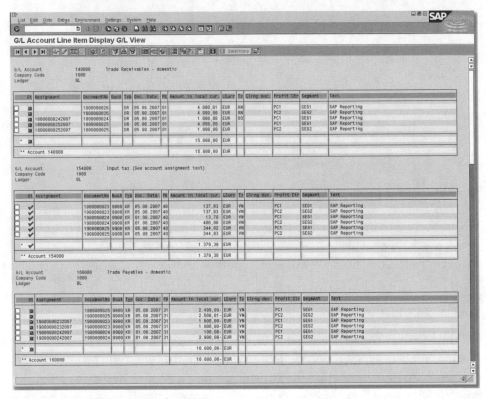

Figure 12.2 ALV Classic List Display Layout

The ALV grid control display is more flexible than the ALV classic list and looks similar to a spreadsheet. Figure 12.3 shows the same report output in the ALV grid control list. Switching between two displays is possible in some of the financial reports. For example, you can switch between the displays by navigating to the **Settings** menu and selecting the **Switch list** option in the G/L Account Line Item Display G/L View report.

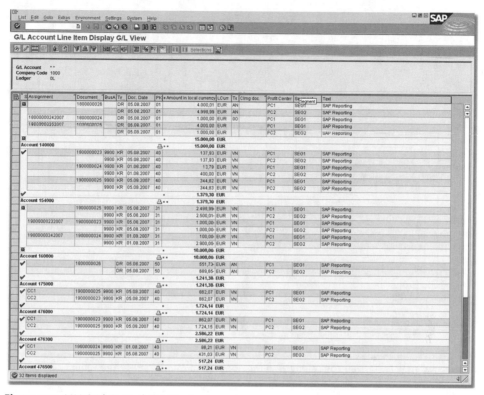

Figure 12.3 ALV Grid Control List Display Layout

Now let's examine how you control the view of the list. You can access the ALV functions using either the toolbar buttons or the menu path. Figure 12.4 shows the standard ALV toolbar buttons along with the application menu path for the same function. Note that some of the buttons in the toolbar are not highlighted, as they are application-specific functions of the G/L Account Line Item Display G/L View report and not functions found in every ALV list.

Below we explain each of the highlighted functionalities, starting from the right side of the ALV control toolbar.

▶ **Filtering**

Filtering is a function that allows you to display only records that have certain values or patterns. For example, you can restrict the profit center characteristic to PC1 by selecting the profit center column, clicking on the **Set Filter** button, and inputting PC1 into the dialog box.

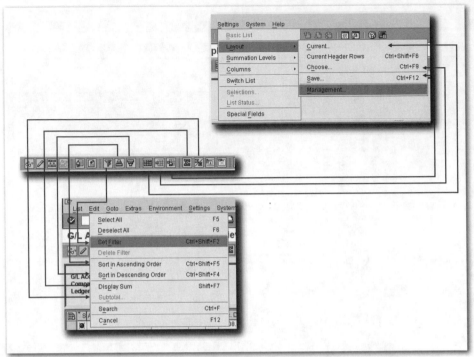

Figure 12.4 ALV Toolbar Buttons along with the Application Menu Path to the Same Function

▶ **Sort Ascending**

With this function you can sort one or more columns in ascending order by selecting the columns and clicking on the **Sort in Ascending Order** button. If you click on the **Sort in Ascending Order** button without selecting a column, a dialog box will appear with all the fields available, where you select the fields for sort ascending.

▶ **Sort Descending**

With this function you can sort one or more columns in descending order by selecting the columns and pressing the **Sort Descending Order** button. If you press the **Sort in Descending Order** button without selecting a column, a dialog box will appear with all the fields available, where you select the fields for sort descending.

▶ **Change Layout**

The change layout function allows you to change the columns displayed in the list. Use this function to add or remove columns or change the order in which they are displayed.

▶ **Select Layout**

With this option you can select a layout that was saved without running the report again.

▶ **Save Layout**

Use this option to save your layout for later use. Layouts created can be used by all users unless they are defined as user-specific layouts.

▶ **Display Sum or Summation**

You can use the display sum or summation function to create totals of value columns.

▶ **Subtotal**

This is a function for analyzing totals for different dimensions in the report. With this function you can subtotal the values in the sum column based on other columns. You can also have multiple subtotals. Figure 12.5 illustrates subtotal functionality per Segment and Account along with the dialog box where you choose the characteristics that you want to subtotal.

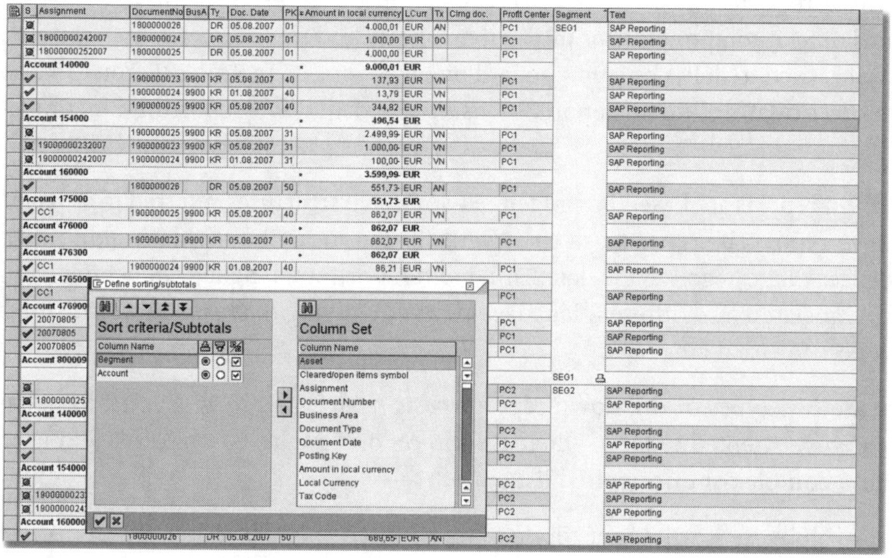

Figure 12.5 Subtotals per Segment and Account

In the ALV grid control display you can move columns using the drag and drop technique. Select a column that you want to move, click and hold the mouse button, move the column to the desired place, then drop the column by releasing the mouse button.

ALV for Web Dynpro tool

ALV for Web Dynpro tool is used to display lists that use Web Dynpro technology. POWER (*Personal object work entity repository*) lists use or leverage ALV for Web Dynpro tool. POWER lists structure the list of business objects and allow specific activities based on these objects. We cover POWER lists in Chapter 15.

12.1.2 Drilldown Reporting

With drilldown reporting, SAP provides an interactive information system to let you evaluate the data collected in your application. The information system is capable of analyzing all the data according to any of the characteristics that describe the data and any key figures that categorize the data. For example, you can display a number of objects for a given key figure or a number of key figures for a given object. In addition, the system lets you carry out any number of variance analyses such as plan and actual comparisons, fiscal year comparisons, comparisons of different objects, and so on.

Drilldown reporting is a cross-application generic tool used in the information systems of SAP components for interactive reports and multidimensional analysis. The tool is used to deliver many standard financial reports in SAP ERP. You can also create your own drilldown reports by using the drilldown reporting functionality.

Drilldown reports are based on predefined SAP table structures referred to as *report* and *form* types. The reports use characteristics that describe the data, along with key figures that categorize the data. Drilldown reports are language dependent and can be translated into different languages without having to create a separate form and report for each language.

There are two types of drilldown reports: *basic reports* and *form reports*. Basic reports are list-oriented reports, whereas form reports are based on forms and used for more complex and formatted list output.

Standard delivered drilldown reports are assigned to transactions in the corresponding SAP ERP component. It is also possible to access all drilldown reports for a specific SAP ERP component via a single transaction. For example, all new G/L drilldown reports can be accessed via Transaction FGI0, which is not listed under the SAP ERP application menu path. Table 12.2 summarizes the important transactions for drilldown reports in SAP ERP Financials components. For example, if you use the new G/L, you can use the report/form types listed in the second column of the table and create your drilldown reports with Transaction FGI1.

Component	Report/Form Types	Execute Report Transaction	Create Form Transaction	Create Report Transaction
FI-AR	Display balances Line item analysis	FDI0	FDI4	FDI1
FI-AP	Display balances Line item analysis	FKI0	FKI4	FKI1
Classic FI-GL	Financial statement analysis Financial statement key figures Balance display Financial statement analysis from cost of sales ledger Key figures for cost of sales ledger	FSI0	FSI4	FSI1
New FI-GL	Reporting for Table FAGLFLEXT Payables according to G/L account assignment Receivables according to G/L account assignment	FGI0	FGI4	FGI1
FI-SL	SL totals tables	FXI0	FXI4	FXI1
EC-CS	Consolidation tables	CXR0	CXR4	CXR1
CO-PC	Summarization tables	KKO0	KKO4	KKO1
CO-PC-ACT	Summarization tables	KKML0	KKML4	KKML1
IM	Appropriation requests Investment programs	IMD0 IMC0	IMD4 IMC4	IMD1 IMC1
CO-PA	Profitability reports Line items reports	KE30	KE34 KE94	KE31 KE91
PS	Project reports Summarization reports for projects	CJE0	CJE4	CJE1
FSCM	TRM operative/parallel: for a given date TRM operative/parallel: for a given period	TRM0	TRM4	TRM1
FSCM-TRM-MR	Market risk management	JBW0	JBW4	JBW1

Table 12.2 Important Drilldown Report Transactions for SAP ERP Financial Components

Drilldown Reporting Example

In Chapter 2 we cover cash flow statement reports, which are drilldown reports that are hard-coded to financial statement version INT. In other words, these reports only work for company codes using the SAP-delivered financial statement version INT. In this section we show you how to copy the form and the report of the *Cash Flow (Direct Method) report* and modify the financial statement version and the financial statement items according to your organization. With this example, you will understand how the drilldown reports are structured and learn how to define your own drilldown reports. The Cash Flow (Direct Method) report has form 0SAPRATIO-04, and its report technical name is 0SAPRATIO-04. If you want to create a form-based drilldown report, the first step is to create the form. In our example, we create a custom form by copying the form 0SAPRATIO-04.

Create Form

You can copy the existing form by using the Transaction FS15. To copy the existing form, select the reference form to be copied (0SAPRATIO-04) and Click on the **Copy** button, as shown in Figure 12.6. When you click on the **Copy** button, the system will ask you for the name of the target form to be created. In our example, we will create the form ZSAPRATIO-04.

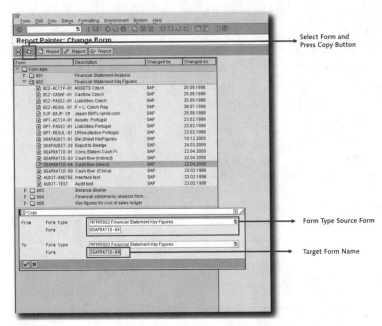

Figure 12.6 Copy Form 0SAPRATIO-04 to ZSAPRATIO-04

Form determines the content and structure of a report. The same form can be used by multiple reports. When you define a form, you need to specify the type of the form. There are three types of forms: one axis without key figure, one axis with key figure, and matrix (two axes). *Types of* forms with one axis only consist of one dimension that is in either columns or rows. Matrix forms contain both columns and rows and are the type of forms mostly used in financial reports.

The form ZSAPRATIO-04 is a typical example of a matrix report. It has two columns that show the balance sheet values for the current and previous year (see Figure 12.7). Each row contains characteristics that restrict values in the columns or simply text. For example, the first row (1) Sales collection is a text-only item, whereas rows such as sales revenue and material costs contain characteristics that restrict values in the cells. A cell is an intersection of columns and rows. Cells can have a special processing type such as a calculation formula. You can edit columns, rows, and cell elements by double-clicking on the corresponding elements. Also, by clicking on the *Drilldown List* button, you can simulate the display of the form as a drilldown list.

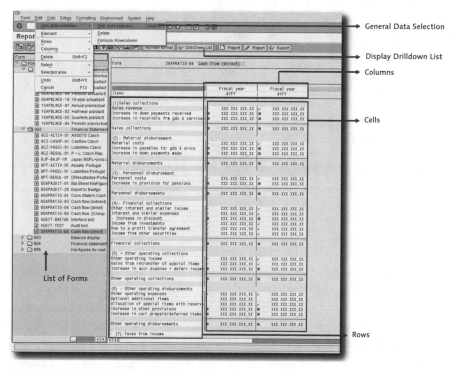

Figure 12.7 Matrix Form ZSAPRATIO-04

General Data Selection and Row Item Definition

To use the form for your cash flow statement, you have to change the financial statement version from INT to your financial statement version in the **general data selection** and change **financial statement (FS) items** according to your financial statement items in rows (see Figure 12.8). Once you complete the changes, click on the **check** and **confirm** buttons and save your form.

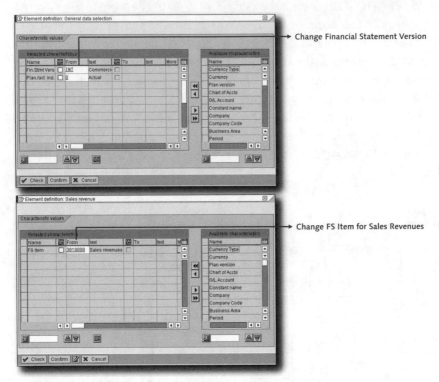

Figure 12.8 General Data Selection and Row Item Definition of Form ZSAPRATIO-04

Create the Report

Once you change the financial statement version and update all financial statement items in the rows of the form, your form will be ready and listed under form type 002 (Financial Statements Key Figures) in the list of forms area. You can then create your cash statement report based on the form you created by using Transaction FSI1. In our example, we created the **ZSAPRATIO Cash flow (direct)** report based on form **ZSAPRATIO-04** under the **Financial Statement Key Figures** report type (see Figure 12.9).

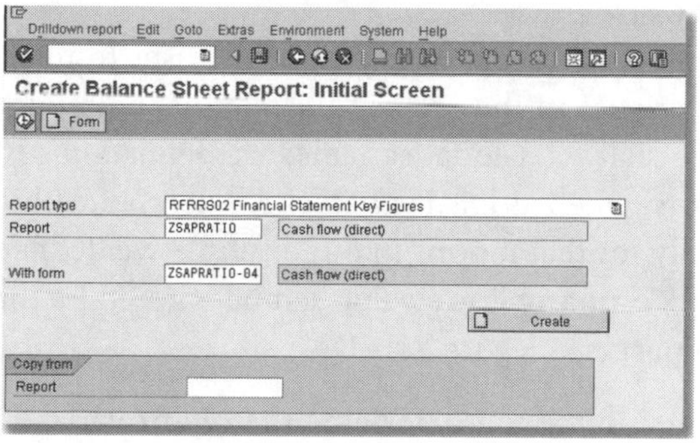

Figure 12.9 Create Report ZSAPRATIO

Navigation Characteristics

When defining the report, you select the report's navigation characteristics from the available characteristics. These characteristics will be available for navigation and filtering when the report is executed. To select the navigation characteristics, select the desired characteristics from the **Char. list** and use the arrow to move the selected characteristics to the left side of the screen, as illustrated in the **Sel. characteristics** box (see Figure 12.10). On the left side of the screen you can see the drilldown reports listed under **Report type**. For example, report **ZSAPRATIO** is created and listed under report type **002 (Financial Statements Key Figures)**.

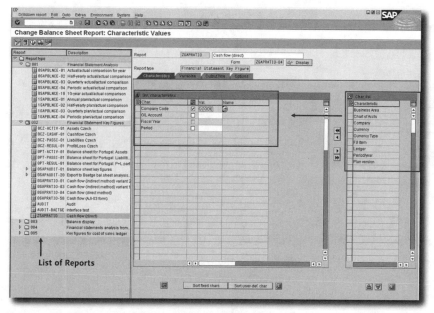

Figure 12.10 Select Characteristics for Report ZSAPRATIO

Report Variables, Output Type, and Options

In the report definition you can also define variables to enable the user to interactively enter values for the characteristics in the selection screen of the report. Variables are defined on a global or local level. Global variables are defined in customizing and can be used in all reports, whereas local variables are defined within the report definition and are used only for that report. In our example we defined the local variable CCODE so that the **Company Code** value can be entered by the user in the selection screen of the report (see Figure 12.11).

In the **Variables** tab of the report definition, you determine the report variables and identify whether they can be entered in the selection screen and determine whether the variables are a required or optional entry (see Figure 12.11, highlight 1). In our example, both **Company Code** and **Fiscal year** can be entered in the selection screen of the report. The company code is set as an optional entry, whereas fiscal year is set as a required entry.

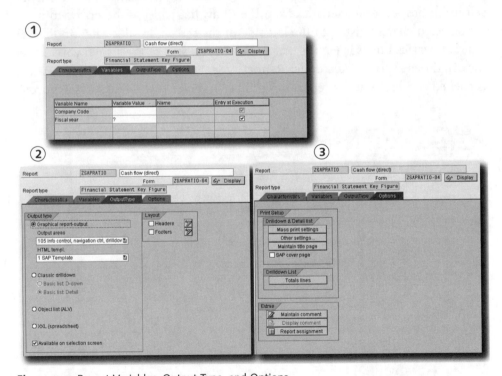

Figure 12.11 Report Variables, Output Type, and Options

You can control the report output in the OutputType tab of the report definition (highlight 2). The following output types are available for drilldown reports:

▶ **Graphical report output**
Graphical report output is the new output type of the drilldown reports. With this type several views of the report data are displayed at the same time, such as drilldown list, detail list, and graphic display.

▶ **Classic drilldown**
Classic drilldown output is the conventional report output, which is particularly preferable for the output of a large volume of data.

▶ **Object list (ALV)**
With this output type all characteristic values for report lines are displayed. Object list output type is suitable when you want to analyze a small amount of data with a flat structure.

▶ **XXL (spreadsheet)**
This output type is preferable when you transfer the report to the extended export of lists (XXL) for offline processing using spreadsheet programs.

By selecting the option **Available on selection screen**, you can choose the **output type** in the selection screen of the report. The option type selected in the report definition is defaulted when executing the report. If you want to restrict the report to only one output type, uncheck the **Available on selection screen** checkbox.

In the **Options** tab, you can set up the print parameters and extras (highlight 3). In the **Print Setup** section, you control the level of detail for mass printing of the drilldown, detail lists, and maintain title page. In the **Extras** section, you assign receiver reports that can be called up via the report/report interface from the report output. For example, you can assign the Line Items report to display the line items of a selected cell in the output of the report. Note that the receiver report must contain variables that are filled in from the sender report to properly set up a report/report interface.

Once you have defined the report variables, output type, and options, your report is ready for use. Figure 12.12 shows an example of the report output of ZSAPRA-TIO in graphical report-output type.

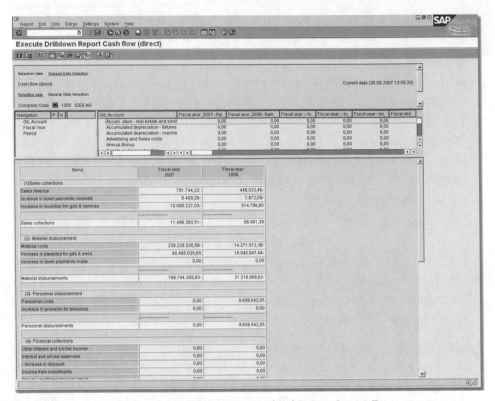

Figure 12.12 Output of the Report ZSAPRATIO in Graphical Report-Output Type

---

Data collection for drilldown reporting

In some of the SAP ERP components, in order to use drilldown reports, you need to collect the data from other database tables. A typical example of this is product drilldown reports for cost object controlling, where you need to run the data collection transactions that will collect data from the database tables into the drilldown reporting tables. In this case, to collect data for the product drilldown in the CO-PC component, you need to execute Transaction KKRV (Program RKKRVBC0).

12.1.3 Report Painter and Report Writer

Report Painter and Report Writer are two very comprehensive reporting tools within the SAP ERP reporting landscape. They are especially useful in the financial area to build your own reports. They allow easy and flexible report definition and can be used effectively with the other reporting analytical tools.

Both Report Painter and Report Writer offer interactive navigation within the hierarchy for objects with a hierarchical structure, such as cost center and cost element. For objects without a hierarchical structure in SAP ERP, *sets* are used to create hierarchies and groupings. This is especially useful for reporting on segment, G/L account, functional area, and so on.

If you analyze the reports in the financial area, you will recognize that a significant proportion of the financial reports are designed with Report Painter and Report Writer tools. For example, many standard reports in management accounting (CO) are Report Painter or Report Writer reports. The same applies to reports in the profit center accounting component (EC-PCA).

Comparing Report Painter and Report Writer

The Report Painter and Report Writer reporting tools are often used together. The main reason is that Report Painter has been developed based on the functionalities of Report Writer, and these reporting tools share functions and some of the reporting components such as report group. Usually, Report Painter and Report Writer create the same report output under the same data set.

Figure 12.13 shows report definition and report output examples of Report Painter and Report Writer. As shown in the figure, Report Painter uses a graphical report structure, which forms the basis for your report definition and displays the rows and columns as they appear in the report output. Report Writer has a complex report definition structure, but it has the same report output. Thus, as a general rule, because Report Painter includes most of the functions available in Report Writer and is simpler and more intuitive to use, Report Painter is recommended instead of Report Writer. Report Writer does not add great value on top of Report Painter, provided that it is technically possible to define the report with the Report Painter tool. Let's examine how to create a report with the Report Painter tool by creating an example report. In our example, we will create a financial statement report that shows the balance sheet and profit and loss for two reporting time frames.

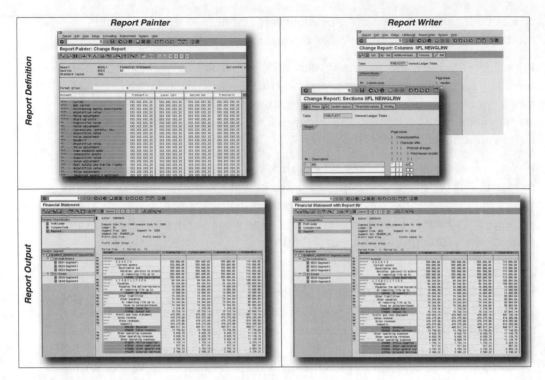

Figure 12.13 Report Definition and Report Output Examples of the Report Painter and Report Writer Reporting Tools

Technical Information of a Report

A good starting point for learning the Report Painter tool is to review and examine the definition of the standard Report Painter reports delivered in SAP ERP and understand how they are defined and populated with data. You can check whether a report is designed with the Report Painter tool or not by checking the technical information of the report. This can be checked from either the selection screen or the report output. To check the technical information, follow the menu path **Environment • Technical Information** (see Figure 12.14). If a report has a table, library, and report group in the environment dialog box, this means the report has been designed using either Report Painter or Report Writer.

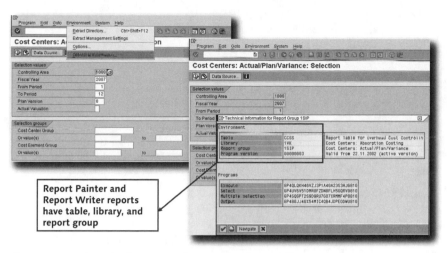

Figure 12.14 Technical Information of Report Painter and Report Writer Reports

By clicking on the library name or report group from the dialog box, you can navigate to the report component definition. We examine the Report Painter and Report Writer components later in this section. Note that if you check the technical information of the Report Painter and Report Writer reports from the output of the report, the report name also appears in the environment box. From there, by double-clicking on the report name, you can examine the definition of the report and determine whether the report is a Report Painter or Report Writer report. The report definition view of both reporting tools is illustrated in Figure 12.13.

Report Painter Menu Path

You can reach the report painter menu path by following the application menu path **SAP Menu • Information Systems • Ad Hoc Reports • Report Painter**. Figure 12.15 shows the Report Painter menu path with some of the important transactions. As shown in the figure, the Report Writer menu path is also listed under the Report Painter menu path, as both reporting tools share the reporting components and functions. Let's take a closer look at the reporting components and functions of the Report Painter tool. Note that Report Painter is recommended instead of Report Writer, provided that it is technically possible to define the report with the Report Painter tool.

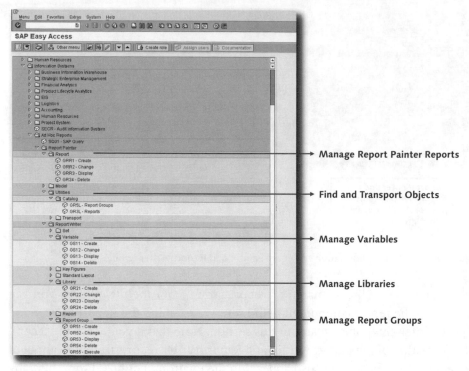

Figure 12.15 Report Painter Menu Path

Report Painter Components and Functions

Figure 12.16 is a schematic diagram summarizing the key components of report painter. Note that the same components are also used in the Report Writer reporting tool. Reporting *libraries* are connected to the reporting tables. Each report is created based on the structure of the library and assigned to a report group. Report groups are then assigned to transactions.

We will now take you through each of these components:

▸ **Reporting table**

Report Painter reports can only be defined based on reporting tables. If there is no reporting table available for the data you want to report on, you cannot define reports with the Report Painter reporting tool. You can check the existing reporting tables by using Transaction GRCT. Note that this transaction is not included in the application or configuration menu path. You need to type in the transaction to check the existing reporting tables. Figure 12.17 shows some of the important financial reporting tables in SAP ERP 6.0. For example, the reporting table for the new G/L totals is FAGLFLEXT. In addition to standard reporting tables, you can create your own reporting tables by defining custom views or using Logistic Information System (LIS) structures.

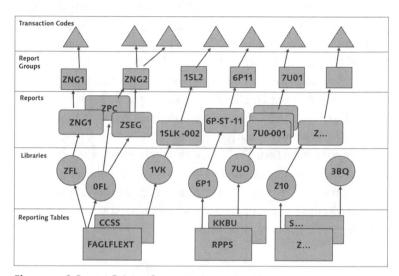

Figure 12.16 Report Painter Components

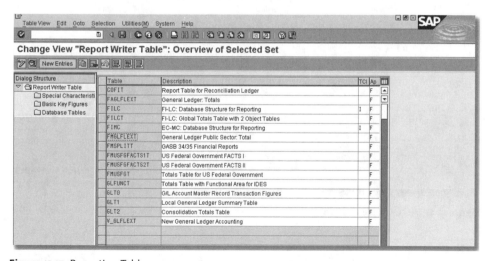

Figure 12.17 Reporting Tables

▶ **Library**

A library is a collection of characteristics, basic key figures, and key figures selected from a reporting table. *Characteristics* are dimensions such as account, cost center, and company code. *Basic key figures* are fields containing numerical values such as amount and fiscal year. Key figures consist of basic key figures and characteristics, for example, period nine debit amount. SAP ERP provides predefined libraries in the system, but you can also create your own libraries. Note that the name of the library cannot start with a number. Figure 12.18 shows an example of a predefined library, 0FL, which is delivered for the new G/L. Each library is linked to only one reporting table. In our example you can see that library 0FL is linked to the FAGLFLEXT reporting table. Characteristics, basic key figures, and key figures of a library are defined based on the corresponding reporting table. Receiver reports of the Report Painter reports can be assigned to **Report-report interface** at the library level. As we explained earlier, the report-report interface allows you to call other reports from the output of your report data. You can also assign **Authorization group** to reports at the library level. Note that **Report-report interface** and **Authorization group** can also be assigned to reports in the report groups.

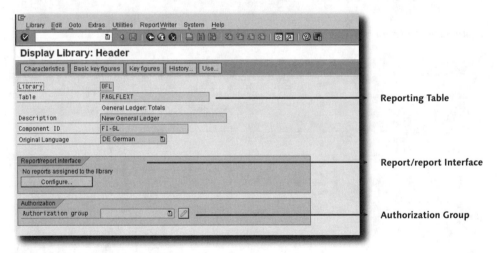

Figure 12.18 An Example of a Library

▶ **Report**

Report Painter reports are defined based on the structure of libraries. A report consists of rows, columns, and general data selection. Each report is assigned to a report group in order to be executed. We explain how to define a Report Painter report in the next section.

▶ **Report group**
As the name suggests, report groups group together reports from one library that use similar data but present it in different forms. Typically, each report is linked to just one report group.

▶ **Transaction**
A transaction is a combination of characters forming a code for a business task. A report group is assigned to the transaction so that they are called up from the menu tree or the command field.

Now that we have explained the Report Painter components, let's look at how to define a Report Painter report.

Define Report Painter Report

Report Painter uses a graphical report structure, and the report definition looks almost like the final output of the report. Figure 12.19 illustrates an example of a Report Painter report definition. The Report Painter reports have rows, a leading column, general data selection, columns, and a values block.

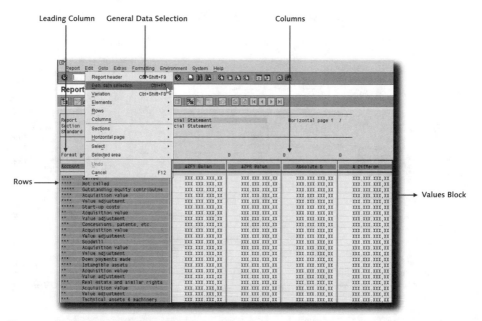

Figure 12.19 Report Painter Report Definition

You can create your own Report Painter report by executing the following steps:

- ▸ Define the leading column and rows of the report.
- ▸ Define the columns of the report.
- ▸ Define the general data selection criteria.
- ▸ Assign the report to a report group.

Let's go through each step to create a Report Painter report. To create Report Painter reports, follow the application menu path **Information system • Ad Hoc Reports • Report Painter • Report • Create (Transaction GRR1)**.

Define Leading Column and Rows of the Report

The first step is to define the leading column and rows of the report. Report rows contain characteristic values or formulas. The leading column is the first column and contains the rows. The Report Painter tool uses the leading column to access the rows. By double-clicking on the rows, you can define rows and the leading column. Figure 12.20 shows an example of row definition. In our example, we selected account number characteristic for the rows. You can select other characteristics from the available characteristics shown on the right side of the dialog. To restrict characteristic values, you can use hierarchies, values, or variables for hierarchies and values. You can change the leading column heading text by selecting the button highlighted with **Lead Column Text** in the figure.

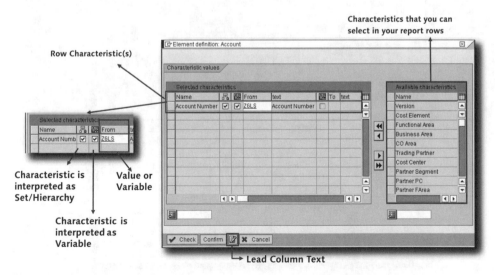

Figure 12.20 Report Row Definition

Using variables makes reports more flexible because the user can select the values of the characteristic in the selection screen of the report. In our example we selected set variable ZGLS for the account number characteristic. This means the set or values of the account number characteristic can be selected by the user in the selection screen of the report. A *set* is a group or hierarchy of the characteristic values. Sets are defined for the characteristics without hierarchies or grouping in SAP ERP. Figure 12.21 shows an example set for the characteristic segment. You can use Transaction GS01 to create sets.

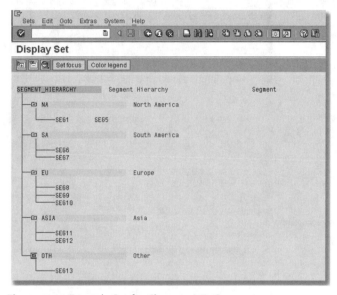

Figure 12.21 Example Set for Characteristic Segment

Financial statement versions in Report Painter

Although G/L accounts have a hierarchical structure called the financial statement version in SAP ERP, you cannot use them in Report Painter reports. You need to create sets for the G/L account characteristic to display the G/L accounts in a hierarchical structure in Report Painter reports. Note that you can control the debit and credit display when defining sets, as it is in financial statement versions. We cover how to control the debit and credit display in financial statement versions in Chapter 2.

When a report is executed, the system replaces the variable with values entered by the user or with values calculated by the system. There are three types of variables: value variable, set variable, and formula variable. Value variable is a placeholder for individual values of a characteristic such as company code. Set variable is a placeholder for a set such as G/L account set and segment set. Each formula variable represents a formula. For example, you can set up a variable for calculating the next period (next period = current period + 1). Figure 12.22 shows an example of value variable for the characteristic period and set variable for the characteristic segment. You can use Transaction GS11 to create report variables.

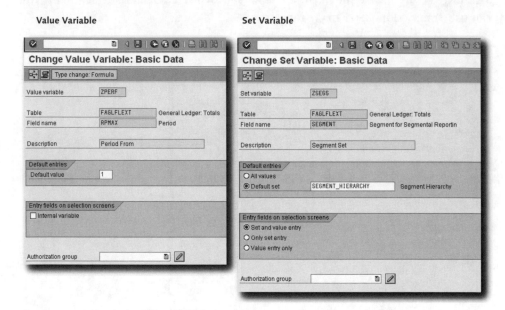

Figure 12.22 Example for Value and Set Variables

Define Columns of the Report

The next step is to define the columns of the report. Columns contain a combination of a basic key figure with or without restricting characteristic values. To define a column you need to double-click on the column header and select the basic key figure option. Figure 12.23 shows the definition of column for basic key figure **HSL Local Currency** without characteristic value restriction. When restricting characteristic values, you can use hierarchies, values, or variables for hierarchies and values. You can change the column heading text by selecting the button highlighted with **Column Text** in the figure.

Define General Data Selection

Now that we have defined the columns of the report, the next step is to define the general data selection. In the general data selection, the data for the whole report is restricted. When restricting characteristic values, you can use hierarchies, values, or variables for hierarchies and values. Figure 12.24 shows an example of general data selection. In our example, we selected the characteristics **Company Code**, **Ledger**, **Period**, **Record Type**, **Segment**, and **Profit Center** in the general data selection and defined a variable for each characteristic. Only the characteristic **Record Type** does not have a variable, and instead the value 0 is restricted for the whole report. The value 0 for characteristic record type is actual data, which means that only actual data will be displayed in the report output, and users will not be able to select value type in the selection screen of the report.

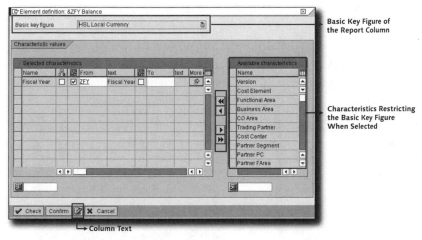

Figure 12.23 An Example of Column Definition

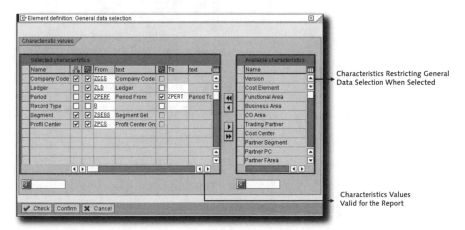

Figure 12.24 An Example of General Data Selection

Assign Report to a Report Group

Once you define the rows, columns, and general data selection, you need to assign it to a report group. To assign the report to a report group, follow the menu path **Environment • Assign Report Group** when you are in the report definition. Alternatively, you create the report group and assign the report to a report group in the report group definition.

Assign Report Group to a Transaction

After you define the report group, you can assign the report group to a transaction. Figure 12.25 shows the definition of the report group and the assignment of a report to a report group along with the definition of a report transaction. For example, we assigned our report NEWGL1 Financial Statement report to **Report Group NGL1** and **Transaction ZNGL1**. To define report transaction and assign the report group to the report transaction you can use Transaction SE93.

Report Group Definition

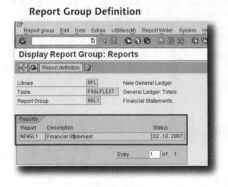

Transaction Code Definition

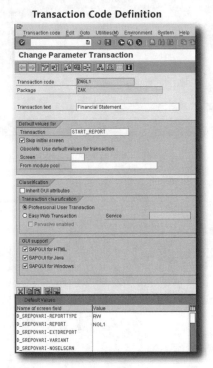

Figure 12.25 Definition of the Report Group and Report Transaction

Executing a Report Painter Report

Figure 12.26 illustrates the report output of our example Report Painter report, which shows the financial statement in local currency with account balances in year 2007 and 2006 and the variance. On the left side of the figure, you can see the characteristics available for variation (highlight 1) and the available variation options for the characteristic segment (highlight 2). Variations let you navigate the report output interactively. For example, you can navigate and analyze your new G/L segments with variation functionality. When navigating between segments, the values change accordingly. Variation is possible for the variable characteristic defined in the general data selection. You can define variation by following the menu path **Edit • Variation** in the report definition. In addition to variation, the Report Painter reporting tool provides many other powerful functions. For example, you can trigger the report/report interface and call up a report assigned to the report by double-clicking on cells. Another good example for Report Painter tool functionality is the Microsoft Excel integration. Highlight 3 shows the office integration options button in the application toolbar. Selecting office integration, you can execute the report in Microsoft Excel.

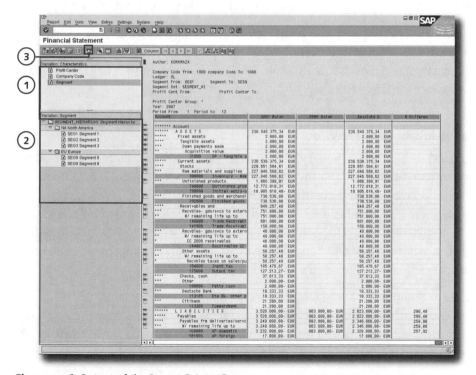

Figure 12.26 Output of the Report Painter Report

12.1.4 SAP Tools for Queries

SAP delivers tools for queries that enable you to query data from one or more database tables. The output of a query is a list that can be displayed in various formats. There are three different query tools that are similar to each other and generate similar reports: SAP Query, QuickViewer, and InfoSet Query. These tools are designed to meet various reporting requirements.

▶ **SAP Query**
SAP Query is the classic reporting tool that enables the query of data from one or more database tables and generates lists, statistics, and ranked lists.

▶ **QuickViewer**
The QuickViewer tool is aimed at relatively inexperienced users, to enable them to easily create QuickViews. QuickViews are the same as queries. The Quick-Viewer tool can be considered as a simplified version of SAP Query tool.

▶ **InfoSet Query**
InfoSet Query was originally used only for SAP Human Capital Management (SAP HCM) queries. It is now possible to use this tool for developing queries in other SAP ERP components, including SAP ERP Financials components.

The output of SAP Query can be in various formats, including ALV, ABAP list, display using SAP graphics, display as table, display as spreadsheet, display as rich text format, and download to a flat file. You can save the output of an SAP query as an extract for later retrieval.

Components of SAP Query Tool

Before exploring the SAP Query tool in detail, let's examine its components and how they are related to the other SAP components (see Figure 12.27). There are three important components of the SAP Query tool: *Queries*, *InfoSets*, and *User Groups*. These components are contained in two query areas: *standard* and *global*. Components of the SAP Query tool are client specific when they belong to a standard area, whereas they are client independent when they belong to a global query area.

Queries are built on InfoSets, which are collections of database table fields. You can either use existing predelivered InfoSets or create your own. Figure 12.28 shows the definition of predelivered InfoSet /SAPQUERY/AM01 used for Asset Accounting (AA) reporting. Note that we cover AA reporting in Chapter 6.

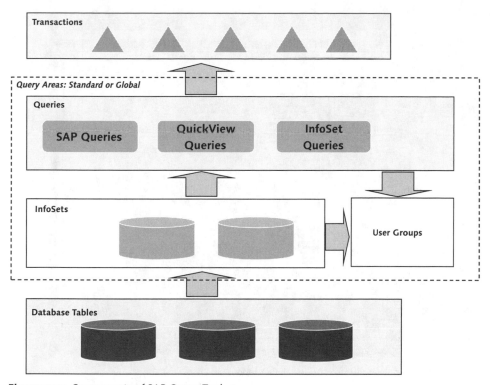

Figure 12.27 Components of SAP Query Tool

Highlight 1 shows all data fields that can be selected for use in the InfoSet. In this example, fields from logical database ADA are displayed. Logical databases are special ABAP programs that retrieve the data and make them available to application programs. A number of predelivered logical databases can be used when defining InfoSets (note that you can use Transaction SE36 to view all available logical databases). To limit the number of fields that are displayed when creating a query, only the necessary data fields are transferred via the drag-and-drop technique in the **Field Group/data fields** area (highlight 2), where they are arranged into logical field groups, that is, **10 General data**. If you select a field in **Field Group/ data fields**, data field details will be displayed in the highlight 3. For example, we selected the **Asset class** field in **Field Group/data fields**, and asset class field details are displayed in the highlight 3. Here you can change the text of the field if you need to display a different name in the query output, provided that you are in the change mode of the InfoSet.

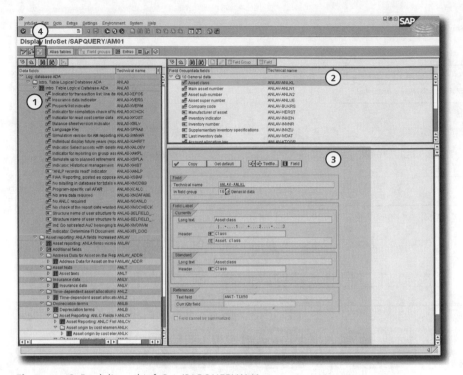

Figure 12.28 Predelivered InfoSet /SAPQUERY/AM01

As we mentioned earlier, you can create your own InfoSets. This can be done either by copying existing ones or creating one from scratch. Once you create the InfoSet, you need to generate it by pressing the **Generate** button, as shown in highlight 4.

InfoSets as DataSources

InfoSets are also used when creating generic data sources in SAP ERP to extract data from SAP ERP to SAP NetWeaver BI. The generated extract structure of the DataSource corresponds to the InfoSet.

User groups are used to group together users with similar query tasks to perform. Each user of a user group can execute queries within that group. SAP users can change and create queries within their user group if they have the relevant authorization role. Users can be assigned to one or several user groups. To manage user groups, access the **Environment** menu in Figure 12.28 and select **User Groups**. InfoSets are assigned to user groups, and all InfoSets covering one task area are assigned to one user group. The users can only define queries in the InfoSets assigned to their user groups.

SAP Query Management Functions

To access the SAP Query management functions, follow the application menu path **SAP Menu • Information Systems • Ad Hoc Reports • SAP Query (Transaction SQ01)**. Once you have accessed the SAP Query transaction and switched to **/ SAPQUERY/AM user group**, you will see the screen displayed in Figure 12.29. To switch to another user group, click on the **Select Other User Group** button in the application toolbar. At the bottom of the figure each button in the application toolbar is indicated. All queries belonging to the selected user group are listed in the list. The InfoSet to which the queries are assigned is displayed on the right side of the list. By using the **Environment** menu, you can switch query areas and manage InfoSets and User Groups. From the query management area, you can create, display, change, and view the description of the queries. In addition, you can go to QuickViewer and InfoSet Query by using the corresponding query management buttons.

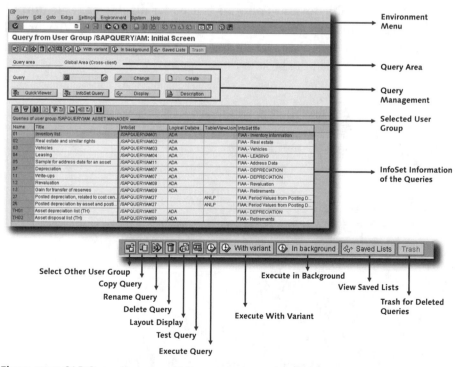

Figure 12.29 SAP Query Management Screen

From the application toolbar, you can use query functions for the selected query. To select a query, double-click on the name in the list or write the name in the **Query** box. Query functions such as copy, rename, delete, display layout, test, execute, execute with variant or execute in background can be applied to the selected query. In addition, the generated query list can be viewed using the **Saved List** button, and queries deleted by mistake can be retrieved from the trash.

Definition of a Query

Let's examine the definition of a query 01 Inventory List, which we explained in Chapter 6. To view the definition of the query, use **Change** or **Display** in the query management area (see Figure 12.29). If you select the **Change** button, the **Title, Format** of the query inventory list will appear on the screen, as illustrated in Figure 12.30. Here you can specify the title of the query. In the lines for the **Notes**, query notes are entered to describe the user of the query. The setting of the **List format** and the query output **Table format** are also specified in the definition of the query. For example, the number of columns per line is set at 133, and the number of the table format columns is set at 83 in the **definition of inventory list** query. Note that **Table format Columns** is used for **display as table output format**, whereas the number of columns per line is used for **SAP List Viewer** and **ABAP List** output formats. Other available output formats that you can use when defining queries are listed at the bottom of the figure.

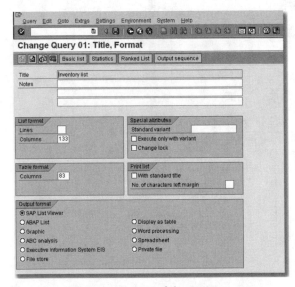

Figure 12.30 Title and Format of the Query

The **Special attributes** section in Figure 12.30 allows you to specify standard report variants for the query, restricts the query to be executed only with variant, and prevents users from changing the query by using **Change lock**. **Print list** controls the output of the query to include a standard title if the check box **With standard title** is selected. From the **Goto** menu, you can assign a receiver report that can be called up from the output of the query by double-clicking on an output cell.

By pressing the right arrow button in the application toolbar you can view field groups. Field groups are defined in the InfoSet of the query. Refer to **Field groups** of the query 01 Inventory List displayed on the left side of Figure 12.31. There are three fields groups for this query: **General data**, **Time-dependent data**, and **Asset values**. Field groups are used to group fields into logical groups to make the handling of the fields easier in the query definition, and they are defined at the InfoSet level. With the arrow buttons on the application toolbar, you can move between the query definition screens. If you click on the right screen you can see the field groups/fields screen shown on the right side of Figure 12.31.

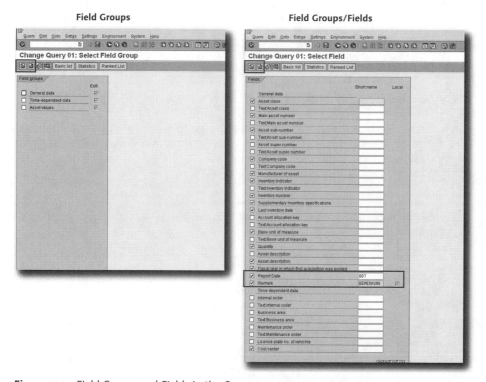

Figure 12.31 Field Groups and Fields in the Query

Here it is possible to define fields that are special for the query and do not exist in the definition of the InfoSet. Such derived fields are called *local fields*. Local fields are indicated with a check box under the column **Local**. You can define, change, and view local fields from the edit menu in the field groups/fields screen. For example, the **Remark** field with the short name **BEMERKUNG** is a local field. One of the screens is designated for query selections. Let's have a close look at the query selection screen.

Define Query Selections

Figure 12.32 shows the screen where you select the fields for which you want to have additional selection criteria. However, if you are working with a logical database, as in our example, there is typically no need to make selections in this screen because selections have already been defined for a number of fields through the logical database. You can check the logical database structure using the **Database structure function** in the **Environment** menu. By selecting the highlighted **Basic list** button in the application toolbar screen, you can display the query layout design.

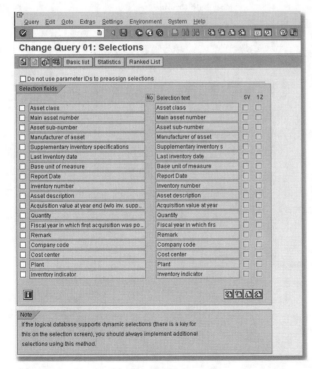

Figure 12.32 Query Selection Fields

Query Layout Design

Figure 12.33 shows the query definition in Graphical Query Painter, which is a visual query design tool used to construct the sub lists for a query. These sub lists are classified as basic list, statistics, and ranking lists of the query. You can switch to the classical query list design by selecting **Settings function** in the **Settings** menu shown in Figure 12.32. Graphical Query Painter is also used for defining QuickViews in the layout mode.

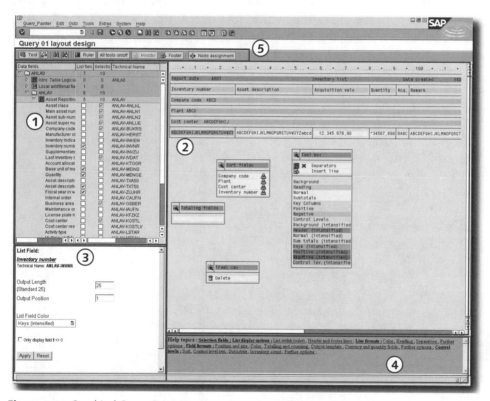

Figure 12.33 Graphical Query Painter

The Graphical Query Painter consists of a screen divided into four windows, which are highlighted with numbers from 1 to 5 in Figure 12.33. The screen in highlight 1 shows all the fields available for the query organized in tree form. The fields used in the list are highlighted and have the **List fields** check box selected. If the field is also in the selection screen of the query, the check box under the **Selection** column is checked. The technical names of the available fields are also displayed.

Highlight 2 shows the list layout, including sample data to help you see and configure the list structure. Highlight 3 shows the screen with information about the list element currently selected. In our example, we selected the **Inventory number** field. You can modify the output length, position, and display color of the selected field in this screen. Highlight 4 shows the screen with links to the help documentation or any error message and warnings. Highlight 5 shows the application toolbar where you can execute query functions such as test or check definition.

Queries are assigned to the transactions. The query transaction definition and the assignment of the query transaction to a query is carried out using Transaction SE93. In our example, the Inventory List report is assigned to Transaction S_ALR_87011979. Refer to Figure 12.34 for the definition of query Transaction S_ALR_87011979.

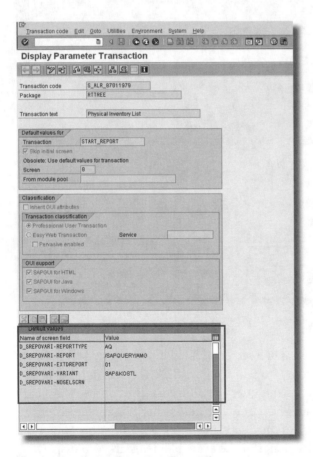

Figure 12.34 Assign Query to a Transaction

12.1.5 ABAP Custom Reports

In the preceding sections, we have given you an overview of the different report development tools available in SAP ERP and SAP R/3. These tools do not necessarily require technical knowledge of programming or, in particular, programming with SAP's programming language ABAP™, which can be used to build custom reports. Using ABAP for custom reports is costly and resource consuming, and requires ongoing maintenance and a significant amount of testing compared to other reporting tools, which we have covered in previous sections. Thus, the decision to use ABAP for custom reports requires careful evaluation. The best practice dictates that ABAP should only be used after all other reporting tools have been explored. However, using ABAP for custom reports is unavoidable in some cases, and you need to ensure that these cases are well defined and integrated into your overall reporting strategy. The reporting features and functions of ABAP are well beyond the scope of this book. You need to refer to online help documentation to find more about ABAP report design.

12.2 Summary

In this chapter we explained the SAP ERP reporting tools to guide you through reporting tools functions and capabilities for financial reports. All SAP ERP reporting tools covered in this chapter are used in various report developments, and each of them has its own features and capabilities. We explained the reporting tools with non-customer specific examples so that you can easily replicate them in your own system to build your own reporting solutions, or simply use them as a learning example. With the basic but solid knowledge that you gain in this chapter, you will be able to take your skills further and master the area you are most interested in.

The purpose of this chapter is to provide an overview of SAP NetWeaver BI reporting tools for those who have little or no experience with reporting tools. We cover the capabilities of SAP NetWeaver BI reporting tools with the aim of giving you a guide to creating and formatting your own reports.

13 SAP NetWeaver BI Reporting Tools

SAP NetWeaver BI provides various reporting capabilities and provides flexible reporting and analysis tools. The business content offers a full suite of predefined queries for each financial component. You can use these queries as references to create your own reports in SAP NetWeaver BI. In previous chapters we have covered the main integration points between SAP ERP and SAP NetWeaver BI to generate financial reports on time and accurately. In addition, we have explained the business content queries delivered within SAP NetWeaver BI. In this chapter we examine each SAP NetWeaver BI reporting tool.

13.1 SAP NetWeaver BI Business Explorer Suite

The SAP NetWeaver BI Business Explorer (BEx) suite provides flexible reporting and analysis tools for strategic analysis and decision-making support within a business. These tools include SAP BEx Query Designer, SAP BEx Web Analyzer, SAP BEx Analyzer, SAP BEx Web Application Designer, SAP BEx Report Designer, and SAP BEx Broadcaster. With these tools you can evaluate data at various levels of detail and from different perspectives in various outputs such as Web, SAP NetWeaver Portal, and Microsoft Excel. The SAP BEx Suite is a collection of programs, tools, and plug-ins for analyzing and evaluating data. The SAP BEx Suite overview is illustrated in Figure 13.1. Compared to previous releases, SAP BEx contains many new and revised reporting and analysis functions. The SAP BEx Suite makes the reporting process easy and is suitable for all types of information workers. For example, analysts and controllers need advanced analysis functionalities and ad hoc data exploration capabilities, executives and decision-makers require more tailor-made information via an easy and intuitive user interface with options of further analysis if needed. Some information workers, for example, customers and partners who are not directly involved in the business activities of the enterprise just need a snapshot of the information they need. The SAP BEx Suite offers services for all types of information workers.

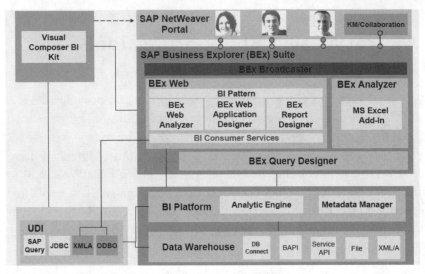

Figure 13.1 SAP Business Explorer Suite (Source: SAP AG)

In this section we focus on the SAP BEx Suite reporting tools and give you an overview, providing useful examples of their usage, functions, and capabilities. We specifically look at the following reporting tools:

▶ **SAP BEx Query Designer**
SAP BEx Query Designer is a powerful tool to analyze the dataset of the SAP NetWeaver BI by defining queries for InfoProviders. It is the central tool for all kinds of OLAP and multidimensional reporting queries. With SAP BEx Query Designer, queries are designed once and reused many times by other SAP NetWeaver BI components. Navigation and evaluation of the InfoProvider to which the query belongs is based on the InfoObjects and reusable query elements.

▶ **SAP BEx Web Analyzer**
The SAP BEx Web Analyzer is a standalone web application for data analysis

on the Web. With SAP BEx Web Analyzer, you can execute analysis on data providers such as query, query view, or InfoProvider. The results are displayed in Microsoft Internet Explorer or other web browsers.

▶ **SAP BEx Analyzer**

The SAP BEx Analyzer is an analytical, reporting, and design tool embedded in Microsoft Excel. Queries created in the SAP BEx Query Designer are analyzed in Microsoft Excel spreadsheets.

▶ **SAP BEx Web Application Designer**

SAP BEx Web Application Designer is a component used to create web applications using generic OLAP navigation. Web applications are displayed in Internet browser tools such as Internet Explorer and are called up via URL.

▶ **SAP BEx Report Designer**

SAP BEx Report Designer is a tool used to generate formatted reports, called SAP NetWeaver BI Enterprise reports. Business-specific layouts can be easily printed either as hard copy or PDF. They are displayed on the Internet via URL.

▶ **SAP BEx Broadcaster**

SAP BEx Broadcaster is the tool used to pre-calculate and distribute information to information workers via email, portal, printer, and other communication means.

Let's take a closer look at each reporting tool.

13.1.1 SAP BEx Query Designer

SAP BEx Query Designer is a powerful tool to analyze the dataset of SAP NetWeaver BI by defining queries for InfoProviders. SAP BEx Query Designer is the central tool for all kinds of OLAP and reporting queries, with which queries are designed once and reused many times. By selecting and combining InfoObjects (characteristics and key figures) or reusable query elements (such as structures) in an SAP BEx query, you can determine the way in which you navigate through and evaluate the data in the selected InfoProvider.

To start the SAP BEx Query Designer in your Windows operating system, select **Start • Programs • Business Explore • Query Designer** (see Figure 13.2).

Figure 13.2 Starting BEx Query Designer

Once you enter the client, your user name, and password, SAP BEx Query Designer appears on your screen (see Figure 13.3). The SAP BEx Query Designer user interface is intuitive and easy for users to become familiarized with.

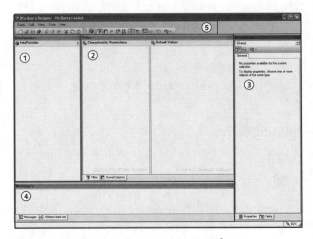

Figure 13.3 BEx Query Designer User Interface

We can divide the query designer user interface into five areas. Highlight 1 shows the InfoProvider area of the query. Once you select the required **InfoProvider**, all available InfoProvider objects (dimensions, key figures, structures) are displayed here in a tree structure. Highlight 2 shows the **Characteristic Restrictions** and **Default Values** area. Characteristic restrictions defined in this area are valid for the entire data set of the query. The default values for the characteristics set here are valid for the filter values of the view of the result set that can be changed by the user once the query is executed. By using the **Rows/Columns** tab at the bottom of highlight 2, you can navigate to the Rows/Columns view of the query. Highlight

3 shows the **Properties** area in the BEx Query Designer. In the **Properties** area, you can make changes to the properties of the selected objects in the query. With the **Tasks** tab, you can list tasks relating to the selected query object. Highlight 4 at the bottom of the screen is the **Messages** window, where information messages are shown. **Where-Used List** provides information related to the use of the query object. None of the highlighted areas are filled in Figure 13.3, as we have not opened or created a query yet. Highlight 5 shows the SAP BEx menu bar and the application toolbars.

There are three application toolbars in SAP BEx Query Designer: standard, view, and exit. The functions included in the application tool bar are also available in the menu bar and supported by shortcut keys. For example, the shortcut Ctrl + N can be used to create a new query. Let's take a closer look at the functions available in the toolbars of SAP BEx Query Designer.

SAP BEx Query Designer Toolbars

Figure 13.4 shows the query designer standard toolbar (highlight 1) and view toolbar (highlight 2), with their button functions highlighted.

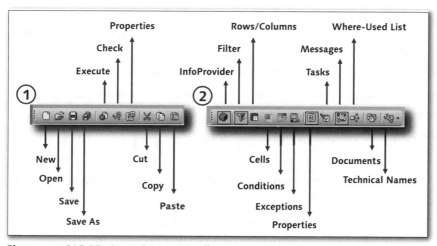

Figure 13.4 SAP BEx Query Designer Toolbar

The standard toolbar buttons and their functions are as follows:

- New: Used to create a new query.
- Open: Used to open an existing query.

- Save: Used to save a query.

- Save As: Used to save the query with a new name.

- Execute: After you have defined and saved a query, this function is used to display the query results in SAP BEx Web Analyzer. SAP BEx Web Analyzer presents the query in an Internet browser such as Internet Explorer.

- Check: This function is used to check the definition of the query.

- Properties: This function enables you to display and change the properties of the queries. For example, you can change the description of the query or display options for the output of the results.

The view toolbar buttons and functions are as follows:

- InfoProvider: Shows the content of the InfoProvider upon which the query is based.

- Filter: Shows the filter area of the query.

- Rows/Columns: Shows the rows/columns area of the query.

- Cells: Shows the cells area of the query. It is active only for queries with two structures.

- Conditions: With this function, you can define the conditions for a query. Once you press the button, a new tab for conditions is created in highlight 2 in Figure 13.3. Conditions are meant for the analysis of data that is most relevant. By defining conditions, you can filter out the irrelevant data.

- Exceptions: This function enables you to define exceptions for the query. Exceptions are used for detecting deviations and creating alerts.

- Properties: By selecting the **Properties** button, you can analyze the properties area.

- Tasks: Tasks provide an overview of the functions available when working on the query.

- Messages: By pressing the **Messages** button, you can check system messages, warnings, and other information. From the context menu of the message, you can jump up to the error or get help on the message and make corrections.

- Where-Used List: Shows the use of the query in other objects.

- Documents: Shows the explanation of the message screen.

- Technical Names: Shows or hides the technical names of the query components.

Creating a Query in SAP BEx Query Designer

Now that we have explained the toolbars, we will show you how to create a query with SAP BEx Query Designer. In our example, we will create a financial statement report showing the balance sheet and profit and loss for two reporting time frames. After selecting the **New Query** button from the standard toolbar and the **Find** button from the **New Query** dialog, the initial screen of SAP BEx Query Designer will appear on your screen (see Figure 13.5). You can search the InfoProvider on which you will build the query by specifying the search string in the **Search Method** box, as shown in Figure 13.5. We found the FI-GL virtual InfoProvider by searching for V10 in the technical names of the InfoProviders. Once the search is completed, the InfoProviders' names found are listed at the bottom of the dialog. In our example, only one InfoProvider, 0FIGL_V10, is found. Select the 0FIGL_V10 InfoProvider and click on the **Open** button in the **New Query** dialog. Note that business content InfoProviders with which you can create financial statements are explained in Chapter 2.

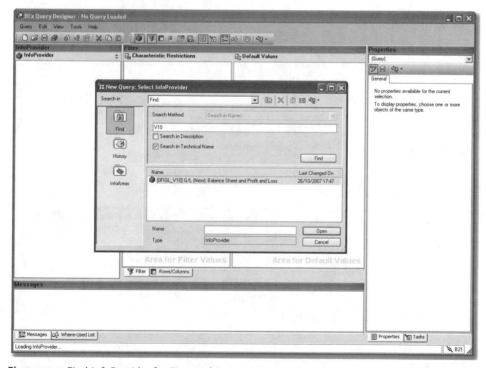

Figure 13.5 Find InfoProvider for Financial Statements

Define Characteristic Restrictions

After you click on the **Open** button in the **New Query: Select InfoProvider** dialog box, the InfoProvider's **Key Figures** and **Dimensions** appear in the InfoProvider area of the SAP BEx Query Designer interface (see Figure 13.6, highlight 1). The objects in the query can be moved from this area into the query area by using drag and drop. For example, the **Company code** dimension is dragged and dropped into the **Characteristic Restrictions** area in the filter section. You can restrict a characteristic to single characteristic values, value ranges, hierarchy nodes, or characteristic value variables by double-clicking on it or via the context menu (right-click menu). Highlight 2 shows these restricting options along with the **History** option, which displays recently used values. With characteristic restrictions, only the filtered data set is available in the output of the query. In our example, we selected **Company Code** as the characteristics restriction (highlight 3). This means the company code dimension must be specified by the user in the selection screen of the query. To complete the configuration of the characteristics restrictions, click on the **OK** button (highlight 4).

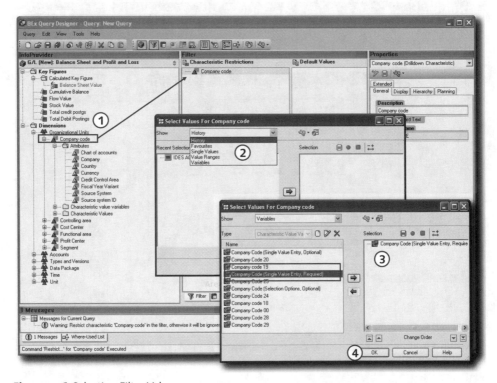

Figure 13.6 Selecting Filter Values

In addition to company code restriction, we also defined restrictions for the characteristics **Fiscal Year Variant**, **Currency Type**, and **G/L Account**, as shown in Figure 13.7. Note that you don't need to finalize the query definition to be able to save the query. After we defined the characteristics restrictions, for example, we saved the query with the description "Financial Statement" and technical name "ZFINSTAT100" under the **SAP Financial Reporting** folder. You can create and organize your folders under **Favorites**.

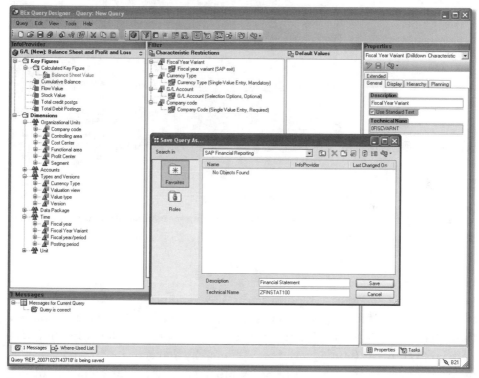

Figure 13.7 Save the Query ZFINSTAT100

Now that we have defined characteristic restrictions, let's define the rows and columns structure of the query. **Rows/Columns** represents the display of the query when it is executed. The representation is shown in the intersection of query columns and rows called the **Preview** area (see Figure 13.8). InfoObjects can be moved to rows and columns using the drag-and-drop technique.

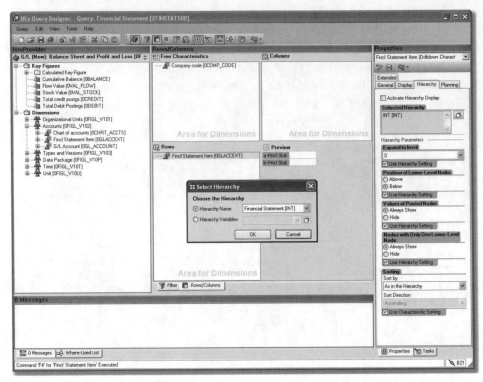

Figure 13.8 Define Rows of the Query

Define Rows

In our example, we want to report balance sheet and profit and loss statement for the two selected reporting time frames. Thus, we moved the **Financial Statement Item (0GLACCEXT)** InfoObject into the rows of the query. In the properties of **Financial Statement Item**, you can select hierarchy and activate hierarchy display. In the **Properties** area, you can specify other parameters for hierarchy display such as level of hierarchy expansion, position of lower-level nodes, characteristic sorting options, and so on.

Define Columns

The next step is to define the columns of the query. If you move a key figure from the InfoProvider screen area into the rows or columns of the query definition, a structure appears in the Query Designer. *Structures* are the basic framework of the axes in a query. They can be in either rows or columns or in both rows and columns. There are two types of structures: key figure structures and characteristic structures. The structural components of key figure structures are based on the key figure selections (basic key figures, restricted key figures, and calculated key figures). Characteristic structural components do not have key figure selections.

The setup of the structures is important because they determine the sequence and the number of key figures or characteristic values in the columns and rows of the query. The system allows you to create up to two structures. If you use two structures, a table with fixed cell definitions is created. Having two structures is a prerequisite for defining exception cells. You can override cell values created implicitly at the intersection of two structural components. Structures can be reused in other queries based on the same InfoProvider. To do so, they have to be saved in the InfoProvider. However, note that changes made to these reusable structures affect all queries in which they are used. In our example, we moved the **Balance Sheet Value** BILANZWERT calculated key figure to the **Columns** area, and the structure **Key Figures** was automatically created. Notice that in the **Preview** area, our first column is shown as **Balance Sheet Value** (see Figure 13.9).

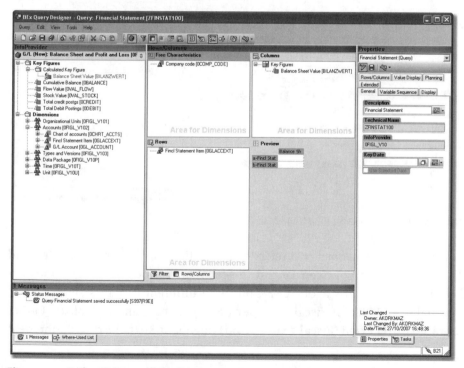

Figure 13.9 Define Columns of the Query

To have year comparison in the financial statement, you need to create a second structure. To do so, you can use the context menu in the **Columns** area (see Figure 13.10, highlight 1) and select **New structure**. In our example, we named the new structure "period." Once you define the new structure, select **New Selection** in the context menu of the new structure (highlight 2). When you click on the new selection, the **Change Selection** dialog box appears, as shown in Figure 13.11.

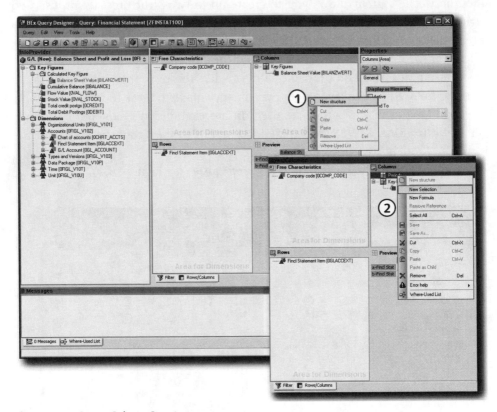

Figure 13.10 Query Column Structure

In our example, we defined two selections: selection for the **Fiscal year/period** and selection for **Comparison Period (Fiscal Year/Period)**. Both selections are based on the characteristic 0FISCPER but with different variables selected. We used variable 0I_FPER for **Fiscal year/period** (highlight 1) and variable 0I_FPER2 for **Comparison Period (Fiscal Year/Period)** (highlight 3). In the description field for both selections, we used *text variables* so that reporting and comparison periods are displayed in the header of the columns depending on the user selection. Text variables represent a text and can also be used in the descriptions of queries and calculated key figures in addition to the structural components. In query definition, text variables are selected by clicking on the button indicated by highlights 2 and 4.

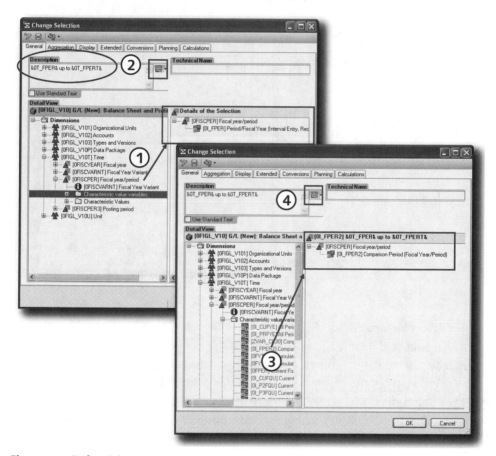

Figure 13.11 Define Selection

Define Formula

By defining formulas in the structures, you can recalculate the key figures. Basic key figures, restricted key figures, and calculated key figures can be included in the formula definition. In our example, we defined the formula with the description **Variance**. Formulas can be defined by using the context menu (Figure 13.12, highlight 1). The formula we defined is based on subtracting the comparison period from the reporting period (highlight 2).

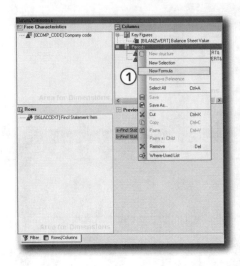
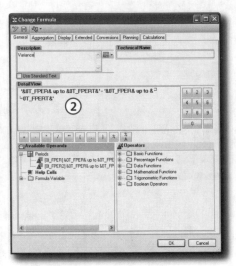

Figure 13.12 Define Column Formula

Define Free Characteristics

Free characteristics enable navigation within the query. Free characteristics do not appear in the initial drilldown of the query; however, they can be included in the drilldown after the query is executed. We defined **Company code** (0COMP_CODE), **Segment** (0SEGMENT), and **Profit Center** (0PROFIT_CTR) as free characteristics. Once you complete the query definition, you need to check and save it. A complete financial statement query example created in SAP BEx Query Designer is illustrated in Figure 13.13.

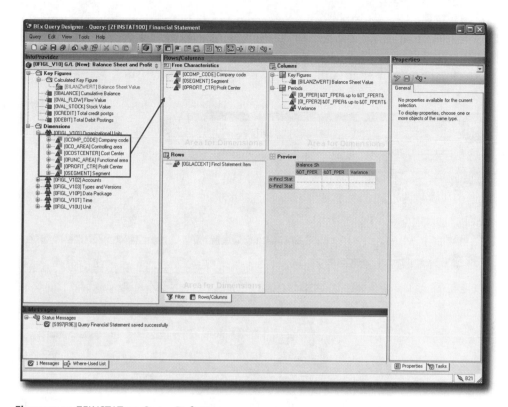

Figure 13.13 ZFINSTAT100 Query Definition

Executing a Query with SAP BEx Web Analyzer

The queries designed with SAP BEx Query Designer can be executed with SAP BEx Web Analyzer. To execute a query from SAP BEx Query Designer, click on the **Execute** button in the standard toolbar. The query will be executed in SAP BEx Web Analyzer, and the portal will be shown using a URL.

Figure 13.14 shows the **Variable Entry** screen and the output of the query in SAP BEx Web Analyzer. In the **Variable Entry** screen of the query, you specify variable values. In our example, we selected **Company Code** 1000 (IDES AG), **Currency Type** 10 (company code currency), **Period/Fiscal Year** 009.2007 to 011.2007, and **Comparison Period** 006.2007 to 008.2007 (see highlight 1). You can save the variable entries as a variant that can be called up later. After you click on the OK button, the query result is shown (highlight 2). The query data is displayed in a table with a navigation pane. You can navigate in the report output using the context menu or the drag-and-drop technique. The context menu provides various functions depending on the cell context and web item used. The drag-and-drop technique can be used to drill down by using free characteristics.

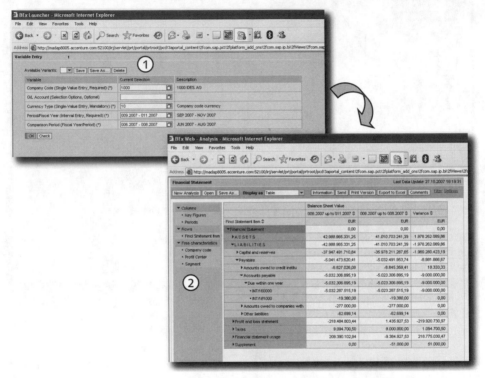

Figure 13.14 Variable Entry Screen and the Output of the Query in SAP BEx Web Analyzer

SAP BEx Web Analyzer has many other functions available in the application toolbar. For example, you can use the information broadcasting functions to broadcast your analyses, create printable versions of the output, or export report output to Microsoft Excel. Also, you can save the data view generated from the navigation as a query view by selecting the **Save View** function in the context menu, and you can save the ad hoc analysis by clicking on the **Save As** button in the application toolbar. Note that when the query view is saved, only the data view is saved, and when the ad hoc analysis is saved, the entire web application is saved.

In addition to SAP BEx Web Analyzer, queries designed by SAP BEx Query Designer can also be executed in SAP BEx Analyzer. You can find examples of SAP BEx queries executed in Web Analyzer in Chapters 2 through 7. In Chapters 9 and 10, we show query output examples in SAP BEx Analyzer.

Queries are used as a data provider for design items in the SAP BEx Analyzer. In SAP BEx Web Application Designer, they are used as a data provider for web items. In the next sections we show you how to use the query ZFINSTAT100 in these applications and give you an overview of their important functions.

13.1.2   SAP BEx Analyzer

SAP BEx Analyzer is an analytical reporting and design tool embedded in Microsoft Excel. With SAP BEx Analyzer, queries created in SAP BEx Query Designer are analyzed in Microsoft Excel spreadsheets. Analysis can be performed by using the context menu or the drag-and-drop technique, enabling navigation within queries. Despite the lack of some options available with SAP BEx Web Analyzer, SAP BEx Analyzer is a very popular reporting tool, particularly for financial analysts and controllers.

With SAP BEx Analyzer, you can design the interfaces for your queries by inserting design items (controls) such as *analysis grids*, *dropdown boxes,* and *buttons* into your Excel workbook. In this way you can transform your workbook into a query application.

SAP BEx Analyzer has two modes: *analysis mode* and *design mode*. Both modes have their own dedicated toolbar and menu path. Analysis mode is used for executing OLAP analyses on queries, whereas design mode is used for designing the interface for query applications in Microsoft Excel.

Like other SAP BEx components, you start SAP BEx Analyzer in your Windows operating system by choosing **Start** • **Programs** • **Business Explore** • **BEx Analyzer** (see Figure 13.2). This starts Microsoft Excel with the **BEx Analyzer** Menu, the **BEx Analysis Toolbox**, and the **BEx Design Toolbox**, as illustrated in Figure 13.15.

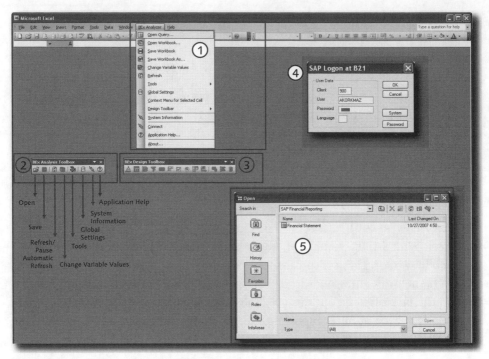

Figure 13.15 SAP BEx Analyzer Excel Menu, Toolboxes, and Open Query Command

SAP BEx Analyzer Analysis Mode

In analysis mode of SAP BEx Analyzer, you can navigate query results and interact with the results to generate different views. You can access analysis functions either from the **BEx Analyzer** menu (see Figure 13.15, highlight 1) or the **BEx Analysis Toolbox** (highlight 2). All functions available on the menu are also available in the toolbox.

To execute a query in SAP BEx Analyzer, you need to open the query. To open a query, you can either use the **Open Query** function on the BEx Analyzer menu (highlight 1) or click on the open command button in the **BEx Analysis Toolbox** (highlight 2). After entering your user name and password (highlight 4), you can select the query in the **Open** query dialog box (highlight 5). In the **Open** query dialog box, there are five methods to select a query. We selected our query using the **Favorites** selection method. Let's explore the analysis functions of SAP BEx Analyzer that are illustrated in highlights 1 and 2:

▶ **Open**

With this function you can open workbooks or queries.

▶ **Save**

This function is used to save workbooks and views, either with their existing names or new names. It is also possible to save the current navigation state (view) of the data provider.

▶ **Refresh/Pause Automatic Refresh**

With this function, you can control the refresh status of the query. This is a toggle function that is used to start and pause the refresh.

▶ **Change Variable Values**

This function is used to change the variable values in an open query.

▶ **Tools**

You can access other tools from within SAP BEx Analyzer via the tools function. For example, you can create a new query, edit the current query, start SAP BEx Broadcaster, start SAP BEx Report Designer, start SAP BEx Web Analyzer, and so on.

▶ **Global Settings**

With this function, you can configure global settings, which are defaults valid for the whole application rather than for individual workbooks.

▶ **System Information**

With this toggle function, you can connect to a system if you are not already connected. If you are already connected to the system, you can view the system information dialog box and execute functions such as disconnecting from the system.

▶ **Application Help**

With this function, you can access application help and SAP BEx Analyzer's about dialog box.

Variable Selection

Now that we have given you an overview of the analysis functions of SAP BEx Analyzer, we can further explore the analysis functions with our example query. Once you click the **Open** button, the query variable selection screen appears (see Figure 13.16). Here you should enter the required variable values. We selected **Company Code** 1000 (IDES AG), **Currency Type** 10 (company code currency), **Period/Fiscal Year** 009.2007 to 011.2007, and **Comparison Period** 006.2007 to 008.2007. You can save the variable entries as variants that can be called up later (highlight 1). In addition, you can personalize variables permanently by assigning a value to them so that you do not have to repeatedly make the required settings for a variable. You can personalize variables by using the button shown in highlight 2. Once the variable selection is completed click on the **OK** button.

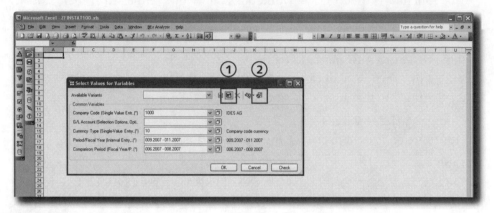

Figure 13.16 Variable Selection

Analysis Example

Our example **Financial Statement** query output in SAP BEx Analyzer is shown in Figure 13.17. In SAP BEx Analyzer, query results are displayed in the analysis grid design item as **Table** (highlight 1). Within this grid, you can navigate using the context menu and the drag-and-drop technique or icons such as expanding and collapsing hierarchies. In addition, you can execute OLAP functions such as filtering, drilling, and sorting characteristics and key figures in rows and columns of the analysis grid.

There are three buttons in the SAP BEx Analyzer workbook: **Chart**, **Filter**, and **Information**. When you click on the **Chart** button (highlight 2), analysis grid design items are shown as a chart. If you click on the **Chart** button again, you switch back to the result table view of the analysis grid. By clicking on the **Information** button (highlight 4), you display query-related information such as **Author** and **Query Description**. Clicking on the **Information** button again hides the information area. Clicking on the **Filter** button (highlight 3) displays query components such as free characteristics, key figures, and structures to the left of the result table. Note that the filter area is based on the navigation pane design item, which we cover in the design mode section. By using the context menu on the required query component in the filter area, you can use filters for that query component. For example, we selected filter value for the characteristic **Segment** (highlights 5 and 6).

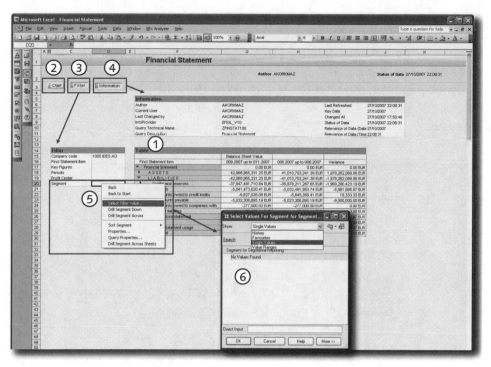

Figure 13.17 Query Display and Functions in SAP BEx Analyzer

Once the filter value or values are selected, the result table is updated and the filter value appears to the right of the corresponding query component in the **Filter** area. In our example, we restricted the characteristic **Segment** with the value **SEG1** (see Figure 13.18).

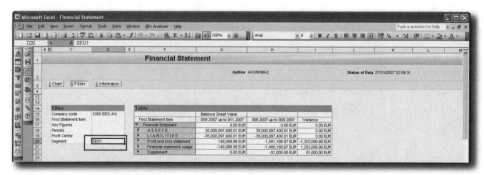

Figure 13.18 SAP BEx Display of Query with Segment Filter

In SAP BEx Analyzer, the same function can be performed in several ways. For example, drilldown OLAP functions can be performed from either the context menu or using the drag-and-drop technique. A good example for the drilldown OLAP function is to drill down on a characteristic. By using the context menu on a query component in the **Filter** area, you can drilldown on **Segment** characteristic (see Figure 13.19). The result table of the query is updated according to the segments.

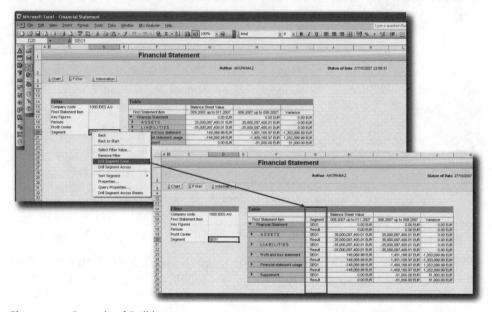

Figure 13.19 Example of Drilldown

Drilldown via Drag and Drop Technique

To drilldown the query to a specified characteristic using the drag-and-drop technique, you need to click on the characteristic in the **Filter** area and drag and drop it to the desired position in the result table. In our example, we defined additional drilldown by the **Profit Center** characteristic using the drag-and-drop technique (see Figure 13.20).

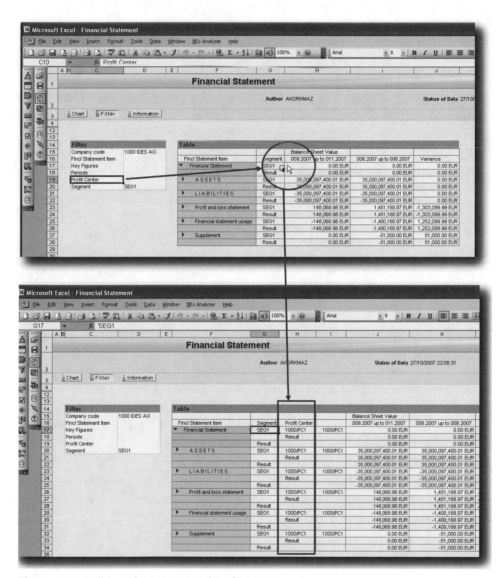

Figure 13.20 Drilldown by Segment and Profit Center

Context Menu of SAP BEx Analyzer Analysis Mode

In the analysis mode of SAP BEx Analyzer, you can use the context menu to navigate query results and generate different views. After executing OLAP analysis, you may need to restore the initial result view of the data when the query or workbook was first opened. This is achieved by using the **Back to Start** function, which undoes all navigational steps and reverts to the saved view. Figure 13.21 shows the available context menu options with the **Back to Start** option highlighted.

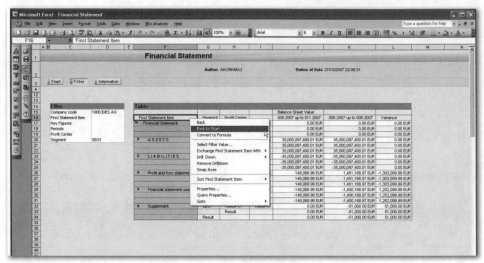

Figure 13.21 Context Menu SAP BEx Analyzer Analysis Mode

You can save workbooks on the server so that other users can open and analyze data saved in your workbook later. You can also save workbooks locally on your computer and refresh them later on with the latest data from the InfoProvider. In addition, you can call the SAP BEx Broadcaster to pre-calculate and distribute workbooks. To call the SAP BEx Broadcaster, follow the menu path **Tools • Broadcaster** in the **Analysis Toolbox**. Note, however, that the broadcasting option is only available when the workbook is open in SAP BEx Analyzer. It is not available when the query is open in SAP BEx Analyzer.

SAP BEx Analyzer Design Mode

SAP BEx Analyzer design mode provides tools for designing workbooks based on queries. With SAP BEx Analyzer design mode, your workbook appears as a collection of design items that you can configure to influence navigation and OLAP analysis in analysis mode. The most important design items are the *analysis grid design item* and *navigation pane design item*. The analysis grid design item is used to display the query results (table), and the navigation pane design item (filter) enables you to navigate in the result set and perform analysis. With the design mode, you can create powerful applications without the need for technical programming skills, and you can use Microsoft Excel functions in the workbook such as formatting, inserting additional worksheets, creating charts, and so on. The workbooks can be saved on either the server or local machine. Before designing our SAP NetWeaver BI application with SAP BEx Analyzer design mode, let's have a closer look at the design functions. The design function buttons of the SAP BEx Analyzer Design toolbox are highlighted in Figure 13.22.

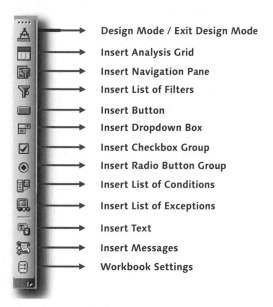

Figure 13.22 SAP BEx Analyzer Toolbox

► **Design Mode / Exit Design Mode**
With this toggle function, you can switch between SAP BEx Analyzer modes.

► **Insert Analysis Grid**
This function enables you to insert an analysis grid design item that displays the query results in a table.

► **Insert Navigation Pane**
With this function, you can insert a navigation pane design item that enables access to dimensions in the query for navigation and analysis.

▶ **Insert List of Filters**

With this function, you can insert a list of filters design item that lists all currently active filters set on selected dimensions in query results.

▶ **Insert Button**

With this function, you insert a design item that executes an assigned command.

▶ **Insert Dropdown Box**

With this function, you insert a dropdown box design item that lists assigned items in a dropdown list from which you can select a value.

▶ **Insert Checkbox Group**

With this function you can insert a checkbox group design item that lists assigned items in a checkbox group from which you can select one or more values from the list.

▶ **Insert Radio Button Group**

With this function, you can insert a radio button group design item that lists assigned items in a radio button group.

▶ **Insert List of Conditions**

With this function, you can insert a list of conditions design item that lists all conditions defined in the query and allows you to activate and deactivate them.

▶ **Insert List of Exceptions**

With this function, you can insert a list of exceptions design item that lists all exceptions defined in the query and allows you to activate and deactivate them.

▶ **Insert Text**

With this function, you can insert a text design item that allows you to display query text elements.

▶ **Insert Messages**

With this function, you can insert a messages design item that displays messages related to the workbook.

SAP BEx Application Example

Now that we have given an overview of SAP BEx Analyzer design functions, let's start designing our SAP BEx application example. You need to start SAP BEx Analyzer and click on the **New** button to create a new empty workbook (Figure 13.23, highlight 1). The next step is to insert design items in the workbook. To do so, click on the cell where you want to insert the results table in the empty workbook and click on the **Insert Analysis Grid** button (highlight 2). Right-click on the analysis grid item and access the **Properties** function (highlight 3). This step opens the **Analysis Grid Properties** dialog, where you configure the analysis grid (highlight 4). Here you have three tabs where properties of the analysis grid are configured:

▶ The **General** tab, where you can configure data provider, cell range, and behavior of the analysis grid

▶ The **Clipping** tab, where you configure whether to clip or scroll the grid display

▶ The **Associated Charts** tab, where you can link Microsoft Excel charts to the analysis grid

To display the data provider data in the analysis mode, you need to assign a data provider to the analysis grid. You can create a data provider by clicking on the **New** button next to the **Data Provider** dropdown box (highlight 5).

Figure 13.23 Creating the BEx Analyzer Application and Inserting an Analysis Grid

Once you have clicked on the **Data Provider** button, the **Create Data Provider** dialog box appears (see Figure 13.24, highlight 1). Here you assign **Query/Query View** and make configuration settings such as **Provide the Result Offline** and **Reference the View**. By selecting the **Provide the Result Offline** option, you can view the data in your result set without connecting to the server. By selecting the option **Reference the View**, you retrieve the original navigational state saved in the query on the server for this design item the next time you open the workbook.

In our example, we assigned query **ZFINSTAT100** to the data provider **DP_1** (highlight 2). After we click on the **OK** button, the data provider DP_1 appeared in the **Data Provider** dropdown box (highlight 3). Finally, we configured clipping to be **Full Size** for both **Horizontal** and **Vertical** clipping (highlight 4). Therefore, the result table will not be clipped. Clicking on **OK** completes customization of the analysis grid **GRID_1** (highlight 5).

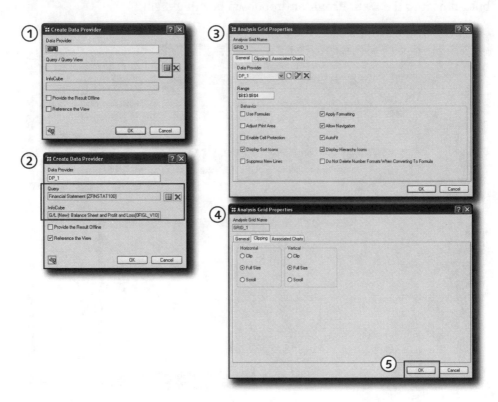

Figure 13.24 Settings of the Analysis Grid

Exit Analysis Mode

Now that we have defined the analysis grid, let's exit the design mode and see what the result table looks like. To exit the design mode and switch to analysis mode, click on the **Exit Analysis Mode** button in the BEx Design toolbox (see Figure 13.24, highlight 1). Depending on the query, the data may not be displayed directly in the analysis mode and you will get the following message: There are variables; change variable values (highlight 2). To change the variable values, click on the **Change Variable Values** button in the BEx Design toolbox (highlight 2). After that, you can enter the values for the variables that appear in the **Select Values for Variables** dialog box (highlight 3). Clicking the **OK** button updates the result table.

Figure 13.25 Exit the Design Mode and Select Values for Variables

After the result table is updated (see Figure 13.26, highlight 1), you can save the workbook. To save the workbook, use the **Save Workbook As** command in the BEx Design toolbox (highlight 2). In our example, we entered "Financial Statement 1" in the **Description** box and clicked on the·**Save** button (highlight 3). The workbook is saved, and the description of the workbook is updated in the window header.

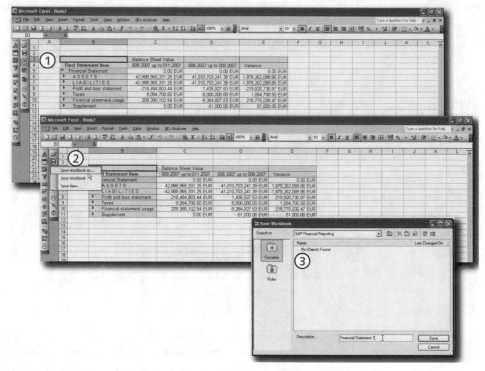

Figure 13.26 Display of the Output Grid and Saving the SAP BEx Workbook

Insert Text Elements

In SAP BEx Analyzer design mode, you can insert and configure the display of text elements that you want to show in the workbook. For example, you can insert text for query description, query technical name, author, InfoProvider, and any global filters configured in the query. To insert a text design element in the workbook, use the **Insert Text** command from the BEx Design Toolbox (see Figure 13.27, highlight 1). You can configure the properties of the text design element by right-clicking and selecting the properties from the context menu. After that, the **Text Properties** dialog box appears (highlight 2). There are three tabs in the text properties dialog box:

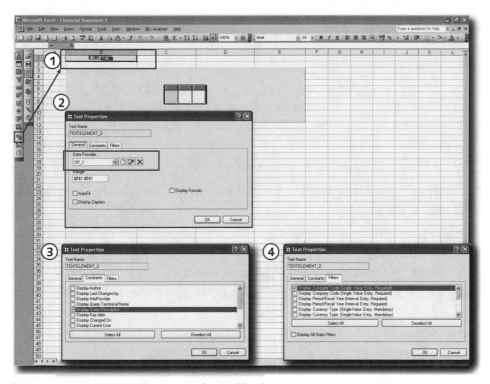

Figure 13.27 Inserting Text Elements in the Workbook

▶ **General**

In the **General** tab, you can configure the data provider for the text element, cell range, and display properties such as **AutoFit** and **Display Caption**. For TEXTELEMENT_2, we selected the data provider DP_1, which we defined in the Analysis Grid configuration step (highlight 2).

▶ **Constants**

In the **Constants** tab, you can select a list of text constants for the output of the query. We selected the constant **Display Query Description** (highlight 3).

▶ **Filters**

In the **Filters** tab, you can determine a list of filters to restrict the output of the query. We selected the filter **Display Company Code (Single Value Entry, Required)** (highlight 4).

Insert Navigation Pane

The navigation pane design item enables you to navigate in the result set and perform OLAP analysis. To insert a navigation pane design element in the workbook, use the **Insert Navigation Pane** command from the BEx Design Toolbox (see Figure 13.28, highlight 1). You can configure the properties of the navigation pane design element by right-clicking on the object and selecting the properties from the context menu or by just clicking on the object. After that, the **Navigation Pane Properties** dialog box appears (highlight 2).

Navigation Pane Properties has four tabs: **General**, **Dimension**, **Display Settings**, and **Clipping**.

▶ **General**

In the **General** tab, you can configure the data provider for the navigation pane, cell range, and display properties such as **AutoFit** and **Display Caption**. For the navigation pane **NAVPANEL_3** we assigned the data provider DP_1, which was already defined in the Analysis Grid configuration step (highlight 2).

▶ **Dimensions**

In the **Dimensions** tab, you can select the dimensions to display in the navigation pane. We selected all available dimensions and moved them to the **Selected Dimensions** box (highlight 3).

▶ **Display Settings**

In the **Display Settings** tab, you can configure settings related to the display of the navigation pane.

▶ **Clipping**

In the **Clipping** tab, you can configure whether to clip or scroll the navigation pane display.

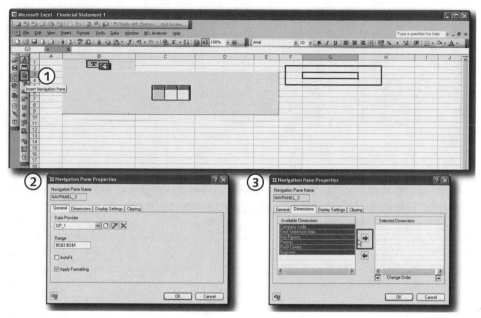

Figure 13.28 Insert Navigation Pane

Once it is configured, the navigation pane appears as shown in Figure 13.29, highlight 1. You can use all navigation functions within the navigation pane. We selected filter value **SEGMENT1** for the characteristic **Segment**, and the result table was refreshed according to this filter value (highlight 2). Note that the text elements we inserted also appear in column B above the analysis grid.

Now that we have explained SAP BEx Analyzer analysis and design modes, we can explore web-based reporting and application development using SAP BEx Web Application Designer. Compared to SAP BEx Analyzer, SAP BEx Web Application Designer is much faster and provides better design options.

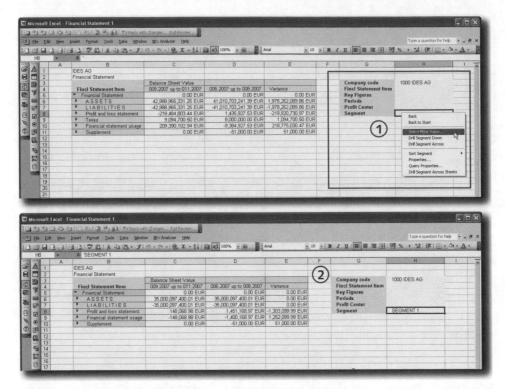

Figure 13.29 Select Filter Value for Segment in the Navigation Pane

Report-Report Interface (RRI)

The report-report interface (RRI) enables you to jump from a SAP NetWeaver BI query to jump target that can be within or outside SAP NetWeaver BI system. The calling query is called sender and the jump target is called receiver. The jump target can be another SAP NetWeaver BI query, web address, SAP NetWeaver BI Java Web Application, SAP ERP report and transaction. The jump target delivers more information using parameters of the sender as selection criteria.

In SAP BEx Web application and SAP BEx Analyzer you can call assigned jump targets from the context GoTo menu. To set up the RRI in a SAP BEx Query or SAP BEx Web Application you first have to make the necessary settings with sender-receiver assignment. To set up this functionality follow the SAP Menu of SAP NetWeaver BI: Business Explorer • Query • Jump Target (Transaction RSBBS). Here you assign the sender and receiver on a query level or on an SAP NetWeaver BI InfoProvider level. You also need to set up parameters for receiver that uses input variables which are filled from the selection conditions and the element definitions of the cells highlighted in the sender query.

13.1.3 SAP BEx Web Application Designer

SAP BEx Web Application Designer allows you to use generic OLAP navigation for the SAP NetWeaver BI data in web applications. With SAP BEx Web Application Designer, you can develop web applications and publish them in the portal SAP BEx Information Broadcaster or execute them in SAP BEx Web Analyzer. The web applications generate HTML pages with SAP NetWeaver BI objects that retrieve information from SAP NetWeaver BI data providers. SAP NetWeaver BI objects that are used in SAP BEx Web Application Designer are called web items. In the following sections we give you an overview and an example of how to create a web application with SAP BEx Web Application Designer.

Like other SAP NetWeaver BI BEx components, you start the SAP BEx Web Analyzer in your Windows operating system by selecting **Start • Programs • Business Explore • BEx Web Application Designer** (see Figure 13.2). Once you log on to the system, the initial of **BEx Web Application Designer** screen appears (see Figure 13.30).

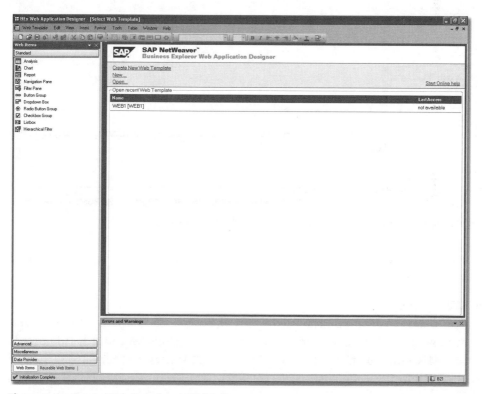

Figure 13.30 Create Web Template Initial Screen

The structure of a web application is formed with a web template. From the initial screen of SAP BEx Web Application Designer, you can create a new web template, open a template, or open a recent web template. When creating a new template, you can use web template patterns or create a blank template. If you select the **Create New Web Template** option, the default view of the SAP BEx Web Application Designer will appear, as shown in Figure 13.31.

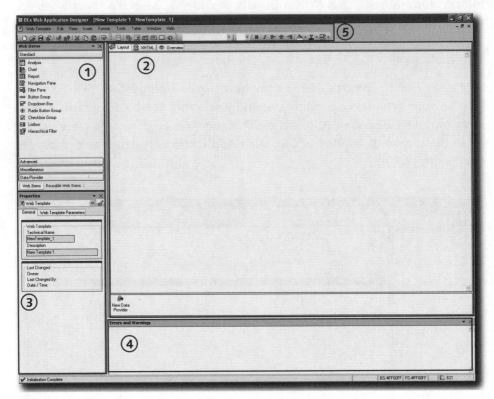

Figure 13.31 Default View of the SAP BEx Web Application Designer

The initial default view of the SAP BEx Web Application Designer can be divided into four screen areas:

▶ **Web Items**
The web items that you can use in your web application are listed in the **Web Items** area, which is classified into three subsections: **Standard**, **Advanced**, and **Miscellaneous**. Highlight 1 in Figure 13.31 shows the **Standard** section of the **Web Item** screen area.

- ▶ **Web Template**

  In this area, you can see the web template that you edit when designing your web application (highlight 2). At the top of the **Web Template** screen area are three tabs that provide different view options. These tabs are **Layout**, **XHTML**, and **Overview**. The **Layout** tab shows the web application in visual format, the **XHTML** tab shows the application in XHTML format, and the **Overview** tab shows all web items, data providers, and commands used in web templates.

- ▶ **Properties**

  In the **Properties** area, you define the properties of web templates and web items. In our example, **NewTemplate 1** properties are illustrated in highlight 3.

- ▶ **Error and Warnings Screen Area**

  In this area, you see the errors and warnings generated when the web template is verified.

SAP BEx Web Application Designer has three toolbars: **Standard**, **Insert**, and **Format**. All the functions available in these toolbars are also available in the application menu.

Web Application Example

Now let's start building our web application example by using various web items. We will create financial statement analysis with various web controls and navigation options. In the basic design of our web template, we will use HTML table layout and position the web items into the table cells. To insert a table, click on the **Insert Table** button highlighted on the Insert Toolbar in Figure 13.32. The table has two **Rows** and two **Columns**, and the table layout is shown in the **Edit HTML Element** dialog box.

When building your web application, you can use the items available in the **Web Items** area. The web items can be inserted into the **Web Template** area using the drag-and-drop technique. Let's start with inserting the Analysis web item. The Analysis web item is similar to the analysis grid design item of SAP BEx Analyzer, which shows the data provider as a table in the web application. We inserted an Analysis web item into the lower-right cell of the table layout (see Figure 13.33, highlight 1). The name of the analysis is automatically generated as **ANALYSIS_ITEM_1**. The next step is to assign a data provider to **ANALYSIS_ITEM _1**. To do so, click on the **New** button shown in highlight 2. The **New Data Provider** dialog box appears with generated data provider name **DP_1** in the **General** Box. The next step is to define the data provider type by assigning the query ZFINSTAT100 to the data provider DP_1 (highlight 3). This can be done either by typing the query "technical name" in the text box or selecting the **Select Query** button indicated by highlight 4.

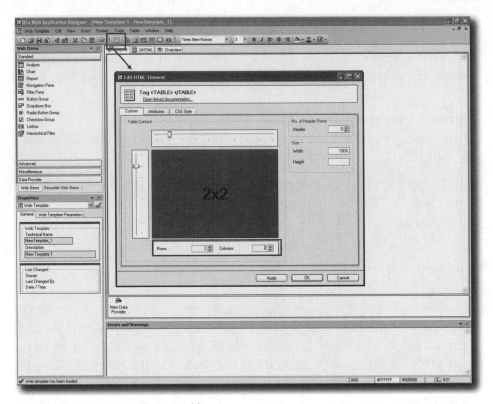

Figure 13.32 Insert HTML Element Table

After configuring the analysis table, we saved our web template with the description "Financial Statement" and technical name "ZFINSTATWEB100." Once the Web template is saved, the description and technical name appear in the header bar of the **SAP BEx Web Application Designer** window (see Figure 13.34). As a next step we added other web items to our web application, using the drag-and-drop technique. For example, we added the **Information Field** web item (**INFO_FIELD_ITEM_1**) to the upper-left cell of the layout table (highlight 1). In the same way, we inserted a Check Box Group item (**CHECK_BOX_GROUP_ITEM_1**) to the upper-right cell of the layout table (highlight 2). We also inserted a Navigation Pane web item (**NAVIGATION_PANE_ITEM_1**) to the lower-left cell of the table (highlight 3). As we mentioned earlier, properties of each web item can be configured in the **Properties** area when the web item is selected in the layout area. In our example, the **INFO_FIELD_ITEM_1** web item is selected and its properties are displayed in the **Properties** screen area (highlight 4). We configured InfoProvider-specific information to be displayed where we specified the display of the **Query Description**, **InfoProvider Name**, **Last Refresh Time**, and **Author**.

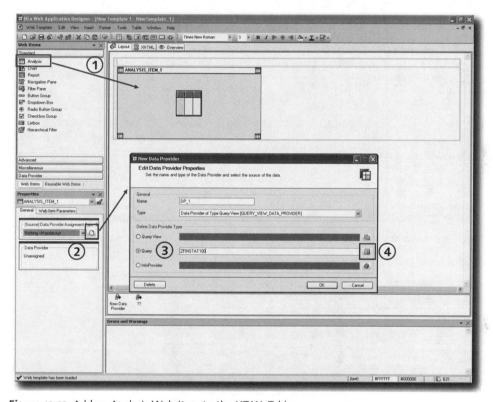

Figure 13.33 Add an Analysis Web Item to the HTML Table

The corresponding properties of **NAVIGATION_PANE_ITEM_1** and **CHECK_BOX_GROUP_ITEM_1** are displayed in Figure 13.35. Note that the data provider is assigned in the **Data Binding** part of the **NAVIGATION_PANE_ITEM_1** box is **DP_1**. The **Data Binding** of **CHECK_BOX_GROUP_ITEM_1** is the characteristic **Segment (0SEGMENT)** of the data provider **DP_1**.

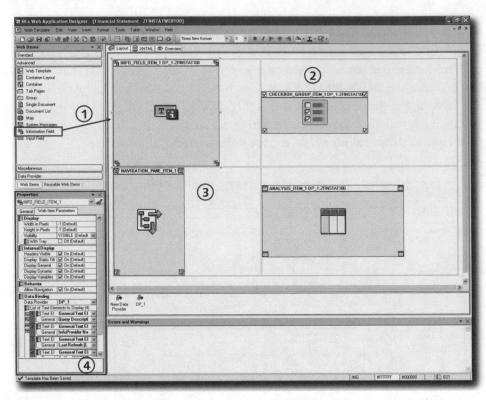

Figure 13.34 Adding an Info Field, Navigation Pane, and Checkbox Group to the Template

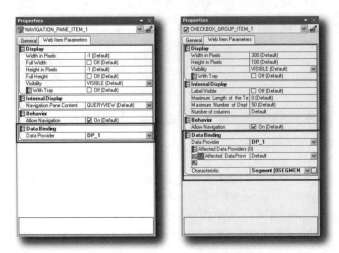

Figure 13.35 Navigation Pane and Checkbox Group Properties

Now let's execute our web application template in the enterprise portal. To execute the web application template, either use the **Execute** button in the Standard Toolbar or use the menu **Web Template** and then select **Execute**. The display of our web template Financial Statement (ZFINSTATWEB100) is illustrated in Figure 13.36.

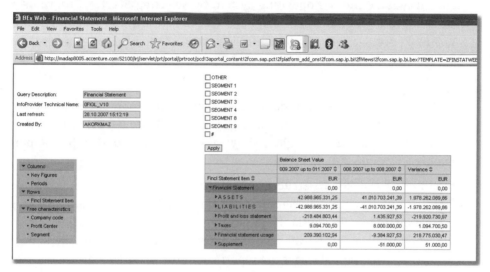

Figure 13.36 ZFINSTATWEB100 Web Template Display in the Enterprise Portal

Note that the examples given to explain the concept and overview of SAP BEx Suite reporting tools should be regarded as an overview of the available options and functions and do not include all the options and capabilities of the tools.

Now that we have explained SAP BEx Web Application Designer, we will explore the SAP BEx Report Designer tool.

13.1.4   SAP BEx Report Designer

SAP BEx Report Designer is a tool used to generate formatted reports, called SAP NetWeaver BI Enterprise reports. With SAP BEx Report Designer, business-specific layouts can be easily printed either as hard copy or PDF or displayed on the Web. The data binding for the SAP BEx Report Designer report is provided by data providers (queries and query views). The layout and formatting of the report can be adapted to various report output requirements. With the SAP BEx Report Designer tool, you no longer need to use third-party or in-house developed solutions for formatted report outputs.

Like other SAP NetWeaver BI BEx Suite components, you start the SAP BEx Report Designer in your Windows operating system by selecting **Start • Programs • Business Explore • BEx Report Designer** (refer to Figure 13.2). The initial view of SAP BEx Report Designer is shown in Figure 13.37, divided into three screen areas:

▶ **Design Area**
The design area is where you design and display the report schematically. In the design area, report elements such as the page header, footer, and report sections are displayed. Highlight 1 shows the design area of SAP BEx Report Designer.

▶ **Field Catalog and Report Structure Area**
In this area you switch between **Field Catalog** and **Report** structure by using the corresponding tabs. In the **Field Catalog** tab, all query fields, filters, variables, and text elements for the report data provider are displayed. The **Report** structure hierarchically displays the report components. Highlight 2 shows the **Field Catalog** tab of this area.

▶ **Formats and Properties Area**
In this area you switch between **Formats** (Format Catalog) and **Properties** by using the corresponding tabs. The Format Catalog provides an overview of the formats used in the report. In the **Properties** tab, properties of the report elements are configured. Highlight 3 shows the **Formats** tab of this area.

The Application menu and Standard and Format toolbars are indicated by highlight 4.

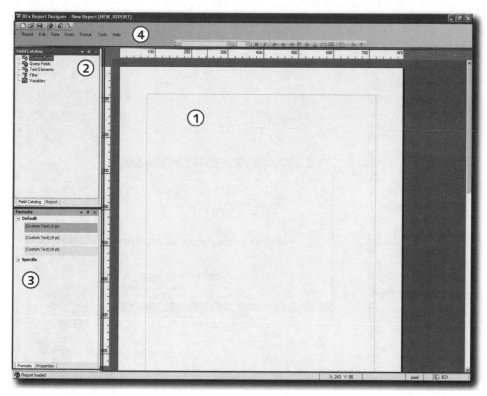

Figure 13.37 SAP BEx Report Designer Initial View

Example Report with SAP BEx Report Designer

Now let's explore the SAP BEx Report Designer functions and capabilities by creating an example report. We will build a cost center formatted report with a graphic and publish it in the Enterprise Portal. Note that you can also publish your reports in SAP NetWeaver Portal. The first step is to insert a data provider in the design area. This can be done either from the Report menu or by using the context menu of the design area's blank page. In our example, we used the context menu (see Figure 13.38, highlight 1) and selected the query **0COOM_C02_Q0003 (Cost Center: Plan/Actual Situation)** as the data provider (highlight 2).

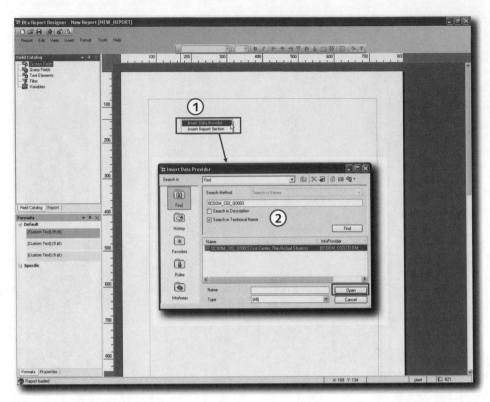

Figure 13.38 Insert Data Provider

After configuring the data provider, we saved our report with the description "Cost Center: Plan/Actual Situation" and technical name "ZCO100." Once the report is saved, the description and technical name appear in the header bar of the **BEx Report Designer** window. The data provider is displayed schematically in the design area (Figure 13.39).

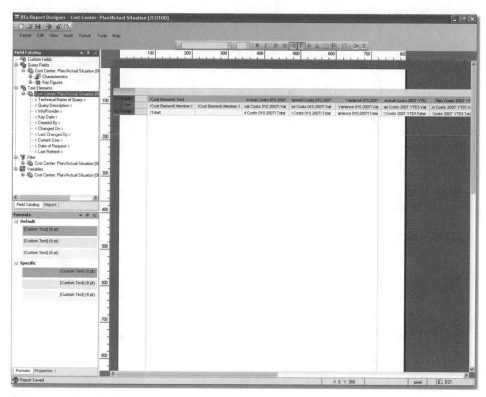

Figure 13.39 Data Provider 0COOM_C02_Q0003

Insert Graphic (Chart)

The next step is to configure the graphics. We inserted a new report section where we placed the graphic. The inserted report section had no data binding on its own. Then we manually adjusted the cell size of the report section to fit the graphic size. The adjusted report section is indicated by highlight 1 in Figure 13.40. With the use of the context menu of the report section we selected the **Insert Graphic** function. After that, the **Edit Chart** dialog box of the chart designer appeared, where you can edit the chart using the chart designer tool by clicking on the **Next** button and configuring the chart options (highlight 2).

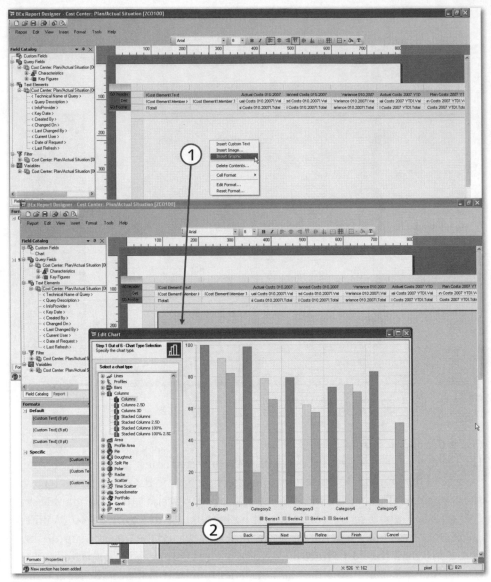

Figure 13.40 Insert Chart

You can use the context menu in the design area on various report items. The options in the context depend upon the report items selected. You can also access the same functions by using the menu bars and toolbars and the other screen areas of the Report Designer, enabling you to edit report elements and design your report.

For example, you can format cells, rows, columns, and so on with the context menu. The context menu of the data provider column is displayed in highlight 1 of Figure 13.41. Highlight 2 indicates the **Report** structure that hierarchically displays the report components, including the Chart that we inserted in **Report Section**.

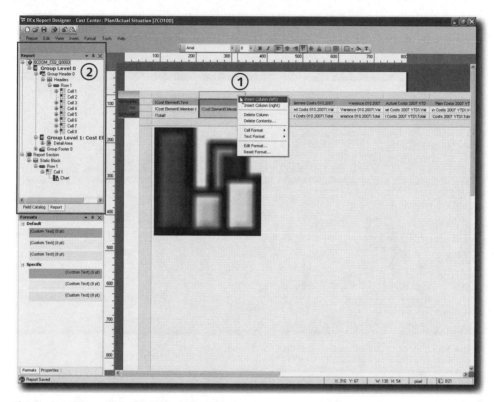

Figure 13.41 Formatting the Report Elements

Execute and Print the Report

To execute the report in the Enterprise Portal, select the **Execute** command from the **Report** menu. The report will be displayed in the standard web template for reports in the portal. An example of report output is shown in Figure 13.42. In our example, we assigned the **Cost Element** dimension to **476100 Travel Cost**. The graphic of the result set is displayed below the data provider element in the report section where we inserted it.

You can print the report by using the menu of the Report Designer and selecting the **Print Version** command from the **Report** menu. The report is then automatically converted to a PDF document that can be saved or printed. You can also print the report from the portal by pressing the **Print Version** button (see Figure 13.42). In addition, you can publish reports in SAP NetWeaver BI roles, iViews in the portal, or via SAP BEx Broadcaster by using the publish function of the **Report** menu.

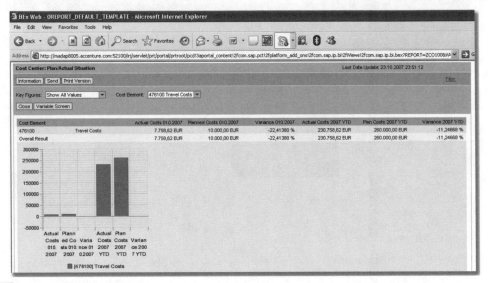

Figure 13.42 Report Output with Filter on Cost Element 476100

Now that we have explained SAP BEx Report Designer, we will explore the SAP BEx Broadcaster tool used for distributing business intelligence results via various means. In the next section we provide you with an overview and example of using the SAP BEx Broadcaster.

13.1.5 SAP BEx Broadcaster

Information broadcasting enables business intelligence content to be distributed to a wide range of recipients. The SAP BEx Broadcaster tool is used to distribute business intelligence content by email, Enterprise Portal, SAP NetWeaver Portal, print, and so on. The email distribution can be pre-calculated content with historical data or containing links to the live data. The tool is used to distribute reports on a regular event-driven basis. It is based on the principle of pushing or streaming the information to the information workers. The SAP BEx Broadcaster can be called in several different ways from SAP NetWeaver BI Business Explorer Suite tools. These are:

▶ **SAP BEx Query Designer**
Follow menu path **Query • Publish • BEx Broadcaster**.

▶ **SAP BEx Analyzer**
In the Analysis Toolbox, follow the menu path **Tools • Broadcaster**.

▶ **SAP BEx Web Application Designer**
Follow menu path **Web Template • Publish • BEx Broadcaster**.

▶ **SAP BEx Web Analyzer**
In the context menu, choose **Broadcast and Export • Broadcast E-Mail, Broadcast to Portal**, or **Broadcast to Printer** (Figure 13.43, highlight 1).

▶ **SAP BEx Report Designer**
Follow menu path **Report • Publish • BEx Broadcaster** (highlight 2).

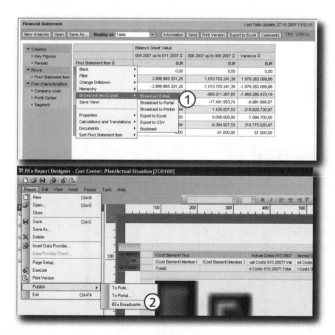

Figure 13.43 Calling SAP BEx Broadcaster

Now let's broadcast the report we created with SAP BEx Report Designer in the previous section. Once you call the SAP BEx Broadcaster from SAP BEx Report Designer, SAP BEx Broadcaster is executed as a web application in Internet Explorer. You can use SAP BEx Broadcaster with or without the wizard. Highlight 1 in Figure 13.44 shows the initial screen of SAP BEx Broadcaster. Here we need to specify the object for which we want to create broadcasting settings. In our example we selected the **Report** option from the dropdown list. You can also create broadcasting settings for **Query**, **Web Template Name**, **Query View**, and **Workbook**. After that, click on the **Create New Setting with the Wizard** button to call the Broadcasting Wizard.

The Broadcasting Wizard is a very easy and intuitive tool to use. It guides you though the broadcasting process with step-by-step screens in which you specify the broadcasting settings. Highlight 2 shows the first out of four steps in the Broadcasting Wizard, which is **Determine Basic Settings**. Here we set **Distribution Type** to **Broadcast E-mail**. And as shown in highlight 3, we set **Output Format** to **Online Link to Current Data**. The receiver of the report receives an e-mail with an embedded hyperlink pointing to the report. After the **Continue** button is clicked, highlight 4 shows **Enter E-mail Message**. Here you enter the **E-Mail Addresses** of the recipient(s), the **Subject**, **Importance**, and the **Content** of the message, and click on the **Continue** button.

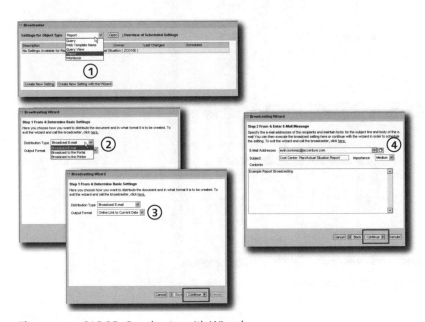

Figure 13.44 SAP BEx Broadcaster with Wizard

In the next step we specify **Technical Name** and **Description** for our broadcast settings (Figure 13.45, highlight 1). After pressing the **Continue** button, **Step 4 from 4: Determine Scheduling Details** is displayed (highlight 2). Here you specify the frequency of the broadcasting. We have selected weekly broadcasting and the **Next Start** at 29.10.2007 at 08:30:00. After that you need to click on the **Schedule** button to schedule the broadcast. Finally, we have to specify the **General Link Generation** settings (highlight 3). Here you specify settings for **Variable Assignment** and **Exceptions**. We determined the variable assignment from **Variant cc2** and select exceptions option **No Include**. Therefore, the report is pre-calculated with variant cc2, regardless of whether exceptions occur.

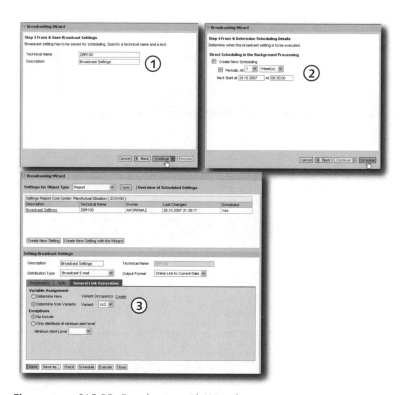

Figure 13.45 SAP BEx Broadcaster with Wizard—1

The information worker receives an email with an embedded hyperlink enabling access to the report by simply clicking on the link. Because a variable variant was configured in the broadcasting settings, the email recipient does not see the variable selection of the report. Therefore, after the required user name and password authentication, the pre-calculated report results are shown to the user in the portal. Figure 13.46 shows an email with an embedded hyperlink broadcasted in our example.

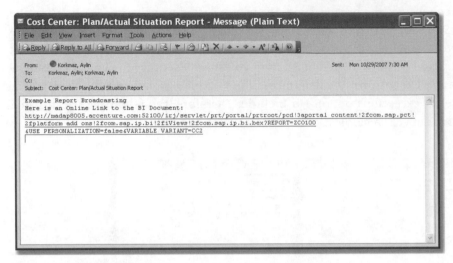

Figure 13.46 Broadcast by Email

> **Reporting Agent**
>
> As of SAP NetWeaver 2004s, SAP BEx Broadcaster covers functions of the previous broadcasting tool called SAP BW Reporting Agent. SAP BW Reporting Agent can still be used, but only with queries and web templates in the SAP BW 3.x format. SAP BEx Broadcaster should be used instead of SAP BW Reporting Agent.

13.2 Summary

In this chapter we explained the SAP NetWeaver BI BEx reporting tools to guide you through reporting tools functions and capabilities for financial reports. All SAP NetWeaver BI reporting tools covered in this chapter are used in various report developments, and each of them has its own features and capabilities. We explained the reporting tools with non-customer specific examples so that you can easily replicate them in your own SAP NetWeaver BI system to build your own reporting solutions, or simply use them as a learning example. Note that the examples given to explain the concept and overview of SAP BEx Suite reporting tools should be regarded as an overview of the available options and functions and do not include all the options and capabilities of the tools.

This chapter deals with organizational performance and information worker applications. We first look at financial compliance, which is heavily focused upon SAP GRC Access Control and SAP GRC Process Control. After that, we explain SAP's new Corporate Performance Management (CPM) strategy, focus on the features and capabilities of new CPM applications, and explain the evolution of SEM solutions to CPM solutions. The last section of the chapter covers SAP solutions for information workers. We specifically cover SAP xApp™ Analytics composite applications, Duet™, and SAP Interactive Forms software by Adobe.

14 Organizational Performance and Information Worker Applications

"The Business User organization will establish SAP as the market leader in innovating and delivering new business application categories, and making processes relevant to all information workers in an organization. In doing so, we will help best-run companies become more nimble, efficient, and responsive by leveraging existing application investments and extending business processes to high-value information workers and organizational performance management."[1]

With this vision, SAP AG has started a series of initiatives on organizational performance and information worker applications to empower its customers' information workers. These initiatives provide competitive organizational benefits to SAP customers such as improved organizational performance, process cost reduction, better compliance, greater employee productivity, and increased employee retention.

How do these new applications fit into your organization's overall solution architecture? Figure 14.1 illustrates SAP's unified solution architecture that works with all of the enterprise applications used to support business processes. The main application categories are: the SAP Business Suite family of business applications,

---

[1] Doug Meritt, *Business User Organization Overview Session*, SAPPHIRE® 2007.

organizational performance applications, and information worker applications. This architecture is built on an enterprise service-oriented platform and enables the use of industry-specific content and analysis. The solution supports the holistic financial management concept, seamlessly connecting information workers, business processes, analytics and controls, and compliance functions across the enterprise and beyond, which is increasingly important for CFOs.

In previous chapters we have covered the strategies for maximizing financial reporting capabilities and explained the best practices for simplifying, streamlining, and automating financial and management reporting in SAP ERP Financials business suite application. In this chapter, we focus on organizational performance and information worker applications and explain how your organization can benefit from these new initiatives. We first look at SAP solutions for governance, risk, and compliance (SAP solutions for GRC) and SAP solutions for performance management. Then we explain SAP solutions for information workers with the focus on SAP xApp Analytics composite applications, Duet and SAP Interactive Forms.

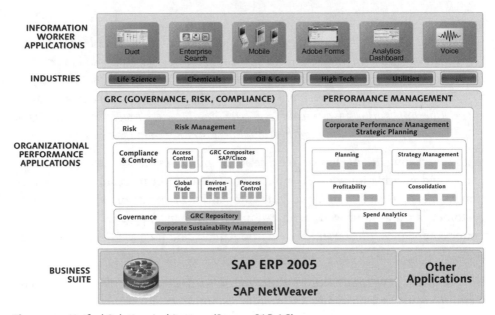

Figure 14.1 Unified Solution Architecture (Source: SAP AG)

14.1   Governance, Risk, and Compliance

Governance, risk, and compliance are three important concepts for the economic health of organizations. At the turn of the century, significant and massive failures in financial reporting, governance practices, and risk prevention created the need for sustainable improvement in these areas. As a result, governance, risk, and compliance concepts have been transformed into the number one business priority for organizations.

The *governance* of an organization can be defined as a system of managing the corporate strategic objectives and directing the means of attaining those objectives.

Businesses and organizations today are faced with a number of different internal and external *risks*. It is important to assess these risks and impacts upon your corporate strategy so that you can make better-informed decisions. The risks posed by the inadequate management and reporting of financial data can lead to severe consequences for corporations and their senior executives in achieving organizational objectives, so it is important to evaluate opportunities and compliance with legislative requirements. Examples of these risks include inaccessibility of records, inaccuracy of data, lack of credibility of information, and incomplete records and information.

Organizations are controlled by numerous mandates and regulations, such as the Sarbanes-Oxley Act (SOX) in the United States, which put pressure on organizations to identify, manage, and quickly adapt to new and existing *compliances*. Adding to growing pressure from financial markets and demands from stakeholders, these requirements have increased the corporate-wide focus upon governance, risk, and compliance (GRC). GRC has become an intrinsic part of the financial reporting landscape of organizations. GRC is also a top priority as business leaders increasingly understand that a small operational control weakness can significantly impair corporate performance.

SAP governance, risk, and compliance (GRC) technology foundation provides integration with existing SAP and non-SAP applications to manage corporate governance, risk management, and regulatory compliance.

The applications of GRC technology foundation offer a holistic, integrated, and automated approach for managing governance, risk and compliance. Figure 14.2 illustrates a schematic view of the GRC technology foundation applications.

Figure 14.2 SAP GRC Technology Foundation (Source: SAP AG)

The applications are classified into three categories. Let's take a closer look at the applications in each category.

Governance

▸ The SAP GRC Repository is the application where GRC content is centrally recorded. This includes corporate policies, compliances, mandates, control frameworks, risks, and controls library.

▸ The SAP GRC Corporate Sustainability Management application enables you to promote the profile and brand of the company by analyzing and disclosing corporate initiatives to improve global economic, social, and environmental conditions.

Compliance and Controls

▸ The SAP GRC Access Control application enables monitoring, testing, and enforcing access and authentication controls across the enterprise. It also enables segregation of duties (SoD) requirements and has preventive controls for access and authorization risks.

▶ The SAP GRC Process Control application allows organizations to automate the monitoring, testing, assessment, remediation, and certification of enterprise-wide business processes and GRC composites.

▶ GRC Composites SAP/Cisco has been jointly developed with Cisco for customer-specific business process impacts. It enables data privacy protection across the entire IT infrastructure. For example, unauthorized emails containing sensitive information are blocked and actioned.

▶ The SAP GRC Global Trade Services enables compliance with trade export and import regulations, expedited cross-border transactions, and the optimum use of trade agreements.

▶ The SAP Environmental Compliance application enables compliance with environmental product safety regulations.

Risk

▶ SAP GRC Risk Management enables collaborative process management for enterprise risk planning, identification, analysis, response, monitoring and reporting.

Now that we have explained the SAP GRC technology foundation applications, let's look at the GRC business drivers.

14.1.1 GRC Business Drivers

The massive failures in financial reporting, governance practices, and risks prevention at the turn of the century, along with SOX and other regulations, are the main business drivers for GRC. These regulations have important effects upon enterprise business processes, infrastructure, system controls, and reporting. Figure 14.3 shows the main GRC business drivers: financial compliances, trade management, and environment regulations. In addition to these business drivers, the GRC concept and tools are extensively developed and promoted by leading enterprise consulting and software companies.

In this chapter, we only focus on financial compliance, which is heavily affected by SOX Sections 302 and 404. Section 302 states that CEOs and CFOs must personally sign off on their company's financial statements. Section 404 mandates that well-defined and documented processes and controls be in place for all aspects of company operations that affect financial reports.

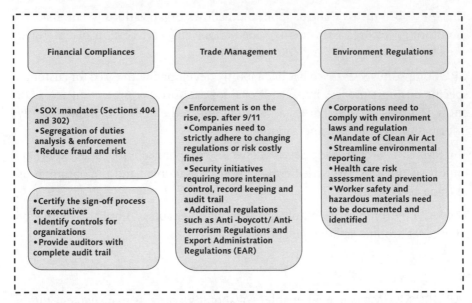

Financial Compliances	Trade Management	Environment Regulations

- • SOX mandates (Sections 404 and 302)
- • Segregation of duties analysis & enforcement
- • Reduce fraud and risk

- • Certify the sign-off process for executives
- • Identify controls for organizations
- • Provide auditors with complete audit trail

- • Enforcement is on the rise, esp. after 9/11
- • Companies need to strictly adhere to changing regulations or risk costly fines
- • Security initiatives requiring more internal control, record keeping and audit trail
- • Additional regulations such as Anti-boycott/ Anti-terrorism Regulations and Export Administration Regulations (EAR)

- • Corporations need to comply with environment laws and regulation
- • Mandate of Clean Air Act
- • Streamline environmental reporting
- • Health care risk assessment and prevention
- • Worker safety and hazardous materials need to be documented and identified

Figure 14.3 GRC Business Drivers (Source: SAP AG)

SOX Sections 302 and 404

SOX Section 302 requires CEOs and CFOs to certify quarterly and annual reports to the SEC, including making representations about the effectiveness of specified controls and procedures over financial reporting, operations, and compliance. Section 404 requires that the annual report include a report by management on the effectiveness of internal controls, including documentation of control design and effectiveness testing, disclosure of any material weaknesses, and attestation by external auditors. Further periodic disclosure requirements are covered under Section 302.

SOX responsibility is not only within U.S. borders. The internal controls required by SOX must be implemented by companies publicly traded on U.S. exchanges. Before the SAP GRC technology foundation applications, SAP had already built controls into SAP ERP and SAP NetWeaver BI to meet the requirements set by SOX Sections 302 and 404. In Chapters 2 to 11 we walked through the requirements of international accounting standards and explained the functionalities of how to meet with these regulations in SAP ERP to generate financial reports that fairly present in all material respects the financial condition and results of operations. We also explained controls, particularly, built-in system and reporting controls, that you can deploy to avoid any material weaknesses in financial reporting. Refer to Table 14.1 for an overview of available control categories and the controls in SAP ERP.

So how do the SAP GRC technology foundation applications add value on top of your existing controls? In the following sections we closely examine SAP GRC Access Control and SAP GRC Process Control to give you insight into how you can increase financial compliance with these applications.

SAP ERP Control Category	SAP ERP Controls
Inherent controls	► Integrated balance postings ► Real-time online data and document principle ► Monitor postings for review and approval ► System retained, transactions, program change, and configuration history ► Internal controls structure monitoring
Configurable controls (built-in system controls)	► Check references such as three-way match in logistic invoice verification ► Mandatory and system populated fields ► Master data controls ► Customizable system messages automatically triggered after certain events occurred ► Workflow ► Automated integrated postings with predefined posting keys and accounts
Reporting controls	► Timely closing process monitoring activities ► Delivered standard reports contained in easily accessible report tree ► Context-sensitive help ► eXtensible Business Reporting Language (XBLR) reporting capability ► System supplied audit capabilities (audit trials, change document log, document flow)
Security controls	► Flexible user access and permissions to program transactions, tables, and fields ► Authorization management, including segregation of duties via comprehensive authorization mechanism ► Detection and prevention of unauthorized access ► Tools to promote efficient, effective creation and maintenance of user profiles and roles

Table 14.1 SAP ERP Controls

14.1.2 SAP GRC Access Control

SAP GRC Access Control is an application for monitoring, testing, and enforcing access and authorization controls across the enterprise. It not only detects the authorizations or SoD risks, but also has embedded preventive controls. SAP GRC Access Control is based upon the former SAP Compliance Calibrator by Virsa Systems. The SAP GRC Access Control application provides an end-to-end access control application that is *business driven*, providing robust *audit management* functions. It is a cross-enterprise ready application; in other words, companies no longer need to deploy different compliance software for each business function or enterprise application.

Figure 14.4 shows a schematic view of the SAP GRC Access Control application. The SAP GRC Access Control addresses the areas of access control management, user management, role management, privileged user access, and reporting and controls management.

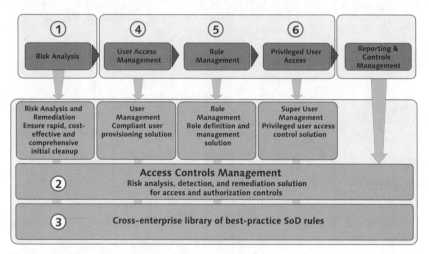

Figure 14.4 SAP GRC Access Control

Many companies have already implemented SoD and access controls in their systems before SAP GRC Access Control had been launched. Perhaps the most important question is Why do you need another application on top of your existing access control software? Do you need to restart your access control project with the SAP GRC Access Control? In this section we focus on what you can build on top of your existing access control applications rather than explaining how to set up an access control process in your organization.

The SAP GRC Access Control leverages the existing SoDs and access controls that you have already built and generates a risk analysis report. This is very important. The roles of the profiles are changed, people move to other roles in the organization, and SoD is overlooked over the time. Many companies believe they have prevented SoD issues, but often when we carry out analysis, we recognize that some users have more access than they should have, which causes SoD issues and associated risks. By using the Risk Analysis and Remediation function (see Figure 14.4, highlight 1) in the SAP GRC Access Control, you can analyze authorization and access data from your existing systems and generate risk analysis reports. These reports are used to assess the access and authorization risks to help create improvements in the SoD and access control area. Once you remediate the risks, the Access Controls Management function (highlight 2) is constantly used for risk analysis, detection, and remediation solutions for access and authorization controls. The SAP GRC Access Control has a Cross-enterprise Library of Best-practice SoD Rules to address SoD compliance for core processes such as procure to pay and order to cash (highlight 3).

Let's continue with the other functions in SAP GRC Access Control.

User Management Function

Organizations are constantly hiring new employees, and employees move between different positions within organizations. With the user management process relying on spreadsheets, MS Word forms, or email approvals, these changes can often be overlooked, causing access risks. For example, when an accounts payable clerk is promoted and needs new system access, request forms are filled, emails sent, and new access is given, but often the security team overlooks taking away his existing access. After a certain time, employees may end up with significant access, causing SoD risks, access risks, and compliance issues. The GRC User Access Management function (highlight 4) enables fully compliant user provisioning throughout the employee lifecycle and prevents SoD issues and access violations. System-controlled workflow is utilized to route the request and approvals to back up approvers and prevent any delays caused when the primary approvers are not available or do not action the request.

Our experience has shown that many companies have an approval process in place, but usually it is based on emails and spreadsheets, with little control. Therefore, auditing and tracing back unauthorized access requests and approvals is very difficult and time-consuming. With the SAP GRC User Management application, you can overcome these issues.

Role Management Function

The SAP GRC Access Control enables centralized role design, testing, and maintenance, resulting in manual error elimination and the use of best practices. With the GRC Access Role Management function (highlight 5), you can easily give role ownership back to business process owners, rather than keep them with the basis team. System workflow automates the role creation, role assignment, and approval process, while keeping track of all the process steps involved.

The role management application enables business process owners to define roles and automatically collaborate with the basis team. With the role management function, business process owners can analyze all the roles in which a particular transaction is used or compare role definitions to the way that roles are used in SAP applications. Once the roles are defined, they can be created easily. The application leverages profile-generating functionality (Transaction PFCG). It offers several historical role reports to help business role owners with their year-end attestations. Thus, business role owners can easily prove to the auditors that all users only have the roles they are supposed to have.

Super User Management Function

The last function of the SAP GRC Access Control application is GRC Super User Management (highlight 6). How can the organization give users super user access to the systems without violating compliance and creating unnecessary risks? SAP GRC Access Control resolves this problem with the so-called *super user ID*, or *firefighter ID*, which is a user ID that has access to transactions that users cannot access with their user ID. The firefighter ID is completely traceable, maintainable, and auditable. With the firefighter or super user ID, you can still do the tasks that are urgent and outside of your daily process responsibility. Once these tasks are complete, you leave the firefighter ID and return to your normal user ID. All the transactions you executed and the tasks you performed are properly recorded, and the process owners are informed simultaneously. Thus, there is always an audit, and risks are remedied. Web-based reporting enables business process owners and auditors to analyze and monitor firefighter logs and usage across systems.

Now that we have explained SAP GRC Access Control, which is pretty much related to SOX Section 302 and requires strong effective access and authorization controls in place, let's take a closer look at SAP GRC Process Control, which deals with SOX Section 404. As previously mentioned, Section 404 requires companies to document their business processes, identify risks and define controls to mitigate them, and regularly demonstrate the effectiveness of those controls.

14.1.3 SAP GRC Process Control

The SAP GRC Process Control application allows organizations to automate the monitoring, testing, assessment, remediation, and certification of enterprise-wide business processes. Many organizations implement process controls without using integrated GRC process control solutions, for example, purchase order release strategy or document parking and approval process. As we mentioned earlier, all these controls are configured and built in the SAP environment. The SAP GRC Process Control application leverages the existing controls and adds value and automation to process control.

Let's examine a real-life example to illustrate how SAP GRC Process Control can add value on top of your existing controls built in your SAP Business Suite. In one of our projects, we had a process control stating that all journals with a dollar value greater than US $10,000 had to be approved by the accounting supervisor. We had a situation where the accounting clerk had to make the closing payroll journals with an approximate value of US $200,000, but his approver was not able to approve because she did not have access to the system. A workaround solution was found, and the accounting clerk posted 20 documents without approval instead of one document with approval. This is, of course, not a normal practice, and the supervisor was aware of the postings, but from a compliance perspective these kinds of practices are a violation of the controls. The SAP GRC Process Control application is based on automatically detecting such practices and performing a number of other controls to ensure that the processes are running smoothly as designed and that violations are prevented.

Some organizations rely on manual activities using nonintegrated Word or Excel to document complex business processes and controls. Relying on manual activities to document complex, ever-changing business processes and controls is not effective and is likely to result in errors. Identifying the risks and process weaknesses, reusing the controls, and even updating the documents becomes a challenge if you use a manual tracking solution for documenting your business processes and controls. With SAP GRC Process Controls, you can automate the monitoring, testing, assessment, remediation, and certification of enterprise-wide business processes and overcome these challenges.

Let's take a closer look at how SAP GRC Process Control works. The application process has four steps: *document*, *test*, *monitor*, and *certify*. Figure 14.5 shows the SAP GRC Process Control steps.

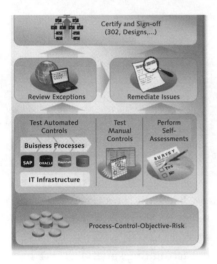

Figure 14.5 SAP GRC Process Control (Source: SAP AG)

Document

The first step of process control is to document processes, associated controls, and risks. In one of our projects, process documentation was managed in a shared network folder, causing version and update problems that were causing critical weaknesses. On another occasion, a process documentation project was completed, and the key person knowing all the process control interrelations moved to another position, so finding the right version of the process documents became a challenging activity. The SAP GRC Process Control application solves these kinds of challenges and allows you to put all of your documentation in one place and manage the documentation process in an integrated way. The application is integrated with SAP GRC Repository, which creates a library of all process documentation and the associated risks and controls for the whole enterprise so that you can centralize enterprise control management. The repository supports version controls, so documents are updated using a check-out and check-in process with versioning control in place. The SAP GRC Repository is integrated with compliance frameworks (e.g., SOX, JSOX, HIPPA), providing integrated reporting functionality across all governance matters (see Figure 14.6).

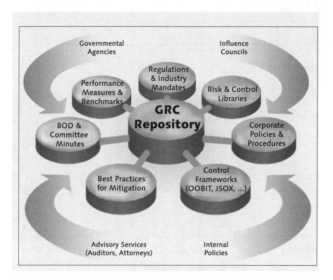

Figure 14.6 GRC Repository (Source: SAP AG)

Test

The testing of controls is the next step of the SAP GRC Process Control process. A control is a policy, directed by an organization's management that supports compliance objectives in efficient and effective processes, the reliability of financial reporting and disclosures, and the application of mandates and regulations. Using automated and manual controls enables preferred employee behavior and optimizes business processes, as well as ensuring that your organization meets compliance mandates on time.

There are two types of controls: automated and manual. *Automated controls* are defined by rules, which are a set of parameters that check the accuracy of a control. You define these rules based on your organization's policies and guidelines and assign them to a control. Rules provide the flexibility of setting up compliance processes under different business environments. The SAP GRC Process Control application provides predefined rules called *master controls and rules* that you can use, or you can configure your own rules and assign them to a control. Rules are defined using the rule designer tool (see Figure 14.7).

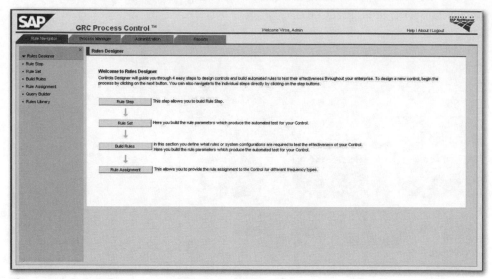

Figure 14.7 SAP GRC Process Control Rule Designer

With the delivered and customized rules, SAP GRC Process Control prevents risks by closely monitoring key areas in subledgers, G/L, and financial consolidation, enabling you to reduce manual controls and ensure the accuracy of financial results. Currently, there are approximately 90 delivered master controls for procure to pay, reconcile to pay, and IT basis process areas. An example of an automated control in the procure-to-pay process is the prevention of a duplicate invoice check or determining lost vendor cash discounts.

Upon automated control set up, test frequency, source, category, and type are defined (e.g., for the duplicate invoice check), and controls are tested automatically.

Manual controls are defined by test scripts. The SAP GRC Process Control supports manual control activities by using workflow-driven procedures. First, the manual tests and test plans are defined. Activities are assigned to test responsible users over workflow and through hierarchies. The tests and the documentation of test results are carried out manually.

The SAP GRC Process Control supports making surveys to check the effectiveness of controls in addition to automatic and manual control tests. This is achieved by *performing self-assessment*. The surveys are important because business processes change over time, and the compliance team has to evaluate that the controls are still valid and serving the purpose they were designed for. The surveys are designed in a flexible way and can be scheduled and directed to the employees. They also include reference information and instructions guides.

Monitor

Monitoring is the next step of the SAP GRC Process Control process. It consists of two parts: *review exceptions* and *remediate issues*. SAP GRC Process Control enables you to monitor and review exceptions and prevent them from turning into material weaknesses. You have visibility into all GRC activities using the monitoring functions provided. For example, you can use the heat map, which shows control exceptions and potential problems to allow fast and efficient action. To fix control exceptions, you can use the centralized remediation workbench, which allows you to create necessary business cases. A business case does not simply state the failure, but also acts as a repository of how this failure will be remedied. As a result, all remedial actions are tracked, documented, and measured. The results of all reports can be exported to PDF and spreadsheet output.

Certify and Sign-off

The certify and sign-off process is the last step of process control. SAP GRC Process Control formalizes the certification and sign-off process by providing a framework where a bottom-up hierarchical approach is adopted. For example, the account manager from the accounting department in one location signs off, and then the treasury manager from the same location signs off, which then rolls up to finance management, and so on. The sign-off process and hierarchy depends upon the organizational structure and type of your organization. Ultimately, the sign-off process rolls up to the CEO and CFO of the organization. This process step of SAP GRC Process Control supports SOX Section 302 certification. This is an online sign-off process, where the sign-off status is monitored through dashboards and reports to ensure that executives are kept informed of progress.

Now that we have explained SAP GRC technology foundation applications, let's look at SAP solutions for performance management.

14.2　Corporate Performance Management

The CPM solution provides an integrated and unified solution for managing performance management activities within the organization. It is composed of a set of applications that cover the full cycle of CPM activities, including defining strategy and managing execution; budgeting, planning, and consolidation; and modeling and optimizing profitability management. To provide a cutting-edge CPM solution, SAP has extended its performance management offerings with the applications developed by Pilot Software, Acorn, and OutlookSoft and provided new branded applications: SAP Strategy Management, SAP Business Planning and Consolidation (SAP BPC), and SAP Business Profitability Management application by Acorn (SAP BPM) (see Figure 14.8).

CPM provides a solution for linking strategic objectives with the organization's budgeting, planning, and reporting processes. The SAP solutions for performance management integrated with the SAP Business Suite family of business applications and SAP solutions for GRC enables a holistic financial management approach, which is increasingly important for CFOs. The SAP solutions for performance management will be integrated into the core SAP NetWeaver BI platform for both front-end and backend in the future.

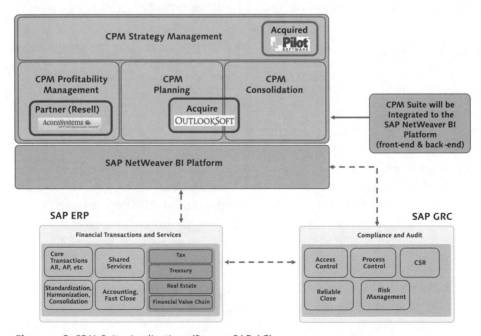

Figure 14.8 CPM Suite Applications (Source: SAP AG)

Let's take a closer look at each of the CPM applications.

14.2.1 SAP Strategy Management

SAP Strategy Management (formerly known as PilotWorks) was first released in the second quarter of 2007 after SAP's acquisition of Pilot Software in February 2007. SAP Strategy Management is now SAP's scorecard and strategy management application.

Organizations often do not have a consistent approach or tool to effectively communicate the strategies set by senior executives across the organization. This can result in a communication gap, leaving employees without fully understanding the organizational strategy and creating risk of insufficient priority and goal setting. The SAP Strategy Management application addresses this problem by providing a collaborative environment and process for strategic planning available at all levels of the organization. Strategic plans are easily connected to initiatives, targets, performance measures, and individual employees, enabling employees at all levels to set their priorities and goals and increase overall organization performance.

The starting point of the solution is to transform written plans into collaborative documents, where employee goals are defined, discussed, and updated. To make things easier, the collaborative documents contain rich contextual visualization that explains the key objectives of the organization. For example, employees can better understand the metrics used to measure their performance against organizational objectives. Managers are encouraged to collaborate with employees and motivate them while tracking, monitoring, and managing operational performance.

The SAP Strategy Management is fully integrated with the SAP BPM as well as the SAP BPC. Some of the capabilities provided with this integration are as follows:

- Performance scorecards are driven by actual and plan figures provided by planning and consolidations.
- Strategic initiative budgets are driven by planning and forecasting.
- Strategic objective performance scoring is based on profitability analysis.

Because a comprehensive, detailed analysis of SAP Strategy Management exceeds the scope of this book, we only provide an overview of this new solution. Note that the SAP SEM-BSC balance scorecard solution of SEM has been retired.

14.2.2 SAP Business Profitability Management

The SAP BPM application provides a solution that enables organizations to rapidly improve profitability by utilizing time-driven activity based costing (ABC). Time-driven ABC is simpler and less costly to implement than traditional ABC. It is based on the principle that *cost driver rates* can be based on the practical *capacity of the resources* supplied. Time-driven ABC needs only two calculation parameters to calculate activity driver rates: unit cost of supplying capacity and time required to perform an activity.

The application is based on business process modeling and calculations. It provides flexible analysis of costs and profitability by characteristics such as line of business, customer, product, branch, location, channel, segment, order, and transaction. In the SAP BPM, these dimensions are called *assets*. Another important term in the SAP BPM is *performance measures*. Performance measures are *revenue*, *direct and indirect cost*, *net operating profit (NOP)*, and *capacity*.

The business profitability results in SAP BPM are generated with these four performance measures. The indirect cost performance measure is itemized as activity costs. This itemization includes activity cost, units, and rate. The profit and loss statement can be generated at the corporate and at each asset level and its categories and is used to analyze cost drivers. An example of a Net Profit by Customer report in SAP BPM is shown in Figure 14.9.

Another important feature of SAP BPM is to create a relationship between assets, called *cost-to-serve*. The concept of cost-to-serve plays a critical role when margin analysis is inadequate for informed decision-making. For example, when the enterprise resells goods, it is important to get the end-to-end profitability across the entire lifecycle of each transaction and not only at the marginal level (i.e., selling price minus cost of goods). In SAP BPM, you can create a relationship among customer, order, vendor, and product. Customers place orders. Orders contain line items with products. Vendors supply products. This relationship allows reporting and analyzing of customer profit based not only on the products they purchase, but also on how they purchase the products, which reflects the cost-to-serve concept. With cost-to-serve profitability reporting, you can identify that a high-margin customer is not as profitable as reported on the marginal level, because higher cost activities are associated with the sales (i.e., special expedited daily deliveries).

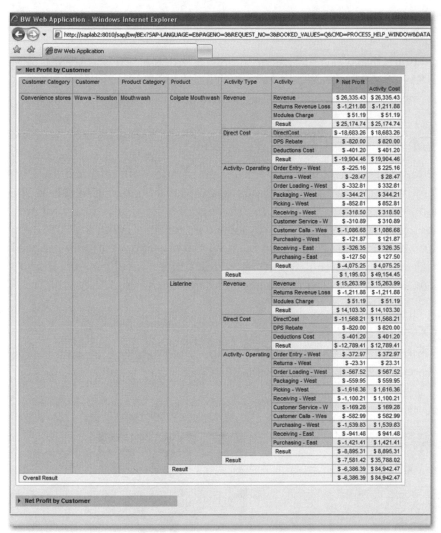

Figure 14.9 Net Profit by Customer (Source: SAP AG and Acorn)

The data can be extracted from SAP and non-SAP systems to SAP BPM for profitability analysis. The assets' characteristics are analyzed using the SAP BPM engine. The cost is assigned to the assets using Excel, such as formula cost equations that simulate the business process. Note that the characteristics are found in either the master data records or transactional data. The profitability information from SAP BPM can be used for costing analysis, determining staffing levels, and supply chain costing. It can be visually reported in SAP NetWeaver Enterprise Portal role-based dashboards. In addition, it can be integrated into the SAP Strategy Management and the SAP BPC.

The integration to NetWeaver BI will be improved with the next release, SAP BPM 7.0. With SAP BPM 8.0, the cost drivers can be leveraged in planning and the solution will support enhanced modeling and simulation.

14.2.3 SAP Business Planning and Consolidation

In June 2007, SAP AG acquired OutlookSoft Corporation and renamed the OutlookSoft software as SAP Business Planning and Consolidation (SAP BPC). The main reason for this acquisition was to deliver a more flexible and easy solution to carry out corporate planning and consolidation activities. With SAP BPC, you can perform bottom-up and top-down financial and operational planning, as well as financial consolidation and reporting, without heavy involvement of the IT department. It offers strong integration with Microsoft Office.

Financial Consolidation Reporting

With the introduction of SAP BPC, SAP now offers two solutions for consolidated financial reporting: SAP BPC and SAP SEM-BCS (see Figure 14.10).

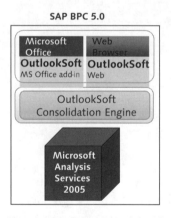
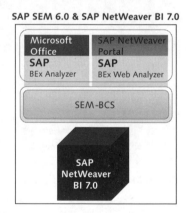

Figure 14.10 SAP's Consolidated Financial Reporting Offerings (Source: SAP AG)

That said, many SAP customers have already implemented SAP SEM-BCS or previous SAP products for consolidation reporting and want to understand how they can improve their consolidation financial reporting in line with SAP's strategic direction. Should they continue to use SAP SEM-BCS or plan to migrate to SAP BPC? What is SAP's future direction with these two solutions for consolidated financial reporting? In this section, we first concentrate on SAP BPC capabilities and then explain the new feature available for SAP SEM-BCS with enhancement packages, which can be optionally installed and activated, and compare these two solutions and explain the future direction of SAP financial consolidation reporting.

> **Note**
>
> Note that we cover SAP SEM-BCS, SAP's self-made consolidation solution and reporting, in Chapter 11.

SAP BPC Reporting Capabilities

With the SAP BPC application, you can meet all your legal and management consolidated reporting requirements. The main features of SAP BPC are outlined below:

▶ Legal and management consolidation functionalities such as currency conversion, intercompany unit elimination, journal entries, allocations, and so on.

▶ Compliance with international accounting standards such as IFRS and U.S. GAAP

▶ Compliance with the SOX

▶ Standard consolidated financial statements such as balance sheet statements, profit and loss statements, and cash flow statements

SAP BPC is based on Microsoft SQL server and Microsoft Analysis Services. Users can create their own reports via MS Excel and web browsers without heavy involvement of the IT department, in contrast to SAP SEM-BCS. Users can use all MS Excel functionalities for the formatting of reports. SAP BPC provides predelivered report templates and context-sensitive functionality and information in the context-sensitive action pane.

One of the important features of SAP BPC is to leverage business process flows (BPFs), which are structured processes that span multiple groups, deliverables, and activities. BPFs enable you to associate workflows within a process and increase control and consistency. The SAP BPC reports are part of BPFs; in other words, they are integrated in the process. BPFs guide users step by step to execute the process and monitor reports easily. This mechanism increases users' productivity.

SAP BPC provides packaged the BPFs Annual Budget, Capital Expenditures, Consolidations, Monthly Financial Reporting, and more. Figure 14.11 shows an example of a Monthly Financial Process: BPF to Do List. In this example, the reports such as currency impact, consolidating, adjustments, monthly package, and data audit are integrated with the consolidation review step. Once you complete the steps in the BPF, you can set the status as complete.

In addition, SAP BCS provides *insight dashboards* for monitoring and analyzing data. The solution provides *automated variance analysis*, which does not require any configuration. Automated variance analysis enables you to quickly find explanations for variances and make risk-adjusted plans based on a precise understanding of risk probabilities.

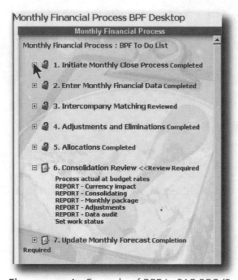

Figure 14.11 An Example of BPF in SAP BPC (Source: SAP AG)

In addition, based on the configured correlation methods such as linear and non-linear regression, the solution provides a capability to correlate any relationship of data with other data within the application, called *predictive analytics* functionality. It enables you to produce more accurate plans and budgets and incorporate real-time actual data with historical data for effective forecasting.

Another important feature of SAP BPC is its integration with Microsoft Office tools. SAP BPC supports Microsoft Word and PowerPoint in addition to Excel. For example, you can publish your report in Microsoft Word and PowerPoint.

SAP BPC offers many reporting publishing capabilities. For example, you can distribute reports with email, HTML, PDF, and hard copy. In addition, dimension hierarchy (customer, product, etc.)–based delivery is possible.

With the next release, which is SAP BPC 7.0, the solution will be integrated with SAP GRC Process Control application. Additional BPFs will also be introduced.

Now that we have covered SAP BPC, let's look at the other consolidated reporting tool, SAP SEM-BCS. Note that we cover SAP SEM-BCS in detail in Chapter 11. Here we only examine the new functionalities and capabilities, which can be optionally installed and activated with enhancement package 2.

SAP SEM-BCS Capabilities Available with Enhancement Packages

As mentioned in Chapter 11, SAP SEM-BCS 6.0 is strongly integrated with SAP ERP and SAP NetWeaver BI. The solution reporting capabilities are based on the reporting tools in the SAP BEx suite. Thus, the report development requires IT and business intelligence involvement.

Two new functionalities are delivered in the area of the consolidated financial reporting of SAP SEM-BCS with enhancement package 2:

▶ Restatement of financial results
▶ Status and control information

Restatement of Financial Results
In today's regulated environment, there might be a requirement of the *restatement* of data because of a new law, a change in accounting standards, or a new requirement of management reporting in an organization. With the restatement functionality, it is possible to adjust the posted data without changing the original data records. For example, your organization may need to regroup the financial statement items or reorganize the consolidation unit hierarchy. With the restatement functionality, you can define a data slice that corresponds to the delta between actual and restated data. You can collect the data either manually or automatically to data slice and carry out validations, currency translation, and balance carry forward and customer-defined tasks.

In SAP NetWeaver BI reports, you can select the **reporting mode** as **restatement** on the selection screen and analyze **historical value**, **impact of restatement**, and **final result of restatement** for consolidated financial statement reports.

Status and Control Information

Status and control information functionality enables you to define SAP NetWeaver BI queries to report on the status of the consolidation monitor. In other words, you can use the status information of the consolidation monitor in SAP NetWeaver BI queries. Status analysis is also available in SAP BEx Analyzer, web applications, and in SAP xApp Analytics composite applications. Doing so, you can analyze the percentages of tasks blocked, initial state, and so on. You can also display the status information in tabular or graphical form.

Comparison of SAP BPC and SAP SEM-BCS

The main differences between SAP BPC 5.0 and SAP SEM-BCS 6.0 are illustrated in Table 14.2.

SAP BPC 5.0	SAP SEM-BCS 6.0
Less involvement of IT department	Heavy involvement of IT department, particularly in the configuration and reporting
Less technical and more user friendly	More technical and complex than SAP BPC 5.0
Planning and consolidation applications are fully integrated	Integration with SAP NetWeaver BI Integrated Planning requires additional effort and configuration
Consolidation is managed via BPFs, in which consolidated financial reports are integrated	Consolidation is executed via a consolidation monitor, which does not contain consolidation financial reports
Not integrated with SAP NetWeaver BI; integration with SAP NetWeaver BI will be available with the SAP BPC 7.0 release	Fully integrated with SAP NetWeaver BI, SAP ERP, and SAP Solution Manager
No support for calculation of unrealized profit in inventory and assets	Supports calculation and postings of unrealized profit in inventory and assets, as well as calculation and postings of profit in assets and fair value adjustments in accordance with international accounting standards. It also supports the calculation and postings of fair value adjustments
Full audit trail detail without automatically created reports	Detailed audit logs and creation of journal entries for automated postings

Table 14.2 Comparison of SAP BPC 5.0 and SAP SEM-BCS 6.0

> **Note**
>
> Note that both solutions support accounting for long-term investments in accordance with the purchase, equity, and proportionate methods of consolidation.

Up until now we have explained the main features of SAP BPC, the new functionalities you can install and activate to improve consolidated financial reporting with SAP SEM-BCS, and the main differences between SAP BPC 5.0 and SAP SEM-BCS 6.0. Perhaps the most important question is Which one is preferable? Both solutions offer advanced consolidated reporting features. SAP will combine these two solutions for robust financial consolidation reporting as part of their corporate performance management strategy. The next release, which is SAP BPC 7.0, will be integrated with SAP NetWeaver BI. After that, SAP will merge these two solutions based on SAP NetWeaver BI. SAP BPC 8.0 will offer Duet workflow integration. Refer to Figure 14.12 for SAP's consolidated financial reporting roadmap. SAP will protect the investment made by its customers choosing either solution so that you don't need to reinvest in the product.

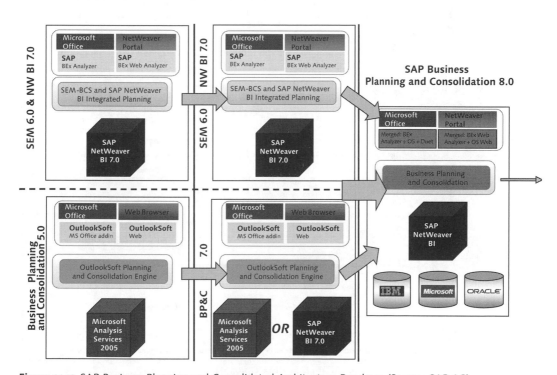

Figure 14.12 SAP Business Planning and Consolidated Architecture Roadmap (Source: SAP AG)

What about planning? SAP recommends using SAP BPC to all customers who have not implemented SAP planning solutions. As we mentioned earlier, SAP BPC 7.0 will integrate with SAP NetWeaver BI. SAP BPC 8.0 will further integrate with the SAP NetWeaver BI Integrated Planning (IP) engine. Note that SAP SEM-BPS in SAP NetWeaver is in maintenance mode, and SAP NetWeaver BI Integrated Planning is the future planning engine.

14.2.4 Evolution of SEM Solutions to CPM Solutions

With the CPM suite, SAP offers a next-generation corporate performance management solution. The evolution of SEM solutions to CPM solutions is illustrated in Figure 14.13. As illustrated in the figure, the SAP SEM-BSC solution is retired. All customers are encouraged to move to SAP Strategy Management. This move is facilitated by the migration utility. SAP recommends that all customers who have not implemented any SAP planning solutions use SAP BPC for planning, which will leverage the SAP NetWeaver BI IP planning engine. The next-generation consolidation solution will be SAP BPC. Going forward, all new customers are encouraged to use SAP BPC.

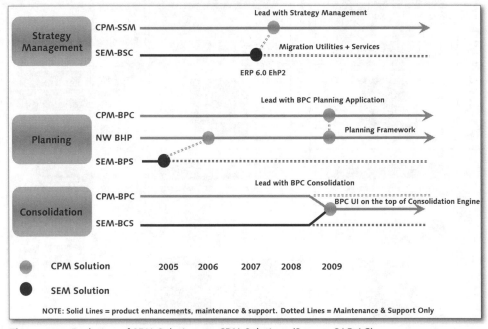

Figure 14.13 Evolution of SEM Solutions to CPM Solutions (Source: SAP AG)

Business objects and SAP

In October 2007, SAP AG announced its planned acquisition of Business Objects, which is an established business intelligence and CPM software vendor. SAP announced that Business Objects will operate independently within the SAP Group. As a result of this friendly takeover, SAP and Business Objects will offer the industry's most comprehensive portfolio of business performance and optimization solutions for companies of all sizes. Customers that use or plan to purchase business objects will have their investment protected and will continue to benefit from the continuous improvement of the product.

SAP AG has announced that both companies together intend to offer high-value solutions for process- and business-oriented professionals. The solutions will be designed to enable companies to strengthen decision processes, increase customer value, and create sustainable competitive advantage through real-time operational business intelligence.

14.3 Information Worker Applications

Information workers are an organization's employees whose main objective is to use information for problem solving and making wiser business decisions. They perform cognitive, creative, and non-repetitive tasks. For example, employees such as managers, planners, sales people, and controllers can be classified as information workers. According to a study by the McKinsey Global Institute, a typical information worker spends:

► 40% of the day searching for relevant information

► 40% of the day coordinating resources

► Only 20% of the day on value-added activities

Using information workers' time effectively and increasing their productivity and accomplishments is a critical success factor for the organization. Searching for information and coordinating resource tasks have to be made more efficient so that information workers can spend more time on value-added activities. Therefore, solutions that give information workers easy access to the information they need when they need it and facilitate team collaboration processes are absolutely paramount for leading organizations today. Information workers need a solution that has the following goals:

► Combine information with the relevant business processes and provide decision-making guidance

▶ Establish a firm data foundation to ensure integrated, consistent, timely information and metrics

▶ Provide instant access to collaboration tools when executing the process, enabling communication to make timely, informed decisions

▶ Apply new business insights to business processes on an ongoing basis to improve efficiency, lower risk, and improve business performance

SAP offers advanced solutions for information workers, helping them achieve all of these goals. Solutions empower people by delivering personalized business context through familiar user environments; including Microsoft Office, mobile devices, and the Web (see Figure 14.14). The information worker applications are built on enterprise service-oriented architecture.

Figure 14.14 Information Worker Applications (Source: SAP AG)

14.3.1 Enterprise Service-Oriented Architecture

Service-oriented architecture enables the existing functionality of enterprise applications to be presented as *services*. By using these services as building blocks, companies can build new applications to extend the scope and functions of their business processes. Services are not necessarily generated from one technical domain and can be rendered from various systems. Therefore, the new applications are built without dependencies upon underlying technical domains. However, while service-oriented architecture has many advantages, it also has some drawbacks—manual build effort, low reusability, and lack of governance—that were eradicated with the introduction of *enterprise service-oriented architecture (enterprise SOA)*. Figure 14.15 illustrates the evolution from service-oriented architecture to enterprise service-oriented architecture. Enterprise SOA provides the capability to add business semantics (i.e., standards, compliance, interfaces, documents for data exchange) to Web services. This capability is based on the *Enterprise Services Repository (ES Repository)*, where predelivered Web services, business semantics, tools, and frameworks are stored and can be used to build composite applications.

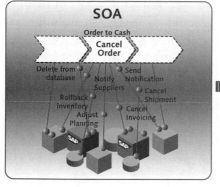

Figure 14.15 From Service-Oriented Architecture to
Enterprise Service-Oriented Architecture (Source: SAP AG)

Enterprise services are the main part of enterprise SOA. An enterprise service consists of Web services combined with business logic. A *Web service* is a mechanism encapsulating the functionality of an application and exposing that functionality through a platform-independent interface. Enterprise services are similar to Web services, but they are structured and fully harmonized across SAP solutions. They provide simplification and flexibility.

SAP delivers enterprise SOA capabilities on the SAP NetWeaver 7.0 platform. Enterprise SOA simply enables the convergence of applications and infrastructures. Composite applications such as SAP xApp Analytics, SAP Interactive Forms, and Duet use the enterprise SOA to integrate with underlying applications and infrastructure. Let's take a closer look at these composite applications. We first examine SAP xApp Analytics, which are composite applications that access all needed data and functions using enterprise services.

14.3.2   SAP xApp Analytics

By analytics we mean the extensive use of data, statistical and quantity analysis, explanatory and predictive models, and fact-based management to drive decisions and actions.[2]

This quotation succinctly describes the meaning of analytics. In most companies, information workers spend a high percentage of their time either searching for

---

[2]*Competing on Analytics*, Harvard Business School Press.

relevant information or coordinating resources. The objective of directing information workers to value-added activities can be achieved with solutions that effectively combine business processes and analytics and encourage collaboration. SAP xApp Analytics are information worker applications that can be deployed to achieve this objective.

SAP xApp Analytics are composite applications that can access information and functions by using enterprise services. They are built on the SAP NetWeaver platform and leverage the functionalities of existing enterprise application components. The power of SAP xApp Analytics lies in their ability to seamlessly integrate analysis, transactions, and collaborative steps in the overall network. SAP xApp Analytics are intuitive applications and provide information workers with up-to-date, accurate, and relevant information at the right time so they can make informed decisions. SAP xApp Analytics also provide a collaborative environment within the network. If a decision requires additional input, the user can communicate with all the relevant process participants, stakeholders, and strategic decision makers. By applying analytics down to the process level with SAP xApp Analytics, organizations enable all individuals within the enterprise to spend their time on value creation.

SAP has built in prepackaged best-business practices into SAP xApp Analytics to help maximize value and increase usability. SAP xApp Analytics support both industry and cross-industry functions and can be enhanced or modified to fit your organization. You can also create your own SAP xApp Analytics. Let's examine the functionalities of SAP xApp Analytics with a content example.

SAP xApp Analytics Investment Approval Example

SAP xApp Analytics Investment Approval is a typical SAP xApp Analytics that combines the investment approval process and investments analytics into a single screen. It provides users with quick access to the details of appropriation requests, financial analysis, and program position values as well as overall values distribution. With the benefits of getting all the necessary information, the user can easily make a decision about investment approval. In other words, the user does not have to swap between different systems to get additional information or spend time searching for the required information to make the analysis for an investment approval decision.

In addition, SAP xApps Analytics can integrate with the backend system at the transactional level. Once the user takes action (approve, reject, or send back) in

SAP xApp Analytics Investment Approval the actions are updated in the backend system simultaneously. Let's take a closer look at this example step by step so you can understand how to leverage SAP xApp Analytics to apply analytics down to the process level in your organization. The SAP xApp Analytics Investment Approval composite application screen consists of four frames:

▶ Work list of the Appropriation Request

▶ Details to Appropriation Request

▶ Yearly Values Distribution

▶ Overall Values Distribution

Work List of Appropriation Request

The first frame of the SAP xApp Analytics Investment Approval is the work list that shows the **Appropriation Requests** to be approved. An example of a work list is illustrated at the top of Figure 14.16.

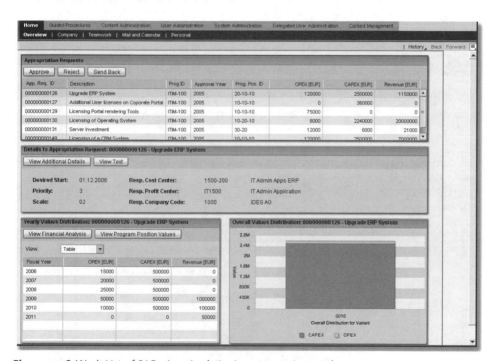

Figure 14.16 Work List of SAP xApp Analytics Investment Approval

As shown in the figure, the work list displays the appropriation request ID, description of the appropriation request, program ID, approval year, program position ID, OPEX, CAPEX, and revenue amounts. Note that the work list can be personalized so that only the information relevant for the user is shown in the work list. Above the work list are three action buttons (**Approve**, **Reject**, and **Send Back**) that we explain later.

Detailed Information on Appropriation Request

The frame below the work list provides detailed information on the selected appropriation request. In our example, we selected the appropriation request **149 Licensing of a CRM System**. Once you select the appropriation request, the detailed information sections are updated according to the selected appropriation request (see Figure 14.17). The **Details to Appropriation Request** section shows the basic information on the master data of the selected appropriation request. For example, you can see the Desired start, Resp. Cost Center, Resp. Profit Center, Priority, and so on. The **View Additional Details** and **View Text** buttons allow you to check further information.

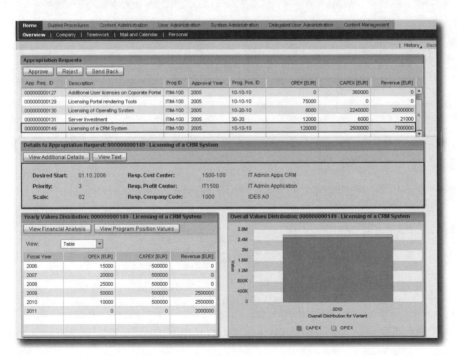

Figure 14.17 Select the Appropriation Request

If you click on the **View Additional Details** button, a dialog box appears in the screen showing you the additional information, such as the values of the *user fields* where you can keep appropriation request details. Figure 14.18 shows an example of the **Additional Information** dialog box.

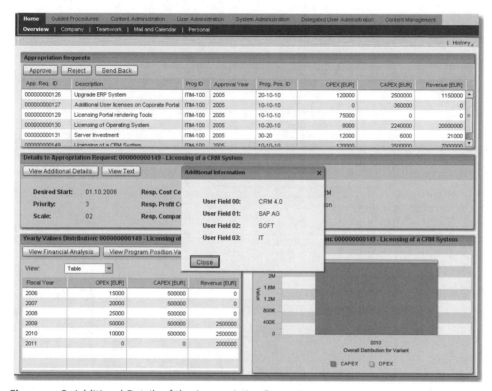

Figure 14.18 Additional Details of the Appropriation Request

If you close this box and select the **View Text** button, another dialog box appears displaying the text entered in the appropriation request master data (see Figure 14.19). Here you can see textual details that describe the context of the investment, such as the purpose of the investment and the expected benefits.

Yearly Distribution Values of Appropriation Request

The frames at the bottom of the SAP xApp Analytics Investment Approval provide financial information on the investment. On the left side of Figure 14.18 you can see the Yearly Values Distribution frame, which shows the plan values of the appropriation request by years. You can display the values either as a chart or table. In the previous figures, the values are displayed in table format. Selecting the **Chart** option from the **View** dropdown box displays the figures as a chart (see Figure 14.20).

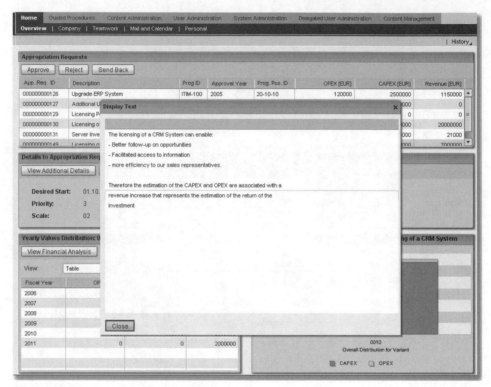

Figure 14.19 Display Text of Appropriation Request

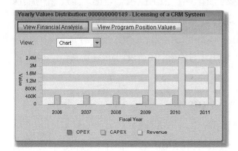

Figure 14.20 Financial Analysis as Chart

Clicking on the **View Financial Analysis** button opens a dialog box showing the results of the back-end calculation. Figure 14.21 illustrates an example of a **Financial Analysis** dialog box, which shows the discount cash flow rate, internal return rate, net present value, payback period, and value date of the investment.

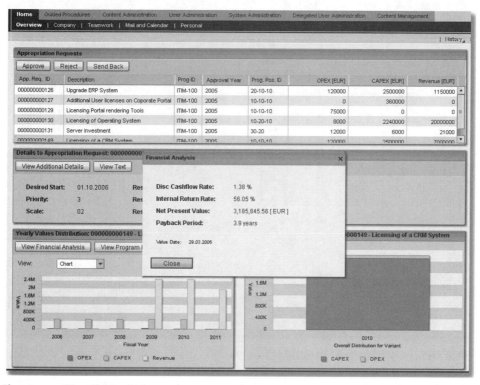

Figure 14.21 Financial Analysis

If you close this box and click on the **View Program Position Values** button, you can carry out a detailed analysis of the program position to which the appropriation request belongs. Here you can analyze the plan values of the program position, the values of all appropriation requests, and the values of approved appropriation requests by fiscal year. In our example, the appropriation request licensing of the CRM system is assigned to program position 10-10-10 and program ITIM-100.

Figure 14.22 shows the detailed plan values for program position 10-10-10 by fiscal year in version IM1.

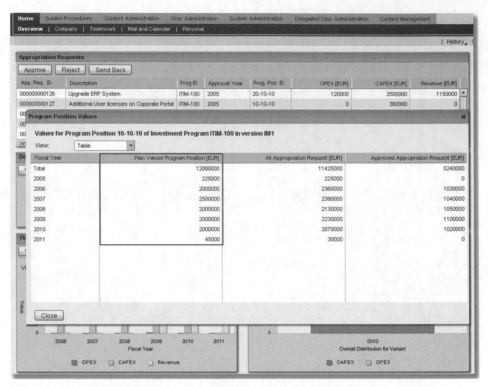

Figure 14.22 Program Position Values in Table View

Like financial analysis, you can switch from table view to chart view by selecting the **Chart** option from the **View** dropdown box. Figure 14.23 shows the program position values as a chart. With the visual charts and graphics, you can easily analyze the values of the program position values.

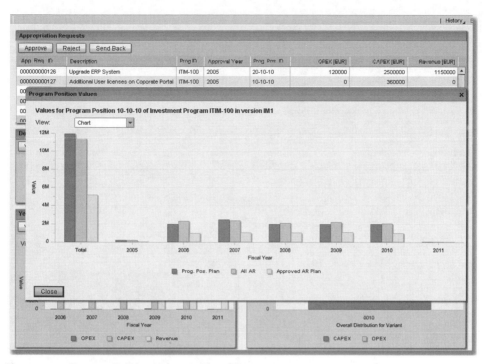

Figure 14.23 Program Position Values in Chart View

Overall Values Distribution

The last frame of the SAP xApp Analytics Investment Approval is the **Overall Values Distribution**, where you can analyze the distribution of CAPEX (capital expenditures) and OPEX (operating expenditure). You can compare the overall values with the yearly values on the same screen. Figure 14.24 illustrates the **Overall Values Distribution**.

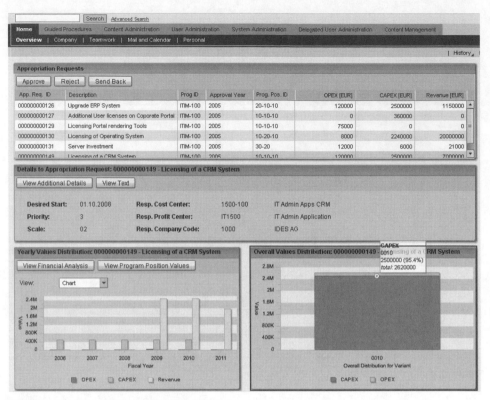

Figure 14.24 Overall Values Distribution

Make a Decision on the Approval

Now that you have completed the analysis of your appropriation request, you can make a decision and take action. As per the business process design, the possible actions are available as transactional elements enabling the user to complete the process. Rather than stepping outside the process to access the backend system, you can select the relevant transactional element for your decision in the SAP xApp Analytics composite applications. In our example, the transactional elements are represented by the **Approve**, **Reject**, and **Send Back** buttons at the top of the screen. By clicking the relevant button, you can approve the investment, reject it, or send it back to request more information or refine the scenario. After selecting the transactional element corresponding to your decision, a dialog box called

Action Confirmation appears, prompting you to confirm your action. In our example, we approved the request. The message **Are you sure you want to approve the appropriation request 000000000149?** appears on the action confirmation dialog box (see Figure 14.25).

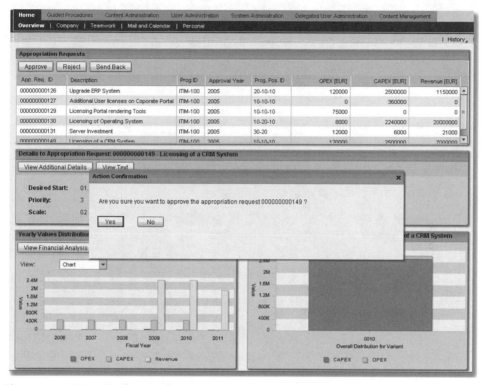

Figure 14.25 Action Confirmation

By selecting **Yes** you can approve your action. After that, a message appears either confirming that the action has been processed in the backend system or displaying any problems that could have occurred in the backend. In our example, we approved the appropriation request in the backend system successfully. The work list is then actualized, and the approved appropriation request disappeared from the work list, as shown in Figure 14.26.

As you see in this example, SAP xApp Analytics enable you to take analytics down to processes and provide the right information to information workers at the right time.

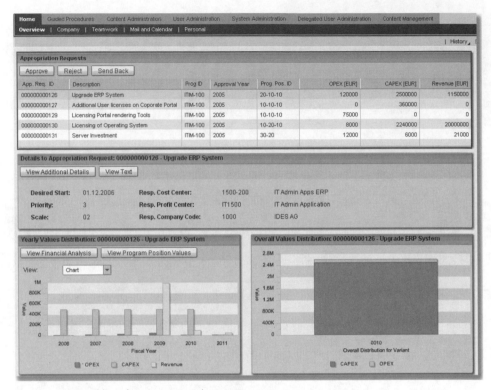

Figure 14.26 Worklist after Approving the Investment

Business Benefits of SAP xApp Analytics

The main benefits of SAP xApp Analytics are as follows:

▶ With SAP xApp Analytics you can simplify and streamline the processes by reducing the manual steps and increasing collaboration.

▶ Users can make better-informed decisions and take actions aligned with the corporate strategy.

- SAP xApp Analytics offer visualization features, such as interactive charts, that help analyze information.

- With SAP xApp Analytics, users spend less time on non–value-added tasks, so enterprises can use human resources for more cognitive and value-added tasks.

- The predefined content of SAP xApp Analytics allows employees to leverage best-practice business analysis for their specific areas.

- With SAP xApp Analytics, your organization can react faster as the conditions change and react better in today's competitive environment.

SAP NetWeaver Visual Composer

SAP xApp Analytics are based on SAP NetWeaver Visual Composer, which is a web-based modeling tool. SAP NetWeaver Visual Composer is delivered as an integral part of the Enterprise Portal usage type in SAP NetWeaver 7.0 SP08 and higher. SAP NetWeaver Visual Composer provides a development environment where you can customize, build, and deploy composite applications without coding. As mentioned earlier, SAP provides pre-built analytics business packages, which enable you to easily customize and deploy the business model. The modifications such as changing application logic and visual layout require minimal technical background. SAP NetWeaver Visual Composer enables the seamless integration of SAP and non-SAP and integrates OLTP and OLAP data.

> **Organizational performance applications and SAP xApp Analytics**
>
> SAP xApp Analytics are an important part of developing dashboards for organizational performance applications and will continue to play an important role in the development of future dashboards for these applications.

Now that we have explained SAP xApp Analytics, let's have a look at Duet, which is another innovative information worker application. Duet offers reporting and process interaction for users working within Microsoft Office. With Duet, reports can be triggered from Microsoft Office and displayed within Microsoft Office.

14.3.3 Duet Reporting

The ability to produce reports integrated with Microsoft Office products has been demanded by users for a long time. Two industry leaders, SAP and Microsoft, collaborated and produced their first joint product, Duet, which offers SAP reporting and process interaction for users working within Microsoft Office. With Duet, Office users do not need to directly access SAP to generate reports and analytics or use functions such as purchase order approval and budget monitoring. Within Duet, the report format and the requested actions are presented in a form that is intuitive for the users to learn and use, improving overall productivity and enabling better decision-making. Other important benefits of Duet are reduced employee training costs and easy user adoption.

Let's consider a real-life case that shows the benefit of using Duet. When you request your manager to approve a new purchase order (PO) for an investment project, he needs to evaluate the budget, commitments, and actual report. For that purpose, he either has to execute the report or request the output. Depending on the reporting landscape, he needs to log-on to SAP ERP, SAP NetWeaver BI, or SAP NetWeaver Portal and find the relevant reports for budget approval, which may take time and effort. Sometimes he is too busy to find or execute the report, so your PO can be hanging in workflow without approval for days or weeks, or there is a risk that the PO will be approved without budget review. Duet overcomes this kind of daily challenge by enabling the reports to be available to decision-makers with the tools regularly employed during a normal business day, in this case Microsoft Outlook. With Duet, your manager has the budget report available with a PO approval request so that he can make the decision and action when he reads the PO approval email (see Figure 14.27).

Note
Note that alerting to Microsoft Outlook uses the same rules in Manager Self-Service, which we cover in Chapter 15.

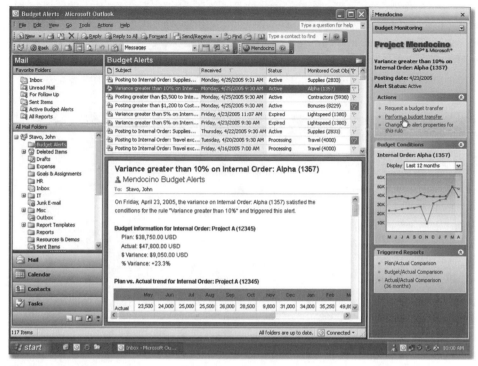

Figure 14.27 Budget Monitoring in Duet (Source: SAP AG and Microsoft Outlook)

Duet is a powerful tool because it makes critical decision-making reports available in Microsoft Office tools such as Microsoft Outlook, Microsoft Excel, and Microsoft Word. The extensive reporting and analytics capabilities of Duet enable you to access the latest information contained in SAP ERP and SAP NetWeaver BI and make it available within the Microsoft Office environment. By using Duet, all Microsoft users can benefit from SAP reports and processes without the need to log-on to SAP systems or get formal SAP training.

With Duet, you can schedule reports to be delivered at a specified time to your Microsoft Office Outlook or directly executed within Outlook. Reports are delivered as emails and contain report data and attached files. Information security is based on the security profile of Outlook users in the source system from which the reports are retrieved.

With Duet, you can use the reports offline and distribute the reports to other users. In addition, you can customize analytics and transactional reports as well as open the reports in Microsoft Excel for further analysis. Figure 14.28 shows an example of a report delivered with Duet into Microsoft Outlook. By clicking on the **Open in Excel** button, the report can be exported into Microsoft Excel. **The Send Report** button is used to distribute the report to other individuals. You can get additional information on the report by clicking on the **Report Details** button.

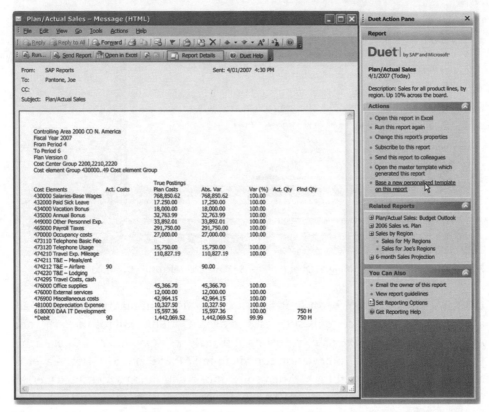

Figure 14.28 Duet Report Example Email in Microsoft Outlook (Source: SAP AG and Microsoft Outlook)

Duet Reporting Folder

With Duet, a folder called Duet Reporting is generated in addition to your other folders in Microsoft Outlook (see Figure 14.29, highlight 1). Let's take a closer look at the components of the Duet Reporting folder.

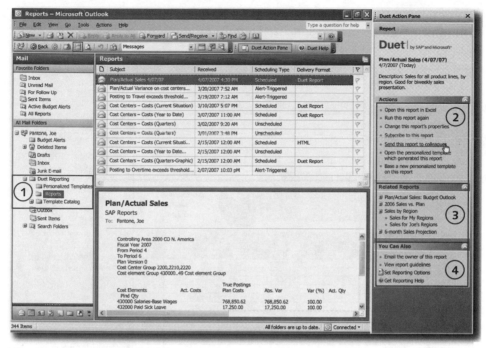

Figure 14.29 Duet Reporting with Microsoft Outlook (Source: SAP AG and Microsoft Outlook)

The Duet Reporting folder contains three subfolders:

▶ **Reports**
The reports folder contains all the reports you have run.

▶ **Template Catalog (and its subfolders)**
The template catalog folder is composed of subfolders that contain catalog report templates. Each subfolder corresponds to a specific report category that you are authorized to run. The standard catalog templates are read only and should not be changed or deleted. You can only save any change to the standard catalog template as a personalized report template under the personalized templates folder.

▶ **Personalized Templates Folder**
The personalized templates folder contains personalized report templates, which are created based on standard catalog report templates that are available under the subfolders of the template catalog folder. By using Microsoft Excel features, you can format and structure reports according to your preferences.

For example, you can format the cells and add formulas or charts. Figure 14.30 shows an example of a personalized template.

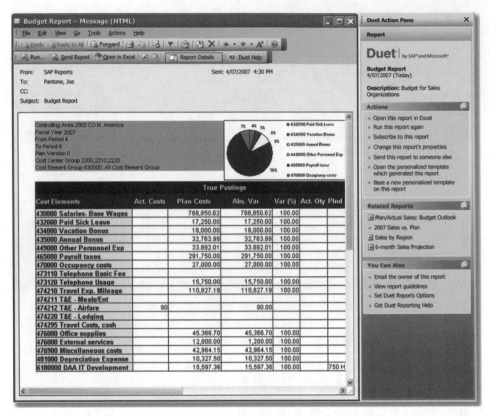

Figure 14.30 Personalized Template (Source: SAP AG and Microsoft Outlook)

Duet Action Pane

You can control the execution of reports with the functions of the Duet Action Pane. The Duet Action Pane opens automatically when you open personalized or catalog report templates or reports. Through the Duet Action Pane, you can take specific actions on the report. For example, you can open the report in Excel, send the report to colleagues, subscribe to the report, and change the report's properties (Figure 14.29, highlight 2). The Duet Action Pane also enables you to access related reports and other links (highlight 3). In addition, you can email the owner of the report, view the report guidelines, set reporting options, and get reporting help (highlight 4).

Executing a Report with Duet

Both transactional and analytical reports can be delivered automatically to the reports folder in Microsoft Outlook using Duet. You can either run reports on demand or schedule them to be delivered at a specified time. There are four steps to execute a report using Duet:

▶ Use the Microsoft Outlook Find feature to search a report that you want to run in the subfolders of the template catalog.

▶ Double-click on the catalog report template name to open it.

▶ Click on the **Run** button on the Duet toolbar or schedule it in the Duet Action Pane.

▶ Reports are delivered as emails to the reports folder in your Microsoft Office Outlook.

Duet security

Duet uses SAP's security roles and authorizations so that access to the reports is controlled through SAP user authorization. In other words, only authorized users can access reports in Duet. In addition, the forwarding options of Duet reports can be controlled. It is possible to control Duet report options: forwarding allowed, forward as a file, forward as a file and template, or forward as a template. The receiver of the report should have the required role and authorization to receive the report.

Duet Reporting Homepage

Duet provides a reporting overview with its reporting folder homepage, which is shown in Figure 14.31. On the reporting homepage you can, for example, see a calendar of your scheduled reports and the available reports for subscription and check recently executed reports. You can reach the Duet Reporting homepage by clicking on the Duet Reporting folder. The Duet Reporting homepage gives you an overview of your Duet reports and analytics. You can switch to monthly view and customize the reporting overview homepage.

Figure 14.31 Duet Reporting Homepage (Source: SAP AG and Microsoft Outlook)

System Requirements for Duet Reports and Analytics

Duet requires Windows Exchange Server 2003 and Microsoft Office 2003/2007. Reports can be delivered from SAP ERP 2004 or SAP ERP 6.0, as well as from SAP NetWeaver BI 3.5 or 7.0. The SAP R/3 reports can only be delivered to Duet via SAP NetWeaver BI. You cannot receive R/3 reports directly from Microsoft Outlook using Duet.

With every new version and value package, Duet supports more and more SAP scenarios, accessing and controlling SAP business processes and reports via the MS Office environment, with the security of the robust SAP controlled authorization. Microsoft and SAP collaborated and embedded analytical capabilities in Microsoft Office.

14.3.4 Adobe Products

Collaboration between SAP and Adobe created SAP Interactive Forms, enabling you to create online and offline interactive forms in Adobe Portable Document Format (PDF). Today millions of documents are created and circulated in Adobe's PDF format. The format itself is very powerful, and the PDF files look exactly like the original file. The collaboration started in 2002 with the initiative to develop solutions accelerating productivity and extending the reach of SAP solutions within an enterprise and beyond corporate firewalls. As a result, Adobe engagement technologies such as SAP Interactive Forms, applications developed with Adobe Flex and conferencing with Adobe Acrobat Connect add significant value to new and existing SAP implementations.

SAP Interactive Forms

Paper-based forms and hardcopy report or information printing are expensive and environmentally unfriendly. Other factors, such as the cost or energy of distributing forms and letters and associated labor and form processing costs, are encouraging organizations to move to more environmentally friendly and economic solutions. Governments, organizations, regulatory bodies, and various agencies are increasingly trying to reduce their costs and help the environment by adopting paperless technologies.

In December 2006, the SEC approved the Notice and Access rules, allowing companies to furnish proxy materials to shareholders using the Internet. The SEC has proposed that these rules become mandatory over the following two years and include shareholder reports and prospectuses. These new rules will significantly reduce printing and provide companies with a more cost-effective means to undertake their own proxy solicitations.

SAP Interactive Forms are a simple and intuitive interface solution, increasing the usability of data capture and data reporting. They can be used with a wide variety of SAP applications. PDF forms and documents are integrated into business processes to increase user productivity. Forms can be completed online or offline, accessing and updating data in SAP applications. SAP Interactive Forms are integrated and delivered as part of SAP NetWeaver. There are approximately 900 print forms (non-interactive) and 60 interactive forms delivered with SAP ERP. These forms can be used as templates when creating your own forms with SAP

NetWeaver Developer Studio. SAP delivers integrated development environments to customize forms.

Adobe Flex

SAP enterprise SOA's separation of presentation from business logic and objects eases the integration of Adobe Flex solutions. Adobe Flex provides organizations with application development tools that simplify the development of rich Internet applications (RIAs) and allow seamless integration with enterprise services.

With Adobe Flex, organizations can use the business processes and information from their SAP platforms to create RIAs. Adobe Flex applications enable information workers to make better decisions by using dynamic charts, visualizations, and information dashboards. In addition, analytics can be enriched with voice, animations, and video elements.

14.4   Summary

In this chapter we first examined SAP's solutions for GRC from a financial reporting perspective, with the focus on financial compliance, which is heavily based on SAP GRC Access Control and SAP GRC Process Control. After that we explained SAP solutions for performance management, which consists of SAP Strategy Management, SAP BPM, and SAP BPC applications. In the last section we covered three important information worker applications that can be deployed to increase the effectiveness of financial reporting, as well as to take down the analytics to processes. We first focused on SAP xApp Analytics, which are an important part of developing dashboards and provide the right information to users at the right time with powerful functionalities such as visual reporting and graphical user interface. After that we focused on Duet, which enables the analysis and reporting of financial and business data within Microsoft Office and which millions of people use throughout their working day. Finally, we examined the use of SAP Interactive Forms and Adobe Flex applications.

It is important to keep your reporting strategy and approach up to pace with SAP's future direction for financial reporting. In this chapter we walk through the future direction of SAP financial reporting and explain the enhancement package for SAP ERP with the focus on new functions and capabilities. We specifically focus on simplified financial reporting innovation and the new features for reporting.

15 Future Direction of SAP Financial Reporting

SAP ERP offers flexible enterprise reporting tools and provides reporting capabilities within each component. Reporting is available through standard reports or reporting tools including SAP List Viewer, Drilldown Reporting, Report Painter and Report Writer, SAP Query, and ABAP™. In addition, SAP NetWeaver BI Business Explorer (BEx) Suite provides flexible reporting and analysis tools for strategic analysis and decision-making support within a business. These tools include BEx Query Designer, BEx Analyzer, BEx Web Analyzer, BEx Web Application Designer, and BEx Report Designer.

Each reporting tool has its own functions and features, and you can create reports with different functionalities using these tools. Let's take an example of a financial statement report. In Chapter 2, we explained that SAP ERP provides two standard financial statements for balance sheets and income statements: new financial statement and classic financial statement. The new financial statement is a drilldown report, whereas the classic financial statement is an ABAP report; both have ALV reporting functions. In Chapter 12, we showed how to create financial statement reports using the Report Painter tool, which can be easily converted to a Report Writer report. We used the financial statement report example to show the capabilities of SAP NetWeaver BI BEx Suite reporting tools in Chapter 13. As you can see, many reporting tool options are available in SAP software. Which ones are right for your enterprise?

There is no simple and straightforward answer to this question. The reporting strategy depends on many factors such as the reporting architecture of your organization, existing applications, human factors, and the nature of the report. Thus, we cannot simply say that reporting tool A is better than reporting tool B. Each reporting tool offers diverse capabilities that you can utilize, and SAP will continue to support and improve each of them.

Although it is important to understand the capabilities of reporting tools, getting the right information to information workers at the right time and accurately, and integrating business processes with reporting is of utmost importance in today's fast-changing business environment. Deploying visual reporting, graphical user interfaces (UI), and dashboards and using intuitive visual interface capabilities is becoming more important each day. This is where the SAP xApp Analytics composite applications play an important role. With SAP xApp Analytics, users can understand the trends, analyze the financial situation, and make an informed decision.

SAP AG will constantly increase the features and capabilities of reporting and analytics. What is expected is that the capabilities and constant innovation in reporting and analytics will expand across every part of the enterprise in the future. In this chapter, we examine the new reporting features for financial reporting available with the enhancement package for SAP ERP.

Let's first look at SAP enhancement package for SAP ERP, which is different than the release strategy that we are familiar from the previous releases of SAP ERP.

15.1 SAP Enhancement Package for SAP ERP

As of SAP ERP 6.0, SAP introduced the enhancement package strategy called SAP Enhancement Package for SAP ERP. With this strategy, SAP will develop new functionalities by means of enhancement packages and release them for SAP ERP 6.0 on a regular basis. Each enhancement package is designed to improve a specific set of business scenarios and includes new functionalities as well as the functionalities introduced with prior enhancement package. Note that support packages will continue to be released separately, and you need to apply them separately.

The enhancement packages are optionally installed and activated in SAP ERP 6.0. With this strategy, SAP customers can select the relevant enhancement package based on their business needs and deploy the new functionalities faster and easier.

With the enhancement package for SAP ERP, SAP customers are able to choose and implement the particular capabilities of an enhancement package. Only the selected part of the enhancement package is installed and activated in your system. The functional clusters that you can choose to implement within the enhancement package are called *business functions*. Each SAP enhancement package includes several business functions. SAP ERP enables you to choose and install specific business functions within the enhancement package with the functionality called *switch framework*, which is available with SAP NetWeaver 7.0 (refer to note activation of business functions). There will be no user interface (UI) or process change until a business function is activated in the system. This strategy provides the following benefits:

▶ Costs are reduced by installing and activating only selected business functions.

▶ Testing is only required for the activated business functions. You can also simplify the testing with predelivered business function templates.

▶ Change of management activities and training is only needed for the activated business functions.

▶ No disruption of the running the business occurs.

Activation of business functions

Activation of business functions is performed with the use of activation switches. Activation of the required business function is executed via the first node in the customizing or by using Transaction SFW5. The available business functions are activated by selecting the corresponding switch. After activation of a business function, new SAP ERP menu entries, new fields on the application interfaces, and new customizing nodes automatically appear in the system.

The new functionalities in the enhancement packages are designed to improve the following areas:

▶ Simplification

▶ Functional capabilities

▶ Industry-specific capabilities

▶ Enterprise services

Next we take a closer look at each of these improvement areas and explain the new concepts introduced with the enhancement package for SAP ERP.

15.1.1 Simplification

The simplification category includes the new functionalities that are developed to streamline and simplify business processes, interfaces, as well as implementations. The simplification category is classified into three subcategories.

Simplification of Implementation

The functionalities and capabilities in this category are intended to simplify implementation. SAP offers special upgrade services to simplify upgrades. For example, SAP ERP Solution Browser enables customers to evaluate and assess the value of upgrades by comparing functionalities and capabilities between their target release and their current release.

UI Options for a Simplified User Experience

This category contains the functionalities and capabilities that are intended to increase users' productivity by simplifying their tasks. Our experience has shown that productivity is typically decreased if a user has to swap between different applications. One of the important offerings for UI options for a simplified user experience is *UI clients*, which provides a single point of entry for different applications. Let's look at some UI client examples:

▶ SAP NetWeaver Portal is a client for browser-based access to SAP applications. The SAP NetWeaver Portal infrastructure allows UI services for multisystem access to applications and transactions from backend systems, including SAP and non-SAP.

▶ SAP NetWeaver Business Client is an alternative client to SAP NetWeaver Portal that provides fast access to web applications. SAP NetWeaver Business Client is available with the enhancement package 2 for SAP ERP 6.0.

▶ Duet™ enables you to access business processes and the latest information contained in SAP ERP and SAP NetWeaver BI and makes it available within the Microsoft Office environment.

▶ SAP Interactive Forms software by Adobe offers form-based tasks to be carried out by customers and partners who are not directly involved in the business activities of the enterprise. These forms are available in the areas of Employee Self-Services, Manager Self-Services, SAP ERP Financials, SAP ERP Human and Capital management, and other SAP Business Suite applications.

Another offering for a simplified user experience is SAP NetWeaver Enterprise Search, a search engine that enables information workers to access all the information they need on time. SAP NetWeaver Visual Composer, used for SAP xApp Analytics composite applications, is another example of this category.

Process and UI Simplification

This category contains the functionalities and capabilities that support users in their business roles. *Roles* are used to manage the authorization of users for tasks and comply with the segregation of duties. Roles are also used in SAP NetWeaver Portal to manage users' access to applications and transactions.

SAP ERP introduced a new concept called *work center* for managing roles in SAP NetWeaver Portal. A role consists of work centers that gather together the activities for a specific task. Work centers provide role-based alerts, work lists, monitors, and so on, so that users can take the right action. Roles and work centers are delivered with *business packages* in SAP ERP. Note that business packages are available for SAP ERP Financials, SAP ERP Human and Capital management, and other SAP Business Suite applications.

Let's take an example of the business unit analyst role, which is available with the business package for Business Unit Analyst (mySAP ERP). The business unit analyst role includes mainly planning and reporting activities. With this role business unit analysts perform activities within a single point of access portal page. The business unit analyst role portal page combines information with the relevant business processes and provides integrated, consistent, timely information and metrics to users from a single point of entry. Figure 15.1 shows an example of portal page for business unit analyst role with the work centers **Work Overview**, Planning, and Master Data. Highlight 1 shows the view where the business unit analyst can navigate between the work centers. In our example Work Overview is selected. The Business unit analyst works on planning activities, such as planning preparation, development of planning guides; collects information from line managers; and performs plan data changes. In his **Worklist**, the business unit analyst receives configurable alerts for budget overruns, postings that exceed a given threshold, and critical postings (highlight 2). Selected alerts can be acknowledged or forwarded. The **Key Figure Monitor** view displays monitors that track aggregate key figures available for analysis (highlight 3). Here the business unit analyst can define views and personalize KPIs. He can access reports within a hierarchy that makes transparent the relationships between profit centers, cost centers, orders, and projects and makes it easy to navigate through many objects. Highlight 4 shows the **My Profit Centers—Actual/Plan/Variance—Balance Sheet Accounts** report displayed as a **Column Chart**. The portal page also enables the business unit analyst to instantly collaborate with colleagues (highlight 5). The availability status of peers is clearly visualized with colors. In addition, the business unit analyst can use service link to start **Related Services** such as rules on critical variances or critical postings (highlight 6).

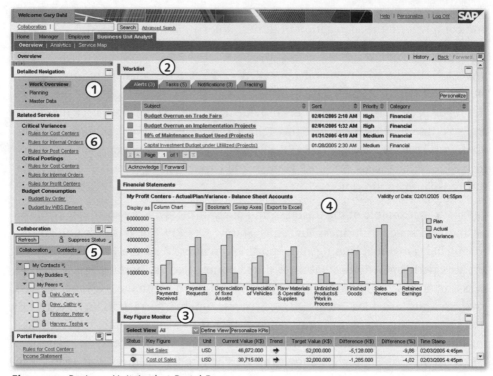

Figure 15.1 Business Unit Analyst Portal Page

SAP Solution Manager includes details of how to implement all roles. You can activate all the content for the business package including SAP NetWeaver BI content via the Solution Manager. See the folder **Roles for the SAP NetWeaver Portal** that includes the content for the Business Unit Analyst business package in Figure 15.2 and Figure 15.3.

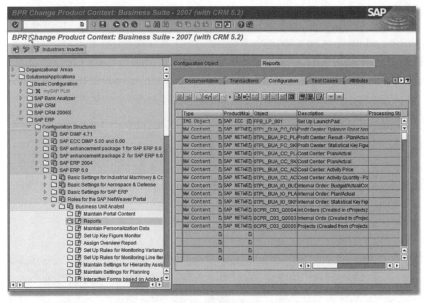

Figure 15.2 Maintain Portal Content for Business Unit Analyst

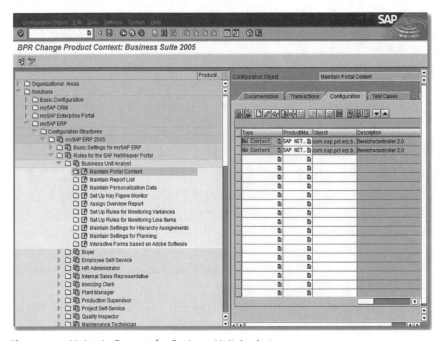

Figure 15.3 Maintain Reports for Business Unit Analyst

Automatic Roles

SAP ERP provides a set of standard roles called *automatic roles*, which includes all transactions and reports in SAP ERP. The SAP ERP 6.0 support pack 8 contains over 300 sample roles for SAP ERP, including many automatic roles for financials. Depending on business needs, customers can modify or enhance the automatic roles and evolve automatic roles into work centers.

One of the main objectives of automatic roles is to enable all ERP applications available in SAP NetWeaver Portal. Figure 15.4 shows an example of an automatic role with a transaction upload. The folder **Information System** for Cost Center Accounting in SAP ERP has been uploaded to the portal with text and icons added. All that will happen if you click on the link is that you start a transaction for the report.

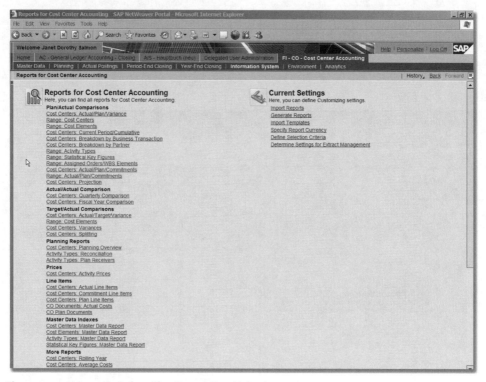

Figure 15.4 Automatic Role with a Transaction Upload

With the use of automatic roles, you can extend the transaction calls, in other words, automatic roles, with other reporting options. The automatic roles enable the complete SAP ERP content to be available in SAP NetWeaver Portal. Users can reach reports and transactions that they are authorized to view from a single point of entry called a reporting launchpad. You can include reporting launchpads in all roles to provide a consistent user experience across different sorts of reports. Figure 15.5 is an example of an analytics reporting launchpad in which you can include a link list allowing the user to start reports from SAP ERP, SAP NetWeaver BI, SAP xApp Analytics, or URLs.

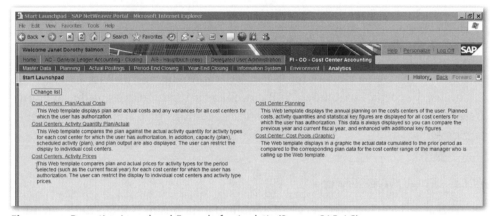

Figure 15.5 Reporting Launchpad Example for Analytic (Source: SAP AG)

Self-services is another example of a process and UI simplification category. Information workers can manage their information as well as use transactions and reports via self-services such as Employee Self-Service (ESS) and Manager Self-Service (MSS), which run in both SAP NetWeaver Portal and SAP NetWeaver Business Client.

> **Automatic roles**
>
> SAP ERP 6.0, SP08 includes over 300 sample roles for SAP ERP Core including many automatic roles for SAP ERP Financials. A complete list of the delivered roles is contained in SAP Note 1000291. You can use the new functions to upload your own roles from SAP ERP to portal content directory. With SAP ERP 6.0, you can also upload icons and descriptions.

15.1.2 Functional Capabilities

This category includes the new capabilities that are relevant for all industries in SAP ERP Financials, SAP ERP Human Capital Management (SAP ERP HCM), and other SAP Business Suite applications regardless of industry. For example, the enhancement package 3 for SAP ERP Financials includes new standard reports and a migration tool to transform traditional profit center reports to the new G/L. Note that we cover the new functional capabilities delivered with the enhancement package 2 for consolidated financials reporting in Chapter 14.

15.1.3 Industry-Specific Capabilities

This category includes new capabilities that are relevant to a particular industry. This is especially important for SAP customers that use industry-specific solutions such as SAP for Oil & Gas (SAP for O&G), SAP for Media, and SAP for Retail. With the industry-specific capabilities, SAP customers using industry-specific solutions are able to select new functionalities and capabilities that are relevant to their implementations.

15.1.4 Enterprise Services

Enterprise services are Web services combined with business logic and semantics that are used to support business processes. Enterprises services are the core element of Enterprise Service-Oriented Architecture (enterprise SOA), which enables convergence of applications and infrastructure. Enterprise services may range from very simple lookup Web services to more complex and composite services. Services such as customer credit check and vendor balance confirmation are examples of enterprise services. Enterprise services enable you to use SAP solutions together with composite applications provided by SAP customers or partners. The main benefits of enterprise services are to enable organizations to continuously improve business processes, create reusable application components, and use innovative composite applications. Enterprise services are used to integrate applications such as Duet and as basis for building SAP xApp Analytics. Note that we cover Duet and SAP xApp Analytics in Chapter 14.

Now that we have explained the enhancement package for SAP ERP, let's take a closer look at SAP's Simplified Financial Reporting innovation, which is first available with the enhancement package 3. Note that SAP will continue to develop financial reporting capabilities in future enhancement packages. Refer to Figure 15.6 for a schematic view of the enhancement packages for SAP ERP 6.0.

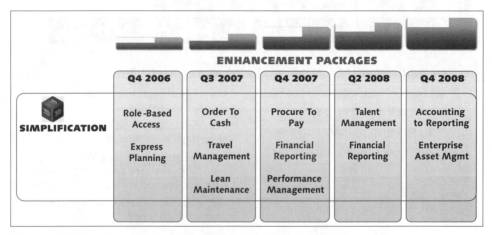

ENHANCEMENT PACKAGES

	Q4 2006	Q3 2007	Q4 2007	Q2 2008	Q4 2008
SIMPLIFICATION	Role-Based Access	Order To Cash	Procure To Pay	Talent Management	Accounting to Reporting
	Express Planning	Travel Management	Financial Reporting	Financial Reporting	Enterprise Asset Mgmt
		Lean Maintenance	Performance Management		

Figure 15.6 Enhancement Packages for SAP ERP 6.0 (Source: SAP AG)

15.2 Simplified Financial Reporting

SAP's simplified financial reporting innovation is to classify reports into five scenarios for simplification and increase the effectiveness of financial reporting. The scenarios are as follows:

▶ Simple list reporting

▶ Multidimensional and graphical analysis

▶ Formatted reporting

▶ KPI monitoring and scorecarding

▶ Analytical applications and composites

The financial reports are first categorized into three scenarios: simple list reporting, multidimensional and graphical analysis, and formatted reporting for both front-end and backend scalability. Refer to Figure 15.7 and Figure 15.8 for schematic views of reporting scenarios and tools, along with UI unification and front-end and back-end scalability.

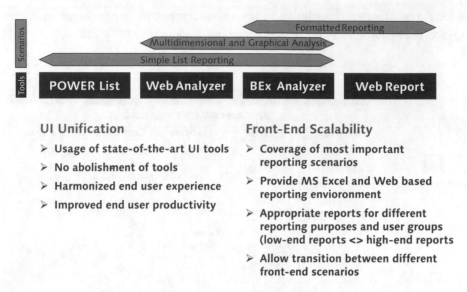

Figure 15.7 Simplified Reporting—UI Unification/Front-end Scalability (Source: SAP AG)

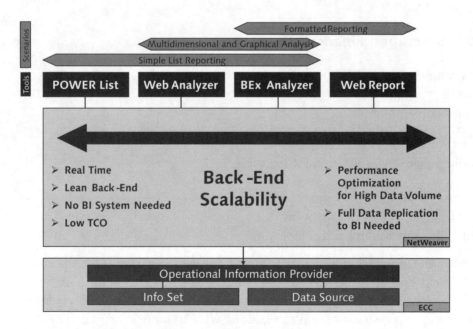

Figure 15.8 Simplified Reporting—Back-end Scalability (Source: SAP AG)

We now take a closer look at each reporting scenario and explain the reporting architecture for simplified reporting.

15.2.1 Simple List Reporting

The simple list reporting scenario contains reports that are executed and displayed as POWER Lists or SAP NetWeaver BI queries executed either with SAP BEx Web Analyzer or SAP BEx Analyzer reporting tools. Note that we covered SAP BEx Web Analyzer and SAP BEx Analyzer in Chapter 13. *Personal object work entity repository (POWER) list* is a new term introduced in SAP ERP 6.0. POWER lists structure the list of business objects and allow specific activities based on these objects. POWER lists use or leverage Web Dynpro SAP List Viewer technology. First POWER lists are available for these reports with the enhancement package 3 in SAP ERP 6.0. Figure 15.9 shows an example of a POWER list for a simple list reporting scenario.

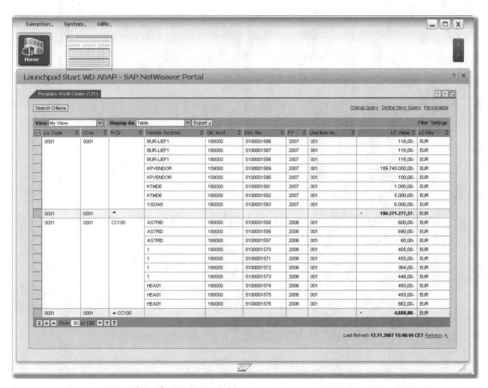

Figure 15.9 POWER List of Profit Center Payables

Note that POWER lists for operational reporting are built on operational data providers (either an InfoSet query or DataSource), and the operational POWER lists use a feeder class to extract data, for example, all sales orders or all customer master records, to allow you to perform actions on these objects. POWER lists use Web Dynpro ALV technology.

15.2.2 Multidimensional and Graphical Analysis

The multidimensional and graphical analysis scenario contains reports executed with SAP BEx Web Analyzer and SAP BEx Analyzer. Figure 15.10 shows an example of an SAP NetWeaver BI query executed from SAP NetWeaver Business Client.

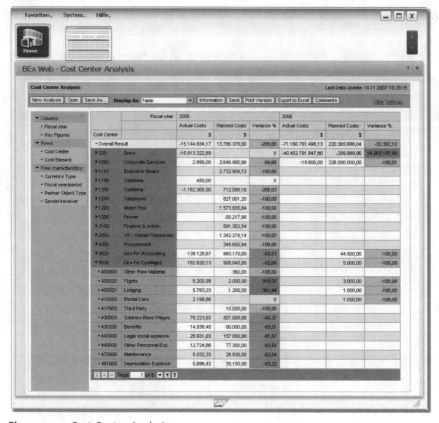

Figure 15.10 Cost Center Analysis

Multidimensional reports are mainly built with drilldown reporting in SAP ERP and built on InfoProviders in SAP NetWeaver BI. The multidimensional reports delivered with the enhancement package 3 enable SAP customers to use SAP NetWeaver

BI front-end either against replicated data in SAP NetWeaver BI or via direct access against data directly in the SAP ERP back-end (without SAP NetWeaver BI persistency of transactional data in SAP NetWeaver BI). The delivered SAP NetWeaver BI queries can be switched between these different data access options.

The architecture of simplified reporting and analysis is illustrated in Figure 15.11. With this new architecture, you can build your queries based on SAP NetWeaver BI InfoProviders and use Master Data and Meta Data in SAP NetWeaver BI or build your queries based on Operational Information Providers (InfoSets and Data-Sources) and get data directly from SAP ERP. Note, however, that the option to define an SAP NetWeaver BI query directly based on an Operational Information Provider is not available with the enhancement package 3. At the time we were writing this book, it had not been officially announced in which enhancement package the architecture will be available.

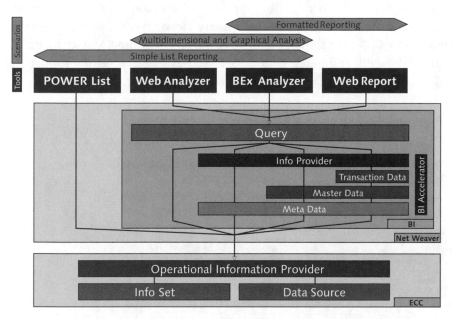

Figure 15.11 Simplified Reporting and Analysis—Architecture (Source: SAP AG)

More real-time reporting is the new trend, eliminating the constant reconciliation effort between SAP ERP and SAP NetWeaver BI, which wastes resources in dealing with the reconciliation of both systems, risking misstatement, and making the wrong decisions. This new architecture gives you the flexibility to report either from data replicated in SAP NetWeaver BI or real time from SAP ERP.

> **Master data with hierarchies**
>
> Although multidimensional SAP NetWeaver BI queries can directly access master data from the SAP ERP backend, hierarchies should be replicated in SAP NetWeaver BI for hierarchical reporting. For example, cost center master data can be accessed in a flat structure directly from SAP ERP, but you need to replicate the cost center hierarchy in SAP NetWeaver BI to display report output with a cost center hierarchy. Whether it will be possible to have hierarchies in SAP NetWeaver BI queries that are based directly on an InfoSet had not been announced when we were writing this book.

15.2.3 Formatted Reporting

Formatted reports, called officially SAP NetWeaver BI enterprise reports, contain reports designed with the SAP BEx Report Designer tool. As we pointed out in Chapter 13, formatted reporting, print-optimized reporting, is used to create business-specific layouts. The data binding for the SAP BEx Report Designer report is provided by data providers (queries and query views). With the enhancement package 3, SAP will deliver formatted financial statements from SAP ERP by using the SAP NetWeaver BI front-end. Figure 15.12 shows an example of a formatted financial statement report as a web report.

Figure 15.12 Formatted Reporting Example

What can you do to prepare your organization for this simplified reporting innovation? We advise you to categorize your existing reports into the scenarios discussed above: list reports, multidimensional reports, and formatted reports. Doing so will help you to decide at a high level which reporting environment is best suited to your business needs.

Report Access

As we mentioned earlier, SAP ERP provides new options for making reports available to users via SAP NetWeaver Portal and SAP NetWeaver Business Client. Figure 15.13 and Figure 15.14 provide reports by financial components in the reporting launchpad of SAP NetWeaver Business Client.

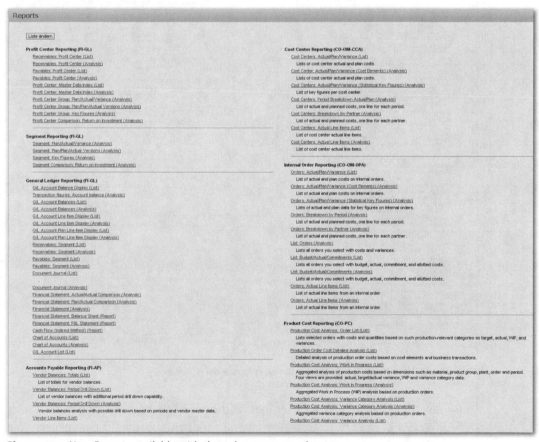

Figure 15.13 New Reports available with the enhancement package 3

Note that Figure 15.13 and Figure 15.14 show the *new financials reporting content* delivered with the enhancement package 3. The launchpad provides a look at what SAP delivered in that area. All the reports included in that launchpad follow the architecture and guidelines we explained when describing the new architecture for simplified financial reporting. These reports can use the new capabilities such as direct access enabled and switch to replicated data if applicable.

> **Note**
>
> SAP NetWeaver Business Client can render automatic roles and work centers.

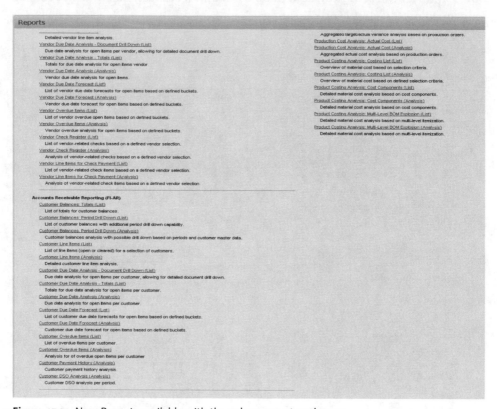

Figure 15.14 New Reports available with the enhancement package 3

In the next section we take a closer look at the MSS business package, which runs in SAP NetWeaver Portal and offers several reporting options for managers. We specifically examine how to customize reporting launchpad, authorization concept for reporting, and setting up personalization.

15.3 MSS Reporting

MSS is a self-employee tool that provides a single point of access to managers via the SAP NetWeaver Portal. You can include existing SAP ERP reports such as standard reports, Report Painter and Report Writer reports, transactions, and queries, as well as SAP NetWeaver BI reports such as queries, web templates, and SAP xApp Analytics in the MSS. Note that you can also embed SAP NetWeaver BI web templates as iViews in SAP NetWeaver Portal. With MSS, managers can easily access the information they need for decision-making in various areas such as cost management and budgeting. MSS provides a single point of entry for calling up reports by using a reporting launchpad, which contains a list of links allowing managers to call up reports from multiple systems, including SAP ERP, SAP NetWeaver BI, SAP xApp Analytics, and the Enterprise Portal. Figure 15.15 shows an example of a reporting launchpad for MSS.

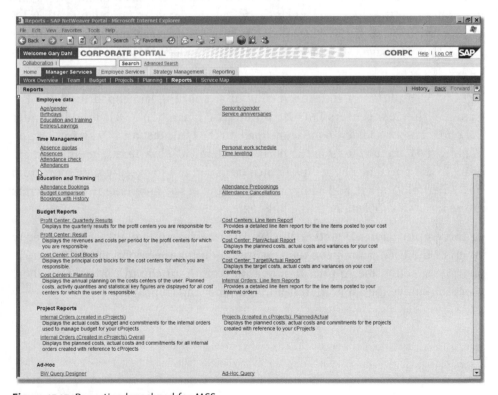

Figure 15.15 Reporting launchpad for MSS

MSS is delivered as a business package for SAP NetWeaver Portal in SAP ERP 6.0. This business package can only be used in combination with SAP ERP 6.0, which contains the implementation guide and all connectors for the MSS. Note that in addition to the MSS business package, you also need to download the SAP ERP Common Parts business package and to maintain the appropriate JCO connections for the Java version. Additional business packages exist for MSS in:

▶ mySAP ERP 2004—in combination with SAP ERP 5.0

▶ Enterprise Portal 5.0 and SAP NetWeaver Portal 6.0—in combination with SAP R/3 releases from 4.0B and SAP BW releases from 2.1C

15.3.1 Setting the Reporting launchpad for MSS

The content of the reporting launchpad is defined in the customizing. To define the content for the reporting launchpad, follow the configuration menu path **Integration with Other mySAP ERP Components • Business Packages/Functional Packages • Manager Self-Service (mySAP ERP) • Reporting • Setup Launchpad**.

Figure 15.16 illustrates the customizing of a reporting launchpad for MSS. For example, the **Cost Centers Line Item Report** (Transaction KSB1) is added under the budget reports folder in the launchpad. In the **Link Test and Descript.** section (highlight 1), the text used in the portal is entered as **Link Text**. The link text appears in the portal as a hyperlink, which users can use to execute the report from the hyperlink. You can add additional text in the description long text to describe the report as a supplement to the link text.

In the **Application—Deactivation by User** section (highlight 2), you specify whether the user can remove the application during the adoption of the launchpad. By selecting the **Applic. Removable from Launchpad** option, you allow users to remove the application from their reporting launchpad.

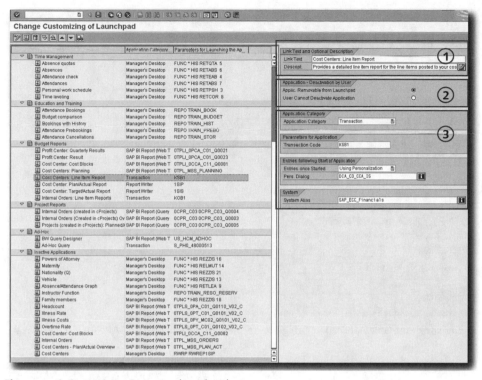

Figure 15.16 Customizing Reporting launchpad

The **Application Category** section (highlight 3) is used to specify the categories, parameters, and system information of the application. The reporting types are selected in the **Application Category** box. You can include the following report types in the reporting launchpad in WebDynpro (WD) Java Version (see Figure 15.17).

▸ SAP NetWeaver BI Report (Query)

▸ Report Writer

▸ Transaction

▸ URL

▸ SAP NetWeaver BI Report (Web Template)

▸ Manager's Desktop

> **Note**
>
> Note that the Manager's Desktop settings are only available in the WD Java version.

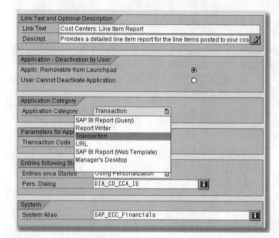

Figure 15.17 Available Application Categories for Reporting launchpad in SAP ERP 6.0 (WD Java)

> **WebDynpro**
>
> WebDynpro (WD) is the development and runtime environment for creating new user interfaces for business applications.

WD ABAP Version of SAP ERP 6.0

In the WD ABAP version of the launchpad of SAP ERP 6.0 support pack 8, you can include the following applications in addition to the applications outlined above:

▸ Portal Page (if launchpad is used in Enterprise Portal)

▸ WD Java Application

▸ WD ABAP Application

▸ KM Document (if launchpad is used in Enterprise Portal)

▸ SAP NetWeaver Visual Composer (if launchpad is used in Enterprise Portal)

▸ InfoSet Query

▸ Object Based Navigation (if launchpad used in Enterprise Portal)

Note that Manager's Desktop settings are only available in the WD Java version; they are not active in the WD ABAP version. Also note that you can create your own roles by using Transaction LPD_CUST as of SAP ERP support pack 8.

The WD ABAP version of SAP ERP support pack 13 also includes entries for SAP BEx Analyzer, SAP NetWeaver BI enterprise reports, and SAP NetWeaver BI 7.0 reports, including web templates and queries.

Conversion of reporting launchpad from SAP ERP 6.0 to SAP ERP 6.0.1

You can convert the reporting launchpad settings from WD Java (SAP ERP 6.0) to WD ABAP (SAP ERP 6.0.1) by using report APB_LPD_LPA_CUST_TO_LPD_CUST. The settings for MSS are role **MSS** and instance **REP**. You need to select these parameters when converting the reporting launchpad from SAP ERP 6.0 to SAP ERP 6.0.1. By selecting a user name in the selection screen of the conversion report, you can also transfer the personalized settings.

Depending on the reporting category that you choose, you identify the report in the **parameters for application** field, such as transaction, report group, the name of the InfoProvider, the name of query, and so on. For example, if you want to add a Report Painter or Report Writer report, you need to specify the report group in the **parameters for application** field. In our example, we specified Transaction KSB1 to add the Cost Centers Line Item report.

Entries following Start of Application (Figure 15.16, highlight 3) is used to control the way reports will start in the portal. There are three options, as illustrated in Figure 15.18:

▶ **In Initial Screen**
The application, for example, the report selection screen, appears without any default parameters. The user specifies the selection parameters of the report.

▶ **Using Personalization**
The application starts with the selection criteria that have been specified in the personalization dialog. For example, you can default the report selection parameters to specific cost centers.

▶ **By Variant**
The initial screen of the application, for example, the selection screen of the report, is predefined with the values identified in the variant.

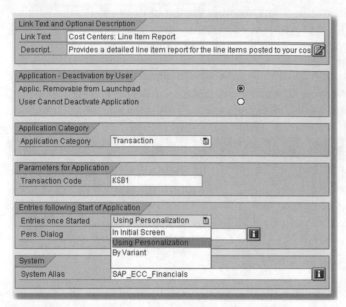

Figure 15.18 Entries Once Started of Applications for MSS

The last step of the reporting launchpad configuration is to determine the name of the system (system alias) for the back-end system in the SAP NetWeaver Portal in which the application is called. The system alias is specified in the **System** field (Figure 15.16, highlight 3).

Once you make all of these steps in the configuration, you can call up the reports from the reporting launchpad. The reports are accessed via the SAP NetWeaver Portal, and you can use features of the reporting tool with which the report is designed. For example, if you call up a Report Painter report, you can use all the features of the Report Painter tool. If you call up a drilldown report, you can use all drilldown reporting functionalities.

> **Active alert settings in MSS**
>
> You can also use MSS for active alerting, which is user defined for the monitoring of critical variances and postings. Active alert is very important for managers who normally do not have time to search a report, run a report, or analyze the results. For example, you can activate alerting to show all postings greater than a specified threshold value for cost centers. The rules for active alerts are set up in customizing. You can set active alerts for cost centers, internal orders, and profit centers. The active alerts are shown in the portal when you log on.

You can also maintain these launchpads using Transaction LPD_CUST. In this case, you need to know the application parameters set in the iView. For example, for MSS, role = MSS and instance = REP.

Now that we have covered how to set up a reporting launchpad, let's look at the financial reporting authorization in MSS.

15.3.2 Financial Reporting Authorization in MSS

One of the important aspects of MSS is to ensure that managers can only report on the financial information they are authorized to report on. This can be achieved with authorization and default personalization settings. To ensure consistent reporting, it is also important to transfer the appropriate authorizations to SAP NetWeaver BI. You can define the authorization for MSS by using the available data in the reporting objects. Let's say you want to set the authorization for cost center reporting in MSS. You want the cost center information to be displayed only by the cost center responsible. Let's first look at how to use the cost center data object when defining the authorization.

In SAP ERP 6.0, the **User Responsible** field is included for all CO objects. In this field, the user ID of the person responsible for the cost object is maintained. Figure 15.19 shows an example of cost center master data in SAP ERP 6.0. You can enter the user ID of the responsible manager of the cost center in this field and generate authorizations based on the cost center master data by using Report FPB_GENERATE_PROFILE_CCMD. Note that SAP ERP provides BAdIs to enhance this report so that you can include organization-specific changes in the automatic profile generation. You can also pull the cost center assignments from the organizational hierarchies in HR. You can use Report FPB_GENERATE_PROFILE_HRORG to generate authorizations based on your HR organizational structure. This program can also be enhanced with BAdIs.

For consistent reporting, it is important to extract authorizations from SAP ERP to SAP NetWeaver BI. You can find an overview of new developments in the area of controlling authorization extract to SAP NetWeaver BI in SAP Note 547533.

Roles that use the personalization dialogs, such as the business unit analyst and MSS, have a separate **Personalization** step in the configuration. This step assigns the personalization parameters (e.g., profit centers, cost centers, and so on) to the users based on the organizational hierarchy and cost center master data. The next section covers how to set up personalization.

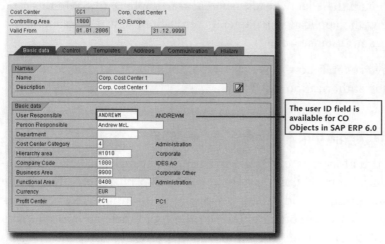

Figure 15.19 Cost Center Master Data

15.3.3 Setting Personalization

Personalization enables you to set defaults automatically for each user. To define personalization, follow the configuration menu path **Integration with Other mySAP ERP Components • Business Packages/Functional Packages • Manager Self-Service (mySAP ERP) • Personalization**.

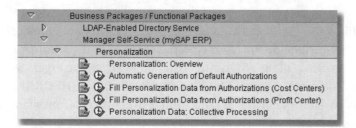

Figure 15.20 Personalization Configuration Menu for MSS

You can generate personalization data based on the authorizations by using **Fill Personalization Data from Authorizations (Cost Centers)** and **Fill Personalization Data from Authorizations (Profit Center)**. Note that if you have assigned orders or projects to a **responsible cost center** in the master data, you can also generate personalization data for orders and projects with the fill personalization data from authorization (cost centers) report. Figure 15.21 shows the selection screen of this report.

Fill Personalization Data from Authorizations (Cost Centers)

User Name	KORKMAZA	to		
Personalization Time Frame		to		

☐ Explode cost center hierarchy
☑ Fill internal orders for area of responsibility
☑ Fill WBS elements for area of responsibility
☑ Test Run

Figure 15.21 Fill Personalization Data from Authorizations (Cost Centers)

In addition to generating authorizations for MSS reporting automatically, you can set defaults in the financial reports by personalization. This can be achieved with the **Personalization Data: Collective Processing** (see Figure 15.20). With this step, you can set defaults for users such as specific cost centers, cost elements, and versions. This step is similar to setting up user settings for controlling reports in SAP ERP (see Figure 15.22).

Personalization dialogs are pre-delivered in the system, for example, DIA_CO_CCA_IS (cost centers, cost elements, activity types, statistical key figures, version, year) and DIA_CO_OPA_IS (orders, cost elements, version, year). If required, you can define new personalization dialogs.

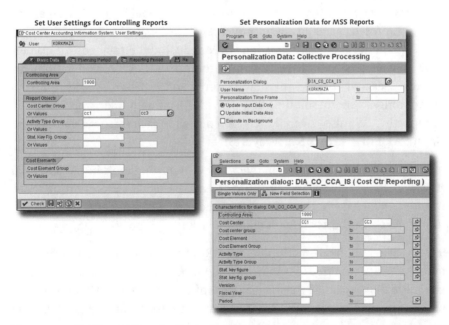

Figure 15.22 Set User Settings for Controlling Reports and Set Personalization Data for MSS Reports

15.3.4 MSS Business Content

Business content includes business packages. You can activate the business content associated with MSS via SAP Solution Manager. By using business content as a starting point, you can benefit from cost savings and reduced time to implementation. Business content for MSS includes portal content, SAP NetWeaver BI content, and IMG settings. For example, the business content includes predefined SAP NetWeaver BI web templates such as Profit Center: Quarterly Results, Cost Center: Cost Blocks (Graphic), and MSS Cost Centers—Plan/Actual Overview.

15.4 Conclusion

SAP provides holistic financial management architecture that consists of the full CFO suite (SAP Business Suite, SAP solution for GRC, SAP solutions for performance management, and SAP solutions for information workers). In this book, we covered the strategies for maximizing financial reporting capabilities and explained the best practices for simplifying, streamlining, and automating financial and management reporting in these applications.

With SAP ERP, SAP has strengthened financial reporting capabilities. Compared to previous releases, many of the modified functions and capabilities, as well as the new features, represent a significant improvement, and, if used correctly, they will increase the quality of financial reporting while reducing the total cost of ownership (TCO). In Chapters 2 to 11 we explained the main design considerations for financial processes and covered the new features and capabilities with the goal of recommending a generic solution that provides leading practices for effective financial reporting. We also covered the key reports for each financial component delivered in SAP ERP and SAP NetWeaver BI.

In Chapters 12 and 13 we provided an overview of reporting tools in SAP ERP and SAP NetWeaver BI for those who have little or no experience with reporting tools. These chapters included brief descriptions of the report components and formatting options, as well as hints and guidelines for creating reports.

Chapter 14 focused on the SAP solutions for GRC, SAP solutions for performance management and SAP solutions for information workers from a financial reporting perspective. We first explained the financial compliance aspect of SAP solutions for GRC, which is heavily focused on SAP GRC Access Control and SAP GRC Process

Control. After that, we explained SAP solutions for performance management and covered the new developments in the area of consolidation, planning, and profitability management reporting. This section was followed by the SAP xApp Analytics, Duet and SAP Interactive forms, which enable organizations to apply analytics down to the process level and provide up-to-date, accurate, and relevant information to information workers for better decision-making and to take actions aligned with business goals set in the corporate strategy.

In this final chapter, we have walked through the future direction of financial reporting and explained SAP's enhancement package strategy, with a focus on the new functions and capabilities. We specifically covered simplified financial reporting innovation and explained the new reporting architecture for reporting.

The journey through *Financial Reporting with SAP* is now complete. You have learned the existing and new reporting functionalities of SAP's applications as well as leading practices for effective reporting. So where have you arrived? You have arrived at a new stage of implementing, using, and enhancing your financial reporting and coping with relentless change, constant system integration, human and organizational factors, and various risks and compliances.

In today's fast-changing business environment, information intelligence and business processes have to be tightly integrated. Business processes integrated with financial reporting and an analytics approach provide the right information to information workers at a time that will undoubtedly increase the competitive advantage of your organization. With the new innovations and capabilities, you can combine all of the necessary information in one place to enable timely decision-making at the right stage of the process. As we mentioned earlier, it is expected that the capabilities and constant innovation in reporting and analytics will only expand across every part of the enterprise in the future.

We hope this book will inspire you to make your financial reporting process more effective with cutting edge technology and continuously improve your reporting and analytics to drive business value and better decision-making, transparency, and compliance while meeting with the business goals set in your corporate strategy.

Author

 **Aylin Korkmaz** is currently a senior manager with the Accenture Finance & Performance Management service line. She has deep process architecture and design skills, and is a leading practitioner in the area of SAP ERP Financials. She has been working in global multi-stream projects for many years, concentrating on the financial and management accounting and underlying business processes. She has extensive experience assisting organizations with process design improvements. Her experience includes full lifecycle Finance ERP programs, business architecture, system integration and finance and accounting operations. She has worked in organizations across many industries, including communications and high technology, automotive, pharmaceutical, manufacturing, utilities, oil and gas.

Index

Get the most out of your SAP ERP Finacials implementation using the practical tips and techniques provided

Achieve operational efficiencies by adopting the process-driven approach detailed through out the book

675 pp., 2008, 79,95 Euro / US$ 79.95
ISBN 978-1-59229-160-1

Optimize Your SAP ERP Financials Implementation

www.sap-press.com

Shivesh Sharma

Optimize Your SAP ERP Financials Implementation

The real work in SAP Financials begins after the implementation is complete. This is when it's time to optimize and use SAP Financials in the most efficient way for your organization. Optimization entails understanding unique client scenarios and then developing solutions to meet those requirements, while staying within the project's budgetary and timeline constraints. This book teaches consultants and project managers to think about and work through best practice tools and methodologies, before choosing the ones to use in their own implementations. The variety of real-life case studies and examples used to illustrate the business processes and highlight how SAP Financials can support these processes, make this a practical and valuable book for anyone looking to optimize their SAP Financials implementation.

Uncover functionality, processes and complete customization details

Master transaction and position management with hedge management

approx. 700 pp., Feb 2008, 99,95 Euro / US$ 99.95
ISBN 978-1-59229-149-6

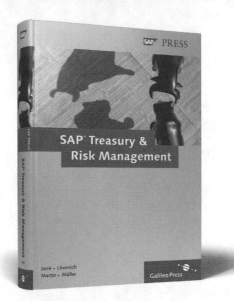

SAP Treasury and Risk Management

www.sap-press.com

Sönke Jarré, Reinhold Lövenich, Andreas Martin, Klaus G. Müller

SAP Treasury and Risk Management

This comprehensive guide introduces you to the functionality and helps you quickly master the usage of SAP Treasury and Risk Management. Learn about the most important customization settings as well as typical use cases and get straightforward solutions to many of the most common problems. With volumes of detailed screenshots, in-depth overviews and practical examples, all components of the tool are covered in detail – from transaction and position management, to risk and performance analyses, to reporting and beyond. Plus, you'll also benefit from expert guidance on interfaces and integration as well as compliance requirements. The book is up-to-date for SAP ERP 6.0.